STEFANO MANFREDI'S ITALIAN FOOD

STEFANO MANFREDI'S ITALIAN FOOD

FAIRFAX BOOKS

ALLEN&UNWIN

FOR MY DAUGHTER ISABELLA

First published in 2013

Fairfax Books, an imprint of
Allen & Unwin
83 Alexander Street
Crows Nest NSW 2065
Australia
Phone: (61 2) 8425 0100
Email: info@allenandunwin.com
Web: www.allenandunwin.com

Cataloguing-in-Publication details are available
from the National Library of Australia
www.trove.nla.gov.au

ISBN 978 1 74331 117 2

Cover and internal design by Sarah Odgers
Index by Jo Rudd
Layout and prepress by Megan Ellis
Printed in China by C&C Offset Printing Co. Ltd

10 9 8 7 6 5 4 3 2 1

CONTENTS

THE REGIONS

INTRODUCTION

WE HAD LEFT BEHIND MORE THAN A COUNTRY WHEN WE GOT OFF THE BOAT FROM ITALY AND WENT TO LIVE IN THE MIGRANT HOSTEL: WE'D LEFT BEHIND AN ENTIRE CULTURE. AND IN DAILY LIFE, THAT CULTURE WAS EXPRESSED IN THE PREPARATION AND EATING OF FOOD. IT WAS A FEELING, TOUCHING, SMELLING CULTURE.

It was 1961 when the Manfredi family – my father Luigi, mother Franca and and brother Franco – arrived in Australia and were dumped in the Bonegilla migrant camp in north-eastern Victoria. Like many thousands of others (by 1971 there would be around 290,000 Italian-born Australians), we'd left our war-torn and economically distressed homeland for a new life.

Home for the Manfredis was and had been for centuries, Gottolengo, a small town in the province of Brescia in the region of Lombardia (Lombardy), roughly 130 kilometres (80 miles) east of Milan and 30 kilometres (18 miles) south of Lake Garda. It is a land rich in produce and food culture.

My grandmother Angelina Pini was one of the finest cooks in the region, and cooked professionally at an *albergo* (small hotel) near Milan. My mother Franca, also a fine cook, would expand on her skills professionally when she came to Australia.

Memories of Angelina and Franca in the kitchen and the food they produced there came with me. Australia at that time, for a variety of reasons, had very little to offer a hungry Italian family. The food at Bonegilla was infamously bad and, ten years before we arrived, had caused a riot among the Italian inmates.

But it was families like ours, and many others from Italy, Greece, Lebanon and other southern European countries, who would, over time, play a major part in the radical changes in the Australian way of eating and drinking.

I grew up, went to university and graduated as a teacher. But it wasn't long before I decided to move from the classroom to the kitchen and, like Angelina, take up cooking professionally. After a series of hard-slog jobs learning the trade, the next step was to open a family restaurant that would bring to my new country the dishes and the flavours of the old.

In 1983, along with Franca, Franco and my then wife (and now business partner) Julie, we opened The Restaurant Manfredi in an obscure back lane in the inner Sydney suburb of Ultimo. Against all the odds it was an almost instant success, introducing a city more used to the tomato-based dishes of southern Italy to the polenta and salamis of the north. The central idea was simple. We had come from a specific cultural background. With this came an attitude to food and the skills used to prepare it. Here we found a new range of produce to use those skills on and to apply that attitude to.

And that remained the basic philosophy for a series of restaurants that won the hearts, minds and palates of Sydney: La Mensa in Paddington, bel mondo in The Rocks and, today, Balla in the Star Casino and Manfredi at Bells, north of Sydney.

In all that time – a time of growth, ferment and change in the Australian food scene, and of the birth of 'modern Australian' food – I've never lost touch with my northern Italian roots.

But in the last ten years, following my fascination with the wines of Italy, I've begun a love affair with the food of all the country's regions. Now, having travelled to them all, eaten their food and tasted their wines, this book has grown from the seed of an idea to a reality. The challenge was to give shape and meaning to the many strands of Italian regional food and that food's natural companion, wine.

This is much more than a recipe book. It is a gastronomic tour of Italy, from the alpine beauty of Trentino-Alto Adige to Arab-influenced Sicilia (Sicily), and from the prehistoric Italici – the first people to occupy the peninsula – to the people who make up the rich culinary tapestry of the present day. It is a long and absorbing history, and an introduction to the landscape and produce of each of Italy's 20 provinces. I hope you enjoy travelling and tasting with me across time, and through the varied and beguiling regions of Italy.

STEFANO MANFREDI

ITALY: A BRIEF CULINARY HISTORY

BY JOHN NEWTON

The first wave of migratory tribes to arrive on what is now known as the Italian peninsula, around the 12th century BCE (Before the Current Era) became known as Italici, from an ancient word meaning 'land of young cattle', or 'land of calves'. This was either descriptive – there were young calves – or a derogatory name used by the Etruscans (who arrived a little later) to disparage their less accomplished southern neighbours. Either way, it can be said that the very name of Italy has a culinary connection.

Little is known of the diet of these early peoples, but it is likely, as in the rest of Western Europe, that between 6000 and 3500 BCE they began to practise agriculture and herding. They domesticated wild herbs, grew crops, and grazed livestock (mainly goats and sheep) using the method known as transhumance (*transumanza*), which is herding the animals to warmer climes in the winter and into the mountains during summer.

Later, three races left indelible marks on the food of Italy: the Etruscans, the Greeks and the Arabs – or, as the latter were called at the time, Moors or Saracens. Three races and, later, one event – the arrival, in the mid-16th century, of the tomato from the lowlands of Peru – were pivotal to the country's cuisine.

THE ETRUSCANS

The first inhabitants of whom we have some knowledge are the group of tribes called the Etruscans, who arrived in about the 11th century BCE and inhabited the area around what is known today as Toscana (Tuscany), then as Etruria.

The Etruscans had linguistic roots in Phoenicia, Turkey and Egypt, but their exact origins are a mystery. Their reputation in the ancient world was for decadence and excess. They ate two meals a day at a time when one was the norm, probably because they were successful farmers who most likely developed rotational cropping and thus grew more food, which had to be eaten. Another reason for their reputation was that, unlike the custom elsewhere, Etruscan women ate with the men at official banquets, and they were reputed to be excellent cooks.

The Etruscans' staples were barley and an ancient wheat called *farro*, which were ground into a gruel called *puls*, an ancestor of today's polenta. They grew hazelnuts, figs, peas, chickpeas, lentils, grapes and olives and were famed for the quality of their olive oil and wine. Their meat was mainly from pigs and chickens but occasionally sheep and cattle, although the cattle were more useful alive, working on the farms.

From the 6th century BCE, the Etruscans began trading and competing with the Greek colonies in southern Italy and with the Phoenicians. The latter would have introduced to the peninsula dates, almonds, pistachios, persimmons and scallions (scallions take their name from the Phoenician town of Ascalon).

MAGNA GRAECIA

Greek civilisation, which rose to power and prominence around the 8th century BCE, was based upon the city-state. So successful were many of these cities that their populations grew to the point where they ran out of land for the younger generation. The solution was to send the young out to find colonies elsewhere. And so, beginning with Pitecusa on the island of Ischia in 770 BCE, southern Italy became Magna Graecia, with Greek cities eventually spreading from Sicilia (Sicily) north to today's Puglia (Apulia) and across to Campania. There are villages in Puglia and Calabria where a dialect of ancient Greek is still spoken.

The Greeks arrived with olives, more grapes, cabbage and onions, plus the advanced agricultural techniques needed to grow them and to make wine and olive oil. For the Greeks, the cultivation of grain and the baking of bread were the distinctive signs of civilisation.

Greek influence can be seen today in Calabria, where orange and lemon blossoms are called by orchardists *zàgara*, a Greek word for flower, and where until recently fishers in Bagnara harpooned swordfish using techniques and tackle similar to those of the ancient Greeks. Greek Sicilia produced the first school for professional cooks, run by Labdacus in the 3rd century BCE. Later, when the Romans ruled Italy, the fame of Sicilian food had spread throughout the Mediterranean world; for the Romans, culinary perfection was *Siculus coquus et Sicula mensa*, meaning 'a Sicilian cook and a Sicilian table'.

The Greek city-states on the Italian peninsula had an unfortunate and ultimately fatal habit of squabbling with each other and their neighbours. While fighting the more powerful Phoenicians and Etruscans, the Greeks employed mercenaries from across the Alps – Celts whose territory spread from present-day Austria to southern Germany. This turned out to be a bad idea. The mercenaries went back home, spread the word on the wealth and timidity of the locals and their abundant lands and, from about the 5th century BCE, began to infiltrate the Po River plains. In the following decades, waves of Celts settled there, pushing the Etruscans back into Toscana.

The invasion did have some good results: the Celts brought with them their pigs as well as their skill at extracting salt and using it to preserve foods. The result was one of Italy's most treasured products, prosciutto, and some of today's best prosciutto is produced around the site of those early Celtic settlements, in Parma.

ROME AND THE ROMANS

While the Greeks and Etruscans had civilisations, they had no nations – only cities. This lack of cohesion was their weakness, and the Romans overran them easily. In a remarkably short time, Rome grew from a loose federation of villages on seven hills around the river Tiber to an empire that ruled most of the known world.

The early Roman diet was similar to that of the surrounding tribes, consisting primarily of farro and barley ground into *puls*. So central was it to their diet that all other foods were known as *pulentarium*, or accompaniments to puls. They also ate pulses, wild herbs, vegetables, cheese, honey, a little meat (mainly fowl, sheep and pig) and, after the 4th century, olives. Cattle were used mostly for agriculture and were sacrificed – and eaten – only for religious ceremonies or celebrations, weddings and births, and then only by the wealthy. Stored food, known as *penus* (which included cured meat), gave its name to the household gods: Penates.

The Romans ate a single main meal, *coena* at midday, and drank *mulsum*, wine mixed with water; the coena was often followed by 'desserts' of cheese and fruit called *secundae mensae*. Breakfast, *ientaculum*, added flatbread to the dessert menu. If there was an evening meal, *vesperna*, it was light and consumed just before going to bed. The people's habit of lying down at table – eating while reclining on their sides – came from Greece via the Etruscans.

After clashes with Carthage, from whose people they learnt new farming and herding techniques, and after establishing outposts on the shores of the eastern Mediterranean, the Romans conquered Spain, Greece, the Middle East, France and Egypt, all in less than two centuries. Such expansion had its problems. The estates – *latifundia* – owned by the richest Romans, which had expanded using slave power, meant that the poorer farmers were unable to compete. Many sold their properties and left for other provinces.

As the Roman Empire advanced and Rome became wealthier, so did Roman cuisine become more and more elaborate. While publicly extolling the virtues of frugality, passing laws aimed at curbing excessive eating, and attributing corruption to gluttony, the reality was that of a society wallowing in excess. (The English word frugality is derived from the Latin *fruges*, the name for the agriculture yield, which was considered the symbol of civilisation.)

In imperial times the midday meal became known as *prandium* and consisted of leftovers from the previous evening meal together with bread and cheese. The main meal, still the *coena*, moved to the evening. Exotic foods and spices, cooking techniques, and recipes from the far-flung corners of the empire converged on Rome. From Gaul, Germany, Iberia, the East and Africa came pepper and cloves, among other spices.

For the Romans, 'sour' meant vinegar, 'sweet' meant honey, and 'salt' meant garum, a fish sauce not unlike modern-day Asian fish sauces; sweet and salt flavours were habitually mixed together. Another common ingredient was silphium, a resin extract from a root that appears to have disappeared in the 1st century, when it was replaced by asafoetida, a gum derived from a Middle Eastern plant known to the Romans as *laserpitium*. During the time of Apicius, fish became fashionable and many of the villas of wealthy Romans incorporated fish ponds.

The urban poor lived in cramped quarters in large apartment blocks called *insulae*, where kitchens were rare for fear of fire. Many ate out in *tabernae*, shops that sold hot meals and wine, and gambling shops and brothels were common. Walking through this hugger-mugger of street life and, often, death, the wealthiest citizens would be followed by slaves carrying food that had been prepared in the homes of their owners.

Another example of the gap between rich and poor was flour. The best white flour, *siligo*, was reserved for the wealthy. Under the emperor Augustus (63–14 BCE), an office, the *annona*, was set up to stabilise grain prices and in times of hardship to distribute free grain.

Pompeii was destroyed by the eruption of Vesuvius in 79, but many of its people, buildings and artefacts were preserved under a layer of volcanic ash. What remains offers a valuable insight into ancient Roman life, including cooking. Kitchens in Pompeii were poorly lit rooms usually at the back of the house, most with only a masonry hearth with a tiled top and a storage area for fuel below. Some houses also had an oven resembling a small pizza oven, with a vent for the smoke to escape. There was usually a basin to hold water and supports for tables. Rich Pompeians often had a choice of dining room: a cold-weather room facing west or a warm-weather one facing east or north to remain in the shade. Many larger houses also had outside dining beneath a pergola, and the Pompeian equivalent of a barbecue: a *craticula* or grid.

The empire began to unravel around the 2nd century for myriad reasons, including two of its pillars: conquest and slavery. The spoils of war dried up, and the slave system inhibited technological progress. Combined with galloping inflation and the excesses already mentioned briefly, this meant that by 350 there had been waves of invasion by the Germans, plus famines and decreasing agricultural productivity. Before his death in 395 Emperor Theodosius split the empire between his two sons: the western empire, centred in Rome, under Honorius and the eastern capital, in Constantinople, under Arcadius.

After a turbulent period of attacks and retreats and short-lived reigns, in 475 Romulus Augustus was named emperor. However, he reigned only from 31 October to 4 September: Rome had a Romulus both at its beginning and at its end.

AFTER THE FALL

The Germans arrived and settled in the countryside, bringing with them rye and barley. They also brought a fermented drink called beer, but the locals did not like it at all and stuck to their wines. Some German nobles started their own *latifundia* (land ownership), and the Roman nobles were pleased to have the German soldiers as peacekeepers. With the collapse of the empire there was no central authority, and many local cultures that had been suppressed by Roman ideology flourished.

A culinary clash was evident between the Roman wine, oil and bread trinity and the German lard, beer and rye: there was some substitution and, no doubt, much rivalry.

When Christianity arrived it adopted the Roman trinity: wine and bread in Holy Communion, oil for ritual.

Socially and politically it was an uneasy time. The German tribes never managed to subdue Constantinople, and in 535, after a 20-year battle, Emperor Justinian I conquered the Goths and also a large part of Italy. He called it Romania, which today's Romagna derives from. In 568, the Longobards or Lombards, another German tribe, captured most of Justinian's territory, leaving to the Byzantines Sicilia, Sardinia, Puglia, Calabria, and Ravenna and surrounds. For 200 years Italy was divided between Byzantine and Lombard culture.

In 751 the Lombards conquered Ravenna and the five cities to its south, from Rimini to Ancona, known as the Pentapolis. The pope seated in Rome called in another Germanic tribe, the Franks, to fight the Lombards, and they invaded northern Italy and conquered most Lombard possessions. In gratitude, and for protection, the pope named their king, Charles the Great (Charlemagne), emperor of the Holy Roman Empire.

The Franks introduced feudalism, a hierarchical system that fixed roles and allegiances and led all the way up to the emperor. His closest allies governed the territories and the nobles owned the farms; the *latifundia* system was integrated, the peasants worked the land and a tithe was extracted from each area and sent to the emperor. The peasants were taxed by the noble whose farm they worked, and all were expected to fight in his armies. Such a system entrenched and amplified class and cultural distinctions. The mostly Germanic nobles ritualised hunting, and roast or grilled meat – the bounty of the hunt – was the core of their diet. As with the Romans, celebratory feasts and banquets were organised and conferred status on both the giver and the guests. Drinking – and wine was back in fashion – was a large part of these events, although the wine was not very well made and was diluted with water to mask the taste.

The peasants ate cereals, pulses, fruit and vegetables grown in their own orchards and market gardens on unclaimed land, and made soups of cabbage, beet, fennel, leek and onion in hearth pots that would simmer all day. Cured pork was common but beef was rare, as oxen were used to pull carts and cows were milked for cheese.

This feudal system was to last in northern and central Italy until the 11th century, when the Frank territories south of the Alps broke away from France and Germany and, in time, became local states in the modern sense of the word. In the south, the Byzantine empire struggled to remain in control – a struggle that would ultimately prove futile.

THE ARABS

In the 8th century they swept out of Africa on horseback and rapidly conquered much of the Mediterranean world, these soldiers of the newly minted Muslim religion. They overcame resistance in northern Africa, central Asia, Corsica, Sardinia and Pantelleria; entered Spain in 711; and were only stopped at Poitiers by the Franks in 732. In 827 the Arab state based in today's Tunisia attacked Sicilia and other Mediterranean locations, and in 902 they occupied Sicilia for the first time (but not the last).

Palermo became the Arabs' capital in the western Mediterranean and was soon stuffed with spices. The island was rapidly planted with new crops made possible by the advanced agricultural techniques of the conquerors, who were known in the western Mediterranean as Saracens and in Spain as Moors. Two of the most important new crops were sugar cane and citrus fruit, which replaced the Roman honey and vinegar respectively. But the Arabs also brought with them pomegranates, eggplants (aubergines), rice, saffron, apricots – the list goes on. One

import worth special mention in the Italian context is coffee. Its name is derived from the Arab *qahwah* and it was a substitute for those who were forbidden wine; indeed, it was known as 'the wine of Arabia'.

The Arab invasion of Sicilia and other parts of the south had the same positive social consequences as it did in the Arabs' first 300 years in Spain. The Muslims were at first wise and tolerant rulers: they reduced the heavy taxes charged by the Byzantines, Christians and Jews were free to practise their religions, many of the *latifundia* were broken up and handed to smaller landholders, and agricultural output increased because of improved techniques and technology – especially in irrigation, at which the desert-dwelling Arabs excelled. Sicilia thrived and became part of the extensive Arabic commercial network. Palermo became an important cultural centre.

The feel of Arab Sicilia lingers today, in Palermo especially and in its Capo and Ballaro markets with their overhead awnings and bargaining stallholders. The Arab presence is also still to be found and savoured in Sicilian cuisine: the lemon, almost a symbol of the island, was introduced by them, while the emblematic *pasta con le sarde* with its currants is generally thought to be Arabic in origin. Another influence of the Arabs is eggplant and the many dishes made from it on the island; the preferred variety is known as the Tunisian. It is round and fades from deep purple to lavender to white near the stem.

THE NORMANS

Those same descendents of Scandinavian warriors who settled in France and occupied Britain in 1066 settled in southern Italy and took up the pope's cause against the Saracens. In 1091 they expelled the Arabs and set up a centralised political organisation. But their agricultural skills were nowhere near as developed as those of the people they had driven out, and sugar cane, among other important crops imported by the Arabs, disappeared. In the 13th century Frederick, then king of Sicily and Holy Roman Emperor, attempted to revive the agricultural practices by hiring farmers from North Africa, but to no avail.

This period of Italian history saw advances in metallurgy, which meant better iron for ploughs and increased productivity in agriculture. This in turn led to the growth in wealth of a crucial element in the development of Italian cuisines: the regional cities, or *communi*, which had been a dominant force in Italy since Roman times.

In their book *Italian Cuisine*, Capatti and Montanari write: 'Over the course of the centuries, Italian history had revealed a trait that distinguishes it from the history of other countries, namely the prevalence of strong urban centres throughout the land … Italy's culinary heritage is usually asserted and recognised through reference to city-based identities.' The city, as they point out, represents the surrounding territory, and many emblematic recipes and product names – such as Treviso chicory, parmesan cheese, San Daniele prosciutto, *Bella di Cerignola* olives and pecorino romano – carry the names of the cities that are the production and marketing centres of the region.

It was these provincial cities, with their relatively dense populations and surrounding produce, that were crucial to the development of Italy's national and regional cuisine. And it was not only the exchange of produce and product between city and countryside that contributed to the construction of the cuisine, but also the flow of recipes from the peasant population of the countryside to the wealthier classes in the cities.

The expanding cities resulted in expanding trade, with the stability of the Mongol Empire easing travel and commerce. Marco Polo brought the luxuries of China to Europe, spices made their way to Italian ports, and the wealthy in the cities had time to refine their lives. Art, music and gastronomy all thrived. At the increasingly opulent banquets, pairs of guests would share a bowl, a goblet and a trencher – the latter either a board or a slice of bread to hold solid food. Fingers would be used for solid food and cleaned on the tablecloth, and spoons were used for soups. It was considered impolite to 'double-dip' with the fingers or to spit at table.

What was on the tables of the wealthy was meat: pork, mutton and poultry. Pork fat was used in the south and butter in the north. Olive oil, which was considered more of an Arabic product, was a luxury and mainly produced in the south and in Toscana. In *Food Culture in Italy*, Fabio Parasecoli wryly remarks that 'Vegetables and pulses were still considered too heavy for the delicate stomachs of the nobles' and so were relegated to peasant tables.

In this time of increased gastronomic consciousness there was growing respect for producers and vendors, including flour millers, tavern keepers, butchers and bakers. Others, like *lardaroli* and *salaroli* (lard and salami makers), were not yet afforded the same respect.

DEATH AND REBIRTH

The Black Death, which began in 1347, killed untold numbers in Europe. Barbara Tuchman writes in *A Distant Mirror* that the population of Europe was halved: in Florence alone, it is believed that 65,000 fell victim. Whole villages and arable lands were abandoned as it became increasingly difficult to find labour. The global cooling of the period (now believed to have been caused by a massive volcanic eruption in Indonesia followed by a string of lesser eruptions around the same time), wars, riots and rebellions also meant a slowing in economic expansion. French and Spanish nobles sided with local landowners to tighten the screws on the local farmers.

JEWISH ITALY

There have been Jews in Rome, Sicilia and Sardinia since the 2nd century BCE and they have lived in and around the entire peninsula since then. The earliest and largest populations were in the south, particularly in Sicilia, where the population was 100,000. For 18 centuries they enjoyed a peaceful existence, especially prospering under Arab rule from 831 to 1061.

But in 1492, the Spanish monarchs Ferdinand and Isabella, who then ruled Sicilia, expelled them, as they did all Jews from Spain. The massive migration of Jews from the south to the centre and the north coincided with an influx of Germans and Jewish refugees from Spain and Portugal. This crisis resulted in Jews being segregated in special quarters. Venice was the first city to set aside a Jewish area, near the foundry, the word for which in Venetian dialect was *ghetto*. In Rome, the Jews were also forced into what became known as ghettos after the Spanish ruling.

This 'ghettoisation' forced the Jews into close contact with each other and resulted in distinctive Italian Jewish cuisines that were different in each locality but often identifiable by their Arabic roots. Eggplants were ubiquitous, as were artichokes: the most famous Jewish Italian dish is *carciofi alla giudia* ('Jewish artichokes'), in which artichokes are flattened and deep-fried. Other Jewish/Arabic signatures are garnishes of raisins and pine nuts, sweet and sour flavours, and *cassola*, a ricotta cake sold in Rome. As has been noted, the Arabic influence can still be seen in Italian food today, and much of it has been transmitted by the Jews.

Livorno on the Tuscan coast was the only city in Italy that did not force Jews into ghettos; consequently, it had a large and vibrant Jewish community. It was through Livornese Jews from Tunisia that couscous arrived in Italy, and it is still made in Livorno today. Indeed, the famous fish soup/stew of Livorno, *cacciucco*, is often served poured over a pile of couscous.

During this time of turmoil, Italian culture experienced the Renaissance, which lasted from the 14th century to the 17th century and spread to the rest of Europe. There was a flowering of literature, philosophy, art, science, religion – and gastronomy.

The epicentre of the Renaissance was Florence. As Waverley Root wrote in *The Food of Italy*: 'Florence was the Renaissance. She created it.' And the banquets of the Florentine Renaissance were the most imaginative, artistic and excessive in all of Italy. One dining club (there were many), the Company of the Trowel, invited members to come one night dressed as workmen and asked them to build a house using sugared ricotta as mortar and loaves of bread as bricks while they ate a pedestal full of pies and a column filled with boiled capons and veal!

However, it is simplistic to ascribe nothing but excess to Renaissance Florence. There was also what Root calls 'an innate disposition to sobriety' that attempted to curb the excesses of, say, Lorenzo de' Medici (Lorenzo the Magnificent) – who more or less ruled the Florentine Republic from 1449 to 1492 – with frowns and frugality at home. At the beginning of the 15th century laws were passed, known as sumptuary laws, restricting the kinds and quantities of food that could be served at a single dinner: for example, more than 40 guests were prohibited, and they could only be served 'three courses and trenchers'. Lorenzo flouted the laws by giving five different banquets for a total of 200 guests to celebrate his wedding. In Florence, the Medicis were seen as above the law.

The prevailing Tuscan disposition of the time is summed up in the dour saying *Si stava meglio quando si stava peggio*, meaning 'We were better off when we were worse off'. But there were limits. On the death of Lorenzo, the religious and political reformer Girolamo Savonarola attempted to introduce even more stringent sumptuary laws, among other restrictions on the freedom of the Florentines. They eventually turned on him and, with an irony that would not have been lost on them, roasted him.

The flavours of Renaissance cuisine returned to the medieval notion of artifice, or the mixing of flavours. The nutritional theory of the time deemed a food balanced if it contained all nutritional qualities, and so the perfect dish was one that contained all possible flavours. There was still a vast difference between the wealthy and the poor table – trade and imported foodstuffs and spices were on wealthy tables, and seasonal produce dictated the content of the tables of the poor – but this distinction was given a loftier explanation. 'The difference in diet between the peasants and the upper classes was interpreted as a physical reflection of spiritual distinctions, closely connected with social status', according to Parasecoli.

Popular Renaissance dishes included *torta manfreda*, a tart of liver and a mixture of meats, and *torta di funghi*, a *sformato* of mushrooms with egg, cheese and breadcrumbs soaked in milk.

Sugar at this time was expensive, so it was used lavishly and ostentatiously by the rich. *Malmona* was an orange-flavoured rice pudding typical of the times. The triumph of Arabic sugar over Roman honey was a feature of the Renaissance in Italy, while the Germans and French continued to use honey. Bartolomeo Platina wrote in what was considered the first printed cookbook published in 1472 that 'it would not be a bad thing to add sugar – indeed no dish should refuse sugar'.

The torte or pie, mainly filled with vegetables, was an important item on medieval and Renaissance tables, yet curiously before the Renaissance the crust was used only to hold the contents and was not edible. 'Making this crust edible,' write Capatti and Montanari, 'was an important innovation of Renaissance cooking.'

The Renaissance was stimulated by the rediscovery of ancient Greek and Roman texts, one of which was *Apicius*, published in 1457. This was a boom time for cookbooks: the loftier ones were in Latin while those for the lower orders were in the vulgar languages (which would become dialects) and also in Italian, which was being spoken in the courts of the nobles for the first time. Meanwhile, what were the peasants eating? Pies or torte, as previously mentioned, were popular – in 'infinite varieties', according to Tommaso Garzoni in his 1585 book *The Universal Marketplace of all the Professions in the World* – as were mortadella, salami, sausages of all kinds, and cheese. In the 16th century the poet Ercole Bentivoglio praised the people of Lombardia (Lombardy), 'where the first thing placed on the table is cheese'.

Apart from the tomato, corn or maize – that other American import – was first planted in the Veneto in northern Italy in the 1530s. At first grown as a fodder crop, it soon became popular with small landholders because as a novel crop it wasn't taxed. When the bigger landowners saw the profits in this high-yielding plant, it gradually replaced all other grains except wheat. This was to have tragic consequences when, in the 18th century, a severe famine saw the hardy maize (as polenta) become a survival food for the peasantry in both Italy and Spain. In the Americas corn was eaten whole after the cobs were boiled in water with white lime (calcium carbonate), which boosted the vegetable's levels of calcium, niacin and vitamin B3. Without this treatment, consuming a corn-heavy diet leads to the vitamin-deficiency disease pellagra, and this is what happened in its new home in 1730. Maize was the major food eaten and pellagra was rife, beginning in Spain and spreading to the Po Valley. Only in the first decades of the 20th century, when better economic conditions allowed for better diets, was the problem finally alleviated.

THE FOOD BOOKS OF ITALY

As you would imagine, a country so immersed in food and food culture has, over the years and starting more than 2000 years ago, produced any number of books reflecting the prevailing appetite. Here is a selection of those books, chosen to represent their times. The food books of Italy provide their own culinary journey.

In Greek Sicilia, the famed food poem *The Life of Luxury* was written by Archestratus of Gela, a man of whom Athanaeus (the author of *Deipnosophistae*, or *The Dinner-party Philosophers*, another work of ancient Greek gastronomy) wrote: 'This Archestratus, in his love for pleasures, travelled over every land and seas with precision, in a desire, as it seems to me, to review with care the things of the belly.' Almost nothing is known of Archestratus, other than that he came from Syracuse, or Gela, on the island of Sicilia and his poem is dated to about 330 BCE.

Surviving from the Roman era is the collection of recipes attributed to Marcus Gavius Apicius entitled *De re coquinaria* (*On the Subject of Cooking*). Apicius lived during the 1st century, but the recipes were probably collected between the 2nd and 4th centuries. Reflecting the cuisine of the time, they use a catalogue of 140 spices. While *Satyricon*, believed to have been written by Gaius Petronius during the reign of Nero (54–68), luridly depicts a period of decadence and decline.

The 12th century was a time of war between King Roger II of Sicily and the forces supporting Pope Innocent II. Pope Innocent was also battling a rival for his title, Antipope Anacletus II, in a protracted and complicated struggle that need not bother us here except to introduce Roger II and his championing of the Arab poet, writer and geographer Muhammad al-Idrisi. In *The Book of Roger: Pleasure Excursion of One Eager to Traverse the World's Regions*, published in 1154, al-Idrisi makes the first mention of dried pasta.

The invention of the printing press by Gutenberg in 1444 (the year he set up his first press in Mainz in Germany) facilitated, among other things, the printing and distribution of recipe collections. The volume considered the first printed cookery book, *De honesta voluptate et valetudinae* (*On Honest Pleasure and Good Health*) by Bartolomeo Platina, was published in 1472, perhaps in Rome. It was a collection of 250 recipes, about 240 of which were taken from Maestro Martino's manuscript *Liber de arte coquinaria* (*The Book of the Art of the Kitchen*); about six of the remaining ten were taken from Apicius.

The first recipe using tomatoes was published in 1692 in a Neapolitan book by Antonio Latini: *Lo scalco alla moderna* (*The Modern Steward*). The recipe is entitled *Salsa di pomodoro, all spagnuola* (Tomato sauce, in the Spanish style)

Books of the 16th century, such as *Galateo* by Giovanni della Casa, taught manners and etiquette at table. Curiously, talking openly at table about the magnificent food was forbidden (one could discuss the wine), even though hosts were encouraged to serve elaborate and creative banquets.

Many of the cookbooks of this period were written by *scalchi*, or stewards. A typical volume is *La singola dottrina* (*The Unique Doctrine*), which was first published in 1560 and written by Domenico Romoli, nicknamed Panunto ('oiled bread'). It contained advice on the responsibilities of a steward in a wealthy household, descriptions of the qualities and seasonality of foodstuffs, and a brief treatise on good health. It was in Romoli's book that the term *antipasto*, in its modern sense, was first used.

One exception to the rule of *scalchi* writing cookbooks is a remarkable work by Bartolomeo Scappi, who was a cook in the pope's palace in 1570. It is known in the current translation as *Opera dell'arte del cucinare*, but was originally called *L'arte et prudenza d'un maestro cuoco* (*The Art and Craft of a Master Cook*). In the fourth volume, Scappi set down methods for dealing with the local and imported ingredients that were available in Rome's markets, and recipes using them. Taken as a whole, Scappi's immense work, according to Carpatti and Montanari in their cultural history of Italian food, 'delineates an almost fully realised image of the "Italian" culinary heritage'.

That by the 16th century Italy had a wealth of highly prized regional produce and products is made clear in eccentric Milanese writer Ortensio Lando's curiously named *Commentary on the Most Notable and Outlandish Things Found in Italy and Elsewhere*. Published in 1548, this book is a fictional story of a foreign – the author calls him Aramaic – traveller to Italy. At one point in the story, the traveller finds himself in an inn where the innkeeper becomes a guide to the culinary specialities of the whole country. In 'the rich island of Sicily', the innkeeper tells the traveller, macaroni is 'usually cooked with fat capons and fresh cheeses, dripping all over with butter and milk and flavoured with sugar and cinnamon'.

In Naples, the traveller is told the bread is excellent; in Sorrento, that he will find excellent veal, fresh caciocavallo cheese, ravioli, fish, mushrooms, chestnuts, almond paste, rosewater preserves, biancomangiare (blancmange, but a very different dish to today's, made of shredded chicken breast, sugar, rice and almond milk), thighs of capon and chicken, shoulders of mutton and 'peaches delicious enough to raise the dead'.

'I must not forget to mention that in Bologna,' the innkeeper advises his guest, 'they make the best sausages that man has ever tasted. They are eaten either cured or cooked and are always appetising. Bless the one who invented this sausage; I kiss and worship his virtuous hands.'

Towards the end of the 18th century, cookbooks and booklets emphasising regional cuisine began addressing the home cook – either the housewife or the literate and urbanised servant class working in bourgeois households. Two such publications were *La cuoca cremonese* (*The Cook of Cremona*) published in 1794 and containing a calendar of seasonal foods and chapters dedicated to meat, poultry, fish, vegetables and pastry; and the wordily titled *L'oniatologia ovvero discorso de' cibi con ricete e regole per ben cucinare all'uso moderne* (*Oniatology; or, A Lesson on Foods, with Recipes and Rules for Good Cooking in the Modern Style*), which first appeared in 1785 as a single publication and then three times a year as an 80-page booklet until 1786 – the precursor to food magazines.

In 1771, *La cuciniera piemontese* (*The Piedmontese Woman Cook*), purported to be by 'a female cook from Piedmont who teaches the easy approach to the best methods of preparing dishes both on fast days and ordinary days', was published. It was a notable attack on the dominance of male cooks, and from then on the rivalry between the sexes gained momentum.

Paradoxically, as Italy fought its way through to unification there was an increased interest by chefs and home cooks in local traditions, and regional food became the subject of scholarly interest. In 1891, the famous *La scienza in cucina e l'arte di mangiare bene* (*Science in the Kitchen and the Art of Good Eating*) by Pellegrino Artusi was published. While acknowledging the local source of many dishes and intending to unify Italian cuisine, the author was confused about the origins of some dishes. This book is still used in Italy.

In 1930, Filippo Tommaso Marinetti published *The Manifesto of Futurist Cookery*, whose avowed intent was to overturn entirely the way Italians ate and whose scandalous central tenet was the banning of pasta (see page 11). The manifesto was followed by the *Futurist Cookbook* in 1932, whose recipes were conceits and jokes based on the Futurists' Fascistic embracing of the machine and speed. Somewhere between the slapstick of the Marx Brothers and the surrealism of Marcel Duchamp, it features dishes with names such as 'Italian breasts in the sunshine', 'Chicken Fiat' and 'Aerofood'. Needless to say, this approach did not change the course of Italian cuisine – although Stefano Manfredi did serve a Futurist dinner at The Restaurant in April 1995!

Other imports from the Americas were chillies and peppers (capsicums); the potato, which didn't enter the Italian diet in any important way until the 17th century; and chocolate, which was first thought of as a spice, then a medicine. In the early 17th century chocolate became involved in a religious controversy: could it be drunk during the Lenten fast? The Roman cardinal Brancaccio was called upon to adjudicate in 1662 and pronounced in chocolate's favour, stating that *liquidum non frangit jejunum* ('liquids do not break the fast'). The turkey, first known as 'Indian chicken', also enjoyed some popularity.

The mid-16th century was a period of great prosperity in Europe. New markets for trade were opened in addition to the Americas, and Italian principalities and city-states prospered. Court life reached high levels of sophistication and refinement, and gastronomy was no exception.

The belief that was held for many years and espoused as late as the 1970s by Root that Catherine de' Medici, who married Henri de Valois in 1533 (later Henry II of France), influenced French cuisine with her retinue of imported Florentine chefs has no basis in fact. For one thing, Italian culture was already present in France in the Middle Ages, and vice versa: there was a reciprocity of influences. In Italy, French influences on the court kitchens included greater use of fish, cheese, butter, beef and offal. The goose foie gras that Bartolomeo Scappi mentioned in his work *Opera* was being made by the Jews in Rome even when it had disappeared in the rest of Europe.

Regional dishes, as described extensively by Lando, were well established at this time. For example, Ferrara was renowned for cured sausages, greens, fruits and root vegetables; Reggio, Mirandola and Correggio for quince; and Brianza for a brain sausage, especially accompanied by *offelle* pastries and sprinkled with vernaccia wine from the region, as well

as special little game birds, *verdorini*, grilled on a skewer. There was trout from Lake Como and Val Malenco, shad from Lugarno, ortolans (tiny birds that are now banned from the table) from the Grigioni hills, and chestnuts from Chiavenna. One could turn south-east to Padua for excellent bread, marzemino wine, frogs and small pike; or go to Chioggia for melons and Venice for fish. This partial list shows that nearly 500 years ago the regional specialities of Italy were already well known and loved.

REGIONAL, INTERNATIONAL AND DOMESTIC

Beginning in the 17th century, and perhaps due to stagnating economic conditions caused by the lack of progress in agriculture and manufacturing, there was a retreat among the bourgeoisie to the regional cuisines and local culinary traditions that dominate Italy to this day. Rejecting the complicated dishes and heavy sauces of court cuisine, the middle classes adapted and refined the stronger, simpler flavours of the food of the lower classes.

Politically, Italy in this period was subject to domination by foreign rulers: Austrian Hapsburgs in the north and Spanish Hapsburgs in the south. This had mixed effects. The Po plain, under the Austrian Hapsburgs, underwent an agricultural revolution that involved modern growing techniques and machinery but also the privatisation of lands, which disenfranchised peasants of their land while improving the efficiency of its use.

Some culinary consequences were the Austrian wiener schnitzel that, somewhat refined, became the *cotoletta alla milanese* of Lombardia. From the south came saffron, introduced by the Spanish (and originally the Arabs), which found its place in risotto. Trentino-Alto Adige, which was in and out of Austrian control for centuries, is the part of Italy that was most deeply affected by the food of its rulers, while the food of French-occupied Piemonte (Piedmont) and Valle d'Aosta (the Aosta Valley) is often said to 'speak with a French accent'.

Indeed, at this time the whole of Italy (or at least the middle and upper classes) was influenced by France and French mores. French service, comprising a first course of soups and appetisers followed by main dishes and then desserts, was introduced. The French preference for fresh ingredients, simpler sauces and more distinct flavours gradually weeded out the excessive use of spices and the medieval mixtures of sweet and savoury. This, combined with the already-mentioned bourgeois preference for the simpler and stronger flavours of regional cooking, began to shape what was to become Italian cuisine.

MOVING TO MODERNITY AND UNIFICATION

The process of unification, *il Risorgimento*, began in 1815 with the end of Napoleonic rule and ended in 1870 when the Italian army, commanded by General Raffaele Cadorna, crossed the papal frontier on 11 September, leaving only Vatican City to the pope.

Of enormous importance in the struggle for unification and liberation was the complex and brilliant Giuseppe Garibaldi, whose revolutionary activities began in 1834 and continued sporadically, with sojourns in America and France, until his last unsuccessful attempt at defeating the papal army in Rome in 1867. The biscuit (cookie) named after him, the garibaldi or 'squashed-fly biscuit', a thin oblong sandwich of dry semi-sweet dough glazed on top and encasing a filling of squashed currants, was invented by a Scot, John Carr, to celebrate Garibaldi's 1864 visit to England.

There were other culinary side effects of this turbulent period of internal movement, one being the northward march of pastas with tomato sauce, which followed the troops. When finally installed, the central government, against the prevailing wave of regionalism, also attempted to unify Italian food habits using the military and the school system.

In the homes of the bourgeoisie, what is known as 'Russian table service', in which dishes are presented in sequence to all guests at the same time, overtook French service. The usual sequence, often followed to this day, became *antipasto*, *primo* (usually a soup, pasta or rice dish), *secondo* (meat or fish), *contorni* (side dishes of vegetables) and *dolci*. This sequence was followed in the new restaurants that had seeped across the border from Paris, where they had begun to appear in the 1770s, just before the French Revolution.

The diet of the poor was pretty much the same as it had been in the 18th century, and would not change until after World War II. When they could – famine was widespread – they ate cereals, pulses and vegetables, with meat and fish rarely. It was in the 19th century that many Italians, particularly in the south and north-east, began migrating, especially to the Americas, often to avoid starvation.

INDUSTRY AND FUTURISM

The 20th century brought with it canned vegetables (especially tomatoes), industrially produced dried pasta, more and more cookbooks flying off the presses, and new stoves – first fired by coal, then gas.

And then came a war, World War I, in which for the first time Italians fought together as Italians, and mixed with their compatriots from all over the peninsula. There were food scarcities, but also an interchange of information about the idea of Italy, and of being Italian.

Perhaps most importantly, it was during and especially after World War I that the country entered the industrial age, a period called by some 'Italy's second industrial revolution'.

The breakfast ration for all Italian soldiers in 1916 – dried figs, chestnuts, almonds, walnuts, cheese, olives and sardines or herrings or fresh apple – was augmented in 1917 by coffee and sugar. From then on, the taste of coffee – an industrial product – would be associated with waking up. Other industrial food products that spread across the country after the war were dried pasta, canned meat, salt cod, and cheeses such as provolone and fontina. Capatti and Montanari point out that here we can observe a dual system of values: 'tradition, memory and a sense of roots (and on the other hand) a contemporary emphasis on industry'. From now on, they say, there is a 'high' and a 'low' point of reference, the high being the bourgeois idea of regional food and the low being the industrial mass-produced food of workers' cafeterias, hospitals and other state-run institutions.

Another important industrial move forward was the introduction of chilled storage lockers in butcher shops. Before this, meat had to be sold quickly in warmer months, and could not be stored. Left to hang in a chilled atmosphere, it now appeared to become permanently available.

Two decades of fascism under Benito Mussolini began in 1922, a period that had two major influences on Italian food. Firstly, nationalism presented Italy as a series of idealised gastronomic regions, in perhaps the forerunner of today's popular image of

the country. Artist Umberto Zimelli was commissioned to create a map identifying the 'principal culinary specialisations of the Italian regions'; his map is still reproduced. *La guida gastronomica d'Italia* (*The Gastronomic Guide to Italy*) was published by the Touring Club Italiano in 1931 and presented the country as a topography of culinary delights. 'Learning to eat Italian style', assert Capatti and Montanari, 'was one of the projects of the Fascist regime.'

One of the positive effects of this exaltation of the Italian table was the rediscovery of the south, with the cuisines of Calabria, Basilicata and the whole Mediterranean region receiving more attention. This gave rise to what Capatti and Montanari call 'the myth of the south', an idealisation of the glories and gastronomy of the countries around the shores of the Mediterranean that has culminated in the 'Mediterranean diet' – low in saturated fats and rich in grains, pulses and vegetables – first propounded by American researcher Ancel Keys, who conveniently turned a blind eye to the fats and proteins of northern Italy.

The opposing strand of the Fascist view of food was a passion for modernity and the continued rise of industrial foods. Women were taught more efficient ways to cook – methods that rode roughshod over the slow and time-consuming practices traditionally used for the preparation and transmission of regional foods. The 1926 National Agency for the Scientific Organisation of Work invaded the kitchen and pressed for households to use electric stoves and boilers and aluminium pots and pans. The pasta machine, through which dough is passed and thinned and then cut into strips, was invented. Domestic refrigerators, however, were still rare.

Neither Mussolini nor Italian Fascism survived World War II. After Mussolini's death, the Nazis occupied northern and central Italy and food became very scarce.

Food stamps were distributed but the system did not work, and a black market arose. The arrival of the Americans meant that food once again began to be distributed from the countryside, as well as the chocolate, condensed milk and cookies they brought with them.

HARDSHIP, MIGRATION AND DISPLACEMENT

Postwar reconstruction was slow to take hold in Italy, and while food was not scarce, it was basic. Whether they liked it or not, most Italians were restricted to 'the Mediterranean diet', which used local produce and very little meat. This period of frugality and personal struggle was starkly portrayed by the new stars of Italian neo-realist cinema, including De Sica, Rossellini and Visconti.

Another wave of migration followed the war (and brought Stefano Manfredi and his family to Australia). Internal migration was swept along by rapid industrial growth, with southern farmers and farm workers migrating to the cities of the north to work in the new factories. Consequently, many of the artisanal products revered today were almost lost as their makers clocked on to their new industrial life. Luckily, another revolution, known as Slow Food, began in the late 20th century, which saved many of them.

Some of the events at this time seemed to be in conflict. For example, women moved into the workforce and out of the kitchen, often embracing feminism to reject their role as home providers. This encouraged the use of more industrial pre-prepared foods. At the same time, those southerners moving north who craved their regional products – for example, buffalo mozzarella and salami – imported them and spread their use around the country.

PASTA ASCIUTTA: FROM BEGINNING TO BANNING

Dried pasta, or *pasta asciutta*, was made possible when the Arabs who conquered Sicilia in 902 imported the high-gluten, low-moisture *Triticum durum* to Italy from what was then called Abyssinia and is now Ethiopia. Although fresh pasta (known as *laganon*) was known to the Greeks, the dried version was a huge advance, enabling this quintessentially Italian food to be stored and transported and used on long sea voyages. At the time of Muhammad al-Idrisi's book, *The Book of Roger* (1154), and perhaps even well before then, pasta was being manufactured in Sicilia and exported to Calabria. Over time it became a staple, but more than that, an emblematic Italian food.

The 1930s saw an unprecedented assault on an Italian tradition from an unlikely source: Futurist artist, poet and polemicist Filippo Marinetti. Marinetti's Futurism was a movement whose manifesto was outlined in a cookbook comprising recipes that were almost totally uncookable – and if not uncookable, certainly inedible. They were poetic and erotic fantasies aimed at promoting such credos as 'the aesthetics of the machine' and 'liberation from aesthetic terror'.

Most scandalously, Marinetti and the Futurists called for 'the abolition of *pasta asciutta*' (but, curiously, not of fresh pasta), which, it was claimed, was '40 per cent less nutritious than meat, fish or pulses, [and] ties today's Italians with its tangled threads to Penelope's slow looms and to somnolent old sailing ships in search of wind'. Needless to say, the Italian people paid little attention to such an outrageous agenda.

The 1980s saw two imports, one not so influential and one with major ramifications for Italy and the world. Nouvelle cuisine arrived from France but never really made an impact among the Italians, who on the whole remained faithful to their culinary roots. And fast food arrived from America, McDonald's being the first to land.

FOOD WARS

The Slow Food movement (see also page 351) has done much to rekindle interest in regional and artisanal food in Italy. But there is an opposing force that, through its sheer size, may prevail, as it appears to be doing in the rest of the world: the supermarket chain.

The first supermarket in Italy opened on 13 April 1957 in Milan, and by 2012 there were 26 supermarket chains in the country. However, there is a strong and numerous opposing force at work. Not long before that first supermarket opened, in 1951, Italy had 951,382 stores and small businesses catering to the public; 801,837 of these had only one or two employees. Today, these 'Mama and Papa stores' still play an important role. 'Italians were accustomed to small shops, and friendly relations with the shopkeeper,' says Emanuela Scarpellini, associate professor at the University of Milan and an expert on the history of the Italian supermarket. 'It was part of the social tissue of everyday life. You knew the shopkeeper and he knew you.'

Currently, the small foodstore and grocery sector represents 60 per cent of the existing selling space in Italy, compared to 20 per cent in Spain, 13 per cent in the UK and 19 per cent in Germany and France. But since 1991, over 30 per cent of these small stores have closed. The question that has to be asked is: how much do Italians want to keep their small local stores in the face of economic hardship? In other words, how much is a food culture worth? Or alternatively, does Italy want to remain Slow and small?

AGRICULTURE IN THE 21ST CENTURY

In 1999, Italy's agricultural sector employed under 6 per cent of the working population, except in the southern regions of Basilicata, Calabria and Molise, where it accounted for just over 20 per cent of local employment. The decline in agriculture is in line with all other western European countries and is due specifically to the effects of the Common Agricultural Policy (CAP) of the European Union (EU), which ensures that subsidies and incentives are offered in order to sustain prices and guarantee a certain level of income to farmers.

With only 5 per cent of its land under cultivation, Italy is not self-sufficient in agricultural products. And yet it enjoys an abundance of agricultural resources, productivity is high, and the Mediterranean climate ensures that a variety of products are available for both internal consumption and external markets. Italy is a world leader in olive oil production and a major exporter of rice, tomatoes and wine. An increasing number of consumers have turned towards organically grown produce, especially after the BSA or 'mad cow disease' scare.

Today Italy concentrates on quality in the dairy-farming sector, exporting only a handful of distinctive and high-quality cheeses such as parmesan, mozzarella and gorgonzola rather than entering the mass-produced arena. Fruit is grown almost exclusively in the south, with most of the oranges and lemons coming from Sicilia. Apples grow in Trentino-Alto Adige. But the real strength of Italian agriculture is the production of olives, wine and tomatoes.

ITALIAN FOOD TODAY

Italy in the 21st century has entered the modern world, with all that world's positive and negative aspects. Domestically, longer hours and more women in the workforce mean more short cuts in the kitchen. On the other hand, Italian families have responded to the pressures of work versus life by having fewer children in order to maintain their living standards. And we can only hope that Italian men go to the kitchen for more reasons than just to stir the polenta!

At the time of writing, there is a contraction in the number of meals eaten outside the home because of financial pressures: instead of going to lavish restaurants, Italian families will opt for a good pizza with friends or a family meal at a nearby osteria.

There has been no diminution in the love of Italians for their own food – every few months, an internet or newspaper poll reveals that the majority of Italians would feel anxious or uncomfortable if deprived of pasta for even a few days. (So much for Marinetti.) To protect their culinary culture, there is a continuing struggle within the country against the forces of globalisation. With Slow Food at the forefront, along with farmers and ordinary Italians, the fight against genetic modification and the proliferation of outlets such as McDonald's continues, with some success: Italy has one-third the number of McDonald's outlets of Britain, France and Germany.

Generally, it could be said of current Italian cuisine that simplicity has replaced the austerity of the Italian diet of yesteryear. As noted in this history, the bourgeoisification of regional cuisines that began in the 18th century has continued to the present day and, as is the case in China, regional cuisines are the haute cuisines and no court or metropolitan culinary idiom has gained the upper hand. Even the movement in the rest of the world towards 'molecular gastronomy', or what is called in Italy *cucina moderna*, has had limited success. Italians, as always, prefer their own traditional food.

Perhaps the apogee of Italian cuisine today is to be found in that style of eating house

PROTECTED FOODS

Two other innovations adopted in Italy are designed to improve the quality of its food and wine.

The European Union's 1992 regulation 2081 allowed for the registration of products as *Designazione d'Origine Protetta* (DOP, meaning Protected Designation of Origin) or *Indicazione Geografica Protetta* (IGP, meaning Protected Designation of Geographic Origin). It protects the integrity of local and artisan foods and gives the buyers of these foods a guarantee as to their authenticity. In addition, it protect the holders of the designations from the fraudulent use of their product names. For example, the makers of the designated Parmigiano Reggiano were able to stop cheesemakers in Wisconsin, USA from using their name. In 2003 additional foodstuffs, including bread, pasta, biscuits, vinegar and many others, were able to apply to register.

Many years earlier, in 1963, a similar system was adapted from the French for Italian wines (see the Wine History section).

called the osteria. Here you will find best-quality local produce transformed into simple regional dishes by cooks who understand the way the food should taste, and hospitable service, often with the entire staff coming from one family. Even in these difficult times, the osteria will offer a carefully calibrated balance between quality and price.

It is the simplicity of Italian food that appeals – not just to the Italians, but to the rest of the world's people, for whom it remains one of the most popular cuisines. It can now be revealed that the real reason for writing this book is to get you to go to Italy and to eat and drink your way around it, because that is where you will taste *la vera cucina italiana*. Until then, you have Stefano Manfredi's recipes. *Buon appetito!*

ITALIAN WINE GRAPE VARIETIES

Wine production in Italy predates the Etruscans. When the Greeks arrived, they were so astounded at the proliferation of grapes that they called the land Enotria: the land of the vine.

Italy produces a lot of wine. It grows more grapes than any other country and accounts for almost a quarter of the world's wine exports. When it comes to indigenous grape varieties, Italy has hundreds. As recently as 20 years ago the number was thought to be around 2000, but with modern DNA testing this number has contracted. In many cases the same grape was found to have several different names according to local dialects.

According to a recent study of the 1368 known grape varieties (see *Wine Grapes* by Jancis Robinson, Julie Harding and José Vouillamoz, published in 2012), Italy has more than a third, with 377. France comes in next at 204, then Spain (84), Greece (77), Portugal (77) and Germany (76). The figure for Italy does not include the many non-native vines that have been planted, such as chardonnay, the cabernets, syrah and pinot noir.

So making sense of the wines of Italy can seem a daunting task, but two points can be made to help give some assurance. Firstly, no other wine-producing nation has improved its wines across the board as dramatically as Italy has in the last 20 years. This means that when you choose an Italian wine, its quality will almost always be good (and often will be great), which was not the case that long ago. Secondly, Italy has so many grape varieties, styles and tastes that its wines represent an unparalleled taste adventure.

It would be impossible to cover every grape variety here, so I've highlighted the most important as well as some of my favourite emerging varieties. The following list will give you a sense of the vast landscape of Italian wine, with the ultimate aim of encouraging you to try something different. The future looks very bright for Italian wines as a new generation of young winemakers rediscover old varieties and use new (and old) techniques to add to an already exciting repertoire.

WHITE WINES

Arneis

Native to the red-wine-dominant region of Piemonte, traditionally arneis was grown dotted throughout vineyards of nebbiolo and barbera and was often used to soften red wines in much the same way as the French use viognier to soften syrah. It was pioneers such as Ceretto, with their benchmark Blange, who developed it into one of Piemonte's premier whites. Typically arneis is fruity with hints of grapefruit and apple and a slight smokiness.

Carricante

Up until the middle of last century, this native Sicilian variety was planted throughout the island. Tastes changed and carricante fell so out of favour that it is now confined primarily to areas of higher elevation to the east and south of Mount Etna, 950–1050 metres (3117–3445 feet) above the base of the volcano. It is noted for its wonderful acidity and a certain minerality, which contribute to quite remarkable longevity.

Catarratto

Most catarratto is fairly bland, and for this reason it is used in Marsala and the vermouth houses of Piemonte. But there are several high-quality clones, including catarratto ammantidatu, catarratto fimminedda, catarratto bagascedda and catarratto mattu, that when treated with care and respect in the vineyard and winery can produce rich, spicy and mouth-filling wines that recall the beeswax-like characters associated with viognier.

Chardonnay

Chardonnay has been in Italy since the early 1950s. It is the tenth most planted grape, at around 12,000 hectares (29,650 acres), but accounts for only about 1.8 per cent of total Italian wine production. It has adapted to most climates in Italy, as it has to climates throughout the rest of the wine world. Most interesting from an Italian viewpoint is chardonnay's use in blending with local varieties such as grechetto, friulano and even inzolia.

Cortese di Gavi

Along with Arneis, Gavi is the other well-known dry white wine of Piemonte. The area in which it grows was once part of the city-state of Genoa and is influenced by Liguria's Mediterranean climate. It is a difficult grape that ripens unevenly, but when made well the wine ranges from light and refreshing with a chalky minerality to more concentrated apple and peach flavours.

Falanghina

Falanghina's home, where it is thought to have originated, is the Falerno del Massico DOC zone along the coast just north of Naples. Typically falanghina is juicy with a touch of pine resin on the finish, but it can also have floral tones, especially citrus blossom. Often it is blended with other grapes of the region, most notably greco, verdeca and coda di volpe.

Fiano di Avellino

Fiano is perhaps the most interesting white grape of Campania. At its best it is grown around the mountain town of Avellino, near densely wooded slopes. It has flavours of nuts (pine nut and hazelnut) with a persistent aroma of mountain herbs and a slight smokiness. In the best examples, fiano develops an intangible but perceptible 'wild' or 'feral' quality, in a good way. The best examples are medium-bodied and lower in alcohol than many modern whites.

Friulano

The full name of this grape is tocai friulano. Its origins are uncertain, but some say it came from Hungary's Tokaj wine region. It is considered a distant relative of sauvignon blanc. Today it is cultivated primarily in the three northern regions of Friuli, Veneto and eastern Lombardia. It is in the first of these regions that it finds its purest expression as well as its name, producing fleshy wines with flavours of peach, pear and almond.

Garganega

This is the important white grape of the provinces of Verona and Vicenza and the key grape for soave. Garganega is thought to have ties to the large trebbiano family, thus placing it squarely with the ancient Etruscans.

It matures late and has a thick, dark-yellow, almost red skin when fully ripe. Its principal aromas are of almonds and white flowers, and the best examples can age well. It blends very well with trebbiano and chardonnay. See page 27 for information on sweet wine made using garganega.

Gewürztraminer

There are discordant views as to the origin of this aromatic grape, which is also called traminer. The German ampelographer Goethe suggested its origins were around the town of Tramin (now Termeno) in Italy's Alto Adige region (formerly part of Austria). Others suggest it came from the French Alsace region. In any case, it is dispersed throughout the world as one of the noble varieties. In Italy it is grown predominantly in Alto Adige, where it attains a purity of freshness, spice and good acid to finish.

Greco di Tufo

Greco, as the name suggests, was brought by the Greeks to Italy, specifically the south, 2500 years ago. It is now planted widely in the regions of Puglia, Campania and Calabria. Perhaps its finest expression is the Greco di Tufo DOC zone in high vineyards around Avellino, north of Naples. Here it achieves certain qualities akin to riesling in minerality, citrus notes and a touch of kerosene.

Grillo

Grillo is the traditional grape used to make Marsala. It is grown predominantly in western Sicily in a triangle roughly bordered by Palermo in the north, Menfi in the south and Marsala in the west. A crisp wine with good acidity, it is lightly textured with good fruit sweetness, and finishes dry and clean.

Grüner Veltliner

Another of the Austrian-connection varietals, Grüner Veltliner's parents include traminer and an obscure, almost extinct variety called St Georgener-Rebe. It is Austria's most-planted variety and in Italy is predominantly grown in Alto Adige. The best examples come from steep, high-altitude vineyards in the most northerly DOC zone and are characterised by pure rich fruit, complex minerality and sword-like acidity, all in perfect balance.

Kerner

One of Kerner's parents is German riesling; the other is schiava grossa, a native of the ex-Austrian part of Italy: the autonomous region of Alto Adige. It is a recent invention (1969) named rather obscurely after Justinus Kerner, a 19th-century writer of drinking songs. Unlike in Germany, where it suffers from a crisis of identity, Kerner's small but high-quality presence in Italy is made into full-flavoured, delicately spiced dry wines.

Malvasia

Though the name Malvasia has its roots in the Greek Peloponnesian city of Monovasia and a famous wine from Malta, it is nonetheless a general title that includes many unrelated vines, both white and red. The vines can, however, be grouped into two distinct categories: those with light aromatics that recall moscato, and those with less perfume. Either way, in the hands of a skilled vigneron malvasia can sing many tunes – still, sparkling and sweet.

Müller-Thurgau

Much more famous in its German homeland, Müller-Thurgau can be exceptional in the Italian Alpine regions of Trentino and Alto Adige. The grape does very well at high altitudes of more than 500 metres (1640 feet). Grown at these heights, Müller-Thurgau develops exotic aromas of dried stone fruits, flowers and mountain herbs, all the while maintaining freshness and crisp acidity.

READING ITALIAN WINE LABELS

There are two basic categories that all EU countries use: Quality Wines and Table Wines. After that, in Italy it gets a little more complicated.

Italy's first laws governing the quality of its wines were introduced in 1900. Then, in 1963, a law was passed that defined 'quality' and 'table' and introduced the concept of controlled origin. In 1992, these rules were revised and are what you will find in use today.

The system defines such variables as the geographic area of an appellation, the grapes permitted to be used and what proportions are admitted for each variety of grape in a blend, etc.

These are the designations, starting with the lowest quality:

- *Vino da Tavola* (Table Wine)
- IGT (*Indicazione Geografica Tipica*, meaning Typical Geographic Indication)
- DOC (*Denominazione di Origine Controllata*, meaning Appellation of Controlled Origin)
- DOCG (*Denominazione di Origine Controllata e Garantita*, meaning Appellation of Controlled and Guaranteed Origin).

The bottom designation of the pyramid, Vino da Tavola, means only that the wine is made in Italy. T used to mean an ordinary wine for local consumption, but times change (see below). At the top of the pyramid, DOCG is the full bottle, the *garantita* is a guarantee of quality, denoting that the wine has been tasted, but this is not always reliable.

Other words you may see on bottles, allowed by some appellations for wines made using particular production techniques, are:

- *Classico* (Classic) – a wine produced in the most typical and renowned area of the appellation
- *Superiore* (Superior) – a wine having a percentage of alcohol by volume higher than the normal requirement for the appellation
- *Riserva* (Reserve) – a wine that has gone through a longer ageing process than the normal requirement for the appellation.

Here's where it gets a little complicated. You may have heard of the Super Tuscans – a name for wines made in Toscana whose makers didn't like the restrictions placed on them by a DOC and opted for Vino da Tavola so they would be freer to use the grapes they wanted in the proportions they wanted to blend them, for example. These wines, especially in the Chianti region, were for some time infinitely superior to DOCG wines. But the law has moved ahead to put these super Vino da Tavola wines back in the system by introducing a new category, IGT (*Indicazione Geografica Tipica*, meaning Typical Geographic Indication). This category, covering wide production areas, allows winemakers more freedom in their choice of grapes and production methods, and producers of quality wines are being attracted to it.

Finally, here are a few abbreviations reserved for special wines:

- VSQPRD (*Vino Spumante di Qualità Prodotto in Regione Determinata*, or Quality Sparkling Wine Produced in Determined Region) – a quality sparkling wine produced in a determined appellation-of-controlled-origin area
- VLQPRD (*Vino Liquoroso di Qualità Prodotto in Regione Determinata*, or Quality Fortified Wine Produced in Determined Region) – a quality fortified wine produced in a determined appellation-of-controlled-origin area
- VFQPRD (*Vino Frizzante di Qualità Prodotto in Regione Determinata*, or Quality Slightly Sparkling Wine Produced in Determined Region) – a quality slightly sparkling wine produced in a determined appellation-of-controlled-origin area.

The problem with all these legal appellations, in Italy as elsewhere, is that some producers adhere only to the minimum requirements. The best way to guarantee excellence is the name of the producer – and that is something you have to learn for yourself by frequent, careful and assiduous tasting. Not really a hardship!

There are books to help you on your journey. Two of the best of them are *Vino Italiano: The Regional Wines of Italy* and the two volumes by Nicholas Belfrage.

Nosiola

Nosiola is the Trentino region's one true native grape variety. Its name seems to be derived from the Italian nocciola, or hazelnut, which is one of the characteristic flavours of the finished wine. It is grown principally in the area north of Lake Garda and produces fresh, low-acid wines with lemon-apple-hazelnut flavours and a particularly refreshing mineral finish.

Passerina

Once widely planted in its native Le Marche region, the passerina grape fell out of favour in the 1960s and saw a steep decline. In the past 15 years there has been a concerted effort by a handful of winemakers to replant, especially around the southern province of Ascoli Piceno. The wines show good aromatic intensity with floral tones and high but balanced acidity.

Pecorino

Another variety of eastern central origin, pecorino was kept from extinction (just) in old vineyards at the foothills of the Macerata and Ascoli Piceno provinces in the Le Marche region. Also grown in neighbouring Abruzzo, the wines can show complex aromatics of anise with a savoury, almost salty palate, making them an excellent accompaniment to seafood.

Pigato

As with many of Italy's indigenous grapes, the origins of pigato are disputed. Some claim it is a relative of vermentino, others that it is a native of Castelli Romani and was brought to Liguria by Caesar's legions. Some say it was imported from Greece, while others relate it to arneis. It is grown almost exclusively on the coast of Liguria's Riviera di Ponente, where it produces robust and fruity wines. The best of these have an extraordinary freshness and seem to explode on the palate with a profusion of citrus peel and herbs.

Pinot Bianco

Pinot bianco, called pinot blanc in its native France, has its roots in Burgundy. It is planted widely throughout northern Italy but, apart from use in the occasional franciacorta sparkling blend, is only really taken seriously by producers in Friuli and Alto Adige. With good reason: pinot bianco does well grown on prime cool-climate hillsides, where it produces wines with delicate perfume, good minerality and weight on the palate, and the ability to age well.

Pinot Grigio

A member of the large family of pinot grapes that includes noir, blanc, meunier, auxerrois and teinturie, to name a few, pinot grigio was introduced from its native France, where it is called pinot gris, in the early 1800s. The popularity of Italian pinot grigio throughout the world in the past 15 years has seen its plantings increase in the three major northern growing regions: Veneto, Friuli and Alto Adige. Its wide success appears to be down to less skin contact compared to French Alsace versions, which keeps the wine lighter in body and avoids the copper colour.

Prosecco

This charming sparkling wine, a traditional favourite aperitivo of Venetians (and Italians generally), has conquered the world. It is made from prosecco grapes (though 15 per cent of other varieties is allowed) grown in nine provinces situated in the regions of Friuli-Venezia Giulia and the Veneto. The grand cru of prosecco comes from the Cartizze vineyard, 300 metres (984 feet) above the valley floor near the town of Valdobbiadene. The Cartizze wines tend to have more structure and complexity and can accompany antipasti and salumi.

Ribolla Gialla

This native Friulian variety is grown almost exclusively in the Collio and Colli Orientali that border Slovenia. Plantings continue eastwards over the border. In total less than 100 hectares (247 acres) is under vine, but the best of the wines are eagerly awaited each vintage. Subtle on the nose with dried fruits and nuts on the palate, there are hints of honey with a perfectly balanced acidity to finish.

Riesling

Think of Italian wines and riesling would be well down the list, if it were on it at all. But all across the northern regions producers are finding out that this variety has considerable potential. As you would expect, riesling is grown in greater quantities in Italy's Germanic enclave of Alto Adige. The best examples declare an admiration for those of Mosel but at the same time have a minerality and terroir that are uniquely Italian.

Roscetto

The only 100 per cent roscetto wine that we know of is produced by the Falesco winery, situated 70 kilometres (43 miles) north of Rome near the border with Umbria. Owner and winemaker Riccardo Cotarella says it is an ancient local variety that is probably related to greco, because locally it is also known by that name; however, recent DNA profiling has discounted this relationship. It is also known as rossetto as the grapes turn a light rose when ripe. Falesco Farentano consistently produces a wine with a sumptuous nose and a creamy, rich and complex body. Jancis Robinson, in *Wine Grapes*, describes it as 'a rich but very well-balanced varietal wine, reminiscent of a top-notch Saint-Aubin'.

Sauvignon Blanc

Simply called sauvignon in Italy, this variety has its roots in Bordeaux, France but more famously produces wines in Sancerre and Loire as well as many parts of the New World. Sauvignon is immediately recognisable for its distinctive aromatics. In Italy the best examples come from the northern regions of Friuli and Alto Adige and are almost exclusively vinified without the use of oak.

Sylvaner

Thought to have originated in Transylvania, which at one time was part of the Austrian Empire, sylvaner is a cross between traminer and the obscure Österreichisch-Weiß ('Austrian white'). A grape that is in decline in Germany and France's Alsace region, it has found an ideal home in Alto Adige's Isarco Valley, where it produces a medium-weight, lightly aromatic wine with a steely backbone and fresh minerality.

Timorasso

A wine made from timorasso appears to have been highly prized by Leonardo da Vinci. This native vine was once grown widely in the regions of Liguria, Piemonte, Lombardia and Emilia-Romagna. Rediscovered in the mid-1980s, it is now confined mostly to the Colli Tortonesi DOC zone in Piemonte, from Alessandria and east to the border of Lombardia. With care in the vineyard and winery, timorasso can produce well-structured white wines with floral and honey notes on the nose, subtle minerality and fresh acidity on the palate with good length. These wines can age well.

Trebbiano d'Abruzzo

The trebbiano family of vines is the most cultivated white wine group in Italy, but on the whole it produces wines that are at best simple and mediocre. It is present to a greater or lesser extent in almost 80 DOCs, both white and red, as a blending component. However, the central Italian regions of Emilia-Romagna and Abruzzo Trebbiano produce wines of great structure and texture that are complex and long-lived.

Verdicchio

Once upon a time this native varietal of the Le Marche region was made into verdicchio wine in industrial quantities and exported by the shipload in fish-shaped bottles. A little more than a generation ago, however, some small producers began experimenting with low yields and concentrating their efforts on quality. The two DOC zones are the larger Verdicchio dei Castelli di Jesi, occupying the rolling hills west of the major port of Ancona, and Verdicchio di Metalica, further west in higher, mountainous terrain. Great verdicchio has a sour fruit quality on the nose and palate that is reminiscent of tart apples, quince and, often, lime. On the finish there is a bitter-almond nuttiness that seems to define verdicchio.

Verduzzo Friulano

Native to the Friuli-Venezia Giulia region, verduzzo friulano (not to be confused with the inferior Sardinian verduzzo trevigiano) grows in the eastern Veneto but produces higher-quality fruit in Friuli, most notably in the Colli Orientali. While it is most often made into delicious and distinctive sweet wines, a few producers vinify verduzzo as a dry wine with good complexity that is rich but also soft as it ages and has a good to great depth of flavour and characteristic bitter almond on the finish.

Vermentino

The best bet as to how this grape came to Italy is via the 400-year occupation of Sardinia by the Spanish. Vermentino has emerged to be not only Sardinia's star white wine but also highly regarded on the mainland, especially western Toscana in the Bolgheri province and the hills around Lucca. It is grown in Australia as producers and public alike love it for its salty, savoury flavours that go so well with seafood.

Vernaccia di San Gimignano and Oristano

The name vernaccia applies to a disparate group of vines scattered in various regions. The most famous and distinctive is vernaccia di San Gimignano, which is grown around the comune of the same name in the province of Siena in central Toscana. It is crisp, elegant and floral, finishing with a note of bitter almond. Vernaccia di Oristano, from the western side of the island of Sardinia, is not related to its Tuscan namesake. It is made in an oxidative style, like a dry sherry, and is heavily influenced by four centuries of Spanish rule. It is a rarity outside Sardinia, but worth seeking out.

Vitovska

Vitovska has been cultivated in the province of Trieste in north-eastern Italy for as long as anyone can remember. It is thought to be native to that area as well as to neighbouring Slovenia and is one of the most exciting of all new-wave Italian white grapes, producing some outstanding wines. But 'new wave' is probably misleading – the protagonists making wines from vitovska are at the forefront of the natural wine movement. The wines can show an astounding array of flavours and scents, including tropical fruits, stone fruits, flowers, citrus, beeswax and smoke. They are able to accompany a much wider range of foods than other white wines.

Zibibbo

Zibibbo is part of the large moscato or muscat family and is also known as muscat of Alexandria. The Arabs introduced the grape to the island of Pantelleria when they occupied Sicilia between 827 and 1061. Ordinarily zibibbo is made into the sweet moscato di Pantelleria, where the grapes are dried by the sirocco, a hot wind that blows across from the Sahara. There are, however, a few producers who make zibibbo as a dry wine. It is generally given a lot of skin contact, which imparts tannins, body and flavour. There are flowers, especially orange blossoms, on the nose, with the shock of a mineral-dry palate and good acidity. When made well, these wines are some of the most striking and characterful one can hope to experience.

RED WINES

Aglianico and Aglianico del Vulture

Aglianico is an ancient grape variety thought to have arrived with the Greeks around 700–600 BCE. It is grown primarily in the southern regions of Campania, Basilicata, Puglia and Molise and loves sun and heat (it has found its way to Australia with promising results). Grown on the slopes of the extinct volcano of Monte Vulture in northern Basilicata, the grape known as aglianico del Vulture produces wines of the highest quality. Often the vineyards are located on lava channels known as pozzolane. The wines produced here are unique, with intensely aromatic, rich, ripe fruit. They are full-bodied with firm but fine tannins and acidity, and the ability to age for many years.

Barbera

As far as native red varieties go, barbera is the second most planted after sangiovese. It is grown in the regions of Piemonte, Lombardia and Emilia-Romagna and is a favourite emerging variety in Australia. It is in Piemonte, barbera's spiritual home, that it achieves the highest quality. In the rolling hills of Monferrato, the Langhe and the province of Asti, barbera produces sublime wines that range from deep ruby to almost pure purple and are high in acid with fine, silky tannins.

Cabernet Sauvignon

It's thought that the cabernet family – sauvignon, franc, merlot, petit verdot and malbec – has been in Italy since around 1835. In 1877 the cabernets were catalogued as part of the varieties grown in the famous wine university at Conegliano, in the northern Veneto. Today cabernet sauvignon is planted primarily in the northern regions as well as in Toscana. Close-planted, high-density vineyards that favour quality have been a feature only since the early 1980s; they are now maturing and wines from these plantings are excellent. The two wines that are to a large extent responsible for the quality revolution in Toscana of the late 1970s and early 1980s are both blends containing a measure of cabernet sauvignon: the great sassicaia (cabernet sauvignon/franc) and tignanello (sangiovese/cabernet sauvignon/franc) have been inspirations for generations of winemakers throughout Italy.

Cannonau

Cannonau is what most people know as grenache, a grape of Spanish origin that the Spaniards brought to the island of Sardinia. It is the most-planted black grape on the island, taking up 20 per cent of all vineyards. Having been cultivated on the island for several centuries, cannonau has taken on its own peculiar regional characteristics. At its best it produces wines with soft fruit characters such as raspberry and strawberry. It can have spicy/peppery tones and a soft, smooth palate.

Carignano del Sulcis

There is conjecture as to the origins of carignano. Some believe it to have originated in North Africa, perhaps Algeria or Tunisia, then making its way to Spain and France before coming to Sardinia. Others suggest its origins are in Asia Minor, and that it was brought by the Phoenicians to ancient Carthage in North Africa, then to Sardinia, and then Spain and France. It is a grape that loves the coast, especially in the south-western part of Sardinia known as Sulcis.

Carignano thrives on heat and poor, sandy soils. It produces a wine that is silky, almost creamy, with great concentration and ripe dark berry fruits.

Cesanese

Cesanese is the Lazio region's main red grape. The name is derived from the village of Cesano in the Castelli Romani, south of Rome. There are two main types: the larger-berried and more widespread cesanese comune, and the small-berried, higher-quality cesanese di affile. This latter clone produces its best wines in the DOC zone of Cesanese di Olevano Romano, around the beautiful town of Olevano Romano, and the DOCG zone of Cesanese del Piglio around the towns of Anagni and Piglio. It is a frustratingly difficult grape to ripen properly, but in the hands of a skilled maker it produces a medium-bodied wine with velvety tannins and a wonderful perfume recalling mulberries and lychees.

Corvina blend

Corvina is the major of the trinity of grapes used for a series of four important red wines made in the province of Verona, just north of the city (the other two are rondinella and molinara, though other varieties can be used in a small percentage). The first and simplest is valpolicella, which is made in varying styles from light to medium-bodied. The same combination of grapes can be picked late, laid on straw mats to dry for over 100 days and then vinified into full-bodied, complex and long-lived amarone. The pressings (seeds, skins, etc.) left over from making amarone are added to an amount of valpolicella wine for an extended maceration to produce a wine known as ripasso, which is somewhere between the two parent wines. Finally there is recioto, the original centuries-old ancestor of the other three. Grapes for recioto are left to raisin even more than amarone. During vinification the conversion of sugar to alcohol is arrested at a certain point to produce a massively rich, sweet red wine of wonderful complexity.

Dolcetto

After nebbiolo and barbera, dolcetto is the next red in the Piemonte hierarchy. Rarely found in Italy outside its native region, it produces brilliantly coloured red wines – they are almost purple – with moderate tannins, soft and supple body and, from the top estates, good complexity and a long finish. In Australia dolcetto has some important plantings, most notably at Best's in Victoria's Great Western region: Henry Best planted the first dolcetto here in the 1860s.

Frappato

The origins of frappato are not precise, though recent DNA studies have linked it to sangiovese. It is grown almost exclusively in the province of Ragusa in south-eastern Sicily and is most often blended with nero d'Avola to make cerasuolo di Vittoria, where it brings abundant perfume. In rare cases it is made as a straight varietal, such as Arianna Occhipinti's elegant and beautifully perfumed example.

Groppello

Groppello is a rare grape grown almost exclusively on the western shores of Lake Garda, on the Lombardia side in the province of Brescia, east of the city. It produces a wine of considerable character, with flavours of fruit and intense sweet spice, good firm acidity and firm but balanced tannins. More often it is blended with barbera, croatina and other black grapes to produce the local Riviera del Garda Bresciano DOC.

Lagrein

Recent DNA parentage analysis has pointed to Val Lagarina in Trentino as the origin of lagrein and a noble lineage including teroldego, pinot and syrah. Grown mainly in

Alto Adige and Trentino, it needs a warm site to set fruit and ripen properly. The best wines have intense colour and pronounced red and black berry flavours. Tannins are soft with occasional sweet fruit, and the wine is less savoury than typical Italian reds.

Lambrusco

There is an immense difference between the industrially made lambrusco that is sold in enormous amounts worldwide and the carefully nurtured, charming wines made by a few maestros. Lambrusco is not one grape, though the parent made its way from the Apennine Mountains to settle around the city of Modena, famous for Ferrari and balsamic vinegar. The three principal grapes are the red-stemmed grasparossa, the delicate sorbara and the salamino, the latter so called because its bunches are shaped like little salami. These are wines made for prosciutto and salumi in general.

Merlot

Originally from the Gironde area of south-west France, merlot is particular to the zone of Bordeaux, where it is blended with the cabernet family in Saint-Emilion and made as a pure varietal in Pomerol to produce some of the great reds of the world. Merlot has been in Italy's Trentino and surrounding regions since the late 1800s, but some of the most successful modern wines are made further south in the warmer climate of Toscana.

Merlot blend

Just as in its native Bordeaux, where it is blended with complementary grapes, so too in Italy merlot is used in a melange for its rich, round and generous qualities. In Toscana winemakers have found that it marries extremely well with sangiovese as both grapes bring differing profiles to the blend. As well as traditional Bordeaux blends, some winemakers are opting for more eclectic mixes.

Montepulciano d'Abruzzo

The montepulciano grape bears no relation to the town of the same name in southern Toscana. Its confusion with sangiovese was only sorted out in 1875, but suffice to say that these two grapes account for most of the quality red wines of central Italy. Montepulciano's home is the warmer east coast, with the region of Abruzzo as the centre, extending south to Puglia and north to Romagna. Montepulciano grape skins are rich in polyphenols and require a relatively short maceration to produce soft, fruity reds. Longer maceration releases fine tannins that produce wines of complexity, structure and longevity.

Nebbiolo

Nebbiolo is the grape responsible for some of the greatest red wines of Italy and indeed the world. In Piemonte it makes both barolo and barbaresco – two denominations with countless variations and nuances depending on vineyards and producers. Nebbiolo is extremely temperamental if not grown on a favourable site. It can have high acidity and tough, hard tannins in the hands of inexperienced winemakers, but when good it is capable of poetry, producing wines of meditation and contemplation that age for many decades. In terms of vineyard area it occupies a small fraction, a total of about 200 hectares (494 acres), across Piemonte, Lombardia and Valle d'Aosta. It is bottled in Piemonte as a straight varietal as well as making up various denominations, such as boca and gattinara from the northern provinces. Diverse too are the styles from the Lombardia region's Valtellina province at the foot of the Alps. After trial and error, Australia has found good sites in Victoria's King Valley and Bendigo, and South Australia's Adelaide Hills and McLaren Vale. Others are currently being explored for their potential with nebbiolo.

Nerello Mascalese

A native of Sicilia's east coast, the best nerello mascalese is grown between 350 and 1000 metres (1148 and 3280 feet) up Mount Etna's flanks in terraced, high-density alberello vineyards. The soil is black, volcanic, rich in minerals and poor in humus. There are vines over 100 years old that predate phylloxera, the blight that devastated many of Europe's vineyards in the late 1800s, and there is evidence that grapes have been grown here since ancient times. It is an astonishingly unique terroir where the grapes have acclimatised to a very stressful environment. Nerello mascalese makes up 80 per cent of the Etna DOC, with the remainder being nerello cappuccio. The wines produced are high in alcohol but elegant and powerful, showing great minerality and structure.

Nero d'Avola

Sicilia's most planted black grape by a long way, nero d'Avola has found homes all over the island. As its name suggests, it produces wines that are inky black. Along with high sugar levels and firm acidity that is not reduced by malolactic fermentation, it is the perfect grape for blending with lower-acid varieties such as nerello mascalese and frappato, and even white grapes such as inzolia. Recently there has been a trend to blend nero d'Avola with syrah, with encouraging results.

Nero di Troia

This grape is supposedly named after the city of Troia in northern Puglia, the region forming the 'heel of the boot'. Legend has it that the Greek hero Diomedes, who destroyed the ancient city of Troy, founded Troia. Confined to northern Puglia, above Bari, nero di Troia can produce excellent dark ruby wines with notes of vanilla and dried flowers and strawberry/raspberry scents.

Pignolo

A native of Friuli, pignolo was well on the way to extinction before a small group of passionate viticulturists rescued it from cuttings found in the Abbey of Rosazzo. Wines produced from this scrappy, almost feral-looking vine are highly distinctive, often exhibiting shyness before finally opening up with a palate laden with spice and dark fruit. They have very good ageing potential.

Pinot Nero

This distinguished native of France's Burgundy area is notoriously fickle and very difficult to make good (let alone great) wines from. Pinot nero, as it is called in Italy, prefers a cool climate. To that extent the most successful pinot nero is being made in the north, in Alto Adige predominantly, with a handful of producers in Piemonte as well as some further south in Toscana.

Primitivo

After much conjecture, DNA tests appear to have concluded that primitivo is the same grape as the one the Americans call zinfandel. It probably came to Puglia via the Dalmatian coast across the Adriatic. The primitivo grape relishes warm climates and has done particularly well in Australia. Wines are rich and full bodied, laden with spices such as black pepper, cloves and anise.

Rebo

This grape is named after Dr Rebo Rigotti, who perfected the merlot/teroldego cross at the the Istituto Agrario di San Michele all'Adige, the famous viticultural research centre in the region of Alto Adige. It has come down from the mountains to find its perfect home around the picturesque western shores of Lombardia's Lake Garda. Here it produces wines of deep ruby with scents of ripe red fruits and a touch of spice on the finish.

Refosco

Refosco is one of those old Italian varietals that is in the process of getting a modern makeover in both the vineyard and the winery. Native to the northern region of Friuli, refosco has traditionally been made as a simple quaffing wine but a handful of producers quietly believe it to be the region's grape of the future. In the right hands refosco gives up wines with a rich and chunky stewed-fruit palate rounded off with peppery notes. They have the potential to age well.

Sagrantino

Sagrantino is responsible for some of the most outstanding wines produced in its native region of Umbria. Its principal area is around the comune of Montefalco, with a mere 670 hectares (1656 acres) planted. This grape is considered one of the most tannic of all, but it produces wines of great intensity and concentration together with a capacity to age. The wines are characterised by their violet-black colour, and a bouquet that has aromas of red fruits and cinnamon overlaid with deep earthy notes.

Sangiovese

Sangiovese dominates the wines and vineyards of central Italy and is found in practically all the red wines of Toscana, Umbria and Le Marche. Not only is it made as a pure varietal, but it is also a fundamental component of many blends. It is thought that sangiovese was used by the ancient Etruscans to make their wines. The family is broken into two: sangiovese grosso and sangiovese piccolo. The former is considered the quality branch, producing the two celebrated clones of Brunello di Montalcino and Vino Nobile di Montepulciano. The classic aromas of sangiovese are floral (violets and roses) and red fruits (mulberry, plum and amarena cherry), but once it is matured in large or small oak, there can be vanilla, liquorice, chocolate and coffee.

Sangiovese blend

Sangiovese is supremely suited to blending with other grapes. Traditionally these have been other local red varieties (and once upon a time whites), such as canaiolo, black malvasia, colorino, ciliegiolo and alicante. But with the arrival of the French Bordeaux gang, sangiovese has shown that it can adapt nicely. The first wine to showcase this latter blend possibility was tignanello, whose appearance shook the entire wine industry not only in Toscana but also in Italy generally.

Sangiovese Grosso

I've given this clone of sangiovese its own category simply because it produces wines that exhibit characteristics different from its parent. In the zone where it is grown, sangiovese grosso is simply called brunello and the wine produced is the famous Brunello di Montalcino. In terms of consistently high quality, brunello is the greatest expression of the pure sangiovese grape – albeit with some notable exceptions coming from Chianti Classico Riserva, Vino Nobile di Montepulciano and IGTs.

Schioppettino

In its native region of Friuli, schioppettino is also known as ribolla nera. It is one of a number of local varieties that were destined to disappear until they were resurrected by a handful of small producers. It is notoriously difficult to work with, low in alcohol and capable of citrus-like levels of acidity. In the hands of a good producer it is mauve–red with primary aromatics of wild blackberry and raspberry. With age it develops woodland scents with musk and underbrush.

Syrah

Syrah (or shiraz) is the offspring of the grape varieties dureza (red) and mondeuse blanche (white), a conclusion reached using modern DNA testing a little over a decade ago. The location of syrah's parents has led to the assertion that the grape originated in France's northern Rhône. In Italy it is gaining in significance. While it is rarely bottled as a straight varietal, it is used primarily to blend, especially with nero d'Avola in the south.

Teroldego

The origins of this grape variety are unknown, but when grown on the gravelly soils (made from alluvial detritus) of the Campo Rotaliano plain in Trentino, teroldego wines can reach levels of elegance, complexity and harmony like very few others. They have a striking, intense, almost impenetrable black colour. On the nose they smell of raspberries and blueberries, while the palate has tones of plum and dark chocolate and tannins are ripe, soft and sweet.

Red varietal blends

Blending is not just a grab bag of disparate varietals thrown together: when done with skill, it is an affirmation of a master palate at work. There are examples of obscure varietals that add complexity, richness or spice to a blend – for example, rarities such as marzemino in a menage with merlot and rebo, or teroldego and lagrein married together. These are blended wines that are unique, not only expressing terroir but also the skill of the master blender.

SWEET WINES

Albana di Romagna

This ancient variety goes back to Roman times. Albana is grown almost exclusively in the Apennine foothills between Bologna and Rimini, and the highest-quality wines come from the provinces of Faenza and Forlì. Though the Albana di Romagna DOCG comes in four styles ranging from dry to passito, it is the sweet end of the spectrum where the grape is most interesting. Sweet wines can come from grapes that are late-harvested and then dried or infected on the vine with noble rot.

Brachetto

This aromatic red variety is grown almost exclusively in eastern Piemonte. While it was once thought to be the French Provençal grape braquet, ampelographers now believe the two grapes are not related. Brachetto's most notable wine is brachetto d'Aqui, a charming, low-alcohol, sweet bubbly that has perfumes of flowers and raspberries. It is thought of as a red moscato d'Asti.

Corvina and Carmenere blend

Corvina is the dominant grape in recioto, the original centuries-old ancestor of the dry valpolicella and amarone wines. But among the other grapes allowed in small measure is the obscure Bordeaux variety carmenère, which is related to cabernet franc. Grapes for recioto are left to raisin for several months; during vinification the conversion of sugar to alcohol is arrested at a certain point to produce a massively rich, sweet red wine of wonderful complexity.

Garganega

This is the important white grape of the provinces of Verona and Vicenza and the key grape for soave. As a late-picked sweet wine, namely recioto di soave, it is rich and honeyed with scents of caramel, peach and banana held tightly by refreshing acidity. See page 17 for information on white table wines made using garganega.

Malvasia

Malvasia has been grown on the volcanic Aeolian Islands, especially Salina and Lipari, off the north-eastern tip of Sicilia for as long as can be remembered. The dry heat and volcanic soil produce grapes that are left to late-ripen and then made into either naturale or passito wines. For the former the grapes are simply late-picked and made into a sweet wine, while for the latter they are late-picked and then dried further on mats under the sun. It is this passito, tasting of dried apricots and orange marmalade, that is highly prized.

Moscato

There is nothing more delightful after a meal than a refreshing, palate-cleansing moscato d'Asti. This low-alcohol (5.5 per cent) fragrant, lightly frothing wine smells of roses, musk and a field of white flowers. The style was first developed in the early 17th century by Giovan Battista Croce, who pioneered a method of reducing refermentation to retain a measure of sugar in a wine.

Primitivo

DNA tests appear to have concluded that primitivo is the same grape as the one the Americans call zinfandel. It relishes warm climates and has done particularly well around the ancient town of Manduria. As well as a table wine (see page 25), the DOC provides for sweet naturale and liquoroso versions.

Picolit

Native to Friuli, picolit gets its name from the small bunches the vine produces (in Italian, small is piccolo). This is due to an inherent defect in the vine that prevents it from pollinating its bunches completely. Each bunch has few grapes and these individual fruits mature to an incredible sweetness, producing a particularly delicious wine.

Trebbiano blend

The production and sale of vin santo ('holy wine') was documented in merchants' logbooks of the early Renaissance. Trebbiano and malvasia grapes are late-picked and then laid on straw mats in well-ventilated buildings until the grapes shrivel. Once the wine is made, it is put into small barrels to undergo a controlled process of oxidation and concentration lasting a minimum of three years and often five or even ten years.

Verduzzo Friulano

Native to the Friuli-Venezia Giulia region, verduzzo friulano grows in the eastern Veneto but produces higher-quality fruit in Friuli, most notably in the Colli Orientali. The most famous is ramandolo, which comes from a tiny subzone high up in north-eastern Friuli. The distinctive sweet wines are rich with a great depth of flavour and a characteristic bitter almond on the finish. See page 21 for information on white table wines made using this grape.

THE ITALIAN KITCHEN

EQUIPMENT

There are obvious accoutrements that all modern kitchens need to have, no matter the type of cuisine, but the Italian kitchen needs a few essentials and optional extras to make it an authentic cucina.

A good selection of knives and learning how to sharpen and maintain them is essential. A basic range begins with a paring knife, a medium-sized vegetable knife, a large chef's knife, a boning knife for meat and a filleting knife for fish.

For pots and pans, start with a 15–20 litre stockpot and a couple of smaller 5 litre saucepans. A wide braising pan with a lid is very handy as is a heavy casserole for slow cooking. One large heavy based frypan and a couple of skillets should round off a basic battery.

Mezzaluna

This is a curved half-moon-shaped blade with knobs on either end. It is used for quick chopping by rocking the blade back and forth and when mastered can save time.

Parmesan knife (sometimes called a wedge)

This makes cutting a chunk of the hard cheese easy and less dangerous.

Mortar and Pestle

For preparations such as pesto and salsa verde the result is better, with regard to both taste and texture, if you use a mortar and pestle. They are also quicker to wash than a food processor which many people often prefer because it seems quicker.

Ricer

A sort of large garlic press that is essential to make classic potato gnocchi. You can also use it to make mash potato.

Pasta Making

- Pasta Machine for the serious Italian cook
- Wooden-handled metal scraper for used for scooping dry dough quickly from your work surface
- Scallop-edged cutting wheel for trimming pasta sheets and ravioli
- Large brush for sweeping away excess flour
- Smaller brushes for applying egg wash
- Chitarra, a guitar-like box, for hand-cutting pasta that results in chewy, textured spaghetti (this is optional).
- Cutters of various sizes are needed for making ravioli, cappelletti, tortellini and the like. There are also regional pasta cutters such as the beautiful wooden corzetti moulds from Liguria.

THE PANTRY

The Italian pantry needs to contain specific items. Though the list below is certainly not exhaustive, from it you can begin to cook from this book. As you explore the recipes, your Italian pantry will grow.

Extra virgin olive oil

It's the ultimate oil – nothing else comes close for sheer natural goodness and the flavour of the Mediterranean. It has to be extra virgin: anything less has undergone industrial extraction processes that use some fairly harsh chemicals. Don't be afraid to cook with it. Both shallow-fried and deep-fried foods benefit from the fact that this oil has never been heated, which means that all its antioxidants are intact. Keep different olive oils in small quantities for different uses. Olive oil that is soft and gently fruity is good for everyday cooking and dressing delicate salads, while spicy, tangy oil is better for more robust dishes, such as hearty soups, meats and shellfish. (For more information on olive oil, see page 32.)

Vinegar

Good red or white wine vinegar, together with extra virgin olive oil, is all that is needed to dress Italian-style salads. Look for single-grape-variety vinegars, such as barolo, moscato and barbera, to add different nuances to dishes. Balsamic vinegar is excellent in sauces and as a final note for grilled meats and vegetables as well as strawberries – but use the best you can afford. Vincotto or saba is boiled grape must and can be used in desserts as well as savoury dishes such as roast duck or suckling pig. (For more information on vinegars, see page 168.)

Preserved tomatoes

Tomatoes are used extensively in Italian cuisine but are only in season and in peak condition for a short time. Therefore, three basic preparations have been developed so tomatoes can be used all year round: peeled whole or in pieces (pelati), puree (passato or passata) and paste (conserva or concentrato). While the first two can be used in place of fresh tomatoes, tomato paste (also known as concentrated puree) should be used sparingly – a teaspoon in sauce and a tablespoon in a pot of minestrone.

Prosciutto

Great Italian Prosciutto di Parma, San Daniele or the many regional styles like Sicilian Prosciutto dei Monti Nebrodi or Campanian Prosciutto di Pietraroja have a sweetness and elegance to their flavour firstly because of the quality of the pigs and secondly the way they are cured. Their taste is fine and complex, the salt almost imperceptible and the fat porcelain white. While good prosciutto is always good to have on hand to serve as an impromptu snack, it's also good to cook with.

Cheese

The essential cheese for the Italian and, increasingly, Australian kitchen is either Grana Padano or its regal cousin, Parmigiano Reggiano. The first is generally less expensive because it has been aged for a shorter period, but both can be used for grating, in cooking, in salads or as part of a cheese course. Freshly made ricotta is also indispensable. Other useful Italian cheeses are fresh mozzarella, taleggio, gorgonzola, fontina and pecorino.

Ricotta

Ricotta is made by heating whey until the remaining milk solids rise to the surface in creamy little lumps. These lumps are skimmed off and transferred to perforated baskets to drain. After three or four hours the ricotta is ready to use. Fresh, creamy ricotta can be enjoyed for breakfast, drizzled with good honey. But it is also delicious in many traditional preparations such as spinach and ricotta gnocchi, lasagna, cannelloni, ricotta cakes or simply crumbled through pasta.

Pasta

A few packets of dried durum-wheat pasta will save time and effort when preparing last-minute meals. Choose supermarket brands on price, but artisan pastas rely on particular wheat, a particular extrusion method and slow drying for superlative flavour.

Other necessary alimentary bits and pieces that need to be on stand-by in your pantry or fridge include:

- good anchovies in small jars
- capers in salt rather than vinegar (the ones in salt taste better)
- breadcrumbs, preferably homemade
- various types of olive, which can be snacked on as well as used in dishes
- dried porcini mushrooms for using in risotto, soup, braises and sauces
- Italian rice for making risotto, arancini and rice soup
- polenta (cornmeal) as an alternative to bread and a must for osso buco (see also pages 34 and 41)
- beans and pulses such as lentils, borlotti beans, cannellini beans and chickpeas
- a small piece of pancetta (air-dried pork belly)
- saffron for use in risotto and other dishes
- couscous

ITALIAN EXTRA VIRGIN OLIVE OIL

I have for years been trying to figure out the source of the often-propagated misinformation that you should not heat olive oil, you should not cook with olive oil and, above all, you should not deep-fry with olive oil because it burns. Many cookbooks, magazines and food writers have perpetuated these untruths and continue to do so.

While researching this book, I came across a section in *The Physiology of Taste* by Brillat-Savarin, which was first published in 1825. It's in Meditation VII: Theory of Frying: 'Experience tells us that olive oil should only be used with things which are soon cooked, and which do not demand too high a temperature, because prolonged ebullition develops an empyreumatic and disagreeable taste produced by a few particles of pulp, which can, being impossible to be gotten rid of, carbonize.'

Nothing could be further from the truth. Cooks of the Mediterranean have known for centuries that olive oil is wonderful not only to eat in its raw state but also as a cooking medium, even when deep-frying.

But don't take my word for it – let's have a look at the facts. The critical consideration when using any oil for cooking is its smoke point, or the point at which an oil begins to break down and form nasty substances that can be harmful and cause the food cooked in it to taste rather unpleasant. Here is what the International Olive Oil Council says about deep-frying with extra virgin olive oil: 'When heated, olive oil is the most stable fat, which means it stands up well to high frying temperatures. Its high smoke point (410°F or 210°C) is well above the ideal temperature for frying food (356°F or 180°C). The digestibility of olive oil is not affected when it is heated, even when it is re-used several times for frying.'

Olive oil has always been a world apart from other cooking oils. Firstly, it has always exquisitely expressed its terroir – that great French word that, when applied to wine, means the expression of its soil and particular microclimate. I'm not talking about blended olive oils here but about the traditional provincial pressing, the true expression of the land. What makes olive oil different from other oils is its diversity and the expression of the land from which it comes. One never hears of a sesame oil coming from a certain region or a peanut oil exhibiting nuances and complexities. In fact, some seed oils – for example, grapeseed and sunflower – are used by cooks precisely because they are neutral and merely the medium through which food is cooked. They are industrial products extracted using chemical solvents and heat, whereas extra virgin olive oil is simply extracted by pressing the juice of the olive.

The idea of using a neutral oil is totally foreign to traditional Italian cooking – and indeed to Mediterranean cooking. Imagine using an ingredient that adds absolutely nothing to the flavour or texture of a dish. The reason olive oil is used is because it tastes so good.

But theory is no substitute for practice. In Verona in April 1988, at VinItaly, I witnessed a group of highly regarded Italian olive-oil producers deep-frying chips in extra virgin olive oil. They wanted to make the point that even the most severe cooking method, deep-frying, gives better results if you use extra virgin olive oil. The chips were spectacular.

Most Italians have grown up cooking with the first-pressed oil of the olive. Their mothers, grandmothers and great-grandmothers used it – mine did. It is one of the essential flavours that make Italian cooking genuine and authentic.

ITALIAN BREAD

In 2001 McDonald's opened an outlet in the centre of Altamura, an Italian town of 65,000 people that is a short drive south of Bari in the region of Puglia. After changes in management, and trying to attract custom with special offers and children's parties, the store was forced to close due to a lack of interest from the locals. This is a familiar story all over Italy, where good fast food at reasonable prices has been around for centuries.

It's not that the people of Altamura had a problem with fast food – it was simply that the fast food offered by McDonald's couldn't compete with their traditional, centuries-old version. After all, the town had been founded in the 5th century BCE and their cuisine was built around the wholesome, wood-fired local sourdough bread made with durum-wheat flour. So their preferred fast food was typically a panino with any of the huge choice of fillings – for example, mortadella, fresh mozzarella or scamorza cheese, eggs, basil and tomato – or fèdda, a local version of bruschetta in which the bread is toasted, drizzled with olive oil and covered in chopped tomatoes.

Panini, bruschetta and focaccia, as well as the ever-present pizza, are now part of fast-food culture around the world. Bruschetta can be found almost everywhere, even in small country towns, and focaccia has officially entered Australian English through the *Macquarie Dictionary*.

Ciabatta

It looks like a long slipper, and that is the meaning of its name. This bread is for those who like maximum chewy crust and minimum fluffy white stuff. It is great toasted, a wonderful soup bread and excellent cut into fingers, brushed with olive oil and garlic and then grilled.

Panino

Panino is the ultimate snack or lunch bread. 'Do you want to grab a panino?' seems to be asked more and more these days. A panino is any small, hand-sized bread. It comes long, round or rose-shaped and when filled, it turns into a meal.

Focaccia

The classic focaccia originated in Genoa. It is typically large and rectangular and tastes of delicate olive oil, which is used in its preparation. It is chewy, soft, savoury, crumbly and crunchy all at the same time.

Lingue di suocera

Literally meaning 'mother-in-law's tongue', this is a crisp flatbread typically 10–15 cm (4–6 in) wide, rounded at each end and up to 50 cm (20 in) long. It is delicious as a snack with dips. Originally from Piemonte, imported and local varieties are now available.

Carta di musica

Literally meaning 'music paper' after the noise it makes when chewed, this is a Sardinian speciality; locally it is also called pane carasau.

ITALIAN FLOUR GRADING

So you're ready to make focaccia using that Italian recipe and it asks for soft wheat '00' flour. What does this mean?

Italian flour grades follow a system that defines particle size, amount of husk and whole grain that remain after sifting, and wheat type if necessary. In the '00' category, some flour is milled for pasta while other flours are milled for biscuits, bread or pizza. Generally speaking, coarser-grained '0' flour will result in a coarser crumb in whatever is baked. Grade '000' is very fine and mostly used for delicate pastry work.

There are also different types of flour. The two main types are soft wheat, and hard or durum wheat. The latter is often referred to as semolina in Italy and can be identified by its pale-yellow colour.

It is paper thin, 40 cm (16 in) in diameter, crisp and tasty, and great with cheese.

POLENTA

When we opened our first restaurant in 1983, I wanted the menu to include many of the dishes that my mother cooked for us. After all, it was her food and my grandmother's food that inspired me to open a restaurant in the first place. Back then, this maize or cornmeal gruel was rarely seen on restaurant menus. I remember that my mother was hesitant about offering polenta (cornmeal) because traditionally it was associated with poverty and famine. How times change! Today polenta enjoys a much higher status and specialist polenta 'flours' are well worth seeking out. My view on 'instant polenta' is that while it is convenient, for supreme flavour and texture there's no beating making it with traditional flours (see below). To get really good results, polenta must be cooked long and slow. To achieve the very low heat required, I use a simmer mat between the heat source and my saucepan. (See page 41 for basic polenta cooking techniques.)

Soft wheat flour is most often used for fresh pasta that includes eggs; it is easy to work with. Durum or hard wheat flour is used to make dry pasta and certain distinctive types of Italian bread.

In the restaurant we have on hand many types and grades of wheat flour for all sorts of baking requirements. Along with the grading, the Italian flour label will stipulate usage such as 'pane e pizza' meaning bread and pizza, or 'biscotti' meaning biscuits.

Plain flour (also known as all-purpose flour) is almost the same as soft wheat '00' Italian flour and can be substituted. However, to get closer to the mark, search for Italian flour (especially when making pizza) as the right flour is essential and this is often the element that is missing.

White polenta

Made from white maize grown in the Veneto, this polenta is delicately flavoured, finely textured, and good with fish and shellfish dishes.

Polenta di Storo

From an old variety of maize called marano that is grown around the town of Storo in the region of Trentino-Alto Adige, this polenta is old gold (dark yellow) in colour and coarsely textured and has a creamy, rich flavour with a tang of radicchio-like bitterness at the end.

Polenta taragna

Popular in the mountainous Valtellina area of northern Lombardia, this polenta is made with coarse-ground buckwheat. Its big, rich taste goes well with parmesan, gruyere or other mature cheeses stirred through, and it is excellent with braised sausages.

Ottofile di Langa

This bright-yellow maize takes its name from the eight rows of kernels on each cob. An old variety grown in the Langa area of Piemonte, it comes as coarse or fine and its sweet flavour is excellent in a range of dishes.

ITALIAN LENTILS

Lentils (*Lens esculenta*) have been eaten by people in the Middle East for about 8000 years, though their exact origin is unknown. Their cultivation began a thousand years after wheat and barley and two to three thousand years before olives, figs, dates and grapes. Their shape, a double convex, inspired ancient astronomers and physicists to name the disc-shaped pulses 'lens', and their Latin name survives to this day.

Two thousand years ago, Apicius dedicated an entire chapter in his cookbook to pulses. He lists recipes for lentils with mussels; lentils with chestnuts; lentils with spices, herbs, honey and vinegar; and a soup made with barley, lentils, peas and chickpeas. A similar soup called haraira or harira is eaten in Morocco to end Ramadan, the month of fasting.

The lentil has always been a 'food for the people' and at times in history has been looked down upon as lowly fare. However, 100 grams of this 'poor man's meat' contains 25 grams of protein. To get the same amount of protein from beef, you would have to consume 134 grams. Of all the dried pulses (with the exception of the soya bean), lentils contain the most protein; they also contain 54 per cent carbohydrate, vitamins A and B, iron and calcium.

Before cooking, lentils need to be meticulously sorted to make sure there are no small stones hiding among them. The stones have a way of looking just like the lentils but of course they do not soften once cooked – so set aside a little time to sort your lentils so that nobody chips a tooth.

Unlike other dried pulses such as beans and chickpeas, lentils do not need to be soaked before cooking, and they generally have a shorter cooking time. They should be washed to rid them of dust and dirt, but soaking them for an extended length of time will cause them to ferment and germinate, which adversely affects their flavour. Proponents of soaking suggest that it makes them more tender and digestible, but in fact it makes them so soft that they fall apart when cooked, losing both flavour and texture.

Cooked lentils soak up enormous quantities of liquid in proportion to their size, so if they end up being a little dry, add some hot broth to moisten them before serving. (For a basic lentil recipe, see page 40.)

As a general rule, 1½ cups of lentils, once cooked, will swell to about twice their volume. They are delicious on their own with grated parmesan or as an accompaniment to boiled pork knuckles, stuffed pig's trotters or poached fish.

Most regions of Italy use lentils, and there are specific varieties grown throughout.

Castelluccio di Norcia lentils

Perhaps the best known of Italy's lentils are grown in Umbria, in high altitudes in the Sibillini Mountains, bordering Le Marche. Castelluccio lentils are protected by IGP (Indicazione Geografica Protetta – Protected Geographical Indication). They are relatively small and range in colour from pale yellow to brown. They have a particularly thin skin that makes them quite quick to cook, but they retain their form. The flavour is delicate and sweet.

Onano lentils

Grown in the volcanic, sandy soils around the town of Onano, province of Viterbo, about 80 km north of Rome, highly regarded Onano lentils are light brown tending to grey and sometimes a deep rosy-yellow. They were almost extinct in the 1960s but today, under the Presidio Slow Food, they have survived in small plots. Increasingly organically grown, they are finding markets in Italy and beyond. The texture is creamy and velvety, with scents of hay and camomile.

Santo Stefano di Sessanio lentils

These tiny lentils (only 3 mm in diameter) have been grown since ancient times at elevations of up to 1000 metres on the slopes of the Gran Sasso mountain of Abruzzo. They are particularly laborious to cultivate because they mature at different times according to the altitude. These lentils are chestnut brown and plump with a deep, rich flavour, and are also part of the Presidio Slow Food.

Ustica lentils

Grown on the volcanic island of Ustica, about 50 km north of Palermo in the Tyrrhenian Sea, these small lentils are light brown and have very thin skin that disappears once cooked to produce tiny lozenges of silky-smooth cream, packed with flavour. They are produced without chemicals or artificial fertilisers, and the few remaining producers are protected by the Presidio Slow Food.

VSEFUL ITALIAN FOOD TERMS

abbacchio: a milk-fed lamb less than two
months old (the general term for lamb
is **agnello**)

acciuga: anchovy

aceto: vinegar

acetosa: sorrel

acqua: water

affettato: something sliced, usually referring
to sliced cured meats (the plural is *affettati*)

affogato: from *affogare*, which literally means
'to drown'; in Italian gastronomy it is
used figuratively in the past tense to mean
poached or smothered, e.g. affogato al caffe
describes ice cream over which hot coffee
has been poured

agliata: garlic sauce

aglio: garlic

aglio e olio: much-loved quick condiment
of garlic sautéed in extra virgin olive oil,
sometimes with the addition of chilli and/
or parsley

agrodolce: literally meaning 'sour-sweet';
in Roman times a combination of sweet
and savoury ingredients but in modern
Italian cooking usually an addition of sugar
and vinegar

antipasto: literally meaning 'before the meal',
these hot and cold 'tastes' are meant to
tantalise, and in a classic meal they precede
the soup

aragosta: spiny lobster

arborio: perhaps the most well known of the
more than 20 rice varieties grown in Italy

arrosto: roast, roasted

assaggio/assaggiare: taste/to taste
or sample

astice: lobster

autunno: autumn

bacalà, baccalà: salt cod

bacio: literally means 'kiss', plural *baci*; *baci
di dama* are chocolate-covered almond or
hazelnut cookies

basso: literally means 'low' or 'short'
(however, note that the word for a short
coffee is *ristretto*)

bavarese: Bavarian cream, bavarois

bianco: white; in cooking, *in bianco* usually
means not the presence of anything white,
but the absence of anything red

biscotti: biscuits (cookies)

biscottini: small biscuits (cookies)

bollito misto: a classic northern Italian dish
of an assortment of mixed boiled meats
accompanied by condiments, such as salsa
verde and mustard fruits

caponata: a Sicilian mixture typically
consisting of eggplant (aubergine), celery,
onion, tomato, pine nuts and olives
held together with extra virgin olive oil,
caramelised sugar and vinegar

carnaroli: a type of Italian rice; considered
one of the best varieties, if not the best

carpaccio: a dish consisting of raw fish or,
originally, raw beef with a dressing

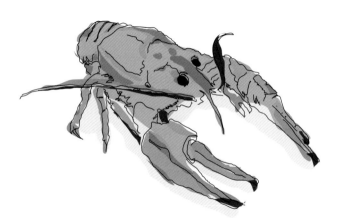

ciabatta: literally means 'slipper'; a flat, wide bread

crostini: small slices of toasted bread

frittata: an Italian omelette

mascarpone: commonly referred to as a cheese, but strictly speaking is more correctly a triple cream because it is derived from milk

moscato: refers to an aromatic grape of the muscat family, a sweet sparkling wine from Piemonte, and various fortified wines such as moscato di Pantelleria from Sicilia

osso buco/ossobuco: note the spelling: two 's' and only one 'c' (never a double 'c'); braised shin or knuckle of veal that has been cut to reveal the bone marrow, the most coveted part of the dish

panettone: a northern Italian Christmas cake, now very popular in Australia

panforte: literally 'strong bread'; a spiced fruit and nut 'bread' from Siena

panna cotta: a famous sweet from Piemonte made with cream and flavourings and set with gelatine

piccante: piquant, spicy; usually includes chilli or pepper

polpettine: little patties or rissoles

rucola: rocket, arugula, ruchetta; a spicy leaf

sbrisolona: polenta shortbread typical of the Milan-Brescia-Mantua area of northern Italy

sformato: turned out from a mould

spaghettini: long pasta; thinner than spaghetti

tagliatelle: 5 mm (¼ in) wide ribbon pasta

tartufo: literally means 'truffle' but can refer to chocolate or gelato truffles

timballo: a round mould used to form food; in French it is timbale

trifolati: literally meaning 'cooked like truffles'; classic preparations are mushrooms, zucchini (courgettes) and veal kidneys sautéed in extra virgin olive oil with onions, garlic and parsley

vialone nano: another Italian rice variety, shorter and quicker to cook than rice

zabaglione: a mixture of egg yolks and flavourings; known by the French as *sabayon*

BASIC TECHNIQUES

ARTICHOKES

Choosing artichokes is like choosing any other vegetable: they should look good. They must be firm and have no blemishes, and their heads should be full and tight.

To prepare artichokes, you need a saucepan of cold water with the juice of a lemon squeezed into it. The lemon will stop the artichokes from discolouring. Using a sharp paring knife, take the top 2–3 cm (¾–1¼ in) of the artichoke clean off, then begin paring around the heart until you reach the tender inner leaves. Leave about 4–5 cm (1½–2 in) of stalk at the base – this part is delicious when cooked – and trim away any leaves. As each artichoke is prepared, place it in the saucepan with the acidulated water.

You will notice that the artichokes float and the topmost ones sit above the water. Place a dinner plate on them – its weight will submerge them so they don't discolour. Bring the water to the boil, then turn down to a simmer and cook until the artichokes are tender. They are perfectly cooked when a sharp knife penetrates with just a hint of resistance.

Drain the artichokes of all their cooking water and let cool completely. Any rough outer leaves can be easily removed and the stem trimmed. Preserve them by storing in jars under olive oil, or slice and serve them in a salad.

POMEGRANATES

The pomegranate is not an easy fruit to deal with. The juice is contained in the pulp that surrounds the many seeds, which are held together by pith and skin. It takes patience and commitment to handle a pomegranate, because it can be very messy.

Perhaps the simplest way is to start with the juice. To extract the juice efficiently and with a minimum of splatter, use a sturdy, lever-type citrus juicer. If you don't have a juicer, put the pomegranate on your workbench and roll it around, pressing firmly with the palm of your hand. The fruit will become soft as the seeds release the juice around them. Slit the skin carefully over a bowl and squeeze out the juice.

Getting to the seeds can be a chore if you are a novice, especially prying them off the bitter pithy membrane that holds them in place. A good technique is to quarter the pomegranate, then immerse each quarter one at a time in a bowl of water and pull the skin back to free the seeds. Most of the pith will float and can be scooped off. Drain through a sieve and the seeds will be left intact.

Once you have mastered the techniques of recovering the juice and seeds, pomegranate dishes, both sweet and savoury, can be easily prepared.

TOMATO FILLETS

Bring a saucepan of salted water to the boil and plunge in the ripe tomatoes for 20–30 seconds depending on their size. Transfer to a bowl of iced water for 5 minutes, then peel, halve and remove and discard all the seeds. All that should be left is peeled, hollow tomato halves. Cut each half into 2 pieces, then cut each quarter into strips of a size suitable to your needs. The tomato fillets will keep for 2–3 days if refrigerated.

PHEASANT, GUINEA FOWL, DUCK AND PIGEON

These game birds have always been popular in central and northern Italy. Along with duck, partridge and other smaller birds such as quail, in times past they were hunted during the autumn season. While it is still possible to get wild-caught game, these days it is mostly the farmed varieties that are available. The birds are usually sold already gutted and with their innards removed, but if you can buy the livers and hearts they are an added bonus.

All of these birds are essentially the same as chicken to prepare but their flesh is generally a little denser and the colour is darker, adding to the meat's flavour. To prepare a pheasant or other game bird for roasting, cut the legs at the knee joint, cut the wings at the first joint from the breast, and remove the neck. (Don't throw these pieces away as they can be used to make excellent stock.) Wash the stomach cavity and dry well using a clean cloth. The bird is now ready for roasting or braising whole.

SLOW COOKING (SOUS-VIDE)

Sous-vide is a method of slow-cooking food in sealable plastic bags at low temperatures in a water bath. First, preheat the oven to 65°C (150°F). Put your seasoned meat in a sous-vide bag or other airtight, sealable plastic bag, then remove the air from the bag and seal. Pour water into a deep, wide ovenproof bowl to fill by two-thirds and put the bowl in the oven for at least 30 minutes so the water reaches the same temperature as the oven. Put the sealed and airless plastic bags in the oven into the preheated water bath, making sure they are submerged – you may need to put a plate on top – and slow-cook according to the recipe instructions.

COOKING LENTILS

For a delicious basic recipe, wash and drain 1½ cups of lentils. In a saucepan, heat a little olive oil and gently fry a carrot, a stick of celery, a leek and 4–5 cloves of garlic, all cut into bite-sized pieces – this should take only a minute or so. Add 4 cups of chicken broth or water and 1 cup of dry white wine. Bring to the boil, then add the lentils and simmer until they are tender – this should take about 35 minutes to 1 hour depending on their size. I like leaving them a little al dente because I enjoy the texture. To finish, season with salt and pepper and a good handful of freshly chopped parsley.

COOKING DRIED BEANS

Whether you are using cannellini or borlotti beans, the method is the same. Soak 1 cup (200 g/7 oz) dried beans overnight in plenty of cold water, then drain and rinse. Pick out and discard any discoloured beans and put the rest in a saucepan. Cover with cold water and discard any beans that float. Bring to the boil, then turn down to a simmer, cover and cook for 1½–2 hours until the beans are tender. Tip the beans and their cooking liquid into a container and let cool. Once cooled, the beans can be stored in the refrigerator for a few days.

COOKING CHICKPEAS

Put 1 cup (200 g/7 oz) dried chickpeas and a sprig of rosemary in a large bowl and pour in cold water to cover. Let soak for at least 10 hours, then drain and put the chickpeas and rosemary in a saucepan. Pour in cold water to cover, add a little salt and bring to the boil. Immediately turn the heat down and simmer for about 1½ hours until the chickpeas are tender. Let cool in the cooking water.

COOKING POLENTA

Bring 1 litre (35 fl oz) water and 2 pinches of salt to a rolling boil, then whisk in 200 g (7 oz) of polenta (cornmeal) in a gradual fine stream. Once it is all in, let the mixture come to the boil and begin to thicken. Cover and turn down the heat to very low (a simmer mat helps). Cook for 1–1½ hours, stirring with a wooden spoon every 20 minutes. For soft polenta, use a spoon dipped in water to scoop the cooked soft polenta directly from the saucepan to serve. Alternatively, turn out the polenta onto a large wooden board. It will spread and set. Cut into slices with cotton twine by running the twine under the polenta and bringing it up at your desired size of slice. Use a spatula to lift the slices onto a plate. Leftover polenta can be stored in the refrigerator. Cut it into pieces and fry in olive oil or butter to serve with mushrooms or braised meat.

MAKING GNOCCHI

To begin to make gnocchi, you must choose the correct potatoes. Even individual potatoes from the same variety will have different properties according to their age and origin. Dry, old roasting potatoes are best for gnocchi; avoid new-season spuds.

Cook them in their skin in a little water or steam them, in both cases with the lid on – this limits the amount of moisture they will retain. Once they are tender, take them from the pan and allow them to cool enough to be handled and peeled. They must still be warm to hot. Put them through a ricer or *schiacciapatate* (not a food processor) and form a pile of potato on your work surface. Make a well in the middle so the pile resembles a volcano.

For every kg (2 lb 4 oz) of potato, add to the well a handful of plain (all-purpose) flour, a little grated nutmeg, a spoonful of grated parmesan, a pinch of salt and 2 egg yolks. The egg yolks must be added last so that they don't come into direct contact with the potato's remaining heat. Knead all the ingredients together and allow to rest for 5 minutes.

Take a little of the mixture and form it into a long 'sausage' 3 cm (1¼ in) in diameter. Using a knife, cut the sausage into 3 cm (1¼ in) lengths. Form each gnocco by using your thumb to run it along the back of a fork. This is the perfect design as the ridges from the fork will hold the sauce and the indent on the other side, formed by your thumb, assures even and quick cooking. You can also use a ribbed wooden gnocchi paddle to achieve the classic gnocchi shape. Boil a large amount of salted water and add the gnocchi. As they cook they will come to the surface. Drain and serve with your desired sauce.

BASIC RECIPES

PASTA

BASIC EGG PASTA
PASTA ALL'UOVO

INGREDIENTS

4 cups (600 g/1 lb 5 oz) plain
(all-purpose) flour or '00'
Italian soft wheat flour

6 eggs

METHOD

Pile the flour on your work surface and make a well in the centre. Crack the eggs into the well and mix using your fingers to form a dough that is neither too sticky nor too dry. If it is too wet, work in more flour. (It is always better to make the initial mixture too wet rather than too dry, as it is easier to add flour to a wet mixture than egg to a dry one.) Once the dough comes together but is still not smooth, begin to roll it through your pasta machine at its widest setting. Fold it and roll it again at the widest setting, then keep rolling and folding until the dough is smooth and uniform. Now bring the roller setting down a little at a time and roll until the dough is at your desired thickness. Cut into the required shape.

SERVES 8

EGG-WHITE PASTA
PASTA AL BIANCO D'UOVO

INGREDIENTS

4 cups (600 g/1 lb 5 oz) plain
(all-purpose) flour or '00'
Italian soft wheat flour

6 egg whites

½ teaspoon salt

METHOD

Pile the flour on your work surface and make a well in the centre. Add the egg whites and salt to the well and mix using your fingers with enough water to make a dough that is neither too sticky nor too dry. If it is too wet, work in more flour. Roll the dough through your pasta machine to your desired thickness, then cut or shape as required.

SERVES 8

CHITARRA PASTA
PASTA PER LA CHITARRA

INGREDIENTS

250 g (9 oz) plain (all-purpose)
   flour or '00' Italian soft
   wheat flour
150 g (5½ oz) hard wheat flour
4 eggs

METHOD

Pile the flour on your work surface and make a well in the centre. Crack the eggs into the well and mix using your fingers to form a dough that is neither too sticky nor too dry. If it is too wet, work in more flour. Roll the dough through your pasta machine until about 3 mm (⅛ in) thick, 12 cm (4½ in) wide and 25 cm (10 in) long. Flour the pasta sheets and put them one at a time on the chitarra wire. Roll a rolling pin along to press the dough through.

SERVES 6

CORZETTI PASTA
CORZETTI

INGREDIENTS

375 g (13 oz) plain
   (all-purpose) flour or '00'
   Italian soft wheat flour
2 eggs
100 ml (3½ fl oz) dry white
   wine
30 ml (1 fl oz) extra virgin
   olive oil

METHOD

Pile the flour on your work surface and make a well in the centre. Crack the eggs into the well, add the wine and olive oil and mix using your fingers to form a dough that is neither too sticky nor too dry. If it is too wet, work in more flour. Once the dough comes together but is still not smooth, begin to roll it through your pasta machine at its widest setting. Fold it and roll it again at the widest setting, then keep rolling and folding until the dough is smooth and uniform. Now bring the roller setting down and roll the dough to about 2 mm (¹⁄₁₆ in) thick. Use a corzetti cutter and moulds to form the pasta.

SERVES 4-6

PICI PASTA
PICI

INGREDIENTS

2 cups (300 g/10½ oz) '00'
    soft wheat flour

50 ml (1½ fl oz) white wine

2–3 tablespoons extra virgin
    olive oil

METHOD

Pile the flour on your work surface and make a well in the centre. Add the wine and a pinch of salt to the well and mix using your fingers with enough tepid water to make a smooth, soft dough. Knead well either by hand or by rolling repeatedly through the widest setting of your pasta machine until soft and malleable but not sticky. Rest for 20–30 minutes in a bowl covered by a clean cloth. Roll out the dough to about 5 mm thick, then cut it into strands about 5 mm wide. Brush the strands with a little olive oil and rub one at a time between your palms to make long 3 mm (⅛ in) thick strands that resemble fat spaghetti. Lay on a floured tray to dry until you are ready to cook.

SERVES 4–6

TACCONI PASTA
TACCONI DI FAVE

INGREDIENTS

200 g (7 oz) broad-bean flour

200 g (7 oz) '00' soft wheat
    flour

4 eggs

METHOD

Combine the flours well and tip into a pile on your work surface. Make a well in the centre and crack in the eggs. Mix using your fingers to form a dough that is neither too sticky nor too dry. If it is too wet, work in more soft wheat flour. Once the dough comes together but is still not smooth, begin to roll it through your pasta machine at its widest setting. Fold it and roll it again at the widest setting, then keep rolling and folding until the dough is smooth and uniform. Now bring the roller setting down and roll the dough to about 2 mm (1/16 in) thick. Cut into 6 cm × 1 cm (2½ in × ½ in) strips.

SERVES 6–8

TESTAROLI PASTA
TESTAROLI

Testaroli gets its name from the testo, a shallow flat pan with a low-domed lid. There are two cooking processes involved in making testaroli: first it is cooked like a flatbread in the pan, and then it is cut up and cooked in boiling salted water. Traditionally, the testo pan is put on coals and covered with the heated lid so both sides cook together, but it takes a lot of skill and the right pan to do this. It is believed that the original testaroli, which date back to Roman times, were made with farro, one of the ancestors of modern wheat. If farro flour is not available, use all '00' flour.

INGREDIENTS

2 cups (300 g/10½ oz) '00'
    soft wheat flour
200 g (7 oz) farro flour
extra virgin olive oil

METHOD

Sift the flours together into a large bowl, then slowly mix in 450 ml (16 fl oz) water until there are no lumps left. Add 2 pinches of salt and 1 tablespoon olive oil and mix through. It should be the consistency of pancake batter. Let sit for 30 minutes. Heat a testo pan or a small wide frying pan to very hot and add 1 tablespoon oil. Move the oil around the pan to coat evenly, then ladle in testaroli mixture to a thickness of 2–3 mm (¹⁄₁₆–⅛ in). Cook for a minute or so on each side, then remove from the pan and set aside. Repeat until all the mixture has been used. Once it is cool enough to handle, cut the testaroli into 5–6 cm (2–2½ in) squares and set aside until you are ready to cook it again in boiling salted water.

SERVES 8–10

UMBRICELLI PASTA
UMBRICELLI

INGREDIENTS

3 cups (450 g/1 lb) '00' soft
    wheat flour
5 egg whites
2–3 tablespoons extra virgin
    olive oil

METHOD

Pile the flour on your work surface and make a well in the centre. Add the egg whites and a pinch of salt to the well and mix using your fingers with enough tepid water to make a smooth, soft dough. Knead well either by hand or by rolling repeatedly through the widest setting of your pasta machine until soft and malleable but not sticky. Rest for 20–30 minutes in a bowl covered by a clean cloth. Roll out the dough to about 5 mm (¼ in) thick, then cut it into strands about 5 mm (¼ in) wide. Brush the strands with a little olive oil and rub one at a time between your palms to make long 3 mm (⅛ in) thick strands that resemble fat spaghetti. Lay on a floured tray to dry until you are ready to cook.

SERVES 6

BASIC RECIPES

BREAD

STARTER CULTURE FOR BREAD AND PIZZA
LIEVITO MADRE

As with any cooking, starting with the best-quality ingredients is of utmost importance. This is particularly relevant when it comes to something as basic as flour. There are so many available for different uses, whether for bread, biscuits, pizza or pastries. Each producer offers specific flours for a diverse range of products. For this starter culture, my personal preference is for organic stone-milled flour such as Mulino Marino from Piemonte or Molino Quaglia from the Veneto. The more commercial, machine-milled Caputo from Campania is also very good and much easier to find outside Italy than some other types.

INGREDIENTS

plain (all-purpose) flour

1 tablespoon raw honey

1 tablespoon extra virgin
   olive oil

METHOD

Combine 200 g (7 oz) flour and 100 ml (3½ fl oz) water with the honey and olive oil to form a dough. Put the dough in a bowl, cut a cross on the top and cover with plastic wrap. Leave for 3 days and then mix in 200 g (7 oz) more flour and 50 ml (1½ fl oz) water. Keep this process going for 3–4 weeks, 'feeding' the dough every 2–3 days until it looks stringy and full of air pockets. This means that the yeast is active and the culture can be used. Store in the refrigerator, covered, and use as required to make bread or pizza bases. After using part of the culture, refresh it with more flour and water. As it matures it will become 'stronger' and can be kept active indefinitely.

PASTRY

SHORTCRUST TART PASTRY
PASTA FROLLA

It is typically used when the contents and the pastry have to be cooked at the same time.

INGREDIENTS

350 g (12 oz) plain (all-purpose) flour
70 g (2½ oz) caster (superfine) sugar
½ teaspoon baking powder
grated zest of 1 lemon
170 g (6 oz) cold unsalted butter, cut into 1 cm (½ in) cubes
1 × 65 g (2¼ oz) egg
1 egg yolk
¼ cup (60 ml/2 fl oz) thick (double) cream

METHOD

Put the flour, sugar, baking powder, lemon zest and a pinch of salt in a food processor. Pulse to combine well, then add the cold butter cubes and pulse repeatedly until the mixture resembles sand. In a separate bowl, whisk together the egg, egg yolk and cream. Add this mixture to the food processor and pulse until the mixture forms a ball. Form the dough into a disc, wrap in plastic and refrigerate for 3–4 hours before rolling out.

MAKES enough for 2 × 24 cm (9½ in) tarts

SHORTCRUST TART PASTRY NO. 2
PASTA FROLLA 2

Blind baking requires a double handling process where the pastry is baked first with weights on it to stop it from puffing up. You use this technique when you are making a pie or tart where the filling requires no baking, such as when filling the pie with pastry cream and fruit.

INGREDIENTS

500 g (1 lb 2 oz) plain (all-purpose) flour, sifted
285 g (10 oz) unsalted butter, cut into 2 cm (¾ in) cubes and softened
130 g (4½ oz) caster (superfine) sugar
½ cup (50 g/1¾ oz) almond meal
2 eggs
seeds from ½ vanilla bean

METHOD

Put half the flour in the bowl of an electric mixer fitted with a paddle attachment and turn the mixer on at its lowest setting. Add the butter, sugar, almond meal, eggs, vanilla seeds and a pinch of salt and mix until it comes together. Add the remaining flour and beat at a low setting until the mixture forms a rough dough. Shape into a disc, wrap in plastic wrap and refrigerate for at least 8 hours before rolling out.

MAKES enough for 2 × 24 cm (9½ in) tarts

BASIC RECIPES

STOCKS

BEEF BROTH
BRODO DI MANZO

You can adjust this recipe to make small or large quantities. If you are making 4–5 litres (7–9 pints) you start with 700 grams (1 lb 9 oz) of chicken or quail carcass then 700 grams (1 lb 9 oz) of beef blade and 1.4 kg (3 lb) of beef breast.

INGREDIENTS

2 parts by weight beef breast
   (punto di petto) or brisket
1 part by weight beef blade
   (shoulder)
1 part by weight chicken or
   quail carcasses
1 carrot, chopped into
   5–6 pieces
1 onion, peeled and halved
1 celery stick, cut into
   3–4 pieces

METHOD

Put all the ingredients in a large saucepan or stockpot and pour in 8 litres (14 pints) of cold water to cover by 3–4 cm. Bring to the boil, then immediately turn the heat down and simmer gently uncovered for 3 hours, skimming off any impurities that form on the surface. Strain carefully through a double layer of muslin (cheesecloth) and let cool before refrigerating.

MAKES about 4.5 litres (7–9 pints)

CHICKEN BROTH
BRODO DI POLLO

INGREDIENTS

2 chicken carcasses
4 chicken necks
6 chicken feet
1 carrot, chopped into
   5–6 pieces
1 onion, peeled and halved
1 celery stick, cut into
   3–4 pieces
1 handful parsley stems

METHOD

Wash the chicken well and pat dry. Put all the ingredients in a large saucepan or stockpot and pour in 6 litres (10½ pints) of cold water. Bring to the boil, then immediately turn the heat down and simmer gently uncovered for 2 hours, skimming off any impurities that form on the surface. Strain carefully through a double layer of muslin (cheesecloth) and let cool before refrigerating.

MAKES about 3.5–4 litres (6–7 pints)

QUAIL STOCK OR BROTH
BRODO DI QUAGLIA

Quail carcasses can be frozen and used later to make this stock. You will need approximately 8–10 quail carcasses to make this quantity.

INGREDIENTS

quail carcasses, well washed

1 onion, chopped

1 carrot, cut into 2 cm pieces

2 celery sticks, cut into
    2 cm pieces

2 garlic cloves, peeled

3–4 parsley stems

METHOD

Put all the ingredients in a large saucepan or stockpot and pour in 8 litres (14 pints) of cold water. Bring to the boil, then immediately turn the heat down and simmer gently uncovered for 3 hours, skimming off any impurities that form on the surface. Strain carefully through a double layer of muslin (cheesecloth) and let cool before refrigerating.

MAKES 4–5 litres (7–9 pints)

VEGETABLE BROTH
BRODO VEGETALE

INGREDIENTS

1 small white onion, diced

1 celery stick, diced

1 garlic clove, thinly sliced

1 small carrot, diced

4 fennel tops, chopped

150 g ripe tomatoes, peeled,
    seeded and diced

1 small leek, white part only,
    thinly sliced

2 cloves

2 bay leaves

1 handful parsley stalks

METHOD

Pour 3 litres cold water into a large saucepan or stockpot and add all the ingredients. Bring to the boil on medium heat, then turn the heat down and simmer gently uncovered for 2 hours, skimming off any impurities that form on the surface. The stock should be clear and bright. Turn off the heat and leave to settle for 30 minutes, then strain through a fine sieve, discarding the solids. Season with salt. Use as a base for soup, risotto or vegetable, seafood or meat dishes.

MAKES 1.5–2 litres (2½–3½ pints)

FISH BROTH
BRODO DI PESCE

INGREDIENTS

1.5 kg (3½ lb) fish bones,
    including head

1 large brown onion, peeled,
    cut into quarters

1 carrot, peeled, cut into
    6–8 chunks

1 celery stick, cut into
    6–8 pieces

1 handful of parsley stalks

METHOD

Wash the fish carcass and place it, along with the vegetables, in a 10–15 litre (21–32 pints) stockpot and add 8 litres (17 pints) cold water. Bring to the boil, reduce heat and simmer gently uncovered for 90 minutes. Keep skimming the top of the water as scum appears. Take off the heat and leave for 30 minutes. Strain the liquid through a double layer of muslin. Let it cool and refrigerate or freeze.

MAKES 5–6 litres (10½ – 12½ pints)

SAUCES

BÉCHAMEL SAUCE
SALSA BESCIAMELLA

INGREDIENTS

1 cup (250 ml/9 fl oz) milk

30 g (1 oz) butter

30 g (1 oz) plain (all-purpose) flour

4 tablespoons finely grated Parmigiano Reggiano

white pepper

METHOD

Heat the milk in a saucepan until warm. In a separate saucepan, melt the butter on medium heat, then whisk in the flour and cook until the mixture forms a thick paste. Add the warm milk a little at a time, whisking constantly, until the mixture starts to boil. Remove from the heat, then whisk in the Parmigiano Reggiano and season with salt and white pepper. Cover with plastic wrap and set aside to cool.

MAKES about 1½ cups (375 ml/13 fl oz)

TOMATO SAUCE
SALSA POMODORO

INGREDIENTS

⅓ cup (80 ml/2½ fl oz) extra virgin olive oil

1 onion, finely diced

2 garlic cloves, minced

1 pale inner celery stick, finely chopped

650 g (1 lb 7 oz) tin tomatoes, mashed

METHOD

Heat the olive oil in a frying pan and gently fry the onion, garlic and celery until translucent. Add the tomato and season with a couple of pinches of salt and some pepper. Stir well and simmer until the sauce thickens and most of the water has evaporated.

MAKES about 2 cups (500 ml/17 fl oz)

PESTO
PESTO

These days there are many types of pesto, including rocket (arugula) pesto, walnut pesto and coriander pesto. But for me, pesto will always first and foremost be the emerald-green and pungent salsa made with sweet basil. Pesto gets its name from the pestle used to pound the basil in a mortar with the rest of the ingredients. This 'hand method' is in my opinion still the best method of making pesto: it results in a much smoother, creamier texture. Even so, using a food processor will give satisfactory results.

INGREDIENTS

60 g (2¼ oz) pine nuts, toasted
2 garlic cloves, peeled
1 cup basil leaves
½ cup (125 ml/4 fl oz) extra
    virgin olive oil
6 tablespoons grated
    Parmigiano Reggiano

METHOD

Put the pine nuts, garlic and a good pinch of salt in a mortar and pound until everything has broken down to a paste. Add the basil and pound, then add the olive oil a little at a time, mixing until smooth and the desired consistency. Stir in the Parmigiano Reggiano and add more salt if necessary.

MAKES a little over 1 cup (250 ml/9 fl oz)

BASIC RECIPES

SWEET SAUCES

RUNNY CUSTARD
CREMA INGLESE

INGREDIENTS

200 g (7 oz) caster (superfine) sugar

12 egg yolks

1 litre (35 fl oz) thin (pouring) cream

1 teaspoon natural vanilla extract

METHOD

Whisk the sugar and egg yolks until pale and forming a ribbon. Heat the cream almost to the boil, then whisk the cream into the egg mixture. Put on medium heat and stir continuously until the custard coats the back of a spoon. Transfer to a bowl, add the vanilla and let cool.

MAKES 2 litres (70 fl oz)

MASCARPONE CREAM
CREMA DI MASCARPONE

INGREDIENTS

2 egg whites

⅓ cup (75 g/2½ oz) caster (superfine) sugar

300 g (10½ oz) softened mascarpone

1 teaspoon natural vanilla extract

METHOD

Whisk the egg whites until soft peaks form, then slowly add the sugar while still whisking. Once firm peaks form, fold in the mascarpone and vanilla. Use to accompany cakes, tarts and biscuits or to fill a sponge.

MAKES about 2 cups

THE REGIONS

1 Piemonte
2 Valle d'Aosta
3 Lombardia
4 Trentino-Alto Adige
5 Veneto
6 Friuli-Venezia Giulia
7 Liguria
8 Emilia-Romagna
9 Toscana
10 Umbria
11 Le Marche
12 Lazio
13 Abruzzo e Molise
14 Campania
15 Puglia
16 Basilicata
17 Calabria
18 Sicilia
19 Sardegna

ABRUZZO E MOLISE

ABRUZZO AND MOLISE

UNTIL 1970, ABRUZZO AND MOLISE WERE ONE REGION. THEY ARE STILL LOOKED AT THAT WAY TODAY IN A CULINARY SENSE, SO I WILL LEAVE THEM TWINNED BUT DEAL WITH THEIR GEOGRAPHY SEPARATELY.

Abruzzo is known as the ceiling of the Apennines – the summit of Gran Sasso, the highest point in the ranges, rises to 1900 metres (6200 feet). It lies south of Le Marche and east of Lazio; its western border is about 50 kilometres (31 miles) from Rome. Its twin, Molise, is to the south, and both share a coastline with the Adriatic. Molise, the second smallest region of Italy after Val d'Aosta, is east of Lazio and north of Campania and Puglia. Between them they cover some 15,000 square kilometres (5800 square miles).

Abruzzo is also known as the green heart of Italy. Half of its area was declared a national park in 1872 and is still maintained as such. Here can be found Marsican brown bears, Apennine wolves, Abruzzo chamois and many other wild animals. Given the wildness of the environment and the difficulty of penetrating it – there was only one road in and out in the early 20th century – Abruzzo had a reputation as a home for bandits and

brigands, a fact celebrated by a dish called pecora alla brigante, or brigand-style sheep.

The climate is cold and, by contrast, the food is hot, with chilli being widely used. As it is so mountainous, the emphasis in the cuisine is on protein: the region is famed for its sheep and goat recipes, and in Molise goat is stewed in rosemary, sage and chilli. Herds of cattle are also grazed to produce the cheeses of the region, and the Abruzzese are known for their fondness for cooking with local cheeses. These include pecorinos from Farindola, Atri and Penne; scamorza, a fresh or smoked cheese; and the cow's-milk fior di latte from Boiano. Grapes, olives and almonds are grown in the valleys, and potatoes, maize and sugar beet in Avezzano, the main industrial commercial and agricultural region.

Alongside the brigands and bandits in the Abruzzese mountains were the charcoal-burners, the carbonai. They gave their name to a secret society of freedom fighters known

56

as the Carbonari, who played a large part in the unification (the Risorgimento), and to a dish known and loved around the world: pasta alla carbonara. Deep in the forest, charcoal-burners always had a hunk of guanciale (cured pork cheek) and some goat's or sheep's cheese, and could raid a nest for a quail egg: apart from pasta, these are the ingredients of a carbonara.

Another local creation that has conquered the world is pasta alla chitarra, which is made using a pasta cutter shaped like a guitar – the sheets of pasta are pushed through to provide square-cut strands.

Saffron is grown in Navelli, inland and on a high plateau. It was introduced to the region by a Dominican monk around 1300 and is used in many Abruzzese dishes, in making pasta alla chitarra and in recipes for goat and sole. Dominicans in the Gran Sasso grow saffron to this day; it is a lucrative crop for them, fetching as much as €10,000 a kilogram.

Just about every town has its specialities: Campotosto is renowned for its pork products, Navelli for its chickpeas and saffron, Capestrano for its white beans, and so on. One speciality with links to the Spanish is prosciutto aquilano, the prosciutto of L'Aquila, which has been cured according to the Spanish method for 500 years. There could also be a Spanish link to the salcicce di fegato, or pig's liver sausage, which includes orange peel in its recipe.

Abruzzese chefs are celebrated for their judicious use of herbs and spices – not just saffron but, as mentioned, chilli and wild mountain herbs, including thyme and rosemary. The Val di Sangro in the province of Chieti has supplied the world with many distinguished chefs.

Celebrated fish dishes from the coast include scapece, a local form of the Spanish escabeche – a fried then pickled fish flavoured with the local saffron, with Persian and Arabic origins. This ancient method of preserving fish is also seen in the Venetian dish pesce en saor. The wonderfully named polpi in purgatorio – octopus in purgatory – is cooked with olive oil, tomato, garlic and large quantities of chilli powder.

With regard to wine, Abruzzo is one of the regions that is struggling to overcome a reputation for industrial wines – a reputation that, in the past, was not unfounded as the region was dominated by huge cooperatives. The chosen grape for the whites of Abruzzo is trebbiano, and most of the wine made from it – the trebbiano d'Abruzzo – is on the whole high in acid, faintly floral and inoffensive. When chilled, it can be just the thing for the highly spiced local dishes. Some makers are lifting Abruzzo's game and producing wines with an eye to the international market, blending their trebbiano with more forceful partners such as chardonnay.

The best-known red wine of the region is montepulciano d'Abruzzo, named for the grape. The best montepulciano comes from the north, around Teramo, although the vast bulk of it comes from the hotter southern end, mostly the province of Chieti. When you fly Alitalia, your little screw-top bottle of red contains montepulciano d'Abruzzo.

When made as a rosato (rosé), montepulciano is called cerasuolo, or cherry-red, and is a very good and dry example of the style. Again, it is fine with the spicy regional dishes. Like most wines of this type, it is best drunk young and chilled.

Also made in the region is a digestive by the name of centerbe, meaning '100 herbs' – one of which is the wormwood used in absinthe. Tasting more like bitter medicine than a liqueur, it is beloved of the Abruzzese.

There are three DOC zones in Molise, and they all make white, rosé and red wines from, respectively, trebbiano and montepulciano grapes. The white falaghina and red aglianico are also widely planted.

ABRUZZO E MOLISE
ANTI-PASTI

MUSSEL AND CHILLI CROSTINI
CROSTINI CON COZZE E PEPERONCINO

Antipasti can be either cold or hot and, as in this case, 'soupy'. While I prefer this as an antipasto, it can easily become a substantial first course by leaving each slice of bread whole.

INGREDIENTS

4 large slices of bread, 1 cm (½ in) thick, each cut into 3

2 tablespoons white wine vinegar

½ cup (125 ml/4 fl oz) extra virgin olive oil

1 kg (2 lb 4 oz) mussels, scrubbed and de-bearded

⅓ cup (80 ml/2½ fl oz) dry white wine

2 bay leaves

2 garlic cloves, thinly sliced

2 red chillies, seeded and finely sliced

1 tablespoon chopped parsley

METHOD

Sprinkle the bread with the vinegar. Heat half the olive oil in a wide frying pan and fry the bread on each side until golden and crisp. Drain on paper towels. Put the mussels in a large saucepan with the wine and bay leaves. Turn the heat to high and put the lid on. Once the mussels have steamed open (4–5 minutes), remove them from the pan. Take the meat from the shells and discard the shells. Strain the cooking liquid through a couple of layers of muslin (cheesecloth) or a fine sieve to extract any grit. Heat the remaining oil in the frying pan and gently fry the garlic and chillies for 30 seconds or so. Don't let the garlic colour. Add 1 cup (250 ml/9 fl oz) of the strained cooking liquid to the pan and turn the heat up a little. Simmer for 3–4 minutes. Turn the heat off, add the mussels and parsley, check for salt and add a couple of turns of pepper. Put the bread into bowls and ladle some mussels and their liquid on top.

SERVES 12   WINE: Molise Greco

ORANGES WITH ANCHOVIES
ARANCE E ALICI

Good oranges – and lemons, for that matter – are often eaten skin and all in Italy because the skin contains the fruit's essential oils and therefore has the most flavour. But if you are going to eat the skin, I would advise that the fruit be from an organic orchard. The unusual combination in this recipe works because the contrast between sweet, salty and fishy is so good.

INGREDIENTS

3–4 oranges (preferably organic), well washed

160 g (5¾ oz) best-quality anchovy fillets in oil, drained

½ cup thinly sliced rocket (arugula)

⅓ cup (80 ml/2½ fl oz) extra virgin olive oil

METHOD

Slice 1 cm (½ in) off both ends of each orange. Cut the oranges into 2 mm (1/16 in) slices and place on a large serving plate, just overlapping each other. Scatter the anchovy fillets evenly over the orange slices. Sprinkle the rocket around, season with salt and dress with the olive oil.

SERVES 4–6   WINE: Pecorino

ABRVZZO E MOLISE

SKATE, TOMATO AND BASIL SALAD
INSALATA DI RAZZA

INGREDIENTS

1.5 kg (3 lb 5 oz) skate wings
   on the bone, skin left on
1 brown onion, thinly sliced
12 ripe cherry tomatoes,
   halved
½ cup basil leaves, chopped
⅓ cup (80 ml/2½ fl oz) extra
   virgin olive oil

METHOD

Put the skate in a large saucepan of salted water and bring to the boil. Turn the heat down and simmer until the fish is cooked – the time will depend on how thick the wings are. You can tell if the skate is cooked by pulling some of the flesh aside using a knife and fork to reveal the middle – the flesh should come off the cartilage easily. Once the fish is cooked, remove all the skin. Pull the flesh off the centre cartilage in small pieces, and toss into a bowl with all the other ingredients. Season and serve hot or cold.

SERVES 6–8   WINE: Molise Greco

CUTTLEFISH WITH SPRING PEAS
SEPPIE E PISELLI

INGREDIENTS

½ cup (125 ml/4 fl oz) extra
   virgin olive oil
1 large brown onion, thinly
   sliced
2 cups (310 g/11 oz) freshly
   shelled peas
¾ cup (180 ml/6 fl oz) dry
   white wine
2 garlic cloves, minced
600 g (1 lb 5 oz) cuttlefish
   or small squid, cleaned
   and cut into 5 mm × 5 cm
   (¼ in × 2 in) strips
½ cup chopped parsley

METHOD

Heat 2 tablespoons of the olive oil in a frying pan over medium heat and lightly fry the onion until it is just coloured. Add the peas and wine, increase the heat and let bubble for 3–4 minutes, by which time the peas should be cooked and the liquid reduced to a few tablespoons. Transfer the peas and liquid to a bowl, wipe out the pan and heat the rest of the oil on medium–high heat. Add the garlic and fry until just golden. Turn the heat up to full, add the cuttlefish and parsley and stir for 2–3 minutes until the cuttlefish turns pearly white. Add the peas and their liquid and cook for 2 more minutes. Season and serve with crusty bread.

SERVES 6   WINE: Passerina

PORK SALAD
INSALATA DI MAIALE

Throughout Italy, seemingly unusable bits of animals are made into tasty dishes such as this. As a child I remember devouring all manner of peculiar animal parts, including a wonderful salad of calf tendons that was made by simmering the cartilage in water with celery, carrots and onions until the tendons were tender. After setting them aside to cool, the gelatinous remains were sliced into thin strips. Some finely sliced raw onion was added and the salad was dressed with good olive oil and vinegar and tossed with rocket or radicchio. This salad can still be bought in food shops of Milan and elsewhere, sold by weight.

INGREDIENTS

4 pig ears

4 pig trotters

⅓ cup (80 ml/2½ fl oz) red wine vinegar

2 celery hearts, cut into 3 mm (⅛ in) slices

1 garlic clove, minced

1 red chilli, seeded and finely sliced

⅓ cup (80 ml/2½ fl oz) extra virgin olive oil

juice of 2 lemons

METHOD

Prepare the ears and trotters by scraping any hair off with a sharp knife. Carefully burn off any difficult hairs using a blowtorch. Wash the ears and trotters well and put in a saucepan with the vinegar and abundant salted water. Bring to the boil, then turn down to a simmer and cook for 2½ hours until the cartilage is tender. It will firm up as it cools. Once it is cool enough to handle, separate the trotter cartilage from the bone and cut into bite-sized pieces, along with the ears. Put in a bowl while still warm and add the celery, garlic and chilli. Dress with the olive oil and lemon juice and season.

SERVES 6–8   WINE: Molise Falanghina

LENTIL PUREE WITH CROSTINI
CROSTINI CON PUREA DI LENTICCHIE

INGREDIENTS

2⅓ cups (500 g/1 lb 2 oz) lentils, well washed

1 celery stick, cut into 1 cm (½ in) slices

1 carrot, cut into 1 cm (½ in) slices

1 potato, cut into 2 cm (¾ in) dice

1 brown onion, sliced

1 ripe tomato, chopped

¼ cup parsley

¾ cup (80 g/2¾ oz) grated parmesan cheese

½ cup (125 ml/4 fl oz) extra virgin olive oil

6 slices day-old bread

METHOD

Put the lentils in a saucepan and cover with water. Bring to the boil, then turn down to a simmer and cook, covered, for 30 minutes or more (depending on the type of lentil) until tender. Drain. Put the celery, carrot, potato, onion and tomato in a saucepan and cover with water. Bring to the boil, then turn down to a simmer and cook until the vegetables are soft. Add the lentils and parsley and bring back to the boil, then turn down to a simmer again and cook for 10 minutes. Puree using a Mouli or food processor, then add the parmesan and season. Heat half the olive oil in a frying pan and fry the slices of bread on both sides until golden. Drain on paper towels. Serve the lentil puree on the crostini with a drizzle of the remaining oil.

SERVES 6   WINE: Trebbiano d'Abruzzo

ABRVZZO E MOLISE
PRIMI

FISH SOUP VASTO-STYLE
BRODETTO VASTESE

Vasto is a fishing town on the Adriatic coast in the province of Chieti in southern Abruzzo. The story of how this dish came about starts with the local fishermen heading past the town's abundant vegetable gardens each day on their way to work. On returning, they would sell their catch on the beach and any fish or shellfish left over would be carried home, back past the same gardens. The fishermen and farmers would trade not only produce but also ways of preparing it. And so the brodetto started to evolve. It was always the smaller, less desirable fish and shellfish that were left over and it is these 'lesser' and ultimately more sustainable ingredients that are essential in the soup's preparation. All up, 13 different types of seafood are traditionally used – not all at once, because it depends on the season, but typically 6–8 are used. The tomatoes traditionally used are a ribbed variety called mezzotempo, which are grown in the area. The soup is usually cooked in a terracotta pot and is unusual because it doesn't begin with a soffritto (frying aromatic vegetables in olive oil). Similarly, if the fish in the ingredients list are not available, you can use whatever is in season and available at your local fishmonger.

INGREDIENTS

1 × 200 g (7 oz) gurnard, scaled and gutted

1 scorpion fish, scaled and gutted

200 g (7 oz) skate wings, cut into 8 pieces

300 g (10½ oz) cuttlefish, cleaned (keep the tentacles)

1 × 150 g (5½ oz) red mullet, scaled and gutted

6 whole mantis shrimps

6–8 mussels, scrubbed and de-bearded

200 g (7 oz) clams (vongole)

2 kg (4 lb 8 oz) ripe tomatoes, cut into large cubes

1 green bull's horn capsicum (pepper), cut in half and seeded

4 garlic cloves, each cut into 5–6 pieces

½ cup parsley leaves

½ cup basil leaves

70 ml (2¼ fl oz) extra virgin olive oil

METHOD

Prepare the fish and seafood, trimming any fins from the fish. Put the tomatoes, capsicum, garlic, parsley, basil and olive oil in a wide, heavy-based saucepan or flameproof casserole dish. Add a couple of good pinches of salt and bring to the boil. Turn down to a low simmer and cook for 15 minutes. Begin to add the seafood with the larger things first, such as the gurnard and scorpion fish, then 5 minutes later the cuttlefish, red mullet and shrimps. Keep spooning the sauce over the fish as it cooks but don't stir – if you do, the fish will break up. Cook for 10 minutes, then add the mussels and clams and cook for 2–3 minutes until the shellfish have opened. Check the seasoning and add a little more salt if necessary. Take the soup to the table in the pan and serve in bowls, accompanied by toasted bruschetta.

SERVES 6–8   WINE: Trebbiano d'Abruzzo

QUAIL AND FARRO SOUP
ZUPPA DI QUAGLIE E FARRO

INGREDIENTS

¼ cup (60 ml/2 fl oz) extra virgin olive oil

2 large brown onions, diced

6 garlic cloves, each cut into 3–4 pieces

1 celery heart (including the tender light-green leaves), sliced

1 bay leaf

350 g (12 oz) boiling (waxy) potatoes, diced

250 g (9 oz) tinned tomatoes, mashed

½ cup (100 g/3½ oz) pearled farro, rinsed

2 litres (70 fl oz) quail broth (see page 49) or chicken stock

250 g (9 oz) spinach, washed and chopped

10 quail breasts, each cut into 4–5 pieces

freshly grated parmesan cheese

METHOD

Heat the olive oil in a large, heavy-based saucepan. Add the onions, garlic, celery and bay leaf. Lightly fry the vegetables for 2–3 minutes, making sure they don't colour. Add the potatoes and tomatoes and stir. Add the farro and broth, then raise the temperature and bring to the boil. As soon as it boils, turn down to a simmer and add a couple of good pinches of salt. Cook for 20–25 minutes until the farro has softened. Add the spinach and quail breasts and simmer for 5 minutes. Season and serve with plenty of parmesan and crusty bread.

SERVES 10   WINE: Trebbiano d'Abruzzo

FARRO IS A GRAIN SIMILAR TO PEARL BARLEY AND HAS A LONG CULINARY HISTORY. FOR CENTURIES IT FED THE MEDITERRANEAN AND NEAR EASTERN POPULATIONS AND THE ANCIENT ROMANS USED IT TO MAKE BREAD, PORRIDGE AND SOUP BEFORE WHEAT BECAME MORE READILY AVAILABLE. IT HAS AN UNUSUAL FLAVOUR (SOMEWHERE BETWEEN RICE AND COUSCOUS) AND A FIRM, CHEWY TEXTURE. IT IS A VERY VERSATILE GRAIN WHICH CAN BE USED IN SOUPS, SALADS AND STEWS. MOST GOOD ITALIAN DELICATESSENS, HEALTH FOOD SHOPS OR SPECIALTY FOOD STORES SHOULD STOCK IT.

CHILLED MUSSEL AND TOMATO SOUP
ZUPPA FREDDA DI COZZE AL POMODORO

INGREDIENTS

1 kg (2 lb 4 oz) mussels,
   scrubbed and de-bearded
½ cup (125 ml/4 fl oz) extra
   virgin olive oil
2 garlic cloves, crushed
1 cup basil leaves, thinly sliced
1 kg (2 lb 4 oz) ripe roma
   (plum) tomatoes, peeled
   and chopped

METHOD

Put the mussels in a large saucepan with ¼ cup (60 ml/2 fl oz) water on a high heat and cover. Once the liquid comes to the boil, remove the lid and stir gently with a wooden spoon. Replace the lid and keep cooking for a minute or two until the mussels have opened. Strain, keeping the juices. Remove the mussel meat and discard the shells. Put the mussel meat in the refrigerator until needed. Strain the mussel juice again, this time through two layers of muslin (cheesecloth) or a clean tea towel (dish towel) so that any grit is removed. Put the strained juice in the refrigerator. Heat 2 tablespoons of the olive oil in a frying pan over moderate heat and add the garlic and basil. Stir for a minute or so, then add the tomatoes. Season with a couple of good pinches of salt and simmer for 10–15 minutes to thicken. Add the mussel juice and bring to the boil. Simmer for 10 minutes, then remove from the heat and season. Cool a little before chilling in the refrigerator. Serve cold in soup bowls with the mussel meat on top and the remaining oil drizzled over.

SERVES 6   WINE: Molise Falanghina

MUSSEL, TOMATO AND CELERY SALAD
INSALATINA DI COZZE, POMODORO E SEDANO

INGREDIENTS

1 kg (2 lb 4 oz) mussels,
   scrubbed and de-bearded
½ cup (125 ml/4 fl oz) dry
   white wine
2 fresh oregano sprigs
250 g (9 oz) cherry tomatoes,
   halved
1 celery heart, thinly sliced
   (including the tender
   light-green leaves)
2 baby cos (romaine) lettuces,
   trimmed
⅓ cup (80 ml/2½ fl oz) extra
   virgin olive oil
juice of 1 lemon
3–4 tablespoons parsley
   leaves

METHOD

Put the mussels in a large saucepan, add the wine and oregano, turn the heat to high and put the lid on. Cook for 2 minutes, shaking the pan every 30–40 seconds to help the mussels to open. Remove from the heat. Drain the liquid into a bowl, then strain it through fine muslin (cheesecloth) or a clean tea towel (dish towel). Put the strained cooking liquid into a small saucepan. Bring to the boil and reduce by two-thirds. Meanwhile, remove the mussel meat from the shells, discarding the shells and any unopened mussels. Put the cherry tomatoes in a large bowl with the mussel meat and celery. Chop each lettuce lengthways into 6 wedges and add to the bowl. Make a dressing by mixing the olive oil, the lemon juice and mussel liquid to taste. Dress the salad and season, then add the parsley and toss. Serve on a platter or in individual bowls.

SERVES 6   WINE: Pecorino

BRAISED PRAWNS WITH BROAD BEANS AND POLENTA
POLENTA CON GAMBERI E FAVE

Polenta is now prepared throughout the peninsula and is just as good with seafood and vegetables as it is with meat. Cooked polenta should be soft but not runny. The longer it is cooked, the thicker and more flavoursome it will be.

INGREDIENTS

- 1 cup (190 g/6¾ oz) polenta (cornmeal)
- ¼ cup (60 ml/2 fl oz) extra virgin olive oil
- 1 small brown onion, finely diced
- 2 garlic cloves, minced
- 12 × 400 g (14 oz) tinned tomatoes, drained
- 1 cup (185 g/6½ oz) double-peeled broad beans
- 1 cup basil leaves, roughly torn
- 500 g (1 lb 2 oz) raw banana or king prawns (shrimp), peeled and deveined

METHOD

Put 1.25 litres (44 fl oz) water in a saucepan and add a couple of good pinches of salt. Bring to a rolling boil. Slowly pour in the polenta and stir constantly with a whisk until it comes away from the sides of the saucepan. Reduce the heat to a simmer and put the lid on the saucepan. Cook for 20–30 minutes, giving the polenta a good stir every 5 minutes with a wet wooden spoon. Meanwhile, heat the olive oil in another saucepan and lightly fry the onion and garlic until soft. Mash the tomatoes roughly using a fork and add to the pan. Season with 2–3 pinches of salt and simmer for 10 minutes. Add the broad beans and basil to the tomato mixture. Stir and simmer for 3–4 minutes, then add the prawns and simmer for 5 minutes until the prawns are cooked. Season with pepper and more salt if necessary. Pour the polenta onto a wooden board or into individual plates and spoon the prawns over the top to serve.

SERVES 6   WINE: Molise Falanghina

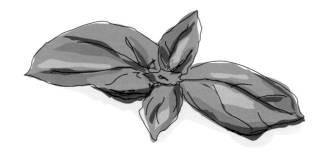

BRAISED PRAWNS WITH BROAD BEANS AND POLENTA

SCALLOPS WITH PARMESAN FENNEL
CAPESANTE E FINOCCHIO AL PARMIGIANO

INGREDIENTS

2 small–medium fennel bulbs

juice of 1 lemon

1 tablespoon white wine vinegar

2–3 knobs butter

150 g (5½ oz) Parmigiano Reggiano, grated

fine white pepper

18 large scallops, cleaned

2 tablespoons extra virgin olive oil

100 ml (3½ fl oz) thin (pouring) cream

2 tablespoons finely snipped chives

METHOD

Preheat the oven to 200°C (400°F). Trim the fennel bulbs by removing the tough outer layer as well as most of the base. Cut each bulb into 16 slices and put in a saucepan with plenty of water, the lemon juice and the vinegar. Bring to the boil, then turn down and simmer for 10–12 minutes until tender. Drain, pat dry and lay in a baking tray. Drop the butter around the fennel. Top with 100 g (3½ oz) of the Parmigiano Reggiano and season with a little salt and white pepper. Bake for 5–8 minutes until golden. Meanwhile, sprinkle the scallops with a little salt. Heat the olive oil in a large frying pan and, just as it begins to smoke, sear the scallops for 1 minute on each side depending on how thick they are. Once they're well browned, remove the pan from the heat. Whip the cream to soft peaks. Put it in a saucepan on medium heat and whisk in the remaining Parmigiano Reggiano until it melts and the mixture begins to bubble. Arrange the fennel and scallops on serving plates, then spoon on the cream sauce. Finish with the chives.

SERVES 6   WINE: Pecorino

PORK RIND WITH CELERY HEARTS AND POTATOES
COTENNE, SEDANO E PATATE

INGREDIENTS

200 g (7 oz) pork rind, cut into finger-length strips

2 tablespoons extra virgin olive oil

1 brown onion, finely chopped

1 celery stick, finely chopped

1 carrot, finely chopped

1 bay leaf

1 sage sprig

1 rosemary sprig

2 garlic cloves, crushed

ground chilli

1 cup (250 g/9 oz) tinned tomatoes

2 celery hearts, thinly sliced

8 small new potatoes, cut into bite-sized pieces

METHOD

Bring a saucepan of water to the boil. Plunge the pork rind into the boiling water and simmer for 1½ hours until tender. Drain and rinse. Heat the oil in a heavy-based saucepan or flameproof casserole dish and gently fry the onion, celery stick and carrot until just browned. Add the bay leaf, sage, rosemary and garlic. Season with pepper and ground chilli. Stir in the pork rind, tomatoes, celery hearts and potatoes. Add a ladleful of water and simmer for 1 hour. Season with salt. Serve in bowls with crusty bread.

SERVES 6   WINE: Sangiovese or Nero d'Avola

FARRO WITH WILD GREENS
FARROTTO

In Abruzzo the wild greens used in farrotto are rucola (rocket/arugula), various types of witlof (chicory and endive), borage, lamb's lettuce (corn salad), dandelion, and others that may not have an English name – such as rosole and cacigni. Use any salad greens both sweet and bitter, as substitutes.

INGREDIENTS

300 g (10½ oz) mixed salad greens

½ cup (125 ml/4 fl oz) olive oil

1 small leek, white part only, chopped

1 red onion, finely chopped

2 garlic cloves, crushed

1 cup (200 g/7 oz) pearled farro, rinsed

100 ml (3½ fl oz) dry white wine

½ cup chopped parsley

4 dried tomatoes, chopped

2 or more red chillies, seeded and chopped

METHOD

Bring 1.5 litres (52 fl oz) lightly salted water to the boil and plunge in the salad greens. Once the water comes back to the boil, simmer for 4 minutes. Drain the greens and keep the water. Heat the olive oil and lightly fry the leek and onion. Add the garlic and farro and stir for a minute or so. Remove the garlic and discard. Add the wine and cook until it has evaporated. Slowly add a ladleful of reserved cooking water, as if you were making risotto. Keep adding ladlefuls of liquid until the farro is cooked – this will take 30–40 minutes, depending on how al dente you like it. Remove from the heat and stir in the blanched greens, parsley, tomatoes and chillies. Season, then serve.

SERVES 4   WINE: Trebbiano d'Abruzzo

ABRVZZO E MOLISE
SECONDI

FLOUNDER WITH OLIVES AND LEMON
PLATESSA IN PADELLA CON OLIVE E LIMONE

INGREDIENTS

2 whole flounder, gutted and
skinned, heads removed

⅓ cup (50 g/1¾ oz) plain
(all-purpose) flour

⅓ cup (80 ml/2½ fl oz)
extra virgin olive oil

1 garlic clove, minced

20 good-quality small black
olives, pitted

1 small lemon, well washed
and cut into 6–8 slices

½ cup chopped parsley

METHOD

Dredge the flounder in the flour so both sides are well dusted. Tap off any excess. Heat 3 tablespoons of the olive oil in a large frying pan on a medium heat. Add the flounder and cook for 90 seconds–2 minutes on each side. (Cook the fish one at a time if your pan is not large enough. Keep the first cooked flounder warm in a 100°C/200°F oven as you fry the second.) The fish should take 90 secounds to 2 minutes a side to cook. Once done, put the fish on warm serving plates. Tip the oil out of the pan and discard. Heat the remaining oil in the same pan. Add the garlic and fry gently until soft. Add ½ cup (125 ml/4 fl oz) water and the olives, lemon and parsley. Turn up the heat and evaporate the liquid until just a few tablespoons are left. Season the sauce, then spoon it over the flounder to serve.

SERVES 2   WINE: Pecorino

PRAWNS AND MUSSELS WITH
CAULIFLOWER AND ROAST GARLIC CREAM
GAMBERI E COZZE AL CAVOLFIORE AGLIATO

INGREDIENTS

1 garlic bulb

50 g (1¾ oz) butter

500 g (1 lb 2 oz) cauliflower,
cut into florets and chopped

1 kg (2 lb 4 oz) mussels,
scrubbed and de-bearded

½ cup (125 ml/4 fl oz) dry
white wine

pinch of saffron threads

2 tablespoons extra virgin
olive oil

1 kg (2 lb 4 oz) raw prawns
(shrimp), shelled and
deveined

METHOD

Preheat the oven to 150°C (300°F). Roast the whole garlic bulb for 15–20 minutes until tender. Remove from the oven, let cool and then remove and peel each clove. Chop each clove carefully into 3–4 pieces and set aside. Heat half the butter in a frying pan and gently fry the cauliflower for 10–12 minutes. Don't let it burn – add a few spoonfuls of water as needed. Once the cauliflower is soft, remove and puree with the remaining butter using a food processor or stick blender. Season the cauliflower and mix in the roasted, chopped garlic pieces, then set the puree aside. Put the mussels in a large saucepan with the wine and saffron. Turn the heat to high, cover with the lid and cook for 2–3 minutes until the mussels open. Give the saucepan a good shake to help the process along. Strain the cooking liquid through a couple of layers of muslin (cheesecloth) or a fine sieve to extract any grit. Remove the mussel meat from the shells and discard the shells. Rest the mussel meat in the strained cooking liquid. Heat the olive oil in a wide frying pan and fry the prawns for 1–2 minutes until just cooked. Season. To serve, spoon the cauliflower cream onto serving plates and top with the prawns and mussel meat.

SERVES 8   WINE: Cerasuolo Rosé

GRILLED SKATE WITH BRAISED BORLOTTI BEANS
RAZZA ALLA GRIGLIA CON BORLOTTI IN UMIDO

Skate is a common fish in many parts of the world. It has a unique flavour and texture. If it can't be found, use fillets from white-fleshed fish such as bream or snapper.

INGREDIENTS

- 2 cups shelled fresh borlotti beans or 2 × 400 g/14 oz tins borlotti beans, drained and well washed
- 4 small or 2 large skate wings (about 1.2 kg/2 lb 12 oz in total)
- ½ cup (125 ml/4 fl oz) extra virgin olive oil
- 4 French shallots, finely diced
- 2 garlic cloves, minced
- 250 g (9 oz) ripe tomatoes, diced
- 2 teaspoons thyme leaves
- 1 teaspoon chopped fresh oregano
- 4 tablespoons finely chopped parsley
- lemon wedges

METHOD

If using fresh borlotti beans, put them in a saucepan with plenty of cold water. Bring to the boil, cover and lower the heat, then simmer for 25–30 minutes until tender. Allow to cool in the liquid, then drain. Meanwhile, use a small sharp knife to remove the skin from the skate wings, exposing the soft flesh. A central line of cartilage separates the top fillet from the bottom fillet. Cut along one side of the cartilage to remove one fillet, then the other. If the fillets are large, cut them into manageable pieces. In a large frying pan, heat ⅓ cup (80 ml/2½ fl oz) of the olive oil. Lightly fry the shallots and garlic until soft. Add the tomatoes, thyme, oregano and 2–3 pinches of salt, mix well and simmer for 15 minutes. Add the beans and mix well, then add the parsley and simmer for 10 minutes. Check for seasoning. Heat the remaining oil on a barbecue grill plate or in a large, heavy frying pan. When the oil is hot, cook the skate for a few minutes on each side, depending on the thickness. Serve with the braised beans and lemon wedges.

SERVES 4   WINE: Trebbiano d'Abruzzo

PAN-FRIED LAMB CUTLETS WITH PECORINO AND ROSEMARY
COSTOLETTE D'AGNELLO IMPANATE

To dry your own breadcrumbs, leave leftover bread in a paper (not plastic) bag for a few days on the kitchen bench or in a cupboard, then put through a food processor.

INGREDIENTS

12 lamb cutlets

2 cups dry breadcrumbs

1 cup (100 g/3½ oz) grated aged pecorino cheese

handful rosemary leaves, finely chopped

½ cup (70 g/2½ oz) plain (all-purpose) flour

2 eggs, well whisked

¼ cup (60 ml/2 fl oz) extra virgin olive oil

lemon wedges

METHOD

Place each lamb cutlet between two pieces of plastic wrap and flatten using a rolling pin with moderate pressure. In a bowl, combine the breadcrumbs, pecorino, rosemary and a pinch of salt and pepper. Mix well. Spread the flour on a plate, pour the eggs onto another plate, and spread the crumb mixture on a third plate. Heat the olive oil in a wide frying pan. Dust each cutlet with flour, then coat with egg and finally crumbs before frying on both sides until golden. Serve with wedges of lemon.

SERVES 4

WINE: Molise Aglianico

PECORINO IS THE TERM USED TO DEFINE ITALIAN CHEESES MADE FROM 100 PER CENT SHEEP'S MILK. PECORINO ROMANO IS ONE OF THE MOST ANCIENT TYPES OF CHEESE AND WAS PART OF THE DIET OF ROMAN SOLDIERS. THE CHEESE IS STILL MADE USING TRADITIONAL METHODS AND ITS PRODUCTION IS LIMITED TO THE ISLANDS OF SARDINIA, LAZIO AND IN THE TUSCAN PROVINCE OF GROSSETO. PECORINO IS DRY-SALTED BY HAND NUMEROUS TIMES AND THEN AGED FROM EIGHT MONTHS TO ONE YEAR. THE LONG AGING TIME CREATES THE STRONG AND SALTY TASTE AND HARD TEXTURE. THE LONGER THE PECORINO IS AGED THE SHARPER AND SMOKIER THE FLAVOUR BECOMES. IT IS A GREAT ALTERNATIVE TO PARMESAN AS A GRATING CHEESE OVER PASTA AND IN STEWS OR AS A CHEESE TO FINISH A MEAL WITH PEARS AND FIGS.

ROAST LEG OF SPRING LAMB WITH ROSEMARY AND GARLIC
COSCIA D'AGNELLO ARROSTO CON TESTE DI AGLIO E ROSMARINO

Lamb leg is best roasted on the bone as the flavour is better. Have your butcher cut the shank bone at the top so it is neat. Leave some fat on the leg – it will melt and baste the meat as it roasts.

INGREDIENTS

2 × 750 g–1 kg (1 lb 10 oz–
   2 lb 4 oz) legs of lamb
½ cup (125 ml/4 fl oz) extra
   virgin olive oil
4 large rosemary sprigs
3 garlic bulbs, halved
   crossways

METHOD

Preheat the oven to 230°C (450°F). If the lamb legs have come straight from the refrigerator, leave them out for 15 minutes or so to lose the chill – they will cook more evenly if they are at room temperature. Rub the legs with salt and pepper and most of the olive oil, then put in a roasting tin on top of a couple of sprigs of rosemary each. Sprinkle the cut sides of the garlic bulbs with the remaining oil and add them to the tin. Roast for 25–40 minutes, depending how you like your lamb. For medium-rare, allow about 25 minutes per kg (2 lb 4 oz); for medium, allow about 35 minutes per kg. Turn the legs every 10 minutes and baste with the juices. When they are cooked, remove from the oven and leave to rest in the tin for around 10 minutes, covered but not sealed with foil. Resting is important to let the muscles relax and the juices inside 'set'. Remove roast garlic cloves from their skin and mix with pan juices. Serve the lamb sliced off the bone with the pan juices and soft, creamy garlic and roast potatoes (see page 101 for recipe).

SERVES 6   WINE: Montepulciano d'Abruzzo

ROAST LEG OF SPRING LAMB WITH ROSEMARY AND GARLIC

LAMB AND RICOTTA POLPETTE IN HERB AND TOMATO SAUCE
POLPETTE DI AGNELLO E RICOTTA

Polpette is the Italian word for patties. The lamb and ricotta mixture has to be rested overnight; otherwise, the polpette will be dry and won't hold together.

INGREDIENTS

700 g (1 lb 9 oz) minced (ground) lamb

300 g (10½ oz) ricotta cheese

1 cup (100 g/3½ oz) grated parmesan cheese

100 g (3½ oz) unsalted butter

⅔ cup (170 ml/5½ fl oz) extra virgin olive oil

1 large brown onion, finely chopped

4 garlic cloves, minced

3 teaspoons ground cumin

1 teaspoon ground chilli

1 teaspoon ground fennel seeds

4 tablespoons chopped fennel tops

4 tablespoons chopped rosemary leaves

½ cup chopped parsley

20–30 g chives, finely snipped

2 tablespoons chopped tarragon

100 g (3½ oz) pine nuts

2 large eggs, whisked

100 g (3½ oz) dry breadcrumbs

HERB AND TOMATO SAUCE

1 kg (2 lb 4 oz) ripe or tinned tomatoes

⅓ cup (80 ml/2½ fl oz) extra virgin olive oil

3 French shallots, finely chopped

2 garlic cloves, minced

¼ cup chopped basil leaves

¼ cup chopped parsley leaves

½ cup (in total) mixed chopped chives, oregano, fennel tops, tarragon and marjoram

METHOD

In a large bowl, mix the lamb, ricotta and parmesan. Heat 20 g (¾ oz) of the butter and 2 tablespoons of the olive oil in a frying pan and gently fry the onion and garlic for a couple of minutes until soft. Add the spices, fennel tops, herbs and pine nuts and gently mix and fry for 4–5 minutes. Remove from the heat and let cool. Add the eggs and breadcrumbs to the lamb and cheese mixture, then add the cooled onion-spice-herb mixture. Season and mix the lot well with your hands so that everything is incorporated evenly. Cover and refrigerate overnight.

To make the herb and tomato sauce using fresh tomatoes, bring a large saucepan of salted water to a rolling boil. Meanwhile, score a shallow cross into the base of each tomato. Carefully plunge the tomatoes into the boiling water for 30 seconds. Remove with a slotted spoon and put in a bowl of iced water for a minute or so. Peel the skin from the tomatoes, cut them in half and squeeze out and discard the seeds. Roughly chop the flesh and put into a bowl. Heat the olive oil in a saucepan and gently fry the shallots and garlic for a couple of minutes until soft. Add the tomatoes and bring to the boil. Turn down to a simmer and add the herbs and a couple of good pinches of salt. Simmer for 15–20 minutes until the sauce is thick. Season and set aside.

Form each polpette by scooping a heaped tablespoon of lamb mixture into your hands and pressing it into the form of a patty. Fry the polpette in batches. For each batch, heat 20 g (¾ oz) of the remaining butter and 1½ tablespoons of the remaining oil until foaming, then cook until well browned on both sides. Simmer the polpette in the herb and tomato sauce for 10 minutes.

SERVES 8 with approx. 750 ml (25 fl oz) sauce   WINE: Cerasuolo d'Abruzzo

GRILLED PORK FILLET WITH BRAISED FARRO
FILETTO DI MAIALE ALLA GRIGLIA CON FARRO

INGREDIENTS

1 × 1.2 kg (2 lb 12 oz) pork fillet

½ cup (125 ml/4 fl oz) extra virgin olive oil

1 small leek, white part only, cut in half lengthways and thinly sliced

2 celery sticks from centre of bunch, diced

1 small carrot, diced

1 garlic clove, minced

8 sage leaves

leaves from 1 small rosemary sprig, chopped

100 g (3½ oz) pearled farro, rinsed

1 cup (250 ml/9 fl oz) dry white wine

4 tinned tomatoes, mashed

METHOD

Trim the pork fillet of any silver skin and slice the fillet into medallions about 2 cm (¾ in) thick. Place on a tray and refrigerate until needed. Heat 2 tablespoons of the olive oil in a large saucepan and lightly fry the leek, celery, carrot, garlic, sage and rosemary for a couple of minutes. Stir continually so the leek and garlic don't colour. Add the farro and stir well for a minute. Add the wine and tomatoes and a couple of good pinches of salt. Simmer for 20 minutes until the farro is cooked and only a small amount of liquid is left. If the pan dries out during cooking, add a little water. Once cooked, remove from the heat and season. Heat the remaining oil on a grill (barbecue or chargrill pan) or in a large frying pan. Season each pork medallion with salt and cook at a high heat for 30–45 seconds on each side. Rest for 5 minutes. Serve the pork with the braised farro.

SERVES 6   WINE: Montepulciano d'Abruzzo

RABBIT WITH CHICKPEAS AND ROCKET
CONIGLIO IN CASSERVOLA

INGREDIENTS

⅓ cup (80 ml/2½ fl oz) extra virgin olive oil

1 white onion, diced

6 garlic cloves, roughly chopped

1 × 1.2–1.5 kg (2 lb 12 oz– 3 lb 5 oz) rabbit, jointed

150 ml (5 fl oz) dry white wine

2 cups (400 g/14 oz) cooked chickpeas

500 g (1 lb 2 oz) rocket (arugula), chopped

¼ cup (60 ml/2 fl oz) red wine vinegar

1 cup chopped parsley

METHOD

Heat the olive oil in a large, heavy-based saucepan. Fry the onion, garlic and rabbit pieces until brown. Add the wine, chickpeas, rocket and a couple of pinches of salt. Stir, then cover and simmer for 1 hour. Add the vinegar and parsley, and season. Rest for 10 minutes before serving.

SERVES 4   WINE: Cerasuolo d'Abruzzo

STUFFED TOMATOES WITH CHICKPEAS
POMODORI RIPIENI

INGREDIENTS

8 ripe tomatoes

20 g (¾ oz) unsalted butter

⅔ cup (170 ml/5½ fl oz) extra virgin olive oil

6 French shallots, finely diced

2 garlic cloves, minced

8 anchovy fillets, drained and chopped

2 tablespoons salted capers, well washed, drained and roughly chopped

¼ cup chopped parsley

½ cup basil leaves, roughly torn

2 tablespoons chopped tarragon leaves

2 tablespoons sultanas (golden raisins)

80 g (2¾ oz) fresh breadcrumbs

¼ cup (40 g/1½ oz) pine nuts, toasted

2 cups (400 g/14 oz) cooked chickpeas

6 tablespoons grated parmesan cheese

METHOD

Cut the top centimetre (½ in) off each tomato, reserving these pieces as little 'hats'. Using a teaspoon, scoop out the insides of each tomato, taking care not to damage the walls. Put the scooped-out flesh in a bowl and set it aside with the hollowed-out tomatoes and 'hats'. Preheat the oven to 160°C (320°F). Heat the butter and 3 tablespoons of the olive oil in a large frying pan and gently fry the shallots and garlic for a couple of minutes until soft. Add the anchovies, capers and herbs and fry gently for another couple of minutes. Add 3 more tablespoons of the oil, the sultanas and the breadcrumbs and fry gently for another minute or so until all is well incorporated. Transfer the mixture to a bowl and let cool a little. Add the pine nuts and season. Fill each tomato with this mixture, gently but firmly pressing into the cavities. Place the stuffed tomatoes in a roasting tin and put their 'hats' on. Mix the chickpeas with the scooped-out tomato flesh and the remaining oil. Season, mix well and scatter around the stuffed tomatoes. Sprinkle the parmesan over the chickpea mixture and bake for 15 minutes. Remove the 'hats' and bake for another 10 minutes until well browned. Delicious either hot or cold.

SERVES 4   WINE: Biferno Rosé

ABRUZZO E MOLISE DOLCI

ABRVZZO E MOLISE

GRAPES PRESERVED IN GRAPPA
UVA SOTTO GRAPPA

In the Molise city of Campobasso, the local white pezzutella grape is used. It is difficult to find outside the zone, but firm, large thomson seedless or white muscatel grapes can be substituted. They have to be very fresh.

INGREDIENTS

800 g (1 lb 12 oz) large, firm white grapes

⅔ cup (150 g/5½ oz) caster (superfine) sugar

1 cinnamon stick

1 litre (35 fl oz) grappa or other spirit

METHOD

Using sharp scissors, cut each grape from the bunch, leaving about 1 cm (½ in) of stem attached. Wash the grapes carefully. Dry well and leave on a tray for 3 hours so they lose any trace of moisture from their skins. In a 2 litre (70 fl oz) glass preserving jar, layer the grapes a few at a time with the sugar. Put the cinnamon stick carefully down the middle of the grapes. Leave for 3 hours to macerate, then pour in the grappa so it covers the grapes. Seal the jar and leave in a cool cellar or cupboard for at least 2 months. Serve with creams or custard or bake into pies, tarts and cakes. Excellent also with duck or pork. The grappa will retain the flavour of the grapes and turn into a wonderful liqueur.

MAKES about 2 litres (70 fl oz)

CHERRIES IN MONTEPULCIANO
CILIEGIE AL MONTEPULCIANO

INGREDIENTS

1 teaspoon anise seeds

1 teaspoon black peppercorns

3 cups (750 ml/26 fl oz) Montepulciano wine

1 cup (220 g/7¾ oz) caster (superfine) sugar

500 g (1 lb 2 oz) cherries, pitted

METHOD

Tie the anise seeds and peppercorns in a small piece of muslin (cheesecloth). Put in a saucepan with the wine, sugar and 125 g (4½ oz) of the cherries and bring to the boil. Reduce the heat to very low and simmer for 1 hour. Strain the liquid, discarding the muslin bag. Press the cooked cherries through a fine sieve to extract all the juice. (Keep these cherries and swirl them through vanilla gelato later.) Put the juice in a saucepan over heat and reduce by a third, then pour the hot liquid over the uncooked cherries. Cool before use. Serve with ricotta or vanilla gelato.

QUINCE JELLY
GELATINA DI MELE COTOGNE

This jelly is great with fresh ricotta or on toast, or served with a sharp cheese such as aged pecorino.

INGREDIENTS
6 quinces, well washed
caster (superfine) sugar
juice of 1 lemon

METHOD
Cut each quince into 6 wedges, leaving the skin and core intact. Put in a saucepan and pour in 2 litres (70 fl oz) water, adding a little more if necessary to cover. Bring to the boil, then put on the lid, reduce the heat to low and simmer for 1 hour. The quinces should be soft. Line a wide sieve or a colander with clean muslin (cheesecloth) or linen. Put the sieve over a bowl and gently pour in the quinces and their cooking liquid. Leave for 5–6 hours to drain completely. Gather the liquid, measure the amount and put in a saucepan. For every litre of liquid, add 700 g (1 lb 9 oz) caster sugar. Add the lemon juice and bring to a rapid boil. After 5 minutes, take a teaspoon of the boiling jelly and drop it onto a cold, slightly inclined plate. If it sets as it cools, then it's ready. If not, keep boiling until the jelly passes the test. Transfer to sterilised preserving jars.

MAKES about 3 litres (5¼ pints)

GRAPE-SKIN JAM
LA SCRUCCHIATA ABRUZZESE

This jam is traditionally made at harvest time with Montepulciano d'Abruzzo grapes. Their skin is exactly the right thickness to give the jam its signature texture. You can substitute thinner-skinned black grapes. Scrucchiata is excellent as a jam in its own right or with a sharp cheese such as aged pecorino.

INGREDIENTS
2 kg (4 lb 8 oz) de-stemmed
    Montepulciano d'Abruzzo
    grapes
200 g (7 oz) sugar

METHOD
Wash the grapes well, taking care not to bruise them. Gently dry the fruit, then, using your fingers, squeeze the juice from each grape into a bowl. Put the grape skins in a separate bowl. Sieve the grape juice carefully to remove any seeds. Combine the sieved juice with the skins and the sugar in a flameproof casserole dish, heavy-based saucepan or jam pot and bring to a simmer on a low heat. Cook for at least 2–3 hours until reduced by two-thirds, stirring every few minutes to make sure the jam doesn't stick and burn at the bottom. Transfer to sterilised preserving jars.

MAKES about 1 litre (35 fl oz)

BAKED CHESTNUT MOULD
BUDINO DI CASTAGNE

INGREDIENTS

450 g (1 lb) chestnuts

3 eggs

120 g (4¼ oz) caster (superfine) sugar

80 g (2¾ oz) butter, softened

finely grated zest of 1 lemon

900 ml (30 fl oz) milk

1 teaspoon natural vanilla extract

3 tablespoons fine dried breadcrumbs

METHOD

Preheat the oven to 180°C (350°F). Using the tip of a sharp knife, score each chestnut by cutting a shallow cross on the flat side. Put the chestnuts in boiling water for 15 minutes. Peel as soon as they are cool enough to handle (they are easier to peel when still warm), making sure both the skin and the fine inner pellicle are removed. Press the chestnut flesh through a potato ricer like you would potatoes for gnocchi. Cream the eggs, sugar and 60 g (2¼ oz) of the butter together and add to the pureed chestnuts with the lemon zest, milk and vanilla. Mix thoroughly. Grease a 2 litre (70 fl oz) capacity pudding basin (mould) with the remaining butter and dust with the breadcrumbs. Pour in the batter and bake for 30 minutes. Cool to room temperature before turning out onto a serving plate. Serve with crema inglese (see page 52).

SERVES 6 WINE: Moscatello di Castiglione Passito

MANDARIN PUDDINGS
TORTINI AL MANDARINO

INGREDIENTS

250 g (9 oz) unsalted butter

530 g (1 lb 2½ oz) sugar

1 teaspoon natural vanilla extract

4 eggs

2 cups (300 g/10½ oz) plain (all-purpose) flour

2½ teaspoons baking powder

¾ cup (180 ml/6 fl oz) milk

finely grated zest of 2 lemons

400 ml (14 fl oz) fresh mandarin juice

24 fresh mandarin segments (3 segments per pudding)

whipped cream

METHOD

Preheat the oven to 180°C (350°F). Butter and sugar 8 dariole or small ring moulds (100 ml/3½ fl oz). Cream the butter and 1½ cups (330 g/11½ oz) of the sugar, then add the vanilla, 2 whole eggs and 2 egg yolks. Reserve the 2 whites. Sift the flour, baking powder and a pinch of salt, then add to the mixture. Mix in the milk and zest. Whisk the 2 egg whites to soft peaks and fold into the mixture. Almost fill the moulds with mixture, then put in a baking dish and pour in water so it comes at least halfway up the sides of the moulds. Bake for 15–20 minutes until a skewer inserted into the puddings comes out clean. Meanwhile, put the remaining sugar in a saucepan and heat until it is light caramel. Carefully add the mandarin juice and boil for 5 minutes. Remove the puddings from the oven and while they are still hot, prick their surface and pour some of the syrup into each one. Allow to cool a little, then turn out and serve with mandarin segments and cream. Add a little more syrup if needed.

SERVES 8 WINE: Liquore di mandarini (mandarin liqueur)

MANDARIN PUDDINGS

BASILICATA

BASILICATA

ALSO KNOWN AS LUCANIA, BASILICATA BORDERS CAMPANIA TO THE WEST, PUGLIA TO THE NORTH AND EAST, AND CALABRIA TO THE SOUTH. IT HAS ONE SHORT, SOUTH-WESTERN COASTLINE ON THE TYRRHENIAN SEA BETWEEN CAMPANIA AND CALABRIA, AND A LONGER ONE TO THE SOUTH-EAST ON THE GULF OF TARANTO ON THE IONIAN SEA BETWEEN CALABRIA AND PUGLIA. ACCORDING TO THE 'ITALY AS BOOT' ANALOGY, BASILICATA IS THE INSTEP. IT COVERS SOME 10,000 SQUARE KILOMETRES (3850 SQUARE MILES) AND HAS A POPULATION OF ABOUT 600,000.

The original name of the province, Lucania, comes from the Latin lucus, meaning 'woods'. It tells us that once, before indiscriminate deforestation, this was a land of forests. It also has mountains, and thus, unlike easily traversed Puglia, a wild and difficult terrain – which made it a haven for those looking for a hiding place, including Christians escaping the rise of Islam in Africa, and dissidents from Turkey. It was also a land of great poverty and hardship, as portrayed by Carlo Levi in his book *Christ Stopped at Eboli*. The name Basilicata, from the Greek basilikos, refers to the Byzantine rulers who arrived in the sixth century.

Here you will find a peasant cuisine, simple and full-flavoured with liberal use of chilli. The chilli was seized upon as soon as it arrived as a cheap substitute for the expensive spices few could afford, and used to season bland pulse and grain dishes. Basilicata gave the world penne all'arrabbiata ('angry penne'), made with tomato, pancetta, onion, garlic, chilli and pecorino cheese; and pollo alla potentina (chicken Potenza style), which contains liberal doses of chilli. Another much-loved fiery product is sugna piccante: lard with chilli, fennel and salt (some recipes call for suet rather than lard), which is spread on bread and cooked in dishes such as cavalfiore piccante (spicy cauliflower).

Cured sausages are made from the local black pigs, of which there is at least one on every farm. The spicy sausages of Lucania – made even before the chilli arrived – were admired by the ancients, from Apicius to

Horace, the latter of whom was born on the border of what was then Lucania and Puglia. The best known of these sausages is lucanica, a name used today to describe any spicy sausage made in the manner of those from Basilicata (and which is curiously close to the Greek word for pork sausage, loukanika). Others are the sopressate of Lagonegro and the pezzenta ('beggar's sausage') from the mountains, made of the leftovers from the slaughter: head, lung, liver and veins. It got its name because it was eaten by the poorest people.

Basilicata is known for its fine cheeses, most notably caciocavallo podolico, which is made from the milk of the (still) semi-wild podolica cattle that roam the mountains. A soft cheese called burrino is made from whey and matured in a caciocavallo skin, sometimes with a sliver of sopressata inserted in it. There are also many goat's and sheep's cheeses, most notably the casieddu di Moliterno, a soft goat's cheese strained through ferns and flavoured with a herb called nepitella.

Lamb and kid are eaten widely, and both can be used for capozzelle – the head cooked on a spit. In Potenza, lamb chops are cooked with olives, and lepre alla cacciatora is hare cooked in a hunter's sauce of garlic, sage, rosemary, ginger and tomatoes. Vegetable dishes include ciaudedda, where potatoes, young artichokes and broad beans are slowly sweated in lard and olive oil with onions and pancetta, and ciammotta, in which eggplants (aubergines), potatoes and peppers are fried separately and then with chopped tomatoes and garlic.

What emerges is a portrait of a hearty, full-flavoured cuisine that epitomises Capatti and Montanari's observation in *Italian Cuisine: A Cultural History* that 'the culture of hunger can be transformed into culinary pleasure'.

The only wine-producing area in Basilicata is the ominously named Mount Vulture, and vines are planted in the rich volcanic soil in its shadow in what is, in spite of its position in the deep south, one of Italy's coolest wine-producing areas.

Aglianico is the indigenous grape variety and Aglianico de Vulture the DOC zone, which extends beyond and away from the mountain to the north. The bad news is that there is not much of this delicious and distinctive wine to be had; it has therefore achieved cult status, to be tracked down and hoarded (it does need time to show its best side). Some large producers are moving in, and expansion looks likely – it can only be hoped that quality does not suffer.

As far as white wines go, some foreign grapes have intruded in recent years – chardonnay and pinot bianco, for example – taking advantage of the climate. Malvasia and moscato are other more traditional grapes found here, but at the time of writing they were being made into simple vini di tavola and sold only locally.

BASILICATA ANTI-PASTI

OVEN-CURED BLACK OLIVES
OLIVE INFORNATE

This way of curing olives appears to have been first done in Italy in the Basilicata region. Today the famous olives have been classified and protected by Slow Food Presidio. They are made around the Ferrandina hills in the province of Matera, using a large olive variety called Majatica that is allowed to ripen totally to a violet black before being cured.

INGREDIENTS

2 kg (4 lb 8 oz) fresh large
  black olives

1 tablespoon coarse salt

extra virgin olive oil

1 teaspoon dried oregano

1 teaspoon ground chilli

METHOD

Using a small sharp knife, slit each olive 2–3 times lengthways. Put the olives in a large bowl and pour in water to cover. Leave for 12 days, changing the water 3 times a day. Preheat the oven to 120°C (250°F). Drain the olives, then wash and dry well, put on a baking tray and sprinkle with the salt. Bake for 30 minutes, then cool completely. Put in sterilised jars with the oregano and chilli and pour in olive oil to cover. If proper sterilisation techniques are followed, they will keep indefinitely. To serve, lightly fry a little chopped garlic, then spoon some cured olives into the pan and gently heat before serving with grated pecorino cheese and crostini.

SERVES 20   WINE: Dry moscato

MIXED GREENS AND OLIVE CALZONE
CALZONE DI ORTAGGI E OLIVE

INGREDIENTS

1 tablespoon extra virgin olive
  oil, plus extra for brushing

1 kg (2 lb 4 oz) mixed greens –
  such as beetroot (beet)
  leaves, cime di rapa (broccoli
  raab), borage and nettles

½ cup black or green olives,
  pitted and chopped

2 small red chillies, chopped

250 g (9 oz) ricotta cheese

100 g (3½ oz) grated pecorino
  cheese

½ quantity basic focaccia dough
  (see page 285)

METHOD

Preheat the oven to 175°C (345°F) and grease a baking tray with the olive oil. Wash and trim the greens. Bring a large saucepan of salted water to the boil and plunge in the greens for 3–4 minutes, then drain and let cool. Squeeze out as much water as possible and roughly chop. Put in a bowl with the olives, chillies, ricotta and pecorino, season and mix well. Roll out the focaccia dough to a 5 mm (¼ in) rectangle and, keeping the sheet in one piece, put half of it on the baking tray. Spread the stuffing on the half that is on the tray, leaving a 2 cm (¾ in) border. Fold the other half of the dough over the filling and pinch together at the border to seal. Brush the surface with oil and bake for about 30 minutes.

SERVES 8–10   WINE: Fiano

CHILLIES STUFFED WITH EGGPLANT, GARLIC AND CAPERS
PEPERONCINI RIPIENI

INGREDIENTS

2 garlic bulbs

18 golf-ball chillies

⅓ cup (80 ml/2½ fl oz) extra virgin olive oil

600 g (1 lb 5 oz) eggplants (aubergines)

1 handful parsley, finely chopped

36 large capers, rinsed and chopped

METHOD

Preheat the oven to 180°C (350°F). Put the garlic bulbs on a baking tray and bake for 20–30 minutes until soft, then transfer to a plate and let cool. Leave the oven on. Cut off the top of each chilli at the stem, just under the shoulder. Using a small spoon, scoop out all the seeds and membrane, taking care not to pierce the skin. Put the chillies on the baking tray, sprinkle with 1 tablespoon of the olive oil, season and roast for 10–15 minutes until the skins have softened a little. Set aside to cool. Put the eggplants directly on a gas flame and, using tongs, turn until charred and soft (or roast in the oven until soft). Let cool, then scoop out the flesh and put it in a sieve to drain. Discard the skin. Cut the roast garlic bulbs in half and squeeze the flesh into a bowl. Add the eggplant flesh, parsley and remaining oil and mash using a fork. Season and stir in the capers. Fill the chillies with the eggplant mixture and serve.

MAKES 18   WINE: Vulcanello bianco

FRITTATA WITH BORAGE AND CHILLI
FRITTATA AL PEPERONCINO

Borage grows wild in many parts of Italy. It has a beautiful blue flower which can be used along with the leaves. Simple, fresh ingredients at their peak typify the frugal cuisine of Basilicata. Frugal it may be, but this almost-forgotten region of Italy is one of my favourites for food and wine.

INGREDIENTS

2 cups borage leaves

8 eggs, lightly whisked

2 tablespoons grated pecorino cheese

2 red chillies, seeded and finely chopped

2 tablespoons extra virgin olive oil

METHOD

Bring a saucepan of salted water to the boil, throw in the borage and cook for 2 minutes. Drain and let cool, then squeeze out as much water as possible and chop. Add to the eggs with the pecorino and chillies, season lightly and mix well. Heat the olive oil in a 20 cm (8 in) frying pan on high heat until just starting to smoke. Pour in the egg mixture and cook until done on the bottom, lifting the edges continually using a spatula so the raw mixture fills the space (this traps air and makes the frittata light and fluffy). Turn the frittata onto a plate, then slide it back into the pan uncooked side down and cook for 2–3 minutes until the centre feels done. Slide the frittata onto a plate and let cool for a couple of minutes, then cut into wedges to serve.

SERVES 8   WINE: Malvasia di Ripolla

BRAISED OYSTER MUSHROOMS
CARDONCELLI IN UMIDO

Cardoncelli mushrooms grow wild in Basilicata and going hunting for them is a cherished pastime. They have a grey cap with prominent gills underneath. Note that mushroom-gathering in the wild should only be undertaken with someone who knows the territory and its mushrooms, as there are many that are poisonous. Commercially grown oyster mushrooms can be substituted here.

INGREDIENTS

650 g (1 lb 7 oz) cardoncelli or oyster mushrooms, trimmed

½ cup (125 ml/4 fl oz) extra virgin olive oil

4 garlic cloves, minced

150 g (5½ oz) tomato fillets (see page 40)

2 tablespoons finely chopped parsley

2 pinches ground chilli

6 tablespoons coarse breadcrumbs

METHOD

Cut any large mushrooms into 2 or 3 pieces. Heat ⅓ cup (80 ml/2½ fl oz) of the olive oil in a large frying pan and add the garlic and mushrooms. Fry on medium heat, stirring continuously, until the mushrooms soften. Add the tomato fillets, parsley, chilli and a couple of pinches of salt and simmer for 5–6 minutes until the mixture thickens. Remove from the heat and season, then transfer to a serving plate. Wipe out the pan and add the remaining oil. Add the breadcrumbs and lightly toast on medium heat, stirring. Sprinkle the breadcrumbs on the mushrooms and serve at room temperature.

SERVES 8   WINE: Chardonnay Martino

GOLF BALL CHILLIES ARE SMALL ROUND CHILLIES DESCRIBED PERFECTLY BY THEIR NAME. THEY ARE GREAT FOR STUFFING. A CALABRIAN FRIEND CALLS THESE CHILLIES 'SATAN'S KISS'. IT'S MEDIUM-HOT, AROUND SIX ON A TEN-POINT HEAT SCALE BUT WHEN PREPARED PROPERLY THAT HEAT IS DIMINISHED TO A PRICKLE ON THE LIPS AND TONGUE. THE HEAT IN CHILLIES IS FOUND IN THEIR VEINS AND CELLS BUT NOT, AS COMMONLY BELIEVED, IN THE SEEDS. SCOOP OUT THIS PITH AND YOU'VE REMOVED A GOOD DEAL OF THE HEAT.

BASILICATA
PRIMI

WHITE FISH AND FLAT BEAN SOUP
MINESTRA DI PESCE E FAGIOLONI

The fish used here can be any non-oily white fish, such as snapper, dory, bream or whiting. Dutch pole beans can be substituted for the Roman flat beans.

INGREDIENTS

600 g (1 lb 5 oz) white fish fillets, skin off and bones removed

1 large brown onion

¼ cup sage leaves

2 tablespoons extra virgin olive oil

150 ml (5 fl oz) dry white wine

300 g (10½ oz) flat green beans, trimmed and cut into 1 cm (½ in) pieces

2 tablespoons finely chopped parsley

chilli oil

METHOD

Cut the fish into bite-sized pieces and refrigerate until you are ready to cook. Finely mince the onion and sage together. Heat the olive oil in a large saucepan and add the onion/sage mixture. Fry gently for 2–3 minutes, stirring regularly, until soft and aromatic. Add the wine, turn up the heat and boil until the liquid has evaporated. Pour in 1 litre (35 fl oz) water and add the beans, then bring to the boil. Reduce the heat and simmer for 8 minutes. Add the fish, parsley and a couple of good pinches of salt and simmer for 2–3 minutes until the fish is just cooked. Add salt (if needed) and a little chilli oil and serve.

SERVES 4-6 WINE: Malvasia

ORECCHIETTE LUCANA STYLE
ORECCHIETTE ALLA LUCANA

Orecchiette (literally 'little ears') are common in both Puglia and Basilicata, albeit prepared in different ways. They are made using durum wheat semolina and water and are exported all over the world. Lucana or Lucania is the other name for Basilicata and was the region's official name between 1932 and 1947.

INGREDIENTS

⅓ cup (80 ml/2½ fl oz) extra virgin olive oil

1 red onion, finely chopped

2 garlic cloves, minced

2 red chillies, finely chopped

300 g (10½ oz) yearling beef shoulder, minced

450 g (1 lb) fresh or tinned tomatoes, chopped

10 basil leaves

400 g (14 oz) dried orecchiette pasta

100 g (3½ oz) grated pecorino cheese

METHOD

Heat the olive oil in a large frying pan and lightly fry the onion, garlic and chillies for a minute, stirring. Add the beef and a couple of good pinches of salt, stir and fry gently for 3–4 minutes. Stir in the tomatoes, then turn the heat down to very low and simmer for 60–70 minutes. If the mixture becomes too dry, add a little water. Stir in the basil and check for seasoning. Cook the pasta in plenty of boiling salted water until al dente, then drain and toss with the sauce. Serve with the grated pecorino.

SERVES 4 WINE: Rosso di Roccanova

LAGANE PASTA AND CHICKPEAS
LAGANE E CECI

One of the most popular dishes of the region, lagane e ceci can be found in various permutations throughout Basilicata. Chickpeas are sometimes replaced with dried beans and baccalà is sometimes added, as are vegetables such as the famous cruschi peppers of Senise (see page 94). Lagane are traditionally made with durum wheat flour, though there are modern versions that use soft wheat flour. The root word, laganum, is Roman in origin; lasagna is derived from it, as are many dialect permutations, including lane, lahane, lajanelle and laganedde.

INGREDIENTS

1 cup (200 g/7 oz) dried chickpeas

1 rosemary sprig

⅓ cup (80 ml/2½ fl oz) extra virgin olive oil

3 garlic cloves, thinly sliced

2–3 red chillies, minced

200 g (7 oz) tin tomatoes, mashed

1 quantity basic pasta dough (see page 42)

100 g (3½ oz) grated pecorino cheese

METHOD

Put the chickpeas in a large bowl with the rosemary and pour in cold water to cover. Let soak for at least 10 hours, then drain and put the chickpeas and rosemary in a saucepan. Pour in cold water to cover, add a little salt and bring to the boil. Immediately turn the heat down and simmer for about 1½ hours until the chickpeas are tender. Drain, reserving about ½ cup (125 ml/4 fl oz) of the cooking liquid and discarding the rosemary. Put the chickpeas and reserved cooking liquid in a large saucepan and add the olive oil, garlic and chillies. Cook for 2–3 minutes, then add the tomatoes and a couple of good pinches of salt. Simmer for about 30 minutes. Meanwhile, roll out the pasta dough to 3 mm (⅛ in) thick and cut into 8 cm × 2 cm (3¼ in × ¾ in) ribbons. Cook in plenty of boiling salted water until al dente, then drain. Check the chickpea mixture for seasoning and adjust if necessary. Remove from the heat, add the pasta and mix carefully for 2–3 minutes. Serve with the grated pecorino.

SERVES 6   WINE: Malvasia

RICOTTA RAVIOLI WITH PORK RAGÙ
RAVIOLI DI RICOTTA AL RAGÙ

The small town of Castelmezzano is nestled in the Dolomiti Lucane national park in Basilicata's mountainous heart. I first tasted these ravioli at Al Becco della Civetta, a wonderful restaurant that looks out on the enormous mountain the town is precariously built upon. If you want to make this dish for vegetarians, simply use a fresh tomato salsa (see page 50) instead of the ragù Potenza style.

INGREDIENTS
250 g (9 oz) ricotta cheese (preferably made from sheep's milk)

3 eggs, lightly whisked

2 tablespoons grated pecorino cheese, plus extra for serving

½ cup finely chopped parsley

400 g (14 oz) basic pasta dough (see page 42)

2 cups (500 ml/17 fl oz) ragù Potenza style sauce (see page 101)

1 teaspoon chilli flakes

METHOD
Combine the ricotta, eggs, pecorino and parsley in a bowl and season. Roll out the pasta to a 2 mm thickness and cut out discs 4–5 cm (1½–2 in) in diameter. Put a small teaspoon of the ricotta mixture in the centre of a disc and cover with another disc, pressing the edges together to seal. You may need to brush a little extra whisked egg on the edge. Repeat until all the pasta and filling have been used. Gently heat the ragù. Bring a large saucepan of salted water to the boil and cook the ravioli – if you have just made them, they will take only a minute or two to cook. Drain and put on serving plates, dress with the ragù and serve with grated pecorino and chilli flakes.

SERVES 4–6   WINE: Aglianico del Vulture

CIME DI RAPA, BROAD BEANS AND POTATO
CIME DI RAPA CON FAVE E PATATE

This dish uses cime di rapa (broccoli raab) but this can be replaced with other greens, such as chicory, various sweet and bitter lettuces, or nettles. You could also use spinach, beet leaves or silverbeet (Swiss chard).

INGREDIENTS
300 g (10½ oz) shelled broad beans

2 potatoes, cut into 3 cm (1¼ in) cubes

½ cup (125 ml/4 fl oz) extra virgin olive oil

1 kg (2 lb 4 oz) cime di rapa (broccoli raab), trimmed and cut into 6 cm (2½ in) pieces

METHOD
Put the beans and potatoes in a saucepan and pour in cold water to just cover. Add a couple of pinches of salt and 2 tablespoons of the olive oil and bring to the boil. Turn the heat down, cover and simmer gently for 45 minutes until the vegetables are falling apart and have absorbed most of the water. Meanwhile, bring a large saucepan of salted water to the boil and plunge in the cime di rapa. Blanch for 3–4 minutes, then drain well, toss with the remaining olive oil and season. Puree the beans and potatoes using a stick blender or food processor and add a little more salt and some pepper. Serve hot with the cime di rapa on top.

SERVES 6   WINE: Rosato di Acerenza

BRAISED BEANS WITH ONIONS AND BEETROOT
BORLOTTI IN UMIDO CON BIETOLE

If fresh borlotti beans are unavailable, use 2 × 400 g (14 oz) tins of borlotti beans. Drain them well and add them towards the end with the parsley.

INGREDIENTS

16 small beetroots (beets), trimmed

⅓ cup (80 ml/2½ fl oz) extra virgin olive oil

1 large brown onion, diced

2 garlic cloves, minced

12–16 small brown onions, peeled

1 cup (250 ml/9 fl oz) dry white wine

½ cup (125 ml/4 fl oz) tomato passata

1 cup shelled borlotti beans

½ cup breadcrumbs

¼ cup grated pecorino cheese

½ cup chopped parsley

METHOD

Put the beetroots in a saucepan and pour in cold water to cover well. Bring to the boil, then turn the heat down and simmer for 15 minutes or so until tender but not soft. Let cool in the cooking liquid, then rub off the skins and halve or quarter the beetroots depending on their size. Set aside. Heat half the olive oil in a large frying pan and gently fry the diced onion, garlic and small whole onions for a minute or two. Add the wine, tomato passata and beans and bring to the boil. Add a couple of pinches of salt, then turn the heat down and simmer for 25–40 minutes until the beans are tender. Meanwhile, heat the remaining oil in a frying pan and gently toast the breadcrumbs until golden. Cool a little, then mix with the pecorino. Once the beans are cooked, add the parsley and beetroots, season and serve with the toasted pecorino crumbs sprinkled on top.

SERVES 4

WINE: Matera Greco

THE MARBLE-PATTERNED **BORLOTTI BEAN** BELONGS TO A LARGE GENUS WITHIN THE LEGUME FAMILY, WHICH INCLUDES BEANS, PEAS, LENTILS AND CLOVER AND ALFALFA. LEGUMES HAVE PLAYED AN IMPORTANT ROLE IN HUMAN HISTORY AND ALSO CULINARY HISTORY BECAUSE THEY ARE SO VERSATILE. THEY CAN BE DRIED, STORED AND USED AS FOOD IN WINTER AND THEY CAN ALSO BE GROUND INTO FLOUR AND MADE INTO PASTES AND USED TO THICKEN DISHES.

BRAISED BEANS WITH ONIONS AND BEETROOT

BRAISED VEGETABLES
VERDURE STUFATE

Vegetables in Basilicata are second to none for freshness and flavour, with many local markets selling only what is in season. This dish is a celebration of the flavours of the territory. It can be served on its own as a first course or to accompany a second course of meat or fish.

INGREDIENTS

350 g (12 oz) eggplant (aubergine), cut into 2 cm (¾ in) cubes

2–3 good pinches coarse salt

160 ml (5¼ fl oz) extra virgin olive oil

3 large red onions, cut into 5 mm (¼ in) rings

4 garlic cloves, minced

250 g (9 oz) zucchini (courgettes), cut into 5 mm (¼ in) rounds

200 g (7 oz) red or yellow capsicums (peppers), seeded and cut into 3 cm (1¼ in) squares

180 g (6½ oz) ripe tomatoes, chopped

½ cup chopped parsley

½ cup basil leaves

METHOD

Put the eggplant in a colander and toss with the salt. Leave for 40 minutes, then rinse and pat dry. Heat the olive oil in a large flameproof casserole dish and add the vegetables one at a time so the oil doesn't lose its heat. First add the onions and garlic. Mix, then add the zucchini and mix again. Add the capsicums and mix, then add the eggplant. Mix well and fry on high heat for a minute, then add the tomatoes and a couple of good pinches of salt. Turn the heat down to low, mix well, cover and cook for 3–4 minutes. Remove the lid, add the parsley and basil and simmer for 10 minutes until the vegetables are tender and the sauce has reduced. Check for salt and add a few turns of pepper. Turn off the heat and let rest for 10 minutes before serving with crusty bread.

SERVES 4–6   WINE: Malvasia del Vulture

BASILICATA
SECONDI

POTENZA-STYLE CHICKEN
POLLO ALLA POTENTINA

Potenza is the capital of the Basilicata region and this is a typical local way of cooking chicken. It uses rendered pork fat, or strutto. Strutto is used all over Italy, on its own or in conjunction with olive oil. If you are unable to find it, substitute butter.

INGREDIENTS

1 × 1.6 kg (3 lb 8 oz) chicken, jointed into 8 pieces

30 g (1 oz) rendered pork fat (strutto)

¼ cup (60 ml/2 fl oz) extra virgin olive oil

150 ml (5 fl oz) dry white wine

1 brown onion, thinly sliced

2 garlic cloves, minced

1 teaspoon chilli flakes

200 g (7 oz) tomato fillets (see page 40)

2 tablespoons finely chopped parsley

1 cup basil leaves

roast potatoes (see opposite)

METHOD

Wash the chicken pieces well and pat dry. Heat the pork fat and olive oil in a flameproof casserole dish on medium heat and add the chicken. Cook, turning and gradually adding the wine. Wait until each portion of wine evaporates before adding the next. When you have used all the wine, the chicken pieces should have browned. Add the onion and garlic and stir for a minute or two until they are soft. Add the chilli flakes, tomato fillets, parsley, basil and a couple of good pinches of salt. Stir, then cover, turn the heat down and simmer gently for 40 minutes. Add the roast potatoes, mix well and cook, covered, for a further 5–8 minutes. Serve.

SERVES 4   WINE: Aglianico

RAGÙ POTENZA STYLE
RAGÙ ALLA POTENTINA

This delicious ragù should be made in a large batch as it provides suitable leftovers to be used in many dishes. It's an unusual preparation because the meat is cooked in one piece and served separately as a second course. The sauce can be used to dress pasta such as bucatini or strangolapreti (literally 'priest chokers').

INGREDIENTS

1 × 800 g (1 lb 12 oz) piece pork shoulder, trimmed of excess fat

80 g (2¾ oz) pecorino cheese

2 garlic cloves, minced

1 teaspoon chilli flakes

½ cup chopped parsley

½ teaspoon grated nutmeg

100 g (3½ oz) pancetta, thinly sliced

60 g (2¼ oz) lardo, chopped

50 ml (1½ fl oz) extra virgin olive oil

100 ml (3½ fl oz) dry white wine

750 g (1 lb 10 oz) tin tomatoes, mashed

METHOD

Butterfly the pork shoulder open so it is roughly rectangular, then use a meat tenderiser to beat it to an even thickness. Grate half the pecorino and dice the rest. Combine the diced pecorino with the garlic, chilli, parsley and nutmeg. Spoon the pecorino mixture onto the meat, leaving a 3 cm (1¼ in) border. Cover with the pancetta, then roll up and secure with butcher's twine. Heat the lardo and olive oil in a flameproof casserole dish and brown the meat well, turning often and splashing with the white wine. Once the wine has evaporated, add the tomatoes, 2–3 good pinches of salt and a couple of turns of pepper. Simmer gently for about 2 hours, turning the meat 90 degrees every 30 minutes. Add a little water if the dish looks too dry. Once cooked, remove the meat to a serving dish and pass the sauce through a Mouli or a fine sieve. Serve the meat as a second course. Toss the sauce with pasta to serve separately with the grated pecorino.

SERVES 6–8   WINE: Aglianico del Vulture

ROAST POTATOES WITH ROSEMARY
PATATE ARROSTITE AL ROSMARINO

INGREDIENTS

1 kg (2 lb 4 oz) roasting potatoes, cut into 3 cm (1¼ in) chunks

⅓ cup (80 ml/2½ fl oz) extra virgin olive oil

2 tablespoons rosemary leaves

METHOD

Preheat the oven to 220°C (430°F). Put the potatoes in a baking dish (use 2 dishes if necessary so they aren't piled on top of each other) and toss with the olive oil. Season well with salt and toss so the potatoes are completely coated. Roast for 30 minutes, carefully turning every 15 minutes so that the potatoes become crisp and golden on all sides. Add the rosemary, then cook for 5–10 minutes until the potatoes are tender. Serve as a side dish for roast meats or fish.

SERVES 6

ROAST POTATOES AND TOMATOES WITH CRUSCHI PEPPERS
PATATE ALLA LUCANA CON PEPERONI CRUSCHI

Peperoni cruschi are a little-known speciality of Basilicata, hard to find outside the region. They are made using a variety of sweet red pepper grown around the town of Senise. The peppers are threaded and dried, then the stems are discarded and the peppers are fried carefully in extra virgin olive oil and drained. The word cruschi is onomatopoeic and describes the sound made as the peppers are eaten. They taste extraordinarily sweet and rich. Traditionally served as part of an antipasto with salumi, cheeses and vegetables, they are also added to orecchiette and strascinati pasta with cacioricotta cheese, or crumbled onto roast potatoes.

INGREDIENTS

½ cup (125 ml/4 fl oz) extra virgin olive oil

500 g (1 lb 2 oz) potatoes, cut into 5 mm (¼ in) slices

80 g (2¾ oz) cacioricotta cheese (or pecorino cheese), grated

400 g (14 oz) brown onions, cut into 5 mm (¼ in) slices

350 g (12 oz) ripe tomatoes, peeled and cut into 5 mm (¼ in) slices

2 tablespoons breadcrumbs

1 teaspoon dried oregano

4 whole peperoni cruschi

METHOD

Preheat the oven to 165°C (330°F) and grease a baking dish with 1 tablespoon of the olive oil. Line the dish with potatoes, then season and scatter on some of the cacioricotta. Add a layer of onions, season and add cacioricotta as before. Add a layer of tomatoes, season and add cacioricotta. Repeat until all the vegetables and cheese have been used (you will have 2 or 3 layers). Scatter with the breadcrumbs and oregano and drizzle on the remaining olive oil, then bake for 50–60 minutes until brown. Crumble the cruschi peppers on top to serve.

SERVES 8   WINE: Aglianico

CACIORICOTTA IS HALFWAY BETWEEN CHEESE AND RICOTTA. IT IS MADE THROUGHOUT THE SOUTH BUT ESPECIALLY BASILICATA, PUGLIA AND CAMPANIA, PREDOMINANTLY USING SHEEP OR GOAT'S MILK. THE CHEESES ARE MADE BY GENTLY PRESSING THE CURDS INTO 8-12 CM HOOPS AND THEN DRY SALTING BEFORE MATURING. THEY ARE READY TO BE USED IN 5-6 DAYS AND CAN BE GRATED OR FLAKED FOR COOKING, SEASONING OR JUST AS A TABLE CHEESE WITH BREAD, TOMATOES AND OLIVES.

POTATO, BEAN AND LAMB STEW
SPALLA D'AGNELLO IN UMIDO

I like to make this with leftover lamb roast. If fresh borlotti beans are unavailable, use dried beans that have been soaked overnight in plenty of cold water.

INGREDIENTS

300 g (10½ oz) yellow-fleshed potatoes (e.g. desiree, kipfler or nicola), chopped into 2–3 cm (¾–1¼ in) pieces

1 brown onion, chopped

1 leek, white part only, chopped

½ celery heart, chopped

2 garlic cloves, peeled

1 tablespoon rosemary leaves

½ cup (125 ml/4 fl oz) extra virgin olive oil, plus extra for drizzling

300 g (10½ oz) shelled borlotti beans

400 g (14 oz) leftover roast lamb (shoulder or leg), cut into bite-sized pieces

1 tablespoon chopped parsley

METHOD

Put the potatoes in a bowl of cold water until needed. Put the onion, leek, celery, garlic and rosemary in a food processor and pulse until finely chopped but not liquid. Heat half the olive oil in a large saucepan and add the chopped vegetables. Stir and cook on medium heat for 2–3 minutes until softened. Drain the potatoes and add to the pan along with the beans. Keep stirring and frying for a couple of minutes, then pour in cold water to cover by about 3 cm (1¼ in). Stir and bring to the boil, then immediately turn the heat down to very low and simmer gently for 3 hours, stirring every so often and adding a little water if the pan is too dry. Stir in the lamb and simmer for 30 minutes, then add the parsley, season and ladle into bowls. Drizzle with a little oil and serve.

SERVES 6　　　　　　　　　　　　WINE: Aglianico del Vulture

BASILICATA
DOLCI

FIG AND WALNUT BISCUITS
BISCOTTI CON FICHI E NOCI

The preparation of these biscuits (cookies) is based on feel. They have no added sugar and everything relies on the figs – the variety, how ripe they are and how much flour they will absorb.

INGREDIENTS

1 kg (2 lb 4 oz) soft ripe figs, stems removed
plain (all-purpose) flour
chopped walnut pieces
1 tablespoon extra virgin olive oil

METHOD

Put the figs in a saucepan and pour in 2 litres (70 fl oz) water. Bring to the boil, then immediately turn the heat down to very low and simmer for 20–25 minutes. Avoid overcooking the figs to the point of them falling apart. Preheat the oven to 180°C (350°F). Transfer the figs to a large bowl and mix with enough flour to obtain the consistency of shortcrust pastry. For every ⅔ cup (100 g/3½ oz) of flour you have used, add 50 g (1¾ oz) walnut pieces. Mix well and then form into a ball. Grease your hands with the olive oil and coat the pastry so it is easier to roll. Roll out the pastry to a rectangle about 5 mm (¼ in) thick and cut into 2 cm × 6 cm (¾ in × 2½ in) fingers. Bake for 10–15 minutes until golden.

MAKES about 50   WINE: Moscato

PEACHES PRESERVED IN SWEET WHITE AGLIANICO
PESCHE NEL AGLIANICO PASSITO

Aglianico bianco passito is a sweet white wine. If you can't find it, use a late-picked riesling or semillon.

INGREDIENTS

6 peaches
90 g (3¼ oz) sugar
3 cups (750 ml/26 fl oz) aglianico bianco passito
1 cinnamon stick

METHOD

Put all the ingredients in a saucepan and bring to the boil. Turn the heat down and simmer gently for 3 minutes. Peel the peaches under cold water, then cut each peach into 8 segments and return to the poaching liquid. Transfer the peaches and liquid to a sterilised preserving jar and seal. If proper sterilisation techniques are followed, they will keep indefinitely. Serve with gelato, cakes or whipped cream.

CHESTNUT AND RICOTTA FILLED PASTRIES
CALZONI DI CASTAGNE E RICOTTA

INGREDIENTS

300 g (10½ oz) chestnuts, scored

100 ml (3½ fl oz) milk

120 g (4¼ oz) caster (superfine) sugar

seeds from 1 vanilla bean

3 tablespoons thick (double) cream

150 g (5½ oz) ricotta cheese

2 cups (500 ml/17 fl oz) extra virgin olive oil

icing (confectioners') sugar

PASTRY

250 g (9 oz) plain (all-purpose) flour

40 ml (1¼ fl oz) extra virgin olive oil

1 heaped tablespoon caster (superfine) sugar

½ cup (125 ml/4 fl oz) dry white wine

METHOD

To make the pastry, put the flour on your work surface and make a well in the centre. Add the olive oil, sugar and a pinch of salt, then add the wine a little at a time as you bring the walls of the well into the centre using your fingers. Once the dough comes together in a mass that is not too sticky or too wet, work it until smooth. Add a little more flour if it is too sticky. Shape into a flat disc and wrap in plastic wrap, then refrigerate for at least 30 minutes.

Boil the chestnuts for 30 minutes, then peel and pass through a sieve or ricer. Bring the milk almost to the boil in a saucepan. Add the chestnut puree, sugar, vanilla seeds and cream and simmer for 10–15 minutes until thickened. Cool, then mix in the ricotta.

Roll out the dough to a rectangle about 2 mm (¹⁄₁₆ in) thick and cut strips about 8 cm (3¼ in) wide. Starting about 1 cm (½ in) from the end of each strip, put teaspoons of ricotta mixture 4 cm (1½ in) apart on one side. Fold the pastry over to cover the stuffing as if making ravioli, then cut into 4 cm (1½ in) squares to form the calzoni. Heat the olive oil to 160°C (320°F) in a frying pan. To test the temperature of the oil, throw in a cube of bread – when the oil is ready, the bread will turn golden brown in 30 seconds. Fry the calzoni in batches until lightly golden, then drain on paper towels. Cool and dust with icing sugar to serve.

MAKES about 40   WINE: Moscato

ORANGE CAKE
TORTA DI ARANCIA

INGREDIENTS

30 g (1 oz) unsalted butter

200 g (7 oz) caster (superfine) sugar, plus extra for dusting

1 large orange, well washed and dried

3 eggs

1 × 7 g (¼ oz) sachet powdered yeast

2 cups (300 g/10½ oz) plain (all-purpose) flour

½ cup (125 ml/4 fl oz) extra virgin olive oil

1 vanilla bean, split and seeds scraped

METHOD

Preheat the oven to 170°C (340°F). Grease a 24 cm (9½ in) cake tin with the butter and dust with the extra dusting sugar. Cut the orange into wedges (leaving the skin on) and remove any seeds. Put the orange wedges in a food processor and puree. Whisk the sugar and eggs together until pale and fluffy. Sift the yeast and flour together and add to the sugar/egg mixture along with the olive oil, vanilla seeds and pureed orange. Pour into the cake tin and knock down on the bench to make sure the mixture is even. Bake for 40–45 minutes until a skewer inserted comes out clean. Cool completely in the tin on a wire rack before unmoulding. Serve as is or with clementine ricotta cream (see page 466).

SERVES 8   WINE: Grottino di Roccanova IGT

SWEET BREAD WITH PRESERVED PEACHES
PANDORATO ALLE PESCHE

Basilicata is perhaps Italy's most underdeveloped region, with most of its towns nestled high on top of mountains. Before fast modes of transport were developed, these towns were isolated, especially during winter. Consequently the region developed a cuisine based on frugality and using everything, including leftover bread. This dish comes from around Matera, home of the ancient cave-dwellers.

INGREDIENTS

6 × 2 cm (¾ in) slices stale bread, crusts removed

160 ml (5¼ fl oz) milk

6 tablespoons apricot jam

100 g (3½ oz) caster (superfine) sugar

2 eggs

6 peaches preserved in sweet white aglianico (see page 105)

100 ml (3½ fl oz) extra virgin olive oil

METHOD

Soak the bread in half the milk. Meanwhile, heat the remaining milk until hot but not boiling. Add the apricot jam and stir until dissolved and let cool. Whisk the sugar and eggs until pale and creamy, then add the milk/jam mixture and stir. Using a spatula, dip the soaked bread into the egg mixture. Transfer the bread to a plate and pour over any remaining egg mixture. Leave to soak for 1 hour. Remove the peaches from their syrup and slice thinly. Heat the olive oil in a wide frying pan until a bit of the egg mixture sizzles when dropped in. Gently fry the bread until golden, turning once. Drain on paper towels, then serve topped with the peaches.

SERVES 6   WINE: Aglianico bianco passito

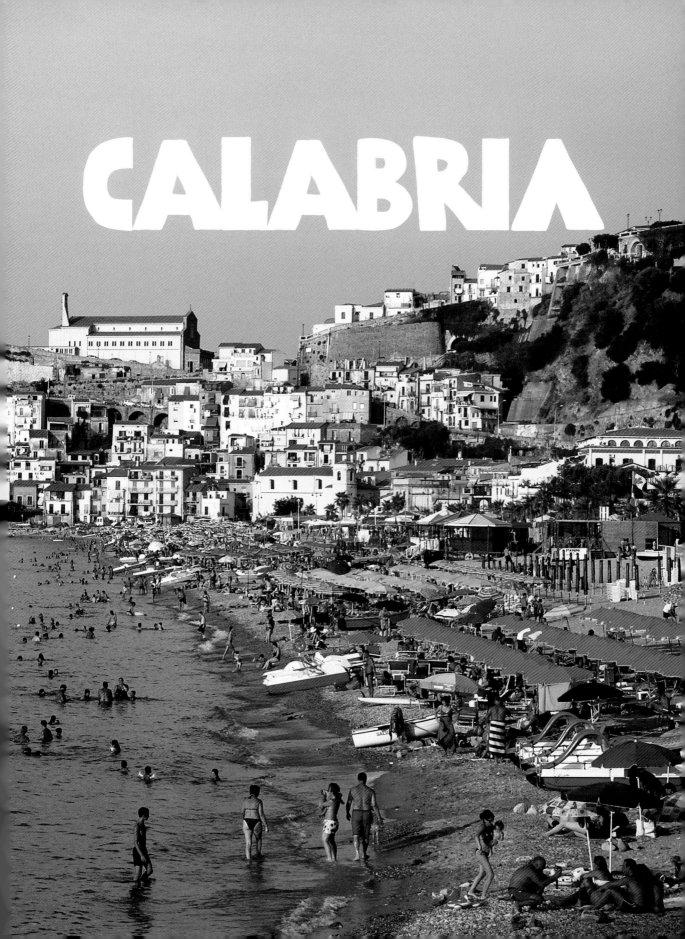

CALABRIA

THE PENINSULA THAT FORMS THE 'TOE' OF ITALY LIES SOUTH OF BASILICATA AND NORTH-EAST OF THE ISLAND OF SICILY. IT HAS COASTLINES TO THE WEST ON THE TYRRHENIAN SEA AND TO THE EAST ON THE IONIAN SEA, COVERS JUST OVER 15,000 SQUARE KILOMETRES (5800 SQUARE MILES), AND HAS A POPULATION OF AROUND TWO MILLION.

It is somewhat of an irony that one of the poorest of the Italian regions was once home to the Greek city of Sybaris, whose name is the origin of the word sybaritic, meaning 'devoted to luxury'. Having been conquered by the city of Croton, home to the abstemious Pythagoras, Sybaris is no more.

Calabria was the most Greek of the Greek regions of Italy, and today there are traces of Greek in food words in the Calabrian dialect. There is also a sizeable Albanian population in the province of Cosenza, whose descendants can be identified by their blonde hair. Many other peoples invaded, fought over and ruled Calabria after the Greeks bowed to Roman rule, including the Moors, the Byzantines, the French and the Spanish.

The terrain is diverse. It is three-quarters mountainous, and in the north the vast Sila plateau, at 500 metres (1640 feet), has dense forests, glades and streams and the snow stays on the ground until May or June. Moving south, where the toe is narrowest,

both seas are visible. The Ionian coast, once you leave the sea, is arid, while there are some rich plains on the Tyrrhenian side and around Cosenza there is intensive cultivation.

Indeed, Calabria is a major food producer. It is rich in citrus fruits and vegetables – especially eggplant, of which many varieties (including asmara, nubia and larga morada) grow. It is the eggplant that has given Calabria its most famous dish, melanzana parmigiana, although the parmesan cheese used in the original dish was made not in Parma but by Calabrian monks in Cistercian dairies.

The citrus of Calabria is worth noting, for every citrus fruit you have ever heard of – and some you haven't – grow here, including two varieties worthy of special mention. Citron, a large, oval, knobbly green to yellow fruit, is used not for its flesh or juice but for its fragrant rind, which is candied and used in panforte and on cheese plates. Bergamot, which looks like a large green lemon, produces an essence that is used in making perfume and added to Earl Grey tea. Eighty per cent of the world's bergamot is grown in Calabria, but how it got there and where it came from is something of a mystery.

Calabria is also Italy's second largest producer of olive oil after Puglia. The oil is used not just for cooking and dressing but also for conserving local produce.

Pasta is an important food in Calabria. Spaghetti con lumache (spaghetti with a snail sauce) is a speciality of Cosenza, while sagne chinne is dialect for stuffed lasagna. A local version of stuffed tomatoes, rigatoncelli con pomodori, uses a pasta called ditalini rugati in the stuffing: it is cooked and mixed with parsley, mint, garlic, pepper and olive oil.

As befits a poor province, Calabria's best-known dishes are simple and rustic, such as sursuminata (scrambled eggs with tomatoes) and ova chi curcuci (fried eggs with pork crackling). Curiously it is the only place in Italy outside of tourist hotels where a substantial breakfast is eaten, in the form of murseddu: lamb or kid offal cooked in a pie-dish-like bread container. Its name is probably derived from the Spanish word for breakfast, almuerzo, which is itself a loan word from Arabic, as indicated by the prefix 'al'.

Another noteworthy local product is nduja (sometimes 'nduja), a word apparently derived from the French andouille, a sausage made from pork intestines. Nduja uses the same ingredients as andouille in paste form, with liberal amounts of chilli. How the connection was made no one knows – although at a guess, as andouille comes from the Latin inductilis, meaning 'made by insertion', it's more than likely nduja comes from the same Latin root.

The main source of protein in this region with its feet in two seas is fish. It provides the fishermen with a choice of two places to hunt, depending on catch and weather, and fish lovers with a greater variety to choose from. »

SCYLLA AND CHARYBDIS

At the port of Scylla, on the narrow body of water between Calabria and Sicily known as the Straits of Messina, there is a rock. Opposite, on the Sicilian side, is a whirlpool, which was known in ancient times as Charybdis.

In Greek mythology, these two features became sea monsters. Scylla was a sea nymph loved by Poseidon, the sea god. Poseidon's wife Amphitrite poisoned the waters in which Scylla bathed; this turned her into a six-headed beast with three rows of sharp teeth in each head who struck out and grabbed sailors from ships that passed too close. Charybdis was also a sea nymph, the daughter of Poseidon. It was Zeus who transformed her into a dangerous whirlpool.

Ships sailing the straits were almost certain to be destroyed by one or other of the two monsters. In the Odyssey, Homer says that Circe told Ulysses to sail closer to Scylla as she could only take sailors, which she did. The reality was that once a ship was sucked down by the whirlpool characterised as Charybdis, there was no hope – whereas if a ship struck the rock Scylla, there was a chance of being saved.

The legend arose because of the dangers of sailing through the straits, where treacherous currents change direction at random and only the best sailors can navigate safely.

All year round, sardines and herrings are caught in the straits between Scylla and Charybdis, but between May and June the swordfish arrive, on their way to warmer southern waters to lay their eggs. In the port of Bagnara a swordfish festival is held on the first Sunday in July, and huge dishes of pennette pasta in a sauce of scozzetta, made from the flesh found under the neck of the swordfish, is served. In the main piazza, guests eat raw swordfish.

Other local seafood dishes include fritters of jujume, or sea anemones; tuna (also caught in the straits) simply spitted and grilled over a wood fire, then sprinkled with lemon juice and olive oil; and red mullet fried and sprinkled with lemon juice and oregano. Herring are often fried in oil with garlic and chilli until reduced to a paste, and then spread on thick slices of bread.

Wine has been produced in Calabria since ancient times on the small amount of scattered arable land suitable for viticulture. Many wines still made there trace their ancestry back to Greek and Roman times when the wines of Calabria were highly prized: the Greeks named it Enotria, the land of wine. In *The Food of Italy*, Waverley Root claimed that, at least in his time (the book was published in 1971), he had heard of but not tasted a wine called Transfigurato di Seminara (Seminara is a small province north of Bagnara) that was still made the Roman way – that is, put in jars and smoked.

But that was then. Now, of the hundred million litres of wine produced in Calabria annually, only 8 per cent is considered good enough for bottling, and about 75 per cent of that comes from the one area: around Cirò, the DOC on the Ionian coast.

The two main indigenous grapes used to make white wines are montonico and greco, with greco being the dominant partner. Wines from both grapes are best drunk young.

Only two DOCs are worth mentioning for reds: Librandi and Cirò, whose vineyards at fairly high altitudes make use of the local gaglioppo grape to make wines best described as jammy. In Librandi, they add cabernet sauvignon to the gaglioppo, which has a softening effect.

One outstanding Calabrian wine is Greco di Bianco, a rare Italian dessert wine made from the grape and in the DOC of the same name. Some say the grape was planted by the Greeks in the 7th century BCE.

The other notable DOCs are Savuto and Scavigna. The rest, as Nicholas Belfrage writes in *Brunello to Zibibbo*, 'are obscure, not to say virtually non existent'.

CALABRIA
ANTI-
PASTi

MARIA CIPRI'S PICKLED EGGPLANT
MELANZANE SOTT'OLIO DI MARIA CIPRI

INGREDIENTS

as many eggplants
(aubergines) as you want
to preserve

white wine vinegar

garlic cloves, cut into slivers

basil leaves

extra virgin olive oil

METHOD

Peel the eggplant, then cut lengthways into 5 mm (¼ in) thick slices. Cut these slices into 5 mm (¼ in) straws. Toss the eggplant straws in fine salt (allow a good pinch per eggplant) until they are well covered. Put them in a container and press them down using a heavy weight. Let sit for 24 hours. Squeeze excess liquid out of the eggplant and wash the salt off well with white wine vinegar. Cover the eggplant with more vinegar and let soak for about 5 hours. Drain, then squeeze really well and pat dry. Toss with slivers of garlic (allow 1 garlic clove per eggplant) and some basil leaves (5 leaves per eggplant), then put in sterilised glass jars and cover with olive oil. Store in a cellar or cool pantry. The pickled eggplant will keep for at least 1 year.

WINE: Ciro Rosato

MUSHROOMS IN OLIVE OIL
FUNGHI SOTT'OLIO

INGREDIENTS

1 kg (2 lb 4 oz) assorted
mushrooms, chopped

1 litre (35 fl oz) white wine
vinegar

extra virgin olive oil

METHOD

Trim any browning areas on the mushrooms using a sharp knife, and use a brush to remove any dirt. Put the mushrooms in a wide, flat sieve. Bring the vinegar and 1 teaspoon of salt to the boil in a saucepan, then plunge in the sieve of mushrooms. Hold them under the liquid for 3 minutes. Drain and transfer to sterilised preserving jars. Cover with olive oil, then seal and store in a cool place. Will keep for three weeks.

SERVES 8–10

WINE: Fiano

PICKLED RED ONIONS
CIPOLLA DI TROPEA SOTT'ACETO

INGREDIENTS

4 large red onions, peeled
   and halved
1 cup (250 ml/9 fl oz) red wine
   vinegar
50 g (1¾ oz) sugar
2 tablespoons extra virgin
   olive oil
1 tablespoon finely chopped
   parsley

METHOD

Slice the onions very thinly and put into a wide, shallow ceramic dish. Bring the vinegar, sugar and ½ cup (125 ml/4 fl oz) water to the boil in a saucepan, then immediately pour the boiling liquid onto the onions. Let cool to room temperature. Drain and use immediately, or leave in the liquid – the onions will become tastier over a few days. To serve, drain the onions and squeeze out any remaining liquid. Dress with the olive oil and parsley and season to taste. Serve as an accompaniment to barbecued meat or seafood, or as an addition to a summer salad. Pickled red onions will keep for 3–4 weeks.

SERVES 6   WINE: Fiano di Avellino

MARINATED GRILLED EGGPLANT ROLLS
INVOLTINI DI MELANZANE ALLA GRIGLIA SOTT'OLIO

INGREDIENTS

2 large eggplants (aubergines),
   washed and cut lengthways
   into 5 mm (¼ in) slices
100 ml (3½ fl oz) extra virgin
   olive oil, plus extra for
   storing
½ cup (125 ml/4 fl oz) red wine
   vinegar
1 cup chopped fresh bread,
   crusts removed
2 tablespoons capers, rinsed
2 fennel fronds, chopped
2 mint sprigs, chopped
4 tablespoons chopped parsley
1 teaspoon dried oregano
1 tin tuna (185 g/6½ oz) in olive
   oil, drained and broken up
3 anchovy fillets, chopped
1 red chilli, seeded and chopped
2 tablespoons white wine
   vinegar

METHOD

Preheat a barbecue or chargrill pan. Brush the eggplant slices with some of the olive oil, sprinkle with salt and grill until golden brown. Arrange side by side on a tray and splash on the red wine vinegar. Put the bread, capers, herbs, tuna, anchovies and chilli in a bowl. Season with salt and mix in the white wine vinegar and remaining oil. Fill each eggplant slice with this stuffing (not too much) and roll up. Arrange in a bowl and pour in oil to cover. Cover the bowl and store in the refrigerator. The eggplant rolls will keep for 7–10 days.

SERVES 6-8   WINE: Greco

PUMPKIN FRITTERS
FRITTELLE DI ZUCCA

INGREDIENTS

500 g (1 lb 2 oz) pumpkin
(winter squash), unpeeled
and cut into pieces

2 large eggs, lightly whisked

1 garlic clove, minced

3 tablespoons chopped
parsley

4 level tablespoons plain
(all-purpose) flour

4 tablespoons grated
pecorino cheese

1 cup (250 ml/9 fl oz) extra
virgin olive oil

METHOD

Steam the pumpkin over a little water until tender. Remove and discard
the skin and mash the flesh using a fork. In a large bowl, combine the
eggs, garlic, parsley, flour and pecorino to obtain a smooth paste. Mix in
the mashed pumpkin and season. Heat the olive oil in a frying pan and
drop in tablespoons of pumpkin mixture. Cook until golden, then drain on
paper towel. Sprinkle with salt if desired and serve hot as a snack.

SERVES 6–8   WINE: Greco

ROASTED BLACK OLIVES
OLIVE NERE INFORNATE

*This is a traditional Calabrian way of curing ripe black olives. The roasted olives can be made into excellent
olive paste, serve as a great addition to an antipasto, or just be eaten as a snack.*

INGREDIENTS

5 kg (11 lb) large fresh black
olives, well washed

250 g (9 oz) coarse salt
(not rock salt)

extra virgin olive oil

METHOD

Make 2–3 cuts in each olive using a sharp knife. Put the olives in a
large plastic or ceramic tub and cover with plenty of cold water. Leave
for 10 days, changing the water twice a day. This will remove most of
the bitterness. Preheat the oven to 120°C (250°F). Drain the olives, dry
well and arrange on baking trays in a single layer. Scatter the salt over
and mix it through. Roast for 20–30 minutes until the olives wrinkle and
dry. Sprinkle with olive oil and transfer to sterilised preserving jars. Seal
and put into a large saucepan. Cover the jars completely with water,
then boil for 20 minutes to sterilise further. The roasted olives will keep
indefinitely if stored in a cool dry place.

WINE: Fiano di Avellino

STUFFED ZUCCHINI
ZUCCHINE IMBOTTITE

Calabrians would say these zucchini (courgettes) are 'mbuttunate instead of imbottite. Wherever you go in Italy, you'll come across dishes, places and people with a 'standard' Italian name as well as a name in the local dialect. 'Nduja is a spreadable salami. It's very hot as there is a large amount of dried chilli mixed in. The 'nduja can be left out of this recipe, if desired. Mozzarella can also be substituted if caciocavallo isn't available.

INGREDIENTS

6 young zucchini (courgettes), each about 12 cm (4½ in)

2 cups finely chopped fresh white bread crusts removed

2 eggs, whisked

2 garlic cloves, minced

4 tablespoons finely chopped parsley

¾ cup (80 g/2¾ oz) grated pecorino cheese

100 g (3½ oz) pork sausage, casing removed

1 tablespoon 'nduja (optional)

½ cup (125 ml/4 fl oz) extra virgin olive oil

50 g (1¾ oz) caciocavallo cheese, grated

METHOD

Plunge the zucchini into boiling water for 3–4 minutes. Remove and let cool, then cut in half lengthways. Carefully scrape out the pulp, creating a good deep cavity. Squeeze the pulp in a clean tea towel (dish towel) to get rid of as much liquid as possible. In a bowl, combine the zucchini pulp, bread, eggs, garlic, parsley, pecorino, sausage and 'nduja (if using). Season well and mix thoroughly. Stuff the zucchini with this mixture, pressing it in securely using the palm of your hand. Heat the olive oil in a wide frying pan and fry the zucchini, stuffing-side down, until brown. Turn the zucchini over and cook the skin side for 1–2 minutes. Serve with the caciocavallo and tomato and chilli salsa (see page 119).

SERVES 6

WINE: Cirò Bianco

CALABRIA
PRIMI

CHILLI SALSA
SALSA DI PEPERONCINO

The heat in chillies is due to a family of alkaloids called capsaicinoids, which are found in varying amounts in the chillies' veins and cells but not, as is commonly believed, in the seeds. The largest concentration of heat in chillies is in the pithy membrane that encloses the seeds. Scoop out this pith and you've removed a good deal of the heat – however, there will be just enough left to make it interesting.

INGREDIENTS

1 tablespoon coriander seeds

40 small hot chillies,
   stalks removed

4 garlic cloves, roughly
   chopped

½ cup (125 ml/4 fl oz) extra
   virgin olive oil

METHOD

Put the coriander seeds in a large mortar and pound gently until crushed. Chop the chillies and add to the mortar with the garlic. Add 1 teaspoon of salt and pound for 3–4 minutes. Add the olive oil and continue pounding gently for 8–10 minutes until you have a homogenous, red–orange paste. This can be done in a food processor but will result in a different texture. The salsa is hot so use with care. Serve in small ramekins to accompany barbecued fish or shellfish, sausages or beef, or simply as a spread on toasted bread.

MAKES 250 ml (8 fl oz)

TOMATO AND CHILLI SALSA
SALSA AL POMODORO E PEPERONCINO CALABRESE

It's difficult to find Calabrian dishes that are free of chilli. Even if a recipe doesn't contain the hot pepper, the Calabrian table will offer salsa, ground chilli or fresh chilli to add. This is the Italian region noted for fiery food, and their chillies are potent but fruity. If you can find Calabrian dried ground chilli for this dish, all the better but other hot chilli will also suffice.

INGREDIENTS

2 kg (4 lb 8 oz) good-quality
   Italian pelati (canned or
   bottled tomatoes)

⅓ cup (80 ml/2½ fl oz) extra
   virgin olive oil

1 brown onion, thinly sliced

2 garlic cloves, minced

½ cup basil leaves, sliced

1 teaspoon ground Calabrian
   chilli, or other hot chilli

METHOD

Put the tomatoes in a bowl and mash using a fork. Heat the olive oil in a saucepan and lightly fry the onion and garlic for a couple of minutes, stirring constantly and taking care they don't colour. Add the tomatoes and a couple of pinches of salt. Simmer very slowly until the mixture is dense and there is little liquid left. Pass the salsa through a sieve to remove any seeds. Return the sieved salsa to the saucepan and simmer on a very low heat for 5 minutes, constantly stirring. Add the basil and chilli, mix well for a minute and then transfer to a bowl to cool. Toss the salsa with pasta, or serve it with eggplant (aubergine) dishes or grilled (broiled) or barbecued sausages or spread on bread.

MAKES 2 litres (70 fl oz)

CUTTLEFISH WITH SALSA PICCANTE
SEPPIE CON SALSA PICCANTE

INGREDIENTS

500 g (1 lb 2 oz) ripe
    tomatoes, peeled,
    seeded and chopped into
    1 cm pieces
juice of ½ lemon
1–3 chillies, chopped
1 garlic clove, minced
good handful basil leaves,
    chopped
140 ml (4¾ fl oz) extra virgin
    olive oil
1 eggplant (aubergine), cut into
    2 cm (¾ in) cubes
250 g (9 oz) cuttlefish or
    squid, bodies cut into 4 cm
    (1½ in) squares, tentacles
    halved

METHOD

Combine the tomatoes, lemon juice, chilli, garlic and basil. Season, then add ¼ cup (60 ml/2 fl oz) of the olive oil and stir well. Leave to sit for 1 hour. Heat half the remaining oil on a grill or in a frying pan and cook the eggplant until browned and softened. Season with salt and allow to cool. Heat the remaining oil in a heavy-based frying pan and fry the cuttlefish squares and tentacles on high heat until golden. Serve on the salsa with the eggplant scattered over.

SERVES 4   WINE: Cirò Rosato

GRILLED PRAWNS IN LEMON LEAVES
GAMBERI ALLA GRIGLIA IN FOGLIE DI LIMONE

The south-western coast of Italy is famous for the quality of its citrus, especially the lemons. Citrus leaves contain oils that are full of flavour, and this simple dish makes full use of this unlikely ingredient.

INGREDIENTS

12 large raw prawns (shrimp),
    peeled and deveined
24 large lemon leaves, well
    washed and dried
½ cup (125 ml/4 fl oz) extra
    virgin olive oil
2 garlic cloves, minced
1 tablespoon chopped parsley
1 teaspoon chopped fresh
    oregano
1 tablespoon chopped black
    olives
1 red chilli, seeded and minced
juice of 1 lemon

METHOD

Salt and pepper the prawns lightly. Using toothpicks, secure each prawn between 2 lemon leaves. Make a salsa by combining ⅓ cup (80 ml/2½ fl oz) of the olive oil with the garlic, parsley, oregano, olives, chilli and lemon juice. Heat the remaining oil on a grill, chargrill pan or barbecue and cook the prawns for about 30 seconds on each side. Remove the toothpicks and arrange the lemon leaves on a serving plate. Put the prawns on top of the leaves, spoon on the salsa and serve warm.

SERVES 4   WINE: Greco

CUTTLEFISH WITH SALSA PICCANTE

EGGPLANT CANNELLONI
CANNELLONI ALLE MELANZANE

INGREDIENTS

TOMATO, LEEK AND CHILLI SAUCE

¼ cup (60 ml/2 fl oz) extra virgin olive oil

1 leek, white part only, thinly sliced

2 garlic cloves, minced

400 g (14 oz) ripe tomatoes, chopped

1 teaspoon dried chilli flakes

handful parsley, chopped

⅓ cup (80 ml/2½ fl oz) extra virgin olive oil

3 large leeks, white part only, thinly sliced

2 garlic cloves, minced

250 g (9 oz) ricotta cheese

1 cup (100 g/3½ oz) grated parmesan cheese

12 cannelloni sheets (see basic pasta dough on page 42)

1 eggplant (aubergine), cut into 5 mm (¼ in) slices and grilled (broiled) or roasted

250 g (9 oz) mozzarella cheese, sliced

extra grated parmesan cheese

METHOD

To make the sauce, heat the olive oil in a large frying pan. Fry the leek and garlic for 30 seconds, then add the tomatoes and chilli and simmer for 8–10 minutes. Add the parsley and season. Keep simmering until the sauce thickens, then remove from the heat and set aside.

Heat the olive oil in a frying pan and gently fry the leeks and garlic until soft. Transfer to a bowl and mix with the ricotta and parmesan. Season. Bring a large saucepan of salted water to the boil. Meanwhile, preheat the oven to 180°C (350°F). Cut the pasta sheets into 12 rectangles measuring 6 × 10 cm (2½ × 4 in), then cook immediately in the boiling water. Drain the pasta sheets and spread them on wet tea towels (dish towels). Spoon some ricotta mixture onto each pasta sheet, then divide the eggplant evenly among the sheets and roll each one into a log. Spread ½ cup (125 ml/4 fl oz) of the tomato sauce in a baking dish. Arrange the cannelloni in the dish and spread another ½ cup sauce on top. Add the mozzarella and a sprinkle of extra parmesan. Season. Bake for 15 minutes and serve straight from the oven with more parmesan.

SERVES 6 (sauce makes 300 ml (10 fl oz))   **WINE:** Greco

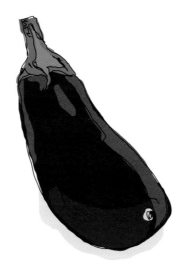

EGGPLANT CANNOLI
CANNOLI DI MELANZANE

INGREDIENTS

3 eggplants (aubergines),
     cut lengthways into 5 mm
     (¼ in) slices
2 teaspoons sea salt
200 ml (7 fl oz) extra virgin
     olive oil
1 cup (250 ml/9 fl oz) tomato
     sauce (homemade or
     store-bought passata)
½ cup basil leaves, chopped

BÉCHAMEL SAUCE

1 cup (250 ml/9 fl oz) milk
30 g (1 oz) butter
¼ cup (30 g/1 oz) plain
     (all-purpose) flour
4 tablespoons finely grated
     parmesan cheese
white pepper

METHOD

Sprinkle the eggplant slices with the salt, put them in a strainer and set aside for 30 minutes. Meanwhile, make the béchamel sauce. Heat the milk in a saucepan until warm. In a separate saucepan, melt the butter over medium heat. Whisk the flour into the butter and cook until it forms a thick paste. Add the warm milk a little at a time, whisking constantly, until the mixture starts to boil. Remove from the heat and whisk in the parmesan. Season with salt and white pepper. Set aside to cool. Preheat the oven to 180°C (350°F). Drain the eggplant, wash off the salt and pat dry immediately with a clean tea towel (dish towel). Heat the olive oil in a wide frying pan until it begins to smoke. Fry the eggplant, turning once, until golden. Drain on paper towels. Spread 1 tablespoon béchamel onto each eggplant slice along with 2–3 basil leaves and roll up. Put the rolls in a baking dish and spoon the tomato sauce over. Bake for 15–20 minutes and serve hot.

SERVES 4–6   WINE: Cirò Rosato

PAN-FRIED TURNIP TOPS WITH CHILLI
CIME DI RAPA AL PEPERONCINO

INGREDIENTS

800 g (1 lb 12 oz) cime di rapa
     (broccoli raab, turnip tops),
     well washed and dried
⅓ cup (80 ml/2½ fl oz) extra
     virgin olive oil
2 garlic cloves, crushed
1 hot red chilli, minced
½ cup (125 ml/4 fl oz)
     vegetable stock or water
1 teaspoon chilli flakes

METHOD

Cut the cime di rapa into manageable lengths, if necessary. Heat half the olive oil in a large frying pan. Lightly fry the garlic until it begins to colour, then remove from the pan and discard. Put the chilli in the pan and fry for a few seconds, then add the cime di rapa and a couple of good pinches of salt. Stir well and add the stock. Bring to the boil, then simmer for about 5 minutes until the rapa stems are tender but still a little firm. Season if necessary. Transfer to a serving plate, scatter the chilli flakes on top and drizzle with the remaining oil.

SERVES 6 (or 8 as an accompaniment)   WINE: Cirò Rosso

CALABRIA
SECONDI

SALT COD WITH BRAISED CAULIFLOWER
BACCALÀ AL CAVOLFIORE

Baccalà is a salted and air-dried fish. Traditionally Atlantic cod is used. It has to be soaked in cold water for several days and the water must be changed 2–3 times a day, depending on the salt content of the fish. In Italy the cod can be purchased already soaked.

INGREDIENTS

500 g (1 lb 2 oz) baccalà, soaked (see recipe introduction)

100 ml (3½ fl oz) extra virgin olive oil

1 small brown onion, diced

1 celery heart, diced

2 garlic cloves, minced

pinch of fennel seeds

1 cauliflower, separated into florets

½ cup (125 ml/4 fl oz) dry white wine

2 ripe tomatoes, chopped

2 tablespoons chopped parsley

60 g (2¼ oz) plain (all-purpose) flour

METHOD

Put the baccalà in a saucepan and cover with cold water. Bring to the boil, then carefully remove the fish. Allow to cool and pat dry. Cut into bite-sized pieces. Heat ¼ cup (60 ml/2 fl oz) of the olive oil in a large frying pan and gently fry the onion, celery, garlic and fennel seeds for a couple of minutes. Add the cauliflower and turn up the heat. Stir continually for a minute, then add the wine and simmer for 3 minutes. Add the tomatoes and parsley, season lightly and simmer for 10 minutes until the cauliflower is cooked. Remove from the heat. Dust the baccalà pieces with the flour and fry in the remaining olive oil until golden on all sides. Serve the baccalà with the braised cauliflower.

SERVES 4   WINE: Greco

SOLE FILLETS IN TOMATO AND CAPSICUM SAUCE
SOGLIOLE AL SUGHETTO

INGREDIENTS

¼ cup (60 ml/2 fl oz) extra virgin olive oil

600 g (1 lb 5 oz) sole fillets

1 brown onion, thinly sliced

2 garlic cloves, minced

2 red capsicums (peppers), cored and thinly sliced

1 teaspoon thyme leaves

200 g (7 oz) ripe tomatoes, peeled and chopped

METHOD

Heat the oil in a large frying pan, then lightly fry the flounder for 30 seconds a side. Transfer to a plate. In the same pan, fry the onion, garlic and capsicums for 2 minutes until soft. Add the thyme and tomatoes and simmer for 5 minutes. Season, mix well and return the flounder to the pan. Spoon the sauce over the fish so it is covered as much as possible, then simmer for another minute and serve.

SERVES 4   WINE: Greco di Bianco

BARBECUED GARFISH WITH LEMON, GARLIC AND PARSLEY

BARBECUED GARFISH WITH LEMON, GARLIC AND PARSLEY
AGUGLIE ALLA GRIGLIA

INGREDIENTS

6 lemon wedges

8 × 150 g (5½ oz) whole garfish, gutted and scaled

½ cup (125 ml/4 fl oz) extra virgin olive oil

juice of 2 lemons

4 tablespoons finely chopped parsley

2 garlic cloves, minced

100 g (3½ oz) mixed salad leaves

METHOD

Using 2 of the lemon wedges, rub vigorously in each of the fish cavities. Take each garfish's long nose, bend the body around and jab it into the tail end, making the fish into a ring. (If necessary, make a hole in the tail end using the point of a thin sharp knife to help with inserting the nose.) Put the fish on a tray and set aside. In a bowl, combine ⅓ cup (80 ml/2½ fl oz) of the olive oil with the lemon juice, parsley and garlic. Add 2–3 pinches of salt and a couple of turns of pepper. Spoon a little of this mixture onto each fish, keeping some for the final dressing. Heat a barbecue grill plate and sprinkle the remaining oil over it. Grill the fish for about 2 minutes on each side, then season with a little more salt and pepper. Scatter the salad leaves on 4 serving plates. For each diner, arrange 2 fish on the salad leaves with a lemon wedge, and dress with the remaining parsley mixture.

SERVES 4   WINE: Greco

CALABRIAN-STYLE GRILLED TUNA
TONNO ALLA CALABRESE

INGREDIENTS

½ cup (125 ml/4 fl oz) extra virgin olive oil, plus 2 tablespoons extra for tuna steaks

1 brown onion, finely chopped

3 garlic cloves, minced

8 anchovy fillets, chopped

150 g (5½ oz) button mushrooms, sliced

300 g (10½ oz) ripe tomatoes, chopped

2 fresh oregano sprigs, chopped

150 g (5½ oz) pitted black olives

250 g (9 oz) tin tuna, drained

½ cup chopped parsley

6 × 150 g (5½ oz) tuna steaks

METHOD

Heat the olive oil in a frying pan and lightly fry the onion, garlic, anchovies and mushrooms for 4–5 minutes until soft. Add the tomatoes, oregano and olives and simmer for 5 minutes. Add the tuna and parsley and simmer for 15–20 minutes, stirring, until the tuna has broken up. Season to taste. Heat extra olive oil on a grill and sear the tuna steaks for 1 minute on each side. Spoon the tuna sauce over the steaks and serve.

SERVES 6 (sauce makes enough for 10 or more)   WINE: Cirò Bianco

CALABRIA

SWORDFISH WITH RED ONIONS
PESCE SPADA ALLE CIPOLLE DI TROPEA

INGREDIENTS

⅓ cup (80 ml/2½ fl oz) extra virgin olive oil

2 large red onions, thinly sliced

200 ml (7 fl oz) red wine

2 bay leaves

20 g (¾ oz) butter

4 × 200 g (7 oz) swordfish steaks

2 garlic cloves, crushed

1 tablespoon grappa

½ cup chopped parsley

METHOD

Heat the olive oil and lightly fry the onions for 3–4 minutes until transparent. Add the red wine and bay leaves and simmer until the onions are creamy and all the liquid has been absorbed or has evaporated. In a separate large frying pan melt the butter and fry the swordfish on both sides for 1 minute. Add the garlic and flame by adding the grappa. Keep lightly frying for a couple of minutes, then add the onions from the other pan. Cook for 2 more minutes and turn off heat. Add the parsley, season and serve.

SERVES 4   WINE: Cannonau

LAMB CUTLETS COSENZA STYLE
COSTOLETTE D'AGNELLO ALLA COSENTINA

INGREDIENTS

16 lamb cutlets

⅓ cup (80 ml/2½ fl oz) extra virgin olive oil

1 brown onion, minced

1 garlic clove, minced

2 red capsicums (peppers), seeded and thinly sliced lengthways

400 g (14 oz) ripe tomatoes, peeled and thinly sliced

120 g (4¼ oz) green olives, pitted

½ cup chopped parsley leaves

METHOD

In a large, heavy-based frying pan, sear the cutlets in 30 ml (1 fl oz) of the olive oil until well browned on each side. Transfer to a plate. Heat the remaining oil in the pan and lightly fry the onion and garlic for a minute, continually stirring. Add the capsicums and continue to stir and fry on medium heat for another minute. Add the tomatoes, olives, parsley, a couple of good pinches of salt and 3–4 turns of pepper. Stir and bring to the boil. Turn down the heat and simmer for 10 minutes. Adjust the seasoning if necessary, then add the lamb cutlets and any juices that have collected on the plate. Turn off the heat, stir everything together and let rest for 5 minutes before serving.

SERVES 4   WINE: Gaglioppo

SEARED BEEF SKIRT WITH GRILLED ARTICHOKES AND LEMON
FESONE ALLA GRIGLIA CON CARCIOFI E LIMONE

Beef skirt is a highly prized cut in Italy. It is part of the large breast flap that covers the ribs and encloses the belly. There is an 'outside' skirt, which is very good, but the prize is a wedge-shaped strip called the 'inside' skirt. Its flavour is superlative. It's readily available, but you'll have to find a good butcher.

INGREDIENTS

600 g (1 lb 5 oz) beef skirt (inside, if available)

4 artichokes, trimmed and cooked (see page 39)

150 g (5½ oz) green beans, trimmed

2 garlic cloves, minced

2 anchovy fillets, chopped

1 cup chopped parsley leaves

1 cup chopped fresh oregano leaves

juice of 1 lemon

300 ml (10½ fl oz) extra virgin olive oil

METHOD

Trim the fat from the beef but leave a thin skin on both sides. Put on a plate, cover and allow to reach room temperature. Cut the artichokes into wedges.

Bring a saucepan of salted water to the boil and blanch the beans for 3 minutes. Drain and keep warm. In a bowl, combine the garlic, anchovies, parsley, oregano, lemon juice and 1 cup (250 ml/9 fl oz) of the olive oil. Heat a flat barbecue grill or a frying pan and add 1 tablespoon of the remaining oil. Season the beef, then sear for 30–45 seconds on each side. Transfer to a warm plate or leave on the hot grill. Heat the remaining oil and grill the artichokes until golden brown. Remove and discard the skin from the beef, then cut the meat across the grain into 5 mm (¼ in) slices. Put on a plate with the artichokes and beans. Drizzle with the oregano and lemon dressing, season and serve.

SERVES 4   WINE: Cirò Rosso

CALABRIA DOLCI

CLEMENTINE LIQUEUR
LIQUORE ALLE CLEMENTINE

This recipe uses clementines that are not totally ripe because the part of the fruit that is used is the skin, as it contains the essential oils, and these oils are at their most potent when the fruit is almost ripe.

INGREDIENTS

14 firm clementines, still with some green patches

2 cups (500 ml/17 fl oz) 90-proof alcohol, vodka or gin

1⅓ cups (300 g/10½ oz) sugar

2 cups (500 ml/17 fl oz) filtered or spring water

METHOD

Wash and dry the clementines. Using a sharp knife, cut off the peel, taking care not to include any white pith. Put the peel in a jar with the alcohol, seal tightly and store in a cool dark place for 10 days. Strain the liquid through a double layer of muslin (cheesecloth) and discard the peel. Put the sugar and water in a saucepan and heat, stirring, until the sugar has completely dissolved. Turn off the heat and let the liquid cool completely. Mix with the alcohol and pass through a double layer of muslin. Pour into a 1 litre (35 fl oz) capacity bottle and seal. Use after 6 months.

MAKES about 1 litre (35 fl oz)

CALABRIAN HONEY BISCUITS
MOSTACCIOLI

These festive biscuits (cookies) are often shaped like fish, people (especially saints), horses and assorted other animals. Ammonium bicarbonate, which has been replaced by baking powder in modern pastry, is said to render a lighter, crisper texture and does not have the aftertaste of baking powder.

INGREDIENTS

20 g (¾ oz) unsalted butter

500 g (1 lb 2 oz) plain (all-purpose) flour

1 tablespoon ammonium bicarbonate or baking powder

500 g (1 lb 2 oz) honey

2 egg yolks, whisked

METHOD

Preheat the oven to 190°C (375°F) and grease a baking sheet with the butter. Sift the flour and ammonium bicarbonate together to make a mound on your work surface. Make a well in the middle. Put the honey in a stainless steel bowl and soften over a saucepan of boiling water. Once the honey is runny, pour it into the well and combine with the flour to produce a dough that is not too soft and not too firm. It should not be sticky. If it is sticky, add a little more flour. Roll out the dough to a thickness of about 1.5 cm (⅝ in). Use your favourite cookie cutter to shape the biscuits, then lay them on the baking sheet so they are not touching each other (about 2 cm/¾ in gaps). Bake for 20 minutes. Remove each biscuit from the baking sheet, brush all over with egg yolk and put on a wire rack to cool. The biscuits will keep for months if stored in an airtight container.

QUANTITY around 40 biscuits depending on the cutter used

WINE: Greco di Bianco

CLEMENTINE TEACAKE
TORTA DI CLEMENTINE

Clementines are a variety of the mandarin. They are easy to peel, usually seedless and have a sweet flavour which is often less acidic than other citrus fruits, such as oranges. Other mandarin varieties could be substituted in this recipe.

INGREDIENTS

1 clementine

2 eggs

125 g (4½ oz) unsalted butter

¾ cup (165 g/5¾ oz) caster sugar

225 g (8 oz) self-raising flour

150 ml (5 fl oz) cream, whipped

4 tablespoons grated dark chocolate

CANDIED CLEMENTINES

6 clementines, well washed

500 g (1 lb 2 oz) sugar

METHOD

To make the candied clementines, preheat the oven to 150°C (300°F). Trim about 5 mm (¼ in) from each end of the clementines. Cut the fruit into 5 mm (¼ in) slices, removing any seeds. Lay the slices in rows in a baking dish, each row slightly overlapping the next. Put 2 cups (500 ml/17 fl oz) water and the sugar in a saucepan and bring to the boil. Lower the heat and simmer for 2 minutes until the sugar has dissolved. Pour the sugar syrup gently over the clementine slices so they are covered. Cut a piece of baking paper slightly smaller than the baking dish and randomly prick it all over using a sharp knife (this will allow the moisture to escape). Lay the paper on top of the fruit, then cover the baking pan with foil. Bake for 50 minutes–1 hour until the clementine slices are translucent. Remove the foil and bake for a further 30–40 minutes until the syrup has thickened. Remove from the oven and cool before using. The candied clementines will keep for weeks if refrigerated in the syrup in an airtight jar.

Bring a saucepan of water to the boil and put the whole clementine in. Place a small plate or similar on top of the clementine to hold it under the water, and poach it for 45 minutes. Drain and let cool. Preheat the oven to 190°C (375°F) and butter a 22 cm (8½ in) round or square cake tin. Cut the clementine in half and remove the seeds. Put the fruit in a food processor with the eggs and pulse until smooth. Add the butter, sugar and flour and process for 2 minutes until smooth, then pour into the cake tin. Bake for 30–35 minutes until a skewer inserted into the centre comes out clean. Cool in the tin for 5 minutes before turning out onto a wire rack. Serve slices of the teacake at room temperature decorated with the cream, chocolate and candied clementines.

SERVES 8–10   WINE Clementine Liqueur Limoncello

MULBERRY AND ALMOND TORTA
TORTA DI MORE DI GELSO E MANDORLE

INGREDIENTS

300 g (10½ oz) mulberries, de-stemmed

⅔ cup (150 g/5½ oz) caster sugar

1 egg

150 g (5½ oz) softened unsalted butter, diced

1½ cups (150 g/5½ oz) almond meal

1 cup (150 g/5½ oz) self-raising flour

1 teaspoon freshly grated nutmeg

1 teaspoon natural vanilla extract

icing (confectioners') sugar

METHOD

Preheat the oven to 180°C (350°F). Grease and flour a 22 cm (8½ in) springform non-stick or silicone cake tin. Toss the mulberries with a couple of tablespoons of the sugar in a bowl and set aside. Beat the remaining sugar with the egg and butter in an electric mixer until smooth. Add the almond meal, flour, nutmeg and vanilla and mix on a low speed for a couple of minutes until thoroughly incorporated. You may need to stop the mixer and scrape the sides of the bowl. Put half the mixture into the cake tin. Let it settle, then tip in the mulberries. Cover with the remaining batter and bake for 1 hour until a skewer inserted into the centre comes out clean. Remove from the oven and let cool completely in the tin before unmoulding. Sprinkle the top with icing sugar to serve.

SERVES 8   WINE: Greco di Bianco

CAMPANIA

CAMPANIA

THE SECOND MOST POPULOUS REGION OF ITALY, WITH ABOUT SIX MILLION INHABITANTS, CAMPANIA IS ON THE WEST COAST ON THE TYRRHENIAN SEA, WITH LAZIO AND MOLISE TO THE NORTH AND PUGLIA AND BASILICATA ON ITS WESTERN BORDER. ITS CAPITAL CITY IS NAPLES, AND OVER THE CENTURIES IT HAS BEEN SUBJECT TO RULE BY THE GREEKS, ROMANS, SPANISH, LOMBARDS, BYZANTINE EMPIRE, FRENCH AND ARAGONESE.

If it were not for this fertile province and its teeming capital city, we would not have two of the planet's favourite Italian foods: mozzarella di bufala (buffalo-milk mozzarella) and, in spite of much of the world thinking it American, pizza. Indeed, a form of pizza – without tomato, which would have to wait another 1500 years – was eaten in Pompeii. Today, the gold standard for pizza is the approval of the Associazione Verace Pizza Napoletana, which bestows approval only on those pizzerias that make pizza according to their very strict rules, which prescribe the flour used to make the dough, the method of cooking, and the toppings.

The natives of Campania and Naples have always had an interest in food 'transcending by far the simple necessity of sustaining life', as Waverley Root, author of *The Food of Italy*, put it. Once again, we find evidence for this in the petrified town of Pompeii, in the Street of Abundance, where a bakery was found containing 81 loaves sold on 24 August in the year 79. Not far from Pompeii can be found what may well have been the first oyster hatchery, if not in the world (the Chinese may have that distinction) then certainly in the western world.

In 1787, in his book *Italian Journey*, Goethe wrote of a feast, or cuccagna, he witnessed in Naples: 'At such times ... a feast is celebrated, in which five hundred thousand people vow to outdo each other ... Crowds of donkeys laden with vegetables, capons and young lambs are driven to market ... every year a policeman, accompanied by a trumpeter, rides through the city and announces how many thousand oxen, calves, lambs, pigs etc. the Neapolitans have consumed.'

Apart from the cuccagna, the food culture of Campania is mainly that of bread, pasta and pizza, and the cornucopia of fresh produce grown there. Campania has always had luxuriantly rich, loose, black volcanic soil as well as a natural fertiliser: seaweed.

Even today it supplies much of the produce for both Naples and Rome, producing fruit including pears, apples, figs, cherries, melons, pomegranates, quinces and tomatoes; vegetables including beans, cabbage and broccoli; and olives. Along the Amalfi coast south of Naples, where the cliffs rise up from the sea, oranges and lemons grow and vines cling to the steep slopes.

Mozzarella came about because the marshy strip between Rome and Naples suited buffalos rather than cows. Although they produce only five to seven litres a day (compared to up to 40 from dairy cattle), the unique characteristics of the milk from the buffalo – rich in fat and protein, a high ratio of solids – mean that it makes sublime mozzarella, which is best eaten in its natural state, as in the famed insalata caprese from the island of Capri, or in carrozza (meaning 'in a carriage') – between two slices of bread (crusts removed), dipped in egg and fried in butter.

Although the sea supplies abundant fish, molluscs, shrimps and crabs, the cuisine of the islands in the Gulf of Napoli – Ischia and Capri among them – is not marine-based. In fact, the major dish from Ischia is based on the rabbit: bucatini are pierced so that a rabbit sauce made with garlic, herbs, red wine, tomatoes and olive oil is absorbed into the centre of the pasta. There is a seafood pasta dish on Capri, spaghetti ai totani, that has a sauce of squid.

Speaking of pasta, it is impossible to speak of the cuisine of Naples without mentioning maccheroni. By the 18th century the city was the capital of dried pasta and the Neapolitans were known as mangiamaccheroni, or macaroni-eaters. But that was plain macaroni, cooked in water containing a little salt and pork fat. Although the first recipe for tomato sauce was published in an Italian cookbook in 1692, the first tomato sauce to be served with macaroni didn't hit the streets of Naples until 1844 – and even then it was a far cry from today's version, being made with reconstituted dried tomatoes cooked in butter or pork fat. Tomatoes, when they arrived, were cultivated in Campania sooner than anywhere else in Europe, and one variety, san marzano, is the premium tomato for canning today.

Campania was once the vineyard of the Romans and home to the imperial favourite: a white wine called Falernian, made from an unknown grape. The region continued to produce wines beloved of many, including the papacy of the 16th century, and then quality dropped, reaching a low in the 20th century. But what was once great can be restored to greatness, and no region has more potential to climb again than Campania.

As matters stand today in terms of quality, one wine grape dominates Campania: aglianico, whose name may derive from the Latin word Hellenicum, meaning Greek (or not, even though the grape is agreed to be of Greek origin). There are variations depending upon the region in which the grape is grown, two being aglianico de Taurasi and aglianico amaro. Although amaro means 'bitter', in this instance it refers to acidity.

The best-known wines of the region are those named Lacryma Christi (the tears of Christ). These are white wines made with a variety of local grapes, the best of which is Lacryma Christi del Vesuvio. This name derives from the legend of Lucifer, who, caught in the act of stealing a piece of paradise, was caught and fell into the Bay of Naples along with a troupe of rebellious angels. The stolen piece of paradise became the island of Capri, and the fallen angels turned the area around Naples into a realm of such wickedness that Christ dropped a tear on Vesuvius, watering the vines on the slopes of the volcano.

RABBIT ITALIAN STYLE

I've always loved the way Italians cook rabbit. No matter which region of Italy you travel through, it has countless ways of preparing them. The most famous rabbit in Italy comes from the island of Ischia in this region.

Whenever I see rabbit on a restaurant menu my choice is made – maybe it's curiosity or the thrill of finding a new way to prepare this extraordinarily versatile meat. It's light like chicken but so much better in quality, unless you compare it to a properly raised hen.

Rabbit can be cooked every which way. Italian rabbit dishes reflect local styles and products that define particular cities or provinces, and sometimes families. For example, at the Osteria di Rubbiana near Modena, rabbit braised in balsamic vinegar has been prepared by the Pedroni family since 1861.

In the north-western wine and truffle city of Alba at the Osteria dell'Arco, rabbit is pot-roasted with aromatic vegetables and continually bathed with Arneis, the local white wine. Moving east in a direct line to the beautiful Valtellina area north of Milan, Osteria del Crotto, in the town of Morbegno, prepares rabbit pieces wrapped in the local lardo affumicato (smoked and cured lard) and flavoured with mountain thyme.

On the island of Ischia, at the northern end of the Bay of Naples, lives Italy's most famous rabbit, coniglio da fossa. It is raised in 3–4 metre caves that extend outwards into its warrens. Its meat is firmer and profoundly tastier than that of cage-raised rabbits. On Ischia, these rabbits are not just food but a symbol of celebration and an agricultural act. They are included in Slow Food's 'Presidia', a collection of the most important products in the world.

On the island, at the restaurant Il Focolare di Loretta e Riccardo D'Ambra, the rabbit is prepared by browning pieces in local olive oil for 20 minutes or so. They are transferred to a terracotta oven dish and splashed with white wine. Tomatoes, garlic, parsley, basil, thyme, rosemary and chilli are added with a little vegetable broth. The rabbit is baked until tender and brought to the table in its roasting dish.

The seemingly endless diversity of preparing rabbit in Italy is astonishing. In the port city of La Spezia it is done with olives and pine nuts; Perugia prepares it with artichokes; in the ancient Sicilian city of Siracusa it is prepared alla stimpiratura, with aromatic vegetables and flavoured with the local wild mint; and the Abruzzese city of Teramo stuffs it with eggs, fennel, herbs and the local pecorino cheese. On and on it goes. I would love to do a rabbit-eating tour of Italy!

CAMPANIA
ANTI-
PASTI

NEAPOLITAN 'BAGELS'
TARALLI AL FINOCCHIETTO

Taralli are produced in various central and southern regions, including Puglia, Calabria, Campania, Basilicata, Lazio, Molise and Sicilia. I love them all, but the best I've tasted were at Gennaro Esposito's restaurant, Torre del Saracino, at Vico Equense on the Sorrentine Peninsula, south of Naples. Gennaro gets his savoury, fennel-flavoured taralli di Agerola from Fausto Naclerio, who makes them at his Naclerio bakery in the small town of Agerola, not far from the restaurant. If you are ever around Sorrento and the Amalfi Coast, I highly recommend a visit to Gennaro's wonderful restaurant and Fausto's bakery.

INGREDIENTS

2 cups (300 g/10½ oz) plain (all-purpose) flour

1⅓ cups (200 g/7 oz) durum wheat flour

2 level teaspoons salt

200 ml (7 fl oz) dry white wine

½ cup (125 ml/4 fl oz) extra virgin olive oil

1 tablespoon fennel seeds

METHOD

Combine the flours in a large bowl and make a well in the centre. Dissolve the salt in the wine by mixing, then add to the flour along with the olive oil and fennel seeds. Mix everything together using your hands. Once it comes together, put the dough on your workbench and knead for 15–20 minutes until smooth. Put in a small bowl, cover with a clean tea towel (dish towel) and let rest for 30 minutes. Preheat the oven to 170°C (340°F) and line 2–3 baking trays with baking paper. Cut chunks from the piece of dough and roll them as though you were making gnocchi. Next, cut gnocchi-sized pieces from the rolls weighing about 8 g (⅙ oz) each and roll these into smaller rolls about 1 cm (½ in) in diameter and 8 cm (3¼ in) long. Fold forming a loop with the ends crossing each other, then lay the taralli on a clean tea towel. Bring a large saucepan of salted water to the boil and cook 10–15 taralli at a time. Once they come to the surface, remove using a slotted spoon and drain on clean tea towels. Arrange the poached taralli on the baking trays so they aren't touching each other. Bake for 25 minutes until golden. Let cool completely before using. They will keep in an airtight container for 2–3 weeks. Can be served with antipasto.

MAKES around 100

CRUMBED MOZZARELLA
MOZZARELLA IMPANATA

Just as it's not the norm to put buffalo mozzarella on pizza in Naples, this dish is made with the firmer fior di latte mozzarella, made with cow's milk. Try to find Mediterranean dried oregano for this recipe, as it has a distinctive flavour.

INGREDIENTS

400 g (14 oz) mozzarella
    fior di latte
3 tablespoons plain
    (all-purpose) flour
3 eggs, whisked
8 tablespoons fine
    breadcrumbs
200 ml (7 fl oz) extra virgin
    olive oil
1 teaspoon dried oregano

METHOD

Cut the mozzarella into 5 mm (¼ in) slices. If the balls are large, you may need to cut each one in half and then slice them. Dust each slice with flour, dredge in egg and finally coat with breadcrumbs. Heat the olive oil in a frying pan and fry the mozzarella until golden brown on both sides. Drain on paper towels and sprinkle with oregano and salt before serving hot.

SERVES 6   WINE: Coda di Volpe

WHITEBAIT FRITTERS
FRITTELLE DI BIANCHETTI

INGREDIENTS

1⅓ cups (200 g/7 oz) plain
    (all-purpose) flour
2 garlic cloves, minced
2 tablespoons grated
    Grana Padano
2 eggs
1 tablespoon chopped parsley
1 tablespoon small fresh
    oregano leaves
400 g (14 oz) whitebait
200 ml (7 fl oz) extra virgin
    olive oil

METHOD

Put the flour in a bowl and add the garlic, Grana Padano, eggs, parsley and oregano. Add a couple of good pinches of salt and 2–3 turns of pepper, then mix everything together to form a batter. Cover and let sit for 3 hours. Pat the whitebait dry with paper towels, then mix it into the batter. Pour the olive oil into a saucepan to give a depth of 2 cm (¾ in). Heat the oil, then drop in tablespoons of batter, making sure not to fry too many at a time. Once golden, drain on paper towel, sprinkle with salt and serve.

SERVES 6–8   WINE: Greco di Tufo

DEEP-FRIED ZUCCHINI FLOWERS FILLED WITH FOUR CHEESES
FIORI DI ZUCCHINI AI QUATTRO FORMAGGI

Zucchini flowers come in both male and female forms. The male is perhaps more delicate, held by a thin stem only. Female flowers are a little sturdier, nourished by the baby zucchini attached. Both are good stuffed – even the female with the nascent fruit attached. That little zucchini on the end provides a functional, edible handle. Cheese works particularly well. Either deep-fried, braised in a sauce or roasted, the cheese melts but is contained by the blossom membrane.

INGREDIENTS

1⅓ cups (200 g/7 oz) plain (all-purpose) flour

⅔ cup (170 ml/5½ fl oz) ice-cold water

150 g (5½ oz) ricotta cheese

200 g (7 oz) provola cheese, grated

150 g (5½ oz) mozzarella cheese, cubed

100 g (3½ oz) Grana Padano, grated

2 tablespoons chopped anchovy fillets

24 zucchini (courgette) flowers

1 cup (250 ml/9 fl oz) extra virgin olive oil

METHOD

To make the batter, use a fork to mix the flour and water to form a rough, lumpy, fairly runny mixture. Rest this while you are preparing the rest of the dish. Make the filling by combining the cheeses and the anchovies. Season. If you are using female flowers with baby zucchini attached, trim the ends of the zucchini. If you are using male flowers, trim the stems. Carefully open the flowers and spoon in a little of the filling. Gently close the flowers by lightly pressing the petals together. Heat the olive oil in a large frying pan until it is about to smoke, then dip the filled zucchini flowers in the batter and allow any excess to run off. Fry the flowers in the oil until golden. Remove from the pan and drain on paper towels, then season and serve with garden greens.

SERVES 8–10   WINE: Falerno del Massico Bianco

ZUCCHINI FLOWERS
AS COOKS, WE'RE FOREVER CONSTRUCTING WAYS OF HOLDING FOOD TOGETHER IN NEAT PARCELS. AFTER ALL, WE LIKE PORTABLE FOOD, ESPECIALLY WHEN WE CAN EAT THE WRAPPER. THE ZUCCHINI (COURGETTE) FLOWER IS PERFECT: THE BLOSSOM IS DELICATE BUT STRONG ENOUGH TO FILL, EVEN WITH A MOIST STUFFING.

DEEP-FRIED ZUCCHINI FLOWERS FILLED WITH FOUR CHEESES

CALAMARI WITH OLIVES, CAPERS AND ASPARAGUS
CALAMARI CON OLIVE, CAPPERI E ASPARAGI

INGREDIENTS

1 kg (2 lb 4 oz) calamari, cleaned

¼ cup (60 ml/2 fl oz) extra virgin olive oil

2 garlic cloves, minced

20 small black pitted olives

1 tablespoon small capers in olive oil (or salted capers, rinsed)

6 asparagus spears, cut into bite-sized pieces

100 ml (3½ fl oz) dry white wine

1 tablespoon chopped parsley

3 tablespoons fresh breadcrumbs

METHOD

Using a sharp knife, cut the calamari flesh into matchsticks. Pat dry using paper towels or a clean tea towel (dish towel). Cut the tentacles into similar-sized pieces and pat dry. Heat the olive oil in a wide frying pan on high heat. Add the calamari and garlic, mixing with a wooden spoon. Stir in the olives, capers and asparagus, then add the wine. When it has evaporated, add the parsley and breadcrumbs. Stir for 30 seconds, then turn off the heat and season. Serve warm or at room temperature.

SERVES 6–8   WINE: Irpinia Coda di Volpe

OCTOPUS TERRINE
POLPO IN TERRINA

INGREDIENTS

1 × 2.5 kg (5 lb 8 oz) whole octopus, head and beak removed

1 brown onion, roughly chopped

1 carrot, roughly chopped

1 celery stick, roughly chopped

1 lemon, washed and cut in half

2 garlic cloves, minced

3–4 chillies, seeded and finely chopped

½ cup finely chopped parsley

juice of 1 lemon

1 cup (250 ml/9 fl oz) extra virgin olive oil

METHOD

Put the octopus in a saucepan and cover with cold water. Add the onion, carrot, celery and lemon. Bring to the boil, then turn the heat down, cover and simmer for about 1 hour until the octopus is tender. Remove the octopus from the water and let sit for 5–6 minutes to cool a little. Discard the vegetables and lemon. While the octopus is still warm, gather the tentacles together and wrap the octopus tightly into a log using plastic wrap. Refrigerate overnight so that its natural gelatine binds it. When you are ready to serve, combine the garlic, chillies, parsley, lemon juice and olive oil and season. Unwrap the octopus and, using a sharp knife, cut 1 cm (½ in) slices. Serve with the dressing.

SERVES 8–10   WINE: Greco di Tufo

BROAD BEANS WITH ROAST TOMATOES AND PECORINO
FAVE, POMODORI ARROSTITI E PECORINO

INGREDIENTS

500 g (1 lb 2 oz) broad beans, double peeled

6 ripe roma tomatoes, halved

½ cup (125 ml/4 fl oz) extra virgin olive oil

2 cups lamb's lettuce (corn salad) or other lettuce cut into bite-sized pieces

100 g (3½ oz) pecorino cheese, shaved

METHOD

Preheat the oven to 170°C (340°F). Blanch the broad beans in boiling salted water for 30 seconds. Drain and let cool on a plate or tray. Put the tomatoes in a baking dish, drizzle with 2 tablespoons of the olive oil, season and roast for 15–20 minutes. Toss the lettuce gently with the beans and the remaining olive oil and season. Put the salad on a serving plate and arrange the tomatoes, cooled to room temperature, on top. Scatter the pecorino over and serve.

SERVES 8   WINE: Coda di Volpe

CAMPANIA
PRIMI

PACCHERI WITH SEA URCHINS AND BUFFALO MOZZARELLA
PACCHERI CON RICCI DI MARE E MOZZARELLA DI BUFALA

Paccheri is one of my favourite pasta shapes. It's a large, thick tube that squashes once cooked. If you love al dente pasta, this is the one to use: it has a chewy texture and holds sauce on its surface but also traps it inside. The town of Gragnano, south-east of Naples, has long been famous for both its wheat and its pasta. If you can't source paccheri, a large macaroni can also be used.

INGREDIENTS

roe from 10 very fresh sea
  urchins, chopped
½ cup tomato fillets
  (see page 40)
1 garlic clove, minced
1 tablespoon chopped parsley
pinch of dried oregano
½ cup (125 ml/4 fl oz) extra
  virgin olive oil
20 paccheri di Gragnano
250 g (9 oz) buffalo
  mozzarella, cut into 1 cm
  (½ in) cubes

METHOD

Put the urchin roe in a stainless steel bowl that fits snugly over a saucepan. Chop the tomato fillets and add to the urchin roe with any liquid on the chopping board. Add the garlic, parsley, oregano and olive oil. Pour about 3 cm (1¼ in) water into your saucepan and bring to a simmer, then turn the heat down to the lowest setting. Put the bowl over the saucepan and heat slowly. Meanwhile, cook the paccheri in abundant salted boiling water. Drain, then put in a bowl with the mozzarella and season lightly with salt. Mix and distribute among 4 serving bowls. Dress with the warm urchin sauce.

SERVES 4

WINE: Costa d'Amalfi Furore Bianco
(Falanghina & Biancolella blend)

ROAST TOMATOES WITH BUFFALO MOZZARELLA AND PESTO
POMODORI ARROSTITI CON MOZZARELLA E PESTO

INGREDIENTS

6 ripe tomatoes
150 ml (5 fl oz) extra virgin
  olive oil
1 cup basil leaves
60 g (2¼ oz) pine nuts, toasted
2 garlic cloves
6 tablespoons grated
  parmesan cheese
mixed salad leaves
6 slices buffalo mozzarella

METHOD

Preheat the oven to 180°C (350°F). Using a sharp knife, remove the woody part at the stem end of each tomato. Cut into the flesh at the stem end making a 2 cm (¾ in) hole. Put the tomatoes on a baking tray and put 1 teaspoon of the olive oil into each cavity. Season and roast for 10–15 minutes until soft but not split. Remove from the oven and set aside. Put the basil, pine nuts, garlic and a good pinch of salt into a large mortar and pound until broken down to a paste. Add the remaining oil and mix. Mix in the parmesan and adjust the seasoning if necessary. To assemble the dish, arrange the salad leaves on serving plates, then add a slice of buffalo mozzarella and a roast tomato. Drizzle plenty of pesto over and serve.

SERVES 6

WINE: Fiano di Avellino

SPRING GARLIC AND EGG SOUP
MINESTRA DI AGLIETTI

INGREDIENTS

¼ cup (60 ml/2 fl oz) extra
    virgin olive oil

cloves from 6 spring garlic
    bulbs, thinly sliced

5 tablespoons tomato passata

3 eggs, whisked

100 g (3½ oz) grated
    parmesan cheese

4 slices sourdough or country-
    style bread, crusts left on,
    toasted

METHOD

Gently heat the olive oil in a saucepan, then add the garlic. Cover the
pan and lightly poach the garlic until it is transparent and soft but not
coloured. Turn the heat up to medium, add the tomato passata and
simmer for 5 minutes. Add 2 cups (500 ml/17 fl oz) water and bring to
the boil. Combine the eggs and parmesan in a bowl, then mix into the
simmering soup for a couple of minutes. Season and serve with the
toasted bread.

SERVES 4   WINE: Falerno del Massico Bianco

LAGANELLE AND CHICKPEA SOUP
LAGANELLE E CECI

*Laganelle are long, wide ribbons of pasta not unlike fettuccine. They are made with hard wheat semolina
and water rather than plain flour and eggs, and are thicker than fettuccine, so they take a lot longer
to cook. A good durum wheat, wide-ribboned pasta such as pappardelle can be substituted.*

INGREDIENTS

1 cup (200 g/7 oz) chickpeas,
    soaked overnight in plenty
    of cold water

160 ml (5¼ fl oz) extra virgin
    olive oil

350 g (12 oz) laganelle

2 garlic cloves, minced

2 tablespoons finely chopped
    fresh oregano

ground chilli (optional)

METHOD

Drain the chickpeas well, then wash them and discard any skin that
comes off. Drain, then put into a large, heavy-based saucepan and cover
with cold water to a level of 6 cm (2½ in) above the chickpeas. Add
½ cup (125 ml/4 fl oz) of the olive oil and bring to the boil. Immediately
turn the heat down to low and cover the pan. Simmer very gently for
2–3 hours until the chickpeas are tender. If the water gets low, add
a little boiling water. Stir in the laganelle and simmer, covered, for
10 minutes. Meanwhile, heat the remaining oil in a small frying pan and
lightly fry the garlic for 30 seconds. Once the pasta is cooked, tip in
the oil and garlic from the frying pan and add the oregano. Season and
serve hot with a sprinkling of ground chilli if desired.

SERVES 6–8   WINE: Costa d'Amalfi Bianco

SALAD OF BUFFALO MOZZARELLA AND ROAST BEETROOT WITH WALNUT SALSA

INSALATA DI MOZZARELLA DI BUFALA E BARBABIETOLE AL FORNO CON SALSA DI NOCE

Campania has been famous for its walnuts for over 2000 years. Even today, the provinces of Naples, Salerno, Caserta, Avellino and Benevento account for the majority of Italy's walnut production. The walnuts of the Sorrentine Peninsula are picked when underripe to make the delicious Nocino liqueur.

INGREDIENTS

16 small red and golden beetroots (beets), trimmed and well washed

2 tablespoons extra virgin olive oil

250 g (9 oz) buffalo mozzarella

100 g (3½ oz) lamb's lettuce (corn salad)

WALNUT SALSA

200 g (7 oz) walnuts

3 garlic cloves, minced

½ cup (80 g/2¾ oz) capers, rinsed and finely chopped

1 cup finely chopped parsley

150 ml (5 fl oz) extra virgin olive oil

juice of 1–2 lemons

METHOD

To make the walnut salsa, finely pulse the walnuts and garlic in a food processor. Add the capers and parsley, then stir in the olive oil to achieve a thickish sauce. Season and add lemon juice to taste. Mix well and set aside. Preheat the oven to 190°C (375°F). Put the beetroots in a roasting tin, drizzle with the olive oil and toss well to coat. Season and roast for 20–25 minutes until tender. Allow to cool to room temperature, then cut in half and arrange on a serving tray. Tear the mozzarella into pieces and arrange among the beetroots. Arrange the lamb's lettuce around and drizzle the walnut salsa over before serving.

SERVES 4   WINE: Greco di Tufo

SPRING GARLIC IS THE TERM USED FOR YOUNG GARLIC THAT HAS FORMED SMALL BULBS BUT HAS YET TO GROW TO THE SIZE WHERE IT'S PULLED FROM THE GROUND AND HUNG TO DRY. NOT AS INTENSE OR CONCENTRATED IN FLAVOUR AS THE DRIED STUFF, SPRING GARLIC IS SWEET AND JUICY. IT IS USUALLY AVAILABLE THROUGHOUT SPRING AND IS A JOY TO USE IN THE KITCHEN.

ROCKET AND RICOTTA LASAGNETTE
LASAGNETTE DI RUCOLA E RICOTTA

A lasagnetta (pronounced lah-sah-NYET-ah) is a small lasagna that is usually individually made and freeform rather than baked in a large dish. The plural is lasagnette. It's important to use large, spicy rocket (arugula) leaves in this dish rather than small-leafed 'wild' rocket, which has little flavour.

INGREDIENTS

600 g (1 lb 5 oz) broad-leafed rocket

¼ cup (60 ml/2 fl oz) extra virgin olive oil

2 French shallots, finely diced

2 garlic cloves, minced

250 g (9 oz) ricotta cheese

8 tablespoons grated parmesan cheese

12 tablespoons tomato passata or sugo

24 × 7–8 cm (2¾–3¼ in) square pasta sheets, cooked

4 best-quality tinned tomatoes, halved

METHOD

Preheat the oven to 200°C (400°F). Roughly chop the rocket, stalks and all, into 3–4 cm (1¼–1½ in) pieces. Heat 2 tablespoons of the olive oil in a wide frying pan and gently fry the shallots and garlic for a minute, stirring, until transparent. Add the rocket, turn up the heat and cook for 3–5 minutes until tender. Season, stir and remove from the heat. Drain the rocket in a sieve, then divide into 3 piles. Combine the ricotta and 6 tablespoons of the parmesan in a bowl and season lightly. Divide into thirds. In a baking dish, smear 2 tablespoons of the tomato passata in 6 separate positions to make bases for the lasagnette. Add a pasta sheet to each base, then use one-third of the ricotta mixture among the 6 lasagnette and then one-third of the rocket. Repeat twice until all the ricotta mixture and rocket have been used, then finish with a pasta sheet on top. Carefully remove and discard the seeds and pulp from the tomato halves, then cut each half lengthways into 3. Top each lasagnetta with 4 tomato slices. Scatter the remaining parmesan on top and drizzle with the remaining olive oil. Bake for 15 minutes and serve hot.

SERVES 6   WINE: Fiano di Avellino

ROCKET AND RICOTTA LASAGNETTE

SPAGHETTI AND BUFFALO MOZZARELLA FRITTATA
FRITTATA DI SPAGHETTI E MOZZARELLA DI BUFALA

This is another dish that demonstrates the frugality of Italian cooking: it uses leftover spaghetti. If there is no leftover spaghetti, cook about 300 g (10½ oz) spaghetti and use that.

INGREDIENTS

6 eggs

100 g (3½ oz) grated parmesan cheese

2 cups leftover cooked spaghetti

2 tablespoons extra virgin olive oil

150 g (5½ oz) buffalo mozzarella, thinly sliced

METHOD

Start with two bowls and crack 3 eggs into each. Put half the parmesan in each bowl and season lightly. Using a fork, whisk until well combined. Add half the spaghetti to each bowl and mix. Heat 1 tablespoon of the olive oil in a 20 cm (8 in) heavy-based frying pan over medium–high heat until the oil starts to smoke. Pour one of the bowls of egg mixture into the pan and cook for 1–1½ minutes, using a spatula to lift the edges continually as the frittata cooks so that raw mixture fills the space (this will trap air and make the frittata light and fluffy). Slide the half-cooked frittata onto a plate and set aside. Heat the remaining oil and cook the second bowl of mixture as you did the first. Scatter the mozzarella on the uncooked top of the second frittata in the pan, then turn the first frittata from the plate into the pan, uncooked side down. Cook for about 2 minutes. Turn off the heat and let the frittata rest for a minute before serving. Cut into wedges and serve with a green salad and ripe tomatoes.

SERVES 4   WINE: Costa d'Amalfi Bianco

CAMPANIA
SECONDI

FISH AND TARALLO SOUP
ZUPPA DI TARALLO AL FINOCCHIETTO E PESCE

This recipe is adapted from a dish by Neapolitan chef Gennaro Esposito. The fish used has to be very fresh. Experiment with any type of oily fish that are available at your fishmonger if the ones in the ingredients list aren't available.

INGREDIENTS

½ cup (125 ml/4 fl oz) extra virgin olive oil, plus extra for finishing

1 tablespoon minced brown onion

1 tablespoon minced celery

1 teaspoon minced carrot

1 sprig oregano

4 taralli al finocchietto (see page 140)

600 ml (21 fl oz) vegetable broth (see page 49)

1 × 200 g (7 oz) ribbonfish fillet, cut into 6

1 × 200 g (7 oz) swordfish fillet, cut into 6

1 × 300 g (10½ oz) bonito fillet, cut into 6

1 × 200 g (7 oz) mackerel fillet, cut into 6

1 tablespoon garum

6 anchovy fillets

2 teaspoons tomato paste (tomato puree)

4 tablespoons pitted and chopped green olives (preferably Sicilian Nocellara del Belice variety)

METHOD

Heat 50 ml (1¾ fl oz) of the olive oil in a large saucepan and lightly fry the onion, celery and carrot for a couple of minutes. Add the oregano and taralli that have been broken up and crumbed. Stir on very low heat for 15 minutes or so until the taralli crumbs have toasted. Add the vegetable broth and a couple of good pinches of salt. Simmer gently for 1 hour. Meanwhile, marinate all the fish except the anchovies for 40 minutes in 50 ml (1¾ fl oz) of the oil and half the garum. Heat the remaining oil in a wide frying pan and fry the fish pieces on both sides until golden. Using a stick blender, whisk the soup until smooth. Check for seasoning and if necessary adjust with a little more salt and freshly cracked pepper. Distribute the fish evenly among 6 large bowls, then add the anchovies, tomato paste, olive fillets and remaining garum. Ladle hot soup into each bowl and finish with a little oil.

SERVES 6   WINE: Fiano di Avellino

GARUM IS ITALY'S FISH SAUCE. IT'S MADE IN A SIMILAR WAY TO THAI FISH SAUCE, USING TUNA OFFAL, SARDINES OR MACKEREL THAT ARE SALTED AND STACKED IN LAYERS IN WOODEN BARRELS. THE BARRELS ARE CLOSED AND PLACED IN THE SUN TO FERMENT THE FISH FOR A FEW MONTHS AND THEN THE CLEAR, GOLDEN LIQUID CALLED GARUM IS DRAWN OFF, READY FOR USE.

GRATIN OF RED MULLET
TRIGLIE GRATINATE

INGREDIENTS

160 ml (5¼ fl oz) extra virgin
 olive oil

1 kg (2 lb 4 oz) red mullet
 fillets, boned, skin on

2 cups dry breadcrumbs

2 garlic cloves, minced

1 teaspoon dried oregano

1 tablespoon capers, chopped

4 tablespoons chopped
 black olives (preferably
 Gaeta variety)

½ cup tomato fillets
 (see page 40)

1 tablespoon chopped parsley

METHOD

Preheat the oven to 210°C (410°F). Use 2 tablespoons of the olive oil
to grease a baking dish that will fit the red mullet fillets in one layer
but not touching each other. Put the fillets, skin side down, in the dish.
Mix the remaining oil in a bowl with the breadcrumbs, garlic, oregano
and capers, and season. The crumbs should just stick together – if
they don't, add a little more oil. Cover each fish fillet with a thin layer
of crumb mixture. Scatter the olives and tomato fillets in the spaces
between the fish. Bake for 5–6 minutes, then transfer to plates, sprinkle
with the parsley and serve immediately.

SERVES 6   WINE: Falanghina del Beneventano

PAN-FRIED SEA BREAM WITH POMEGRANATE
FILLETTO DI ORATA IN PADELLA AL MELOGRANO

INGREDIENTS

600 g (1 lb 5 oz) bream fillets,
 skin removed

2 tablespoons finely chopped
 parsley

2 tablespoons finely chopped
 coriander (cilantro) leaves

1 tablespoon finely chopped
 thyme

3 pomegranates

2 tablespoons red wine
 vinegar

½ cup (125 ml/4 fl oz) extra
 virgin olive oil

2 cups chopped curly endive

METHOD

Cut the bream fillets into roughly 2 cm (¾ in) pieces. Combine the herbs
in a large bowl with a couple of pinches of salt. Add the bream and toss
so that the fish is well coated. Refrigerate until needed. Meanwhile, juice
2 of the pomegranates and remove the seeds from the third. Make a
dressing with the pomegranate juice by mixing it with the vinegar and
⅓ cup (80 ml/2½ fl oz) of the olive oil. Scatter the endive on a serving
platter or individual plates. Heat the remaining oil in a frying pan until
just smoking, then add the bream and fry for a few seconds on each
side. Remove from the heat and season. Arrange the fish on the endive,
sprinkle with the dressing and scatter the pomegranate seeds over.

SERVES 4   WINE: Greco di Tufo

155

BRAISED BUFFALO IN AGLIANICO
BRASATO DI BUFALA ALL'AGLIANICO

While buffalo mozzarella is famed all over the world, buffalo meat is also eaten in Campania. It is typically leaner than beef, having less intramuscular fat; however, it has more fat around the muscles – this is easily removed. The same cut of beef can be substituted for the buffalo in this recipe.

INGREDIENTS

1 kg (2 lb 4 oz) buffalo meat from the shoulder blade

3 garlic cloves, cut lengthways into 3

600 ml (21 fl oz) Aglianico (or other full-bodied red wine)

100 ml (3½ fl oz) extra virgin olive oil

1 red onion, chopped

1 celery heart, chopped

1 carrot, chopped

2 rosemary sprigs

½ cup whole basil leaves

40 g (1½ oz) unsalted butter

METHOD

The night before you plan to serve the dish, stud the piece of meat all over with the garlic slivers. Tie with butcher's twine to keep the meat together. Sprinkle with salt and put in a flameproof casserole dish that just fits the meat. Pour the wine over, cover and leave overnight in the refrigerator. The next day, put the casserole dish on a low heat and simmer covered for 1 hour, turning the meat once. Meanwhile, heat the olive oil in a separate large flameproof casserole dish and lightly fry the onion, celery and carrot for 10 minutes or so, adding a couple of pinches of salt and stirring constantly with a wooden spoon. Add the meat and its cooking liquid carefully. Add the rosemary and basil and simmer for 1 hour, turning the meat every 15 minutes. Once cooked (the meat should pull apart with a fork), remove the meat carefully and keep hot in a 140°C (285°F) oven. Strain the vegetables, keeping the liquid. Remove and discard the rosemary. Using a Mouli or food processor, puree the vegetables. Simmer the cooking liquid until reduced to about 200 ml (7 fl oz), then add the vegetables and heat gently. When ready to serve, cut the meat into 1 cm (½ in) slices and put on serving plates. Whisk the butter into the sauce and add freshly cracked pepper. Check for salt, then spoon the sauce over the meat.

SERVES 6–8   WINE: Aglianico

RABBIT ISCHIA STYLE
CONIGLIO ALL'ISCHITANA

Italy's most famous breed of rabbit, coniglio da fossa, lives on the island of Ischia, at the northern end of the Bay of Naples, in caves that extend outward into warrens. Its meat is firmer and tastier than that of cage-raised rabbits.

INGREDIENTS

⅓ cup (80 ml/2½ fl oz) extra virgin olive oil

1 × 1 kg (2 lb 4 oz) rabbit, jointed

10 garlic cloves, peeled

2 cups (500 ml/17 fl oz) dry white wine

12 basil leaves

1 × 6 cm (2½ in) thyme sprig

1 × 6 cm (2½ in) rosemary sprig

¼ cup chopped parsley

1 chilli, chopped

10 tinned tomatoes, mashed

METHOD

Heat the olive oil in a flameproof casserole dish and fry the rabbit pieces and garlic, keeping everything moving, for 10 minutes until well browned. Add the wine and allow it to evaporate completely. Add the remaining ingredients, season and simmer for 20 minutes until the rabbit is cooked. To check if cooked pierce the hind leg of its thickest point to see if tender. Add a little water while cooking if the dish gets too dry.

SERVES 4   WINE: Ischia Rosso

FENNEL GRATIN WITH FENNEL SAUSAGES
FINOCCHI GRATINATI CON SALSICCE

INGREDIENTS

3–4 fennel bulbs

1 small lemon, halved

½ cup (125 ml/4 fl oz) extra virgin olive oil

150 g (5½ oz) fresh breadcrumbs

150 g (5½ oz) provolone cheese, coarsely grated

100 g (3½ oz) Grana Padano, finely grated

8 pork and fennel sausages

METHOD

Preheat the oven to 170°C (340°F). Trim the outer layers off each fennel bulb, leaving only the tender heart. Bring a large saucepan of salted water to the boil, add the lemon and blanch the fennel for 4–5 minutes. Drain and cool. Cut each bulb lengthways into 8 pieces. Using 2 tablespoons of the olive oil, grease a baking dish. Arrange the fennel evenly in the dish. In a bowl, mix the breadcrumbs, provolone and Grana Padano with a couple of pinches of salt and pepper. Sprinkle this mixture evenly over the fennel and drizzle 2 tablespoons of the oil over. Bake for 25 minutes. Fry the sausages in the remaining oil and present on a serving plate with the fennel.

SERVES 4   WINE: Irpinia Rosso

CAMPANIA
DOLCI

ALMOND AND ORANGE BISCUITS
BISCOTTI ALLE MANDORLE E ARANCIA

INGREDIENTS

150 g (5½ oz) blanched almonds

100 g (3½ oz) candied orange peel

85 g (3 oz) unsalted butter

120 g (4¼ oz) caster (superfine) sugar

40 g (1½ oz) plain (all-purpose) flour, sifted

2 tablespoons tepid (just warm) milk

METHOD

Preheat the oven to 140°C (285°F). Put the almonds on a baking tray and roast lightly for 6–8 minutes. Remove from the oven and let cool. Increase the oven temperature to 250°C (480°F) and grease the baking tray with butter or line with baking paper. Put the almonds in a food processor with the candied orange peel and pulse until finely ground. In a bowl, beat the butter and sugar together until smooth and creamy. Add the flour and milk and mix until well incorporated. Add the almond/orange mixture and mix well. Using a teaspoon, put equal-sized amounts of batter on the baking tray, leaving plenty of room between the dollops. Bake for 6–7 minutes. Remove from the oven and cool completely on the tray. They will keep for 2 weeks if stored in an airtight container.

MAKES 30–35   WINE: Orange liqueur such as Petrone Liquore all'Arancia

RUM BABAS
BABÀ AL RHVM

This simple, light version is adapted from a recipe by British baker Dan Lepard. The babas can be made ahead of time and heated in a microwave before soaking and serving.

INGREDIENTS

100 ml (3½ fl oz) warm milk

1½ teaspoons dried yeast

1 cup (150 g/5½ oz) plain (all-purpose) flour

1 egg

1 egg yolk

1½ teaspoons caster (superfine) sugar

¾ teaspoon fine salt

50 g (1¾ oz) softened unsalted butter

6–8 teaspoons dark rum

whipped cream

SYRUP

600 g (1 lb 5 oz) caster (superfine) sugar

6 thin strips of pith-free lemon zest

1 vanilla bean, split lengthways

METHOD

Rinse the bowl of an electric mixer with boiling water and wipe dry, then add the milk, yeast and ⅓ cup (50 g/1¾ oz) of the flour. Stir well and leave for 15 minutes until foamy. Add the remaining flour, egg and yolk, sugar and salt and beat for 2 minutes. Finally, add the butter and beat for 2 minutes. Cover the bowl and leave in a warm place until the dough has doubled in size. Butter 5–6 × 100 ml (3½ fl oz) capacity muffin moulds (or 20 × 30 ml/1 fl oz dariole moulds). Half-fill the moulds with dough, then set them aside for the dough to rise further. Preheat the oven to 190°C (375°F). When the dough has reached the top of the moulds, bake for 25 minutes until a skewer inserted comes out clean. Meanwhile, make the syrup by heating 2 cups (500 ml/17 fl oz) water in a saucepan with the sugar, lemon zest and vanilla bean and simmering for 5 minutes. Remove the babas from the oven and unmould. Put them in a large deep bowl and pour the hot syrup over. Sit a plate on the babas to keep them dunked under the syrup. Cool. Serve the babas split in half with a little rum drizzled on top and some whipped cream.

SERVES 5–6, depending on moulds   BEST SERVED with espresso

159

NEAPOLITAN DOUGHNUTS
GRAFFE

Originally a Christmastime speciality, graffe (also called zeppole) can now be found in cafès all over Naples. They are eaten for breakfast with espresso. Don't use new potatoes that have a lot of moisture in them for this recipe. Older, dry potatoes are better, like the ones used to make gnocchi.

INGREDIENTS

300 g (10½ oz) potatoes (see recipe introduction), unpeeled

½ cup (125 ml/4 fl oz) milk

25 g (1 oz) fresh yeast

60 g (2¼ oz) caster (superfine) sugar, plus extra for dredging

500 g (1 lb 2 oz) strong flour

finely grated zest of 1 lemon

1 teaspoon light-coloured honey (such as orange-flower or acacia)

3 eggs, lightly whisked

100 g (3½ oz) softened unsalted butter

extra virgin olive oil for frying

METHOD

Put the potatoes in a saucepan with plenty of water and bring to the boil. Cover, turn down to a simmer and cook until tender. Remove from the pan and let cool a little, then remove and discard the skin. Put the potatoes through a ricer into a large bowl or mash well. Heat the milk until warm (not hot) and pour into a bowl. Add the yeast and half the sugar and mix to dissolve. Add 1 cup (150 g/5½ oz) of the flour and mix well so there are no lumps. Cover the bowl with plastic wrap and let rise for 50 minutes until the dough has doubled in size. Meanwhile, to the bowl containing the potato, add the lemon zest, honey, eggs, the remaining sugar and flour, and a pinch of salt. Add the risen dough and combine until smooth. Finally, work in the butter. Transfer the dough to your work surface and knead for 10–12 minutes until shiny and elastic. Put back in the bowl and cover with plastic wrap, then leave for 2 hours or so until doubled in size. Transfer the dough to a floured work surface and work it into an even cylinder about 8 cm (3¼ in) in diameter. Cut 2 cm (¾ in) pieces (approximately 60 g/2¼ oz each) off the cylinder. Flatten each piece and then work a hole into the middle to shape into the classic doughnut. Put on a tray lined with a clean tea towel (dish towel), cover with another tea towel and let rise for 1 hour. Heat a couple of centimetres deep of olive oil in a frying pan to 180°C (350°F). Fry 3–4 graffe at a time, depending on the size of your pan, until golden on the bottom, then turn and cook the other side. Drain on paper towels and dredge in caster sugar while still warm. Eat warm or cold.

MAKES about 20   WINE: Fiano Passito

LEMON PIE
TORTA AL LIMONE

This recipe was given to me by Caterina Nuzzo from the small town of Cancello, near Naples.

INGREDIENTS

PASTRY

500 g (1 lb 2 oz) plain
  (all-purpose) flour, sifted

300 g (10½ oz) sugar

200 g (7 oz) unsalted butter, cut
  into small cubes

2 eggs

1 egg yolk

finely grated zest of 1 lemon

400 g (14 oz) sugar

100 g (3½ oz) potato flour
  (or potato starch), sifted

2 egg yolks

finely grated zest of 2 lemons

½ cup (125 ml/4 fl oz) lemon juice

icing (confectioners') sugar

METHOD

To make the pastry, put the flour and sugar in the bowl of a food processor. Turn on and add the butter 1 cube at a time. Add the eggs, egg yolk and lemon zest and pulse until they have been incorporated and the mixture forms balls. Shape the pastry into a rough disc, wrap in plastic wrap and refrigerate for at least 2 hours. Meanwhile, combine the sugar and potato flour in a bowl. Mix in the egg yolks, lemon zest and lemon juice, then add 1 litre (35 fl oz) water and whisk everything together into a smooth liquid. Pour into a saucepan on low–medium heat and stir continuously until the mixture thickens to a smooth cream. Remove from the heat and let cool completely. Preheat the oven to 180°C (350°F). Roll out half the pastry to fit a 28 cm (11¼ in) tart tin. Fill with the cooled cream, then cover with the remaining rolled-out pastry. Bake for 40–45 minutes until golden. Remove from the oven and cool completely before refrigerating. Best eaten cold. Dust with icing sugar to serve.

SERVES 8   WINE: Limoncello

LEMON PUDDING
LIMONCINI

INGREDIENTS

4 eggs

250 g (9 oz) unsalted butter,
  plus extra for greasing

530 g (1 lb 2½ oz) caster
  (superfine) sugar, plus
  extra for dusting

1 teaspoon natural vanilla
  essence

2 cups (300 g/10½ oz) plain
  (all-purpose) flour

2½ teaspoons baking powder

¾ cup (185 ml/6 fl oz) milk

finely grated zest of 2 lemons

200 ml (7 fl oz) lemon juice

100 ml (3½ fl oz) limoncello

whipped cream

METHOD

Preheat the oven to 180°C (350°F). Grease 8 × 100 ml (3½ fl oz) dariole moulds with butter and dust with sugar. Separate 2 of the eggs. Beat the butter and 1½ cups (330 g/11½ oz) of the sugar together until creamy, then add the vanilla, 2 whole eggs and 2 yolks, reserving the 2 whites. Sift in the flour, baking powder and a pinch of salt, then mix in the milk and zest. Whisk the 2 egg whites to soft peaks and fold into the mixture. Fill the moulds with batter to about 1 cm (½ in) from the top. Put the moulds in a baking dish and pour in boiling water to come two-thirds up the sides of the moulds. Put the baking dish carefully into the oven, then reduce the temperature to 180°C (350°F) and bake the limoncini for 25 minutes. Meanwhile, bring the lemon juice and remaining sugar to the boil. Remove from the heat and add the limoncello. Release the limoncini from their moulds. If you are serving them later, they can be refrigerated and reheated in the microwave or oven. If serving immediately, prick the tops 4–5 times using a skewer and pour 2 tablespoons of the warm syrup onto each limoncino. Serve with fresh whipped cream.

MAKES 8   WINE: Limoncello

FROZEN PRICKLY PEAR SOUFFLES

FROZEN PRICKLY PEAR SOUFFLES
SOFFIATI DI FICHI D'INDIA

This dish is based on a recipe from Neapolitan chef Alfonso Iaccarino. It can be made with prickly pears of any colour.

INGREDIENTS

10 prickly pears, peeled

2 eggs, separated

3 tablespoons caster (superfine) sugar

1 cup (250 ml/9 fl oz) cream, whipped

SUGAR SYRUP

100 g (3½ oz) caster (superfine) sugar

METHOD

Make the sugar syrup by heating 100 ml (3½ fl oz) water with the caster sugar. Once it boils, remove from the heat and let cool, then set aside. (Any sugar syrup left over after making this recipe can be refrigerated indefinitely.) Puree 8 of the prickly pears in a food processor. Transfer to a sieve over a bowl and strain, discarding the seeds. Set aside the juice. Put the egg yolks in a bowl with 2 tablespoons of the sugar. Whisk continuously over a simmering saucepan of water for about 5 minutes until fluffy and thick, like zabaglione or custard, then set aside to cool. Beat the egg whites to soft peaks, add the remaining sugar and keep whisking until stiff peaks form. Gently fold in the cream, the cooled yolk/sugar mixture and half the prickly pear juice, until evenly incorporated. Ladle into 6 × 150 ml (5 fl oz) round moulds and put in the freezer for at least 4 hours. When you are ready to serve, mix ⅓ cup (80 ml/2½ fl oz) of the sugar syrup with the remaining prickly pear juice. Cut the remaining prickly pears into wedges. Unmould the soufflés by dipping the bases quickly in hot water. Spoon a little syrup over and serve with the prickly pear wedges.

SERVES 6 WINE: Fiano Passito

PRICKLY PEAR LOOKS LIKE A SMALL BARREL ABOUT 6–8 CENTIMETRES (2–3 INCHES) LONG. TAKE CARE WHEN HANDLING THE FRUIT BECAUSE THE FINE HAIRS CAN LODGE IN YOUR SKIN. HANDLE THE FRUIT WITH A GLOVED HAND. PEELING IS EASY. CUT OFF EACH OF THE ENDS USING A SHARP KNIFE. MAKE A SLIT SKIN-DEEP DOWN THE LENGTH OF THE FRUIT AND PEEL THE SKIN AWAY FROM THE PULP. PRICKLY PEAR FRUIT CAN RANGE FROM RED TO DEEP YELLOW AND IS SWEET AND JUICY.

EMILIA-ROMAGNA

EMILIA-ROMAGNA

ONE OF THE RICHEST AND MOST DEVELOPED REGIONS IN EUROPE, THE 22,000-PLUS HECTARES (85 SQUARE MILES) OF EMILIA-ROMAGNA SPRAWL ACROSS THE ITALIAN PENINSULA WITH ACCESS TO THE ADRIATIC TO THE EAST AND THE MEDITERRANEAN TO THE WEST. EMILIA-ROMAGNA IS BORDERED BY LIGURIA TO THE WEST, LOMBARDIA AND VENETO TO THE NORTH, AND TOSCANA AND LE MARCHE TO THE SOUTH.

Emilia-Romagna is nearly half plains, a quarter hilly and a quarter mountainous. The mountains stretch north to south-east for 300 kilometres (186 miles), with three peaks over 2000 metres (6500 feet).

The name of the province derives from two great roads of ancient Rome: Via Emilia, which still exists as State Route 9, and Via Romeo, the Road of the Pilgrims. Emilia-Romagna is the centre of Italy's racing and sports car culture, being home to Maserati, Ferrari, Lamborghini, De Tomaso and motorcycle maker Ducati. Culturally and historically it is represented by the Romanesque in Modena, the Gothic in Bologna, the Byzantine in Ravenna and the Renaissance in Ferrara. The entire city of Ferrara is a jewel of the Renaissance.

Such a rich cultural background promises – and delivers – a similar cuisine. Two of the most famous cured pork meats in Italy, derived from the foraging pigs of the Po Valley, come from Emilia and Romagna: prosciutto from Parma and culatello from Zibello. And then

there is what is perhaps the most famous cheese on the planet: Parmigiano Reggiano, the whey from which is fed to the pigs that produce the prosciutto. Nothing is wasted!

The other great meat of the region is mortadella. Produced in copious and inferior quantities in the rest of the world, the mortadella of Bologna is a magnificent creation made of finely chopped pork that is kneaded to a paste, highly and idiosyncratically spiced (each maker has a mixture), and packed tightly in the skin of a whole suckling pig with such artistry that the incision where the meat is inserted is invisible unless you lift the foreleg and look beneath it. According to Waverley Root in *The Food of Italy*, this is a trick that was known to the ancient Romans.

There are two possible origins of the name mortadella: firstly, from the fact that the meat was pounded to a paste using a mortar and pestle (mortaio in Latin), and secondly, that it comes from an ancient Roman sausage flavoured with myrtle berries known as farcimen mirtatum. In America, mortadella is called bologna and pronounced 'baloney' – a reference to its origin. Where the saying 'a lot of baloney', meaning 'nonsense', comes from is unclear.

The other emblematic product of the region is the balsamic vinegar of Modena. It originated in the Middle Ages, when it was considered a remedy for the plague. The best of Modena's aromatic vinegars are among the most expensive liquids on the planet.

Many Italian cities have been bestowed with nicknames, but only Bologna, the capital of the province, has two: Bologna La Grassa, meaning 'the fat one', and Bologna La Dotta, 'the learned one'. It earned the latter for its university, which was the first in Europe, and the former for its cuisine. 'One eats more in Bologna in a year than in Venice in two, in Turin in five and in Genoa in twenty,' wrote Ippolito Nievo in his book *The Confessions of an Italian*, published in 1867. The la grassa nickname might also refer to the fact that in Bologna three cooking fats are used: olive oil, butter and lard – and not just any butter, but some of the best butter in Italy, burro di panna.

The pasta of Bologna is renowned, firstly because of the quality of the soglia (semolina flour) used to make it and secondly because of the skill of its makers. Tortellini, according to many, is the pasta della pasta. Root quotes a Bolognese poet who wrote 'if the first father of the human race was lost for an apple, what would he have done for a bowl of tortellini?' Proper tortellini is stuffed with a paste of prosciutto, mortadella, veal, parmesan and a pinch of nutmeg, which is pressed into the pasta and rolled into a ring shape that suggests to the Bolognese a woman's navel – a resemblance that has inspired much poetry and literature.

Mention of the word Bolognese, and harking back to the desecration of mortadella in the world outside, Bologna brings us to what is perhaps the most famous non-Italian Italian dish in the world: spaghetti bolognese, also known as spag bol. This ubiquitous global standby is, in reality, a corruption of a superb sauce, ragù bolognese – a slowly simmered sauce of, among many other things, finely chopped pork and veal and the budelli (intestines) of chicken. It is served most typically not on spaghetti, but on green tagliatelle, the pasta being coloured by the addition of chopped spinach to the dough.

The region is a great producer of tomatoes, sugar beet, peas and beans, while the Po River supplies carp, tench and pike. The Comacchio lagoons of Romagna are home to eels that are caught using complex reed traps known as lavorieri and then spit-roasted, or smoked and spit-roasted, or roasted over coals; they are especially prized eating on Christmas Eve.

The best-known wine of Emilia-Romagna is another local product that has been thoroughly debased by export: lambrusco. Root is one of many writers who regard this wine as mediocre at best ('perilously close to vinegar'), but there is good lambrusco. If you cannot find it where you live, you may have to go to Bologna for it.

Four DOCs are designated for lambrusco, producing secco, amabile and dolce versions. There is even a white version, called lambrusco in bianco. For full-bodied versions, look for the lambrusco grasparosso di Castelvetro, and for more elegant styles, the lambrusco di Sorbara.

Fourteen of the region's 21 DOCs produce dry white wines, but they are for the most part undistinguished.

The major red wine grape is sangiovese, which, some researchers contend, first grew in Romagna. Be that as it may, the sangiovese wines of the region are not to be compared with those of Toscana. In the Colli Bolognesi some producers are making a name with wines using the cabernet sauvignon grape, and in Colli Piacentini pinot noir is enjoying success.

Also produced in this rich and varied region are the liqueurs sambuca and nocino, the latter of which is made from green walnuts.

TRADITIONAL BALSAMIC VINEGAR

There is a tradition all over Italy where grape must – the juice collected when grapes are first pressed – is boiled until it becomes syrupy and concentrated. Depending where you are, this wonderful sweet condiment is called saba, vincotto or mostarda di uva. It is used as a final dressing on sweet dishes such as baked figs or apples, and as an accompaniment to mature cheeses such as Reggiano or Gorgonzola.

Perhaps the greatest tradition of this kind is achieved when the boiled-down grape must is allowed to undergo an alcoholic fermentation and then, with the introduction of a 'mother', encouraging an acetic transformation before being allowed to age gracefully.

While it is a simple and inexpensive matter to buy balsamic vinegar in a shop or supermarket, what you are often getting is young vinegar coloured with caramel. It is the ageing process that transforms the immature must into the precious, complex-flavoured condiment called Aceto Balsamico Tradizionale.

Made around the northern Italian city of Modena, it starts off life as boiled must in a 100 litre barrel, where it undergoes fermentation and acetification. After a year some is put into a smaller barrel and each year after that a little is transferred to progressively smaller barrels. A series may contain as little as three or as many as 20 or more barrels made of different types of wood, each imparting different characteristics.

Chestnut, for example, gives the typical dark mahogany colour to the must; sweetness is often achieved from cherry wood; juniper provides a particular resinous aroma; mulberry imparts a delicate vanilla note; and oak, considered neutral, is reserved for the final, smallest barrel before the nectar is bottled.

The law states that Aceto Balsamico Tradizionale must be a minimum of 12 years of age. It is subjected to rigorous tastings by an independent panel of experts before it is offered for sale. In any given year, 10–20 per cent of the volume in each barrel is lost to natural evaporation, so by the time it is bottled, it is concentrated and complex like a great aged wine.

All Aceto Balsamico Tradizionale comes in a bottle designed in 1988 by Giorgetto Giugiaro, one of the most influential designers of the 20th century. The shape of the bottle is registered and patented and can only be used by members of the consortium. It holds a mere 100 ml (3½ fl oz) and prices start at around $100 for the minimum 12-year-old to well over $1000 for a stravecchio ('very old') of 100 years.

This may seem extravagant, but a few drops of this extraordinary nectar go a long way. Unlike the aggressive, acidic stuff bottled as balsamic vinegar, Aceto Balsamico Tradizionale is subtle and balanced but concentrated. Try a few drops on a simple dish such as a soft-boiled egg placed on a grilled piece of ciabatta that has been brushed with extra virgin olive oil, and finish with a little salt and pepper.

From there, sprinkle some on a grilled fillet of whiting or any fine white fish. On grilled or roast beef or duck, it lifts the flavour of the meat so it needs nothing else. And to finish, add a teaspoon to some berries and leave them to macerate for an hour; serve them with mascarpone or vanilla gelato for a perfect Italian dessert.

EMILIA-ROMAGNA

ANTI-PASTI

FRIED GNOCCO
GNOCCO FRITTO

Originally from Emilia-Romagna, gnocco fritto is now popular in many parts of Italy. If strutto is not your thing, substitute extra virgin olive oil.

INGREDIENTS

500 g (1 lb 2 oz) plain (all-purpose) flour

12 g (⅖ oz) fresh yeast

1 teaspoon honey

10 g (¼ oz) salt

70 g (2½ oz) pork dripping (strutto) melted

400 ml (14 fl oz) extra virgin olive oil

METHOD

Sift the flour into a bowl. In a smaller bowl, dissolve the yeast and honey in 80 ml warm water, stirring with a spoon. Add a couple of tablespoons of the flour to the dissolved yeast and stir to make a paste. Let rest for 30 minutes. Dissolve the salt in 100 ml (3½ fl oz) warm water. Make a well in the remaining flour and pour in the yeast mixture, pork dripping and salted water. Bring together using your hands until the dough forms one lump. Lightly flour your work surface and knead the dough for 5–6 minutes until smooth, shiny and elastic. Form into a ball and put back in the bowl. Cut a cross on the top of the ball, cover the bowl with plastic wrap and set aside in a warm part of the house (at about 28°C/82°F, if possible) for 3 hours or until it has risen by 50 per cent. Put the leavened dough back on a lightly floured work surface and knead for 2 minutes. Roll out to a thickness of 2–3 mm (¹⁄₁₆–⅛ in) and cut into 8–9 cm (3¼–3½ in) squares. Heat the olive oil to 180–190°C (350–375°F) in a wide frying pan (to test the temperature of the oil, drop in a cube of bread – the oil is ready if the bread turns golden brown in 15 seconds) and fry 4–5 squares at a time. They will puff up and need to be turned once so they are golden brown on both sides. Drain on paper towels. To serve, open each gnocco and put some salumi (such as mortadella, prosciutto or culatello) inside to resemble a mini panino.

MAKES 40–45   WINE: Lambrusco Secco

GNOCCO IS THE SINGULAR FORM OF GNOCCHI AND LITERALLY MEANS, LUMP. THE GNOCCO FRITTO IN EMILIAN CUISINE IS A SMALL, YEASTED BUN THAT IS FRIED RATHER THAN BAKED. IT IS THEN SERVED FILLED WITH ALL MANNER OF ACCOMPANIMENTS, USUALLY THE WONDERFUL PROSCIUTTO OR MORTADELLA PRODUCED IN THE REGION AS WELL AS CHEESES AND VEGETABLES, MUCH LIKE A SANDWICH. DEPENDING ON WHERE YOU ARE IN ITALY THIS GNOCCO FRITTO IS ALSO KNOWN AS CRESCENTINA FRITTA, TORTA FRITTA OR PINZIN.

TOMATO FRITTATA
FRITTATA ROSSA

INGREDIENTS

400 g (14 oz) ripe tomatoes, peeled and seeded

2 tablespoons extra virgin olive oil

1 garlic clove, finely sliced

4 large eggs, whisked

100 g (3½ oz) buffalo mozzarella, broken into pieces

1 teaspoon dried oregano

METHOD

Preheat the oven to 180°C (350°F). Cut the tomatoes into 2 cm (¾ in) cubes. Heat the olive oil on medium heat in an ovenproof frying pan and fry the garlic for a few seconds. Add the tomatoes and a couple of pinches of salt, stir and simmer on medium heat for 10 minutes. Add the eggs and use a spoon to push them gently from the sides of the pan to the middle so they ooze to the bottom. Keep this action going for a few minutes until the eggs cook a little. Remove the pan from the heat and scatter the mozzarella on the frittata. Sprinkle on the oregano and add a couple of turns of pepper. Bake for 5–6 minutes. Serve warm or cold.

SERVES 6   WINE: Sparkling Malvasia

PARMESAN BISCUITS
BISCOTTINI AL PARMIGIANO

Try to use the sharper Reggiano here instead of the milder Grana Padano – the biscuits (cookies) will taste much better.

INGREDIENTS

125 g (3½ oz) butter

1⅔ cups (250 g/9 oz) plain (all-purpose) flour

80 g (2¾ oz) Parmigiano Reggiano, grated

1 egg

METHOD

In a food processor, mix all the ingredients together with a pinch of salt until well incorporated. Do not overwork. Form the dough into a sausage about a 3 cm (1¼ in) diameter and rest in the refrigerator for 1 hour. Preheat the oven to 180°C (350°F). Cut the sausage into circles roughly a 2 mm (1/16 in) thickness and put on a baking tray. Cook for 10–12 minutes until light golden. Allow to cool, then serve or store in an airtight container.

MAKES 30–40   WINE: Malvasia Frizzante

ROAST POLENTA, PARMESAN AND PROSCIUTTO FINGERS
CROSTINI DI POLENTA, PARMIGIANO E PROSCIUTTO

INGREDIENTS
250 g (9 oz) polenta
  (cornmeal)
200 g (7 oz) Parmigiano
  Reggiano, shaved
50 thin slices prosciutto,
  halved lengthways

METHOD
Bring 1.25 litres (44 fl oz) salted water to the boil. Add the polenta in a fine stream, stirring constantly so that no lumps form. Keep stirring until the polenta starts to come away from the sides of the saucepan. Turn down the heat to very low and simmer, covered, for about 25 minutes, stirring well every 5 minutes or so. When the polenta is ready, transfer it to a tray and allow it to set – it should be about 2 cm (¾ in) thick. Preheat the oven to 180–200°C (350–400°F). Once the polenta is cool, cut it into 4 cm × 2 cm (1½ in × ¾ in) 'fingers'. Put a little parmesan on the top and bottom of each finger and wrap with a slice of prosciutto. Arrange on a baking tray and bake for about 15 minutes until the prosciutto is crisp. Serve hot.

MAKES about 100 — WINE: Lambrusco

SPINACH FRITTERS
FRITTELLE DI SPINACI

The best oil to use for frying is always extra virgin olive oil. Do not believe anything to the contrary.

INGREDIENTS
450 g (1 lb) spinach
4 eggs, whisked
80 g (2¾ oz) plain
  (all-purpose) flour
150 g (5½ oz) parmesan
  cheese, grated
300 ml (10½ fl oz) extra virgin
  olive oil

METHOD
Bring a large saucepan of water to the boil and blanch the spinach for a minute. Drain and let cool, then put in a clean tea towel (dish towel) and squeeze out as much water as possible. Roughly chop the spinach and mix well in a bowl with the eggs, flour, parmesan and 1 tablespoon of the olive oil. Season. Heat the remaining olive oil in a frying pan and drop in spoonfuls of the batter. Cook until golden on both sides. Drain on paper towel. Continue until all the batter is used, then sprinkle with a little salt and serve.

SERVES 6–8 — WINE: Malvasia Frizzante

MODENESE FLATBREAD WITH LARDO, ROSEMARY AND GARLIC
BORLENGHI TRADIZIONALE

This traditional flatbread is typically found between the cities of Modena and Bologna – though it is practically unobtainable in nearby Parma, attesting to the localisation of many of Italy's traditional dishes. Its origins are said to be in the burla, the carnival period of the area dating from the 1500s. While these days borlenghi can be found in osterie and trattorie, they remain essentially street or snack food. The filling given here is perhaps the most traditional, but they can be filled with anything.

INGREDIENTS

2 cups (300 g/10½ oz) Italian soft wheat flour type '0'

60 g (2¼ oz) cured lardo, chopped

2 garlic cloves, finely chopped

2 tablespoons finely chopped rosemary

1 small piece of pork back fat or extra virgin olive oil

100 g (3½ oz) Parmigiano Reggiano, grated

METHOD

Put the flour and 2 pinches of salt in a bowl and slowly mix in 3 cups (750 ml/26 fl oz) water, working with a spoon or fork until all lumps have gone. The batter should be fairly runny. Mix the lardo, garlic and rosemary to a soft, spreadable paste. Put a well-seasoned 27 cm (10¾ in) heavy-based frying pan on medium heat and, when hot, oil with the pork back fat. Ladle in about 150 ml (5 fl oz) batter and tilt the pan so the liquid covers the surface. Cook for 1½–2 minutes on each side on medium–high heat, turning using a spatula. There should be a golden lattice-like surface on each side that is crisp on the extremities and a little softer in the middle. (The first borlengo is often not very good as the pan needs a 'practice'.) Pile the finished borlenghi on a hot plate to keep warm, and re-oil the pan surface with the pork back fat before cooking each borlengo. To serve, spread a little of the lardo and rosemary paste on each borlengo and sprinkle with Parmigiano Reggiano. Either roll up or fold into quarters like you would a handkerchief. Serve warm.

MAKES 7   WINE: Lambrusco di Sorbara

EMILIA-ROMAGNA
PRIMI

CHESTNUT AND LEEK SOUP
PASSATO DI CASTAGNE E PORRI

If you'd like to keep this soup meat free, then substitute water for the chicken or veal broth.

INGREDIENTS

500 g (1 lb 2 oz) chestnuts,
   peeled (see page 82)
1.5 litres (52 fl oz) chicken
   or veal broth (see page 48)
3 cups thinly sliced leek
100 g (3½ oz) butter
50 ml (1¾ fl oz) extra virgin
   olive oil
grated parmesan cheese
6 slices country-style bread,
   toasted

METHOD

Put the chestnuts in a saucepan with the broth and leek and simmer gently for about 1 hour. Mix in the butter and olive oil, season and serve with parmesan and toasted country-style bread.

SERVES 6   WINE: Sangiovese di Romagna

SORREL SOUP
ZUPPA DI ACETOSA

INGREDIENTS

2 tablespoons extra virgin
   olive oil
50 g (1¾ oz) unsalted butter
500 g (1 lb 2 oz) potatoes,
   diced
1 large brown onion, diced
2 garlic cloves, sliced
2 litres (70 fl oz) vegetable
   or chicken stock
180 g (6½ oz) sorrel leaves
300 ml (10½ fl oz) thin
   (pouring) cream
2 tablespoons chopped chervil
2 tablespoons chopped
   parsley
4 slices country-style bread,
   toasted

METHOD

Heat the olive oil and butter in a large saucepan and lightly fry the potatoes, onion and garlic for 3 minutes, stirring constantly. Add the stock and sorrel and bring to the boil. Turn down the heat and simmer for 20 minutes. Strain over a bowl, then puree the solids using a food processor. Return the liquid to the saucepan, add the puree and bring back to the boil. Add the cream and season. Stir in the chervil and parsley, and serve with the toasted bread.

SERVES 6   WINE: Pignoletto Superiore

STUFFED PASTA IN BROTH
TORTELLONI IN BRODO

Traditionally tortellini are about half to a third the size of these larger tortelloni, but either way, they are a joy to eat. The trick, as always with Italian food, is to use the best ingredients for both stuffing and broth.

INGREDIENTS

20 g (¾ oz) unsalted butter

80 g (2¾ oz) pork loin, cut into 2 cm (¾ in) cubes

80 g (2¾ oz) veal loin, cut into 2 cm (¾ in) cubes

80 g (2¾ oz) chicken breast, cut into 2 cm (¾ in) cubes

100 g (3½ oz) mortadella

80 g (2¾ oz) prosciutto

100 g (3½ oz) Parmigiano Reggiano, grated, plus extra for serving

pinch of grated nutmeg

4 eggs

1 quantity basic pasta dough (see page 42)

2 litres (70 fl oz) beef broth (see page 48)

METHOD

Heat the butter in a heavy frying pan and fry the pork, veal and chicken for 5–6 minutes, stirring constantly, until browned. Using a mincer, mince the pork, veal, chicken, mortadella and prosciutto. Mix in the Parmigiano Reggiano, nutmeg and 2 of the eggs. Season. Whisk the remaining eggs to make an egg wash. Cut the pasta into 8 cm (3¼ in) squares and put a teaspoon of stuffing in the middle of each square. Starting at a corner facing you, brush the 2 furthest sides of the square with egg wash and fold the 2 nearest sides over to seal. Bring the 2 corners at each end of the long base together to form into a 'hat' shape. Repeat until all the stuffing has been used. Bring the beef broth to the boil and season. Drop in the tortelloni and simmer until cooked. (To test if the tortelloni is cooked, take one out and feel the edge, if it is tender and floppy, they are ready.) Ladle into bowls and serve immediately with extra parmesan on top.

SERVES 6–8   WINE: Colli della Romagna Centrale Sangiovese

GRILLED QUAIL BREASTS WITH PANCETTA
PETTI DI QUAGLIA ALLA GRIGLIA

INGREDIENTS

12 quail breasts

12 thin rashers pancetta

1 tablespoon extra virgin olive oil

good-quality balsamic vinegar

METHOD

Season the quail breasts with a little salt and freshly cracked pepper, then wrap each one tightly with a pancetta rasher. Heat the olive oil on a grill plate or in a frying pan and grill the quail on each side for 1 minute. Rest well. To serve, sprinkle each breast with a few drops of balsamic vinegar.

SERVES 6   WINE: Sangiovese di Romagna

JEWISH-STYLE BRAISED MULLET
CEFALI IN UMIDO ALL'EBRAICA

This is a Bolognese dish that comes from the area's Jewish tradition. It's usually made with Mediterranean mullet, but yellowtail or sea mullet can be substituted.

INGREDIENTS

¼ cup (60 ml/2 fl oz) extra virgin olive oil

1 celery heart, finely chopped

6 anchovy fillets

6 × 250 g (9 oz) mullet, scaled and gutted

½ cup (125 g/3½ oz) tomato passata

juice of 1 lemon

METHOD

Heat the olive oil in a wide frying pan and lightly fry the celery for a couple of minutes. Add the anchovies and lightly fry until they have dissolved. Make sure the celery doesn't burn. Turn the heat up to medium and add the fish, then add the passata and enough water to half-submerge the fish. Add a couple of pinches of salt and bring to a simmer. Simmer for 3 minutes, then turn the fish to cook on the other side. Sprinkle with the lemon juice and carefully transfer the fish to a serving dish. Return the cooking liquid to the boil and reduce by half. Pour over the fish, cover and put in the refrigerator. When the liquid has turned to a jelly-like consistency, serve.

SERVES 4   WINE: Albana di Romagna Secco

'TEGAMINO' OF EGGS AND ASPARAGUS
TEGAMINO DI UOVA E ASPARAGI

Tegamino is an Italian term for the ramekins used to cook this dish. Any small shallow ceramic dish can be used.

INGREDIENTS

16 asparagus spears

2 tablespoons extra virgin olive oil

8 eggs

160 ml (5¼ fl oz) thin (pouring) cream

80 g (2¾ oz) grated parmesan cheese

METHOD

Preheat the oven to 180°C (350°F). Trim the asparagus spears so they will fit into your ceramic dishes (see recipe introduction). Bring a saucepan of salted water to the boil and blanch the asparagus for a minute or two, depending on thickness, until tender but not soft. Grease 4 ceramic dishes (2 cm (¾ in) deep × 15 cm (6 in) wide) with the olive oil and break 2 eggs into each. Add 2 tablespoons cream to each dish and arrange the asparagus on top. Sprinkle the parmesan evenly among the 4 dishes and season. Bake for 10–15 minutes until the eggs have cooked but the yolks are still runny. Serve immediately.

SERVES 4   WINE: Pignoletto

SPAGHETTI AND MEATBALLS
BUCATINI ALL'AMERICANA

The pork fat called for in this recipe is the succulent sort that goes into making sausages and salami – ask your butcher. Bucatini are thick spaghetti with a hole in the middle. I think a thicker-gauge long pasta works better with meatballs.

INGREDIENTS

100 g (3½ oz) day-old bread, crusts removed

⅓ cup (80 ml/2½ fl oz) milk

500 g (1 lb 2 oz) lean pork shoulder

100 g (3½ oz) pork fat (see recipe introduction)

100 g (3½ oz) mortadella

2 tablespoons minced garlic

1 teaspoon finely chopped thyme

1 tablespoon finely chopped sage

2 tablespoons finely chopped parsley

1 teaspoon grated nutmeg

100 g (3½ oz) grated parmesan cheese, plus extra for serving

1 egg, whisked

plain (all-purpose) flour

480–640 g (1 lb 1 oz–1 lb 7 oz) bucatini

TOMATO SALSA

⅓ cup (80 ml/2½ fl oz) extra virgin olive oil

1 brown onion, finely diced

2 garlic cloves, minced

1 small leek, white part only, cut in half lengthways and thinly sliced

1 celery stick from centre of bunch, finely chopped

650 g (1 lb 7 oz) tin tomatoes, mashed

1 teaspoon fennel seeds

METHOD

To make the tomato salsa, heat the olive oil in a frying pan and gently fry the onion, garlic, leek and celery until transparent. Add the tomatoes and fennel seeds. Season lightly. Stir well and simmer until the sauce thickens and most of the water has evaporated. Makes 500 ml (17 fl oz).

Soak the bread in the milk until the liquid has been absorbed. Using a mincer, mince together the pork, pork fat and mortadella. Combine the minced meat with the bread, garlic, herbs, nutmeg, parmesan and egg. Mix well using your hands, taking care to incorporate all the ingredients. Season. (A good way to check the seasoning is to fry a small patty made from the mixture in a frying pan with olive oil, then taste.) Lightly flour your hands and roll the mixture into meatballs roughly 3 cm (1¼ in) diameter. Bring the tomato salsa to a light simmer, then add the meatballs and poach for 15–20 minutes. Cook the bucatini in plenty of salted boiling water and drain. To serve, gently toss the bucatini with the meatballs and tomato sauce and add parmesan to taste.

SERVES 6–8   WINE: Dry Lambrusco

SPAGHETTI AND MEATBALLS

NETTLE AND RICOTTA TORTELLINI
TORTELLINI DI RICOTTA E ORTAGGI

If nettles are not available, use spinach. Spinach may need to be blanched a little more, and make sure it's squeezed well to remove any water. If you don't want to make pasta, you can use fresh wonton squares. The salsa can be used for any pasta (including lasagna), or served with meat or vegetable patties or on toast.

INGREDIENTS

10 cups nettle leaves

400 g (14 oz) ricotta cheese

100 g (3½ oz) grated parmesan cheese

½ teaspoon grated nutmeg

2 cups (300 g/10½ oz) '00' pasta flour or plain (all-purpose) flour

3 large eggs

1 tablespoon extra virgin olive oil

NETTLE, FENNEL SEED AND TOMATO SALSA

⅓ cup (80 ml/2½ fl oz) extra virgin olive oil

1 brown onion, finely diced

2 garlic cloves, minced

1 small leek, white part only, cut in half lengthways and thinly sliced

1 celery stick from centre of bunch, finely chopped

10 cups nettle leaves

650 g (1 lb 7 oz) tin tomatoes, mashed

1 teaspoon fennel seeds

METHOD

To make the salsa, heat the olive oil in a frying pan and gently fry the onion, garlic, leek and celery until transparent. Add the nettle leaves, tomatoes and fennel seeds. Season with a couple of pinches of salt and pepper. Stir well and simmer until the sauce thickens and most of the water has evaporated. Makes 500 ml (17 fl oz).

Bring a large saucepan of salted water to the boil. Drop in the nettle leaves for 30–40 seconds, submerging them well using a spoon, then drain well. Let them cool, then squeeze out as much water as possible. Finely chop and put in a bowl with the ricotta, parmesan and nutmeg. Add 2 pinches of salt and some turns of pepper. Mix well and taste for seasoning. Cover and refrigerate. Now make the pasta. Put the flour on your work surface and make a well, then crack in the eggs and add the olive oil. Using your hands, bring everything together in a mass. Add a little more flour if the mixture is too wet and sticky. Cut the dough into smaller workable pieces so it can be easily passed through your pasta machine. Start at the widest setting and roll through, thinner each time, until about 2 mm (¹⁄₁₆ in) thick. Cut the pasta sheets into 6 cm (2½ in) squares. Fill each square with a heaped teaspoon of nettle/ricotta mixture, then moisten the edges of each square and fold over to enclose the filling and form a triangle-shaped pillow. Press the edges to secure, then join 2 opposite corners to form a little 'hat'. Cook in plenty of salted boiling water until the edges are cooked but still al dente. Drain and toss with the nettle and tomato salsa to serve.

SERVES 10   WINE: Malvasia Rosa Frizzante

EMILIA-ROMAGNA
SECONDI

PAN-FRIED CUTTLEFISH WITH CAPSICUM AND ONION IN BALSAMIC
SEPIE IN PADELLA CON PEPERONI E CIPOLLE AL BALSAMICO

INGREDIENTS

2 red capsicums (peppers),
    seeded and each cut into
    8 strips

2 yellow capsicums (peppers),
    seeded and each cut into
    8 strips

4 red onions, each cut into
    8 wedges

extra virgin olive oil

1–2 tablespoons good-quality
    balsamic vinegar

6 medium–large cuttlefish,
    cleaned, bodies cut into
    bite-sized 'tiles'

METHOD

Preheat the oven to 180°C (350°F). Arrange the capsicums and onions in a baking tray. Sprinkle with olive oil and season. Mix so they are well coated with oil, then bake for about 20 minutes until soft. Remove from the oven, add the balsamic vinegar, mix well and cool to room temperature. Heat a little oil in a frying pan and fry the cuttlefish for about 30 seconds on each side. Season and serve with the peppers and onions (agrodolce).

SERVES 4   WINE: Malvasia

BAKED HAM AND LEEK ROLLS
ROTOLI DI PROSCIUTTO COTTO E PORRI

This simple recipe relies on the quality of the ham. Try to get the best you can find, sliced off the leg.

INGREDIENTS

2–3 large leeks, white part
    only, cut in half lengthways,
    then cut into 5 mm (¼ in)
    half-rounds (you need
    4 cups), plus extra ½ large
    leek for garnish

350 g (12 oz) ricotta cheese

1 teaspoon grated nutmeg

½ cup (50 g/1¾ oz) grated
    parmesan cheese, plus
    3 tablespoons

12 slices best-quality ham

2 tablespoons extra virgin
    olive oil

METHOD

Preheat the oven to 140°C (285°F). Bring a large saucepan of salted water to the boil. Throw in the leek half-rounds and blanch for 2 minutes. Drain well, then scatter on a tray to cool. Combine the ricotta, nutmeg, cooled leeks and the ½ cup of parmesan in a bowl. Season and mix well. Put a couple of spoonfuls of ricotta mixture on each ham slice and roll up, tucking in the sides to seal. Put the ham rolls side by side in a baking dish, spoon the olive oil on top and sprinkle with the remaining parmesan. Bake for 25 minutes. Meanwhile, finely slice extra leek (approximately 6 tablespoons, matchstick-thin) and bring a small saucepan of salted water to the boil and blanch the leek for 30 seconds. Drain and dry well. Arrange the rolls on serving plates and scatter the blanched leek on top.

SERVES 4–6   WINE: Barbera

BEEF SKIRT WITH WHOLE SPRING GARLIC AND BALSAMIC
FESONE ALLA GRIGLIA CON AGLIETTO AL BALSAMICO

INGREDIENTS

600 g (1 lb 5 oz) beef skirt (inside, if available)

8 stems spring garlic or 20 peeled garlic cloves

½ cup (125 ml/4 fl oz) extra virgin olive oil

1 cup (250 ml/9 fl oz) dry white wine

½ cup (125 ml/4 fl oz) white dessert wine

2 tablespoons chopped parsley

1 rosemary sprig

2 teaspoons good-quality aged balsamic vinegar (preferably tradizionale)

METHOD

Trim the beef skirt of fat but leave the thin skin on both sides. Put the beef on a plate, cover and let come to room temperature. Trim the stems from the spring garlic and remove the tough outer layer of skin from each bulb. Heat ⅓ cup (80 ml/2½ fl oz) of the olive oil in a frying pan and brown the garlic, constantly turning so it doesn't burn. Add the dry and sweet wines and bring to a low boil, then cook until the liquid has reduced to about ¼ cup (60 ml/2 fl oz). Add the parsley and rosemary, season and set aside. Heat the remaining oil in a separate frying pan. Season the beef and sear on high heat for 30–45 seconds on both sides. Transfer to a warm plate to rest. To serve, remove and discard the skin from the beef, then slice the meat and arrange on a platter with the garlic and sauce. Finish with the balsamic vinegar.

SERVES 4   WINE: Sangiovese di Romagna Superiore

ACETO BALSAMICO TRADIZIONALE IS MADE AROUND THE NORTHERN ITALIAN CITY OF MODENA AND IS GRAPE MUST WHICH HAS UNDERGONE FERMENTATION, ACETIC TRANSFORMATION AND A MINIMUM TWELVE YEARS OF AGING. WHILE IT IS SIMPLE AND INEXPENSIVE TO BUY BALSAMIC VINEGAR IN THE SUPERMARKET, THIS IS OFTEN VINEGAR THAT HAS BEEN COLOURED AND SWEETENED WITH CARAMEL. IT IS THE AGING PROCESS THAT TRANSFORMS THE IMMATURE GRAPE MUST INTO THE COMPLEX FLAVOURS OF ACETO BALSAMICO TRADIZIONALE.

DUCK BREAST WITH FIGS, LEEK AND VINCOTTO

DUCK BREAST WITH FIGS, LEEK AND VINCOTTO
PETTO D'ANATRA ALLA GRIGLIA CON FICHI, PORRI E VINCOTTO

This dish uses vincotto, which is also called saba. Vincotto is essentially concentrated grape must, and can be used in sweet or savoury dishes.

INGREDIENTS

2 tablespoons extra virgin
   olive oil
1 leek, white part only, cut into
   2 cm (¾ in) slices
2 tablespoons vincotto
6 ripe figs, quartered
1 tablespoon red wine vinegar
4 duck breasts

METHOD

Heat half the olive oil in a large frying pan and gently fry the leek for a couple of minutes until coloured and softened. Add the vincotto and figs and simmer for a minute until the figs are soft. Add the vinegar and remove the pan from the heat. Season the skin side of each duck breast well with a couple of good pinches of salt. Put them skin side down in a separate frying pan, without oil, and fry on medium heat for about 10 minutes. This will crisp the skin and remove most of the fat without overcooking the breast meat. Discard the fat and, keeping the duck skin side down, turn the heat to low, cover the pan and cook for 2 minutes. Uncover, turn the heat up high and cook for 30 seconds. Transfer the duck to the vincotto pan, skin side up. Bring to the boil, then immediately turn off the heat and add a few turns of freshly cracked pepper. Slice the duck and arrange on individual serving plates or a platter with the leek and figs. Mix the remaining oil with the vincotto in the pan and spoon over the top to serve.

SERVES 4

WINE: Gutturnio

BOLOGNESE-STYLE CROQUETTES
CROCCHETTE ALLA BOLOGNESE

INGREDIENTS

60 g (2¼ oz) chicken hearts

50 g (1¾ oz) chicken giblets

120 g (4¼ oz) unsalted butter

200 g (7 oz) veal (leg cut),
thinly sliced

¼ cup (60 ml/2 fl oz) beef
broth (see page 48)

1 × 120–130 g (4¼–4¾ oz)
calf or lamb brain (or
2 smaller brains)

100 g (3½ oz) prosciutto,
sliced

½ cup (125 ml/4 fl oz)
béchamel sauce
(see page 50)

50 g (1¾ oz) dried porcini
mushrooms, soaked,
drained and squeezed
of excess water

100 g (3½ oz) Parmigiano
Reggiano, grated

3 eggs

½ teaspoon grated nutmeg

30–40 g (1–1½ oz) fresh white
truffle, grated (optional)

fine breadcrumbs for coating

METHOD

Trim any excess fat from the tops of the chicken hearts and cut each
into 4 pieces. Trim the chicken giblets, removing any hard casing, and
cut into 1 cm (½ in) dice. Heat 40 g (1½ oz) of the butter in a frying
pan and fry the veal, hearts and giblets for a couple of minutes on
medium heat, constantly stirring, and adding a little beef broth every
30 seconds. Remove the pan from the heat (the broth should have
mostly evaporated) and let cool for 5 minutes. Bring a small saucepan
of salted water to the boil and blanch the calf brain, simmering for
5 minutes or so until firm. Drain. Put the veal, hearts, giblets, brain and
prosciutto through a meat grinder twice, then put the minced meat in
a saucepan with any of the cooking juices from the veal pan. Add the
béchamel and porcini and cook gently, continually stirring, for 5 minutes.
Turn off the heat and mix in the Parmigiano Reggiano, one beaten egg
and nutmeg, then spoon out onto a flat tray to cool completely. Mix in
the truffle (if using) and season well. Wet your hands and shape walnut-
sized pieces of mixture into large flat croquettes. Whisk the remaining
two eggs to make an egg wash. Dredge the croquettes in egg wash and
then in breadcrumbs. Heat the remaining butter in a frying pan and fry
the croquettes until golden. Drain on paper towels and serve hot with a
contorno (side dish) such as cime di rapa with chilli (see page 401) or
with nettle, fennel seed and tomato salsa (page 50).

SERVES 6   WINE: Sangiovese di Romagna

EMILIA-ROMAGNA
DOLCI

FIG AND ROSE PETAL JAM
MARMELLATA DI FICHI E ROSE

INGREDIENTS

100 g (3½ oz) honey

2 cinnamon sticks

4 cloves

1 vanilla bean, split lengthways and scraped

500 g (1 lb 2 oz) figs, roughly chopped

5 g (⅛ oz) dried rose petals

METHOD

Put the honey, cinnamon, cloves and vanilla bean in a saucepan and gently bring to the boil. Add the figs and stir, then turn down the heat and simmer until the mixture is thick and jam-like. Remove from the heat and discard the cinnamon sticks, cloves and vanilla bean, add the rose petals and mix thoroughly. Cool, then transfer to sterilised jars.

MAKES about 500 ml (17 fl oz)

CHESTNUT-FLOUR FRITTERS
FRITTELLE DI CASTAGNE

INGREDIENTS

100 g (3½ oz) sultanas (golden raisins)

500 g (1 lb 2 oz) chestnut flour

80 g (2¾ oz) caster (superfine) sugar

325 ml (11 fl oz) milk

2 tablespoons grappa

½ cup (80 g/2¾ oz) pine nuts

grated zest of 1 lemon

2 egg whites

extra virgin olive oil

icing (confectioners') sugar

METHOD

Soak the sultanas in warm water for 20 minutes, then drain and squeeze out as much liquid as possible. Put the flour and sugar in a large bowl and mix in the milk and grappa to make a smooth paste with no lumps. Mix in the sultanas, pine nuts, lemon zest and a pinch of salt. In a separate bowl, whisk the egg whites to firm peaks. Gently fold the egg whites into the chestnut paste, keeping as much air in the mixture as possible. Heat 2 cm (¾ in) olive oil in a frying pan and fry a few tablespoons of batter at a time, turning gently to cook on both sides until golden. Drain on paper towels, dust with icing sugar and serve warm.

MAKES 50–60   **BEST SERVED** with grappa and espresso

MODENA CAKE
BENSONE

Bensone is the Modena version of the ciambella that is popular in Bologna and Ferrara. It can be made as a simple cake or shaped in 'S' forms or, as is the case here, baked with jam in the centre and then cut into large biscuits (cookies).

INGREDIENTS

1⅔ cups (400 g/14 oz) plain (all-purpose) flour

100 g (3½ oz) potato flour

⅔ cup (150 g/5½ oz) caster (superfine) sugar, plus extra for dusting

2 eggs

180 g (6½ oz) unsalted butter, melted

7 g (¼ oz) dried yeast

⅓ cup (80 ml/2½ fl oz) warm milk, plus extra for brushing

30 ml (1 fl oz) Sassolino anise liqueur (or Sambuca)

½ teaspoon natural vanilla extract

finely grated zest of 1 lemon

150 g (5½ oz) fig and rose petal jam (see opposite page)

METHOD

Preheat the oven to 180°C (350°F) and grease a baking tray with butter or spray with olive oil. Sieve the flours together into a large bowl. In a separate bowl, whisk the sugar and eggs together until pale and fluffy, then mix in the melted butter. In a small bowl, dissolve the yeast in the milk. Combine the flour with the sugar/egg/butter mixture and the yeast and milk. Add the liqueur, vanilla and lemon zest and mix to a smooth, soft dough. Dust your work surface with a little flour and roll out the dough to a rectangle about 1 cm (½ in) thick. Brush any excess flour from the surface of the dough using a pastry brush, then spread the jam over, leaving a couple of centimetres (about 1 in) between the edge of the jam and the edge of the pastry. Fold one outer third into the middle and then fold over the remaining third to form a loaf. Put on the baking tray, brush with the extra milk and sprinkle with the extra sugar. Bake for 40 minutes.

SERVES 8   WINE: Lambrusco Rose

RICE CAKE
TORTA DI RISO

INGREDIENTS

2 cups (500 ml/17 fl oz) milk

200 g (7 oz) Italian rice (such as vialone nano, carnaroli or arborio)

½ cup fine breadcrumbs

60 g (2¼ oz) unsalted butter, plus extra for greasing

⅔ cup (150 g/5½ oz) caster (superfine) sugar

grated zest of 1 lemon

juice of 1 lemon

2 eggs, separated

METHOD

Bring the milk and 1 cup (250 ml/9 fl oz) water to the boil and add the rice. Stir well and simmer gently for 20 minutes or so until the rice has absorbed most of the liquid, stirring regularly to stop the rice from sticking to the bottom of the pan. Remove from the heat and let cool for 15 minutes. Meanwhile, preheat the oven to 170°C (340°F). Butter a 22 cm (8½ in) cake tin and dust well with the breadcrumbs. Transfer the rice to a bowl and mix in the butter, sugar, lemon zest, lemon juice and egg yolks. Whisk the egg whites to form stiff peaks, then fold into the rice mixture. Pour into the cake tin and bake for 40 minutes. Serve with crema inglese (see page 52).

SERVES 6–8   WINE: Cagnina di Romagna

PEACH AND RICOTTA CREAM BISCUITS
BISCOTTI RIPIENI DI PESCHE E CREMA DI RICOTTA

The biscuits (cookies) used in this recipe can be good-quality store-bought ones, or they can be homemade. Remember that the flavours of poached peach and ricotta cream are delicate, so choose biscuits that are delicately flavoured, such as vanilla, lemon or orange. The peach and ricotta cream can also be used to fill cannoli or to layer vanilla sponge.

INGREDIENTS

4 peaches

1 vanilla bean

200 g (7 oz) caster (superfine) sugar

50 ml (1¾ fl oz) thin (pouring) cream

100 g (3½ oz) fresh ricotta cheese

16 biscuits (cookies), around 4–5 cm (1½–2 in) diameter

icing (confectioners') sugar

METHOD

Put the peaches in a wide saucepan so they fit in 1 layer. Add enough water to comfortably submerge the peaches when they are pushed down. Remove the peaches and set aside. Split the vanilla bean lengthways, scrape the seeds from each half and put both pod and seeds in the water. Add ¾ of the sugar. Bring the water to the boil and simmer for 2 minutes, stirring, until the sugar has dissolved. Add the peaches and put a small plate on them to keep them under the liquid. Simmer for 3 minutes, then remove from the heat and, keeping the plate on the peaches, allow them to cool in the liquid. Meanwhile, whip the cream and the remaining sugar to soft peaks, then fold into the ricotta. Once the peaches are cool, remove their skins. Cut the flesh of 2 peaches into small cubes and fold into the ricotta cream. Quarter 2 more peaches and cut into slices. Spoon a generous amount of ricotta cream onto each biscuit, add some slices of poached peach and top with another biscuit. Dust with icing sugar to serve.

SERVES 4   WINE: Sparkling Malvasia Rosa

PEACH AND RICOTTA CREAM BISCUITS

NONNA'S PIE
TORTA DELLA NONNA

Throughout Emilia-Romagna there are many versions of this pie. Some have ricotta in the filling, some don't; some contain candied fruit, some don't – but this variety is typical of popular Italian dishes. Each family has their own recipe.

INGREDIENTS

1 litre (35 fl oz) milk

1 vanilla bean, split and seeds scraped

grated zest of 1 orange

grated zest of 1 lemon

8 egg yolks

250 g (9 oz) caster (superfine) sugar

110 g (3¾ oz) potato flour

200 g (7 oz) pine nuts

icing (confectioners') sugar

PASTRY

500 g (1 lb 2 oz) plain (all-purpose) flour

250 g (9 oz) unsalted butter

4 egg yolks

180 g (6½ oz) caster (superfine) sugar

grated zest of 1 lemon

½ teaspoon natural vanilla extract

METHOD

To make the pastry, put all the ingredients in a food processor and add a pinch of salt. Pulse until the mixture comes together in a ball. Divide the dough into 2 pieces, one about ⅔ and the other ⅓ of the total. Shape each piece into a rough disc, wrap in plastic wrap and refrigerate for at least 3 hours. Meanwhile, put the milk, vanilla (pod and seeds) and lemon and orange zest in a saucepan and bring almost to the boil. Remove from the heat and set aside. Beat the egg yolks and sugar until creamy, then whisk in the flour until smooth. Remove and discard the vanilla bean from the hot milk, then add the milk to the egg mixture and whisk. Return the mixture to a low heat and cook until thick, stirring constantly. Stir in ½ cup (80 g/2¾ oz) of the pine nuts and pour into a bowl to cool. Preheat the oven to 180°C (350°F). Roll out the larger of the 2 pastry discs and use to line a 24 cm (9½ in) flan (tart) tin with sides at least 3–4 cm (1¼–1½ in) high and a removable base. Trim the edges to remove any excess pastry, then fill the pastry case. Roll out the remaining pastry and cover the tart. Trim off any overhang and scatter over the remaining pine nuts. Bake for 30–40 minutes until golden. Cool on a wire rack in the flan tin, then dust with icing sugar and cut into slices to serve.

WINE: Albana di Romagna Passito

STRAWBERRIES IN LAMBRUSCO WITH RICOTTA CREAM
FRAGOLE AL LAMBRUSCO CON CREMA DI RICOTTA

Any medium-bodied red wine will work just as well as lambrusco, as long as it's not too tannic or woody.

INGREDIENTS

500 g (1 lb 2 oz) strawberries

100 g (3½ oz) caster (superfine) sugar

1 cup (250 ml/9 fl oz) lambrusco (such as Lambrusco di Sorbara or Grasparossa di Castelvetro)

2 teaspoons black peppercorns, crushed

1 cup (250 ml/9 fl oz) cream (thin/pouring, thick/double or thickened/whipping)

250 g (9 oz) ricotta cheese

METHOD

A couple of hours before you plan to serve the dessert, rinse the strawberries carefully to remove any sand or dirt. Put them on a clean tea towel (dish towel) and gently pat dry. Hull, then cut into quarters lengthways. Put in a large bowl and sprinkle over 2 tablespoons of the sugar. Using your hands, mix gently but thoroughly so the sugar is distributed evenly. Pour the wine over and, using a large spoon, carefully mix in the crushed peppercorns. Cover and put in the refrigerator until you are ready to serve, stirring occasionally. Meanwhile, whisk the cream with the remaining sugar until soft peaks form. Fold into the ricotta until incorporated. To serve, divide the ricotta cream among glasses or bowls, then spoon on the strawberries and their juices.

SERVES 6

WINE: Lambrusco di Sorbara or Grasparossa di Castelvetro

FRIULI-VENEZIA GIULIA

FRIULI-VENEZIA GIULIA

FRIULI-VENEZIA GIULIA (FVG) NESTLES INTO THE NORTH-EAST CORNER OF ITALY. IT IS BOUNDED IN THE NORTH BY AUSTRIA, TO THE EAST BY SLOVENIA, TO THE WEST BY VENETO AND TO THE SOUTH BY THE ADRIATIC SEA. FVG WAS RULED BY VENICE FROM THE 15TH TO THE 18TH CENTURY, WHEN IT BECAME A PART OF THE AUSTRO-HUNGARIAN EMPIRE. ITS CULTURAL AND CULINARY INFLUENCES ARISE FROM THIS HISTORY, AND FROM ITS PROXIMITY TO SLOVENIA.

FVG is not large – it covers about 7800 square kilometres (3000 square miles) and has a little over a million inhabitants – but it is culturally rich. If it is not as gastronomically varied as other regions (mainly because of the long and snowy winters), there are some noteworthy regional delicacies to be found – not to mention great wines.

Although FVG is extensively cultivated, there's not a lot of arable land as about 40 per cent of the region is covered by mountains. The best agricultural land is the plain of Friuli, where most of the cereal crops, especially corn, are grown. Vegetables are grown around Udine, while on the strip of arid limestone bordering Slovenia, goats and sheep are raised on small farms. The forests abound with game and the two most important cheeses made from the milk of the alpine cattle are montasio and carnia.

It is in FVG that corn made an early entry to Italy as polenta, and the pellagra, a vitamin deficiency disease caused by limited diets with too much corn prepared a particular way, had a devastating impact. Today polenta is still eaten, but not alone. For example, sguazeto, a rich lamb and tomato stew, is served on a bed of polenta. Perhaps the best-known local food product is prosciutto de San Daniele, which can be recognised because the foot of the pig is left on the cured leg. Montasio, a fresh cow's milk cheese, is fried in butter and served with potatoes and onion to make a dish known throughout Italy as frico.

Even in such a small region, there are smaller subregions with their own specialities. Grado, near Gorizia, is known for broéta, a fish soup (the name is dialect for brodetto), and Cormons, another Gorizian town, is celebrated for a pastry called buzolai. In the cuisine of Trieste can be found traces of Hungarian, Greek, Slavic and Jewish cuisines – golas, for example, which is the local version of goulash. The food of Carso, a wine region bordering Slovenia, is heavy and robust. A typical dish is jota triestina, a thick soup of beans, potatoes and cabbage that is often enriched with smoked pork.

The excellent wines of the region are particularly good with the local pork sausages, which include lujanis and muset (the latter of which is the Friulian version of cotechino).

The wines of Friuli, ignored by the wider world for many years (but not by the Italians and Germans), have now been justly elevated to their status as some of Italy's finest whites. The viticulture of the region has to a large extent been taken over by international varieties such as merlot, cabernet franc and sauvignon, but indigenous varieties – especially whites – have survived. These include tocai friulano, verduzzo, ribolla and malvasia istriana. With the reds it is a different story, and only traces of such grapes as refosco and tazzelenghe are found today.

That viticultural takeover and the predominance of white wines – underlines the fact that the wines of this region, although most emphatically Italian, have cultural ties to their neighbours Austria and Slovenia. Of the nine DOC districts in Friuli, the most famous are three that border Slovenia: Collio, parts of Colli Orientali del Friuli, and Friuli Isonzo. As Italian wine expert Nicholas Belfrage points out, all areas are capable of making good wine but some are capable of outstanding wine – even if they don't always deliver.

And then there are the Friulian grappas, as famed for their flavours as for the elegant glass flasks in which they are sold.

FRIULI-VENEZIA GIULIA
ANTI-PASTI

TUNA PRESERVED IN OLIVE OIL
TONNO FRESCO SOTT'OLIO

This ancient method of preserving tuna has been used around the Mediterranean extensively, and in more recent times has resulted in the ubiquitous tinned tuna found in supermarkets. In most cases that 'industrial' canning uses seed oils or highly refined olive oil, but when made in this traditional way, using good extra virgin olive oil, it is on another level.

INGREDIENTS

1 cup (250 ml/9 fl oz) white wine vinegar

1 brown onion, sliced

3 garlic cloves, lightly crushed

1 teaspoon black peppercorns

5 bay leaves

2 kg (4 lb 8 oz) fresh tuna fillet, cut into 2–3 cm (¾–1¼ in) chunks

extra virgin olive oil

METHOD

Pour 2 litres (70 fl oz) cold water into a saucepan and add the vinegar, onion, garlic, peppercorns and bay leaves. Bring to the boil and keep boiling until the liquid has reduced by a third. Carefully add the tuna, then turn the heat down and simmer for 35 minutes. Drain and let the tuna dry on a very clean tea towel (dish towel) for a couple of minutes. Transfer it carefully to sterilised preserving jars and cover with olive oil. Seal and put in a cool, dark place for 30 days. The tuna can be used in salads and sandwiches, to make tuna sauce for vitello tonnato, and as part of an antipasto. Toss with capers, thinly sliced red onion, tomato and rocket (arugula) for a tuna salad.

SERVES 8 WINE: Pinot Grigio

SALT COD WITH GARLIC, PARSLEY AND LEMON
BACCALÀ CONDITO

Baccalà is salted and air-dried cod. It has to be soaked in cold water for several days and the water must be changed 2–3 times a day before using.

INGREDIENTS

400 g (14 oz) baccalà (salt cod), soaked and rinsed (see page 125)

3 garlic cloves

2 cups small parsley leaves

½ cup (125 ml/4 fl oz) extra virgin olive oil

juice of 1 lemon

METHOD

Put the baccalà in a saucepan and cover with cold water. Bring to the boil, then turn down the heat and simmer for 45 minutes–1 hour depending on the thickness of the fish. Remove from the heat and let cool in the cooking liquid. Take the fish carefully from the liquid, then peel off the skin and remove any bones from the flesh. Break the flesh into bite-sized flakes and put in a bowl. Finely chop the garlic and parsley together, then add to the baccalà. Dress with the olive oil and lemon juice. Season, then toss gently and serve with crusty bread or crostini.

SERVES 8 WINE: Ribolla Gialla

CRAB AND SPINACH FRITTATA ROLLS
ROTOLINI DI GRANCHIO E SPINACI

INGREDIENTS

200 g (7 oz) cooked crabmeat

⅓ cup (80 ml/2½ fl oz) extra virgin olive oil

1 brown onion, finely diced

1 small garlic clove, minced

80 g (2¾ oz) spinach

6 large eggs

6 tablespoons finely snipped chives

6 tablespoons grated parmesan cheese

METHOD

Pick through the crabmeat, removing and discarding any shell, then refrigerate until needed. Heat half the olive oil in a frying pan and lightly fry the onion and garlic until translucent but not coloured. Add the spinach and mix until wilted. Remove from heat and mix in crabmeat, season and set aside to cool. To make each frittata, whisk 1 egg in a bowl with 1 tablespoon chives, 1 tablespoon parmesan and a pinch of salt and pepper. Heat some of the remaining oil in a small frying pan on medium–high heat, ensuring the oil covers the entire surface including the sides. Pour the egg mixture into the hot pan and tilt so the mixture covers the pan evenly. Cook for a minute, without turning – the frittata will still be a little creamy on top. Slide the frittata onto a board and top with some spinach and crab mixture, then roll up to a diameter of about 3 cm (1¼ in) and cut into 5 rolls. Serve hot or, even better, at room temperature.

MAKES 30   WINE: Friulano

MONTASIO AND POTATO FRITTATA
FRITTATA DI FORMAGGIO E PATATA

In the local dialect this dish is simply called frico. At its simplest it is made with two cheeses: a young Montasio (about 3 months old) and a carnia stravecchio that has been aged for longer than 18 months (stravecchio indicates that a cheese has been aged for a long time) – plus pork fat, onion and salt and pepper. This version is a modern take on the original. Montasio is a DOP cheese that is perhaps the region's best known. While it is relatively easy to find outside Italy, carnia is not. If you can't find carnia, you can use Montasio exclusively.

INGREDIENTS

150 g (5½ oz) pancetta (smoked, if available), diced

1 brown onion, thinly sliced

750 g (1 lb 10 oz) potatoes, diced

200 g (7 oz) Montasio (about 3 months old), thinly sliced

100 g (3½ oz) carnia stravecchio, grated

METHOD

Put the pancetta in a large flameproof casserole dish and lightly fry on low–medium heat until some of the fat is released. Add the onion and fry for 2–3 minutes until softened. Add the potatoes, a couple of pinches of salt and pepper and 1 cup (250 ml/9 fl oz) water, then cover and simmer for 30 minutes. Remove the lid. There should be very little liquid left – if there is too much, let it reduce. Remove from heat, add the cheeses a little at a time and mix to make a dough. Turn the dough into a 22 cm (8½ in) non-stick frying pan and carefully pour off any excess fat from the pancetta. Fry on medium heat until the bottom is crisp and golden. Cut into slices and serve warm.

SERVES 6–8   WINE: Ribolla Gialla

CRAB AND SPINACH FRITTATA ROLLS

TRIESTE-STYLE ARTICHOKES
CARCIOFI ALLA TRIESTINA

You'll find artichoke preparations similar to this throughout Italy. I include it in this part of the book because I've had the best versions around Trieste. It's important that the artichokes used are firm and not ready to flower. The choke needs to be tender.

INGREDIENTS

1 lemon, halved

8 artichokes

1 cup parsley

6 anchovy fillets

2 garlic cloves

200 g (7 oz) coarse breadcrumbs

100 g (3½ oz) Grana Padano, grated

⅓ cup (80 ml/2½ fl oz) extra virgin olive oil

METHOD

Fill a large bowl with cold water. Squeeze the lemon juice into the water and then add the lemon halves as well. For each artichoke, remove the tough outer leaves and slice off the top 2 cm (¾ in) and the stem, reserving 5–6 cm (2–2½ in) of the stem. Put the artichoke in the lemon water. Gently pull the leaves apart, making sure not to rip any off. Submerge them in the lemon water and soak for 20 minutes. Meanwhile, finely chop the parsley, anchovies and garlic together and mix thoroughly with the breadcrumbs, Grana Padano and a little salt and pepper. Remove the artichokes and their stems from the lemon water. Pat the stems dry, thinly slice them and add to the breadcrumb mixture. Stuff the breadcrumb mixture in between the artichoke leaves, then put the stuffed artichokes in a saucepan in one layer so they fit snugly. Sprinkle them with the olive oil and pour in enough water to just cover. Bring to the boil, then turn down the heat and simmer until most of the water has evaporated. Let cool to room temperature before serving.

SERVES 8   WINE: Collio Pinot Bianco

THE **ARTICHOKE'S** COMMON NAME IS THOUGHT TO BE DERIVED FROM THE LIGURIAN WORD 'COCALI' WHICH MEANS PINE CONE. ARTICHOKES ARE PART OF THE THISTLE SPECIES AND HAVE BEEN CULTIVATED AS FOOD SINCE ANCIENT GREEK AND ROMAN TIMES AND WERE THOUGHT TO BE AN APHRODISIAC. THE EDIBLE PART OF THE ARTICHOKE IS THE BUD THAT FORMS WITHIN THE FLOWER HEAD BEFORE THE PLANT BLOOMS. ONCE THE FLOWER BLOOMS, THE ARTICHOKE BUDS BECOME VIRTUALLY INEDIBLE.

GREEN VEGETABLE FLAN
FRITTATA DI ERBE AL FORNO

This is a speciality of Friuli and is traditionally made using whatever is on hand. It is a quick and easy way to use up leftover greens, such as cime di rapa (broccoli raab), spinach, silverbeet (Swiss chard) or the tops of beetroot (beets) and the like.

INGREDIENTS

2 cups assorted chopped
   greens (see recipe
   introduction)

⅓ cup (80 ml/2½ fl oz) extra
   virgin olive oil

1 small leek, white part only,
   thinly sliced

1 brown onion, thinly sliced

6 eggs, whisked

80 g (2¾ oz) Montasio
   (see page 200), grated

6–8 basil leaves, torn

6–8 sage leaves, chopped

METHOD

Preheat the oven to 180°C (350°F). Bring a large saucepan of salted water to the boil. Plunge in the greens for 2 minutes to blanch, then drain and let cool. Squeeze out as much water as possible and roughly chop the greens. Give them another squeeze and set aside. Heat half the olive oil and lightly fry the leek and onion until soft but not coloured. Combine with the eggs, cheese, herbs and greens, mixing well. Use the remaining oil to grease a flan tin or pie dish and pour in the mixture. Bake for 15–20 minutes until firm, then rest in the tin for 5 minutes before turning out onto a serving plate.

SERVES 6–8   WINE: Tocai Friulano

FRIULI-VENEZIA GIULIA
PRIMI

ASPARAGUS AND BOW-TIE SOUP
MINESTRINA DI ASPARAGI E FARFALLINE

This recipe calls for pasta called farfalline ('little bow ties'), which was one of my favourites when I was a child. It may be difficult to find; if so, substitute any other small shape, such as gomiti ('elbows'), stelline ('little stars') or ditalini ('little thimbles').

INGREDIENTS

tips and stems from 450 g (1 lb) asparagus spears

2 tablespoons extra virgin olive oil

1 small white onion, finely diced

pinch of chopped thyme

150 g (5½ oz) farfalline pasta

1 ripe tomato, peeled, seeded and diced

2 tablespoons finely snipped chives

grated parmesan cheese

ASPARAGUS VEGETABLE BROTH

ends from 450 g (1 lb) asparagus spears (you need about 175 g/6 oz ends), peeled and sliced

1 small white onion, diced

1 celery stick, diced

1 small carrot, diced

1 small leek, white part only, finely sliced

1 garlic clove, finely sliced

4 fennel tops, chopped

150 g (5½ oz) ripe tomatoes, peeled, seeded and diced

2 cloves

2 bay leaves

1 handful parsley stalks

METHOD

To make the asparagus vegetable broth, pour 3 litres (5¼ pints) cold water into a saucepan and add all the ingredients. Bring to the boil on medium heat, then reduce the heat and simmer for 2 hours, skimming any impurities that form on the surface. Turn off the heat and leave to settle for 30 minutes. Strain through a fine sieve, discarding the solids, then season with salt. The stock should be clear and bright and is now ready to use as a base for soup, risotto, or vegetable or meat casseroles. Makes 1.5–2 litres (52–70 fl oz).

Separate the asparagus tips and stems, then cut the stems into 5 mm (¼ in) rounds. Heat the olive oil in a large saucepan and gently fry the onion for a minute. Add the asparagus stem rounds and fry for another minute, stirring. Add the thyme and 1.5 litres (52 fl oz) asparagus vegetable broth. Increase the heat and bring to the boil, then drop in the pasta and cook until al dente. Stir in the tomato and season. Ladle into bowls, scatter with the chives and serve with parmesan.

SERVES 4   WINE: Pinot Grigio

CUTTLEFISH AND TOMATO BROTH
BRODO DI SEPPIE E POMODORO

This dish calls for a little cuttlefish ink. If you're not confident about extracting the ink from fresh cuttlefish when you are cleaning them, you can buy sachets from good providores.

INGREDIENTS

1 kg (2 lb 4 oz) cuttlefish, cleaned (you should have about 700 g/1 lb 9 oz after cleaning)

3 garlic cloves, minced

2 tablespoons finely chopped parsley

¼ cup (60 ml/2 fl oz) extra virgin olive oil

2 tablespoons tomato paste (concentrated puree)

300 g (10½ oz) tin tomatoes, mashed

1 teaspoon cuttlefish ink (optional)

METHOD

Cut the cuttlefish into bite-sized strips and combine with the garlic, parsley and olive oil. Let sit for 5 minutes, then put in a large saucepan and lightly fry for a couple of minutes, stirring. Stir in the tomato paste. Add the tomatoes, cuttlefish ink (if using) and a couple of pinches of salt. Stir, then simmer gently, covered, for 45 minutes. Season and serve with bread or polenta (cornmeal) (see page 41).

SERVES 6   WINE: Friulano

SPAGHETTI WITH CALAMARI AND RADICCHIO
SPAGHETTI CON CALAMARI E RADICCHIO

INGREDIENTS

300 g (10½ oz) calamari, cleaned

2 heads of radicchio or treviso lettuces, tough outer leaves removed

400 g (14 oz) dried spaghetti

⅓ cup (80 ml/2½ fl oz) extra virgin olive oil

2 garlic cloves, minced

200 ml (7 fl oz) dry white wine

2 tablespoons finely chopped parsley

METHOD

Cut the calamari into matchstick-sized strips. Pull the radicchio leaves from the hearts and wash thoroughly, then cut into long strips. Cook the spaghetti in a large saucepan of boiling salted water until almost ready. Meanwhile, heat the olive oil in a large frying pan and fry the calamari, radicchio and garlic on medium heat for 4–5 minutes. Add the drained spaghetti and turn up the heat to full. Add the wine and parsley and cook, stirring, until the liquid has almost all evaporated and the spaghetti has a glossy coating. Season and serve.

SERVES 4   WINE: Vitovska

PAN-FRIED SCALLOPS WITH CAVOLO NERO AND POLENTA
CAPESANTE E CAVOLO NERO IN PADELLA CON POLENTA

INGREDIENTS

200 g (7 oz) cavolo nero (Tuscan kale)

½ cup (125 ml/4 fl oz) extra virgin olive oil

4 French shallots, finely diced

2 garlic cloves, minced

2 red chillies, finely sliced (optional)

1 tablespoon good-quality balsamic vinegar

1 cup (190 g/6¾ oz) polenta (cornmeal)

20 scallops, cleaned

METHOD

Strip the leaves from the cavolo nero, discarding the stems. Chop the leaves into small pieces and blanch in a saucepan of boiling water for 5 minutes. Drain. Heat 2 tablespoons of the olive oil in a frying pan and gently fry the shallots, garlic and chillies (if using) for 2–3 minutes until soft. Add the cavolo nero, turn up the heat to medium and cook for 10 minutes, stirring and adding a few spoonfuls of water every 3–4 minutes to prevent the mixture from drying out. Remove from the heat, season and add the balsamic vinegar and 2 more tablespoons of the oil. Mix well and leave for at least 1 hour. Meanwhile, whisk the polenta into 1 litre (35 fl oz) boiling salted water. Once the polenta has thickened, turn down the heat to very low and cook for 30–45 minutes. When you are ready to serve, reheat the cavolo nero until warm. Heat the remaining oil in a large frying pan on high heat and sear the scallops on both sides for 20–30 seconds. Serve on top of the polenta with the cavolo nero.

SERVES 4   WINE: Ribolla Gialla

CRUMBED SCALLOPS WITH EGGPLANT RELISH

CRUMBED SCALLOPS WITH EGGPLANT RELISH
CAPPESANTE FRITTE CON SALSA DI MELANZANE

INGREDIENTS

18–24 scallops (depending on size), cleaned

1 large eggplant (aubergine)

1 cup (250 ml/9 fl oz) extra virgin olive oil

1 brown onion, finely diced

½ teaspoon sugar

2 teaspoons red wine vinegar

2 ripe tomatoes, diced

3 tablespoons finely chopped parsley

½ cup (75 g/2¾ oz) plain (all-purpose) flour

2 eggs, whisked

1 cup fine breadcrumbs

METHOD

Pat the scallops dry and reserve. Put the whole eggplant on the largest gas ring (hob) on the stove and then light the gas. As the skin chars, rotate the eggplant using tongs until all the skin is black and the flesh is soft. Remove from the flame and let cool, then remove and discard the skin and put the smoky flesh in a sieve over a bowl to drain. Meanwhile, heat 50 ml (1¾ fl oz) of the olive oil in a saucepan and lightly fry the onion and sugar for about 20 minutes, stirring constantly. Add the drained eggplant flesh and turn up the heat a little. Mash the eggplant using a fork and cook for about 10 minutes until it loses much of its liquid. Cool, then mix with the vinegar, tomatoes and 2 tablespoons of the parsley. Season. Put an egg ring in the centre of your serving plates and spoon in some relish. Dust the scallops with flour, dunk in the egg and coat with breadcrumbs. Fry in the remaining oil until golden brown and serve on top of the relish.

SERVES 6

WINE: Rosazzo Bianco

BRAISED SCHOOL PRAWNS IN WHITE WINE AND HERBS WITH POLENTA
GAMBERETTI AL VINO BIANCO E POLENTA

In the old Jewish quarter of Cannaregio in Venice, near the Ponte Tre Archi (Bridge of the Three Arcs), there's a tiny restaurant called Dalla Marisa. It makes an unforgettable gamberetti e polenta – tiny school prawns (shrimp) peeled and braised in white wine and herbs. The quality of the dish is in the masterly way it is cooked as well as the freshness of those meticulously peeled small prawns. This recipe was inspired by that dish.

INGREDIENTS

600 g (1 lb 5 oz) cooked school prawns (shrimp)

100 ml (3½ fl oz) extra virgin olive oil

1 brown onion, thinly sliced

2 cups (500 ml/17 fl oz) dry white wine

4 French shallots, thinly sliced

1 garlic clove, minced

150 g (5 oz) shelled peas, blanched in boiling water for 3 minutes

½ cup mixed herbs (parsley, thyme, tarragon, dill), chopped

1 quantity soft polenta (cornmeal) (see page 41)

METHOD

Peel and devein the prawns, keeping the shells. Heat 2 tablespoons olive oil in a frying pan and lightly fry the onion and prawn shells for 5 minutes, stirring constantly. Add the white wine, turn up the heat and boil it away. Pour in enough water to cover the prawn shells, then simmer for 30 minutes. Strain, keeping the small amount of stock and discarding the shells and onion. Wipe out the pan, then heat the remaining oil and lightly fry the shallots and garlic until soft. Add the prawn stock and turn up the heat. Reduce the liquid by half, then add the peas and simmer for 2–3 minutes. Add the prawns and herbs, season and serve with the polenta (cornmeal).

SERVES 4   WINE: Pinot Bianco

BLACK TRUFFLE, BROCCOLI AND PARMESAN COCOTTE
COCOTTE DI BROCCOLETTI, TARTUFO E PARMIGIANO

INGREDIENTS

1 cup (60 g/2¼ oz) broccoli florets

2 tablespoons truffle butter (see page 335)

8 eggs

160 ml (5¼ fl oz) thin (pouring) cream

shaved black truffle

80 g (2¾ oz) grated parmesan cheese

METHOD

Preheat the oven to 180°C (350°F). Bring a saucepan of salted water to the boil and blanch the broccoli for 2–3 minutes. Drain, cool and roughly chop. Grease 4 ceramic gratin dishes (2 cm (¾ in) deep × 15 cm (6 in) wide) with the truffle butter and break 2 eggs into each. Add 2 tablespoons cream to each and arrange some broccoli on top. Sprinkle the parmesan evenly among the dishes and season. Bake for 10 minutes until the eggs have cooked but the yolks are still runny.

SERVES 4   WINE: Ribolla Gialla

POLENTA WITH BRAISED BROCCOLINI
POLENTA CON BROCCOLETTI

Use good-quality polenta (cornmeal), such as polenta di Storo. To get really good results polenta must be cooked long and slowly. To achieve the very low heat, I use a simmer mat between the heat source and my saucepan. Any leftover polenta can be stored in the refrigerator for a few days.

INGREDIENTS

200 g (7 oz) polenta
    (cornmeal)

350 g (12 oz) broccolini,
    trimmed

¼ cup (60 ml/2 fl oz) extra
    virgin olive oil

1 brown onion, finely diced

2 garlic cloves, minced

1 large eggplant (aubergine),
    peeled and cut into 2 cm
    (¾ in) cubes

100 g (3½ oz) ripe tomatoes,
    peeled, seeded and
    chopped

1 tablespoon capers, rinsed

1 tablespoon red wine vinegar

METHOD

Bring 1 litre (35 fl oz) salted water to a rolling boil and gradually whisk in the polenta in a fine stream. Once it is all in, let the polenta come to the boil and begin to thicken. Cover and turn the heat to very low (a simmer mat helps). Cook for 1–1½ hours, stirring well with a wooden spoon every 20 minutes. Cut the broccolini heads into florets and the stalks into 1 cm (½ in) pieces. Heat the olive oil in a large frying pan and gently fry the onion and garlic until soft. Turn up the heat and add the broccolini and eggplant. Cook for about 2 minutes, stirring constantly, until the vegetables wilt a little. Add the tomatoes and capers and season with a couple of good pinches of salt. Bring to the boil, then turn down the heat and simmer for about 15 minutes until the vegetables are tender. Stir in the vinegar, season and serve with the polenta.

SERVES 6

WINE: Pinot Bianco

FRIULI-VENEZIA GIULIA
SECONDI

BAKED GARFISH ROLLS WITH ROSEMARY AND PROSCIUTTO
AGUGLIE AL PROSCIUTTO E ROSMARINO

INGREDIENTS

juice of 1 lemon

2 garlic cloves, minced

1 tablespoon finely chopped rosemary

8 large garfish fillets

2 tablespoons finely chopped parsley

4 tablespoons lightly toasted breadcrumbs

4 thin rashers prosciutto, halved lengthways

100 ml (3½ fl oz) extra virgin olive oil

METHOD

Combine the lemon juice, garlic and rosemary with a couple of pinches of salt and a few turns of pepper. Put the garfish fillets in a bowl and pour in the lemon mixture. Leave for 30 minutes. Preheat the oven to 150°C (300°F). Combine the parsley and breadcrumbs in a bowl. Remove a fish fillet from the marinade and coat with the breadcrumb mixture. Roll up as tightly as possible, then wrap securely with a piece of prosciutto. Repeat with the remaining fillets, breadcrumb mixture and prosciutto. Arrange the rolls in a baking dish so they fit snugly. Strain the marinade and mix with the olive oil, then pour into the baking dish. Bake for 25 minutes. Serve the garfish rolls with the sauce and your choice of vegetables or salad.

SERVES 4 WINE: Pinot Grigio

FRESHWATER CRAYFISH WITH HERBS AND POLENTA
GAMBERI DI FIUME ALLE ERBE AROMATICHE

The polenta used here should be quite fine and delicate: I would suggest a white polenta or a fine-milled yellow.

INGREDIENTS

2 kg (4 lb 8 oz) live freshwater crayfish

2 tablespoons extra virgin olive oil

1 leek, white part only, cut into 5 mm (¼ in) rounds

2 garlic cloves, minced

8 tinned tomatoes, drained and mashed

½ cup chopped mixed herbs (basil, thyme, marjoram, oregano)

1 quantity soft polenta (cornmeal) (see page 41)

METHOD

Bring a large pot of salted water to the boil and plunge in the crayfish. Once the water comes back to the boil, simmer for 3 minutes, then drain and let cool. Remove the tail meat from the crayfish and crack any large claws. Set aside the tail meat and claws. Heat the olive oil in a saucepan and lightly fry the leek and garlic until soft. Add the tomatoes and season with 2–3 pinches of salt, then stir in the herbs and simmer slowly for 15 minutes. When you are ready to serve, add the crayfish tail meat and claws to the sauce and simmer gently to heat through. Season with more salt (if necessary) and some pepper. Pour the polenta onto a large serving dish or wooden board, or individual plates, and spoon the crayfish and sauce over the top.

SERVES 6 WINE: Ribolla Gialla

ROSEMARY-CRUMBED WHITING FILLETS WITH SALSA VERDE
FILETTI DI MERLANO IMPANATI CON LA SALSA VERDE

INGREDIENTS

4 × 400 g (14 oz) whiting, scaled and filleted, skin left on

150 g (5½ oz) breadcrumbs

½ cup chopped rosemary leaves

⅓ cup (50 g/1¾ oz) plain (all-purpose) flour

2 eggs, whisked

50 ml (1¾ fl oz) extra virgin olive oil

50 g (1¾ oz) butter

lemon wedges

SALSA VERDE

2 slices bread, crusts removed

50 ml (1¾ fl oz) milk

6 cups parsley leaves

2 garlic cloves

6 anchovy fillets

juice of 2 lemons

1 cup (250 ml/9 fl oz) extra virgin olive oil

2 hard-boiled eggs, yolks and whites separated

2 tablespoons salted capers, rinsed

METHOD

To make the salsa verde, soak the bread in the milk for a couple of minutes, then squeeze out any excess milk and put the bread in a food processor with the parsley, garlic, anchovies, lemon juice and olive oil. Add the hard-boiled egg yolks and all but 4 or 5 of the capers. Add a couple of pinches of salt and pepper and pulse to a rough paste. Season and set aside until needed.

Halve each whiting fillet lengthways, removing the bones down the middle by slicing on either side. Mix the breadcrumbs with the rosemary and a pinch of salt and pepper. Dust each whiting piece with flour, then dip into the eggs and press with the crumb mixture. Heat the olive oil and butter in a wide frying pan until foaming, then fry the whiting for a minute on each side until golden. Put the salsa verde in a dipping bowl. Dice the hard-boiled egg whites and put on top of the salsa verde with the reserved capers. Serve the fish with the salsa and plenty of lemon wedges.

SERVES 4–6   WINE: Ribolla Gialla

ROSEMARY IS ONE OF ITALY'S OLDEST AND MOST USED HERBS. IN 300 B.C. THE ETRUSCANS WERE USING ROSEMARY AS AN AROMATIC STUFFING FOR FISH AND THEY BELIEVED THAT IT WOULD WARD OFF EVIL SPIRITS. IT IS EXTREMELY VERSATILE AND CAN BE USED WITH MEAT AND FISH ALIKE, AND VEGETABLES, ESPECIALLY POTATOES. IT IS USUALLY AVAILABLE ALL YEAR AND CAN BE USED FRESH OR DRIED, HOWEVER, IT IS STRONGER IN FLAVOUR WHEN FRESH.

ROAST DUCK BREASTS WITH CELERIAC AND ROAST GARLIC PUREE
PETTO D'ANITRA ARROSTO CON PUREA DI SEDANO RAPA E AGLIO

INGREDIENTS

1 garlic bulb

500 g (1 lb 2 oz) celeriac, peeled and quartered

100 g (3½ oz) butter

6 duck breasts, skin on

METHOD

Preheat the oven to 180°C (350°F). Roast the garlic bulb whole for 15–20 minutes until the cloves have lost their firmness but have not turned to a puree. Meanwhile, simmer the celeriac in water for about 15 minutes until soft, then drain and pulse in a food processor with the butter. Adjust the seasoning. Remove the garlic bulb from the oven and increase the oven temperature to 220°C (430°F). Separate out the garlic cloves, peel them, cut into chunks and fold through the celeriac puree. Sprinkle the duck skin with salt. Heat an ovenproof frying pan and fry the duck breasts skin side down on medium heat for a few minutes to crisp the skin and remove most of the fat. Discard the fat and, keeping the duck pieces skin side down, put the pan in the oven and cook for 6–8 minutes. Remove from the oven and let rest for 5 minutes before serving sliced or whole with the celeriac and garlic puree.

SERVES 6   WINE: Pinot Nero from Oltrepò Pavese

GULASCH GORIZIA STYLE
GULASCH ALLA GORIZIANA

INGREDIENTS

⅓ cup (80 ml/2½ fl oz) extra
    virgin olive oil

1 kg (2 lb 4 oz) brown onions,
    thinly sliced

1.2 kg (2 lb 12 oz) beef shin
    or shoulder, cut into 3 cm
    (1¼ in) cubes

1 teaspoon smoked paprika

1 tablespoon plain
    (all-purpose) flour

200 ml (7 fl oz) tomato salsa
    (see page 50 or page 178)

beef broth (see page 48)

2 bay leaves

2 marjoram sprigs

1 rosemary sprig

METHOD

Heat the olive oil in a large flameproof casserole dish and lightly fry the onions until softened. Add the beef and a couple of pinches of salt and cook, stirring constantly, until browned a little. Add the paprika and flour and keep stirring and frying for 4–5 minutes. Add the tomato salsa and enough beef broth to cover the meat by a couple of cm (1 in). Add the herbs and simmer for 2 hours, half-covered with a lid, until the liquid has reduced slightly and the meat is tender. Add salt (if necessary) and 3–4 good turns of pepper. Let cool and rest overnight in the refrigerator. Reheat the next day and serve with potato gnocchi (see page 359) or fresh or fried polenta (cornmeal; see page 41).

SERVES 6   WINE: Refosco

GORIZIA IS BOTH AN ITALIAN TOWN AND A COMUNE (ADMINISTRATIVE DIVISION) AT THE FOOT OF THE JULIAN ALPS ON THE BORDER WITH SLOVENIA. OF HUNGARIAN ORIGIN, GOULASH IS QUITE A POPULAR DISH IN THIS REGION AND ALSO IN TRENTINO. AS WITH PRACTICALLY ALL DISHES IN ITALY, THERE IS NO ONE AUTHENTIC VERSION BUT RATHER MANY DIFFERENT APPROACHES TO THE THEME. EVEN THE PRINCIPAL MEAT CAN BE VARIED TO PORK, LAMB, GOAT OR EVEN VENISON.

ROAST PORK LIVER WITH CELERIAC
FEGATO DI MAIALE ALLA TRIESTINA CON PUREA DI SEDANO RAPA

Pork net or caul is the thin, fatty membrane that lines the abdominal cavity of a pig. When used in baking or cooking, it melts during the process. You should be able to order it through your local butcher. It may come frozen, in which case it should be thawed in the refrigerator over a couple of days.

INGREDIENTS

400 g (14 oz) celeriac, peeled and cut into large cubes

100 g (3½ oz) unsalted butter

2 tablespoons extra virgin olive oil

1 leek, white part only, cut into 5 mm (¼ in) slices

1 tablespoon white wine vinegar

300–400 g (10½–14 oz) pork net (caul)

1 × 500 g (1 lb 2 oz) pig liver, quartered

8 bay leaves

100 ml (3½ fl oz) dry white wine

METHOD

Simmer the celeriac in water for 12–15 minutes until softened. Drain and pulse in a food processor with the butter, then season and keep warm. Preheat the oven to 220°C (430°F). Heat the olive oil in a frying pan and gently fry the leek until softened but not coloured. Set aside to cool.

Mix the vinegar with 3–4 litres (5¼–7 pints) warm water in a large bowl and add the pork net. After a few minutes it should unravel easily into sheets when pulled apart carefully using your fingers. Cut each pig liver piece into 2 equal pieces, then divide the pork net into 8 squares of a size that can wrap a piece of the liver in a secure parcel. There should be no holes in the squares. Place a bay leaf in the centre of each pork net square, then a piece of liver. Season and add a tablespoon or so of the cooked leek. Roll each parcel up tight and put in a baking dish, bay-leaf side down. Sprinkle with the wine and bake for 8–9 minutes. Remove carefully from the dish and arrange 2 parcels on each plate on top of some celeriac puree.

SERVES 4   WINE: Collio merlot

FRIULI-VENEZIA GIULIA
DOLCI

ESPRESSO BISCOTTINI
BISCOTTINI ALL'ESPRESSO

INGREDIENTS

250 g (9 oz) unsalted butter

125 g (4½ oz) caster
(superfine) sugar

2 teaspoons natural vanilla
extract

2 cups (300 g/10½ oz) plain
(all-purpose) flour

70 g (2½ oz) freshly ground
coffee

½ teaspoon sea salt

METHOD

Cream the butter and sugar using an electric mixer fitted with a paddle
attachment. Beat in the vanilla, then on low speed mix in the flour,
coffee and salt until well combined. Flatten the dough and shape into
a rough rectangle a couple of cm (1 in) thick. Wrap in plastic wrap and
refrigerate for 2 hours. Preheat the oven to 160°C (320°F). Roll out the
dough between 2 sheets of baking paper to a thickness of 5 mm (¼ in)
(this may be easier to do if the dough is divided into 2 or 3 pieces).
Cut into 8 cm × 2 cm (3¼ in × ¾ in) strips and put on a baking tray with
at least 3 cm (1¼ in) between each strip. Refrigerate for 20 minutes.
Bake for about 20 minutes and cool on a wire rack.

MAKES 30–40   SERVE with grappa and espresso

PEACH AND PROSECCO JELLY
GELATINA DI PESCHE E PROSECCO

*This can be made with any sparkling wine, but prosecco is relatively inexpensive, generally of good
quality and a classic match for peaches. Try to find gelatine sheets (rather than powdered gelatine) for
a better result.*

INGREDIENTS

3 cups (750 ml/26 fl oz)
prosecco or other
sparkling wine

100 ml (3½ fl oz) peach
poaching liquid
(see page 371)

10 g (¼ oz) gelatine sheets,
moistened in water

4 poached peaches (see
page 371), peeled and
thickly sliced

METHOD

Bring the prosecco and poaching liquid to the boil in a saucepan, then
remove from the heat. Drain the gelatine sheets and squeeze out any
excess water. Add the gelatine to the hot liquid and whisk to dissolve,
then pour the liquid into a bowl to cool a little. Distribute the peach
slices evenly among 8 serving glasses and pour the warm liquid over.
Put in the refrigerator to set, then serve as is or with vanilla ice cream.

SERVES 8   WINE: Prosecco

QUINCE AND RICE PUDDING TART
CROSTATA DI RISO E MELE COTOGNE

INGREDIENTS

200 g (7 oz) Italian rice (arborio, vialone nano or carnaroli)

100 g (3½ oz) caster (superfine) sugar

1 teaspoon natural vanilla extract

1 litre (35 fl oz) milk

25 g (1 oz) unsalted butter

6 egg yolks

⅓ cup (60 g/2¼ oz) sultanas (golden raisins)

60 g (2¼ oz) candied lemon peel

60 g (2¼ oz) candied orange peel

16 pieces baked quince (see below)

700 g (1 lb 9 oz) sweet shortcrust pastry (see page 47)

2 tablespoons brown sugar

METHOD

Put the rice in a large saucepan with the caster sugar, vanilla, milk, butter and a pinch of salt. Bring to the boil, then turn the heat down, stir well and simmer for 20 minutes or until the liquid has reduced and the rice is cooked. Remove from the heat and let cool for 15 minutes. Preheat the oven to 160°C (320°F). Grease and flour two 20 cm diameter × 3 cm deep (8 in × 1¼ in) tart (flan) tins. Mix the egg yolks, sultanas and candied peel into the rice mixture. Thinly slice the quince into enough pieces to cover each tart. Roll out the pastry and use it to line each tart tin, then spoon in the rice mixture and top with quince slices. Sprinkle the brown sugar over and bake for 20 minutes. Cool to room temperature before serving.

SERVES 12–16   WINE: Albana di Romagna Passito

BAKED QUINCES
MELE COTOGNE AL FORNO

The quantities given here can be multiplied according to how many quinces you have. Keep in mind that the amount of wine should not be automatically multiplied: rather, use enough to just cover the quinces. Gauge your sugar and spice quantities in proportion to the wine.

INGREDIENTS

1 kg (2 lb 4 oz) quinces, well washed and dried

3 cups (750 ml/26 fl oz) white wine

⅔ cup (150 g/5½ oz) caster (superfine) sugar

juice of 1 lemon

2 star anise

1 cinnamon stick

8 black peppercorns

METHOD

Preheat the oven to 100°C (200°F). Cut each quince lengthways into 8 wedges, leaving the skin, seeds and core intact. Put in a baking dish that fits the pieces snugly. Whisk the wine, sugar and lemon juice together, then pour into the dish to cover the quince pieces. If needed, add some water or more wine. Scatter the spices over and cover loosely with foil, then poke some holes in the foil using a skewer. Bake for 8 hours. Remove from the oven and let cool, then peel and core the quince pieces. Serve for breakfast, or for dessert with cream or ice cream, or as an accompaniment for pork and other rich meats.

CHERRIES IN RED WINE WITH PANETTONE
CILIEGIE AL VINO ROSSO CON PANETTONE

For this recipe use red wine that's not too tannic, such as chianti, bardolino or pinot noir.

INGREDIENTS

500 g (1 lb 2 oz) pitted
 cherries
3 cups (750 ml/26 fl oz)
 red wine
⅔ cup (150 g/5½ oz) caster
 (superfine) sugar
2 star anise
6 black peppercorns
8 × 4 cm (1½ in) thick slices
 panettone, cut to fit into
 individual serving bowls
8 scoops vanilla gelato
 (see page 473)

METHOD

Put half the cherries in a saucepan with the red wine, sugar, star anise and peppercorns. Bring to the boil, then turn down the heat and simmer for 1 hour. Strain the cooking liquid, discarding the star anise and peppercorns. Press the juice from the cooked cherries and add to the cooking liquid. Chop the cooked cherries and reserve. Return the cooking liquid to the saucepan and reduce by a third, then pour over the uncooked cherries. Cool before using. (The cherries will keep in a sealed container in the refrigerator for 2 weeks.) To serve, put the panettone pieces in the serving dishes, add some chopped cherries and a scoop of gelato, then spoon some whole cherries and their syrup over the lot.

SERVES 8   WINE: Picolit

LAZIO

LAZIO

BEGINNING IN THE NORTH ON THE EDGE OF THE TUSCAN MAREMMA, LAZIO (ALSO CALLED LATIUM) IS BORDERED TO THE NORTH-EAST BY UMBRIA, WITH A SMALL NODULE STRETCHING EAST PAST ABRUZZO TO NUZZLE INTO LE MARCHE, AND TO THE SOUTH-EAST BY MOLISE AND CAMPANIA. ITS 17,000 SQUARE KILOMETRES (6500 SQUARE MILES) ARE A COMBINATION OF FLAT AND HILLS, WITH A FEW MOUNTAINS TO THE EAST AND SOUTH. IT IS POPULOUS BECAUSE OF ROME, ITALY'S LARGEST CITY WITH ABOUT SIX MILLION RESIDENTS, AND WEALTHY, AGAIN THANKS TO THE CAPITAL.

Of Roman food, Waverley Root stated emphatically in *The Food of Italy*: 'Roman food is Etruscan food'. The Etruscans raised sheep, as did the Latin shepherds on the mouth of the Tiber some 800 years ago. Sheep provided mutton, cheese and ricotta, which the Etruscans enjoyed, as does modern Rome. The Etruscans also raised wheat and wine, beef cattle (the ancestors of the Chianina) and pigs.

But it wasn't always so simple. Come the empire and all food roads led to Rome, with exotic species and spices arriving from all over the known world to feed the feasts (orgies?) that Rome is fondly remembered for. Long after the decline and fall of the empire, in the 16th century Rome was, as Capatti and Montanari remind us in *Italian Cuisine: A Cultural History*, 'not only the capital of Christianity, but still … the capital of the food market' – although by then it was 'centred on the products of the Italian peninsula'.

Indeed, from one form of excess (the emperors) to another (the pontiffs), Rome knew how to have a good time, as long as you were a member of whatever few were privileged: in imperial times that meant all of 200 families, and later, those close to the popes. In *Machiavelli*, Prezzolini wrote of the Renaissance era: 'Rome was caput mundi, the world's latrine, a country of gang wars, imposing ruins, puddles, chronic malaria, general filth, luxury and beggary, hugger-mugger neighbours … To the better contemporaries Rome was Sodom, Gomorrah and Babylon rolled into one … The Pope had his minions, his sons, his concubines …'

Two hundred years later, Rome was the capital of eating out: in the 18th century, 200 inns and 200 hostels along with 100 cafes were recorded (bars offering coffee and alcohol appeared in the 20th century). Because of the overcrowding, the height and 'hugger-mugger' nature of apartment living, many Romans preferred to eat out for fear of fire, so they took their meals in a trattoria sotto casa ('outside the house').

As they did in ancient times, for special events and celebratory feasts Romans will place at the centre of the table some imported luxury, such as caviar or salmon, while sticking to more humble foods for every day, such as zucchini (courgette) flowers, tripe and focaccia.

The most Roman of vegetables is the artichoke, with varieties forming a hierarchy from the purple cimarola down. Artichokes are best, and habitually, simply boiled in water and vinegar and then sprinkled with oil, parsley, mint and salt. There is also the famed Jewish artichoke, carciofi alla giudia, which is pounded flat and plunged in boiling olive oil.

Other emblematic dishes of the Eternal City are the suckling pig roast on a spit, which is the main event at the festival of Noantri ('the rest of us') held every July in Trastevere; and abbacchio, baby lamb either spit-roasted or oven-roasted, with rosemary to make it truly Roman, and usually eaten at Easter, which is the season for baby lambs. A favourite family excursion at Easter is to drive into the country to picnic on a barbecued lamb in the open air.

Then there is saltimbocca ('leap into the mouth'), thin slices of veal seasoned with sage and attached with tiny skewers to slices of prosciutto, braised in butter and Marsala wine; and supplì al telefono, a ball of rice (usually leftover risotto) fried with a piece of provatura (buffalo-milk cheese) inside. Why telefono? Because when you bite into one the melted cheese stretches out like a telephone wire.

There is cotechino, a pork sausage made from various pig's innards and cooked with lentils, which is traditional at New Year; zampone, stuffed pig's feet, also served with lentils; and the uncompromising coratella, the heart, liver, lungs and spleen of lamb heavily peppered and fried in olive oil with onions.

So powerful and omnipresent has been the influence of Rome that there is little in the way of Lazio cuisine outside the city, but for a handful of dishes that are the exceptions that prove the rule. In that area between the Lepini mountains and the Apennines is Ciociaria, and from its capital, Alatri, comes spaghetti alla ciociara, with a sauce of bacon, ham and sausage. From Amatrice, a town on the slopes of the Tronto valley, comes spaghetti all'amatriciana, with a sauce of tomatoes, onions and bacon sprinkled with pecorino cheese; in various forms (most of which are nothing like the original), this dish has become a cliché of suburban Italian food worldwide.

Lazio is a major wine region, with 26 DOC areas. Three of them are Castelli Romani, Frascati and Orvieto, the latter of which Lazio shares with Umbria. The problem with the wines of Lazio, many critics say, is Rome: because it is so close and its tourists drink so much wine uncritically, on the whole producers turn out oceans of lacklustre white wine.

The two names that leap out of the crowded but fairly undistinguished field are frascati, from the DOC of the same name, and Est! Est!! Est!!!, from the Montefiascone DOC on the shores of Lake Bolsena. The former is made mainly from a blend of malvasia and trebbiano, while the latter is made predominantly from the trebbiano grape. There is good frascati, but not much of it, and the same can be said of Est! Est!! Est!!! There are also malvasia del Lazio wines produced, many with bigger flavours than most frascati wines.

Small amounts of white wine are made using semillon, sauvignon blanc, chardonnay and viognier, either in blends or alone.

The indigenous grape, cesanese, is the main red wine grape of the region. Perhaps the best wine made with this variety is the cesanese del Piglio, which is more traditionally made in the frizzante style but lately more and more as a still wine and, in one instance at least, in a blend with syrah.

Red wines are also made with other foreigners, among them sangiovese, cabernet sauvignon, merlot, montepulciano and aglianico.

LAZIO
ANTI-PASTI

ROMAN-STYLE FRIED ARTICHOKES
CARCIOFI FRITTI ALLA ROMANA

INGREDIENTS

2 lemons

6 large artichokes

2 eggs

2 heaped tablespoons plain
(all-purpose) flour

1 cup (250 ml/9 fl oz) extra
virgin olive oil

METHOD

Half-fill a large bowl with cold water. Halve 1 lemon and squeeze
the juice into the water. Using a sharp knife, cut off the end of each
artichoke a third of the way from the top, then peel off the dark outer
leaves until you reach the tender light-green ones. Leave 5 cm (2 in) of
stalk at the base and cut each artichoke into 8 from top to bottom. Put
the artichoke pieces immediately into the bowl of lemon water. Working
with 1 piece at a time, cut out and discard any furry choke from the
centre, then return the piece to the lemon water. Combine the eggs,
flour, 50 ml (1¾ fl oz) of the olive oil and a pinch or two of pepper in a
separate bowl to make a batter. Remove the artichoke pieces from the
lemon water and pat dry with a clean tea towel (dish towel). Pour the
remaining oil into a frying pan to achieve a depth of 2 cm (¾ in) and put
on high heat. Dip the artichoke pieces in the batter, letting any excess
fall back into the bowl. Test the temperature of the oil by dropping in a
piece of artichoke to see if it sizzles. Fry the artichokes in batches and
drain on paper towels. Cut the remaining lemon into wedges. Season
the fried artichokes with salt and serve hot with the lemon wedges.

SERVES 8   WINE: Frascati

CODDLED EGG WITH WINE AND GARUM
VOVO COCCOLATO AL GARUM

INGREDIENTS

160 ml (5¼ fl oz) extra virgin
olive oil

8 very fresh eggs

160 ml (5¼ fl oz) dry white
wine

1 tablespoon garum
(see page 154)

2 tablespoons finely snipped
chives

METHOD

Preheat the oven to 190°C (375°F). Grease 8 small ramekins
(150 ml/5 fl oz) with 1 tablespoon of the olive oil each. Don't worry if
there seems to be too much oil – it's also there for flavour. Break 1 egg
carefully into each ramekin. Add 1 tablespoon of the wine, ½ teaspoon of
the garum and some chives. Put the ramekins in a baking dish and pour
in hot water to come halfway up the sides of the ramekins. Cover with
foil and bake for 15 minutes. Serve straightaway.

SERVES 8   WINE: Ferentano (Roscetto)

BANANA CHILLIES STUFFED WITH CABBAGE
PEPERONI RIPIENI

INGREDIENTS

12 red banana chillies (peppers)

½ small cabbage, finely sliced

1 egg

60 g (2¼ oz) grated parmesan cheese

1 teaspoon thyme leaves

2 tablespoons finely chopped parsley

½ cup diced bread, crusts removed

1 brown onion, minced

2 garlic cloves, minced

2 tablespoons extra virgin olive oil

200 ml (7 fl oz) tomato passata

1 cup fresh breadcrumbs

METHOD

Preheat the oven to 165°C (330°F). Slit the banana chillies carefully down one side. Remove and discard the stem end and all the seeds and pith inside, making sure each chilli remains in one piece. Plunge the cabbage into salted boiling water for 4–5 minutes until tender. Drain and let cool, then roughly chop and put in a bowl. Whisk the egg with the parmesan, thyme and parsley and add to the cabbage along with the bread, onion, garlic and olive oil. Season and mix well. Stuff the chillies with this mixture and arrange in a baking dish, stuffing side up. Add 1 tablespoon of the passata to each chilli and sprinkle with breadcrumbs. Pour water into the baking dish to a depth of 5 mm (¼ in), then bake for 30 minutes. Serve at room temperature.

SERVES 8　　　　　　　　　　WINE: Est! Est!! Est!!! di Montefiascone

CRAB AND BROAD BEAN CROSTINI
CROSTINI DI GRANCHIO E FAVE

INGREDIENTS

2 cups (370 g/13 oz) double-peeled broad beans

160 ml (5¼ fl oz) extra virgin olive oil

200 g (7 oz) cooked crabmeat (blue swimmer, spanner or mud crab)

¼ cup finely chopped coriander (cilantro) leaves

1–2 red chillies, finely chopped

½ cup (125 ml/4 fl oz) lemon juice

4 large slices bread

1 large garlic clove, halved

METHOD

Plunge the broad beans into salted boiling water for 2 minutes until soft. Put ¾ of the beans in a bowl with ½ cup (125 ml/4 fl oz) of the olive oil and use a fork to mash to a rough puree. Add the remaining beans, crabmeat, coriander, chilli and lemon juice and season. Mix gently, keeping the pieces of crab whole. Brush the bread slices with the remaining oil and lightly grill (broil) or toast them, then rub with the cut side of the garlic. Spread the broad bean and crab mixture on the crostini and serve whole or cut into pieces.

SERVES 8–10　　　　　　　　　　　　　　WINE: Frascati

CUTTLEFISH, CANNELLINI BEANS AND PEAS
SEPPIE CON CANNELLINI E PISELLI

INGREDIENTS

1 cup (200 g/7 oz) dried
  cannellini beans, soaked
  overnight in plenty of
  cold water
⅓ cup (80 ml/2½ fl oz) extra
  virgin olive oil
1 garlic clove, minced
1 tablespoon rosemary leaves,
  finely chopped
1 cup (155 g/5½ oz) shelled
  peas
250 g (9 oz) tin tomatoes,
  mashed
600 g (1 lb 5 oz) cuttlefish
  or small squid, cleaned,
  bodies cut into thin strips
2 tablespoons finely
  chopped parsley

METHOD

Drain and rinse the cannellini beans. Pick out and discard any discoloured beans and put the rest in a saucepan. Cover with cold water and discard any beans that float. Bring to the boil, then turn down to a simmer, cover and cook until the beans are tender. Tip the beans and their cooking liquid into a container and let cool. (The beans can be stored in the fridge for a few days at this point, if desired.) Heat the olive oil in a saucepan and gently fry the garlic and rosemary for a minute, stirring to make sure the garlic doesn't colour. Add the peas and tomatoes and a good pinch or two of salt. Simmer gently for 15–20 minutes until the peas are tender. If the pan gets too dry, add a little water. Turn up the heat and add the beans, cuttlefish and parsley. Stir well and simmer briskly for 2–3 minutes until the cuttlefish is just cooked. Season.

SERVES 10–12   WINE: Frascati

PUNTARELLE AND ANCHOVY SALAD
INSALATA DI PUNTARELLE

Puntarelle are part of the chicory family – see page 385 for more information. Serve this salad as part of the antipasto or as an accompaniment to a second-course fish or shellfish dish.

INGREDIENTS

500 g (1 lb 2 oz) puntarelle,
  prepared as on page 385
4 anchovy fillets
1 garlic clove
⅓ cup (80 ml/2½ fl oz) extra
  virgin olive oil
2 tablespoons red wine
  vinegar

METHOD

Once the sliced puntarelle have been in the lemon water for 10–15 minutes (as per preparation instructions), they will have curled up. When ready to serve, drain the puntarelle well and dry using a salad spinner or clean tea towel (dish towel), then put in a large bowl. Put the anchovies, garlic and a couple of good pinches of salt in a mortar and pound to a paste. Add the olive oil, vinegar and a few turns of pepper and mix well with a spoon. Dress the puntarelle, toss well and serve.

SERVES 6–8   WINE: Est! Est!! Est!!! di Montefiascone

LAZIO
PRIMI

EGG RIBBON SOUP
LA STRACCIATELLA

Though this soup is famous the world over, its origins are Roman and in Rome it is always a light soup with just a few ingredients. Its quality depends on the base broth. In neighbouring regions an addition of breadcrumbs and flour is common, but that results in a cloudy soup. In some other parts of the world spinach seems to be a popular adjunct, but I prefer the simplicity and clean flavours of the original ingredients.

INGREDIENTS

6 very fresh eggs

100 g (3½ oz) Parmigiano Reggiano, grated

½ teaspoon grated nutmeg

1.5 litres (52 fl oz) good-quality beef or quail broth (see pages 48 and 49)

METHOD

Whisk the eggs in a bowl with the Parmigiano Reggiano, nutmeg and a pinch of salt until mixed but not frothy. Bring the broth to the boil in a saucepan and then remove from the heat. Whisk in the egg mixture energetically so it's well incorporated. Return the saucepan to the heat and bring the soup back to the boil, whisking. Check for seasoning and serve immediately.

SERVES 6

WINE: Colli Lanuvini white (100% Trebbiano or blended with Malvasia)

RIGATONI WITH THREE CHEESES
RIGATONI AI TRE FORMAGGI

INGREDIENTS

2 tablespoons extra virgin olive oil

10 garlic cloves, minced

½ cup parsley, chopped

1 litre (35 fl oz) tomato passata

600 g (1 lb 5 oz) dried rigatoni

1 small slice fontina cheese

1 small slice gorgonzola cheese

2 tablespoons grated parmesan cheese

½ cup breadcrumbs

METHOD

Gently heat the olive oil in a frying pan and fry the garlic. Once its perfume is evident, add the parsley and stir for a moment. Add a small ladleful of hot water and simmer for 2 minutes, then add the passata, a couple of good pinches of salt and a little cracked pepper and simmer for 10 minutes. Cook the pasta according to the instructions on the pack. Meanwhile, in a small saucepan, gently melt the 3 cheeses with 1–2 tablespoons water. Add the cheeses to the sauce and mix. Drain the pasta and mix thoroughly with the sauce, then put in serving bowls and sprinkle the breadcrumbs on top.

SERVES 6

WINE: Roscetto

TAGLIERINI WITH PORK CHEEK AND MUSHROOMS
TAGLIERINI CON GUANCIA DI MAIALE E FUNGHI

INGREDIENTS

20 g (¾ oz) dried porcini
  mushrooms

80 g (2¾ oz) butter

140 ml (4¾ fl oz) extra virgin
  olive oil

1 leek, white part only, diced

2 garlic cloves, finely chopped

350 g (12 oz) mixed mushrooms
  (your choice of enoki, Swiss
  brown, shiitake, oyster, black
  fungus, king brown, buttons),
  cut into bite-sized pieces

1 cup (250 ml/9 fl oz) white
  wine

½ cup chopped parsley

2 pork cheeks, trimmed of fat
  and sinew

600 g (1 lb 5 oz) dried taglierini
  or spaghetti

grated parmesan cheese

METHOD

Soak the porcini in ½ cup (125 ml/4 fl oz) cold water for 20 minutes, then drain and discard the liquid. Meanwhile, put the butter and 100 ml (3½ fl oz) of the olive oil in a wide frying pan on medium heat. Once the butter has melted, add the leek and garlic and lightly fry for 2 minutes. Add the mushrooms (including the porcini), turn the heat to high and fry for 2 minutes. Pour in the wine and boil for a minute or so, then turn down the heat, add the parsley and simmer for 5 minutes. Turn off the heat and season. Cut the pork into very thin strips about 6 cm (2½ in) long. Heat the remaining oil in a separate large frying pan on medium-high heat and put the pork strips in the pan in 1 layer. Season. When the meat starts to crisp and colour, turn it over to crisp the other side. Add the pork to the mushrooms and stir. Cook the taglierini (or spaghetti) according to the instructions on the pack, drain and toss with the pork and mushrooms. Serve with grated parmesan.

SERVES 6   WINE: Cesanese del Piglio

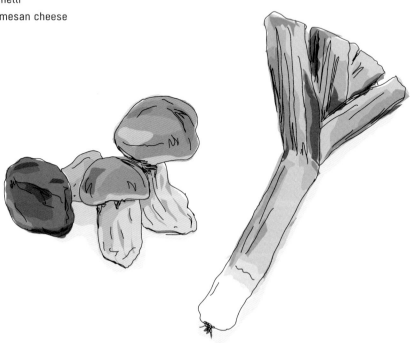

ROMAN-STYLE GNOCCHI WITH ASPARAGUS
GNOCCHI ALLA ROMANA CON ASPARAGI

This recipe calls for gnocchi made with semolina rather than potato. It's believed that gnocchi (literally meaning 'lumps' in Italian) were first made using a simple mixture of flour and water, much like pasta. Potato was introduced much later from the Americas through the so-called 'Columbian Exchange'. Potatoes became the norm for making gnocchi in most of Italy – so much so that Roman food historian and author Livio Jannattoni says he grew up eating the more usual potato gnocchi and only tasted gnocchi alla romana by chance in a dining car on a provincial train. Which version is better? They are both delicious, but there's no doubt that gnocchi alla romana is easier to make. Semolina is the heart of the durum-wheat grain and it is removed before milling the rest of the grain into flour.

INGREDIENTS

250 g (9 oz) asparagus
    spears, trimmed
1 litre (35 fl oz) milk
250 g (9 oz) semolina
2 egg yolks, lightly whisked
100 g (3½ oz) unsalted butter
½ teaspoon grated nutmeg
70 g (2½ oz) grated parmesan
    cheese

METHOD

Bring a saucepan of salted water to the boil and plunge in the asparagus. Cook until tender, then drain and let cool. Cut the asparagus tips to no more than 4 cm (1½ in) long and finely slice the stalks. Set aside. Bring the milk to a gentle boil in a saucepan with 2–3 good pinches of salt, then pour in the semolina in a fine stream, continually stirring with a whisk to stop any lumps forming. Once the mixture has thickened, turn the heat to low and cook for 10–12 minutes, stirring with a wooden spoon. It will thicken quite a lot. Remove the pan from the heat and stir in the egg yolks, butter, nutmeg and half the parmesan. Finally, stir in the asparagus stalks. Pour the hot mixture onto a marble slab or large wooden board to a 1 cm (½ in) thickness and let cool. Preheat the oven to 190°C (375°F) and line 1–2 baking dishes with baking paper. Using a 5 cm (2 in) round pastry (cookie) cutter, cut out the gnocchi and lay them side by side on the baking trays, leaving a small space between each. Halve the asparagus tips lengthways and lay 1 piece on each gnocco. Use a teaspoon to scatter the remaining parmesan over, then bake for 30 minutes. Serve gnocchi hot by themselves or with a tomato sauce.

SERVES 4–6   WINE: Orvieto or Verdelho

RICE WITH REGGIANO, PROSCIUTTO AND MOZZARELLA
RISO AL PROSCIUTTO E MOZZARELLA

INGREDIENTS

400 g (14 oz) Italian rice (carnaroli, arborio or vialone nano)

300 g (10½ oz) mozzarella fior di latte, torn into small pieces

120 g (4¼ oz) Parmigiano Reggiano, grated

60 g (2¼ oz) unsalted butter, thinly sliced

6 rashers prosciutto, cut into thin strips

3 tablespoons chopped parsley

METHOD

Bring 4 litres (7 pints) water and 1 teaspoon salt to the boil in a saucepan. Add the rice, stir and simmer for about 20 minutes until al dente but not chalky. Drain and transfer to a large, warm serving bowl. Immediately stir in the mozzarella and Parmigiano Reggiano so that the cheeses melt evenly. Stir in the butter, prosciutto and parsley, then season with salt and cracked pepper. Serve hot.

SERVES 6   WINE: Cesanese del Piglio

GRILLED PRAWNS WITH TOMATO HORSERADISH SALSA
GAMBERI ALLA GRIGLIA CON SALSA FORTE

INGREDIENTS

⅓ cup (80 ml/2½ fl oz) extra virgin olive oil

2 brown onions, finely diced

2 garlic cloves, minced

1 large green capsicum (pepper), seeded and diced

600 g (1 lb 5 oz) truss tomatoes, peeled, seeded and diced

2 tablespoons red wine vinegar

1 tablespoon tomato paste (concentrated puree)

80 g (2¾ oz) horseradish, finely grated

1 kg (2 lb 4 oz) raw king prawns (shrimp), peeled and deveined

METHOD

Heat half the olive oil in a large frying pan and gently fry the onions, garlic and capsicum for 2–3 minutes until soft. Add the tomatoes and simmer for 10 minutes, stirring frequently. Add the vinegar, tomato paste and a couple of pinches of salt and simmer rapidly until thick. Season and transfer to a bowl to cool to room temperature. Stir in the horseradish. Wipe out the pan and heat the remaining oil. Cook the prawns until they turn red and are cooked through, season and serve with the tomato horseradish salsa.

SERVES 6   WINE: Ferentano

MEATBALL AND BEAN STEW
ZUPPA DI POLPETTE E FAGIOLI

INGREDIENTS

800 g (1 lb 12 oz) dried beans (cannellini, borlotti or tondini), soaked overnight in plenty of cold water

¼ cup (60 ml/2 fl oz) extra virgin olive oil

100 g (3½ oz) prosciutto or pancetta, finely diced

1 brown onion, finely chopped

2 garlic cloves, minced

200 ml (7 fl oz) red wine

15 sage leaves

2 bay leaves

500 g (1 lb 2 oz) tin tomatoes, pureed

MEATBALLS

150 g (5½ oz) minced (ground) pork shoulder

150 g (5½ oz) minced (ground) veal shoulder

2 garlic cloves, finely chopped

1 egg

½ cup (50 g/1¾ oz) finely grated parmesan cheese

½ cup finely chopped parsley

3 good pinches of salt

½ teaspoon fine white pepper

METHOD

Drain and rinse the beans. Pick out and discard any discoloured beans and put the rest in a saucepan. Pour in cold water to cover by 3–4 cm (1¼–1½ in) and discard any beans that float. Bring to the boil, then turn down to a simmer. Cover and cook until the beans are tender and retain their shape (the time will vary according to the dried beans used). Meanwhile, combine all the meatball ingredients, then roll the mixture into balls about 2.5 cm (1 in) in diameter and refrigerate until needed. Drain the beans and let cool. Preheat the oven to 140°C (285°F). Heat the olive oil in a flameproof casserole dish and lightly fry the prosciutto, onion and garlic for 2–3 minutes. Add the wine and cook until the liquid has reduced by half. Add the beans, herbs and tomatoes and season with 2–3 good pinches of salt. Mix well, cover and bake for 1–1½ hours. Add the meatballs to the dish, distributing them evenly and covering them carefully with the liquid. Add some cracked pepper and return the dish to the oven for 15–20 minutes. Serve hot.

SERVES 8–10   **WINE:** Circeo Rosso

PAN-FRIED SWEETBREADS WITH BEANS, CAPERS AND SAGE
ANIMELLE IN PADELLA CON FAGIOLINI, CAPPERI E SALVIA

INGREDIENTS

400 g (14 oz) veal or lamb sweetbreads

1 small carrot, cut into 3–4 pieces

1 brown onion, quartered

1 celery stick, cut into 3–4 pieces

2 tablespoons white wine vinegar

150 g (5½ oz) green beans, trimmed

1 garlic clove, minced

2 tablespoons chopped parsley

¼ cup (60 ml/2 fl oz) extra virgin olive oil

⅓ cup (50 g/1¾ oz) plain (all-purpose) flour

2 eggs, whisked

1 cup breadcrumbs

50 g (1¾ oz) butter

½ cup sage leaves

1 tablespoon capers, rinsed

METHOD

Put the sweetbreads, carrot, onion and celery in a saucepan. Add the vinegar and enough water to cover everything by 3–4 cm (1¼–1½ in). Bring to the boil, then turn down the heat and simmer for 5 minutes if the sweetbreads are small (lamb) or 10 minutes if they are large (veal). Drain and set aside until cool enough to handle. Using a small, sharp knife, trim off any fat, gristle and sinew and peel away and discard the membrane that encases the sweetbreads. This step can be a bit fiddly but is well worth it. Cut the sweetbreads into bite-sized pieces. Plunge the beans into a saucepan of rapidly boiling salted water for 3 minutes. Drain, then put in a bowl and dress with the garlic, parsley and 2 tablespoons of the olive oil. Season and toss well. Dust the sweetbreads with the flour, dredge in the egg and coat in the breadcrumbs. Heat the butter and remaining oil in a frying pan until foaming, then add the sweetbreads to the pan with the sage and capers and fry until golden. Drain on paper towels. Arrange the sweetbreads on the beans and scatter the sage leaves and capers on top to serve.

SERVES 4   WINE: Ferentano

SWEETBREADS ARE THE THYMUS GLANDS OF YOUNG ANIMALS, MOST COMMONLY VEAL AND LAMB. ONCE THE ANIMAL MATURES, THESE GLANDS DISAPPEAR. ONCE POACHED AND CLEANED THEY CAN BE DUSTED WITH FLOUR OR CRUMBED AND THEN FRIED TO A GOLDEN CRISPNESS. FRIED SWEETBREADS SERVED ON TOP OF BUTTERED, FRESHLY SHELLED PEAS OR BROAD BEANS FOR SOME CAN TASTE SIMILAR TO CHICKEN. SWEETBREADS ARE EXCELLENT WITH CREAM SAUCES FLAVOURED WITH MUSTARD, SORREL OR PARMESAN; VERY GOOD ALSO WITH MUSHROOMS AS WELL AS CREAMED SPINACH.

PAN-FRIED SWEETBREADS WITH BEANS, CAPERS AND SAGE

PEAS WITH PROSCIUTTO
PISELLI AL PROSCIUTTO

Once upon a time this was made using strutto (rendered pork fat). If you have access to strutto it is well worth it as it makes the peas rich and creamy. This recipe is best made with tender new spring peas. It is a great first course but can also be served as an accompaniment to meat and game dishes.

INGREDIENTS

160 g (5¾ oz) prosciutto, thinly sliced

2 tablespoons extra virgin olive oil

1 small brown onion, minced

1 kg (2 lb 4 oz) peas (preferably new spring peas), shelled

200 ml (7 fl oz) chicken broth (see page 48)

20 g (¾ oz) unsalted butter

METHOD

Cut off the fatty part of the prosciutto and chop the fat. Cut the prosciutto meat into thin strips and set aside. Heat the olive oil in a frying pan and add the prosciutto fat and onion. Fry lightly until the onion is soft but not coloured. Add the peas and half the broth and bring to a simmer. Add a pinch of salt and stir, then cover and simmer gently for 10 minutes, stirring every now and then and adding more broth as needed. Remove the lid and stir in the butter and the prosciutto strips. Season with a little more salt, if needed, and a couple of turns of pepper. Transfer to a bowl and serve with toasted bread.

SERVES 6   WINE: Roscetto

BAKED ARTICHOKE FLAN
TIMBALLO DI CARCIOFI

INGREDIENTS

12 artichokes

juice of 1 lemon

2 tablespoons extra virgin olive oil

2 spring onions (scallions), thinly sliced

1 tablespoon marjoram leaves

100 ml (3½ fl oz) dry white wine

1 egg

3 egg yolks

100 g (3½ oz) potato, cooked and mashed

1 cup (250 ml/9 fl oz) thin (pouring) cream

60 g (2¼ oz) finely grated parmesan

METHOD

Trim the artichokes until all but the heart and tender leaves remain. Put in a bowl of cold water with the lemon juice. If there is a tough choke in any of the artichokes, remove it entirely. Finely slice the artichokes. When ready to cook, drain the artichoke slices and pat them dry. Heat the olive oil in a frying pan and lightly fry the artichoke slices, spring onions and marjoram until softened. Add the wine and simmer for 5–6 minutes until the liquid is almost all gone. Take the pan off the heat and let cool. Preheat the oven to 180°C (350°F). Transfer the artichoke mixture to a food processor and pulse to a puree. Whisk the egg and egg yolks together, mix with mashed potato, cream and parmesan and add to the puree, then season and spoon into 6–8 ramekins or dariole moulds (150 ml/5 fl oz). Put the ramekins in a baking dish and pour in water to come halfway up their sides. Bake for 20–25 minutes until set. Serve warm with a vinaigrette and salad.

SERVES 6–8   WINE: Circeo Bianco

BAKED PARSNIP AND CAULIFLOWER
PASTINACA E CAVOLFIORE AL FORNO

INGREDIENTS

600 g (1 lb 5 oz) parsnips,
cut into chunks

400 g (14 oz) cauliflower
florets

1 tablespoon red wine vinegar

½ cup (125 ml/4 fl oz) extra
virgin olive oil

60 g (2¼ oz) plain
(all-purpose) flour

1 cup (250 ml/9 fl oz) milk

80 g (2¾ oz) grated parmesan

4 eggs, separated

250 g (9 oz) fresh mozzarella
balls, cut into 1 cm (½ in)
dice

white pepper

½ cup breadcrumbs

1 treviso (radicchio) or other
bitter lettuce, sliced

METHOD

Preheat the oven to 200°C (400°F). Cook the parsnips and cauliflower
separately in boiling water until soft, then puree together in a food
processor until smooth. Transfer to a bowl and mix in the vinegar,
1 tablespoon of the olive oil and a couple of pinches of salt. Heat half the
remaining oil in a saucepan on medium heat and add the flour, whisking
and toasting it for a minute. Add the milk and parmesan and whisk well
for 30 seconds so no lumps form. Remove the pan from the heat and
add the egg yolks, whisking well to incorporate, then add this mixture
to the vegetable puree. Add 200 g (7 oz) of the mozzarella and mix well.
Check for salt and add a little white pepper. Whisk the egg whites to
soft peaks and fold into the mixture. Oil 8 × 150 ml (5 fl oz) ramekins or
1 × 28 cm (11¼ in) tart (flan) tin with the remaining oil and line with the
breadcrumbs. Pour in the cheese and vegetable mixture and bake for
15 minutes if using individual ramekins, or 25–30 minutes for a tart tin.
Cool a little in the dishes or tin before turning out and serving with the
treviso and remaining mozzarella.

SERVES 8   WINE: Grechetto

IT WAS THE ROMANS WHO INTRODUCED
PARSNIPS TO BRITAIN AND GAUL. BECAUSE PARSNIPS
CONTAIN A LOT OF NATURAL SUGAR, A BOILED-DOWN,
HONEY-LIKE SYRUP MADE BY REDUCING PARSNIP
COOKING WATER WAS USED AS A GENERAL SWEETENER.

ROMAN-STYLE BRAISED SPRING VEGETABLES
VIGNAROLA

This is the classic Roman springtime dish, along with abbacchio (spring lamb). If you want to make this recipe your own, just use whatever spring vegetables are available – but the artichokes and peas are essential.

INGREDIENTS

8 baby artichokes (picked before the choke has formed), trimmed

juice of 1 lemon

2 butter lettuces, outer leaves trimmed

½ cup (125 ml/4 fl oz) extra virgin olive oil, plus extra for drizzling

50 g (1¾ oz) pancetta, finely diced

4 spring onions (scallions), thinly sliced

400 g (14 oz) peas, shelled

2 or more chillies, chopped

400 g (14 oz) broad beans, double peeled

1 handful parsley, chopped

1 handful mint, chopped

4 tablespoons shaved pecorino cheese

METHOD

Cut each artichoke into 6 slices and put in a bowl of cold water with the lemon juice. Cut the lettuce into largish pieces. Heat the olive oil in a saucepan and lightly fry the pancetta and spring onions until softened. Drain the artichokes and add to the pan with the peas and ¼ cup (60 ml/2 fl oz) water. Bring to the boil, then add a couple of good pinches of salt and the chillies. Turn down the heat and simmer for about 10 minutes. Add the lettuce and broad beans, stir well and simmer for 15 minutes until the lettuce is tender. Season, then stir in the parsley and mint. Transfer to a serving bowl, drizzle with oil and scatter the pecorino over. Serve with toasted sourdough bread.

SERVES 6   WINE: Est!Est!!Est!!! di Montefiascone

SECONDI

ROMAN-STYLE CHICKEN
POLLO ALLA ROMANA

Chicken in Italy is still considered rather special, so much so that it is represented in relatively few dishes compared to other meats. Italy is among the lowest consumers of chicken in the European Union. Take a walk through an Italian supermarket and look at the chickens available and you will be struck by the good quality of the birds and their presentation as well as their relatively high price. Their crest and wattle and feet are almost always left intact (these give great flavour to broths and stocks) and the colour is different, it's a lot yellower. The choice of birds includes roosters and hens of small and large sizes (above 2 kg/ 4 lb 8 oz) and all the chicken's offal is available, too. Above all, the chicken is much more flavoursome.

INGREDIENTS

1 × 2 kg (4 lb 8 oz) chicken

⅓ cup (50 g/1¾ oz) plain (all-purpose) flour

½ cup (125 ml/4 fl oz) extra virgin olive oil

1 brown onion, sliced

2 garlic cloves, minced

1 celery heart, thinly sliced

1 large red capsicum (pepper), seeded and cut into 1 cm (½ in) slices

1 large yellow capsicum (pepper), seeded and cut into 1 cm (½ in) slices

300 ml (10½ fl oz) dry white wine

250 g (9 oz) cherry tomatoes, halved

200 ml (7 fl oz) tomato passata

1 bay leaf

½ cup chopped parsley

METHOD

Joint the chicken into 8 pieces. Wash well and pat dry, then dredge in the flour. Heat half the olive oil in a large frying pan and fry the chicken until well browned on both sides. Remove and drain on paper towels. Wipe out the pan and heat the rest of the olive oil, then fry the onion, garlic, celery and capsicums on a fairly lively heat for 4–5 minutes, stirring constantly. Pour in the wine and cook until all the liquid has evaporated. Add the tomatoes, passata and bay leaf, stir and cook for 5 minutes. Add the chicken and turn the heat down to low. Add a good pinch or two of salt and a couple of turns of pepper and simmer for 10 minutes, then turn the chicken pieces. If the liquid reduces too much, add some hot water. Test to see if the chicken is done by piercing near the bone with a sharp knife – if the juice runs clear, it's cooked. Add the parsley, check the seasoning and remove the pan from the heat. Rest for 5 minutes before serving.

SERVES 4   WINE: Orvieto

GRILLED LAMB SHOULDER 'ROMAN STYLE' WITH CAVOLO NERO GRATINATO AND SALSA DRAGONCELLO
SPALLA D'AGNELLO AL DRAGONCELLO

Sous-vide is a method of slow cooking food in sealable plastic bags at low-temperatures in a water bath. While there are professional and home vacuum packers and water baths available, these are costly appliances. The improvised setup used in this recipe is very effective.

INGREDIENTS

2 × 1.5–2 kg (3 lb 5 oz–4 lb 8 oz) lamb shoulders, bone in

4 tablespoons extra virgin olive oil

2 rosemary sprigs

600 g (1 lb 5 oz) cavolo nero (Tuscan kale)

1 cup coarse breadcrumbs

100 g (3½ oz) melting cheese (such as gruyere or fontina)

½ cup (50 g/1¾ oz) grated parmesan cheese

50 g (1¾ oz) butter

¼ cup (60 ml/2 fl oz) extra virgin olive oil

1 large brown onion, finely chopped

2 garlic cloves, minced

100 ml (3½ fl oz) thin (pouring) cream

SALSA DRAGONCELLO

2 slices bread, crusts removed

2–3 tablespoons red wine vinegar

2 cups small tarragon leaves

2 garlic cloves

½ cup (125 ml/4 fl oz) extra virgin olive oil

METHOD

Season the lamb shoulders and place each in a separate sous-vide bag with 2 tablespoons of olive oil and a sprig of rosemary. Seal, remove air from bag and cook sous-vide at 65°C (150°F) for 12 hours (see page 40 for sous-vide explanation). Strip the leaves from the cavolo nero and discard the stems. Drop the leaves into a large saucepan of boiling water and simmer for 3 minutes. Drain well, squeezing out any remaining liquid using the back of a ladle or a small bowl, then chop coarsely. Preheat the oven to 200°C (400°F). In a bowl combine the breadcrumbs and cheeses. Put a frying pan over medium heat and add the butter and oil. When they begin to sizzle, add the onion and lightly fry for 3–4 minutes until transparent. Add the garlic and sauté for 1 minute, then add the cavolo nero. Sauté for 2 minutes, add the cream, increase the heat to high and cook until the liquid has evaporated and there is just enough cream to coat the cavolo nero. Spoon the mixture into a baking dish to fit snugly (the mixture should be 3–4 cm/1¼–1½ in deep). Spread the breadcrumb mixture over the top and bake for 20 minutes until golden brown.

Meanwhile, make the salsa dragoncello. Moisten the bread with the vinegar, then put the bread in a mortar with the tarragon, garlic and a couple of good pinches of salt. Pound to a paste, add the olive oil and mix well. Season and add more oil if necessary. Bone the lamb (it will fall away easily), then grill or barbecue whole to form a crust. Cut into chunks and drizzle with salsa dragoncello. Serve with the cavolo nero gratin.

SERVES 6   WINE: Syrah

SLOW-BRAISED BEEF SHOVLDER

GRILLED LAMB LOIN CUTLETS
COTOLETTE D'AGNELLO ALLA GRIGLIA

INGREDIENTS

100 g (3½ oz) fatty part of prosciutto (or bacon fat or pancetta), cut into small cubes

3 garlic cloves

1 small rosemary sprig

1 tablespoon marjoram leaves

16 lamb loin cutlets, at room temperature

METHOD

Put the prosciutto fat in a food processor with the garlic, rosemary and marjoram and blend to a paste (or pound in a mortar). Smear the paste on both sides of each cutlet, season with a little salt and barbecue or grill. Serve immediately with a tomato salad.

SERVES 4   WINE: Cesanese del Piglio

SLOW-BRAISED BEEF SHOULDER
STRACOTTO DI SPALLA DI MANZO

INGREDIENTS

1 carrot

1 celery heart

1 brown onion

4 garlic cloves

1 × 1.5–1.75 kg (3 lb 5 oz– 3 lb 12 oz) piece beef blade, trimmed of fat and membrane

⅓ cup (50 g/1¾ oz) plain (all-purpose) flour

150 ml (5 fl oz) extra virgin olive oil

3 cups (750 ml/26 fl oz) dry white wine

8 tinned tomatoes, mashed

2 bay leaves

1 cup chopped parsley

30–40 French shallots, trimmed

METHOD

Put the carrot, celery, onion and garlic in a food processor and pulse until finely chopped. Dust the beef with the flour. Heat one-third of the olive oil in a large frying pan and cook the beef on medium heat until well browned on both sides. Transfer the meat to a tray. Heat half the remaining oil in the pan on medium heat, then add the chopped vegetables and garlic and fry for 5–6 minutes until softened. Add the meat and turn the heat up to high. Add the wine and tomatoes and bring to the boil, then reduce the heat to very low. Add the bay leaves, half the parsley and 2–3 good pinches of salt. Cover and simmer for 2½ hours. Meanwhile, heat the remaining oil in a wide frying pan and cook the shallots until well browned. Once the beef is cooked, add the shallots and remaining parsley. Simmer, uncovered, for 20 minutes until the shallots are tender. Season with a little more salt if necessary and add a few turns of pepper before serving.

SERVES 8–10   WINE: Cesanese di Olevano Romano

CABBAGE ROLLS WITH OXTAIL AND CHESTNUT
VERZE RIPIENE IN BRODO

INGREDIENTS

1 Savoy cabbage, tough outer leaves discarded

50 g (1¾ oz) butter

1 large brown onion, finely diced

2 garlic cloves, crushed

5 tablespoons finely chopped bone marrow

200 g (7 oz) cooked peeled chestnuts

3 tablespoons chopped parsley

8 tablespoons grated Grana Padano

1 cup stale breadcrumbs

SLOW-COOKED OXTAIL

3 kg (6 lb 12 oz) oxtail, cut into 5 cm (2 in) long pieces by your butcher

2 brown onions, quartered

3 carrots, cut into large pieces

2 celery sticks, cut into chunks

5 ripe tomatoes, halved

2 thyme sprigs

2 bay leaves

1 handful parsley stalks

1 teaspoon black peppercorns

METHOD

To cook the oxtail, put all the ingredients in a stockpot, cover with cold water and bring to a simmer. Simmer covered for about 5 hours or until the meat is falling off the bone. During the cooking, skim off any impurities that rise to the surface. Remove the oxtail from the broth and let cool. Strain the broth through a couple of layers of muslin (cheesecloth) and cool in the refrigerator, then remove and discard the solidified fat that has surfaced. Take the oxtail meat off the bones and shred it. Set the oxtail broth and shredded meat aside.

Carefully remove 8 similar-sized leaves from the cabbage, keeping the leaves whole. (Use the remaining cabbage for another dish.) Blanch the leaves in boiling salted water for 3 minutes, then refresh in cold water. Pat dry and set aside. Heat the butter in a frying pan and lightly fry the onion until soft. Add the garlic and gently fry for 2 minutes. Combine with the bone marrow, oxtail meat, chestnuts, parsley and half the Grana Padano and season well. Add half the breadcrumbs. If the mixture is too moist, gradually add more of the breadcrumbs until you have a relatively dry mixture. Lay the cabbage leaves on a clean work surface. Take 2 tablespoons of the stuffing, shape into a small ball and put on the bottom third of a cabbage leaf. If there is an excess amount of leaf around the sides (which would make the roll too big), trim the leaf to an adequate size. Fold the two sides in and then roll up to make a neat parcel. Repeat using the rest of the stuffing and cabbage leaves. Put the rolls in a heavy-based saucepan so they all fit in one layer, then pour in enough oxtail broth to cover. Bring slowly to the boil and simmer for 10 minutes to warm the rolls. Serve in deep bowls, ladling in some of the broth and finishing with the remaining Grana Padano.

SERVES 4   WINE: Cesanese del Piglio

SAUSAGES BRAISED WITH LENTILS WITH POLENTA
SALSICCIE IN UMIDO CON LENTICCHIE DI ONANO E POLENTA

This hearty dish is perhaps best enjoyed during the colder months. There's a Roman tradition of serving a large board of steaming polenta (cornmeal) topped with all manner of meats, including sausages. When the sausages are braised with lentils, they make the dish even heartier. If you are able to procure the unique Onano lentils for this recipe, it will be all the better.

INGREDIENTS

250 g (9 oz) Onano lentils (or other similar lentils), well washed

800 g (1 lb 12 oz) pork and fennel sausages

¼ cup (60 ml/2 fl oz) extra virgin olive oil

1 brown onion, minced

1 small celery heart, minced

1 carrot, minced

2 garlic cloves, minced

1 tablespoon marjoram leaves

½ cup (125 ml/4 fl oz) dry white wine

200 g (7 oz) tinned tomatoes, mashed

1 quantity cooked soft polenta (cornmeal) (see page 41)

METHOD

Cook the lentils for 15–20 minutes in a saucepan of lightly salted boiling water until almost cooked. Drain, reserving the cooking liquid. Skin 1 of the sausages and finely chop the sausage meat. Heat the olive oil in a large saucepan and lightly fry the chopped sausage meat with the onion, celery, carrot, garlic and marjoram for 2–3 minutes until fragrant. Prick the remaining sausages 2–3 times with a fork and add to the pan. Fry for a couple of minutes, then add the wine. When it has all evaporated, add the lentils and 3 ladlefuls of the cooking liquid. Add the tomatoes and simmer slowly for 15–20 minutes until the sausages and lentils are cooked. If necessary, add more lentil cooking liquid. The result should be a thick, creamy, lentil-laden sauce. Season and serve on freshly cooked soft polenta.

SERVES 6–8   WINE: Cesanese del Piglio

ONANO LENTILS ARE GROWN ON THE VOLCANIC, SANDY SOILS AROUND THE TOWN OF ONANO, PROVINCE OF VITERBO, ABOUT 80 KILOMETRES NORTH OF ROME. THEIR COLOUR IS LIGHT BROWN TENDING TO GREY AND SOMETIMES A DEEP ROSY-YELLOW. THEY WERE ALMOST EXTINCT IN THE 1960S BUT TODAY, UNDER THE PRESIDIO SLOW FOOD, THEY HAVE SURVIVED IN SMALL PLOTS, INCREASINGLY ORGANICALLY GROWN, AND ARE FINDING MARKETS IN ITALY AND BEYOND. THEIR TEXTURE IS CREAMY AND VELVETY, WITH SCENTS OF HAY AND CAMOMILE.

LAZIO
DOLCI

TOZZETTI BISCUITS
TOZZETTI

These are similar to the cantucci of Tuscany. They are a true biscuit in that they are cooked twice.

INGREDIENTS

500 g (1 lb 2 oz) plain (all-purpose) flour

½ teaspoon baking powder

4 eggs

1 egg white

200 g (7 oz) caster (superfine) sugar

150 g (5½ oz) softened unsalted butter

¼ cup (60 ml/2 fl oz) sweet passito wine (such as vin santo, moscato passito or aleatico)

70 g (2½ oz) almonds

70 g (2½ oz) hazelnuts

70 g (2½ oz) pine nuts

grated zest of 1 lemon

1 teaspoon anise seeds

METHOD

Preheat the oven to 180°C (350°F) and line a baking tray with baking paper. Sift the flour and baking powder together onto a clean work surface and make a well in the middle. Beat the eggs, egg white and sugar together, then add to the flour along with the butter. Add the wine, nuts, lemon zest and anise seeds and bring together quickly to form a dough. Shape the dough into a roll about 3 cm (1¼ in) wide and put on the baking tray. Bake for 15–20 minutes, then remove from the oven and let cool a little. Reduce the oven temperature to 120°C (250°F). Using a serrated knife, cut across the roll to make biscuits (cookies) about 1.5 cm (⅝ in) thick. Put the biscuits on 1–2 baking trays and return to the oven to dry out for 5–10 minutes. The biscuits will keep indefinitely in an airtight container.

MAKES 40–50   WINE: Moscato di Terracina

OPEN FIG TART
CROSTATA DI FICHI

INGREDIENTS

1 quantity shortcrust pastry no. 2 (see page 47)

4 egg yolks

⅔ cup (150 g/5½ oz) caster (superfine) sugar

60 g (2¼ oz) plain (all-purpose) flour

2 cups (500 ml/17 fl oz) milk

zest of 1 lemon, removed using a vegetable peeler or sharp knife

100 ml (3½ fl oz) thin (pouring) cream

1 kg (2 lb 4 oz) ripe figs, trimmed and halved

METHOD

Line a baking tray with silicone paper. Roll out the pastry to a rough thickness of 5–6 mm (¼ in). Cut a 28 cm (11¼ in) disc from the pastry and transfer to the baking tray. Refrigerate for 30 minutes. Meanwhile, preheat the oven to 180°C (350°F). Bake the pastry for 20–25 minutes until golden, then let cool. Beat the egg yolks, sugar and flour together until pale and creamy. Bring the milk and lemon zest almost to the boil in a saucepan. Remove and discard the lemon zest, then slowly pour the hot milk, whisking continuously, into the egg/sugar/flour mixture. Return the mixture to the saucepan and cook on a low heat, whisking continually, until the custard thickens. Transfer to a bowl and cool completely. Whip the cream to firm peaks and fold into the cooled custard. Spread the custard evenly onto the pastry using a spatula and gently press in the figs, cut side up. Slice and serve.

SERVES 8   WINE: Aleatico di Gradoli DOC

CHERRY CREAM TORTA
TORTA DI CILIEGIE ALLA CREMA

This recipe is from Enoteca La Torre, a restaurant in the ancient city of Viterbo, 100 km (62 miles) north of Rome.

INGREDIENTS

6 eggs

180 g (6½ oz) sugar

30 g (1 oz) unsalted butter, melted

2 cups (300 g/10½ oz) plain (all-purpose) flour

1 teaspoon baking powder

1 cup (250 ml/9 fl oz) milk

350 g (12 oz) pitted cherries, each chopped into 5–6 pieces

CHERRY CREAM

1 litre (35 fl oz) milk

3 egg yolks

300 g (10½ oz) sugar

130 g (4¾ oz) plain (all-purpose) flour

150 g (5½ oz) pitted cherries

METHOD

Preheat the oven to 170°C (340°F) and butter and flour a 20 cm (8 in) cake tin. Beat the eggs with the sugar until creamy, then add the melted butter, flour, baking powder and milk. Mix well and fold in the chopped cherries. Transfer to the tin and bake for 40 minutes or until a skewer inserted comes out clean. Cool in tin.

To make the cherry cream, bring the milk almost to the boil. Whisk the egg yolks, sugar and flour together, then whisk them into the hot milk and keep cooking and whisking until the mixture thickens. Add the cherries and remove from the heat. Cool. Serve the torta cold with the cherry cream.

SERVES 8   WINE: Moscato di Terracina Amabile

RICOTTA PUDDING
BUDINO DI RICOTTA

Ricotta seems to taste better from Rome southwards – perhaps it's because it's made with sheep's milk. The taste is rich and creamy and needs very little added to turn it into a wonderful dessert. Candied cedro is readily available in continental delicatessens and specialty food shops.

INGREDIENTS

1 tablespoon unsalted butter

1 tablespoon fine rice flour

500 g (1 lb 2 oz) ricotta cheese, as fresh as possible

5 eggs

2 tablespoons plain (all-purpose) flour, sifted

1 tablespoon candied orange peel, finely diced

1 tablespoon candied cedro (citron), finely diced

grated zest of 1 lemon

2 tablespoons white rum

120 g (4¼ oz) caster (superfine) sugar

1 teaspoon ground cinnamon

METHOD

Preheat the oven to 160°C (320°F). Grease a 1 litre (35 fl oz) pudding basin (mould) with the butter and dust with the rice flour. Pass the ricotta through a sieve into a bowl. Separate 4 of the eggs, then add the remaining whole egg and 4 of the yolks to the ricotta and mix thoroughly. Add the flour, candied orange peel and cedro, lemon zest, rum and 100 g (3½ oz) of the sugar. In a separate bowl, whisk the egg whites to firm peaks, then gently fold into the ricotta mixture. Pour the mixture into the mould and bake for 30 minutes. Cool before unmoulding. To serve, dust with the cinnamon and remaining sugar.

SERVES 8   WINE: Moscato di Terracina

LE MARCHE

LE MARCHE

THE MARCHES

THE INLAND BORDER TO THE WEST OF THIS PROVINCE RUNS ALONG THE UMBRIAN APENNINES, EMILIA-ROMAGNA AND THE TINY REPUBLIC OF SAN MARINO TO ITS NORTH, A SMALL INTRUSION OF TOSCANA TO THE NORTH-WEST, AND ABRUZZO AND LAZIO TO THE SOUTH. TO THE EAST, THERE IS A 170-KILOMETRE (105-MILE) STRETCH OF THE ADRIATIC SEA.

Most of Le Marche's 9700 square kilometres (3745 square miles) are mountainous or hilly. Even today, the mountainous nature of the region means it can only be traversed north to south on rough roads. The Holy Roman Empire began (or ended) here, and the name derives from the marquises (marchesi) who governed the areas – the marches – that were border zones.

Although agriculture has diminished in importance since the 1980s in Le Marche, cereals (wheat) are grown and livestock (cattle and sheep) graze in the Sibillini Mountains, and fish from the Adriatic are an important resource.

An amalgamation of influences – a complex history, a population of skilled artisans and craftspeople, a strong intellectual tradition (the University of Urbino dominates that town) and a rich musical heritage (the best accordions are made in the province, and Rossini was a native) – has resulted in a complex and divided cuisine. Inland there is the one labelled by an Italian gastronomic writer as 'rough and ready', but along the coast and in other areas of Le Marche there is complex and intricate food that relies heavily on stuffing, or *in porchetta*.

Everything from olives to wild boars and rabbits is stuffed in Le Marche. Olive ascolane are green olives stuffed with meat and prosciutto, then dipped in flour, egg and breadcrumbs and fried. This is a speciality of the town of Ascoli that has spread around the world. Other stuffed dishes include mutton head and pork rinds, and there are elaborate preparations such as ciarimboli (entrails seasoned with garlic, salt, pepper and rosemary and grilled), and baby snails stuffed with chicken gizzards.

From the 'rough and ready' side of the culinary equation comes what is perhaps the best-known dish of the region, the curiously named vincisgrassi – a lasagna of mushrooms, chicken livers, veal sweetbreads and brains, onions, butter, nutmeg and vin santo. It was invented in 1799 by a chef of the town of Macerata, and named for Prince Alfred zu Windischgrätz, the head of the Austrian occupation forces that were based in Ancona at the end of the 18th century.

From the sea come crocette (sea snails), served in a hot and spicy sauce, and simple grilled fish, or pesce ai ferri all'ancontena – fish grilled in the style of Ancona, which locals swear is the best in Italy.

Verdicchio is the main thing to remember about Le Marche wine. Two of the best known and loved are Verdicchio dei Castelli di Jesi and Verdicchio di Matelica. Given the long coastline and excellent seafood of the province, it doesn't hurt that both these wines make wonderful companions to fish and shellfish of all kinds.

Montepulciano is the dominant red grape, and Rosso Piceno, in the hills above Ascoli Piceno, is the largest production zone. Its wines are made primarily with montepulciano and sangiovese. The other DOCG making magnificent montepulcianos is Rosso Cònero, the home of the 'Super-Marchigiano', which was only promoted to that status (from DOC) in 2004. There is a growing crop of these Super-Marchigianos, usually with an IGT designation and incorporating cabernet sauvignon, merlot and syrah.

The verdicchio of Le Marche was used to make one of the first spumantes in Italy in the 19th century, and good versions are still made in Jesi and Matelica. In addition, there are botrytis-affected verdicchios.

SONG WINES

In 1997, a Rosso Cònero maker, Antonio Terni, decided to name some of his best barrels after the Bob Dylan song 'Visions of Johanna'. He called the wine Visions of J. Having tried some of Terni's wine, Dylan asked Terni to make a wine for him, which he did. Named Planet Waves after a Dylan album, this one was made from montepulciano and merlot. Terni described the wine as 'a Dylanesque cross between the strength of the noble Montepulciano d'Abruzzo and the softness of the Merlot'. The back label carries both Terni's and Dylan's signatures.

LE MARCHE

ANTI-PASTI

FRIED STUFFED ASCOLI OLIVES
OLIVE FRITTE ALL'ASCOLANA

In Le Marche this recipe is made exclusively using the olive variety known locally as tenera ascolana. These are grown around the town of Ascoli Piceno in southern Le Marche and are a particularly tender green olive that is quite large, like a queen or Bella di Cerignola. Though the flavour and texture of Ascolane olives are unique, the recipe can be made with any large green olives. To pit the olives, take a sharp knife and, starting at the stem end, cut around the stone from top to bottom as you would when peeling an apple or orange. Keep close to the stone and remove as much flesh as possible. You should have a single ribbon of olive flesh that can be rolled back up into the shape of the olive. This method is called 'a spirale' or 'in a spiral'. The stuffing is put into the space where the stone was and then the flesh closes around. Once the olive is crumbed it will look round and intact.

INGREDIENTS

150 g (5½ oz) good-quality bread, 1–2 days old, crusts removed

200 ml (7 fl oz) vegetable broth (see page 49)

⅓ cup (80 ml/2½ fl oz) extra virgin olive oil, plus extra for frying

1 small brown onion, chopped

1 celery stick, chopped

1 carrot, chopped

2 garlic cloves, lightly crushed

1 × 200 g (7 oz) beef loin

1 × 200 g (7 oz) veal loin

1 × 150 g (5½ oz) pork shoulder

1 × 150 g (5½ oz) chicken breast

1 cup (250 ml/9 fl oz) dry white wine

9 eggs

150 g (5½ oz) Parmigiano Reggiano, grated

100 g (3½ oz) pecorino cheese, grated

3 tablespoons finely chopped parsley

½ teaspoon grated nutmeg

48 large green olives (preferably tenere ascolane variety), pitted as per recipe introduction

120 g (4¼ oz) plain (all-purpose) flour

200 g (7 oz) fine breadcrumbs

METHOD

Cut the bread into rough cubes and put in a bowl with the vegetable broth. Set aside. Heat the olive oil in a heavy-based casserole dish. Add the onion, celery, carrot and garlic and fry on medium heat for 2 minutes, then add the whole pieces of the various meats and fry for 2–3 minutes until browned. Pour in the wine and cook until half of it has evaporated. Turn the heat to low, cover and cook for 30 minutes. Remove from the heat and let cool. Drain the bread and squeeze out any excess liquid. Put the bread, meat and vegetables through a mincer (or pulse through a food processor) into a bowl. Add 6 of the eggs and the cheeses, parsley and nutmeg. Season and mix until well incorporated. Shape the stuffing into small egg shapes and wrap an olive around each one, pressing lightly to hold in the stuffing. Put the flour, remaining eggs (whisked) and breadcrumbs in 3 separate bowls. Dust the stuffed olives in flour, then dredge in egg and finally coat with breadcrumbs. Do this twice for each olive so that they are 'double crumbed'. Pour oil into a wide frying pan to a depth of at least 3 cm (1¼ in). When the oil is hot enough, drop in a few olives at a time and fry until golden. Drain on paper towels and serve hot.

MAKES 48

WINE: Falerio Colli Ascolani (Trebbiano, Passerina e Pecorino)

PECORINO AND HONEY BREAD
PANE CON PECORINO E MIELE

This is from Maria Pia Cioccoloni's beautiful restaurant and guesthouse, Il Giardino degli Ulivi, in the hamlet of Castelsantangelo which sits in the rolling foothills of the Sibillini Mountains in western Le Marche. Maria mixes traditional dishes with inventive interpretations of the local cuisine. I ate this bread with the special salame di Fabriano, which is made in the province of Ancona and studded with cubes of pearly pork fat.

INGREDIENTS

1 kg (2 lb 4 oz) soft wheat flour
(preferably type '0')

50 g (1¾ oz) fresh yeast

70 ml (2¼ fl oz) extra virgin
olive oil

pinch of sugar

100 g (3½ oz) aged pecorino
cheese, grated

100 g (3½ oz) young pecorino
cheese, cut into 5 mm
(¼ in) cubes

80 g (2¾ oz) light-coloured
honey (such as clover
or acacia)

METHOD

Put the flour on your work surface and make a well in it. Dissolve the yeast in ½ cup (125 ml/4 fl oz) warm water. Add this to the well along with the olive oil, sugar, grated pecorino and a pinch of salt. Add enough water (around 500–600 ml/17–21 fl oz) to make a smooth dough that is not sticky or wet. Knead well for 5–6 minutes until elastic, then incorporate the cubes of pecorino and put the dough in a large bowl. Cover with a damp tea towel (dish towel) and set aside in a warm spot in the kitchen for 5 hours, knocking the dough down 2–3 times during this period. Preheat the oven to 190°C (375°F). Work the honey into the dough (you may need to scatter a little flour on your work surface), then divide it into 8 small, long loaves and put them on baking trays. Cut diagonal slashes on the top of each loaf and let them rise for 15 minutes. Brush with water and bake for 20 minutes until golden.

SERVES 8–10   WINE: Vernaccia di Serrapetrona

GRILLED BORLOTTI-BEAN POLENTA
POLENTA GRIGLIATA AI FAGIOLI

INGREDIENTS

1 quantity soft polenta
(cornmeal; see page 41)

2 tablespoons extra virgin
olive oil

1 brown onion, thinly sliced

150 g (5½ oz) cooked or
tinned borlotti beans

tomato salsa (see page 50 or
page 178)

METHOD

While you are cooking the polenta, heat the olive oil in a separate small saucepan and lightly fry the onion for a few minutes until softened and almost dissolved but not coloured. Add the beans and a couple of tablespoons of water. Season and cook gently until the water has evaporated. A few minutes before the polenta is ready, add the beans, onion and any pan juices to it. Mix well, then turn out into a shallow tray to a depth of 2 cm (¾ in). Let cool and set, then cut into 3 cm × 5 cm (1¼ in × 2 in) rectangles and either grill (broil) or bake until crisp. Serve hot with tomato salsa.

SERVES 8   WINE: Rosso Piceno

GRILLED PEAR AND CACIOTTA
PERE ABATE E CACIOTTA DI MUCCA ALLA GRIGLIA

This is another dish from the beautiful restaurant and guesthouse Il Giardino degli Ulivi (see Pecorino and Honey Bread opposite). The pears used by Maria for this dish are abate, a variety that is grown widely in central Italy. Substitute ripe williams or bosc; they should be soft but still a little firm. The cheese is a typical 20–30-day-old caciotta made from either cow's or sheep's milk, small–medium in size (800 g–1.2 kg), round and made from raw milk. The curds are cooked and pressed into their forms before being salted; the cheese is then aged for a month or so until the flavour is sweet, delicate and slightly acidic. If you can find a Casciotta d'Urbino DOP it is perfect for this dish.

INGREDIENTS

4 pears (preferably abate, but williams or bosc will do), peeled, halved and cored

300 g (10½ oz) caciotta cheese, thinly sliced

METHOD

Heat the grill (broiler) to hot. Choose round serving plates and cut circles of baking paper to fit them, then put the paper circles on baking trays. Cut the pears lengthways into 3 mm slices and arrange on the paper circles to cover the paper. Put the caciotta slices in a single layer on the pears and grill (broil) for a minute or two until the cheese is melted and bubbling. Make sure not to burn the cheese as it will go bitter. Serve hot.

SERVES 8   WINE: Offida Pecorino

SKATE AND CHICKPEA SALAD
INSALATINA DI RAZZA E CECI

INGREDIENTS

1 lemon

1 × 1 kg (2 lb 4 oz) skate wing, skin left on

1 brown onion, quartered

1 celery stick, cut into chunks

1 carrot, cut into chunks

450 g cooked chickpeas

⅓ cup (80 ml/2½ fl oz) extra virgin olive oil

4 tablespoons chopped parsley

2 tablespoons finely snipped chives

1 celery heart, thinly sliced

METHOD

Finely grate the lemon's zest and set aside. Cut the remaining lemon into quarters and put in a saucepan with the skate, onion, celery and carrot. Pour in water to cover. Bring to the boil, then immediately remove from the heat, cover and let cool for about 20 minutes. While the skate is still warm, peel off the skin and strip the flesh carefully from the cartilage. Put the flesh in a bowl with the chickpeas. Combine the olive oil, parsley, chives, celery and lemon zest and add to the skate and chickpeas. Season and mix gently before serving.

SERVES 6   WINE: Offida

WILD HERBS BAKED IN A MOULD
SFORMATO DI ERBE DI CAMPO

Throughout spring and summer people have traditionally gathered wild plants from Italian meadows to use in various dishes. The plants include dandelion (tarassaco), sculpit (sgrizoi), borage, wild rocket, wood sorrel, wild beet leaves and spinach. If wild plants are not available, use spinach, sorrel, and young beet and rocket (arugula) leaves.

INGREDIENTS

30 g (1 oz) unsalted butter, plus extra for greasing

500 g (1 lb 2 oz) mixed leaves (see recipe introduction), well washed and dried

80 g (2¾ oz) pecorino cheese (3–4 months old), thinly sliced

80 g (2¾ oz) Grana Padano, grated

2 eggs, whisked

METHOD

Preheat the oven to 170°C (340°F) and butter a 750 ml (26 fl oz) ovenproof oval ceramic pudding mould with lip. Heat the butter in a large frying pan and add the leaves. Stir using a wooden spoon until the leaves wilt and begin to release liquid. Remove from the heat and mix in the cheeses. Leave for 5 minutes, then add the eggs and season. Transfer the mixture to the mould, then put the mould in a baking dish and pour in water to come halfway up the sides of the mould. Bake for 30 minutes. Remove from the oven and let cool a little, then unmould onto a serving plate. Serve warm or at room temperature.

SERVES 8   WINE: Verdicchio brut

LE MARCHE

PRIMI

OYSTER AND POTATO SOUP
ZUPPA DI OSTRICHE

Ideally, the oysters used here will be freshly shucked and their liquor used to add extra flavour to the soup.

INGREDIENTS

24 freshly shucked oysters, liquor reserved

½ cup (125 ml/4 fl oz) extra virgin olive oil, plus extra for drizzling

1 large brown onion, sliced

2 garlic cloves, minced

½ celery heart, sliced

400 g (14 oz) potatoes, sliced

1 bay leaf

½ cup (125 ml/4 fl oz) dry white wine

white pepper

1 tablespoon chopped parsley

METHOD

Strain the oyster liquor through muslin (cheesecloth) to remove any grit, then set aside. Heat the olive oil in a large frying pan and lightly fry the onion and garlic for a minute or two. Add the celery, potatoes, bay leaf and wine, then turn up the heat and cook until the wine has all but evaporated. Pour in enough water to just cover the vegetables and bring to the boil. Turn the heat down, cover and simmer for 40–50 minutes until the vegetables are soft. Using a fork, roughly mash so that the soup still has texture. Add the oyster liquor and season with white pepper and salt (if needed). Add the oysters and parsley and simmer for a minute until the oysters are barely cooked. Ladle into soup bowls and drizzle with a little oil. Serve with crusty bread.

SERVES 4   WINE: Verdicchio di Matelica

CRAB WITH BROAD BEAN AND OLIVE SAUCE
GRANCHIO CON SALSA DI FAVE E OLIVE

INGREDIENTS

200 g (7 oz) double-peeled broad beans

1 tablespoon extra virgin olive oil

1 small garlic clove, minced

½ cup (125 ml/4 fl oz) thin (pouring) cream

fine white pepper

240 g (8½ oz) cooked crabmeat, picked free of shell

12 small black olives, pitted and chopped

METHOD

Bring a saucepan of salted water to a rolling boil. Throw in the broad beans for 45 seconds, then drain. Heat the olive oil in a small saucepan and gently fry the garlic for a minute, making sure not to let it colour. Add the cream and three-quarters of the blanched broad beans. Bring to a simmer and cook gently for a couple of minutes until the cream has reduced and thickened. Remove from the heat and season with salt and a small pinch of white pepper, then blend in a food processor until smooth. Put a few spoonfuls of sauce on each of 4 serving plates. Place even portions of the crabmeat in the centre, scatter over the olives and remaining broad beans, and serve.

SERVES 4   WINE: Offida Passerina

SPAGHETTI WITH PORK CHEEK AND MUSHROOMS
SPAGHETTI CON GUANCIALE E FUNGHI

Italians don't tend to prepare pork-cheek dishes from the fresh product: they salt-cure and air-dry the cheeks in much the same way as is done for prosciutto. The cured pork cheek, known as guanciale, is then used in classic dishes. Carbonara, for example, should be made using guanciale rather than pancetta — there is a subtle but significant difference in taste. As a fresh cut of meat, it needs to be trimmed of its covering of fat to reveal a triangular piece of flesh with lightly coloured collagen veins. It can be slow-braised whole in much the same way as osso buco or beef cheeks. The result is gelatinous and very tasty.

INGREDIENTS

20 g (¾ oz) dried porcini mushrooms

80 g (2¾ oz) butter

100 ml (3½ fl oz) extra virgin olive oil

1 leek, white part only, cut into 1 cm cubes

2 garlic cloves, finely chopped

350 g (12 oz) mixed mushrooms (Swiss brown, oyster, king brown and button), cut into bite-sized pieces

1 cup (250 ml/9 fl oz) white wine

½ cup chopped parsley

2 pork cheeks, trimmed of fat and sinew

2 tablespoons extra virgin olive oil

600 g (1 lb 5 oz) dried spaghetti

grated parmesan cheese

METHOD

Soak the porcini in ½ cup (125 ml/4 fl oz) cold water for 20 minutes, then drain. Meanwhile, put the butter and olive oil in a wide frying pan on medium heat. Once the butter has melted, add the leek and garlic and lightly fry for 2 minutes. Add the mushrooms (including the porcini), turn the heat to high and fry for 2 minutes. Pour in the wine and boil for a minute or so, then turn the heat down, add the parsley and simmer for 5 minutes. Turn off the heat and season. Cut the pork into very thin strips about 6 cm (2½ in) long. Heat a separate large frying pan on medium–high heat and add the pork in one layer. Season. Once the pork starts to crisp and colour, turn to crisp the other side. Add the pork to the mushroom mixture and stir. Cook the spaghetti in plenty of boiling salted water, then drain and toss with the pork and mushrooms. Serve with grated parmesan.

SERVES 6   WINE: Rosso Colli del Trasimeno

TACCONI PASTA WITH GRASS PEAS, BROAD BEANS AND PORK CHEEK

TACCONI DI FAVE CON CICERCHIA, FAVE FRESCHE E GUANCIALE

Tacconi is a type of pasta from Le Marche that is made with various flours – in this case dried broad-bean flour. Perhaps the most interesting part of the dish from a historical perspective is the use of cicerchia (Lathyrus sativus), an ancient legume native to the Mediterranean that has been grown in central Italy, especially Le Marche, for millennia. Known as the grass pea in English, it is high in protein and grown in many arid parts of the world because it can produce a good crop even in poor soil. There was a slow decline in its production in Italy until recently, when it was rediscovered along with interest in traditional dishes. If cicerchia can't be found, use a small dried bean such as cannellini. The pork cheek used in this dish is cured in much the same way as pancetta. If guanciale is not available, pancetta can be substituted.

INGREDIENTS

150 g (5½ oz) cicerchia (grass peas), soaked in plenty of cold water for 8 hours

⅓ cup (80 ml/2½ fl oz) extra virgin olive oil

1 brown onion, finely chopped

1 garlic clove, minced

120 g (4¼ oz) guanciale (or pancetta), finely diced

200 g (7 oz) ripe cherry tomatoes, quartered

½ cup (95 g/3¼ oz) double-peeled broad beans

½ tablespoon chopped marjoram

1 tablespoon chopped parsley

1 quantity tacconi pasta dough (see page 44)

100 g (3½ oz) Parmigiano Reggiano, grated

METHOD

Rinse the cicerchia well and discard any small skins that have come off. Put in a large saucepan with 4 litres (7 pints) cold water (don't add salt), partly cover and bring to the boil on medium heat. Immediately turn the heat down and simmer for 40 minutes, skimming off any impurities that rise to the surface. Let the cicerchia cool in the cooking liquid. Heat the olive oil gently in a frying pan and add the onion, garlic and guanciale. Fry gently for 2–3 minutes, then add the tomatoes and cook for 5 minutes. Drain the cicerchia, keeping about 150 ml (5 fl oz) of the cooking liquid. Add the cicerchia, broad beans and herbs to the pan and simmer for 10 minutes, adding the reserved cooking liquid as needed. Season. Cook the tacconi in plenty of boiling salted water, then drain and toss with the sauce. Sprinkle on the Parmigiano-Reggiano and serve.

SERVES 6   WINE: Offida Pecorino

POLENTA WITH CLAMS IN WHITE WINE
POLENTA CON VONGOLE IN VINO BIANCO

INGREDIENTS

200 g (7 oz) polenta
(cornmeal)
3 garlic cloves, minced
2 tablespoons extra virgin
olive oil
1 kg (2 lb 4 oz) clams
(vongole)
2 ripe tomatoes, chopped
½ cup chopped parsley
2–3 red chillies, chopped
1 cup (250 ml/9 fl oz) dry
white wine

METHOD

Bring 800 ml (28 fl oz) water and 1 teaspoon salt to a rolling boil. Whisk in the polenta and keep whisking until it thickens. Turn down the heat, cover and simmer for at least 1 hour. Every 10 minutes, stir using a wooden spoon. In a large saucepan, lightly fry the garlic in the olive oil for 30 seconds, making sure it doesn't brown. Add the clams, tomatoes, parsley and chillies, then turn the heat up to high and give the clams a good stir for a few seconds. Pour in the wine and put the lid on the pan for 3–4 minutes. Check that all the clams have opened – sometimes it's just a matter of giving the pan a good shake or stirring them so they have room to open. Remove the clams from the saucepan and take the meat from the shells. Reduce the cooking liquid by half, then return the clam meat to the sauce and season. Spoon the polenta into bowls and serve the clams and sauce on top.

SERVES 6   WINE: Verdicchio dei Castelli di Jesi

POTATOES WITH ONIONS AND PANCETTA
PATATE CON CIPOLLE E PANCETTA

The pancetta in this recipe can be substituted with streaky bacon, or left out entirely if need be.

INGREDIENTS

1 kg (2 lb 4 oz) boiling
potatoes, unpeeled
2 tablespoons extra virgin
olive oil
1 large brown onion, thinly
sliced
2 tablespoons finely sliced
pancetta
1 teaspoon chopped thyme

METHOD

Simmer the potatoes in salted water for 30 minutes or so until tender. Drain and cool a little, then peel and slice thinly. Heat the olive oil in a wide frying pan and fry the onion and pancetta until golden. Add the potatoes and fry until coloured. Squash roughly using a fork, then add the thyme and fry on medium–high heat for about 10 minutes, constantly scraping and stirring so the mixture doesn't catch and burn. You should have a mixture of soft and crispy bits. Season and serve as a side dish with scallops, or roasted or braised meat.

SERVES 6   WINE: Verdicchio if serving with scallops

MUSSELS WITH SNOW PEAS AND PANCETTA
MUSCIOLI CON TACCOLE E PANCETTA

INGREDIENTS

1 kg (2 lb 4 oz) mussels, scrubbed and de-bearded

2 tablespoons extra virgin olive oil

80 g (2¾ oz) pancetta, sliced 3 mm thick, cut into matchsticks

350 g (12 oz) snow peas (mangetout), trimmed and thickly sliced lengthways

1 small leek, white part only, thinly sliced

1 small brown onion, thinly sliced

1 teaspoon minced ginger

1 garlic clove, minced

1 tablespoon finely snipped chives

1 tablespoon finely chopped parsley

METHOD

Put the mussels in large saucepan, cover and bring to the boil on high heat. Shake the pan after 2–3 minutes to help the mussels open. Remove from the heat and strain, collecting the cooking liquid. Strain the liquid through muslin (cheesecloth) to remove any grit or shell. Remove the mussel meat from the shells and set the meat aside. Heat the olive oil in a frying pan or wok, then add the pancetta and fry for 30 seconds on medium heat. Turn the heat up to high and add the snow peas, leek, onion, ginger and garlic. Stir until the snow peas wilt but still have a little 'bite' to them. Stir in the chives and parsley, then add the mussel meat, 100 ml (3½ fl oz) of the cooking liquid, season and stir. Serve immediately.

SERVES 4   WINE: Offida Pecorino

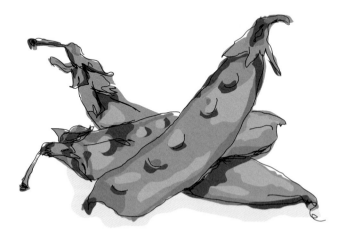

MUSSELS WITH SNOW PEAS AND PANCETTA

FISH CAKES WITH BRAISED CAULIFLOWER
POLPETTE DI PESCE CON CAVOLFIORE IN UMIDO

INGREDIENTS

1 brown onion, thinly sliced

200 g (7 oz) firm-fleshed fish fillets (such as blue eye, whiting or snapper)

200 g (7 oz) raw prawn (shrimp) meat

60 g (2¼ oz) day-old bread, crusts removed

½ cup (125 ml/4 fl oz) clear fish broth (or water)

2 eggs, whisked

2 tablespoons finely chopped parsley

plain (all-purpose) flour

breadcrumbs

extra virgin olive oil

BRAISED CAULIFLOWER

1 small brown onion, finely diced

1 garlic clove, minced

¼ cup (60 ml/2 fl oz) extra virgin olive oil

300 g (10½ oz) cauliflower florets

200 ml (7 fl oz) tomato puree

METHOD

To make the braised cauliflower, lightly fry the onion and garlic in the olive oil until soft. Add the cauliflower and tomato puree, season and simmer until the cauliflower is soft. Meanwhile, finely chop the onion, fish and prawn meat together (don't use a food processor). Moisten the bread a little in the fish broth and add to the fish mixture. Add the eggs and parsley and season, then form into small cakes about 5 cm (2 in) in diameter. Coat the cakes lightly with flour and then gently press breadcrumbs in. Pour olive oil into a frying pan to a depth of 2 cm (¾ in) and heat. Fry the fish cakes until golden brown, turning once, then drain on paper towels and serve with the braised cauliflower.

SERVES 6   WINE: Riesling or verdicchio

LE MARCHE
SECONDI

FISH SOUP FANO STYLE
BRODETTO ALLA FANESE

Fish soups are plentiful all around the Mediterranean and have evolved into separate traditions and recipes by virtue of the spices, herbs and vegetables used in their preparation. There are also differences in the fish used – for example, in the upper Adriatic both saltwater and freshwater fish can be used, whereas in the mid-Adriatic, where Fano sits, the soup is made exclusively with marine species. You'll see species of crustacean here that are rarely used further north, such as the cicala di mare or 'sea cicada', which we would call a bug or slipper lobster. Traditionally the seafood is served separately to its liquid so the guests can pour on the liquid as they please. Use the various leftover fish carcasses to make a broth or stock (see page 49).

INGREDIENTS

1 × 500–600 g (1 lb 2 oz– 1 lb 5 oz) scorpion fish (mahi mahi), filleted

1 × 1 kg (2 lb 4 oz) skate, filleted and skinned

1 × 600–700 g (1 lb 5 oz– 1 lb 9 oz) gurnard, filleted

500 g (1 lb 2 oz) fillets assorted firm-fleshed fish (such as cod, dory and wrasse)

600 ml (21 fl oz) fish broth (see page 49)

160 ml (5¼ fl oz) extra virgin olive oil

1 large brown onion, finely chopped

3 garlic cloves, minced

3 tablespoons tomato paste (concentrated puree)

160 ml (5¼ fl oz) red wine vinegar

420 g (15 oz) cuttlefish, cleaned and cut into 24 small squares

6 scampi, cleaned and left whole

tail meat from 6 bugs (slipper lobsters)

500 g (1 lb 2 oz) red mullet, filleted

4 tablespoons finely chopped parsley

12 slices country-style bread

METHOD

Cut the scorpion fish, gurnard, skate and firm-fleshed fish fillets into even-sized pieces. Pour the fish broth into a saucepan and bring to a simmer. In a wide frying pan, heat the olive oil and lightly fry the onion and garlic until soft. Stir in the tomato paste, vinegar and ½ cup (125 ml/4 fl oz) of the hot fish broth, letting the liquid evaporate and the mixture thicken. Add the cuttlefish and gently cook for 5–6 minutes, continually stirring. Pour in the remaining hot fish broth and turn the heat down to a simmer. Add the firm-fleshed, thick pieces of fish fillet and bring back to a simmer, then add the thinner pieces of fish and bring back to a simmer. Add the scampi, then the bug meat and finally the red mullet. Mix in the parsley and simmer for 2–3 minutes. Remove from the heat and season. The brodetto liquid should be a little thick and very tasty. Distribute the seafood evenly among 6 plates along with 2 slices of toasted bread for each diner. Pour the brodetto liquid into 6 small jugs and give one to each diner to pour on as they please.

SERVES 6   WINE: Verdicchio dei Castelli di Jesi Riserva

SOLE GRATIN
SOGLIOLE GRATINATE

Here is yet another dish that pairs seafood with cheese. I've eaten sogliole gratinate in the beautiful city of Ascoli Piceno. If you happen to be there, go and have an Aperol spritz in the Piazza del Popolo around sunset and watch the square fill with people.

INGREDIENTS

4 × 250 g (9 oz) sole, skin
   removed
⅓ cup (80 ml/2½ fl oz) extra
   virgin olive oil
½ cup parsley, finely chopped
1 garlic clove, minced
4 tablespoons breadcrumbs
4 tablespoons grated
   Grana Padano
lemon slices

METHOD

Preheat the oven to 180°C (350°F). Coat the fish well with the olive oil and put in a baking tray. Combine the parsley, garlic, breadcrumbs and Grana Padano and distribute evenly on each fish. Season with salt and bake for 15–20 minutes. Serve immediately with slices of lemon.

SERVES 4   WINE: Vernaccia di Serrapetrona

CLAMS WITH BRAISED SPINACH
VONGOLE AGLI SPINACI

INGREDIENTS

3 slices good-quality
   country-style bread, cut
   into 2 cm (¾ in) cubes
100 ml (3½ fl oz) extra virgin
   olive oil
500 g (1 lb 2 oz) clams
   (vongole)
100 ml (3½ fl oz) dry white
   wine
2 large garlic cloves, minced
3 French shallots, thinly sliced
200 g (7 oz) spinach, chopped

METHOD

Preheat the oven to 150°C (300°F). Toss the bread with 2 tablespoons of the olive oil and put on a baking tray. Bake for 8–10 minutes until toasted, then set aside. Put the clams in a large saucepan and pour in the wine. Turn the heat to high, put the lid on and bring to the boil. Give the pan a shake and remove the lid. If the clams have opened, turn off the heat; if not, cook a little longer (they should take 2–3 minutes to open). In a wide saucepan, heat the remaining oil and lightly fry the garlic and shallots for a minute until tender. Turn up the heat and add the spinach, mixing well. Cook for 3–4 minutes, then season and transfer to a serving plate. Add the clams (still in their shells) and scatter with the bread to serve.

SERVES 4   WINE: Verdicchio di Matelica

MACERATA-STYLE MEAT LASAGNA
VINCISGRASSI

INGREDIENTS

½ cup (125 ml/4 fl oz) extra
   virgin olive oil

1 kg (2 lb 4 oz) veal and beef
   bones, cut to manageable
   sizes by your butcher

1 cup (250 ml/9 fl oz) dry
   white wine

80 g (2¾ oz) tomato paste
   (concentrated puree)

50 g (1¾ oz) chicken hearts,
   trimmed

60 g (2¼ oz) chicken livers,
   trimmed

60 g (2¼ oz) chicken giblets,
   trimmed

250 g (9 oz) lean pork
   shoulder, minced

250 g (9 oz) veal shoulder,
   minced

200 g (7 oz) chicken thigh
   meat, minced

1 brown onion, finely diced

1 celery heart, finely diced

1 carrot, finely diced

4 cloves

400 g (14 oz) tin tomatoes,
   chopped

60 g (2¼ oz) unsalted butter

1 quantity basic pasta dough
   (see page 42), rolled into
   wide 2 mm (⅟₁₆ in) sheets

1 quantity béchamel sauce
   (see page 50)

grated Grana Padano

METHOD

Heat 2 tablespoons of the olive oil in a large saucepan and brown the
veal and beef bones well, taking care not to burn them. Pour in half the
wine and let it evaporate. Add the tomato paste and stir, then pour in
water to just cover the bones. Bring to the boil, then immediately turn
down the heat and simmer for 1½ hours, skimming off any impurities
that rise to the surface. Strain and put the liquid in a clean saucepan on
medium heat. Reduce until there is about 200 ml (7 fl oz) stock left, then
set aside. Heat 1 tablespoon of the remaining oil in a small saucepan
and fry the chicken hearts, livers and giblets for about 2 minutes until
brown. Let cool a little, then cut into small dice and set aside. In a
larger saucepan, heat the remaining oil on high heat and fry the minced
pork, veal and chicken until brown, continually stirring. Add the onion,
celery, carrot, cloves and a couple of good pinches of salt. Keep stirring
and frying for 2–3 minutes, then add the remaining wine. Let the liquid
evaporate and add the diced chicken offal, tomatoes and reserved
stock. Mix well, then turn the heat down and simmer for 1½ hours. The
sauce should always be a little runny – if it looks like drying out, add a
small ladleful of water. Once cooked, season.

Preheat the oven to 170°C (340°F) and use about a third of the butter
to grease a 36 cm × 24 cm (14¼ in × 9½ in) baking dish that is deep
enough for at least 7–8 layers. To assemble the lasagna, cut the pasta
sheets to fit the length of the baking dish and cook them in plenty of
boiling salted water. Have a large bowl of iced water ready to refresh
the sheets once they come out of the boiling water, then lay them on
clean tea towels (dish towels), ready for assembling. Begin with a layer
of pasta covering the base of the dish, then spoon on some meat sauce,
then béchamel, then a generous amount of Grana Padano. Repeat
until you've used up all the meat sauce, finishing with a layer of pasta.
Sprinkle with Grana Padano and add knobs of the remaining butter. Bake
for 45 minutes until the top is golden and the edges are crisp.

SERVES 6–8   WINE: Rosso Piceno

VINCISGRASSI MORE WIDELY FITS INTO THE LARGE ITALIAN CATEGORY OF PASTA DISHES CALLED PASTA AL FORNO (PASTA BAKED IN THE OVEN). ITS ORIGINS ARE DISPUTED BETWEEN THE CITIES OF ANCONA AND MACERATA. ANCONA TIES THE NOMENCLATURE TO THE POST-NAPOLEONIC CAMPAIGNS AND A CERTAIN AUSTRIAN GENERAL, WINDISCH GRÄTZ, WHO FORMED A RELATIONSHIP WITH THE CITY. VINCISGRASSI IS MADE WITH EGG PASTA SHEETS ABOUT 10 CM (4 IN) WIDE AND AS LONG AS THE BAKING DISH USED. THE FILLING IS MADE WITH VARIOUS MEATS BUT HAS TO INCLUDE LE RIGAGLIE DEL POLLO – ALL THE CHOOK'S INSIDES, INCLUDING GIBLETS, HEARTS, LIVERS AND, OFTEN, COMBS AND WATTLES AS WELL. ALSO, THERE ARE VEAL SWEETBREADS AND BRAINS; MINCED VEAL, YEARLING OR LAMB; AND LOCAL WILD MUSHROOMS. THESE CAN BE PORCINI, CHIODINI, FINFERLI OR ONE OF THE MANY OTHER SPECIES THAT GROW IN THE WOODS OF LE MARCHE. THERE IS A VERY FAMOUS VERSION BY MACERATA CHEF AND WRITER ANTONIO NEBBIA, WHO WROTE IL CUOCO MACERATESE IN 1786. HE USES VEAL SWEETBREADS AND FRESH PORK CHEEKS FOR THE RAGU AND FINISHES WITH PLENTY OF BLACK TRUFFLE. IT IS IN ESSENCE A LASAGNA, ALTERNATING LAYERS OF BÉCHAMEL AND MEAT SAUCE AND WITH THE TOP COVERED WITH GRATED PARMESAN AND KNOBS OF BUTTER; THE DISH IS THEN BAKED.

CHICKEN BRAISED WITH ARTICHOKES
POLLO E CARCIOFI IN UMIDO

INGREDIENTS

1 × 2–2.2 kg (4 lb 8 oz–5 lb)
   chicken, jointed into 8 pieces

¼ cup (60 ml/2 fl oz) extra
   virgin olive oil

3 garlic cloves, crushed

150 ml (5 fl oz) dry white wine

4 large or 6 medium artichokes,
   trimmed (see page 39) and
   each cut lengthways into
   8 wedges

1 egg yolk

juice of 1 lemon

METHOD

Wash the chicken pieces well and pat dry. Heat the olive oil in a frying pan that will fit the chicken pieces in a single layer with a little room between them. Salt the skin of each piece and fry lightly for 8 minutes. Add the garlic and fry a minute longer, then add the wine and scatter the artichokes around. Season, cover and simmer for 35–45 minutes until the chicken is cooked through. Whisk the egg yolk and lemon juice together. Transfer the chicken to serving plates, then mix the egg and lemon into the sauce and check for seasoning. Pour the sauce over the chicken and serve hot.

SERVES 4   WINE: Lacrima di Morro d'Alba

ROAST PIGEONS WITH GREEN OLIVES
PICCIONI CON LE OLIVE

INGREDIENTS

4 pigeons, trimmed

8 slices pancetta

100 g (3½ oz) unsalted butter

1 brown onion, cut lengthways
   into 16 wedges

100 ml (3½ fl oz) dry white
   wine

150 ml (5 fl oz) hot chicken
   or quail broth (see
   pages 48–49)

180 g (6½ oz) green olives,
   pitted

METHOD

Preheat the oven to 180°C (350°F). Wash and dry the pigeons, especially the internal cavity. Season the skin lightly and wrap 2 slices of pancetta around each pigeon, making sure the breast is covered. Use half the butter to smear the pigeons, then put them in a baking dish and bake for 12 minutes. Meanwhile, gently fry the onion segments in the remaining butter for 5 minutes until soft. Add the wine and simmer until it evaporates. Add the broth and olives and continue to simmer gently until the pigeons come out of the oven. Pour the contents of the pan over the pigeons and return the baking dish to the oven for 10 minutes. Check the sauce for seasoning and adjust if necessary. Serve hot.

SERVES 4   WINE: Rosso Conero

LE MARCHE
DOLCI

MANDARIN AND RAISIN COMPOTE
COMPOSTA DI MANDARINO E UVETTA

INGREDIENTS

¾ cup (185 ml/6 fl oz)
  mandarin juice

4 pieces mandarin rind
  (no white pith)

1 cup (170 g/6 oz) seedless
  raisins

65 g (2½ oz) sugar

¼ cup (60 ml/2 fl oz) overproof
  rum (56% alcohol)

2 tablespoons softened
  unsalted butter

METHOD

Put the juice, rind, raisins, sugar and rum in a saucepan and simmer until the raisins are plump (approximately 4–5 minutes). Strain, reserving the raisins and rind. Return the liquid to the saucepan and reduce on medium heat until syrupy (you need about ½ cup/125 ml/ 4 fl oz). Remove the pan from the heat and whisk in the butter. Pour the sauce over the reserved raisins and rind, mix and let cool to room temperature. Use as an accompaniment to panna cotta, gelato, sponge cake and biscotti.

MAKES about 425 ml (15 fl oz)

FRIED LEMON PASTRIES
LIMONCINI FRITTI

INGREDIENTS

1 cup (250 ml/9 fl oz)
  warm milk

60 g (2¼ oz) fresh yeast

3 eggs

500 g (1 lb 2 oz) plain
  (all-purpose) flour, sifted

60 g (2¼ oz) unsalted butter,
  melted

grated zest of 3 lemons

grated zest of 1 orange

320 g (11¼ oz) caster
  (superfine) sugar

extra virgin olive oil

METHOD

Dissolve the yeast in the milk using a fork until it is entirely incorporated. Whisk 2 of the eggs well. Put the flour on your work surface and make a well. Add the milk/yeast, whisked eggs, melted butter and a pinch of salt. Slowly mix by 'pinching' the edges of the well into the liquid a little at a time, eventually making a mass. Knead well until smooth, then rest the dough for about 30 minutes. Meanwhile, mix the lemon and orange zest with the sugar. Roll out the dough to a rectangle 5 mm (¼ in) thick. Scatter the sugar and zest mixture evenly on the dough, leaving a 2 cm (¾ in) border. Whisk the remaining egg and brush the border with it, then roll up the dough into a log and cut 1.5 cm (⅝ in) slices. Pour olive oil into a wide frying pan to a depth of 2–3 cm (¾–1¼ in) and heat. Fry the limoncini on each side until golden (you may need to fry them in 2–3 batches depending on the size of your pan). Drain on paper towels and serve warm.

MAKES 16–18   WINE: Verdicchio dei Castelli di Jesi Passito

HONEY AND ANISEED ROLLS
MARITOZZI CON L'ANICE

The Italian way to start the day is with a brioche and coffee. This recipe is based on a preparation by pastry chef Iginio Massari.

INGREDIENTS

30 g (1 oz) fresh yeast

500 g (1 lb 2 oz) strong bread flour (baker's flour)

125 g (4½ oz) honey

125 g (4½ oz) whisked eggs (approx. 2–3 eggs)

60 g (2¼ oz) egg yolk (approx. 3–4 eggs)

125 g (4½ oz) softened unsalted butter

10 g (¼ oz) salt

GLAZE

150 g (5½ oz) honey

30 g (1 oz) anise seeds

METHOD

Dissolve the yeast in 200 ml (7 fl oz) warm water. Put the flour in the bowl of an electric mixer fitted with a paddle attachment. Add the dissolved yeast, honey, eggs, egg yolk, butter and salt and beat until the mixture comes together. Transfer the dough to your workbench and knead for a few minutes until smooth and elastic. Put in a bowl, cover with plastic wrap and let rise for 2 hours. Knock down the dough and cover again, this time letting it rise for 30 minutes. Knock down again and let rise for a further 30 minutes.

Preheat the oven to 200°C (400°F). Shape the dough into 30 g (1 oz) balls roughly 2 cm (¾ in) in diameter, put on baking trays and leave to rise until doubled in size. Bake for 10–12 minutes until golden, then remove from the oven and let cool. Meanwhile, make the glaze. Put the honey and anise seeds in a saucepan and bring to the boil. Immediately turn off the heat and keep warm. Once the rolls are cool, brush them with the glaze. Serve for breakfast or as an afternoon snack with espresso or caffè latte.

MAKES about 35   WINE: Verdicchio passito

SWEET CHESTNUT RAVIOLI
RAVIOLI DOLCI DI CASTAGNE

This is a typical sweet made for Carnevale and Christmas in Le Marche. Use fresh chestnuts if available, but if not you can use dried chestnuts or frozen, raw and peeled chestnuts. The Meletti aniseed liqueur called for here is from Ascoli Piceno in southern Le Marche and is made with aniseed grown around the town. It will give a specific taste to the ravioli, but if you can't find it, use another anise-based liqueur.

INGREDIENTS

1 kg (2 lb 4 oz) chestnuts, scored (see page 82)

100 g (3½ oz) caster (superfine) sugar

¾ cup (80 g/2¾ oz) best-quality unsweetened cocoa powder

120 ml (4 fl oz) short espresso coffee

120 ml (4 fl oz) Meletti aniseed liqueur (or other anise-based liqueur)

grated zest of 1 lemon

½ cup (50 g/1¾ oz) almond meal

½ teaspoon ground cinnamon

1 quantity corzetti pasta dough (see page 43)

extra virgin olive oil

Icing (confectioners') sugar

METHOD

Put the chestnuts in a saucepan with abundant water and bring to the boil. Turn down the heat and simmer for 15–20 minutes. Drain and let cool, then cut each chestnut in half and scoop out the flesh using a teaspoon. Make sure the pellicle (fine inner skin) is not removed with the flesh. You need 600 g (1 lb 5 oz) chestnut flesh. Pass the chestnut flesh through a fine sieve or Mouli into a bowl. Add the sugar, cocoa, coffee, liqueur, lemon zest, almond meal, cinnamon and a pinch of salt and mix until you have a homogenous firm mixture. Roll out the pasta dough to a thickness of 2 mm (¹⁄₁₆ in) and cut out circles about 9 cm (3½ in) in diameter. Put 1 teaspoon of the chestnut mixture on each circle, just off centre, then flatten out a little using the back of the teaspoon. Fold the dough over to make a half-moon and seal the raviolo tightly by pressing the prongs of a fork on the edge. Heat plenty of olive oil in a frying pan and deep-fry the ravioli a few at a time until the edges turn golden. Remove, drain on paper towels and dust with icing sugar. Serve warm with a little pot of crema inglese (see page 52) to dunk the ravioli into.

MAKES 24–30   WINE: Verdicchio dei Castelli di Jesi Passito

AS COOKS WE NEED TO THINK OF THE CHESTNUT AS A STARCH RATHER THAN A NUT. BECAUSE IT IS HIGH IN CARBOHYDRATE AND LOW IN FAT, IN A CULINARY SENSE IT IS CLOSER TO POTATOES. IT CAN BE USED AS A VEGETABLE OR IN A SOUP, STUDDED IN PIECES THROUGH OR MASHED TOGETHER WITH POTATO OR OTHER FARINACEOUS VEGETABLES. USED IN A STUFFING FOR QUAIL, DUCK OR PHEASANT, IT ADDS A DISTINCTIVE SWEETNESS THAT COMPLEMENTS RICH FLESH.

FIG AND AMARETTO CREAM
CREMA DI FICHI AL AMARETTO

This recipe is based on a dish by Danilo Bei of Ristorante Emilio in the township of Casabianca, province of Fermo, in south-eastern Le Marche. When figs are ripe and have been grown without being sprayed with nasty things, the skin is soft and edible. It is an essential element in this dessert.

INGREDIENTS

6 large ripe figs

1 egg, separated

30 g (1 oz) caster (superfine) sugar

150 g (5½ oz) mascarpone cheese

50 ml (1¾ fl oz) amaretto liqueur

pinch of ground cinnamon

1 teaspoon grated ginger

¼ cup (60 ml/2 fl oz) thin (pouring) cream, whipped to firm peaks

1 teaspoon best-quality unsweetened cocoa powder

METHOD

Wash the figs carefully, taking care not to damage the skin. Cut in half lengthways and carefully scrape out the flesh, keeping the skins intact. Set the skins aside. Mash the flesh using a fork, then set aside. Beat the egg yolk with the sugar until pale and fluffy. Gradually beat in the mascarpone until well incorporated, then mix in the mashed fig, amaretto, cinnamon and ginger. Fold in the cream. Whisk the egg white to firm peaks, then fold into the fig cream. Spoon some fig cream into tall serving glasses, then add a layer of fig skin so it can be seen through the glass. Add some more fig cream, more fig skin and lastly fig cream. Dust with the cocoa to serve.

SERVES 6   WINE: Verdicchio passito

LIGURIA

LIGURIA

THIS TINY CRESCENT-SHAPED COASTAL REGION – AT JUST OVER 5400 SQUARE KILOMETRES (2080 SQUARE MILES) ITALY'S THIRD-SMALLEST PROVINCE – IS BORDERED BY FRANCE TO THE WEST, PIEMONTE TO THE NORTH AND EMILIA-ROMAGNA AND TOSCANA TO THE EAST. ITS NARROW STRIP OF LAND IS SQUEEZED IN BY THE GULF OF GENOA IN THE LIGURIAN SEA ON THE ONE HAND, AND THE ALPS AND THE APENNINES, WHICH MARCH DOWN TO MEET THE SEA, ON THE OTHER; SOME OF ITS MOUNTAINS RISE ABOVE 2000 METRES (6500 FEET).

In spite of their proximity to and powerful relationship with the sea (the Genoese have always been renowned as sailors, with Columbus being perhaps the best known), Ligurians' food generally is land-based, especially herb-based. This could actually be because of the marine presence: Kostioukovich, author of *Why Italians Love to Talk About Food*, suggests that 'once back on land, the sailor has no desire whatsoever to gaze back at the sea'.

One Genoese creation, focaccia, has links to both land and sea: sailors' wives would make the dough the night before a voyage, leave it to rise overnight and bake it the next day, pressing little hollows into the top to take olive oil and sprinkling the focaccia with salt.

Waverley Root, in *The Food of Italy*, claims that there is another Genoese invention that has links to land and sea. The Genoese dialect word from which we get ravioli was, he contends, rabiole, meaning 'things of little value' or leftovers, and since these were valuable on board ship, they would be chopped up, placed between sheets of pasta and served again. This story is given some credence because of another dish that uses large sheets of pasta, mandilli de seta ('silk handkerchiefs') al pesto genovese, the 'silk handkerchiefs' being large sheets of pasta, as used in making ravioli.

This brings us to another Genoese culinary creation: pesto. Although the Genoese were great traders in spices, their cuisine uses very few spices but many aromatic herbs – such as basil. Again, the reason given is that once returned to shore, sailors did not want anything more to do with spices, which they had inhaled all through the long sea voyage; instead, they delighted in the aroma and taste of fresh herbs, which were unavailable at sea. Pesto – made with basil, excellent Ligurian olive oil, Sardinian pecorino, garlic and pine nuts – is not only a sublime sauce but also a good way to preserve basil for use out of season. Along with ravioli, pesto is a Ligurian dish that has travelled the world.

Not all Genoese dishes travel so easily. For example, cappon magro ('fast-day capon') is an elaborate composed salad built on ship's biscuits that are scattered with boiled vegetables – one of which must be salsify – and accompanied by a sauce of capers, green olives and parsley, along with mushrooms, boiled eggs and the finest seafood you can afford.

Owing to its narrow strip of land, Ligurian farming is small-scale and mostly built on terraces. Today the region tends to be what Kostioukovich calls 'a bastion of ecological and ethno-gastronomic "food defenders"'. The scarcity of land is why so many farmers stick to smaller, more humble produce such as herbs, eggs and seasonal vegetables. These local vegetables are seen at their best at Easter in the torta pasqualina, another exquisite Ligurian dish that is best eaten there: a light pastry crust filled with silverbeet (Swiss chard), boiled artichokes, Parmigiano Reggiano, ricotta, fresh oregano, cream, eggs and butter. Local legend has it that when the German philosopher Nietzsche

lived in Genoa, he spent half a day learning how to make this torta.

Fish are not entirely ignored in Liguria. Local delicacies include bianchetti, tiny white fish taken immediately after hatching, lightly poached and served with oil and lemon, or fried, when they are known as rossetti; and exquisite anchovies from the Ligurian Sea, consumed fresh or salted and packed in the local olive oil.

Although not a prolific wine-producing region, the wines of the Cinque Terre – five remote villages on the west coast in the province of La Spezia that until relatively recently were inaccessible by road – are highly regarded. Using the small white grapes rosco, albarola and vermentino, they are made into dry (or, using sun-dried grapes, sweet) white wines. It is the vermentino grape that produces the most characteristic of Liguria's wines, best weathering, as it does, the harsh dry climate and even absorbing some of the herbal nature that characterises Ligurian cuisine.

There are a small number of reds produced, with those made from the rossese grape the most distinctive; ormeasco – the local name for dolcetto – and ciliegiolo are two others worth noting.

If you are in the area, perhaps the best way to start sampling the wines of Liguria is to visit the Enoteca Regionale in the hilltop town of Castelnuovo Magra.

LIGURIA
ANTI-PASTI

SWEET AND SOUR ONIONS
CIPOLLINE IN AGRODOLCE

Use these as part of an antipasto, drained and dressed with parsley and extra virgin olive oil. They are also good with boiled meats, such as tongue, chicken or silverside, and terrines.

INGREDIENTS

1 kg (2 lb 4 oz) small white onions, peeled

40 g (1½ oz) caster (superfine) sugar

1 cup (250 ml/9 fl oz) white wine vinegar

1 long red chilli, halved lengthways

10 black peppercorns

1 bay leaf

METHOD

Bring a large saucepan of salted water to the boil. Plunge in the onions and keep them immersed for 4 minutes using a plate. Drain. Bring the sugar, vinegar, chilli, peppercorns and bay leaf to the boil. Add ½ teaspoon salt and simmer for 3 minutes. Add the onions and turn off the heat. Leave to cool in the liquid overnight, then store in sterilised preserving jars.

SERVES 8   WINE: Colli di Luni

BASIC FOCACCIA
FOCACCIA

With its wonderful local fruity extra virgin olive oil as flavouring, Liguria is famous for soft, fluffy focaccia with a crisp top. This basic recipe can be finished with tomatoes, herbs, olives, capers, or whatever you like.

INGREDIENTS

540 ml (19 fl oz) water

28 g (1 oz) fresh yeast

900 g (2 lb) Italian bread or pizza '00' flour or other strong flour

140 ml (4¾ fl oz) extra virgin olive oil

salt flakes

METHOD

Using a fork, dissolve the yeast in half the (270 ml (9½ fl oz)) tepid (not hot) water. Transfer to the bowl of an electric mixer fitted with a dough hook. Add the flour and 18 g (¾ oz) salt and mix on a low speed, gradually adding the rest of the water and then ½ cup (125 ml/4 fl oz) of the olive oil. Once the dough comes together, increase the speed a little and mix for 5 minutes. Transfer the dough to a lightly oiled work surface and fold and knead for 5 minutes. Return the dough to the bowl, cover and let prove until doubled in size. Line 2 baking trays (32 cm × 44 cm × 2.5 cm/13 in × 17½ in × 1 in) with baking paper. Divide the dough in half and stretch the pieces to fit into the trays. Let prove for 45 minutes–1 hour. Preheat the oven to 210°C (410°F). Dimple the surface of each focaccia using your fingertips, brush with the remaining oil and sprinkle with salt flakes. Bake for 15–20 minutes until golden and cool on a rack.

SERVES 10–15

CAULIFLOWER, BASIL AND OLIVE SALAD
INSALATA DI CAVOLFIORE E OLIVE TAGGIASCHE

INGREDIENTS

1 large cauliflower, cut into bite-sized florets

1 cup basil leaves

¼ cup chopped parsley

10 good-quality anchovy fillets, chopped

3 tablespoons large capers, rinsed and chopped

30 Ligurian taggiasche olives, pitted and chopped

2 long red chillies, seeded and sliced

100 ml (3½ fl oz) extra virgin olive oil

METHOD

Plunge the cauliflower into a saucepan of boiling salted water for 2–3 minutes until tender. Drain and let cool. Meanwhile, tear any larger basil leaves into smaller pieces. In a large bowl, combine the basil, parsley, anchovies, capers, olives and chillies. Pour in the olive oil and add the cooled cauliflower. Season well and toss, mixing everything together well. Serve as a refreshing summer salad.

SERVES 8-10

WINE: Pigato

FRIED MACKEREL
BOGHE A SCABECCIO

INGREDIENTS

12 × 150 g (5½ oz) mackerel, cleaned and gutted

4 tablespoons plain (all-purpose) flour

extra virgin olive oil

2 garlic cloves, gently crushed

2 French shallots, minced

1 large brown onion, thinly sliced

4 sage sprigs

4 bay leaves

150 ml (5 fl oz) white wine vinegar

150 ml (5 fl oz) dry white wine

METHOD

Wash the fish well and pat dry, then dust lightly with the flour. In a frying pan that will fit 6 of the fish snugly, pour in olive oil to a depth of 1 cm (½ in). Heat until the oil is beginning to smoke, then add 6 fish and fry carefully for a minute or so on each side, depending on their size. Drain on paper towels and season with salt. Repeat with the remaining fish. Drain and reserve the oil in the pan for frying other fish later. Heat 2 tablespoons fresh oil in the pan and lightly fry the garlic, shallots and onion for a minute or so until softened and lightly coloured. Add the sage and bay leaves and mix well, then add the vinegar and wine and increase the heat. Once it boils, turn the heat down and simmer for 3 minutes. Meanwhile, put the cooled fried fish in a glass or ceramic container that will fit it snugly in 2 or 3 layers (2 layers of 6 fish, or 3 layers of 4). Pour the hot contents of the frying pan on top. It should cover the fish completely – if not, top up with more vinegar. Cover and refrigerate for 24 hours. Remove fish from the vinegar as needed and serve drizzled with good-quality olive oil.

SERVES 12

WINE: Cinque Terre

CAULIFLOWER, BASIL AND OLIVE SALAD

SPRING SALAD
INSALATA PRIMAVERA

INGREDIENTS

½ cup (95 g/3¼ oz) double-peeled broad beans

1 garlic clove, halved

2–3 large oxheart tomatoes, not fully ripe, cut into bite-sized wedges

2 red capsicums (peppers), thinly sliced

2 spring onions (scallions), halved and thinly sliced

2 cucumbers, peeled and thinly sliced

8 basil leaves, torn into strips

3 anchovy fillets, finely chopped

20 small green olives (Ligurian taggiasche), pitted and chopped

2 tablespoons red wine vinegar

⅓ cup (80 ml/2½ fl oz) extra virgin olive oil

1 hard-boiled egg, cut into 8 wedges

METHOD

Blanch the broad beans in boiling water for 30 seconds, then drain. Rub the inside of a ceramic serving bowl well with the cut sides of the garlic. Discard the garlic. Put the tomatoes in the bowl, then add the vegetables, basil, anchovies and olives and dress with the vinegar and olive oil. Season and toss well. Leave for 15 minutes, tossing every so often. Divide among serving plates and add the egg. Spoon any leftover dressing on top and serve.

SERVES 4   WINE: Rose

MUSHROOMS FRIED IN CHICKPEA BATTER
FUNGHI FRITTI

INGREDIENTS

100 g (3½ oz) chickpea flour (besan)

⅓ cup (50 g/1¾ oz) plain (all-purpose) flour

1 egg, whisked

50 ml (1¾ fl oz) milk

50 ml (1¾ fl oz) cold sparkling mineral water

pinch of grated nutmeg

2 cups (500 ml/17 fl oz) extra virgin olive oil or other frying oil

750 g (1 lb 10 oz) mixed mushrooms (choose from porcini, Swiss brown, oyster, shimeji, king brown), cut into bite-sized pieces

METHOD

Sift the flours into a bowl, make a well in the middle and add the egg, milk, mineral water, nutmeg and a pinch of salt and pepper. Mix well. The batter should be a little runny but not watery (add more water if it is too thick or more flour if too watery). Pour the oil into a frying pan to a depth of 4–5 cm (1½–2 in) and heat to 170°C (340°F). To test the temperature of the oil, drop in a cube of bread – the oil is ready if the bread turns golden brown in 20 seconds. Dip the mushrooms in the batter and shake off any excess. Fry each type of mushroom separately and in small batches so the pan isn't crowded. Drain on paper towels, season lightly with salt and serve.

SERVES 4–6   WINE: Prosecco

LIGURIA

PRIMI

BORAGE AND BROAD BEAN SOUP
ZUPPA DI BORRAGINE E FAVE

INGREDIENTS

4 cups (740 g/1 lb 10 oz)
double-peeled broad beans
or 1 kg (2 lb 4 oz) dried
broad beans

160 ml (5¼ fl oz) extra virgin
olive oil

1 large white onion, thinly
sliced

2 garlic cloves, minced

4 cups borage leaves, well
washed and thinly sliced

2 tablespoons finely chopped
parsley

1 tablespoon tomato paste
(concentrated puree)

2 tablespoons marjoram
leaves

6 thick slices country-style
bread, toasted

METHOD

If using dried broad beans, soak them in plenty of cold water for
2 days before draining and using. Heat half the olive oil in a saucepan
and gently fry the onion and garlic for 10–15 minutes until soft and
transparent. Add the borage, parsley, tomato paste and half the
marjoram. Stir and lightly fry for 2 minutes, then add 2 litres (70 fl oz)
water and bring to the boil. Add the broad beans and a couple of good
pinches of salt. Once the liquid comes back to the boil, turn the heat
down and simmer for 30–40 minutes until the beans are tender and
beginning to break apart. Check for seasoning. To serve, put a slice of
toasted bread in each soup plate and ladle the soup on top. Finish with
a scattering of the remaining marjoram.

SERVES 6   WINE: Colli di Luni

PRAWN, OLIVE AND HAZELNUT SALAD
INSALATA DI GAMBERI, OLIVE E NOCCIOLE

INGREDIENTS

24 cooked king prawns
(shrimp), peeled and
deveined

1 cup (135 g/4¾ oz) hazelnuts,
lightly roasted and chopped

½ cup green olives, pitted and
finely chopped

2 tablespoons finely snipped
chives

2 tablespoons chopped
parsley

1 tablespoon extra virgin
olive oil

1 tablespoon hazelnut oil

1 teaspoon good-quality
balsamic vinegar

juice of 1 lemon

METHOD

Leave the prawns whole or chop each one into 4–5 pieces. Put the
prawns in a large bowl and mix gently with the hazelnuts, olives, chives
and parsley. Combine the oils, vinegar and lemon juice, then add to the
prawns, season and toss gently.

SERVES 6   WINE: Pigato

SALT COD BALLS
POLPETTINE DI BACCALÀ

INGREDIENTS

4 brown onions

2 litres (70 fl oz) milk

1 handful parsley stalks

1 tablespoon black peppercorns

1 kg (2 lb 4 oz) baccalà (salt
cod), soaked and rinsed,
skin on (see page 125)

600 g (1 lb 5 oz) potatoes,
unpeeled

3 eggs, lightly whisked

300 g (10½ oz) provolone
piccante, diced

3 tablespoons chopped parsley

500 ml (17 fl oz) extra virgin
olive oil

60 g (2¼ oz) plain (all-purpose)
flour

2 eggs, beaten

100 g (3½ oz) fine dry
breadcrumbs

METHOD

Slice 2 of the onions, then put in a stockpot with the milk, parsley
stalks, peppercorns and 2 litres (70 fl oz) water. Bring to the boil.
Add the baccalà and simmer for 5 minutes. Remove the pot from the
heat and leave for 5 minutes, then remove the baccalà and set aside.
Discard the liquid and aromatics. Put the potatoes in a saucepan,
cover with cold water and bring to the boil. Cook until soft, then drain,
peel and pass through a ricer or mash into a bowl. Coarsely chop
the baccalà (including the skin) and add to the potato with the eggs,
provolone, parsley and remaining finely chopped onions. Season, mix
well and let cool. Coat with flour, egg wash, breadcrumbs and deep-fry
in 2 cm (¾ in) oil

MAKES about 40   WINE: Vermentino

CORZETTI WITH PINE NUTS
AND MARJORAM
CORZETTI AL BATTUTA DI PINOLI

INGREDIENTS

½ cup (80 g/2¾ oz) pine nuts

3 tablespoons marjoram
leaves

extra virgin olive oil
(preferably Ligurian)

70 g (2½ oz) Grana Padano,
grated

1 quantity corzetti pasta dough
(see page 43)

METHOD

Put the pine nuts and marjoram in a mortar with a couple of pinches of
salt. Begin pounding with the pestle and slowly add enough olive oil to
form a runny cream. Pour into a large warm bowl and mix in the Grana
Padano and a couple of turns of pepper. If the mixture is too thick, add
a little more oil. Cook the corzetti in plenty of boiling salted water until
al dente. Drain, then toss into the warm bowl with the pine-nut cream
and serve immediately.

SERVES 6   WINE: Pigato

POLENTA WITH BORLOTTI AND CAVOLO NERO
POLENTA INCATENATA

INGREDIENTS

250 g (9 oz) shelled fresh or 1.8 kg (4 lb) dried borlotti beans

3 cups finely sliced cavolo nero (Tuscan kale)

1 carrot, finely diced

3 boiling potatoes, sliced

1 brown onion, finely diced

2 garlic cloves, thinly sliced

100 ml (3½ fl oz) extra virgin olive oil, plus extra for drizzling

250 g (9 oz) polenta (cornmeal)

80 g (2¾ oz) Grana Padano, grated

METHOD

If using dried borlotti beans, soak in plenty of cold water for 24 hours and then drain and cook in boiling salted water for 30 minutes. Drain. Put 3 litres (5¼ pints) cold water in a large saucepan and add the beans, cavolo nero, carrot, potatoes, onion, garlic, olive oil and a couple of good pinches of salt. Bring to the boil, then turn down the heat and simmer for 25 minutes. Slowly add the polenta in a stream, stirring so that no lumps form. Simmer gently for 40–45 minutes, stirring often, until the polenta is cooked. It should be quite runny but thick. If the polenta is looking too dense during the cooking, add some warm water. Season and ladle into serving bowls. Sprinkle with the Grana Padano and drizzle with oil to serve.

SERVES 6–8

WINE: Rossese di Dolceacqua

THIS IS A DISH THAT IS POPULAR IN THE **LUNIGIANA** AREA THAT STRADDLES SOUTHERN LIGURIA AND NORTHERN TUSCANY. IT IS AN EXAMPLE OF THE HEART AND SOUL OF ITALY'S MEATLESS CUISINE – A CUISINE DERIVED FROM HARD TIMES WHEN MEAT WAS A COSTLY AND SPECIAL-OCCASION LUXURY. WHILE MEAT IS OBTAINABLE ON A REGULAR BASIS THESE DAYS, THESE MEATLESS DISHES SURVIVE AND CONTINUE TO BE POPULAR SIMPLY BECAUSE THEY ARE SO GOOD.

POTATO AND SAFFRON GNOCCHI WITH CRAB, PEAS AND CHILLI
GNOCCHI DI PATATE E ZAFFERANO ALLA POLPA DI GRANCHIO, PISELLI E PEPERONCINO

The gnocchi can be made up to 3–4 hours ahead of the time you plan to serve them.

INGREDIENTS

1 kg (2 lb 4 oz) unpeeled potatoes, well washed
½ teaspoon saffron threads
50 g (1¾ oz) grated parmesan cheese
2 egg yolks
200 g (7 oz) plain (all-purpose) flour

SAUCE

2 cups (310 g/11 oz) shelled peas
¼ cup (60 ml/2 fl oz) extra virgin olive oil
2 garlic cloves, minced
2 red chillies, seeded and finely chopped
4 tablespoons tomato passata
450 g (1 lb) crabmeat
½ cup chopped basil

METHOD

Put the potatoes in a saucepan with about 3–4 cm (1¼–1½ in) water. Cover and bring to the boil, then turn the heat down and simmer for 25–30 minutes until tender. Meanwhile, soak the saffron threads in 160 ml (5¼ fl oz) hot water. Drain the potatoes and let cool a little, then peel. Pass through a ricer (or finely mash) onto your work surface. Make a well in the centre and add the parmesan, egg yolks, 1 cup (150 g/5½ oz) of the flour and half the saffron water. Season with 3 good pinches of salt and some fine pepper. Bring the lot together using your hands. If the dough seems a little sticky, add more flour. Flour your work surface, then roll a piece of dough into a small sausage about 3 cm (1¼ in) thick. Cut some gnocchi about 2 cm (¾ in) wide. Bring a small saucepan of salted water to the boil and plunge in a couple of the gnocchi. Once they rise to the surface (1–1½ minutes), remove with a slotted spoon and taste: they should be firm but tender. If they are falling apart, the dough needs a little more flour. Shape and cut the rest of your gnocchi and put them on a tray lined with a clean tea towel (dish towel). Cover with another clean tea towel and refrigerate until needed.

To make the sauce, cook the peas in rapidly boiling salted water for 3–5 minutes until tender. Drain. Heat the olive oil in a wide frying pan and gently fry the garlic and chillies for a minute or so. Add the passata and simmer for 30 seconds before adding the crabmeat, basil, peas and remaining saffron water. Simmer gently for 2 minutes, then season with salt and a little pepper and remove from the heat. Cook the gnocchi in a large saucepan of boiling salted water. Once they come to the surface, remove them with a slotted spoon and put on serving plates. Dress with the crab sauce to serve.

SERVES 6–8   WINE: Pigato

TESTAROLI WITH PESTO
TESTAROLI AL PESTO

Testaroli pasta gets its name from the testo, a shallow flat pan with a low-domed lid. There are two cooking processes when making testaroli: first it is cooked like a flatbread in the pan, and then it is cut up and boiled in salted water.

INGREDIENTS

3 boiling potatoes, cut into
1 cm (½ in) cubes

250 g (9 oz) green beans,
trimmed

1 quantity testaroli pasta
dough (see page 45)

8 tablespoons pesto
(see page 51)

grated Parmigiano Reggiano
(optional)

METHOD

Blanch the potatoes in boiling salted water for 1–1½ minutes. Drain and set aside. Blanch the beans in boiling salted water for about 3 minutes, then drain and cut into 3 cm (1¼ in) lengths. Cook the testaroli in plenty of salted boiling water until al dente – the cooking time will depend on the thickness of the pasta. Meanwhile, put the pesto in a warm bowl. When the testaroli are almost cooked, throw the potatoes and beans into the saucepan for a minute. Drain, then toss with the pesto. Add a little Parmigiano Reggiano, if desired, and serve immediately.

SERVES 6   WINE: Vermentino

LIGURIA
SECONDI

PAN-FRIED JOHN DORY FILLETS WITH ROAST SALSIFY

PAN-FRIED JOHN DORY FILLETS WITH ROAST SALSIFY
SAN PIETRO IN PADELLA E SCORZONERA AL FORNO

INGREDIENTS
250 g (9 oz) salsify (or dutch carrots), peeled and cut into 6 cm lengths

juice of 1 lemon

½ cup (125 ml/4 fl oz) extra virgin olive oil

2 tablespoons chopped parsley

8 john dory fillets (total weight about 1.2 kg/2 lb 12 oz)

METHOD
Preheat the oven to 200°C (400°F). Put the salsify in a saucepan of cold water with the lemon juice and a couple of pinches of salt. Bring to the boil, then simmer for 10–15 minutes until tender. Drain and cool a little before patting dry. Heat 2 tablespoons of the olive oil in an ovenproof frying pan and fry the salsify until golden brown. Sprinkle with salt and transfer to the oven. Bake for 10 minutes, shaking the pan to make sure the salsify colours evenly and doesn't burn. Remove from the oven and toss with the parsley and a little salt (if needed) and pepper. Heat the remaining oil in another frying pan and fry the fish. Season and serve with the roast salsify.

SERVES 4 WINE: Riviera Ligure di Ponente Vermentino

BARBECUED SPATCHCOCK WITH HERBS AND RADICCHIO
GALLETTO AI FERRI

If spatchcocks are not available, small chickens cut in half lengthways can be prepared using the same method.

INGREDIENTS
4 × 400–500 g (14 oz–1 lb 2 oz) spatchcocks

½ cup (125 ml/4 fl oz) extra virgin olive oil

1 cup mixed herbs (sage, rosemary, parsley, chives), leaves picked from stems

1 treviso lettuce (radicchio), trimmed and thinly sliced lengthways

cheeks from 4 lemons

METHOD
Lay each spatchcock on your work surface with the cavity of the bird facing you and the legs behind. The backbone is underneath and runs from the 'parson's nose' all the way to the neck, where it protrudes. Using sharp kitchen scissors and starting at the cavity end, cut 1 cm (½ in) to the right of the backbone along the length of the bird. Now cut 1 cm (½ in) to the left of the backbone all the way along and remove the entire backbone and the neck. Wash the birds well, removing any small pieces of bone left from the cutting process, then pat dry and flatten. Preheat a barbecue or chargrill pan to hot. Rub the birds with 2 tablespoons of the olive oil and sprinkle with salt and pepper. Cook for 8–10 minutes on each side. Meanwhile, chop all the herbs together and mix with the remaining oil. When the birds are cooked, put on serving plates with some treviso and lemon cheeks. Spoon the herb dressing over to serve.

SERVES 4 WINE: Vermentino

SEAFOOD AND BARLEY STEW
ORZO ALLA MARINARA

The inspiration for this dish comes from my love of Italian soups and stews. What binds it all together and thickens it is the starch from the soft, round and nutty pearl barley.

INGREDIENTS

1 kg (2 lb 4 oz) mussels, scrubbed and de-bearded

1 kg (2 lb 4 oz) clams (vongole), well washed

⅓ cup (80 ml/2½ fl oz) fruity extra virgin olive oil

4 French shallots, thinly sliced

3 garlic cloves, crushed

½ teaspoon smoked paprika

¼ teaspoon ground chilli

1 teaspoon fennel seeds

1 cup (250 ml/9 fl oz) dry white wine

2 cups tomato passata

3 banana chillies, seeded and halved

1½ cups (300 g/10½ oz) pearl barley, washed

300 g (10½ oz) shelled peas

400 g (14 oz) fish fillets, skinned, boned and cut into bite-sized pieces

250 g (9 oz) calamari, cleaned, bodies cut into thin strips

200 g (7 oz) raw prawns (shrimp), peeled and deveined

1 cup chopped parsley

METHOD

Put the mussels and clams in a large saucepan. Turn the heat to high and put the lid on. Once the shellfish have steamed open (4–5 minutes), remove them from the pan. Take the meat from the shells and discard the shells. Strain the cooking liquid through a couple of layers of muslin (cheesecloth) or a fine sieve to extract any grit. Heat the olive oil in a saucepan and gently fry the shallots, garlic, paprika, ground chilli and fennel seeds for a minute. Add the wine, turn up the heat and boil until there is almost no liquid left. Add the reserved shellfish cooking liquid and the passata, chillies and 1 litre (35 fl oz) water. Bring to the boil, add the barley and simmer for 15 minutes. Add the peas and simmer for 10 minutes, then add the fish, calamari and prawns. Simmer for 5 minutes, then add the mussel and clam meat and parsley, season and stir well. Serve immediately with one piece of banana chilli per person.

SERVES 6   WINE: Riviera Ligure di Ponente Pigato

TAGGIASCHE OLIVE
THIS SMALL OLIVE IS FAMOUS FOR PRODUCING A FINE, ELEGANT OLIVE OIL THAT DOES NOT OVERPOWER DELICATE DISHES AND IS A FEATURE OF LIGURIA'S CUISINE. THE TAGGIASCHE IS ALSO AN OPTIMUM TABLE OLIVE AND IS OFTEN THE OLIVE OF CHOICE WHEN MAKING OLIVE PASTE. THEY RANGE IN COLOUR FROM A DEEP GREEN TO ALMOST BLACK AND HAVE A RELATIVELY LARGE STONE WITH A SMALL AMOUNT OF FLESH SURROUNDING IT.

VEAL LIVER WITH MARSALA AND SWEET AND SOUR ONIONS
FEGATO DI VITELLO CON MARSALA E CIPOLLINE IN AGRODOLCE

INGREDIENTS

500 g (1 lb 2 oz) calf liver, cut into 8 × 5 mm (¼ in) thick slices

2 tablespoons plain (all-purpose) flour

¼ cup (60 ml/2 fl oz) extra virgin olive oil

⅓ cup (80 ml/2½ fl oz) dry Marsala

32 sweet and sour onions (see page 285)

1 tablespoon red wine vinegar

1 tablespoon chopped parsley

METHOD

Lightly dust the calf liver with the flour and sprinkle with a little salt and pepper. Heat 2 tablespoons of the olive oil in a wide frying pan and fry the liver for a minute on each side. Transfer to a warm serving plate. Drain the oil from the pan, then return the pan to the heat. Add the Marsala and onions and reduce until there is about one tablespoon (20 ml/¾ fl oz) of liquid left. Add the vinegar and parsley, season and pour over the liver to serve.

SERVES 4   WINE: Ormeasco di Pomassio

RABBIT COOKED IN CLAY LIGURIA STYLE
CONIGLIO IN TERRACOTTA ALLA LIGURE

INGREDIENTS

160 ml (5¼ fl oz) extra virgin olive oil

1 white onion, diced

6 garlic cloves, chopped

1 × 100 g (3½ oz) piece prosciutto, cut into 1 cm (½ in) cubes

100 g (3½ oz) taggiasche olives (or other small green olives), pitted and halved

30 g (1 oz) pine nuts

1 sprig each of thyme, marjoram, sage and rosemary

1 × 1.2–1.5 kg (2 lb 12 oz– 3 lb 5 oz) rabbit, jointed

2 cups (500 ml/17 fl oz) red wine

¼ cup (60 ml/2 fl oz) good-quality balsamic vinegar

1 cup chopped parsley

METHOD

Preheat the oven to 150°C (300°F). Put a well-seasoned clay braising pot or casserole dish on medium heat and add the olive oil. Fry the onion, garlic, prosciutto and olives until the onion is translucent. Add the pine nuts, herbs (except the parsley), rabbit and 3–4 good pinches of salt and mix well. Add enough wine to almost cover the rabbit, then cover and cook in the oven for 2½ hours. Add the balsamic vinegar, parsley, a little more salt (if necessary) and some freshly cracked pepper. Rest for 5 minutes in the pot before serving.

SERVES 6   WINE: Rosesse di Dolceacqua

LETTUCE ROLLS STUFFED WITH VEAL
LATTUGHE RIPIENE

Lettuce of all sorts is used all over Italy in a number of preparations. At the height of the Roman Empire citizens had access to more than 500 types of edible leaves, ranging from many types of lettuce – such as those of the Lactuca sativa family, which form rosette-like heads (e.g. iceberg) – to weedy leaves such as sorrel, rocket and lamb's lettuce.

INGREDIENTS

10–12 outer iceberg lettuce leaves

1 tablespoon extra virgin olive oil

200 g (7 oz) minced (ground) veal

1 carrot, finely diced

1 brown onion, finely diced

1 tablespoon chopped rosemary leaves

3 tablespoons pine nuts

1 tablespoon marjoram leaves

2 garlic cloves, minced

1 egg yolk

400 ml (14 fl oz) hot chicken broth (see page 48)

60 g (2¼ oz) Grana Padano, shaved

METHOD

Preheat the oven to 180°C (350°F). Blanch the lettuce leaves quickly in simmering salted water so they wilt slightly. Lay them on a clean tea towel (dish towel) to cool and dry. Heat the olive oil in a frying pan and lightly fry the veal with the carrot, onion, rosemary and pine nuts for a few minutes until just cooked. Transfer to a bowl and add the marjoram, garlic and egg yolk. Season and mix well. Cut the lettuce leaves into 18 squares and put a small ball of the veal mixture on each. Roll up to make neat parcels and put in a baking dish. Bake for 15 minutes. Put 3 lettuce rolls in each serving bowl, ladle in some seasoned chicken broth and sprinkle with the Grana Padano to serve.

SERVES 6   WINE: Rossese di Dolceaqua

LIGURIAN ROSEMARY LIQUEUR
LIQUORE AL ROSMARINO

This liqueur is great as a digestive or after-dinner accompaniment for biscotti or castagnaccio (see below).

INGREDIENTS

80 g (2¾ oz) rosemary leaves

2 tablespoons rosemary flowers

peel from 1 large orange (no white pith)

1 litre (35 fl oz) neutral grappa (not highly aromatic)

400 g (14 oz) sugar

METHOD

Combine the rosemary leaves and flowers, orange peel and grappa in a sterilised jar. Seal and put in a dark cellar or cupboard for 1 week. Bring the sugar and 2 cups (500 ml/17 fl oz) water to the boil, then turn down the heat and simmer for 8 minutes. Remove from the heat and cool completely. Add the sugar syrup to the rosemary and grappa infusion, mix well and leave for 2 hours. Strain the liqueur through a couple of layers of muslin (cheesecloth) or kitchen filter paper, then put in sterilised bottles and seal with corks. Leave for at least 1 month before using.

MAKES 1.4 litres (2½ pints)

CHESTNUT FLAN
CASTAGNACCIO

Castagnaccio is made in several versions throughout many regions of Italy. In Tuscany it is strewn with rosemary, and even within Liguria it has variations – for example, in the province of Savona candied mixed peel is commonly added. Chestnuts contain a good amount of natural sugar, and chestnut flour is naturally sweet, so castagnaccio was often made without the addition of extra sugar. If a sweeter result is desired, simply add 80 g (2¾ oz) sugar when working the flour and water together. It's important to use fresh chestnut flour as when it is old it loses its sweetness and becomes rather bitter.

INGREDIENTS

150 g (5½ oz) sultanas (golden raisins)

500 g (1 lb 2 oz) chestnut flour

1.5 litres (52 fl oz) tepid water

100 ml (3½ fl oz) extra virgin olive oil, plus extra for greasing

grated zest of 1 orange

½ cup (80 g/2¾ oz) pine nuts

80 g (2¾ oz) hazelnuts, lightly roasted, skinned and chopped

METHOD

Soak the sultanas in warm water for 30 minutes, then drain and set aside. Preheat the oven to 200°C (400°F). Sift the chestnut flour into a large bowl, then pour in the water a little at a time, mixing with a wooden spoon to attain a smooth, runny mixture. Add the olive oil, orange zest and a pinch of salt. Choose a baking dish that will hold the mixture at a depth of about 2 cm (¾ in) and brush well with oil. Pour in the batter and scatter the sultanas, pine nuts and hazelnuts evenly over. Bake for 30–35 minutes until a crust has formed and the flan has begun to shrivel. Remove and cool completely before cutting into 4–5 cm (1½–2 in) squares.

WINE: Ligurian rosemary liqueur (see above)

CANESTRELLI BISCUITS
CANESTRELLI

These traditional Ligurian biscuits (cookies) are a favourite served with espresso or tea. They are made using a very rich shortcrust base.

INGREDIENTS

425 g (15 oz) plain
(all-purpose) flour
150 g (5½ oz) icing
(confectioners') sugar,
plus extra for dusting
85 g (3 oz) potato flour
465 g (16½ oz) softened
unsalted butter
1 hard-boiled egg yolk

METHOD

Sift the plain flour and put half of it in the bowl of an electric mixer fitted with a paddle. Add the icing sugar and potato flour. Put 2 tablespoons of the butter in a shallow bowl and mash gently using a fork. Crumble the egg yolk into the butter and mash until well incorporated. Add to the flour mixture with the remaining butter. Mix on the lowest setting until the mixture comes together, then add the remaining flour and a pinch of salt and continue to mix. When the mixture comes together, form it into a rough disc, wrap in plastic wrap and refrigerate for at least 24 hours. When you are ready to cook, line baking trays with silicone paper. Roll out the dough to a thickness of 4 mm (¼ in), then cut out using the classic daisy-shaped cutter and make a hole in the centre of each biscuit. Put the biscuits on the baking sheets and refrigerate for 1 hour. Preheat the oven to 180°C (350°F). Bake the biscuits for 15–20 minutes until golden. Cool completely before dusting with icing sugar to serve.

MAKES about 80   WINE: Cinque Terre Sciacchetrà

GENOA CAKE
PANDOLCE GENOVESE

This medieval cake has a grand tradition in Genoa. It is made before Christmas in large quantities so there is enough left over for the Epiphany. It was said that cooks would take the dough to bed with them so it would stay warm and rise better. Pandolce predates Lombardia's more famous panettone and its reputation spread as far as London, where it was adapted and adopted as 'Genoa cake'. It is now a staple of traditional English baking and at country shows, alongside the 'rich fruit cake' competition, there is always a Genoa cake competition. This recipe is for the traditional Ligurian pandolce, not the anglicised Genoa cake. I have only called it 'Genoa cake' here for convenience.

INGREDIENTS

85 g (3 oz) unsalted butter

105 g (3¾ oz) caster (superfine) sugar

6 drops rum essence

6 drops lemon essence

½ teaspoon natural vanilla extract

1 egg

1⅓ cups (230 g/8 oz) sultanas (golden raisins)

75 g (2½ oz) candied orange peel, cut into 5 mm (¼ in) dice

75 g (2½ oz) candied cedro (citron), cut into 5 mm (¼ in) dice

1 tablespoon pine nuts

2 cups (300 g/10½ oz) plain (all-purpose) flour

½ teaspoon baking powder

⅓ cup (80 ml/2½ fl oz) milk

METHOD

Preheat the oven to 180°C (350°F). Beat the butter and sugar until pale and creamy. Add a pinch of salt and whisk in the rum, lemon and vanilla essences. Mix in the egg using a wooden spoon (don't whisk). Add the sultanas, candied orange peel, candied cedro and pine nuts and mix using the wooden spoon until evenly distributed. Sift the flour and baking powder together into a separate bowl, then add to the fruit mixture with the milk. Knead the dough on a lightly floured surface for 10 minutes or so until smooth and even. Shape into a ball and put on a baking tray. Using a sharp knife, slash a triangle on the top. Bake for about 40 minutes or until a skewer inserted comes out clean. Cool before serving. Keeps for 10 days.

WINE: Cinque Terre Sciacchetrà

GENOA CAKE – TRADITIONAL RECIPE
PANDOLCE GENOVESE TRADIZIONALE

Before leavening agents such as baking powder were invented, cakes such as this one achieved their lift through a process involving natural yeast. The starter was fed and kept in a warm place when it needed to be activated, and retired to a cool cellar to 'sleep' when it wasn't needed. Using this method is time-consuming, as the various stages of dough need to rise gradually, but the result is a much moister, airier and altogether better crumb texture than that of cakes made with modern leavening agents.

INGREDIENTS

35 g (1¼ oz) starter culture (lievito madre) (see page 46)

105 g (3¾ oz) caster (superfine) sugar

2 cups (300 g/10½ oz) plain (all-purpose) flour

85 g (3 oz) unsalted butter

6 drops rum essence

6 drops lemon essence

½ teaspoon natural vanilla extract

1 egg

1⅓ cups (230 g/8 oz) sultanas (golden raisins)

75 g (2½ oz) candied orange peel, cut into 5 mm (¼ in) dice

75 g (2½ oz) candied cedro (citron), cut into 5 mm (¼ in) dice

1 tablespoon pine nuts

⅓ cup (80 ml/2½ fl oz) milk

METHOD

Dissolve the starter culture in 50 ml (1¾ fl oz) water, 1 tablespoon of the sugar and ⅓ cup (50 g/1¾ oz) of the flour. Let prove at 39°C (102°F) for 30 minutes. Meanwhile, beat the butter and remaining sugar until pale and creamy. Add a pinch of salt and whisk in the rum, lemon and vanilla essences. Mix in the egg using a wooden spoon (don't whisk). Add the sultanas, candied orange peel, candied cedro and pine nuts and mix using the wooden spoon until evenly distributed. Sift the remaining flour into a separate bowl, then add to the fruit mixture along with the milk and starter culture. Knead the dough on a lightly floured surface for 10 minutes or so until smooth and even. Transfer to a bowl and let prove at 39°C (102°F) for 1 hour. Knock down the dough and knead for 5 minutes, then shape into a ball and put on a baking tray. Let prove at 39°C (102°F) for 20 more minutes. Preheat the oven to 180°C (350°F). Using a sharp knife, slash a triangle on the top of the dough. Bake for 1 hour or until a skewer inserted comes out clean. Coll before serving. Keeps for xx days

WINE: Cinque Terre Sciacchetrà

ROSE SYRUP
SCIROPPO DI ROSE

This concentrated syrup can be used in gelato, cakes, biscuits (cookies) and cocktails. The main rose varieties used to make it are the heavily scented muscosa, rugosa and gallica and Mister Lincoln and David Austins. The flowers need to be fully open and intact, and must be free from pesticides and chemicals. Try not to pick them during or just after rain. Avoid washing them as this will remove their all-important perfume.

INGREDIENTS

200 g (7 oz) fragrant rose
    petals (can be from
    mixed varieties)

2 lemons, halved

sugar

METHOD

Put the rose petals in a large container. Pour 2 litres (70 fl oz) water into a saucepan, add the lemons and bring to the boil. Pour the water and lemons over the rose petals and use a spatula or the like to gently press the petals down into the water, submerging them. Cover the container so that no steam can escape and leave to infuse for 24 hours. Remove and discard the lemons. Line a sieve with 3 layers of muslin (cheesecloth) and set it over a large bowl. Pour in the liquid and petals. When all the liquid has strained into the bowl, gently fold up the muslin around the petals and squeeze to release as much liquid as possible. Discard the petals. Measure the strained liquid and put it in a large saucepan. For every litre (35 fl oz) of liquid, add 1.5 kg (3 lb 5 oz) sugar. Mix, then slowly bring to the boil. Turn the heat down to very low and simmer for 20 minutes. Transfer to sterilised bottles or jars and seal. The syrup will last indefinitely.

MAKES about 3.5 litres (6 pints)

IN AND AROUND THE PROVINCE OF **GENOA ROSES** WERE GROWN IN GARDENS, ABBEYS AND VINEYARDS SPECIFICALLY FOR THE PRODUCTION OF THE FAMOUS ROSE SYRUP. THIS HAPPENS LESS SO THESE DAYS AS ARTIFICIALLY FLAVOURED CONCOCTIONS PROLIFERATE. IN 2000 SLOW FOOD'S PRESIDIO NAMED THE AREA'S ARTISAN-PRODUCED ROSE SYRUP AS ONE OF ITALY'S PRODUCTS WORTH PRESERVING. NOWADAYS, IF YOU LOOK FOR IT, YOU'LL FIND A GROWING NUMBER OF AUTHENTIC ROSE SYRUPS FROM THIS AREA OF ITALY.

RICE PUDDING WITH ROSE SYRUP
BUDINO DI RISO ALLO SCIROPPO DI ROSE

INGREDIENTS

1 cup (250 ml/9 fl oz) milk

150 g (5½ oz) Italian rice (carnaroli, vialone nano or arborio), well washed to remove starch

⅔ cup (150 g/5½ oz) caster (superfine) sugar

2 tablespoons rose syrup, store-bought or homemade (see opposite page)

1 teaspoon orange-flower water

3 tablespoons unsalted pistachio kernels, chopped

METHOD

Put the milk and 1 cup (250 ml/9 fl oz) water in a saucepan and bring to the boil. Add the rice and stir well. Bring back to the boil, then turn the heat down and simmer for 20 minutes, stirring occasionally so the rice doesn't stick to the base of the pan. Once the mixture has begun to thicken, add the sugar, rose syrup and orange-flower water. Simmer and stir for a minute or so, then transfer to 6–8 ramekins and sprinkle with the pistachios. Cover and refrigerate before serving.

SERVES 6–8   WINE: Sciacchetrà

LOMBARDIA

LOMBARDIA

LOMBARDY

BORDERED BY SWITZERLAND TO THE NORTH, TRENTINO-ALTO ADIGE AND VENETO TO THE EAST, EMILIA-ROMAGNA TO THE SOUTH AND PIEMONTE TO THE WEST, LOMBARDIA HOLDS ONE-SIXTH OF ITALY'S POPULATION AND PRODUCES AROUND ONE-FIFTH OF ITS GDP, MAKING IT THE RICHEST AND MOST POPULOUS OF THE COUNTRY'S REGIONS, AND ONE OF THE WEALTHIEST IN EUROPE.

Geographically it can be split into three zones: Alta, the high plains; Bassa, the low plains along the Po River; and the mountains, the highest of which is Presolana at just over 2500 metres (8200 feet). It contains some important and magnificent lakes, including Maggiore, Lugano (shared with Switzerland), Como, Iseo, Idro and Garda, the last of which is Italy's largest and shared with Trentino-Alto Adige. Its capital, Milan, is the industrial, commercial, financial and, some would say, fashion capital of Italy.

The food of Lombardia is a product of the extraordinary variety of peoples who have lived in, conquered or passed through the region, beginning with the Etruscans, who lived in the present town of Mantua. Much later came the Spanish, then the Austrians – two cultures that left their mark on the local cuisine. The Spanish arrived with the saffron found in risotto alla milanese, and the Austrians introduced wiener schnitzel, which was refined to cotoletta alla milanese. The cotoletta is made from a bone-in cutlet rather than an escalope, and dredged only in flour and egg rather than the schnitzel's flour, egg and breadcrumbs.

Lombardia is home to some of the world's favourite Italian foodstuffs and dishes, starting with gorgonzola cheese, which originated in the little town of Gorgonzola, some 20 kilometres (12 miles) north of Milan. It is only one of an enormous number of cheeses from the region, including, but by no means limited to, Grana Padano, mascarpone and taleggio. One reason why so many wonderful cheeses are made in Lombardia is that it has Italy's highest density of cattle.

Not exactly a food, but most definitely a favourite from Italy, the drink Campari was invented in Lombardia at Cafe Zucca in Milan in 1867. The cafe is still there today.

Then there's panettone, the irresistible sweet bread studded with candied citrus peel and raisins that is especially in evidence at Christmas; colomba, the cake served at Easter; and mostarda di Cremona – cooked and concentrated grape must with crushed mustard grains, in which is steeped cherries, plums, figs and pears. Mostarda di Cremona is famously served with bollito misto, an elaborate collection of boiled meats and sauces most often served in Lombardia and Piemonte. Minestrone alla milanese is the famous vegetable soup made using rice rather than, as is done elsewhere, pasta.

There is a very good reason why rice is such an important component of the cuisine of Lombardia. As well as being the premier industrial region of Italy, Lombardia is an important agricultural region, and the arborio and carnaroli rice grown in the Lomellina valley and south-west of Mantua are among the most important agricultural products in Italy. One reason for the province's abundant agricultural production is the excellent water supply from the melting glaciers of the Alps – and the technological superiority of its farms and farmers.

But in spite of – or perhaps because of – the wealth and industriousness of Lombardia and its citizens, there is a great respect for frugality. Leftovers are big in Lombardia, and nothing is wasted. Popular dishes are riso al salto, a sort of fried rice that uses leftover risotto, and meatballs, or polpette. Indeed, the Milanese poet Giovanni Raiberti called Milan 'the capital of meatballs'.

There are 13 winemaking regions in Lombardia. Perhaps the best known is the Valtellina, whose high-altitude vineyards – at 700 metres (almost 3000 feet) – are most famous for their wines made from the nebbiolo grape. ▶▶

THE INVENTED CHEESE

One of the cheeses from Lombardia, far from being an ancient product whose origins are lost in the mists of time, is the result of clever marketing.

In 1906 the entrepreneur Egidio Galbani, a native of Melzo, a small town not far from Milan, designed a cheese to compete internationally with successful French cheeses. It was without the strong odours and flavours associated with the traditional cheeses of Lombardia (such as Grana Padano, taleggio and gorgonzola), soft and creamy – indeed, some might say bland and inoffensive – and was sold using one of the earliest marketing campaigns in the history of modern Italy.

Bel Paese is the cheese, and it took its name from a phrase first used by Dante in his epic poem *Inferno*: 'del bel paese là dove 'l sì suona' (meaning 'that fair land where sì [yes] is heard'). By the time Galbani picked it up, the phrase il bel paese was known throughout Italy as the name of a book by Antonio Stoppani that had been published in 1875 and written in an attempt to give some form and shape to the idea of a unified Italy. The book had been particularly popular among the bourgeoisie of Milan.

Obviously Galbani's campaign was successful: Bel Paese is still on the market and its origins are now lost in the mists of a much shorter time.

The final irony of the story is that Galbani, the company that produces Bel Paese, the cheese originally created to compete against the French, was sold in 2006 to the French dairy conglomerate Lactalis.

While Lombardia may not be as rich in wine as it is in industry, it does produce excellent wines in styles borrowed from elsewhere, including champagne. For the visitor, there is a treasure trove of fascinating and eccentric offerings to be found among its 17 DOC regions. What it lacks in indigenous grapes it makes up for by importing from its neighbours and others grapes such as nebbiolo, barbera and cortese (from Piemonte); marzemino and schiava (from Trentino); and riesling from Germany, lambrusco from Emilia, and so on.

Some of the most notable wines are the metodo-classico-style chardonnays from the Francaciorta DOCG, referred to by Italian wine expert, Nicholas Belfrage as 'indisputably the best in Italy – some would say the best outside Champagne'.

Most of the white wine produced in Lombardia comes from DOCs along the western and southern shores of Lake Garda. It includes those made from trebbiano di Lugana, garganega, and a mix of sangiovese, marzemino, barbera and groppello (the latter of which is one of the few remaining indigenous grapes of the region) used in a spicy local rosé. In Francaciorta they make chablis-style still whites with their chardonnay.

While reds are made throughout the region, the two major DOCs for red wine are Oltrepò Pavese and the Valtellina, the latter being the second most northerly wine region (after Alto Adige) in Italy. Oltrepò Pavese was arguably the country's first region to plant pinot nero (pinot noir), which was originally sold in bulk to spumante and vermouth producers. More recently, their barrel-aged still pinot neros have been turning heads locally. Savvy red-wine drinkers are increasingly looking to this region for good-quality low-price reds: the newer barberas are fuller bodied than in the past, and bonarda is being used more and more to make interesting wine.

Another discovery worth making is nebbiolo from the Valtellina, some of which approaches the body and complexity of the barolos through means such as appassimento (drying the grapes for concentration of flavour), with results reminiscent of the amarones of Barolo.

But that is not all: head east to discover some curious wines, most of which you will have to find on the spot. Near Mantua, for example, in the DOC called Colli Morenici Mantovani del Garda, there is a red of great local reputation made from a blend of merlot, molinara and sangiovese.

LOMBARDIA
ANTI-PASTI

PICKLED LETTUCE
LATTUGA SOTT'ACETO

This recipe demonstrates the frugality of la cucina povera italiana but in doing so also highlights the depth and brilliance that adversity and necessity can bring to cuisine. It is usually made in large quantities because it utilises the excess tough lettuce leaves from a kitchen garden. This recipe is adapted for a domestic situation and can even be halved if necessary.

INGREDIENTS

1 kg (2 lb 4 oz) outer lettuce leaves (any type of lettuce), trimmed and well washed

3 garlic cloves, each roughly chopped into 3–4 pieces

2 bay leaves

red or white wine vinegar

METHOD

Put the lettuce in a large saucepan and cover with water. Bring to the boil and cook for 5 minutes. Drain and let cool, then squeeze out as much liquid as possible. Arrange in sterilised jars and put the garlic and bay leaves randomly in among the lettuce. Pour in enough vinegar to cover well. Using a spoon, press down to force out any trapped air. Seal the jars and put in the refrigerator. The pickled lettuce can be used after 2–3 weeks but is better left for a couple of months or more. To serve, squeeze out any excess vinegar, chop roughly and dress with olive oil, salt and pepper.

SERVES 8–10 as antipasto   WINE: Franc Cuvee

CROSTINI WITH PEPPERS AND ONIONS 'AL AGRODOLCE'
CROSTINI CON PEPERONI E CIPOLLE AL AGRODOLCE

INGREDIENTS

2 red capsicums (peppers), seeded

2 yellow capsicums (peppers), seeded

2 red onions, each cut into 8 wedges

extra virgin olive oil

2 tablespoons balsamic vinegar

6 × 1 cm (½ in) slices good-quality white bread

METHOD

Preheat the oven to 180°C (350°F). Cut each capsicum into 8 strips and put in a baking tray. Add the onions and sprinkle with olive oil, salt and pepper. Mix so the vegetables are well coated with oil. Bake for about 20 minutes until soft. Add the balsamic vinegar, mix well and let come to room temperature. Cut each slice of bread into 3–4 pieces, brush with oil and grill (broil) or toast to make crostini. Put some agrodolce on each crostino and serve.

SERVES 6   WINE: Groppello

PANCETTA CROSTINI WITH TRUFFLE MUSTARD DRESSING
CROSTINI CON PANCETTA E MOSTARDA AL TARTUFO

Mostarda (mustard fruits) are very popular in Lombardia, especially in the provinces of Milano, Brescia and Mantova. While they are generally fruit-based, some producers have begun making truffle mustards using fresh white and black truffles.

INGREDIENTS

⅓ cup (80 ml/2½ fl oz) extra
  virgin olive oil
1 tablespoon red wine vinegar
8 × 1 cm (½ in) slices
  country-style bread
8 slices pancetta
small salad leaves

TRUFFLE MUSTARD

250 g (9 oz) superfine smooth
  mustard
1 × 30 g (1 oz) white or black
  truffle, finely shaved

METHOD

To make the truffle mustard, put the mustard and truffle in a food processor and pulse until well incorporated. Mix half the olive oil with the vinegar and 2 teaspoons of the truffle mustard and season. Brush the bread with the remaining oil and grill (broil) or toast in the oven. Transfer to a serving plate and put a slice of pancetta on each crostino. Add salad leaves and drizzle with the dressing. Refrigerate the remaining truffle mustard for later use. It should keep for 2–3 weeks refrigerated.

SERVES 8   WINE: Franciacorta Brut Rosè

SAVOY CABBAGE AND CHERRY TOMATO SALAD
INSALATA DI VERZA E POMODORI PACCHINI

This is one of my favourite salads from my mother's repertoire. It really does improve in texture and flavour if dressed and left awhile.

INGREDIENTS

¼ Savoy cabbage, tough outer
  leaves and core removed
½ cup (125 ml/4 fl oz) extra
  virgin olive oil
⅓ cup (80 ml/2½ fl oz) red
  wine vinegar
250 g (9 oz) cherry tomatoes,
  halved

METHOD

Finely slice the cabbage and put in a bowl. Add the olive oil and vinegar, sprinkle with 2–3 good pinches of salt and toss well. Leave for 30–45 minutes, giving it a stir occasionally. When you are ready to serve, add the cherry tomatoes and toss with a few turns of pepper.

SERVES 4   WINE: Oltrepo Pavese Crausé

FIGS WITH STRACCHINO AND HONEY
FICHI CON STRACCHINO E MIELE

INGREDIENTS

1 tablespoon light-coloured
honey (such as acacia,
citrus blossom or clover)

¼ cup (60 ml/2 fl oz) extra
virgin olive oil

1 tablespoon red wine vinegar

700 g (1 lb 9 oz) ripe green or
black figs, cut into wedges

250 g (9 oz) soft stracchino
cheese, torn into bite-sized
pieces

150 g (5½ oz) large-leafed
rocket (arugula), torn into
even-sized pieces

¼ cup basil leaves

METHOD

Combine the honey, olive oil and vinegar until smooth. Carefully toss all
the ingredients together, season and serve.

SERVES 4   WINE: Groppello

RAW STURGEON AND RADISH
CRUDO DI STORIONE E RAPANELLO

*Sturgeon is native to north and central Italy and its eggs were a favourite delicacy of ancient Rome. The
flesh is particularly good eaten raw.*

INGREDIENTS

400 g (14 oz) very fresh
sturgeon fillets (or other
white-fleshed fish such as
snapper or kingfish), very
thinly sliced

4 ripe tomatoes, seeded and
finely diced

100 ml (3½ fl oz) extra virgin
olive oil

8 golfball-sized radishes,
trimmed and thinly sliced

2 tablespoons finely snipped
chives

METHOD

Put the fish on a plate, cover and refrigerate until ready to serve. Mix
the tomatoes with 1 tablespoon of the olive oil and season. Interleave
slices of the fish and radish on a serving plate (or individual plates) in
concentric circles. Pile the tomato in the centre, sprinkle the entire dish
with the remaining oil and season. Scatter the chives on top to serve.

SERVES 4–6   WINE: Benaco Bresciano

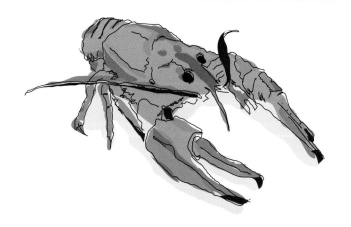

RICE, ASPARAGUS AND FRESHWATER CRAYFISH FRITTERS
POLPETTINE DI RISO, ASPARAGI E GAMBERI DI FIVME

Although these fritters are ideally made with freshwater crayfish, prawns can be substituted. They can also be made with leftover fish or shellfish risotto.

INGREDIENTS

2 kg (4 lb 8 oz) live freshwater crayfish, to yield about 300 g (10½ oz) meat

2 small brown onions

1 celery stick, chopped

1 carrot, cut into 5–6 chunks

140 ml (4¾ fl oz) extra virgin olive oil

300 g (10½ oz) Italian rice (preferably vialone nano)

½ cup (125 ml/4 fl oz) dry white wine

200 g (7 oz) asparagus spears, trimmed, cut into bit-sized pieces

50 g (1¾ oz) unsalted butter

2 tablespoons Grana Padano, grated

white pepper

1 egg

1 tablespoon fine breadcrumbs

plain (all-purpose) flour

coarse salt

1 cup young green chicory leaves, thinly sliced

2 tablespoons red wine vinegar

1 tablespoon extra virgin olive oil

METHOD

Put the crayfish in the refrigerator for an hour or so to slow down their metabolism. Cut 1 of the onions into quarters and finely dice the other. Put 4 litres (7 pints) water in a large saucepan on high heat with the celery, carrot and quartered onion. Boil for 2 minutes, then plunge in the crayfish, pushing them under the water if need be. Let the water come back up to a rolling boil, then turn off the heat. Drain and reserve the cooking liquid. Remove and chop the crayfish tail meat. Put the crayfish carcasses, celery, carrot and quartered onion back in the pan and pour in the reserved cooking liquid. Bring to the boil, then reduce the heat and simmer for 15 minutes. Drain, reserving the liquid and discarding the rest.

Heat 2 tablespoons of the olive oil in a frying pan and lightly fry the diced onion until translucent. Add the rice and toast as if making risotto. Pour in the wine and let it evaporate, then add a few ladlefuls of hot crayfish liquid and proceed as for risotto. About 2–3 minutes before the rice is ready, add the chopped crayfish and the asparagus. When the rice is al dente, remove the pan from the heat, fold in the butter, grated Grana Padano and season with white pepper. Pour into a tray to cool. Mix the cooled rice with the egg and breadcrumbs and form into 4 cm (1½ in) patties. Dust with flour and fry in the remaining oil until golden. Drain on paper towels and sprinkle with coarse salt. Gently toss the chicory with oil and the vinegar and serve with the fritters.

SERVES 10–12   WINE: Lugana

EGGPLANT 'MEATBALLS'
POLPETTINE DI MELANZANA

The Milanese poet Giovanni Raiberti called Milano 'the capital of meatballs'. Anything left over from a previous meal can go into a polpetta or polpettina. It's a good way to avoid wasting food.

INGREDIENTS

500 g (1 lb 2 oz) eggplant (aubergine), cut into 3–4 cm (1¼–1½ in) cubes

100 g (3½ oz) moist breadcrumbs from day-old bread

½ cup (80 g/2¾ oz) pine nuts

30 g (1 oz) Grana Padano, grated

2 garlic cloves, minced

2 small red chillies, minced

2 eggs, whisked

3 tablespoons finely chopped parsley

extra virgin olive oil

⅔ cup (80 g/2¾ oz) fine dry breadcrumbs

tomato passata

METHOD

Bring 2 litres (70 fl oz) water and 1 tablespoon salt to the boil in a large saucepan. Add the eggplant and boil for about 10 minutes, uncovered, until soft, pushing it under the water repeatedly with a wooden spoon as it cooks. Drain, cool and press with a spoon to remove any excess liquid. Chop and put in a bowl with the moist breadcrumbs, pine nuts, Grana Padano, garlic, chillies, eggs and parsley. Blend gently using a fork. Season. Heat a little olive oil in a frying pan until hot and fry a tablespoon of the mixture to check for seasoning. Roll the mixture into 2.5 cm (1 in) balls and put on a tray. If the mixture is too wet to roll easily, add more fresh breadcrumbs. Roll each ball in the dry breadcrumbs to coat evenly. Pour oil into a wide frying pan to a depth of 1 cm (½ in). Turn the heat to medium and when the oil begins to shimmer put a ball in. If it begins to sizzle immediately, the oil is ready. Fry the balls until browned all over. Drain on paper towels. Cool for 10 minutes, then serve with tomato passata.

MAKES about 40   WINE: Franciacorta Rosè

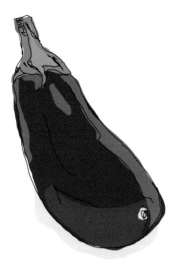

EGGPLANT 'MEATBALLS'

BRAISED FENNEL WITH GORGONZOLA AND WALNUTS
FINOCCHIO, GORGONZOLA E NOCI

This is such a great combination. Often when I don't want to cook, I'll cut some wedges of raw fennel and serve them as is with creamy gorgonzola and walnuts. It works just as well!

INGREDIENTS

4 small–medium fennel bulbs with fronds

½ cup (125 ml/4 fl oz) extra virgin olive oil

1 garlic clove, halved lengthways

100 g (3½ oz) gorgonzola cheese, broken into small pieces

½ cup (70 g/2½ oz) walnut pieces

METHOD

Trim the fennel bulbs by cutting off and discarding the tops (reserve the light-green fronds) and discarding the tough outer layers. Wash well and cut lengthways into 5 mm (¼ in) slices. Heat half the olive oil in a wide frying pan and gently fry the garlic until it starts to colour all over. Remove from the pan and discard. Add the fennel and fry lightly for 10 minutes. Add 1 cup (250 ml/9 fl oz) water and a couple of good pinches of salt, cover tightly and cook on low heat for 10–12 minutes until the fennel is tender. Transfer to serving plates and season with a little more salt (if needed) and some cracked pepper. Dress with the remaining oil and scatter the gorgonzola, walnuts and fennel fronds over to serve.

SERVES 8   WINE: Franciacorta Satèn

BROCCOLI AND RICOTTA BAKE WITH GORGONZOLA SAUCE
BROCCOLI E RICOTTA AL FORNO CON CREMA DI GORGONZOLA

INGREDIENTS

30 g (1 oz) butter

200 g (7 oz) broccoli florets

1 egg

200 g (7 oz) ricotta cheese

⅓ cup (30 g/1 oz) grated parmesan cheese

pinch of grated nutmeg

50 ml (1¾ fl oz) thin (pouring) cream

100 g (3½ oz) gorgonzola or other blue cheese

METHOD

Preheat the oven to 160°C (320°F) and grease a small baking dish with the butter. Steam the broccoli until tender. Transfer to a tray and let cool, then chop finely. Put half the broccoli in a bowl and mix with the egg, ricotta, parmesan and nutmeg. Season. Put the mixture in the baking dish and bake for 20 minutes. Meanwhile, bring the cream to the boil, then reduce the heat to low and add the gorgonzola and remaining broccoli. Stir until the cheese has totally melted, then simmer for 1 minute. Season with a little pepper and serve with the broccoli and ricotta bake.

SERVES 4   WINE: Bardolino

MOREL AND SPRING PEA FRITTATA
FRITTATA DI SPUGNOLE E PISELLI

This is a modern form of frittata in that it is made in a thin, single-serve format. If fresh morels can't be found, dried ones can be substituted, or you can use dried porcini. Both morels and peas are best in spring.

INGREDIENTS

130 g fresh or 30 g (1 oz) dried morel mushrooms

½ cup (80 g/2¾ oz) shelled peas

80 g (2¾ oz) unsalted butter

1 French shallot, finely diced

1 garlic clove, minced

4 eggs

2 tablespoons grated parmesan cheese

2 teaspoons extra virgin olive oil

METHOD

Remove any twigs or dirt from the morels using a soft brush. If using dried morels, soak in plenty of cold water for 15–20 minutes, then drain and pat dry. Bring a saucepan of salted water to the boil and cook the peas until tender. Drain and put in a bowl with half the butter. Season, then mash using a fork, cover and keep warm. Heat the remaining butter in a frying pan and gently fry the shallot and garlic for 30 seconds. Add the morels and fry for 2–3 minutes, stirring constantly. Season and set aside. Whisk 2 of the eggs in a bowl with half the parmesan and a little salt and pepper. Heat half the olive oil in a 15–18 cm (6–7 in) frying pan and pour in the egg mixture. Move it around the pan to cover the bottom. Cook for less than a minute without turning – it should still be a little creamy. Spoon half the morels and peas on top, then transfer to a warm plate. Quickly whisk the remaining eggs and mix with the remaining parmesan. Season, then cook as for the first frittata. Serve immediately, one frittata per person.

SERVES 2  WINE: Chiavennasco Rosato

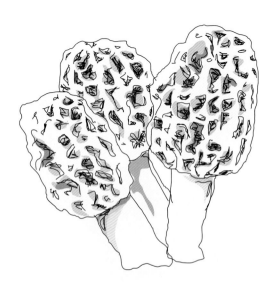

LOMBARDIA
PRIMI

BEAN AND RICE MINESTRONE
MINESTRONE DI RISO E FAGIOLI

This soup uses parmesan rind cut into small pieces, which is delicious as it melts but retains a little chewiness.

INGREDIENTS

60 g (2¼ oz) parmesan rind

¼ cup (60 ml/2 fl oz) extra virgin olive oil

2 brown onions, diced

8 garlic cloves, each cut into 3–4 pieces

1 celery heart (including the tender light-green leaves), sliced

2 large or 4–5 smaller carrots, cut into bite-sized pieces

2 cups chopped Savoy cabbage

2 bay leaves

1 cup fresh or tinned borlotti, cannellini or similar beans

350 g (12 oz) boiling potatoes, diced

200 g (7 oz) tin tomatoes, mashed

100 g (3½ oz) carnaroli rice

150 g (5½ oz) spinach, chopped

1 cup parsley, chopped

grated parmesan cheese

METHOD

Using a sharp knife, scrape off the thin coating of wax on the parmesan rind (it's harmless, but will taste a little strange if left on), then cut the rind into 1 cm (½ in) cubes and set aside. Heat the olive oil in a large saucepan and add the onions, garlic, celery, carrots, cabbage and bay leaves. Lightly fry for 2–3 minutes, making sure the vegetables don't colour. Add the beans, potatoes and tomatoes and stir, then pour in enough water to cover. Bring to the boil and add the rice. Reduce the heat, add a couple of good pinches of salt and stir. Simmer for 20–25 minutes until the rice is cooked. Add the spinach, parsley and parmesan rind and simmer for 5 minutes. Turn off the heat, season and serve with plenty of grated parmesan and crusty bread. The soup is much better the day after cooking.

SERVES 10

WINE: Bardolino

WHEN WE WERE KIDS MY MOTHER WOULD THROW TOGETHER A QUICK **MINESTRINA** WHEN WE WERE HUNGRY. SHE WOULD USE SOME CHICKEN OR MEAT BROTH AS THE BASE OR A COUPLE OF STOCK CUBES, ADDING SOME SPINACH, MUSHROOMS OR OTHER VEGETABLES AND A HANDFUL OR TWO OF RISONE PASTA. IT WAS READY IN 10 MINUTES AND ALL IT NEEDED WAS A DUSTING OF GRATED PARMESAN. THE TERM 'MINESTRINA' MEANS A SMALL SOUP.

FISH-CHEEK SOUP
ZUPPA DI PESCE ALLA GARDESANA

This soup is traditionally made with freshwater lake or river fish, but you can substitute freshwater perch, or saltwater species such as snapper and cod. Fish heads contain a massive amount of flavour and should never be wasted. Choose larger fish heads for convenience as it is easier to extract the meat.

INGREDIENTS

1 × 1.5–2 kg (3 lb 5 oz–4 lb 8 oz) fish heads, fins on, scaled and gilled

1 large brown onion, chopped

1 carrot, chopped

1 celery heart (including the tender light-green leaves), chopped

6 garlic cloves, chopped

6 very ripe tomatoes, chopped

½ cup (125 ml/4 fl oz) extra virgin olive oil, plus extra for drizzling

leaves from a few sprigs of thyme

salt flakes

100 g (3½ oz) parsley, chopped

METHOD

Wash the fish head well, put in a saucepan and just cover with cold water. Bring to the boil, then reduce the heat and simmer for 20–30 minutes until the flesh flakes easily when pulled apart with a fork. Strain, reserving the cooking liquid and the fish head. When the head is cool enough to handle, remove all the flesh and discard the bones and scales. Put the onion, carrot, celery and garlic cloves in a food processor and mince. Transfer to a bowl. Put the tomatoes in the food processor and puree, then pass through a fine sieve. Heat a large saucepan on medium heat and add the oil. When it is hot, add the minced vegetable mixture and fry for 6–8 minutes until lightly coloured. Add the tomato puree, thyme and salt and bring to the boil, then reduce the heat and simmer for 15 minutes. Add enough of the reserved fish stock to achieve a thick soup consistency and bring to the boil. Stir in the fish-head flesh and parsley, season and serve drizzled with oil.

SERVES 8

WINE: Lugana

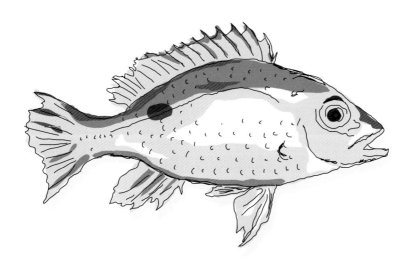

OXTAIL BROTH WITH QUADRUCCI
QUADRUCCI ALLA CODA IN BRODO

INGREDIENTS

2 kg (4 lb 8 oz) oxtail, cut into
  6 cm (2½ in) lengths

1 carrot, chopped

1 brown onion, quartered

1 celery heart, chopped

150 g (5½ oz) bone marrow

1 cup (100 g/3½ oz) grated
  parmesan cheese, plus
  extra for serving

2 garlic cloves

2 cups parsley

½ teaspoon grated nutmeg

3 eggs

1 quantity basic pasta dough
  (see page 42)

½ cup (80 g/2¾ oz) shelled
  peas

100 g (3½ oz) spinach,
  chopped into large pieces

METHOD

Put the oxtail, carrot, onion and celery in a stockpot. Cover with water, bring to the boil and simmer for 2–3 hours until the meat is tender. Strain and reserve the broth. When it is cool enough to handle, strip the meat from the oxtail, making sure no bones are left. Put the meat in a food processor with the bone marrow, parmesan, garlic, parsley, nutmeg and eggs and pulse until well incorporated. Season. You will need ¼ of this mixture to finish the dish. (Freeze the remainder in small quantities to use later.)

Roll out the pasta dough into 2 sheets the width of your pasta machine and 50 cm (20 in) long. Flour your work surface and lay 1 pasta sheet on it. Spread on the oxtail mixture in a thin even layer, then lay the other pasta sheet on top. Use a rolling pin to gently roll the mixture evenly between the pasta sheets. Using a pasta cutter, cut the sheets into 2 cm (¾ in) squares. These are your quadrucci. Bring the reserved broth to the boil, then turn the heat down and add the peas and quadrucci. Simmer for 3 minutes, then stir in the spinach. Season and serve with grated parmesan.

SERVES 6–8   WINE: Garda Classico Gropello

QUADRUCCI IS THE ITALIAN WORD FOR 'LITTLE SQUARES'. QUADRUCCI IS TRADITIONALLY FRESHLY MADE EGG PASTA THAT IS ROLLED OUT FLAT AND CUT INTO SQUARES. YOU CAN MAKE THE SQUARES ANY SIZE YOU LIKE; SMALL QUADRUCCI WILL TYPICALLY BE USED IN SOUPS WHILE THE LARGER SQUARES ARE MORE SUITED TO PASTA DISHES.

PUMPKIN TORTELLI
TORTELLI DI ZUCCA

This dish is eaten on Christmas Eve all across the north of Italy, but Mantova is perhaps its epicentre. It is an old family favourite. The pumpkin (squash) type is important. Butternut pumpkins are not flavoursome enough. Traditionally local Mantovane pumpkins are used, but I've had success with Japanese (kent) as well as Queensland blue varieties. Try to avoid pumpkins that have just been picked – they need to age a little so they lose some of their moisture.

INGREDIENTS

1 × 2.5 kg (5 lb 8 oz) pumpkin (squash)

200 g (7 oz) unsalted butter

1 large brown onion, cut into 1 cm (½ in) cubes

2 garlic cloves, minced

15 apricot kernels

50 g (1¾ oz) amaretti biscuits, crushed

120 g (4¼ oz) mustard fruits (apple, pear or quince), finely chopped

2 good pinches of grated nutmeg

200 g (7 oz) Grana Padano, grated

1 quantity basic pasta dough (see page 42)

½ cup sage leaves

METHOD

Cut the pumpkin into pieces of the same size. Remove and discard the seeds and the soft webbing around them but do not peel – the skin is very important. Steam the pumpkin until tender, then drain and let cool a little. Use a fork (not a spoon) to scrape the pumpkin flesh off the skin – sometimes a pumpkin has woody pieces, and with a fork you can feel these. Put the flesh in a bowl, including the green part near the skin (this is the best part, so try to get as much of it as possible). Put a small amount of the pumpkin in a clean tea towel (dish towel) and squeeze out as much liquid as possible so you are left with dry flesh the consistency of thick paste. Repeat until all the pumpkin has been squeezed.

Heat half the butter in a frying pan and lightly fry the onion until it begins to colour. Remove from the heat and drain off the butter, setting it aside to cool. Discard the onion. Mix the cooled butter and the garlic with the pumpkin. Put the apricot kernels in a mortar with a pinch of salt and grind to a powder. Add this powder to the pumpkin with the amaretti, mustard fruits, nutmeg and half the Grana Padano. Season, then rest in the refrigerator to firm up a little.

Roll out the pasta to 2 mm thick and cut into 9 cm squares. Put a teaspoon of pumpkin mixture in the centre of each square and roll from a corner. Press to seal (you may need to brush the opposite corner with egg wash if the pasta is too dry). Put the tortelli on a tray lined with a clean tea towel (dish towel), making sure they don't touch each other. Cover with another clean tea towel and refrigerate until needed.

Cook the tortelli in rapidly boiling salted water. Remove with a spider (flat sieve) and put on a serving plate. Sprinkle with the remaining Grana Padano and keep warm. Put the remaining butter in a small saucepan and cook until nut-brown, then add the sage leaves and fry until crisp. Spoon the butter and sage over the tortelli and serve immediately.

SERVES 10–12   WINE: Garda Classico Bianco

TAGLIATELLE WITH FRESHWATER CRAYFISH AND SESAME
TAGLIATELLE CON GAMBERI DI FIUME E SESAMO

This is one of my mother's dishes and a favourite in my restaurant repertoire. It is easy to make – though, as always in Italian cooking, the final result depends on the quality of the ingredients.

INGREDIENTS

30 live freshwater crayfish

500 g (1 lb 2 oz) basic pasta dough (page 42), cut to tagliatelle size (approx. 1 cm (¼ in))

½ cup (75 g/2½ oz) sesame seeds, toasted

125 g (4½ oz) butter at room temperature, thinly sliced

100 g (3½ oz) Grana Padano, finely grated

METHOD

Bring a large saucepan of well-salted water to the boil and add the crayfish. When the water returns to the boil, remove the crayfish from the pan. Cool a little, then remove their shells and cut the tails in half lengthways. Cook the tagliatelle in plenty of salted water, then drain and toss with the sesame seeds, butter, crayfish tails and Grana Padano. Season and serve immediately.

SERVES 6   WINE: Chardonnay

PIZZOCCHERI
PIZZOCCHERI

This is a traditional pasta dish from the Valtellina area of northern Lombardy. You can occasionally find ready-made dried pizzoccheri imported from Italy, but it's easy to make your own. Bitto cheese is produced in the alpine areas of Lombardy.

INGREDIENTS

250 g (9 oz) buckwheat flour

1 cup (150 g/5½ oz) plain (all-purpose) flour

300 g (10½ oz) thinly sliced Savoy cabbage

180 g (6 oz) potatoes, sliced

150 g (5½ oz) butter

2 garlic cloves, minced

½ cup sage leaves

250 g (9 oz) Bitto cheese (or fontina), thinly sliced

METHOD

Combine the flours and work in enough water (about 250 ml/9 fl oz) to make a medium-firm dough. Work through a pasta machine into sheets about 2 mm (¹⁄₁₆ in) thick, using more buckwheat flour to keep the dough from sticking, if necessary. Cut into 6 cm × 1 cm (2½ in × ½ in) strips. Put the cabbage and potatoes in a large saucepan of water and bring to the boil. Cook for 15–20 minutes until the vegetables are tender, then drain. Melt the butter in a large frying pan and lightly fry the garlic and sage, taking care not to burn them. Add the cabbage and potatoes and stir through. Cook the pasta, drain and toss into the pan. Add the cheese, season and serve.

SERVES 6–8   WINE: Inferno

VEAL SHANK AND BRUSSELS SPROUTS STEW

VEAL SHANK AND BRUSSELS SPROUTS STEW
ZUPPA DI VITELLO E CAVOLINI DI BRUXELLES

As with any soup or stew, it is better to make this ahead of the intended serving day.

INGREDIENTS

4 veal shanks, well washed

160 ml (5¼ fl oz) extra virgin olive oil

1 large brown onion, chopped

1 celery heart, chopped

3 carrots, chopped

3 garlic cloves, chopped

8 tinned tomatoes, mashed (or 300 ml/10½ fl oz tomato passata)

2 bay leaves

500 g (1 lb 2 oz) brussels sprouts, trimmed and quartered

3 tablespoons chopped parsley

10–20 slices crusty white bread

1 cup (100 g/3½ oz) grated parmesan cheese

METHOD

Put the veal shanks in a large stockpot, pour in about 15 litres (3 gallons) cold water and bring to the boil. Immediately turn the heat down and simmer for 2 hours, skimming any impurities that form on the surface. Turn off the heat and cool the shanks in the liquid. Strain, reserving the stock. Pull the meat from the bones, cut into bite-sized pieces and set aside. Heat half the olive oil in a large saucepan and gently fry the onion, celery, carrots and garlic for 5 minutes, stirring occasionally. Stir in the tomatoes, then add the reserved veal stock and the bay leaves. Bring to the boil, then turn the heat down and simmer for 40 minutes. Add the brussels sprouts, season with 4–5 good pinches of salt and simmer for 20 minutes. Add the veal shank meat, check for seasoning and add a few turns of pepper. Remove from the heat and stir in the parsley. When you are ready to serve, brush the bread with some of the remaining oil and grill (broil) until slightly charred. Generously sprinkle the stew with the parmesan and the remaining olive oil and serve with the toasted bread.

SERVES at least 10

WINE: Groppello

SPAGHETTI WITH SWEET AND SOUR OXTAIL
SPAGHETTI ALLA CHITARRA ALLA CODA IN AGRODOLCE

The spaghetti called for in this dish is made on a traditional chitarra (a wooden, guitar-like pasta maker). If you can't find spaghetti alla chitarra commercially, substitute good-quality thick spaghetti. Bagoss cheese is made in the mountains above the town of Bagolino in the province of Brescia. Its vibrant yellow colour is due to the addition of saffron in the cheese-making process.

INGREDIENTS

2 oxtails, cut into 6 cm (2½ in) pieces

2 large brown onions, cut into 2 cm (¾ in) pieces

3 celery sticks, cut into 2 cm (¾ in) pieces

3 carrots, cut into 2 cm (¾ in) pieces

1 leek, white part only, cut into 2 cm (¾ in) pieces

1 tablespoon black peppercorns

1 bay leaf

1 handful parsley stalks

1 thyme sprig

½ cup (110 g/3¾ oz) caster (superfine) sugar

150 ml (5 fl oz) red wine vinegar

800 g (1 lb 12 oz) dried spaghetti alla chitarra or other thick spaghetti

100 g (3½ oz) grated bagoss cheese or grated parmesan cheese

TO FINISH THE SAUCE

½ cup (125 ml/4 fl oz) extra virgin olive oil

2 leeks, white part only, cut into matchsticks

4 celery sticks from centre of bunch, cut into matchsticks

2 carrots, cut into matchsticks

METHOD

Put the oxtails, vegetables, peppercorns and herbs in a large saucepan and cover with cold water. Bring to the boil, skimming any impurities that rise to the surface, then turn the heat down and simmer covered for 5–6 hours until the oxtail meat is tender and comes off the bones easily. Remove the oxtail pieces from the broth. When they are cool enough to handle, strip the meat from the bones and reserve. Discard the bones.

Strain the stock, discarding the vegetables, and let cool, then refrigerate until cold. Remove the surface fat and strain the stock through muslin (cheesecloth) into a saucepan. Bring to the boil and reduce by three-quarters. Meanwhile, boil the sugar with ¼ cup (60 ml/2 fl oz) water until a golden caramel is formed. Remove from the heat and carefully add the vinegar. Once the mixture has stopped bubbling, put the saucepan on medium heat and simmer, stirring with a spoon, until the sugar has completely dissolved. When the oxtail stock has reduced, add half the vinegar/sugar mixture and then reduce by half again. Taste for balanced seasoning and acidity and add more vinegar/sugar mixture if needed, or a little salt.

To finish the sauce, put the olive oil a wide frying pan over high heat and lightly fry the vegetables for 2–3 minutes until softened. Add the reserved oxtail meat and warm through, then add enough of the oxtail sauce to bind all the ingredients so the mixture is moist. Season and keep warm. Cook the spaghetti in plenty of boiling salted water. Drain and toss with the oxtail sauce and bagoss. Serve immediately.

SERVES 8　　　　　　　　　　　　　　　　WINE: Bonarda

MILANESE-STYLE ASPARAGUS
ASPARAGI ALLA MILANESE

When Julius Caesar added Milano to the occupied territories of the Roman Empire, Valerio Leonte, one of the city's leaders, offered the emperor a meal as a sign of friendship and diplomacy. When a course of steamed asparagus with burnt butter was presented to the Roman guests, the generals were so offended that they drew their daggers. In those times in Rome, asparagus was food for only the most miserable citizens and butter was used only for women's cosmetics. Caesar intervened: 'Who shows the most discourtesy? Who offers the best of what they have to their guests, and who threatens friends and insults them in their own house?' Once the generals had tasted asparagus prepared the Milanese way, they knew they had been served a grand dish rather than an insult. Caesar was so impressed that he asked for the recipe, and when he learned that the butter had been made in Lodi, conferred honorary Roman citizenship on all Lodi's inhabitants.

INGREDIENTS

600 g (1 lb 5 oz) asparagus
  spears, trimmed
125 g (4½ oz) butter
150 g (5½ oz) parmesan,
  grated

METHOD

Immerse the asparagus, base first, in rapidly boiling water and cook for about 3 minutes until tender but still a little al dente. Transfer to a warm serving plate. Meanwhile, put the butter in a small saucepan on high heat and cook until it is nut-brown. Turn off the heat. Sprinkle the asparagus with the parmesan, then spoon on the sizzling butter and serve immediately.

SERVES 4   WINE: Franciacorta Bianco

VEAL KIDNEYS BRAISED IN RED WINE, PARSLEY AND GARLIC
ROGNONCINI DI VITELLO TRIFOLATI

A favourite dish from my childhood, this is relatively easy to make. Care must be taken to cook out the red wine; otherwise, the acidity will overpower everything else.

INGREDIENTS

8 small calf kidneys, trimmed
  and cut into bite-sized pieces
plain (all-purpose) flour
⅓ cup (80 ml/2½ fl oz) extra
  virgin olive oil
2 brown onions, finely diced
4 garlic cloves, minced
100 ml (3½ fl oz) dry red wine
½ cup chopped parsley

METHOD

Lightly dust the kidneys with flour. Heat the olive oil in a frying pan and fry the onions, garlic and kidneys for 3–4 minutes. Add the wine and cook until the liquid has reduced to a sauce. Turn off the heat, add the parsley, season and stir well. Serve on toasted bread or soft, steaming polenta (cornmeal).

SERVES 4   WINE: Oltrepò Pavese Pinot Nero

BROCCOLI AND RICOTTA FLAN WITH TALEGGIO SAUCE
SFORMATO DI BROCCOLI E RICOTTA AL TALEGGIO

Taleggio is a washed-rind cheese from the Taleggio Valley in the mountains above Bergamo. Fairly firm when young, it develops a lovely creamy texture and complex flavours as it ages.

INGREDIENTS

200 g (7 oz) broccoli, trimmed leaving 3–4 cm stem

200 g (7 oz) ricotta cheese

1 egg

100 g (3½ oz) taleggio cheese, diced

¼ cup (25 g/1 oz) finely grated parmesan

METHOD

Preheat the oven to 160°C (320°F). Bring a saucepan of salted water to the boil and cook the broccoli until tender. Drain. Finely chop half the broccoli and combine with the ricotta, parmesan and egg. Season and mix well. Butter 4 individual moulds (150 ml/5 fl oz) and spoon in the mixture, then bake for 15–20 minutes until set (these are the sformati). Meanwhile, pass the other half of the cooked broccoli through a sieve into a small saucepan. Add the taleggio and put the saucepan on a low heat, stirring, until the cheese has melted completely. Remove the sformati from the oven and let sit for 5 minutes before turning out and serving with the taleggio sauce.

SERVES 4   WINE: Lugana Bianco

LEEKS BRAISED WITH PANCETTA
PORRI E PANCETTA

A favourite combination in the northern regions is leeks with prosciutto or pancetta. The sweet and salty flavours go well with bone-dry white wine.

INGREDIENTS

1 kg (2 lb 4 oz) large leeks, trimmed and cut into 10–12 cm (4–4½ in) lengths

50 g (1¾ oz) pancetta, cut into matchsticks

1 small carrot, thinly sliced

1 small brown onion, thinly sliced

1 cup (250 ml/9 fl oz) chicken stock

juice of ½ lemon

20 g (¾ oz) softened butter

METHOD

Bring a large saucepan of lightly salted water to the boil and plunge in the leeks. Simmer for 10 minutes, then drain. Scatter the pancetta, carrot and onion into a baking dish. Lay the leeks on top and pour in the chicken stock. Add a little salt and cover with foil. Bake for 1½ hours. Meanwhile, use a spoon to work the lemon juice and butter together until well incorporated. Transfer the leeks to a plate and whisk the lemon butter into the liquid in the baking dish. Return the leeks to the dish and bake, uncovered, for 5 minutes. Serve hot.

SERVES 4   WINE: Franciacorta Zero Dosage

LENTILS WITH ROAST CAULIFLOWER AND TWO CHEESES
LENTICCHIE E CAVOLFIORE CON DUE FORMAGGI

INGREDIENTS

1 small brown onion, finely chopped

½ celery heart, finely chopped

1 small carrot, finely chopped

1 small leek, white part only, halved vertically and cut into 5 mm (¼ in) slices

extra virgin olive oil

leaves from 1 rosemary sprig, chopped

leaves from 1 thyme sprig, chopped

100 g (3½ oz) castelluccio (or puy) lentils

100 g (3½ oz) ripe roma tomatoes, pureed

2 garlic cloves, minced

1 cup chopped parsley, plus extra for serving

60 g (2¼ oz) grated fontina cheese

60 g (2¼ oz) grated parmesan cheese

½ cauliflower

METHOD

In a large frying pan, lightly fry the onion, celery, carrot and leek in a little olive oil until softened but not coloured. Add the rosemary and thyme and continue to cook, then add the lentils and stir. Add the tomato puree and enough water to cover. Cook for 40 minutes–1 hour until the lentils are tender, adding more water if necessary. Stir in the garlic and parsley and season. Set aside to cool. Preheat the oven to 180°C (350°F) and brush a baking tray with a little oil. Combine the fontina and parmesan in a bowl. Poach or steam the cauliflower until tender. Cool, then cut lengthways into 2 cm (¾ in) slices. Put the slices on the baking tray and cover each slice with cheese mixture. Bake for 10–12 minutes until the cheese has melted. Serve the cauliflower on the braised lentils with a little parsley sprinkled on top.

SERVES 6   WINE: Sassella

LOMBARDIA
SECONDI

ROAST TURKEY WITH A BREAD AND MUSTARD FRUIT STUFFING
PETTO DI TACCHINO RIPIENO

INGREDIENTS

1 × 1.5 kg (3 lb 5 oz) turkey breast (preferably organic), skin on

1 brown onion, finely diced

8 garlic cloves, minced

100 g (3½ oz) butter

2½ cups breadcrumbs

150 g (5½ oz) cooked chestnuts, peeled and chopped

60 g (2¼ oz) mustard fruits, finely chopped

100 g (3½ oz) parmesan, grated

1 cup chopped parsley

¼ cup (60 ml/2 fl oz) extra virgin olive oil

METHOD

Preheat the oven to 170°C (340°F). Make a pocket between the turkey skin and flesh by running your fingers gently under the skin to pull it back, leaving it sealed at the edges of the breast. Lightly fry the onion and garlic in the butter until soft but not burnt. Transfer to a bowl and add the breadcrumbs, chestnuts, mustard fruits, parmesan and parsley. Season and mix well, then use to stuff the turkey breast in the pocket between the skin and flesh. Lightly oil and season the skin, put in a roasting tin and roast for about 1 hour 10 minutes until golden. Remove from the oven, cover loosely with foil and let rest for 10 minutes before carving.

SERVES 8-10 WINE: Rebo

ROAST GUINEA FOWL WITH A BREAD AND TRUFFLE STUFFING
FARAONA ARROSTO, RIPIENO DI PANE E TARTUFO

INGREDIENTS

1 brown onion, diced

4 garlic cloves

50 g (1¾ oz) butter

2 cups breadcrumbs

1 good-sized truffle (40g/1½ oz), shaved and finely chopped

100 g (3½ oz) grated parmesan

1 cup chopped parsley

6 guinea fowl, wings trimmed off at the first joint

TRUFFLE BUTTER

250 g (9 oz) softened butter

1 × 30 g (1 oz) truffle, finely shaved

METHOD

To make the truffle butter, put the butter and truffle in a food processor and pulse until well incorporated. Transfer to a length of plastic wrap and roll up into a log. Refrigerate until needed. Preheat the oven to 250°C (480°F). Lightly fry the onion and garlic in the butter until soft but not burnt. Remove the pan from the heat and melt in 50 g (1¾ oz) of the truffle butter (refrigerate the remaining truffle butter for later use). Transfer to a bowl and add the breadcrumbs, truffle, parmesan and parsley. Season and mix well, then let cool. Stuff the bread and truffle mixture in the pocket between the skin and the flesh of the guinea fowl breasts. Season the skin with a little salt and put the birds in a roasting tin. Roast for 15-20 minutes. To serve, take the breast meat off the bone and cut the legs at the joint.

SERVES 12 WINE: Oltrepò Pavese Pinot Nero

ROAST PHEASANT WITH SAVOY CABBAGE, CHESTNUTS AND RED WINE
FAGIANO ARROSTO AL VINO ROSSO, VERZA E CASTAGNE

INGREDIENTS

3 × 800 g (1 lb 12 oz)
   pheasants, prepared
   for roasting

extra virgin olive oil

1 brown onion, finely diced

100 g (3½ oz) pancetta, finely
   diced

½ Savoy cabbage, trimmed,
   core removed, leaves cut
   into strips

30 cooked chestnuts, peeled
   (see page 82)

RED WINE SAUCE

¼ cup (60 ml/2 fl oz)
   extra virgin olive oil

1 brown onion, chopped

1 celery heart, chopped

10 garlic cloves, chopped

1 cup (250 ml/9 fl oz)
   balsamic vinegar

1.5 litres (52 fl oz) red wine

METHOD

To make the red wine sauce, heat the olive oil in a large frying pan and lightly fry the onion, celery and garlic for a few minutes until softened but not coloured. Add the balsamic vinegar, turn up the heat and reduce by three-quarters. Pour in the wine and reduce by half, skimming any impurities from the surface. Strain through muslin (cheesecloth) and reduce the strained liquid to 1 cup (250 ml/9 fl oz).

Preheat the oven to 250°C (480°F). Rub the pheasants with olive oil, salt the skin and put in a roasting tin. Roast for 15–20 minutes, then transfer to a warm dish (on the stovetop is good) to rest for about 10 minutes, leaving the oven on. Add the red-wine reduction to the roasting tin and mix it with the juices, then put in the oven for 5–6 minutes. Strain again through muslin and keep warm. Heat ¼ cup (60 ml/2 fl oz) oil in a large frying pan and gently fry the onion and pancetta. Add the cabbage and a little salt and stir continuously until the cabbage wilts. Add the chestnuts and simmer until the cabbage is cooked, making sure it retains a little texture. Season. Take the pheasant breast meat off the bone and remove the legs. Serve with the cabbage and chestnuts and the red wine sauce.

SERVES 6   WINE: Bonarda

TO PREPARE A PHEASANT (OR OTHER GAME BIRD) FOR ROASTING, CUT THE LEGS AT THE KNEE JOINT. CUT THE WINGS AT THE FIRST JOINT FROM THE BREAST AND REMOVE THE NECK. DON'T THROW THESE AWAY AS THEY MAKE EXCELLENT STOCK. WASH THE STOMACH CAVITY AND DRY WELL USING A CLEAN CLOTH. THE BIRD IS NOW READY FOR ROASTING OR BRAISING WHOLE.

OSSO BUCO WITH BORLOTTI BEANS
OSSO BUCO E BORLOTTI

When I think of the food of my childhood in northern Italy, I can feel the seasons – each is as clear and defined as black and white. In winter, the fog rising from the fields would distort the world around me. The sounds were muffled and eerie so that they seemed to come from another place, and the physical world was dismembered into pieces of buildings, sections of trees and parts of animals and people, barely visible through the dense whiteness.

When the fog was at its worst, my mother and grandmother would put large black cauldrons of minestrone on the fire and slowly cook osso buco so that the comforting and familiar smell pervaded our home. The food of my family and the comfort contained in those simple dishes still warms my bones and keeps the fog from seeping into my soul.

INGREDIENTS

1 cup (150 g/5½ oz) plain (all-purpose) flour

6 × 5 cm (2 in) thick pieces veal shank from the hind leg, cut across the bone

extra virgin olive oil

4 brown onions, cut into 2 cm (¾ in) chunks

8 ripe roma tomatoes, pureed

dry white wine

2 cups borlotti beans

1 cup chopped parsley

5 garlic cloves, crushed

METHOD

Set aside 1 tablespoon of the flour, then dust the osso buco all over with the remaining flour. Heat olive oil in a frying pan and brown the meat lightly. In a large saucepan, lightly fry the onions in a little oil until translucent but not coloured. Arrange the meat on top of the onions, season lightly, and add the tomatoes and enough wine to just cover the meat. Bring to the boil, then lower the heat, cover, and simmer for 50 minutes. Turn the osso buco, then take ½ cup (125 ml/4 fl oz) of the liquid and mix with the reserved flour. Return this mixture to the saucepan and add the beans, parsley and garlic. Cover and simmer for 30–45 minutes until the meat is tender. Season and serve with steaming polenta (cornmeal).

SERVES 6   WINE: Sforzato

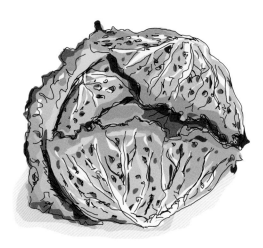

STUFFED RABBIT SADDLE WITH LENTILS
SELLA DI CONIGLIO RIPIENA, LENTICCHIE IN UMIDO

This versatile stuffing can be used to stuff all manner of other things, including veal breast, turkey and even quail.

INGREDIENTS

1 cup sage leaves

1 brown onion, diced

4 garlic cloves, minced

100 g (3½ oz) butter

2½ cups breadcrumbs

50 g (1¾ oz) mustard fruits, thinly sliced

100 g (3½ oz) grated parmesan

1 cup chopped parsley

8 slices prosciutto

2 saddles of rabbit, boned and kept whole

2 tablespoons extra virgin olive oil

BRAISED LENTILS

⅓ cup (80 ml/2½ fl oz) extra virgin olive oil

1 brown onion, finely chopped

½ celery heart, finely chopped

1 carrot, finely chopped

1 leek, white part only, halved lengthways and cut into 5 mm (¼ in) slices

2 garlic cloves, minced

leaves from 1 rosemary sprig, chopped

leaves from 1 thyme sprig, chopped

500 g (1 lb 2 oz) lentils

200 g (7 oz) ripe tomatoes, pureed

1 litre (35 fl oz) vegetable or chicken stock

1 cup chopped parsley

METHOD

Chop half the sage leaves and set the whole leaves aside. Lightly fry the onion and garlic in the butter until soft but not burnt. Transfer to a bowl and add the breadcrumbs, mustard fruits, parmesan, parsley and chopped sage. Season and mix well, then set aside to cool. Lay the prosciutto slices on a clean work surface in 2 sets of 4 so that each slice slightly overlaps the previous one. Put 1 rabbit saddle on each set of prosciutto slices. Distribute the cooled stuffing evenly in the middle of each saddle, making sure that there is just enough stuffing to roll up (too much stuffing will make this difficult). Roll up into tight sausages so that the prosciutto covers the rabbit completely, then wrap tightly in plastic wrap and refrigerate for 2–3 hours. One hour before serving, remove the parcels from the refrigerator and let them come to room temperature.

To make the braised lentils, heat the oil in a large frying pan and lightly fry the vegetables and garlic for a few minutes without colouring them. Add the rosemary and thyme and cook for another minute or two. Add the lentils and stir, then add the tomatoes and pour in enough stock to cover the lentils. Simmer for 30–50 minutes until the lentils are tender, adding more stock if the pan gets too dry. Add parsley, season and keep warm.

Preheat the oven to 200°C (400°F). Remove the plastic wrap from the stuffed rabbit saddles and lay the parcels in a roasting tin. Sprinkle with the olive oil and add the reserved sage leaves. Season and mix well, then roast for 15–20 minutes. Remove from the oven and rest for 10 minutes before slicing and serving with the braised lentils.

SERVES 8   WINE: Oltrepò Pavese Barbera

VEAL TONGUE WITH BAKED SWEET ONIONS AND FENNEL SEEDS
LINGUE DI VITELLO E CIPOLLE ALLA GRIGLIA

INGREDIENTS

2–3 calf tongues, depending on size

1 brown onion, cut into chunks

1 celery stick, cut into chunks

1 carrot, cut into chunks

½ cup (125 ml/4 fl oz) red or white wine vinegar

6 white onions, unpeeled and halved lengthways

2 teaspoons cayenne pepper

2 teaspoons paprika

1 tablespoon fennel seeds

½ cup (125 ml/4 fl oz) extra virgin olive oil, plus extra for dressing

250 g (9 oz) green beans, blanched

150 g (5½ oz) rocket (arugula)

2 tablespoons chopped dried tomatoes

balsamic vinegar

METHOD

Put the tongues, brown onion, celery, carrot and vinegar in a saucepan that is large enough to hold everything comfortably. Cover with cold water and bring to the boil. Turn the heat down, cover tightly and simmer for at least 45 minutes until the tongues are cooked. Prod the thick end of a tongue using a sharp knife – the meat should be tender but still firm, and the tough skin should peel easily. Peel the tongues and put the meat in a bowl, then pour in enough cooking liquid to cover. (As long as they are completely covered by the liquid, they will keep for a week or so in the refrigerator.)

Preheat the oven to 180°C (350°F). Sprinkle the cut sides of the white onions with the cayenne, paprika and fennel seeds. Season and put in a baking dish cut side down. Sprinkle with the olive oil and roast for 15–20 minutes until soft and brown. Meanwhile, cut the tongues into ½ cm (¼ in) slices. Peel the roasted onions and combine with the tongue, beans and rocket. Dress with the dried tomatoes, oil and balsamic vinegar and serve.

SERVES 6   WINE: Bardolino

CELERY PUREE
SEDANO PASSATO

This is a side dish or contorno for grilled (broiled), barbecued or roast meats.

INGREDIENTS

1 garlic bulb

500 g (1 lb 2 oz) celery hearts (including the tender light-green leaves), chopped

100 g (3½ oz) softened butter

2 tablespoons grated Grana Padano

2 tablespoons extra virgin olive oil

METHOD

Preheat the oven to 180°C (350°F). Roast the garlic bulb whole for 15–20 minutes until soft. Separate out the cloves, peel them and put the flesh in a food processor. Bring a saucepan of salted water to the boil and add the celery. Simmer for about 10 minutes until soft, then drain and add to the food processor with the butter, Grana Padano and olive oil. Season and pulse to a smooth puree.

SERVES 6–8

BRAISED TRIPE WITH PEAS
TRIPPA E PISELLI IN UMIDO

The tripe called for in this dish is the 'honeycomb' type, which is available pre-cooked from good butchers. This is a dish from my childhood. Whenever I make it, I'm always transported back to my mother's kitchen.

INGREDIENTS

1 kg (2 lb 4 oz) calf or
   ox honeycomb tripe, pre-
   cooked and well washed

¼ cup (60 ml/2 fl oz) extra
   virgin olive oil

2 brown onions, cut into 1 cm
   (½ in) cubes

2 carrots, halved lengthways
   and cut into 1 cm (½ in)
   slices

1 celery heart, cut into 1 cm
   (½ in) slices

½ cup (125 ml/4 fl oz) dry
   white wine

2 cups (500 ml/17 fl oz)
   chicken stock

2 garlic cloves, minced

½ cup chopped parsley

2 small rosemary sprigs

6–8 basil leaves, torn

100 ml (3½ fl oz) tomato
   passata

2 cups (310 g/11 oz) shelled
   peas

2 chillies, chopped (optional)

grated Grana Padano

METHOD

Cut the tripe into 1 cm × 5–6 cm (½ in × 2–2½ in) strips. Give it another good wash, then drain. Heat the olive oil in a flameproof casserole dish and gently fry the onions, carrots and celery for 2 minutes until fragrant. Add the tripe and fry gently for 5–6 minutes, stirring. Add half the wine and keep stirring and cooking for 5 minutes. Increase the heat and pour in the chicken stock and remaining wine. Bring to the boil, then turn down the heat and simmer for 1 hour. Add the garlic, parsley, rosemary sprigs, basil, passata, peas and chillies (if using), stir well and simmer for 20–30 minutes until the tripe is tender. Season, then turn off the heat and let sit for 15 minutes. Serve hot with grated Grana Padano.

SERVES 6   WINE: Rebo

LOMBARDIA

DOLCI

LATTUGHE
LATTUGHE

One of the most widely known of all Italian sweets is the fried pastries called crostoli. You've seen them – they're brittle, sometimes with edges as sharply patterned and regular as a new postage stamp, and dusted with icing (confectioners') sugar. Bite into one and it will shatter like Murano glass. In my home region of Lombardia, they can be variously called chisoi, ciaccier or manzòle. Of course, in the typical contrary way that is a hallmark of Italy, in my home town they are commonly called lattughe. Up and down the peninsula the same fried pastries, albeit with some slight differences in form or flavouring, are called bugie ('lies'), risòle, galani, sassole ('pebbles'), carafoi, puttanelle, frottole, nastrini ('little bows'), donzellini and even frati fritti ('fried priests'). Who would have thought that a simple mixture of flour, eggs, butter and sugar, with the addition of simple flavourings such as grappa and citrus, could produce so many permutations?

Even though they're all basically the same article, the Italian desire for the expression of the individual leads each pastry maker to respect the original tradition but at the same time confuse and confound it by changing it in every way possible. As if that were not enough, each version is passionately defended as being the authentic, the best-tasting and the most genuine. Crostoli or lattughe, or whatever you call them, are traditionally eaten during the Christmas season. They are festive-looking with their snow-white dusting, and perfect accompanied by grappa and espresso.

INGREDIENTS

5 eggs, separated

¼ cup (55 g/2 oz) caster (superfine) sugar

40 g (1½ oz) butter

30 ml (1 fl oz) grappa

grated zest and juice of 1 lemon

750 g (1 lb 10 oz) plain (all-purpose) flour

1 tablespoon baking powder

500 ml (17 fl oz) duck fat for frying

icing (confectioners') sugar

METHOD

Beat the egg yolks, sugar and butter together. Mix in the grappa, lemon zest and lemon juice. Whisk the egg whites until they form soft peaks, then fold into the mixture. Add the flour and baking powder and work until you have a smooth dough. Roll out into thin sheets using a pasta machine or rolling pin and cut into 8–10 cm × 3 cm (3¼–4 in × 1¼ in) strips. Heat the duck fat in a frying pan to a depth of 2 cm (¾ in). It's hot enough when a piece of the pastry sizzles instantly when dropped in. Gently tie each strip of pastry into a loose knot, then fry until golden brown, turning once. Drain on paper towels. When cool, dust with icing sugar to serve. The lattughe will keep well if stored in an airtight container in a cool place (not in the fridge).

MAKES about 40   WINE: Grappa

CHIAVENNA WILD ANISEED CAKE
TORTA FIORETTO DI CHIAVENNA

This is a local torta from high up in the Valtellina, where they use the very aromatic wild aniseed. I first had it at Mamete Prevostini's restaurant, Crotasc, in the town of Mese, province of Sondrio.

INGREDIENTS

14 g (½ oz) dried yeast

650 g (1 lb 7 oz) plain (all-purpose) flour

6 egg yolks

250 g (7 oz) softened unsalted butter

180 g (6 oz) caster (superfine) sugar

2 tablespoons anise seeds

METHOD

Dissolve the yeast in 200 ml (7 fl oz) warm water, then combine with 200 g (7 oz) of the flour. Cover and let rise for 1 hour. Mix the remaining flour with the egg yolks, 200 g (7 oz) of the butter, 120 g (4¼ oz) of the sugar and a pinch of salt until it reaches the consistency of wet sand. Combine the two doughs and work until well incorporated, then press evenly into a 28 cm (11¼ in) round cake tin (there is no need to grease or flour the tin as the cake won't stick). Cover and set aside to rise for 45 minutes. Preheat the oven to 190°C (375°F). Scatter the remaining sugar on top of the batter, then the anise seeds, and bake for 40–45 minutes or until a skewer comes out clean. Turn off the oven. Melt the remaining butter and brush the cake with it, then return the tin to the turned-off oven for 5 minutes. Serve hot or at room temperature with crema inglese (see page 52) and fresh berries.

SERVES 8   WINE: Vertemate di Mamete Prevostini (passito using 60% traminer aromatico, 40% riesling)

NOUGAT SEMIFREDDO
TORRONE SEMIFREDDO

INGREDIENTS

400 ml (14 fl oz) milk

1 vanilla bean, split and seeds scraped

6 eggs, separated

50 g (1¾ oz) sugar

1 cup (250 ml/9 fl oz) thin (pouring) cream, whipped

300 g (10½ oz) hard Italian almond or hazelnut nougat, chopped

METHOD

Put the milk in a saucepan with the vanilla pod and seeds and bring almost to the boil. Remove from the heat. Once cooled remove the vanilla bean. Beat the egg yolks and sugar together until pale and creamy, then add the hot milk and whisk together. Put the mixture back in the pan and cook on low–medium heat for a few minutes, stirring constantly, until thick enough to coat the back of a spoon. Pour into a bowl to cool. Mix the cream and nougat into the cooled custard. Whisk the egg whites with a pinch of salt until they form stiff peaks, then fold gently into the mixture. Transfer to a small loaf tin or 10 individual moulds, cover and put in the freezer overnight.

SERVES 10   WINE: Moscato d'Asti

POLENTA AND AMARETTO CAKE
AMOR POLENTA

Amor polenta is traditionally made in Milano and west to Varese, where it's simply called dolce di Varese. It has the consistency of tea cake but with a little more texture from the polenta (cornmeal). While it usually includes a rising agent this naturally risen version uses eggs for lift.

INGREDIENTS

300 g (1¾ oz) unsalted butter, melted

½ cup (80 g/2¾ oz) pine nuts

3 eggs

5 egg yolks

225 g (8 oz) caster (superfine) sugar

1 teaspoon natural vanilla extract

zest of 1 lemon

90 g (3¾ oz) hazelnut meal

⅔ cup (45 g/1¾ oz) almond meal

90 g (3¾ oz) plain (all-purpose) flour

75 g (2¾ oz) fine polenta (cornmeal)

50 g (1¾ oz) unsweetened pure hazelnut paste

50 ml (1¾ fl oz) amaretto di Saronno

icing (confectioners') sugar

METHOD

Preheat the oven to 170°C (340°F). Brush the inside of a 38 cm (15 in) half-cylinder tin with 50 g of the butter, then stick the pine nuts onto the butter as evenly as possible. Don't worry if some of them fall. Whisk the eggs, egg yolks and sugar until fluffy, then mix in the vanilla, lemon zest and a pinch of salt. In a separate bowl, combine the hazelnut and almond meal, flour and polenta, then add this to the egg mixture. Combine the remaining butter and the hazelnut paste and stir into the main mixture with the amaretto. Pour into the tin to about three-quarters full so the cake can rise, then bake for 45 minutes or until a skewer comes out clean. Remove from the mould and let cool on a wire rack. Dust with icing sugar, then cut into slices and serve with crema inglese (see page 52) or zabaglione.

SERVES 8–10   WINE: Amaretto di Saronno

LUCIANA'S TIRAMISU
TIRAMISU DI LUCIANA

INGREDIENTS

3 eggs, separated

100 g (3½ oz) caster (superfine) sugar

300 g (10½ oz) mascarpone cheese

400 ml (14 fl oz) strong espresso coffee

⅓ cup (80 ml/2½ fl oz) rum

30 savoiardi (lady fingers)

unsweetened cocoa powder

METHOD

Beat the egg yolks and sugar together until pale. Whisk the egg whites until they form fluffy peaks. Combine the yolk/sugar mixture with the mascarpone and then gradually fold the whites. Combine the coffee and rum. Soak the savoiardi in the coffee/rum mixture, then arrange in 1 layer on the bottom of a small rectangular ceramic dish. Spread on a layer of the mascarpone mixture, then repeat this process until all the savoiardi and mascarpone mixture have been used. Sprinkle with cocoa powder and refrigerate for 4–5 hours before serving.

SERVES 8–10   WINE: Bukkuram Moscato Passito di Pantelleria

RICE PUDDING CAKE
TORTA DI RISO

Puddings and cakes made with rice are common all over Italy, but they are more prolific in areas where rice is grown – such as in the northern strip on the plains below the Alps from Piemonte across to Lombardia, Veneto and Friuli.

INGREDIENTS

3 cups (750 ml/26 fl oz) milk

150 g (5½ oz) Italian rice (such as vialone nano or carnaroli)

4 eggs

½ cup (175 g/6 oz) honey

30 g (1 oz) candied citrus peel, chopped

15 g (½ oz) candied cedro (citron), chopped

30 g (1 oz) pine nuts, toasted

¼ cup (30 g/1 oz) pistachio kernels, toasted, skinned and chopped

30 g (1 oz) hazelnuts, toasted, skinned and chopped

30 g (1 oz) sultanas (golden raisins)

1 teaspoon natural vanilla extract

grated zest of 1 lemon

40 g (1½ oz) softened unsalted butter

METHOD

Heat the milk in a saucepan until almost boiling. Add the rice, then reduce the heat, cover and cook for about 30 minutes, stirring occasionally, until the rice is soft and creamy. Remove the rice from the saucepan and let cool. Meanwhile, preheat the oven to 170°C (340°F) and butter and flour a 25 cm (10 in) cake tin. Whisk the eggs with the honey and stir into the cooled rice. Stir in the candied peel and cedro, nuts and sultanas, then add the vanilla, lemon zest and butter and stir well. Put in the tin and bake for 50 minutes–1 hour until set. Cool a little before unmoulding. The cake will keep for up to 1 week in a sealed container in the fridge.

SERVES 8–10

WINE: Cantrina Sole di Dario (passito using sauvignon, semillon and riesling)

TIRAMISU IS ONE OF ITALY'S MOST FAMOUS DESSERTS. IT IS DIFFICULT TO SAY WHAT A TRULY AUTHENTIC TIRAMISU SHOULD CONTAIN, BUT ON AN ASSESSMENT OF ALL THOSE I'VE TRIED, LUCIANA'S IS HARD TO BEAT. LUCIANA COOKS AT L'OROLOGIO (THE LOCAL TRATTORIA UNDER THE TOWN'S LARGE CLOCK, AS THE NAME IMPLIES) IN THE TOWN OF GOTTOLENGO, WHERE I WAS BORN. OPPOSITE IS HER ORIGINAL RECIPE.

PANETTONE PUDDINGS
SFORMATO DI PANETTONE

INGREDIENTS

½ cup (125 ml/4 fl oz) orange juice

grated zest of 2 oranges

grated zest of 3 limes

60 g (2¼ oz) chopped mixed peel

60 g (2¼ oz) candied cedro (citron), chopped

⅓ cup (60 g/2¼ oz) sultanas (golden raisins), chopped

½ cup (125 ml/4 fl oz) Grand Marnier

½ cup (125 ml/4 fl oz) sugar syrup (see page 163)

6 × 5 g (¼ oz) gelatine sheets

300 ml (10½ fl oz) brandy crema inglese (see below), plus extra for serving

300 g (10½ oz) egg whites

90 g (3¼ oz) sugar

300 ml (10½ fl oz) thin (pouring) cream, whipped

240 g (8¾ oz) panettone, cut into 1 cm (½ in) cubes

250 g (9 oz) flaked almonds, toasted

200 g (7 oz) candied orange peel

METHOD

Put the orange juice, orange and lime zest, mixed peel, cedro, sultanas, Grand Marnier and sugar syrup in a small saucepan. Bring to the boil and reduce by half. Dissolve the gelatine in the hot mixture, then add the crema inglese and let cool. Meanwhile, whisk the egg whites with the sugar until stiff peaks form, then fold into the cooled fruit mixture and cream. Add the panettone. Spoon into 150 ml (5 fl oz) moulds and refrigerate for 3 hours. Serve with brandy crema inglese (cream custard) and the toasted almond flakes and candied orange peel.

MAKES about 12   WINE: Sauvignon Passito

BRANDY CUSTARD CREAM
CREMA INGLESE AL BRANDY

INGREDIENTS

12 egg yolks

200 g (7 oz) caster (superfine) sugar

1 litre (35 fl oz) thin (pouring) cream

1 teaspoon natural vanilla extract

2 tablespoons brandy

METHOD

Whisk the egg yolks and sugar until pale and thick enough to form a ribbon when lifted from the bowl and allowed to fall back in. Heat the cream almost to the boil. Whisk the cream into the egg mixture and return to medium heat, stirring continuously, until the custard coats the back of a spoon. Transfer to a bowl, add the vanilla and allow to cool. Add the brandy when cooled.

MAKES about 1.5 litres (2½ pints)

TORTA SBRISOLONA WITH QUINCE, MASCARPONE CREAM AND VINCOTTO
TORTA SBRISOLONA E MELE COTOGNE AL VINCOTTO

Sbrisolona has always been a sweet of the poor, using basic ingredients that are readily available. Over time, like many other similar things, it has attained a loftier reputation as culinary fashion directs. This polenta (cornmeal) shortbread is available in many pastry shops in Milano, Brescia and the wider Lombardia region.

INGREDIENTS

125 g (4½ oz) plain (all-purpose) flour

80 g (2¾ oz) fine polenta (cornmeal)

1 cup (100 g/3½ oz) blanched almond meal

80 g (2¾ oz) caster (superfine) sugar

1 egg yolk

grated zest of 1 lemon

juice of ½ lemon

1 teaspoon natural vanilla extract

60 g (2¼ oz) softened butter

50 g (1¾ oz) duck fat

100 ml (3½ fl oz) vincotto (or saba) (see page 431)

BAKED QUINCES

6 quinces, peeled and quartered

1 litre (35 fl oz) dry white wine

300 g (10½ oz) sugar

2 cinnamon sticks

8 black peppercorns

MASCARPONE CREAM

2 egg whites

⅓ cup (75 g/2½ oz) caster (superfine) sugar

300 g (10½ oz) softened mascarpone cheese

1 teaspoon natural vanilla extract

METHOD

To bake the quinces, preheat the oven to 100°C (200°F). Put the quinces in a baking dish and pour in the wine. Add the sugar, cinnamon and peppercorns, cover with foil and bake for 6–8 hours until tender. Let cool, then core the quince pieces and thinly slice.

Preheat the oven to 160°C (320°F) and line a baking tray with silicone paper. Combine the flour and polenta, then add the almond meal, sugar, egg yolk, lemon zest, lemon juice and vanilla extract. Mix in the butter and duck fat. Roll out the dough to a thickness of 6 mm (¼ in) and cut with a round 8 cm (3¼ in) cookie cutter. Put on the tray and bake for 30 minutes. Cool on wire racks. (The sbrisolona will keep for 14 days in a sealed container.)

To make the mascarpone cream, whisk the egg whites until soft peaks form, then slowly add the sugar while still whisking. Once firm peaks form, fold in the mascarpone and vanilla. To serve, lay a spoonful of mascarpone cream on each sbrisolona, top with quince slices and spoon on 1–2 tablespoons vincotto.

SERVES 20   WINE: Riesling Passito

PIEMONTE

PIEMONTE

PIEDMONT

UNSURPRISINGLY – EVEN PROSAICALLY – NAMED FROM THE LATIN MEANING 'AT THE FOOT OF THE MOUNTAINS', THIS LARGE (OVER 25,000 SQUARE KILOMETRES, OR 9600 SQUARE MILES) AND CULINARILY RICH PROVINCE IS SURROUNDED ON THREE SIDES BY THE ALPS. IT SHARES BORDERS WITH SWITZERLAND AND VALLE D'AOSTA TO THE NORTH, LIGURIA TO THE SOUTH, A SLIVER OF EMILIA-ROMAGNA TO THE EAST AND FRANCE TO THE WEST. LIKE LOMBARDIA, THE LANDSCAPE RANGES FROM RUGGED PEAKS TO RICE PADDIES ON THE PLAINS.

Piemonte has a population of around four million and its capital, Turin, rivals Milan for supremacy in the north. It is known as the region that gave birth to Italy: the first king of Italy after reunification in 1861 was Piemonte's Vittorio Emmanuele II, and the architect of that unification was the prime minister, Camillo Benso di Cavour.

As in Valle d'Aosta, the house of Savoy reigned here (Vittorio Emmanuele was a Savoy), but unlike Valle d'Aosta, the French also ruled. The result is a patchwork of over 1200 towns and villages and French-based languages – Occitan, Franco-Provençal and Waldensian – as well as Italian. To further complicate and enrich the mixture, Turin has been the capital of two kingdoms, Sardinia and Italy.

The cuisine of Piemonte is divided by the mountains. In the lower altitudes and the larger cities, the food is not very different from that of Lombardia – it is in the north and the mountains that you encounter the true Piedmontese, a cuisine whose most magnificent ingredient is the white truffle, or trifola d'Alba, named for the town at the centre of its provenance. On the first Sunday in October there is a truffle fair in Alba that includes, among other celebratory activities, a procession in which participants carry the season's best truffles, and the choosing of a beauty queen – La Bela Trifolera, the beautiful truffle-seeker. In season, these magnificent fungi are incorporated into fonduta, a fondue-like dish where the cheese is mixed with butter, milk and beaten egg yolks, and the whiter truffles are sliced paper thin and laid on top.

Piemonte produces more than 10 per cent of the rice grown in Italy, and for this reason rice features strongly in its cuisine. Riso alla piemontese contains hard cheese and nutmeg and a meat broth prepared with Barolo wine and white truffle.

A local dish of international renown is the bagna cauda, a hot sauce of anchovies, garlic, butter and olive oil into which are dipped mainly raw vegetables – fennel, cardoons, celery, sweet peppers, raw young artichokes and so on, depending on the season. Another dish using anchovies, and by preference the delicious anchovies of neighbouring Liguria, is vitello tonnato, which has travelled far from its birthplace thanks, perhaps, to the cookbooks of Elizabeth David.

Braised beef with barolo celebrates what is perhaps the greatest of the local wines, and finanziera is a dish of boiled veal sweetbreads and brains, bull's testicles, filone (spinal marrow) and cock's combs with fresh porcini mushrooms. Use of the cuts so often discarded today, and what would have been a foraged item (the mushrooms), reminds us of Capatti and Montanari's observation in *Italian Cuisine: A Cultural History* of the way in which 'the culture of hunger can be transformed into culinary pleasure'.

It isn't possible to leave Piemonte without acknowledging two more local inventions: Nutella, the Ferrero family's challenge to American peanut butter, first marketed in 1964; and vermouth, first distilled in Piemonte in 1786 by Benedetto Carpano. The province is also home to the Slow Food movement and its University of Gastronomic Sciences, both in the town of Bra.

Two names spring to mind when thinking of Piemonte and wine: spumante and barolo (and, to a slightly lesser extent, barbaresco). The spiritual – or vinous – home of the sweet sparkler made from moscato bianco is Asti; and Barolo is the name of a village, a zone and the deeply tannic, hugely flavoured wine made from the nebbiolo grape. Barolo and its cousin barbaresco, produced in their respective DOCGs, are two of the bright stars in the Italian firmament.

With regard to the region's whites, I'll start with those made from arneis, a previously obscure grape that has risen to global prominence, making, as it does, full-flavoured wines with fruit aromas.

The erbaluce is the other dominant white wine grape here, producing much flintier, herbally aromatic wines as well as refreshing passiti. In the Gavi DOC, the cortese grape is employed to make a wine that has been compared, some say extravagantly, to white burgundy. What is Burgundian is the chardonnay, most of which is produced in the Langhe DOC.

Apart from the aforementioned stars, barolo and barbaresco, wines made from an early-ripening grape, dolcetto ('the little sweet one'), are produced in seven Piemonte DOCs; they can be made in a lighter, almost beaujolais style or a rounder and plumper style. Either way, the dolcetti are being held up as the Piedmontese wines of the future.

ITALY GOES SLOW

'An environmentalist who isn't a gastronome is sad. A gastronome who isn't an environmentalist is stupid.'– Carlo Petrini

Carlo Petrini, founder of the Slow Food movement, was born and bred in the little Piedmontese town of Bra, where the Slow Food headquarters are situated today.

At the core of the Slow Food philosophy is this statement from the manifesto: 'We believe that everyone has a fundamental right to the pleasure of good food and consequently the responsibility to protect the heritage of food, tradition and culture that make this pleasure possible.'

The movement, whose motto is now 'Good, clean and fair (food)', has matured into one of the most powerful enemies of industrial food on the planet, and a champion of traditional foods and their producers.

Today, Slow Food can be found globally in small local branches, known as 'conviviums', of which there are, at the time of writing, in excess of 800 worldwide. It also runs biennial world meetings of food communities – farmers, producers, chefs and communicators – called Terra Madre.

PIEMONTE
ANTI-PASTI

VEAL SHANK AND CELERIAC SALAD
INSALATA DI VITELLO E SEDANO RAPA

INGREDIENTS

2 veal shanks, trimmed of
  excess fat and membrane

1 brown onion, quartered

1 celery stick, chopped

1 carrot, cut into chunks

1 small celeriac, peeled
  and cut into 3 cm (1¼ in)
  matchsticks

2 French shallots, finely sliced

2 tablespoons chopped
  parsley

½ cup (125 ml/4 fl oz) extra
  virgin olive oil

¼ cup (60 ml/2 fl oz) red wine
  vinegar

METHOD

Put the shanks in a saucepan and pour in cold water so they are well covered. Add the onion, celery and carrot. Bring to the boil, then turn the heat down and simmer for 45 minutes–1 hour, covered, until the meat is tender. Let the shanks cool in the broth. Drain, keeping the broth to make soup later. Take the meat from the bones and cut into bite-sized pieces, then combine with the celeriac, shallots and parsley. Dress with the olive oil and vinegar, season and serve.

SERVES 6–10   WINE: Monferrato Rosso

TRIPE SALAD
INSALATA DI TRIPPA

INGREDIENTS

500 g (1 lb 2 oz) cooked tripe,
  cut into 6 cm × 5 mm
  (2½ in × ¼ in) strips

1 red onion, minced

1 celery heart (including the
  tender light-green leaves),
  minced

1 medium or 2 small carrots,
  minced

1 large garlic clove

½ cup small parsley leaves

1–2 small hot chillies, seeded
  and finely chopped

¼ cup (60 ml/2 fl oz) red wine
  vinegar (preferably barbera)

150 ml (5 fl oz) extra virgin
  olive oil

METHOD

In a large bowl, combine the tripe, onion, celery and carrot. Finely chop the garlic and parsley together, then add to the tripe mixture with the chilli, vinegar and olive oil. Season and mix well. Set aside for about 1 hour, mixing every so often. Serve at room temperature.

SERVES 8   WINE: Freisa

POACHED YEARLING LOIN IN TUNA SAUCE

POACHED YEARLING LOIN IN TUNA SAUCE
VITELLONE TONNATO

This is a take on the classic Italian dish vitello tonnato (veal in a tuna sauce), using yearling beef instead of veal. The method uses an improvised sous-vide (low-temperature water bath) to cook the yearling – I've found that this results in moist, pink meat with lots of flavour.

INGREDIENTS

800 g (1 lb 12 oz) yearling girello beef (eye of round), cut into 2 pieces

⅓ cup (80 ml/2½ fl oz) extra virgin olive oil

100 ml (3½ fl oz) dry white wine

2 small garlic cloves, crushed

2 bay leaves

2 small parsley stalks

2 cloves

2 teaspoons grated lemon zest

150 g (5½ oz) tin tuna, drained

2 tablespoons capers, rinsed

1 cup (250 ml/9 fl oz) mayonnaise

4 tablespoons finely chopped parsley

METHOD

Pour water into a deep, wide ovenproof bowl to fill by two-thirds. Preheat the oven to 65°C (150°F), then put the bowl in the oven for at least 30 minutes so the water reaches the same temperature as the oven. Meanwhile, put each piece of beef in a sealable (zip lock) plastic bag with 2 tablespoons olive oil, 50 ml (1¾ fl oz) wine, 1 garlic clove, 1 bay leaf, 1 parsley stalk, 1 clove and 1 teaspoon lemon zest. Season and seal, making sure most of the air is squeezed out of the bags before closing. Put each bag in another sealable bag, pressing the air out of the second bag as well before closing. Put the bags carefully in the preheated water bath, making sure they are submerged – you may need to put a plate on top. Cook in the oven for 2 hours. Carefully remove the bowl from the oven and let the meat cool in the water before removing it from the bags. Strain the cooking liquid through muslin (cheesecloth) and thinly slice the beef. To make the sauce, put the tuna and capers in a food processor with 160 ml (5¼ fl oz) of the strained cooking liquid and blend. Whisk this mixture into the mayonnaise and season if necessary. Spread the sauce on serving plates, arrange the meat on top and sprinkle with parsley to serve.

SERVES 6–8 WINE: Grignolino d'Asti

SALSIFY FRITTERS
FRITTELLE DI SCORZONERA

INGREDIENTS

450 g (1 lb) salsify, peeled

juice of 1 lemon

2 large eggs

pinch of white pepper

20 g (¾ oz) butter

2 tablespoons extra virgin
    olive oil

METHOD

Put the salsify in a bowl of water with the lemon juice. In a large separate bowl, whisk the eggs with the pepper and 2 good pinches of salt. Drain the salsify and dry it well with a clean tea towel (dish towel). Using the larger holes on a grater, grate the salsify directly into the egg mixture. Mix well. Heat the butter and olive oil in a 15–20 cm (6–8 cm) frying pan, then drop 50 ml (1¾ fl oz) of batter (use a medicine cup or a small ladle to measure) into the hot oil. The fritter will spread to about 5 cm (2 in). Fry on each side until golden, then drain on paper towels. Repeat until all the batter has been used, season with salt (if necessary) and serve hot.

SERVES 6   WINE: Langhe Bianco

GOAT'S CHEESE, POTATO AND MUSHROOM TERRINE
TERRINA DI CAPRINO, PATATE E FUNGHI

INGREDIENTS

5 large potatoes, thinly sliced

100 g (3½ oz) mushrooms,
    thinly sliced

200 g (7 oz) goat's cheese,
    crumbled or sliced

1 cup chopped parsley

⅓ cup (80 ml/2½ fl oz) extra
    virgin olive oil

50 g (1¾ oz) grated parmesan

METHOD

Preheat the oven to 190°C (375°F). Butter a terrine tin or mould (28 cm (11¼ in) long × 10 cm (4 in) wide) and put in a layer of potatoes, then a layer of mushrooms, then goat's cheese, then parsley. Season and repeat this sequence until the tin is full, finishing with a layer of goat's cheese. Season, then scatter the olive oil and parmesan over and bake for 30 minutes. Serve at room temperature with a salad.

SERVES 8   WINE: Langhe Chardonnay

BAKED JERUSALEM ARTICHOKES WITH CREAM OF BAGNA CAUDA
TOPINAMBUR AL FORNO CON CREMA DI BAGNA CAUDA

Bagna cauda is a staple of Piemontese cooking that is traditionally served as a dip or dressing with seasonal raw and cooked vegetables. This recipe uses the flavours of the famous sauce, with the addition of cream and a little potato flour to thicken, to create a flavoursome 'gratin' baked with the Jerusalem artichokes.

INGREDIENTS

100 g (3½ oz) unsalted butter

100 ml (3½ fl oz) extra virgin olive oil

3 garlic cloves, minced

8 anchovy fillets, chopped

50 ml (1¾ fl oz) thin (pouring) cream

½ teaspoon potato flour

400 g (14 oz) Jerusalem artichokes, peeled and thinly sliced

1 litre (35 fl oz) milk

juice of ½ lemon

METHOD

Preheat the oven to 200°C (400°F). Put the butter, olive oil and garlic in a saucepan and heat slowly for about 8 minutes until the garlic cooks but does not colour. Turn off the heat and add the anchovies, then mix using a wooden spoon until the anchovies have dissolved. Stir in the cream and a little salt. Add the potato flour and whisk well using a fork or small whisk. Put the Jerusalem artichokes and milk in another saucepan with the lemon juice and simmer for 6–7 minutes until tender. Drain and arrange the Jerusalem artichokes in layers in a baking dish. Pour the bagna cauda cream on top and bake for 6–8 minutes until golden. Serve immediately.

SERVES 6–8   WINE: Langhe Chardonnay

PIEMONTE
PRIMI

POTATO GNOCCHI WITH BURNT BUTTER AND SAGE
GNOCCHI AL BURRO E SALVIA

Gnocchi, while a very simple liaison of potato, egg and flour, are very difficult to perfect. Not only are the relative quantities of these three ingredients extremely sensitive and unforgiving to miscalculation, but their form, shaped by hand, also has precise parameters. For this reason a strict recipe will in fact misguide. A chef I once worked with would slavishly follow Swiss chef Frédy Girardet's recipe for gnocchi and wonder why they always resembled rubber bullets.

INGREDIENTS

1.5 kg (3 lb 5 oz) unpeeled roasting potatoes (preferably older potatoes with dry flesh)

200 g (7 oz) plain (all-purpose) flour

150 g (5½ oz) grated parmesan cheese

½ teaspoon grated nutmeg

2 egg yolks

125 g (4½ oz) butter

½ cup sage leaves

METHOD

Cook the potatoes in a little water in a covered saucepan until soft. Peel while still hot, then pass through a ricer (do not put them in a blender or food processor) and allow to cool. Make a well in the centre of the mound of potato and add a handful of the flour, then ½ teaspoon salt, the nutmeg, one-third of the parmesan, and lastly the egg yolks. Fold together towards the centre, gradually adding more flour, until the mixture comes together without being sticky. Remember that the more flour you add, the firmer the gnocchi will be. Let rest for 5 minutes. Roll some mixture into a sausage about 3 cm (1¼ in) in diameter, then cut off a few 3 cm (1¼ in) pieces. Roll each piece on the back of a fork using your thumb and forefinger. Bring a small saucepan of water to the boil and add 3–4 gnocchi. Once they rise, check that they aren't too soft or falling apart. If they are, add more flour to the potato mixture. Shape and cut the remaining gnocchi, then poach in batches in a large saucepan of salted boiling water until they rise to the surface. Remove using a slotted spoon and keep warm on a plate. Meanwhile, put the butter in a small saucepan on high heat until it turns nut-brown. Add the sage and cook for 30 seconds until the leaves are crisp. Sprinkle the gnocchi with the remaining parmesan, then spoon on the sizzling butter and sage to serve.

SERVES 8   WINE: Freisa

LENTIL, CARROT AND TURNIP SALAD WITH HAZELNUT SAUCE
INSALATA DI LENTICCHIE, CAROTE E RAPA CON CREMA DI NOCCIOLE

INGREDIENTS

150 g (5½ oz) lentils

200 g (7 oz) hazelnuts

3 garlic cloves

80 g (2¾ oz) salted capers, soaked and rinsed

1 cup parsley leaves

⅔ cup (170 ml/5½ fl oz) extra virgin olive oil

juice of 1–2 lemons

18 carrots, each cut into 3

12 baby turnips, quartered

1 tablespoon extra virgin olive oil

1 tablespoon small purple basil leaves

METHOD

Bring 2 litres (70 fl oz) water to the boil and add the lentils. Return to the boil, the turn the heat down and simmer for 20–30 minutes until tender but not falling apart. Cool in the cooking liquid. Meanwhile, preheat the oven to 160°C (320°F). Put the hazelnuts on a baking tray and lightly roast for 15–20 minutes. Cool, then rub in a clean tea towel (dish towel) to remove the skin. Put the nuts in a food processor with the garlic and pulse to chop finely. Add the capers and all except 1 tablespoon of the parsley and chop finely, then stir through 150 ml (5 fl oz) of the olive oil to achieve a thick sauce. Season and add some or all of the lemon juice. Mix well. Heat the remaining oil in a frying pan and fry the carrots and turnips until their edges are caramelised, moving them around the pan. Chop the remaining parsley. Spread the sauce on a plate, then the carrots and turnips. Drain the lentils and scatter over, then finish with the parsley and basil. Season and serve.

SERVES 6   **WINE:** Dolcetto

GARLIC AND ANCHOVY LASAGNE
LASAGNE DELLA VIGILIA

This is not what most people would normally consider lasagna – which is the many-layered, cheesy-gooey baked variety of Bologna – but the word refers literally to the pasta sheet used. This version is a delicious combination of unlikely ingredients and is traditionally eaten on Christmas Eve.

INGREDIENTS

150 g (5½ oz) unsalted butter

8–10 anchovy fillets, finely chopped

4 garlic cloves, lightly crushed

500 g (1 lb 2 oz) lasagna sheets (see page 272), cut into 8 cm (3¼ in) squares

150 g (5½ oz) grated parmesan cheese

METHOD

Melt the butter slowly in a large non-stick frying pan over low heat, making sure it doesn't fry. Add the anchovies and garlic and warm them in the butter for 10–15 minutes until the anchovies melt. Remove the garlic and discard. Cook the pasta sheets in plenty of salted boiling water and drain well. Put a lasagna sheet on each serving plate and top with 1 tablespoon of the parmesan and 1 tablespoon of the anchovy butter. Repeat this process twice on each plate and finish with lots of freshly grated pepper. Serve straightaway, passing around grated parmesan for those who want more.

SERVES 6   **WINE:** Gavi

LENTIL, CARROT AND TURNIP SALAD WITH HAZELNUT SAUCE

TURNIP AND HORSERADISH FRITTERS WITH SAUCE GRIBICHE
FRITELLE DI RAPA E RAFANO AL GRIBICHE

INGREDIENTS

350 g (12 oz) turnips, peeled and coarsely grated

80 g (2¾ oz) ricotta cheese

50 g (1¾ oz) fresh horseradish, finely grated

¾ cup coarse breadcrumbs, plus extra if needed

4–5 eggs

fine breadcrumbs

plain (all-purpose) flour

extra virgin olive oil

SAUCE GRIBICHE

2 hard-boiled eggs

1 teaspoon Dijon mustard

½ cup (125 ml/4 fl oz) extra virgin olive oil

1 large or 2 small French shallots, finely chopped

2 tablespoons finely chopped parsley

2 tablespoons chopped tarragon

2 tablespoons finely snipped chives

4 small cornichons (small pickled gherkins), finely chopped

1 tablespoon chopped capers

juice of 1 large lemon

METHOD

To make the sauce gribiche, separate the hard-boiled egg yolks from the whites. Dice the whites. Mash the yolks in a bowl with the mustard, then whisk in the olive oil. Add the whites and the rest of the ingredients and season. Set aside.

Combine the turnips, ricotta, horseradish, coarse breadcrumbs and 2 of the eggs, season and mix well. The mixture should be firm enough to allow you to form a ball in your hand without it falling apart. If the mixture is too wet, add a handful of coarse breadcrumbs. Whisk the remaining eggs in a bowl. Shape the turnip mixture into small patties 3 cm (1¼ in) in diameter. Lightly coat each patty in flour, then beaten egg and then fine breadcrumbs. Pour enough oil into a saucepan to deep-fry the fritters. Heat to frying temperature (175°C/350°F) or until when you put a breadcrumb in the oil it floats and sizzles instantly. Make sure the oil is not too hot. Fry the fritters until golden brown on both sides, then drain on paper towels and serve with the sauce gribiche.

SERVES 6   WINE: Langhe Reisling

SAUCE GRIBICHE
PIEMONTE'S PROXIMITY TO FRANCE IS NOTICEABLE IN THE REGION'S DIALECT AS WELL AS SOME LENDING AND BORROWING IN CUISINE. FRENCH IN ORIGIN, GRIBICHE IS VINAIGRETTE WITH THE ADDITION OF HARD-BOILED EGG, CAPERS AND HERBS BOUND WITH OLIVE OIL. IT TRADITIONALLY ACCOMPANIES BOILED MEATS AND TERRINES AS WELL AS POACHED FISH.

ASPARAGUS WITH BASIL MAYONNAISE
ASPARAGI ALLA MAIONESE DI BASILICO

INGREDIENTS

24 fat asparagus spears, trimmed

1 egg

¼ cup basil leaves

1 tablespoon white wine vinegar

½ cup (125 ml/4 fl oz) extra virgin olive oil (preferably an elegant oil, such as Ligurian)

METHOD

Bring a saucepan of salted water to the boil and blanch the asparagus for a minute or two until tender but still with a little 'bite'. Drain and keep warm. Put the egg, basil, vinegar and a couple of pinches of salt in a food processor. Turn the processor on and add the olive oil slowly, in a fine stream, until the mixture thickens to the desired (like mayonnaise) consistency. You may not need all the oil. Season, then serve the asparagus with the basil mayonnaise.

SERVES 4

WINE: Timorasso

ZUCCHINI FLOWERS FILLED WITH ZUCCHINI AND AMARETTI
CAPONET

This is a take by Osteria dell'Unione in Treiso on a traditional dish called caponet. It usually includes roasted and boiled meats as well as cooked salami and cheese. This meatless version is both simple and unusual. When purchasing your zucchini flowers, note that the female zucchini flowers have the fruit attached whereas the males don't.

INGREDIENTS

500 g (1 lb 2 oz) female zucchini (courgette) flowers

⅓ cup (80 ml/2½ fl oz) extra virgin olive oil

8 amaretti biscuits, crushed

1 level tablespoon unsweetened cocoa powder

2 egg yolks

1 teaspoon caster (superfine) sugar

METHOD

Separate the flowers from the zucchini and set the flowers aside. Wash the zucchini well and trim any woody ends. Cut the zucchini into matchsticks. Heat half the olive oil and fry the zucchini on medium heat for 2–3 minutes until golden, mixing gently with a wooden spoon. Drain and cool on paper towels, then chop roughly and put in a bowl. Add the amaretti, cocoa powder, egg yolks and sugar and mix well. Gently open the zucchini flowers and stuff with the mixture. Pinch the end of each flower with your fingertips to close. Heat the remaining oil in a frying pan and fry the stuffed flowers, turning gently until golden brown. Season with salt and serve immediately.

SERVES 4

WINE: Gavi di Gavi

JERUSALEM ARTICHOKE FLAN WITH GORGONZOLA SAUCE
TORTINO DI TOPINAMBUR

The Jerusalem artichoke is neither from Jerusalem nor an artichoke. While the globe artichoke is essentially a thistle leaf, the Jerusalem artichoke is a bulbous tuber made up of around 50 per cent carbohydrate. It contains no starch or oil and only a tiny amount of protein, so if it is made into a puree it needs to be bound with butter or oil, or mixed with a starchy vegetable such as potato. Another consideration is its tendency to discolour to a dull grey once peeled. To overcome this, simply put the peeled artichokes in a bowl of water with either lemon juice or vinegar. It appears that the plant was present in the Farnese Gardens of Rome, brought there from the New World, and was known as girasole articocco. From Rome it was taken to Britain in the 1600s. The most likely theory for the Anglicised name is that girasole was changed to Jerusalem.

INGREDIENTS

500 g (1 lb 2 oz) peeled Jerusalem artichokes, thinly sliced

600 ml (21 fl oz) milk

3 eggs

½ cup (50 g/1¾ oz) grated parmesan cheese

20 g (¾ oz) butter

100 ml (3½ fl oz) thin (pouring) cream

75 g (2¾ oz) gorgonzola cheese

2 tablespoons brandy or cognac

2 tablespoons finely snipped chives

METHOD

Put the artichokes in a saucepan with the milk and bring to the boil. Turn the heat down and simmer for about 15 minutes until soft. Strain, discarding the milk, and let cool. Preheat the oven to 160°C (320°F). Beat the eggs well with the parmesan and a couple of good pinches of salt and pepper. Add the Jerusalem artichokes and mix well. Butter 4 ramekins (200 ml/7 fl oz) and distribute the mixture evenly among them. Put in a baking dish and pour in water to come halfway up the sides of the ramekins. Bake for 30 minutes. Meanwhile, put the cream and gorgonzola in small saucepan and simmer slowly, stirring, until the cheese has melted. Add the brandy, some pepper and a little salt if needed. Turn the flans out onto serving plates (run a sharp knife around the sides to dislodge) and sprinkle the chives on top. Serve with the sauce.

SERVES 4-6

WINE: Colli Tortonesi Timorasso

PIEMONTE
SECONDI

SOUP OF THE DEAD
ZUPPA DEI MORTI

In Italy, 2 November is the day of the pagan festival known as 'I Morti' – the day of the dead, or All Souls' Day. It is also the Celtic New Year and the festival of warriors, Samhain. It was originally linked to the agricultural year as a feast commemorating a particular point of relative inactivity when the new seeds had been planted and the summer's produce had been harvested. Through this 'gap' between one year and the next, the Celts believed that dead relatives were able to return to their homes to be reunited with their family. Those who had no family were destined to roam the countryside. This is the basis of the American festival of Halloween.

This soup is typical of the area of Piemonte and Lombardia (where I was born) and is used to celebrate the day of I Morti. It is made with beans, chickpeas and farro (Triticum dicoccum), one of the ancestors of modern wheat. The Romans served beans as a sacred dish at funeral banquets, and even filled urns with dried chickpeas and broad beans and buried them with the dead to act as nourishment in the tomb. These days in Italy, soup of the dead is made each year and restaurants and households give generous helpings to the poor, who come by to fill their bowls. It is also left out in tureens on the kitchen table overnight so that the spirits of any dead relatives can take nourishment.

INGREDIENTS

1 cup (200 g/7 oz) dried chickpeas, soaked overnight in plenty of cold water

½ cup (100 g/3½ oz) dried borlotti beans, soaked overnight in plenty of cold water

½ cup (100 g/3½ oz) dried broad beans, soaked overnight in plenty of cold water

150 g (5½ oz) lardo

150 g (5½ oz) pancetta

½ cup (125 ml/4 fl oz) extra virgin olive oil

800 g (1 lb 12 oz) Savoy cabbage, cut into wide strips

½ cup (100 g/3½ oz) pearled farro

2.5 litres (4½ pints) beef broth (see page 48)

15 slices good country-style bread, toasted

250 g (9 oz) fontina cheese, thinly sliced

150 g (5½ oz) grated parmesan cheese

METHOD

Separately drain and rinse the chickpeas and beans, then cook each variety separately. Put the lardo, pancetta and 2 tablespoons of the olive oil in a large saucepan on medium heat and stir until the meat begins to brown. Add the cabbage and mix constantly for a minute or so. Stir in the chickpeas, beans and farro, then pour in the beef broth and bring to the boil. Turn the heat down and cook gently for 30–40 minutes. Preheat the oven to 190°C (375°F). Put 5 slices of the toasted bread in the bottom of a ceramic or cast-iron casserole dish. Ladle in a quarter of the soup and then add a quarter each of the fontina and parmesan. Repeat the layers three times and drizzle the remaining oil on top. Bake for 20 minutes until well browned. Serve immediately.

SERVES 8

WINE: Nebbiolo d'Alba

BEEF CHEEKS BRAISED IN BAROLO WITH PEA PUREE
GUANCIALE DI MANZO AL BAROLO CON PUREA DI PISELLI

INGREDIENTS

6 beef cheeks, membrane
 trimmed

plain (all-purpose) flour

2 brown onions, finely diced

200 ml (7 fl oz) extra virgin
 olive oil

4 ripe roma tomatoes, pureed

2 cups (500 ml/17 fl oz)
 barolo or other full-bodied
 red wine

½ cup chopped parsley

2 garlic cloves, minced

400 g (14 oz) shelled peas

50 g (1¾ oz) butter

METHOD

Dust the beef cheeks with flour, shaking off any excess. Heat ¼ cup (60 ml/2 fl oz) of the olive oil in a frying pan and brown the meat well on both sides. In a saucepan that is wide enough to fit the beef cheeks snugly side by side, lightly fry the onions in ¼ cup of the oil until translucent but not coloured. Arrange the meat on top of the onions and season lightly. Add the tomatoes and pour in enough wine to almost cover the meat. Bring to the boil, then lower the heat and simmer, covered, for 1½ hours. Add the parsley and garlic and simmer for 30 minutes. Turn off the heat and let rest for at least 1 hour. When you are ready to serve, cook the peas in plenty of salted boiling water for a few minutes until tender. Drain, then puree the hot peas with the butter and remaining oil. Season and serve with the beef cheeks.

SERVES 6   **WINE:** Barolo

BRAISED VEAL BREAST WITH ONIONS
PETTO DI VITELLO IN UMIDO

INGREDIENTS

10 brown onions, cut into 1 cm
 (½ in) cubes

3 teaspoons smoked paprika

4 sage leaves, chopped

125 g (4½ oz) unsalted butter

100 ml (3½ fl oz) extra virgin
 olive oil

1.5 kg (3 lb 5 oz) veal breast,
 rolled and tied

300 ml (10½ fl oz) red wine
 (such as barbera)

4 tablespoons chopped
 parsley

METHOD

Put the onions in a large bowl and toss with the paprika and sage. Heat the butter and oil in a large cast-iron casserole dish on low heat. Add the onions and simmer for 2–3 minutes, mixing well. Put the veal on top of the onions and season well. Increase the heat to medium and cook for 10 minutes (don't let the onions brown). Add the wine and parsley, then cover and simmer for 1½ hours until the meat is tender. Remove the meat and keep warm. Strain the onions, reserving the cooking liquid, then pass the onions through a Mouli or fine sieve. Add the onion puree to the cooking liquid and simmer to make a thickened sauce. Slice the veal breast and serve with the sauce.

SERVES 10   **WINE:** Barbera d'Alba

PAN-FRIED BEEF FILLET WITH BRAISED OYSTER MUSHROOMS
FILETTO DI MANZO IN PADELLA CON ORECCHIE D'ELEFANTE

INGREDIENTS

250 g (9 oz) oyster mushrooms, trimmed

⅓ cup (80 ml/2½ fl oz) extra virgin olive oil

3 French shallots, finely chopped

2 garlic cloves, thinly sliced

½ cup (125 ml/4 fl oz) dry white wine

4 tinned tomatoes, drained and chopped

4 tablespoons finely chopped parsley

3 tablespoons black peppercorns or 1 teaspoon cracked pepper

4 × 150 g (5½ oz) × 2 cm (¾ in) thick pieces beef fillet, at room temperature

METHOD

If any of the mushrooms are too big, cut them into bite-sized pieces. Heat ¼ cup (60 ml/2 fl oz) of the olive oil in a frying pan and lightly fry the shallots and garlic until softened. Turn up the heat, add the mushrooms and keep frying and stirring for about 1½ minutes until the mushrooms are soft. Add the wine and keep the heat high until the liquid is almost gone. Add the tomatoes and a couple of good pinches of salt, then turn the heat down and simmer for 5 minutes. Stir in the parsley and peppercorns and simmer for 2–3 minutes, then turn off the heat. Season the beef on both sides with a little salt and pepper. Heat the remaining olive oil in a wide frying pan and when it begins to smoke add the beef. Fry on each side for 30 seconds, then remove the pan from the heat and rest the meat for 2–3 minutes. Serve immediately with the braised oyster mushrooms.

SERVES 4

WINE: Boca

BRUSSELS SPROUTS WITH LEMON
CAVOLO DI BRUXELLES AL LIMONE

This is a contorno or side dish to accompany roast or boiled meats.

INGREDIENTS

500 g (1 lb 2 oz) brussels sprouts, halved and cored

1 tablespoon extra virgin olive oil

juice of 1 lemon

20 g (¾ oz) unsalted butter

METHOD

Slice the brussels sprouts very thinly across the grain. Heat the olive oil on medium heat, then add the sprouts and half the lemon juice. Cook for exactly 1 minute, stirring constantly. Turn off the heat, add the remaining lemon juice and season. Mix the butter through and serve with extra pepper if you wish.

SERVES 6

PIEMONTE
DOLCI

BAKED NECTARINES WITH AMARETTI BISCUITS
NETTARINI AL FORNO

*This simple dessert can be served with vanilla ice cream, whipped or pouring cream, or clotted cream.
Use good-quality amaretti biscuits.*

INGREDIENTS

20 g (¾ oz) unsalted butter at room temperature + 40 g (1½ oz) cold unsalted butter, diced

750 g (1 lb 10 oz) ripe but firm yellow and white nectarines, peeled and cut into 3 cm (1¼ in) chunks

2 tablespoons caster (superfine) sugar

200 g (7 oz) amaretti biscuits, crushed

2 eggs, whisked

METHOD

Preheat the oven to 180°C (350°F) and grease a baking dish with the room-temperature butter. Put the nectarines, sugar and amaretti biscuits in a large bowl. Mix in the cold diced butter, then fold in the eggs. Transfer the mixture to the baking dish and put in the oven on the middle rack. Bake for 1 hour or until browned. Remove and cool a little before serving.

SERVES 4   WINE: Brachetto d'Aqui

BONET
BONET

*This traditional dessert (pronounced boo-NET) from the Langhe area of Piemonte has a basic and constant
ingredient list of eggs, cocoa, caramel and milk, to which other optional ingredients – such as coffee, rum,
amaretti, marsala and the like – can be added.*

INGREDIENTS

6 eggs

360 g (12¾ oz) caster (superfine) sugar

30 g (1 oz) good-quality unsweetened cocoa powder

1 teaspoon freshly ground coffee beans

30 ml (1 fl oz) rum

2 cups (500 ml/17 fl oz) cold milk

METHOD

Preheat the oven to 140°C (285°F). Beat the eggs and 300 g (10½ oz) of the sugar until pale and fluffy. Slowly add the cocoa, coffee and rum, mixing until well combined. Drizzle in the milk and keep mixing until creamy and unified. Set aside. Put the remaining sugar in a small saucepan with 2 tablespoons water and bring to the boil. Keep boiling until the sugar is a golden caramel. Pour half the caramel evenly into a rectangular terrine tin or mould (1–1.2 litres/1½–2 pints capacity). Add 2 tablespoons water to the remaining caramel and dissolve completely to make a sauce. Pour the egg mixture onto the caramel in the tin. Put the tin in a baking dish and pour in water to come halfway up the sides of the tin. Bake for 1 hour. Remove from the oven and let cool before refrigerating for at least 4 hours. Unmould, slice and serve with the caramel sauce.

SERVES 10   WINE: Barolo Chinato

POACHED PEACHES WITH HAZELNUT ZABAGLIONE
PESCHE NEL VINO CON ZABAGLIONE ALLE NOCCIOLE

INGREDIENTS

6 freestone peaches

90 g (3¼ oz) sugar

3 cups (750 ml/26 fl oz) sweet white wine (such as moscato or late-picked riesling)

4 egg yolks

3 tablespoons caster (superfine) sugar

⅓ cup (80 ml/2½ fl oz) hazelnut liqueur

4 tablespoons hazelnuts, roasted, skinned and crushed

METHOD

Put the peaches in a saucepan with the sugar and sweet wine and bring to the boil. Reduce the heat and simmer for 5 minutes. Remove the fruit from the liquid and when cool enough to handle, cut in half and discard the stones. Peel the peaches, then return them to the poaching liquid and let cool. (The poached peaches and liquid can be stored in the refrigerator in a sealed container until needed.) Fill a saucepan about one-third full with water and bring to the boil. In a stainless steel bowl that will fit neatly over the saucepan, whisk the egg yolks, sugar and hazelnut liqueur together until pale and creamy, then whisk in ½ cup (125 ml/4 fl oz) of the peach poaching liquid. Put the bowl over the pan and turn the heat down to a simmer, making sure the bottom of the bowl is not touching the water. Keep whisking for 5–8 minutes until the zabaglione thickens. Transfer to a bowl and let cool. To serve, put 2 peach halves in each serving bowl, spoon over some zabaglione and sprinkle with hazelnuts.

SERVES 6

WINE: Moscato d'Asti

BRUTTI MA BUONI
BRUTTI MA BUONI

Literally translated, these biscuits (cookies) are called 'ugly but delicious'.

INGREDIENTS

5 large egg whites

330 g (11¾ oz) caster (superfine) sugar

400 g (14 oz) blanched almonds, lightly roasted and chopped

pinch of ground cinnamon

METHOD

Preheat the oven to 160°C (320°F) and butter and flour a baking tray. Using an electric mixer fitted with a whisk attachment, whisk the egg whites until foamy. Slowly add the sugar, continuing to whisk, until stiff, shiny peaks form. Gently fold in the almonds and cinnamon. Dollop tablespoons of the mixture on the baking tray 2 cm (¾ in) apart, then bake for 30 minutes. Remove from the oven and reduce the oven temperature to 130°C (270°F). When the temperature has dropped, bake the biscuits for another 10–12 minutes. Cool completely before serving. They will keep for weeks in an airtight container.

MAKES 35–40

SERVE with espresso, macchiato or caffè latte

STONE FRUIT IN RED WINE
FRUTTA DRUPACEA IN VINO ROSSO

This dessert is also good for a weekend breakfast. If Brachetto d'Acqui is not available, use a red wine that is not too big or woody – a medium-bodied dolcetto or sangiovese will do the trick.

INGREDIENTS

½ cup (125 ml/4 fl oz) freshly squeezed orange juice

1 cup (250 ml/9 fl oz) Brachetto d'Acqui or other medium-bodied red wine

2 tablespoons Aurum or Grand Marnier liqueur

2 tablespoons caster (superfine) sugar

1 cinnamon stick

8 black peppercorns

2 lemons

2 yellow peaches

2 white peaches

4 apricots

2 white nectarines

2 yellow nectarines

½ cup mint leaves

METHOD

Strain the orange juice into a large glass or ceramic bowl and add the wine, liqueur, sugar, cinnamon stick and peppercorns. Using a vegetable peeler, peel thin strips from the lemons, making sure not to take any white pith. Add the peel to the bowl and stir well. Peel all the stone fruit and cut into wedges, then add to the bowl along with the mint. Stir well and cover with plastic wrap. Refrigerate for 2 hours before serving.

SERVES 6   WINE: Brachetto d'Acqui

NUTELLA BACI
BACI ALLA NUTELLA

INGREDIENTS

⅔ cup (100 g/3½ oz) plain (all-purpose) flour

90 g (3¼ oz) softened unsalted butter

60 g (2¼ oz) almond meal

60 g (2¼ oz) hazelnut meal

50 g (1¾ oz) sugar

1 teaspoon unsweetened cocoa powder

50 g (1¾ oz) good-quality dark chocolate, chopped

½ teaspoon natural vanilla extract

pinch of salt

80 g (2¾ oz) Nutella

METHOD

Put everything except the Nutella in a food processor and pulse until well incorporated. Wrap tightly with plastic wrap into a log and refrigerate for at least 1 hour. Preheat the oven to 160°C (320°F) and grease a baking tray with butter. Lightly flour your hands, then quickly roll small balls (2.5 cm/1 in diameter) from the log and put them on the tray. Refrigerate for 20 minutes, then bake for 20 minutes. Remove from the oven and let cool on the tray. Spoon a little Nutella on the flat side of 2 baci and gently stick them together. The baci will keep for 1 week if stored in a tightly sealed container in the fridge.

MAKES 40-50   WINE: Barolo Chinato

STONE FRUIT IN RED WINE

GIANDUIA CHOCOLATE TRUFFLES
TARTUFI DI CIOCCOLATO ALLA GIANDVIA

INGREDIENTS

500 ml (17 fl oz) thick (double) cream

500 g (1 lb 2 oz) gianduia (hazelnut) chocolate

500 g (1 lb 2 oz) dark chocolate (70% cocoa solids)

100 g (3½ oz) unsweetened cocoa powder

METHOD

Bring the cream to the boil in a saucepan, then turn down the heat and simmer carefully for 2 minutes. Melt the gianduia in a double boiler. Pour the boiled cream onto the melted chocolate, whisking continuously, and whisk until the mixture is completely homogenous. Cool. Line a large tray with baking paper. Shape the cooled mixture into 2.5 cm (1 in) diameter balls and put on the tray, then refrigerate for about 2 hours until set. Spread the cocoa powder on a plate and melt the dark chocolate in a double boiler. Spear each truffle using a fork and quickly dip it in the melted chocolate, then roll it in the cocoa. Store in a sealed container in the refrigerator. They will keep for 2 weeks well sealed and refrigerated.

MAKES about 100

WINE: Barolo Chinato

GIANDVIA IS A MIXTURE OF FINE CHOCOLATE WITH THE RICH FLAVOUR OF GROUND PIEMONTE HAZELNUTS (TO AROUND 30 PER CENT). HIGH COCOA PRICES IN THE MID 1800S SAW PIEMONTESE CHOCOLATIERS 'STRETCHING' THE CHOCOLATE THEY PRODUCED WITH THE READILY FOUND (AND INEXPENSIVE) LOCAL HAZELNUTS FROM THE NEARBY LANGHE AREA. GENERATIONS OF KIDS GREW UP ON GIANDVIA'S OFFSPRING NUTELLA (ORIGINALLY CALLED GIANDUJOT). THERE ARE SOME CHOCOLATIERS WHO MAKE THEIR OWN AND WHEN IN TORINO AND OTHER PARTS OF ITALY ARE WELL WORTH LOOKING OUT FOR UNDER VARIOUS NAMES SUCH AS CREMA GIANDVIA OR CREMA SPALMABILE. THE HIGHLY REGARDED TUSCAN CHOCOLATE MAKER AMEDEI MAKES AN EXCELLENT VERSION CALLED CREMA TOSCANA.

ESPRESSO, CARDAMOM AND MASTIC PANNACOTTA WITH BANANA TUILES
PANNACOTTA AL ESPRESSO CON BISCOTTINI DI BANANA

This dolce is made up of a layer of espresso pannacotta, a layer of espresso jelly and finally a layer of mastic pannacotta. Mastic is the aromatic resin from the mastic tree. It is used in varnishes, lacquers, adhesives and also as a flavouring in food. It is also known as gum arabic and is readily available. You will need to start this recipe a day ahead.

INGREDIENTS

BANANA TUILES

175 g (6 oz) banana puree

200 g (7 oz) egg whites

30 ml (1 fl oz) thin (pouring) cream

175 g (6 oz) plain (all-purpose) flour

175 g (6 oz) sugar

pinch of salt

30 g (1 oz) glucose

175 g (6 oz) unsalted butter, melted

ESPRESSO PANNACOTTA

1½ cups (375 ml/13 fl oz) thin (pouring) cream

3 tablespoons sugar

1 tablespoon ground espresso

4 cardamom pods

6 g (⅛ oz) gelatine sheets, moistened in water

ESPRESSO JELLY

80 g (2¾ oz) sugar

1 cup (250 ml/9 fl oz) espresso (short black shots)

4 g (⅛ oz) gelatine sheets, moistened in water

MASTIC PANNACOTTA

4 g (⅛ oz) mastic

3 tablespoons sugar

1½ cups (375 ml/13 fl oz) thin (pouring) cream

6 g (⅛ oz) gelatine sheets, moistened in water

METHOD

To make the banana tuiles, combine all the ingredients except the butter. Mix in the butter, then refrigerate for 24 hours. Preheat the oven to 160°C (320°F). Spread the batter in 8 cm (3¼ in) circles on a non-stick baking tray and bake for 5–6 minutes until golden. Cool on wire racks and store in an airtight container while you make the pannacottas and jelly.

To make the espresso pannacotta, put the cream, sugar, coffee and cardamom in a saucepan and bring to the boil. Remove from the heat and cool. Add the gelatine and mix thoroughly, then strain discarding the cardamom and pour into serving glasses to fill by a third. Refrigerate for about 1 hour until set.

To make the espresso jelly, mix the sugar and coffee, then add the gelatine and mix well. Strain and let cool to room temperature. Pour into the serving glasses over the espresso pannacotta layer, then refrigerate for about 1 hour until set.

To make the mastic pannacotta, grind the mastic and sugar together in a mortar. Transfer to a saucepan, add the cream and slowly bring to the boil. Add the gelatine and mix well. Strain and let cool to room temperature, then pour into the serving glasses over the espresso jelly. Refrigerate for about 1 hour until set, then serve with the banana tuiles.

SERVES 10–12   WINE: late-picked Gavi

PUGLIA

PUGLIA

IF THE ITALIAN PENINSULA IS SHAPED, AS POPULARLY IMAGINED, LIKE A BOOT, THEN PUGLIA IS THE HEEL. A REGION OF SOME 19,000 SQUARE KILOMETRES (7300 SQUARE MILES), IT RUNS ALONG THE ADRIATIC SEA TO THE EAST AND THE STRAIT OF OTRANTO AND GULF OF TARANTO TO THE SOUTH. IT FACES GREECE AND ALBANIA ACROSS THE IONIAN AND ADRIATIC SEAS RESPECTIVELY, AND ITS SOUTHERNMOST TIP, THE HIGH HEEL (TO CONTINUE THE IMAGE), IS THE SALENTO PENINSULA. INLAND IT IS BORDERED BY MOLISE TO THE NORTH, CAMPANIA TO THE WEST AND BASILICATA TO THE SOUTH-WEST.

In ancient Roman times, up to a million head of sheep came down from the high plateaux of the Abruzzi to the flat plains of Puglia for winter pasture. It is fitting then that one of the most famous and ancient dishes of the region is calderiella, lamb (sometimes kid) cooked in sheep's or goat's milk in a fat-bellied cauldron – a caldaro, hence the name of the dish – with wild fennel. Waverley Root suggests in *The Food of Italy* that this is the original of the dish condemned by Moses in Exodus 23:19: 'Thou shalt not seethe a kid in his mother's milk'; the same verse is the basis for the kosher prohibition against milk and meat in the same dish. If this is true, it would make calderiella a very ancient dish, and it is not entirely impossible as Puglia,

the heart of Greek Italy, boasts a very old civilisation indeed.

Puglia is flat, and while much grows there under benevolent skies, there is little water. So while it produces a lot – around a third of the olive oil and 30 per cent of the wine in Italy – that produce is not of the best quality. Likewise, it is a supplier of vast amounts of vegetables (including broccoli, tomatoes, cauliflower and chicory), legumes and sun-dried tomatoes. The low cost of its agricultural production is made possible by a supply of cheap (and often illegal) labour from North Africa. Small orchards radiate out from the cities and towns to enable farm workers to return to the cities after a day on the land, and no matter how small that plot, there will always be olives and almonds growing.

A staple of the area is turnip greens, which are incorporated into the most important Pugliese dish: orecchiette pasta served with turnip greens. Good artichokes, such as the thornless mola, grow here, as does lampascioni (*Muscari comosum*), a wild bulb that is boiled and stored in vinegar and sold as baby onions.

Many of the cities of Puglia are 'oil cities' – that is, they give their name to the region's olive oils. They include Bitetto, Castel del Monte, Trani and Barletta. This practice of giving the name of the nearest town to regional produce is common in Italy, and particularly so in Puglia. Olive varieties used to make oil include leccino, frantoio, ogliarola, peranzana, rotondella and garganica.

The table olives of Puglia are also an important industry – the Pugliese love to eat them with the huge round loaves of Altamura bread. The most important table olives are the big, green and fleshy Bella di Cerignola, from the southern part of the province of Foggia, and the coratina.

With such an expanse of coastline, fish and seafood are a significant part of the local cuisine – much more so than meat. The zuppa de pesce gallipolina is a soup from the Salentine town of Gallipoli that features the local fish cernia, a kind of sea bass. A curious local custom is the appetite for raw fish: go to the fish markets and you'll be given a dish of raw cuttlefish or mussels while you're waiting. You'll also find raw octopus and mazzancolle – a large prawn known in Spanish as a langostina – on the table at restaurants. The best-known and loved oyster of the region is from Taranto, and has been known for its excellent flavour since Roman times: the emperor Trajan regulated its culture and collection.

Other seafood dishes are calamaretti in casseruola, a stew of squid and prawns, and alici recanate, an anchovy tart. There are also many recipes for mitili, the Tarantese name for mussels (mussels are as abundant as oysters); perhaps the best known of these is risotto di mitili. An interesting dish dating back to the Spanish occupation of Puglia in the 18th century is tiella, or tiella barese, a rice dish from Bari and a distant relation to paella; it is made with rice, potatoes and, most often, mussels, as tiella de cozze.

Unusually in a country that elsewhere is not much in love with them, potatoes are an important crop in Puglia. As well as in tiella, they're an important ingredient in taiedda, a dish of mussels baked with potatoes from Brindisi.

It's impossible to leave Puglia without mentioning the trulli: conical houses that have no windows, only a ventilation opening at their peak. They date from the 16th and 17th centuries, and were the Pugliese response to avoiding the tax on windows imposed by the Spanish and Bourbon rulers: no windows meant no taxes. They are still lived in today, and rented out to tourists.

Promises, promises: that is the story with southern Italy's wines, and especially so with Puglia's. The province produces about 30 per cent of Italy's wine in volume – twice as much as Australia – and has a high number of DOCs. The huge co-ops that were once content to churn out white vermouth base and blending wines are now being sold, through EU pressure, to producers more interested in quality than quantity – such as Antinori, the Tuscan maker who has bought land at Castel del Monte.

White wines first. The verdeca grape, thought to be a native of the region, is widely planted. While it is mainly used in bulk wines, some from the DOCs Martina Franca and Locorotondo finds its way into bottles that are hard to obtain outside the trulli district. The most interesting DOC wines come from Castel del Monte and Salice Salentino: local rules allow a certain amount of chardonnay to be added to the local grapes, which include taurino and pervine. These are mostly best drunk on the spot.

Two grapes dominate the red wine landscape: the aptly named negroamaro, meaning 'black and bitter', which is the base for 11 DOC reds on the Salento peninsula, and primitivo, a distant relative of the American zinfandel. The tannins in the negroamaro are often softened by the addition of malvasia nera. The negroamaro of the Salento is also used to advantage locally to make flavoursome rosati, which is a splendid accompaniment to the local seafood.

There are some quite rare but very good sweet wines, such as the moscato di Trani, made from moscato bianco, and aleatico di Puglia; the latter is a sweet red wine from the grape of the same name.

Finally, it can be recorded that the presence of Antinori in Puglia is bearing fruit. One of their early wines, inevitably dubbed a Super Puglian, is a blend of negroamaro, primitivo and cabernet sauvignon.

PUGLIA'S OLIVE GROVES

Travelling through Puglia is a delight. A simple detour off the autostrada will take you onto narrow country lanes with olive groves on either side.

White dry-stone walls around a metre high separate the individual groves and each holding is meticulously kept. There are almost a quarter of a million of these individually owned plots in the region.

Puglia produces a lot of olives for both oil and the table. The region is a powerhouse accounting for 40 per cent of all Italian olive oil production (Tuscany is miniscule at around 3 per cent). And the best extra virgin is as good as any produced in Italy.

Puglia also produces the famous Bella di Cerignola olive. It is large and meaty at around 22 mm (¾ in) in average length with a weight of just under 10 g (¼ oz). Even large examples are common and can be more like 40 mm (1½ in) in length and weigh 30 g (1 oz).

This olive is produced in northern Puglia around the town of Cerignola in the province of Foggia. It's exclusively a table olive rather than made into oil and almost always green but occasionally black.

PUGLIA
ANTI-PASTI

CRUSHED BROAD BEANS WITH MINT
FAVE SCHIACCIATE ALLA MENTA

INGREDIENTS

100 g (3½ oz) potato, unpeeled

2 cups (370 g/13 oz) double-
    peeled broad beans

⅓ cup (80 ml/2½ fl oz) extra
    virgin olive oil

1 tablespoon chopped capers

2 tablespoons chopped mint

METHOD

Bring a large saucepan of salted water to the boil and cook the potato until soft, then remove and let cool a little before peeling. In the same water, blanch the broad beans for 2 minutes. Transfer to a bowl with the potato and olive oil. Using a large fork, mash until broken down to a puree. Add more oil if required. Season, then mix in the capers and mint. Use as a topping for crostini or an accompaniment to grilled or roast meats.

MAKES 3 cups   WINE: Fiano

POTATO FOCACCIA WITH TOMATOES AND OLIVES
FOCACCIA PUGLIESE

INGREDIENTS

200 g (7 oz) roasting potatoes
    (such as sebago), unpeeled

12 g (¼ oz) fresh yeast

pinch of sugar

215 g (7½ oz) plain
    (all-purpose) flour

⅔ cup (100 g/3½ oz) durum
    wheat flour

70 ml (2¼ fl oz) extra virgin
    olive oil, plus extra for
    greasing

10 cherry tomatoes, halved

2 tablespoons finely chopped
    pitted green olives

2 tablespoons chopped fresh
    oregano

2 teaspoons coarse salt

METHOD

Cook the potatoes in their skins in 3 cups (750 ml/26 fl oz) water, covered, until soft. Peel and mash, preferably using a ricer, and let cool. Dissolve the yeast and sugar in ½ cup (125 ml/4 fl oz) water, using a fork to mix. Combine 200 g (7 oz) of the plain flour and all the durum wheat flour on your work surface and make a well in the middle. Add the potatoes, yeast, 50 ml (1¾ fl oz) of the olive oil and enough water to make a dough that won't stick to the work surface or your hands. Work the dough by stretching and folding for 5–6 minutes, then put it in a lightly floured bowl and cover with plastic wrap. Leave in a warm spot for 1–1½ hours until more than doubled in size. Preheat the oven to 220°C (430°F). Sprinkle the remaining flour into the bowl and work the dough away from the sides of the bowl for 30 seconds. Liberally oil a 28 cm (11¼ in) round tin and put in the dough. Put the remaining oil on top and, using your fingertips, stretch the dough to fit the pan. Press the tomatoes into the surface, scatter over the olives and oregano and sprinkle with the salt. Bake for 25–35 minutes until golden.

SERVES 8   WINE: Squinzano rosato

POTATO FOCACCIA WITH TOMATOES AND OLIVES

BLACK PEPPER TARALLI
TARALLI AL PEPE NERO

Taralli are produced in various central and southern regions, including Puglia, Calabria, Campania, Basilicata, Lazio, Molise and Sicilia. This is a variation on the recipe in the Campania section for taralli with fennel seed (see page 140).

INGREDIENTS

- 2 cups (300 g/10½ oz) plain (all-purpose) flour
- 200 g (7 oz) durum wheat flour
- 9 g (¼ oz) fresh yeast
- 100 ml (3½ fl oz) dry white wine
- ½ cup (125 ml/4 fl oz) extra virgin olive oil

METHOD

Put the flours in a large bowl, mix thoroughly and make a well in the centre. Dissolve the yeast in 100 ml (3½ fl oz) warm water. In another bowl, dissolve 2 level teaspoons salt in the wine, then add to the flour with the yeast, olive oil and 1 teaspoon cracked pepper. Mix using your hands until the dough comes together, then put it on your workbench and knead until smooth. Put in a small bowl, cover with a clean tea towel (dish towel) and let rest for 20 minutes. Cut chunks from the main piece of dough and roll them as though you were making gnocchi. Cut gnocchi-sized pieces from the roll weighing about 8 g each and roll these into smaller rolls about 1 cm (½ in) in diameter and 8 cm (3¼ in) long. Fold each small roll so the ends cross each other, then rest on a clean tea towel. Once all the taralli have been shaped, let them rise for 10 minutes. Preheat the oven to 180°C (350°F) and line baking trays with baking paper. Bring a large saucepan of salted water to the boil and poach around 10–15 taralli at a time until they come to the surface. Remove using a slotted spoon and drain on clean tea towels. Arrange the poached taralli on the trays so they aren't touching each other, then bake for 20–25 minutes until golden. Let cool completely before using. Serve with antipasto or cheese.

MAKES about 100   WINE: Vermentino

PUNTARELLE PATTIES
POLPETTINE ALLE PUNTARELLE

To prepare puntarelle, remove the leaves from the shoots and cut the shoots lengthways into thin slices. Place the cut shoots into a bowl with lemon water for 2–3 hours to sweeten up. The previously straight stems will curl up. Puntarelle are highly prized from Rome down to Puglia. Outside of Italy this is a new ingredient but look out for it in farmers' markets or continental greengrocers.

INGREDIENTS

1 lemon, halved

400 g (14 oz) puntarelle, trimmed

1 egg, whisked

2 tablespoons grated pecorino cheese

3 tablespoons breadcrumbs

extra virgin olive oil

METHOD

Squeeze the lemon halves into a large bowl of water. Thinly slice the puntarelle clumps lengthways and soak in the bowl of lemon water for 2–3 hours. Drain. Bring a large saucepan of salted water to the boil and plunge in the puntarelle. Once the water comes back to the boil, cook for 3 minutes. Drain and let cool, then squeeze to get rid of any excess water. Roughly chop the puntarelle and squeeze out any further water. Combine with the egg, pecorino and breadcrumbs and season well. Form into patties 4–5 cm (1½–2 in) in diameter. Pour olive oil into a frying pan to a depth of 5 mm (¼ in) and heat. Fry the patties a few at a time, drain on paper towels and serve as part of an antipasto or as a snack by themselves or with a spicy tomato-based sauce.

MAKES about 30   WINE: Verdeca

PUNTARELLE ARE PART OF THE CHICORY FAMILY, BUT INSTEAD OF THE LEAVES IT'S THE TENDER TUMESCENT SHOOTS THAT FORM FROM THE CENTRE OF THE PLANT THAT ARE EATEN. THEY ARE CRISP, FLAVOURSOME GREENS WITH A PLEASANT, SLIGHTLY BITTER TASTE. THEY'RE USED IN SALADS, OR BRAISED WITH GARLIC AND CAPERS BEFORE BEING TOSSED THROUGH PASTA.

BRAISED BROAD BEANS, PEAS AND LEEKS

BRAISED BROAD BEANS, PEAS AND LEEKS
FAVE NOVELLA LESSATE CON PISELLI E PORRI

This dish doesn't require the broad beans to be double peeled as long as they are young and not too big. They just need to be taken out of their pods.

INGREDIENTS

2 leeks, white part only, quartered lengthways

⅓ cup (80 ml/2½ fl oz) extra virgin olive oil

1 brown onion, sliced

2 garlic cloves, minced

2 cups (370 g/13 oz) shelled young broad beans

1 cup (155 g/5½ oz) shelled peas

1 teaspoon chopped marjoram leaves

1 teaspoon chopped fresh oregano leaves

12 ripe cherry tomatoes, halved

½ cup (125 ml/4 fl oz) chicken or vegetable stock

4 tablespoons chopped parsley

METHOD

Cut the leeks into 2 cm (¾ in) pieces. Heat the olive oil in a saucepan and gently fry the onion and garlic for 30 seconds. Add the leeks, stir and fry for 2 minutes, then add the broad beans, peas, marjoram, oregano and tomatoes. Stir and keep frying for a minute until liquid comes out of the tomatoes. Add the stock and a couple of good pinches of salt, then simmer for 20 minutes. Add the parsley and season. Serve at room temperature as part of an antipasto or as a side dish with grilled fish or barbecued meats.

SERVES 4–6 WINE: Verdeca

WHEN **BROAD BEANS** ARE VERY YOUNG (LESS THAN 1 CM (½ IN) LONG) THEY CAN BE COOKED OR EATEN RAW WITHOUT DOUBLE PEELING. DOUBLE PEELING ENTAILS PODDING THEM FIRST, THEN PEELING THE FINE SKIN AROUND EACH BEAN. WHEN BUYING BROAD BEANS MAKE SURE THEY ARE FRESH AND THE PODS GREEN WITH NO BLACK SPOTS OR BLEMISHES. FEEL THE PODS TO MAKE SURE THERE ARE BEANS INSIDE. SOMETIMES THEY WILL LOOK FULL AND DECEPTIVELY SWOLLEN EVEN WHEN THEY ARE EMPTY.

BRAISED ARTICHOKES WITH ONIONS, OLIVES AND CAPERS
CARCIOFI BRASATI

INGREDIENTS

juice of 1 lemon

8 artichokes

⅓ cup (80 ml/2½ fl oz) extra virgin olive oil

2 bulb spring onions (scallions), peeled and quartered

1 garlic clove, minced

2–4 bird's eye chillies, halved lengthways

4 thyme sprigs

350 ml (12 fl oz) dry white wine

12 pitted green olives

2 tablespoons capers, rinsed

METHOD

Put the lemon juice in a large bowl of cold water. Using a sharp knife, cut the top third off each artichoke and peel off and discard any tougher, darker leaves. Cut off the stalk, leaving about 5 cm (2 in) attached. Cut off and discard any leaves attached to the stalk, then cut the artichokes in half lengthways. Put in the lemon water for at least 10 minutes. When you are ready to cook, remove the artichokes from the water and pat dry. Press a pinch of salt into each artichoke on the flat side. Heat half the olive oil in a wide frying pan and lightly fry the artichokes, flat side down, until well browned. Remove to a tray. Add half the remaining oil to the pan and lightly fry the spring onions, garlic and chillies until soft. Return the artichokes to the pan, flat side down, then add the thyme and wine and bring to a low simmer. Add the olives and capers. Simmer for 10 minutes, then flip the artichokes and simmer until the wine has almost all evaporated. Season and drizzle with the remaining oil to serve.

SERVES 6   WINE: Fiano

PUGLIA
PRIMI

OYSTERS BAKED IN THEIR SHELL
OSTRICHE ALLA TARANTINA

INGREDIENTS

24 oysters on the shell

1 kg (2 lb 4 oz) coarse rock
salt

2 tablespoons finely chopped
parsley

4 tablespoons fine
breadcrumbs

50 ml (1¾ fl oz) extra virgin
olive oil

fine white pepper

4 lemon wedges

METHOD

Preheat the oven to 200°C (400°F) and turn on the top griller (broiler),
if available. If the oysters are alive, shuck them and discard the top
shell. Carefully remove any pieces of shell from the liquor surrounding
the oysters. Using the shucking knife, dislodge each oyster by scraping
underneath and against the shell, then turn the oyster so the plump
part is on top. Put the salt on a baking tray and carefully arrange the
oysters on top so the liquor stays in the shells. Sprinkle some parsley,
breadcrumbs and olive oil on each oyster and then a little white pepper.
Bake for 8–10 minutes and serve with the lemon wedges.

SERVES 4   WINE: Vermentino

OYSTER AND SPINACH FRITTATA
FRITTATA ALLE OSTRICHE

INGREDIENTS

2 eggs (preferably very fresh)

1 tablespoon grated parmesan
cheese

8–10 baby spinach leaves

1 tablespoon extra virgin
olive oil

6 oysters

a few fennel fronds

METHOD

Crack the eggs into a bowl and add the parmesan and a pinch of salt.
Whisk lightly using a fork. Bring a small saucepan of water to the boil
and blanch the spinach leaves until just wilted. Drain, cool a little and
squeeze to remove any excess water. Heat the olive oil in a non-stick
18–20 cm (7–8 in) frying pan on medium heat until it begins to smoke.
Add the egg mixture and roll it around the pan so it covers the bottom
and cooks evenly. After about 30 seconds, scatter the oysters and
spinach evenly over the frittata. Cook for a few more seconds until the
frittata firms but is still a little creamy. Season with pepper and transfer
to a plate. Scatter the fennel fronds on top to serve.

SERVES 1   WINE: Locorotondo

OYSTER AND SPINACH FRITTATA

MUSSELS, ZUCCHINI AND EGGS
COZZE, ZUCCHINI E UOVA

This dish from Bari goes against the conventional notion that Italians don't mix cheese and seafood. They do on some occasions, when the result warrants the combination.

INGREDIENTS

¼ cup (60 ml/2 fl oz) extra
   virgin olive oil

1 brown onion, cut into thin
   wedges

300 g (10½ oz) zucchini
   (courgettes), thinly sliced

1 kg (2 lb 4 oz) mussels,
   scrubbed and de-bearded

3 eggs

2 tablespoons grated aged
   pecorino cheese

METHOD

Heat the olive oil in a large saucepan and lightly fry the onion for a minute until soft. Add the zucchini and lightly fry for about 5 minutes, stirring often, then add ¼ cup (60 ml/2 fl oz) water. Add the mussels, turn up the heat and cover the pan. Cook until the mussels have opened. Whisk the eggs in a bowl with the pecorino and pour over the mussels. Turn off the heat and stir well. Season and serve.

SERVES 4   WINE: Castel del Monte Bianco

LINGUINE WITH SEA URCHINS
LINGUINE AI RICCI DI MARE

Sea urchins abound in Puglia, from Brindisi to the Salento Peninsula. Their most popular use is as a condiment with pasta, as here. They must be very fresh.

INGREDIENTS

20 very fresh sea urchins

350 g (12 oz) basic pasta
   dough (see page 42)

2 tablespoons extra virgin
   olive oil

1 French shallot, minced

2 garlic cloves, minced

200 g (7 oz) ripe tomatoes,
   peeled, seeded and
   chopped

6 large green olives
   (preferably Bella di
   Cerignola), pitted and
   chopped

1 tablespoon chopped parsley

METHOD

Wearing gloves and using scissors, hold each sea urchin over a bowl and cut through the shell at the top from the small hole. Make sure you cut only the shell and not the roe. Remove the roe carefully and put in a separate bowl. Once you have cleaned all the sea urchins, strain the liquid into a bowl through a couple of layers of muslin (cheesecloth) and refrigerate. Refrigerate the bowl of roe, too. Roll out the pasta and cut it into linguine. Heat the olive oil in a large frying pan and lightly fry the shallot and garlic until fragrant but not coloured. Add the tomatoes and the olives and simmer gently for 5 minutes or so until slightly reduced. Add the sea urchin liquid and parsley and simmer for a minute. Cook the pasta in boiling salted water until al dente, then drain and add to the frying pan. Toss with the sauce for a minute until well coated. Turn off the heat and add the urchin roe, mixing it carefully through the pasta. Serve immediately.

SERVES 4   WINE: Vermentino

BURRATA WITH TOMATO FILLETS AND ARTICHOKES
BURRATA CON CARCIOFI E FILETTI DI POMODORO

This dish can be prepared with any fresh cheese, including buffalo mozzarella, goat's curd or even ricotta.

INGREDIENTS

juice of 2 lemons

2 artichokes

2 ripe tomatoes, peeled, halved and seeded

⅓ cup (80 ml/2½ fl oz) extra virgin olive oil

1 tablespoon chopped parsley

burrata or other fresh soft cheese

METHOD

Put half the lemon juice in a large bowl of cold water. Using a sharp knife, cut the top third off each artichoke and peel off and discard any tougher, darker leaves. Cut off the stalk, leaving about 5 cm (2 in) attached. Cut off and discard any leaves attached to the stalk, then cut the artichokes in half lengthways and thinly slice. Put in the lemon water for at least 10 minutes. When ready to cook, remove the artichokes from the water and pat dry. Bring a large saucepan of salted water to a rolling boil and plunge in the artichokes for 1½ minutes. Drain and let cool. Cut each tomato half into four small 'fillets'. Dress the artichokes with the remaining lemon juice and the oil and parsley. Season and serve with the burrata and tomato fillets.

SERVES 4   WINE: Verdeca

BURRATA IS A MEMBER OF THE FAMILY OF STRETCHED CURD CHEESES THAT INCLUDE MOZZARELLA. A SHEET OF STRETCHED CURD ABOUT A CENTIMETRE THICK IS FORMED INTO THE REQUIRED SIZE TO FORM AN ENVELOPE; THIS CAN VARY ACCORDING TO THE SIZE OF THE BURRATA. IT IS THEN FILLED WITH STRETCHED CURD STRINGS MIXED WITH CREAM FROM THE WHEY WHILE STILL WARM. THE ENVELOPES ARE TIED AT THE TOP TO FORM LITTLE 'MONEYBAGS'. THE BURRATA ARE THEN DIPPED INTO A BRINE SOLUTION FOR A FEW MINUTES TO SALT THEM BEFORE EATING.

CIME DI RAPA AND RICOTTA GNOCCHI WITH CREAM OF CANNELLINI BEANS
GNOCCHI DI RICOTTA E CIME DI RAPA

The amount of cime di rapa (broccoli raab) leaves and flowering tips needed for this gnocchi will come from about 1.5 kg (3 lb 5 oz) of plant.

INGREDIENTS

200 g (7 oz) cime di rapa (broccoli raab), leaves and flowering tips separated from stems

2 tablespoons extra virgin olive oil, plus extra for drizzling

2 garlic cloves, minced

350 g (12 oz) fresh but dry ricotta cheese

40 g (1½ oz) plain (all-purpose) flour

80 g (2¾ oz) grated parmesan cheese

pinch of grated nutmeg

2 eggs

CREAM OF CANNELLINI BEANS

200 g (7 oz) dried cannellini beans, soaked overnight in plenty of cold water

1 large brown onion, diced

1 garlic clove, thinly sliced

2 ripe tomatoes, chopped

1 handful parsley leaves

METHOD

To make the cream of cannellini beans, drain the beans and put in a large saucepan of cold water. Bring to the boil, then drain again. Return the beans to the pan and cover with plenty of water. Add the onion, garlic, tomatoes and parsley and bring to the boil. Turn the heat down and simmer for 2 hours or so, adding boiling water if the mixture looks dry. Drain, reserving the cooking liquid. Using a stick blender, puree the beans, adding reserved cooking liquid as necessary to achieve a creamy consistency. Season, then set aside and keep warm.

Blanch the cime di rapa leaves and tips in boiling water for a minute. Drain and let cool, then squeeze out as much liquid as possible and roughly chop. Finely chop the stems and lightly fry in a frying pan with the olive oil and garlic until soft. In a bowl, combine the ricotta, cime di rapa leaves and stems, flour, parmesan, nutmeg and eggs. Season. Dust your hands with flour and shape the mixture into balls two-thirds the size of a golf ball. Bring a large saucepan of salted water to the boil and poach the gnocchi for 3–4 minutes until they rise to the surface. Remove from the water quickly using a slotted spoon, drain well and divide among serving bowls, allowing 5–6 gnocchi per person. Put a few tablespoons of cream of cannellini beans in each serving bowl and finish with a drizzle of oil.

SERVES 8–10   WINE: Castel del Monte Chardonnay

CIMI DI RAPA IS ALSO KNOWN A BROCCOLI RAAB AND RAPINI. IT IS PART OF THE TURNIP FAMILY AND RESEMBLES BROCCOLI BUT WITHOUT THE LARGE HEADS. IT HAS A BITTER FLAVOUR AND ALL THE PARTS (THE LEAVES, BUDS AND STEMS) ARE EDIBLE.

BORLOTTI BEAN PUREE WITH OLIVES AND RADICCHIO
PUREA DI BORLOTTI CON OLIVE E RADICCHIO

This is great on its own with chunky toasted bread or as an accompaniment to grilled meat, fish or vegetables.

INGREDIENTS

200 g (7 oz) shelled fresh
  borlotti beans

200 g (7 oz) potatoes,
  unpeeled

160 ml (5¼ fl oz) extra virgin
  olive oil

1 red onion, diced

1 small head of radicchio,
  trimmed and chopped

50 g (1¾ oz) large green
  olives, pitted and chopped

2 tablespoons white wine
  vinegar

METHOD

Put the borlotti beans in a saucepan, cover with water and bring to the boil. Reduce the heat and simmer for 30–40 minutes until tender. Meanwhile, steam the potatoes until easily pierced with a skewer. Drain the beans, reserving 1 cup (250 ml/9 fl oz) of the cooking liquid. Peel the potatoes and mash with the beans and half the olive oil, moistening with a little of the cooking liquid to reach the desired consistency of a thick cream. Heat the remaining oil in a frying pan and gently fry the onion until soft. Add the radicchio and fry until wilted. Stir the onion and radicchio into the puree with the olives and vinegar. Season and serve.

SERVES 6   WINE: Fiano

395

PUGLIA
SECONDI

BREAM IN WHITE WINE
ORATA AL VINO BIANCO

INGREDIENTS

3 × 700–800 g (1 lb 9 oz–
    1 lb 12 oz) bream, cleaned
    and scaled
75 g (2¾ oz) sultanas
    (golden raisins), soaked in
    hot water until plump
1 brown onion, thinly sliced
2 garlic cloves, minced
¼ cup finely chopped parsley
1 bay leaf
300 ml (10½ fl oz) dry white
    wine
300 ml (10½ fl oz) fish stock
    (see page 49)
100 ml (3½ fl oz) extra virgin
    olive oil

METHOD

Fillet the fish, then cut each fillet into 2 pieces, taking the bone line
out at the same time and leaving the skin on. (Use the heads and
carcasses to make fish stock.) Put the fish fillets in a wide flameproof
casserole dish and add all the other ingredients except the olive oil.
Add 2–3 pinches of salt and a couple of turns of pepper. Cover and
leave to marinate for an hour or so. Uncover the pan and bring to the
boil on medium heat. Immediately turn down the heat and simmer for
a minute until the fish is just cooked. Carefully remove the fish from
the pan and put on a warm serving plate. Boil the liquid in the pan until
reduced to about ½ cup (125 ml/4 fl oz). Strain through a sieve lined
with muslin (cheesecloth), then pour over the fish. Splash on the olive
oil and serve.

SERVES 6   WINE: Fiano

SARDINE FLAN
TORTIERA DI SARDE

INGREDIENTS

800 g (1 lb 12 oz) sardine fillets
200 g (7 oz) breadcrumbs
150 g (5½ oz) pecorino cheese,
    grated
leaves from 2 mint sprigs
leaves from 2 parsley sprigs
leaves from 2 oregano sprigs
2 fennel fronds
⅓ cup (80 ml/2½ fl oz) extra
    virgin olive oil, plus extra for
    greasing
3 eggs

METHOD

Preheat the oven to 175°C (345°F). Using sharp scissors, cut the tail
and fins from each sardine. Combine the breadcrumbs and pecorino
in a bowl. Chop the herbs and fennel fronds together and add to the
bowl. Season. Grease a ceramic baking dish with olive oil, sprinkle with
salt and line with the sardines, skin side down. Sprinkle on a layer of
breadcrumb mixture, then another layer of sardines. Continue until all
the sardines and breadcrumb mixture have been used, finishing with a
breadcrumb layer. Sprinkle on the olive oil. Whisk the eggs with a little
salt and pepper and distribute over the top. Bake for 35–45 minutes,
depending on the size of the dish and the number of layers. Cool to
room temperature, then slice and serve.

SERVES 6   WINE: Fiano/Greco blend

BARBECUED JUMBO PRAWNS WITH SALSA PICCANTE
GAMBERONI ALLA GRIGLIA CON SALSA PICCANTE

Nothing beats the taste of cooking on a wood-fired grill. Puglia has a lot of olive wood, which is perfect. Though you'll get best-tasting results cooking over wood, a gas barbecue or grill will work fine here.

INGREDIENTS

16 large raw prawns (shrimp)

⅓ cup (80 ml/2½ fl oz) extra virgin olive oil

SALSA PICCANTE

500 g (1 lb 2 oz) ripe, flavoursome tomatoes, peeled, seeded and diced

juice of ½ lemon

1 chilli, finely chopped

1 garlic clove, minced

leaves from 3 oregano sprigs, chopped

2 tablespoons extra virgin olive oil

2 tablespoons finely snipped chives

METHOD

To make the salsa piccante, combine the tomatoes, lemon juice, chilli, garlic and oregano. Season, then add the olive oil, stir well and let sit for 1 hour. When ready to serve, mix in the chives. Makes 2 cups.

Turn each prawn on its back and use a large sharp knife to 'butterfly' it from top to bottom to expose the meat, taking care not to cut all the way through. Make sure the barbecue is hot and the coals are glowing if using wood. Lightly brush each prawn with olive oil on the meat side. Put on the barbecue, meat side down, and grill for 1–1½ minutes depending on the heat source and the size of the prawns. Turn so the meat is facing up for 30 seconds, then transfer to serving plates. Season lightly and spoon on some salsa piccante. Serve immediately.

SERVES 4   WINE: Bombino Bianco

GRILLED SPATCHCOCK WITH POMEGRANATE
GALLETTO ALLA GRIGLIA CON MELOGRANO

Travel through Puglia in autumn and you see beautiful pomegranate trees with ripe red fruit dotted about the manicured landscape. Getting the juice and seeds out takes a little patience but it's very easy. To remove the juice, put the pomegranate on your workbench and roll it around, pressing firmly with the palm of your hand. The fruit will become soft as the seeds release the juice around them. Slit the skin carefully over a bowl and squeeze out the juice. To remove the seeds, cut the pomegranate in half and then, using the back of a heavy knife, tap each half vigorously over a bowl. The seeds will dislodge easily.

INGREDIENTS

4 × 350–400 g (12–14 oz) spatchcocks

¼ cup (60 ml/2 fl oz) pomegranate molasses

⅓ cup (80 ml/2½ fl oz) dry white wine

1 red onion, thinly sliced

2 tablespoons red wine vinegar

160 ml (5¼ fl oz) extra virgin olive oil, plus extra for cooking

1 cup pomegranate seeds (from 1 large or 2 small pomegranates)

best leaves from 150 g (5½ oz) rocket (arugula)

METHOD

Put each spatchcock on a cutting board, breast up, and put a sharp heavy knife into the cavity. Cut down on each side of the backbone and remove it, along with the neck. The spatchcock will now flatten easily. Season the birds. In a large bowl, mix 2 tablespoons of the pomegranate molasses with the wine. Add the spatchcocks and coat with the mixture. Cover and marinate in the fridge for 2–3 hours. Meanwhile, in a large stainless steel or ceramic bowl, mix the remaining molasses with the onion and vinegar and leave for 1 hour. Whisk the olive oil into the molasses/onion mixture and season. Heat a little oil on a barbecue grill or in a large frying pan and grill or fry the spatchcocks, breast side down, for 7–8 minutes. Turn and cook the other side for 3–4 minutes, then transfer to the bowl with the onion and put the bowl on the barbecue or stovetop to warm through. Mix in the pomegranate seeds and remove from the heat. Put the spatchcocks on serving plates, scatter the rocket around and finish with the warm dressing.

SERVES 4

WINE: Martina Bianco

WHOLE ROASTED SPATCHCOCK WITH BREAD AND HERB STUFFING
GALLETTO RIPIENO AL FORNO

INGREDIENTS

4 spatchcocks

200 g (7 oz) two-day-old good-quality bread, chopped

80 g (2¾ oz) butter

1 brown onion, finely diced

2 garlic cloves, minced

½ cup finely chopped herbs (rosemary, sage, parsley, tarragon)

80 g (2¾ oz) grated parmesan cheese

2 tablespoons extra virgin olive oil

METHOD

Prepare the spatchcocks by trimming each wing at the first joint, then cutting off the neck using a large sharp knife. Chop the end of the drumsticks clean off just below the end joint and cut off the parson's nose. Your birds are now ready to be stuffed. Take them one at a time and position so the head end is facing away from you. You'll see the 2 breasts on top are covered with skin – this skin will lift easily from each end of the breast. Insert your fingers and make a pocket between the skin and breast meat, then put the birds in the refrigerator. Preheat the oven to 190°C (375°F). Pulse the bread in a food processor until crumbly but not too fine. Heat the butter in a frying pan and gently fry the onion and garlic for 2–3 minutes until very tender and aromatic. Remove from the heat and add to the breadcrumbs along with the herbs and parmesan. Add a couple of good pinches of salt and a few turns of pepper. Mix well using your hands so that the butter is worked into the bread. Stuff the spatchcock breast pockets with as much of this mixture as you can without breaking the skin. Put the birds in a baking dish and brush all over with the olive oil. Sprinkle with a little salt and roast for 30–35 minutes. Serve with a green salad or roasted vegetables.

SERVES 4 WINE: Brindisi Rosso

CIME DI RAPA WITH CHILLI
CIME DI RAPA AL PEPERONCINO

This dish is popular around the city of Lecce. Serve it as a contorno or side dish with pork or sausages.

INGREDIENTS

800 g (1 lb 12 oz) cime di rapa (broccoli raab)

⅓ cup (80 ml/2½ fl oz) extra virgin olive oil

2 garlic cloves, crushed

1–2 red chillies, minced

1 cup (250 ml/9 fl oz) vegetable stock or water

1 teaspoon chilli flakes

METHOD

Cut the cime di rapa into manageable lengths if necessary. Heat half the olive oil in a large frying pan and lightly fry the garlic until it begins to colour. Remove and discard the garlic. Add the chilli to the pan and fry for a few seconds, then add the cime di rapa and a couple of good pinches of salt. Stir well and add the vegetable stock. Cover and simmer for 10 minutes, then remove the lid and simmer for about 5 minutes until the cime di rapa stems are tender but still a little firm. Season (if necessary) and transfer to a serving plate. Scatter the chilli flakes on top and drizzle on the remaining olive oil to serve.

SERVES 4–6   WINE: Salice Salentino Rosato

TURNIPS ARE POPULAR IN THE COOLER NORTHERN REGIONS OF ITALY AND ARE USED IN DISHES SUCH AS ROAST DUCK WITH ROAST TURNIPS. IN THE SOUTHERN AREAS, HOWEVER, THE SPROUTING TURNIP TOPS, CALLED CIME DI RAPA (BROCCOLI RAAB), ARE PRIZED AS A LEAFY GREEN VEGETABLE. TURNIP BULBS AND CIME DI RAPA ARE RELATED BUT ARE TREATED AS TWO SEPARATE VEGETABLES IN THE KITCHEN IN MUCH THE SAME WAY AS CELERY AND CELERIAC. THE EDIBLE PARTS ARE THE TENDER LEAVES, THE STEMS AND THE FLOWERING TIPS THAT LOOK A LITTLE LIKE BROCCOLI.

PUGLIA

DOLCI

POMEGRANATE SYRUP
SCIROPPO DI MELAGRANA

The pomegranate is not an easy fruit to deal with. The juice is contained in the pulp that surrounds the many seeds, which are held together by pith and skin. It takes patience and commitment to handle a pomegranate, because it can be very messy. Perhaps the simplest way is to start with the juice, which makes a most wonderful breakfast drink. To extract the juice efficiently and with a minimum of splatter I use a sturdy, lever-type citrus juicer. Getting to the seeds can be a chore for the novice, especially prying them off the bitter pithy membrane that holds them in place. A good technique is to quarter the pomegranate, immerse each quarter one at a time in a bowl of water and pull the skin back to free the seeds. Most of the pith will float and can be scooped off. Drain the water through a sieve and the seeds will be left intact. Once the techniques of recovering both juice and seeds have been mastered, pomegranate dishes, both sweet and savoury, can be easily prepared.

INGREDIENTS

3–4 kg (6 lb 12 oz–9 lb)
  pomegranates
sugar (see method for
  quantity)

METHOD

Halve each pomegranate, taking care to recover any juice. Juice the pomegranates and pass the juice through a fine sieve or muslin (cheesecloth) into a saucepan. For every 2 cups (500 ml/17 fl oz) of juice add 1.1 kg (2 lb 7 oz) of sugar. Bring to the boil, then turn down to a medium boil and stir and cook for 20 minutes. Pour into sterilised preserving jars and seal. Leave for 2 days before using in sweet and savoury dishes where pomegranate syrup or pomegranate molasses is called for.

AS FAR AS GARDEN DECORATION GOES, THE POMEGRANATE IS AS BEAUTIFUL A TREE AS ANY. ITS LIMBS ARE FINE AND NIMBLE WITH LIME-GREEN TO YELLOW LEAVES, AND THE FRUIT – LARGE, ROSEHIP-SHAPED, DULL TO BRIGHT RED SPHERES THE SIZE OF A TENNIS BALL – APPEAR IN AUTUMN AND EARLY WINTER.

WALNUT AND QUINCE BISCOTTINI
BISCOTTINI DI NOCI ALLA COTOGNATA

INGREDIENTS

170 g (6 oz) unsalted butter

125 g (4½ oz) icing
(confectioners') sugar

1 teaspoon natural vanilla
extract

180 g (6½ oz) plain
(all-purpose) flour

75 g (2¾ oz) cornflour
(cornstarch)

130 g (4¾ oz) walnuts, ground

10 teaspoons quince jelly
or grape-skin jam
(see page 81)

METHOD

Cream the butter and sugar, then add the vanilla, flours and ½ teaspoon
salt and mix until well incorporated. Stir in the walnuts and set aside
to rest for about 30 minutes. Preheat the oven to 160°C (320°F). Roll
the mixture into small balls and put them at least 5 cm (2 in) apart
on a baking tray. Using your fingertip, make a little indentation in the
middle of each ball and add ½ teaspoon of the quince paste. Bake for
12–15 minutes until golden brown, cool and serve.

MAKES 25–30   WINE: Aleatico di Puglia Dolce

AUTUMN FRUIT WITH PISTACHIO
FRUTTA D'AUTUNNO AL PISTACCHIO DI BRONTE

Use pistachio kernels from Bronte, Sicily, for the best result.

INGREDIENTS

2 pomegranates

2 teaspoons light honey

2 figs, sliced

2 ripe persimmons, cut into
wedges

2 peaches, peeled and cut into
bite-sized pieces

2 apricots, peeled and cut into
bite-sized pieces

2 plums, pitted and sliced

½ cup red grapes, halved

½ cup green grapes, halved

2 tablespoons pistachio
kernels, roasted and
chopped

METHOD

Remove the juice from one of the pomegranates and the seeds from the
other. Set the seeds aside. Whisk the honey into the pomegranate juice
until dissolved. Layer the fruits in a glass bowl and pour the honey/
pomegranate mixture over the top. Sprinkle with the pistachios and
pomegranate seeds to serve.

SERVES 6   WINE: San Severo Bianco Spumante

WALNUT AND QUINCE BISCOTTINI

CANDIED AND DRIED ORANGE PEEL
SCORZA D'ARANCIA CANDITA O ESSICATA

This can be used for all manner of cakes and as a flavouring for desserts, or mixed with ricotta for cannoli, or added to gelato or grated chocolate. The same method can be used to make candied lemon peel.

INGREDIENTS

oranges
sugar

METHOD

Use a vegetable peeler to peel strips of orange rind, taking care to remove as little as possible of the white pith beneath. To dry the peel, simply thread the strips using a needle and thread and hang them up away from direct sunlight. To candy the peel, thinly slice the strips and put in a saucepan with enough water to just cover. Bring to the boil, then remove from the heat, drain and run under cold water to refresh. Repeat this process twice. The third time, add a mixture of half sugar, half water to cover the peel and bring to a simmer. Keep simmering until the water reduces and a thick syrup is left. Transfer the candied peel and syrup to a sterilised jar and store in the refrigerator.

CANDIED CLEMENTINES
CLEMENTINE CANDITE

INGREDIENTS

14 clementines, well washed
   and dried
750 g (1 lb 10 oz) sugar

METHOD

Cut the clementines lengthways into 4 or 6 wedges depending on their size. Put ⅔ cup (150 g/5½ oz) of the sugar and 550 ml (19 fl oz) water in a large stainless steel saucepan and whisk to dissolve the sugar. Add the clementines and bring to the boil, then turn the heat down and simmer for 5 minutes. Remove from the heat and leave for 12 hours. Add another ⅔ cup sugar and bring to the boil, then turn the heat down and simmer for 5 minutes. Remove from the heat and leave for another 12 hours. Repeat this process 3 more times. After the final time, drain the clementines and put on trays lined with baking paper. Put the trays in a dry, cool, well-ventilated area and leave for at least 24 hours. The candied clementines are then ready to use in cakes and tarts or just to eat as they are. Perfect with bitter chocolate.

WHEAT GRAINS WITH RICOTTA AND VINCOTTO
GRANO AL VINCOTTO

Puglia was once the granary for Rome and it still produces abundant wheat, which is used for bread and flour and as whole grains in both savoury and sweet dishes. Good vincotto and saba are available from providores, though a recipe is provided on page 431.

INGREDIENTS

250 g (9 oz) husked wheat, soaked overnight in plenty of cold water

2 tablespoons honey

⅓ cup (80 ml/2½ fl oz) vincotto or saba

200 g (7 oz) ricotta cheese

80 g (2¾ oz) caster (superfine) sugar

½ teaspoon natural vanilla extract

2 tablespoons candied cedro (citron), finely chopped

METHOD

Drain the wheat well, put in a saucepan and cover with water. Add the honey and bring to the boil, then turn down the heat, cover and simmer for 1–1½ hours until tender. Drain and, while still hot, mix in half the vincotto. Set aside to cool. Put the ricotta in a bowl and stir in the sugar, vanilla and cedro. Serve the dessert in glass or metal cups as you would gelato. First put in a little ricotta, then wheat, then ricotta and then wheat, and finish with ricotta. Drizzle the remaining vincotto over.

SERVES 6   WINE: Aleatico di Puglia Dolce

SARDEGNA

SARDEGNA

SARDINIA

IT IS SARDEGNA'S FATE ALWAYS TO COME AT THE END OF ANY LIST OF THE ITALIAN REGIONS, TO BE THE SECOND-LARGEST MEDITERRANEAN ISLAND AFTER SICILIA (AND BEFORE CYPRUS) AT AROUND 24,000 SQUARE KILOMETRES (9260 SQUARE MILES), AND FOR ITS PEOPLE TO BE BEST KNOWN AS THE ISLANDERS WHO EAT VERY LITTLE FISH OR SEAFOOD.

Sardegna sits beneath Corsica and above Sicilia and is more or less equidistant from the Spanish Balearic Islands to the west and mainland Italy to the east. Geologically it is the oldest of the Italian regions, and historically it is one of the most fascinating, with its 7000 nuraghi (prehistoric stone structures), some of which date from around 1300 BCE.

There are a number of stories about the origin of Sardegna's name. Some think it is after Sardus, the leader of a group that left Libya to settle on the island. According to Homer in the *Odyssey*: 'Of the western barbarians the Sardegnians offered a brazen statue of Sardus, from whom their island took its name. For its size and prosperity Sardegna is equal to the most celebrated islands. What its ancient name was among its original inhabitants I do not know, but the Greeks who sailed there for commerce called it Ichnusa, because its shape was like that of a man's footprint.' Then there is the possibility

that it is named after the Shardanes, one of a number of groups of seafaring raiders who sailed the Mediterranean around 1200 BCE. Legend has it that they migrated to the island and gave it their name.

Either way, Sardegna is the root of the word sardonic, meaning 'bitterly scornful' and said to be derived from the facial convulsions caused by eating a plant growing on the island.

As enigmatic as the origin of the name is the origin of the people. Some linguists have linked the Sardegnian language to that other distinct language, Basque. These hardy people were warriors who resisted the myriad invaders – a who's who of the Mediterranean – who tried to colonise their beautiful island, mainly by retreating to the interior caves and gorges, until the Romans conquered them in 238 BCE. The other important cultural influence was the Aragonese, who were there from 1323 to 1720. The port of Alghero has a strong

Catalan influence and an ancient form of that language is still spoken there.

Sardegnians were wedded to their dense forests and craggy mountains, and were shepherds, hunters, farmers and, sometimes, bandits more often than fisherfolk. There are more sheep and goats here than anywhere else in Italy, and sheep's milk goes to making the island's most sought-after cheese, pecorino sardo. The best pecorino sardo was fiore, meaning 'the flower', which was originally made by shepherds who used a wooden mould that left the imprint of a little flower on the cheese. Today some fiore is still made by hand on the farm, but most is factory made – the flower has been retained but is now imprinted by a metal mould. There is also a soft dolce sardo, and a goat's cheese called feta that is more than likely a remnant of the Greek occupation. Indeed, dozens of different kinds of pecorino are made depending on the season, and the rural calendar is set by them.

There is another cheese so singular, so putrid, that, for a time, EU regulations banned its sale. However, this was circumvented by labelling it as a 'traditional food'. Known as casu marzu, or jumping cheese (or other names depending on which part of the island it comes from), it is said that first you smell it, then you hear it as the maggots crawling from within the cheese jump onto the table!

A far more acceptable and succulent speciality of the island is prosciutto di cinghiale, made from wild boar. Game was once an important component of Sardegnian cuisine, and today, although much of what was hunted in the past is now protected, there are still plentiful wild hares and rabbits.

Harking back to their primitive forest-dwelling past, the most typical cooking technique of the Sardegnians is open-air roasting of whole animals. The fire is traditionally made using twigs of arbutus, lentisk and myrtle and the meat is either spitted above the ground, or smoked and perfumed from the smouldering twigs. The most famous – and outlandish – of these barbecues is the malloru de su sabatteri, the cobbler's bull, where a young bull is stuffed with a kid, then a piglet, a hare and a partridge. The town cobbler sews up this bundle and it is slowly roasted by those who are expert enough to do so.

More usual is porceddu, or suckling pig, cooked using the technique known as carne a càrrarglu ('meat in a hole'). A pit is dug and lined with branches and leaves, heated stones are placed on the bottom and the pig is laid on them, then more heated stones are placed on and the pit is sealed with earth for the meat to cook slowly underground. This technique is reminiscent of the Melanesian luau or the New Zealand hangi. Today, the porceddu is more often cooked in a wood-fired oven.

Wheat, especially *Triticum durum* or hard wheat, is an important crop in Sardegna, where it is made into the distinctive bread called carasau or into carta da musica, a paper-thin bread sold in packs of 20. These crisp breads can be eaten as they are, topped with anything, or sprinkled with water and stuffed and rolled.

The two most typical local pastas are both difficult to make. Filindeu, meaning 'God's threads', are extremely fine spaghetti braided into what look like sheets of woven cloth; they are traditionally eaten with mutton broth and pecorino. Malloreddus is made from flour mixed with saffron and is ribbed and rolled to soak up sauce and hold grated cheese.

Although the Sardegnians have turned their back on the sea, there is seafood – much of it caught by fishers with Spanish and Catalan ancestry. The stretch of coast on the Alghero side of the island is crawling with huge lobsters; they are so abundant that the locals don't eat them, just catch them. Sardegnian octopus is highly prized, as are grey mullet and giant dentex known as lupo marino ('sea wolf'); both of these are cooked over an open fire.

With so little arable land, and with 80,000 hectares (198,000 acres) of vines once supporting a thriving wine industry that was knocked out by phylloxera at the end of the 19th century, it's surprising that Sardegna still has such a significant industry that produces excellent wines. The EU reduced production from around four million to 750,000 hectolitres (1 hectolitre = 100 litres), and this has been beneficial. The remaining producers concentrate on quality, and the best wines are the so-called 'meditation wines' made from grapes such as nasco, malvasia, moscato and vernaccia di Oristano in the categories of dolce naturale, liquoroso dolce and secco.

The most-planted red wine grape is cannonau, which was perhaps brought to the island by the Spanish sometime between the 15th and 18th centuries and has recently been identified as identical to grenache. Carignan is another Spanish migrant; in Spain it is known as cariñena or mazuela. Then there are monica, buvale, cagnulari, pascale di Cagliari and nieddera, as well as nebbiolo and sangiovese.

Among the whites is the perhaps relatively recent arrival vermentino, which thrives in the dry, stony interior. The most planted variety is nuragus, which takes its name from the prehistoric nuraghi, and the main varieties are vernaccia di Oristano, malvasia de Sardegna, moscato bianco, nasco and torbato.

SARDEGNA
ANTI-PASTI

AIR-DRIED MULLET ROE
BOTTARGA

One of the staple seasonings of Sardegna, bottarga is made using the egg sacs (roe) of certain fish. In Sardegna both mullet and tuna roe is salted and air-dried when it is fresh and abundant, and thereby preserved for the rest of the year. It is grated onto many dishes, including salads and pasta, as well as thinly sliced and eaten with grilled bread. I like to eat it with pecorino and a glass of vermentino. The two attached sacs must be very fresh and intact, with no holes, tears or blemishes. Bottarga is available at good delicatessens and providores.

INGREDIENTS

2 kg (4 lb 8 oz) fresh
  mullet roe (see recipe
  introduction)
coarse sea salt
white wine vinegar

METHOD

Wash the roe carefully in cold water, put on clean tea towels (dish towels) and pat dry. Put a 5 mm (¼ in) layer of salt on the bottom of a tub or other container that will hold the roe in one layer without touching each other. Lay the roe on the salt and cover with more salt. Put a tray or chopping board on top and then a weight (a stockpot filled with 2 litres (4 pints) of water will do nicely). Leave in a cool place for 5 hours – the salt will extract the liquid from the egg sacs. Remove the roe from the salt, wash carefully in a solution of water and vinegar at 20:1 and pat dry. Arrange the roe on a wire rack and cover securely with muslin (cheesecloth). Put in the refrigerator for a week, turning once each day. After a week it should be dry enough to hang with butcher's twine between each lobe. We hang ours in a refrigerated coolroom for 4 weeks wrapped in muslin, but it can be hung in a domestic refrigerator as long as the lobes do not touch each other. Check after 2 weeks or so, and once it has darkened to a burnished yellow, cut a little off the end and try it. If you like your bottarga a little drier, leave for 1–2 weeks longer. To preserve the bottarga so it doesn't dry out any more, we vacuum-pack them, 1 double lobe per pack. (If you don't have vacuum-pack facilities wrap tightly in plastic wrap.) The bottarga will last at least until the next season.

FENNEL, CELERY HEART AND BOTTARGA SALAD
INSALATA DI FINOCCHI, SEDANO E BOTTARGA

INGREDIENTS

2 fennel bulbs, trimmed and
thinly sliced

1 celery heart (including the
tender light-green leaves),
chopped

tender inner leaves from
1 head of treviso lettuce or
radicchio, sliced

½ cup (125 ml/4 fl oz) extra
virgin olive oil

juice of 2 lemons

50 g (1¾ oz) bottarga
(see opposite page)

METHOD

Toss the fennel, celery and treviso with the olive oil and lemon juice.
Season, remembering that bottarga is salty. Put in a serving dish and
finely shave the bottarga on top. Serve as a side dish for grilled fish or
as a stand-alone salad as part of the antipasto.

SERVES 4–6   WINE: Vermentino di Gallura Superiore

POACHED EGGS SARDINIAN STYLE
PANE FRATTAU

*Breakfast in Italy is not as lavish as it can be in other countries, nor does it take as long. It's a rapid
affair, mostly involving a sweet cornetto pastry and espresso. But this egg dish could become a classic in
countries where eggs are a staple of the first meal of the day.*

INGREDIENTS

2 tablespoons extra virgin olive
oil, plus extra for drizzling

200 ml (7 fl oz) tomato passata

2 sheets pane carasau broken
into 5–6 pieces

100 g (3½ oz) pecorino cheese
(Sardinian, if possible), thinly
shaved

2 very fresh eggs

METHOD

Heat the olive oil in a frying pan and add the passata and a pinch of
salt. Simmer slowly for 5–6 minutes, then turn off the heat. Pour water
into a separate wide frying pan to a depth of about 3 cm (1¼ in) and
bring to a simmer. Poach the pane carasau a few pieces at a time for
a few seconds until softened. Remove carefully with a wide flat sieve
and drain well, then divide between 2 hot serving plates. Spoon the
reduced passata over the bread and add the pecorino. Poach the eggs,
then drain and put one on each plate. To serve, drizzle a little oil on top
and season.

SERVES 2   WINE: Sparkling Vermentino di Sardegna

SEAFOOD SALAD WITH SARDINIAN FLATBREAD
INSALATA DI MARE E PANE CARASAU

Pane carasau is the flatbread of Sardegna. It's also called carta di musica (music paper) because it looks like sheets of paper. It is made from durum wheat flour and, once cooked, can last for many months. It is complicated to make and is available at good delicatessens, providores and online. The pane carasau that's exported is still mostly made by small bakeries in the traditional way. Flour is mixed with water and yeast and rolled into thin rounds. Piled one on top of the other, they are each separated by cloth to retard the rise. They are cooked in a hot, usually wood-fired, oven where they inflate like a balloon. The two halves are separated into thin sheets and these are then cooked again to lose more moisture and attain their golden colour and crispness. To prepare them for the table, each sheet is sprinkled with good extra virgin olive oil and a little salt. They are placed in a hot oven for a minute or so and then broken into shards and served.

INGREDIENTS

2 litres (70 fl oz) vegetable stock (see page 49)

150 g (5½ oz) octopus tentacles

2 tablespoons extra virgin olive oil, plus extra for dressing

2 garlic cloves, lightly crushed

8 mussels, scrubbed and de-bearded

8 large clams (vongole), scrubbed

dry white wine

150 g (5½ oz) calamari, cleaned and thinly sliced

150 g (5½ oz) cuttlefish, cleaned and thinly sliced

80 g (2¾ oz) celery, cut into matchsticks

2 cups salad leaves (e.g. endive or rocket/arugula)

2 tablespoons grated bottarga (see page 414)

1–2 sheets pane carasau, broken into pieces

METHOD

Bring half the vegetable stock to the boil in a wide saucepan, then reduce the heat and poach the octopus tentacles for about 40 minutes. Let cool in the cooking liquid, then drain and cut into bite-sized pieces. Wipe out the saucepan and set aside. Heat the olive oil in a large frying pan and lightly fry the garlic until soft but not coloured. Add the mussels and clams and a splash of wine, then cover and cook until all the shells are open. Remove from the heat and let cool to room temperature in the cooking liquid. Drain, reserving the cooking liquid. Bring the remaining stock to the boil in the saucepan, then reduce the heat and lightly poach the calamari and cuttlefish for 30 seconds. Let cool in the cooking liquid, then drain and combine with the octopus, clams, mussels and celery. Dress with oil and 2–3 tablespoons of the cooking liquid from the mussels and clams. Season, then put a little salad on each serving plate, add some seafood and bottarga, and top with pane carasau.

SERVES 4   WINE: Vermentino

ARTICHOKE, TOMATO AND EGGPLANT ROASTED WITH FREGOLA, SPRING VEGETABLE SAUCE
ARROSTO DI CARCIOFO, POMODORO E MELANZANA CON FREGOLA

INGREDIENTS

½ small brown onion, chopped

extra virgin olive oil

1 garlic clove, minced

80 g (2¾ oz) fregola (Italian couscous)

pinch of saffron threads

1 litre (35 fl oz) boiling vegetable stock

3 artichokes

juice of 2 lemons

2 small eggplants (aubergines), halved lengthways

2 tablespoons chopped capers

1 tablespoon chopped mint

1 tablespoon chopped parsley

75 g (2¾ oz) buffalo mozzarella, diced

2 tablespoons chopped basil

2 ripe, very good-quality fragrant tomatoes, halved and seeded

3 tablespoons grated pecorino cheese

3 tablespoons toasted pine nuts

1 teaspoon grated lemon zest

2 tablespoons thyme leaves

SPRING VEGETABLE SAUCE

140 ml (4¾ fl oz) extra virgin olive oil

1 red capsicum (pepper), seeded and cut into thin strips

1 baby fennel bulb, sliced

½ small brown onion, chopped

1 carrot, cut into thin strips

1 garlic clove, minced

½ cup (125 ml/4 fl oz) vegetable stock

METHOD

In a saucepan on medium heat, fry the onion in ¼ cup (60 ml/2 fl oz) olive oil until softened. Add the garlic and fry for a minute, then add the fregola, saffron and a little salt. Pour in enough boiling stock to cover the mixture and simmer for 1 minute, then cover, turn the heat off and let steam for 5 minutes. Remove the lid and use a fork to aerate the fregola. Transfer the mixture to a tray, cover loosely and let cool.

Using a sharp knife, cut the top third off each artichoke and peel off and discard any tougher, darker leaves. Cut off the stalk, leaving about 5 cm (2 in) attached. Put in a small saucepan and pour in enough cold water to cover. Add the lemon juice and a good pinch of salt and bring to the boil, then turn the heat down and simmer until tender. Remove from the heat and set aside to cool in the liquid. Preheat the oven to 200°C (400°F). Scoop out ⅔ of the flesh from the eggplants and roughly chop, then cook in a frying pan with a little oil until softened. Remove from the pan and let cool. Put the eggplant shells on a baking tray, season, drizzle with oil and bake for 10 minutes or until tender. Cool.

Distribute the fregola among 3 bowls. Add the capers, mint and parsley to the first bowl and mix, then spoon into the eggplant shells. Add the mozzarella and basil to the second bowl and mix, then spoon the mixture into the tomato halves. Add the pecorino, pine nuts, lemon zest and thyme to the third bowl and mix, then spoon into the artichokes by separating the leaves and stuffing in between. Put all the stuffed vegetables in a baking dish and sprinkle with oil. Add ½ cup (125 ml/4 fl oz) water and bake for 8 minutes.

Meanwhile, make the spring vegetable sauce, heat ¼ cup (60 ml/2 fl oz) of the olive oil in a large saucepan on medium heat. Add the vegetables and garlic and fry until softened. Season, then add the stock and simmer for 3 minutes. Transfer to a food processor, add the remaining oil and puree until smooth. Season and serve with the stuffed vegetables.

SERVES 4

WINE: Vernaccia di Oristano

417

SARDEGNA
PRIMI

TURNIP AND BEAN SOUP
ZUPPA DI RAPE E FAGIOLI

INGREDIENTS

300 g (10½ oz) dried cannellini
    beans, soaked overnight in
    plenty of cold water

2 garlic cloves, minced

2 tablespoons chopped
    parsley

¼ cup (60 ml/2 fl oz) extra
    virgin olive oil

400 g (14 oz) turnips, peeled

6 handfuls chopped day-old
    bread

grated pecorino cheese

METHOD

Drain and rinse the beans, then drain again. In a large saucepan,
lightly fry the garlic and parsley in the olive oil. Add the beans, cover
with water and cook until tender (approximately 40 minutes). Season.
Meanwhile, cook the turnips in simmering water until tender (when
the tip of a sharp knife easily pierces the flesh), then drain, slice and
distribute among 6 bowls. Add a handful of bread to each bowl and
ladle the beans over. Serve with grated pecorino.

SERVES 6   WINE: Carignano del Sulcis Rosato

MULLET AND RICE SOUP
MINESTRA DI MUGGINE E RISO

*Grey mullet is plentiful during the season, when it runs in large schools. Many Sardinian dishes are
traditionally prepared using this fish, especially around Oristano. The egg sacs of the fish are salted and
dried to make bottarga (see page 414). Yellow-eye mullet can also be used.*

INGREDIENTS

500 g (1 lb 2 oz) grey or
    yellow-eye mullet fillets,
    bones removed

3–4 dried porcini mushrooms,
    soaked in cold water

⅓ cup (80 ml/2½ fl oz) extra
    virgin olive oil

2 French shallots, finely diced

4 garlic cloves, sliced

150 g (5½ oz) button
    mushrooms, sliced

150 g (5½ oz) tomatoes,
    peeled and chopped

1 cup (220 g/7¾ oz) Italian
    rice (arborio, carnaroli or
    vialone nano)

½ cup chopped parsley

METHOD

Cut the mullet into bite-sized pieces. Drain and roughly chop the porcini
mushrooms. Heat the olive oil in a large saucepan and lightly fry the
shallots and garlic for a minute or so. Add the button mushrooms and
stir well. Fry for 2–3 minutes until softened, then add the porcini and
tomatoes and stir well. Pour in 4 litres (7 pints) water, bring to the boil
and add the rice and 2–3 good pinches of salt. Stir and simmer for
15–20 minutes until the rice is cooked. Add the fish and parsley, stir
carefully and turn off the heat. Check for salt and add several good turns
of pepper. Stir again and leave for 15 minutes before serving.

SERVES 6   WINE: Vernaccia di Oristano

COUSCOUS WITH ARTICHOKES
FREGOLONE CON CARCIOFI

For this dish I've used large Sardinian couscous, or fregolone sardo, which is more like small balls of pasta than couscous.

INGREDIENTS

1 lemon, halved

4 artichokes

2 tablespoons extra virgin olive oil

1 brown onion, sliced

2 garlic cloves, minced

1 teaspoon fennel seeds

250 g (9 oz) Sardinian couscous (fregolone sardo)

pinch of saffron threads

1 bay leaf

4 ripe tomatoes, seeded and chopped

3 tablespoons finely chopped parsley

METHOD

Fill a saucepan three-quarters full with cold water and squeeze in the lemon. Using a sharp knife, cut the top third off each artichoke and peel off and discard any tougher, darker leaves. Cut off the stalk, leaving about 5 cm (2 in) attached. Put the trimmed artichokes in the saucepan of water and put a plate on top to keep them submerged. Bring to the boil, then turn the heat down and simmer for 10–15 minutes or until the hearts are tender when pierced with a sharp knife. Drain and cool. Trim off any tough leaves and the outer layer of the stem, then cut each artichoke lengthways into 4–6 pieces. Heat the olive oil in a large, deep frying pan and lightly fry the onion, garlic and fennel seeds until the onion is soft. Add 800 ml (28 fl oz) water and bring to the boil, then add the couscous, saffron, bay leaf, tomatoes and 2–3 good pinches of salt. Simmer for about 12 minutes, stirring occasionally, until the water has been absorbed and the couscous is cooked. Add the artichokes and parsley, season, stir well and serve.

SERVES 4   WINE: Vernaccia di Oristano

FREGOLA AND FREGOLONE

FREGOLA IS USED IN VARIOUS DISHES IN PARTS OF SOUTHERN ITALY BUT IT IS MOST AT HOME IN SARDINIA. IT IS SIMILAR TO COUSCOUS IN THAT IT IS MADE FROM FLOUR (IN THIS CASE DURUM WHEAT) AND WATER AND FORMED INTO SMALL BEADS. THE SARDINIAN VERSIONS ARE TAKEN A STEP FURTHER AND LIGHTLY TOASTED. THE LARGER FREGOLONE IS THE SIZE OF A SMALL PEA. BOTH SIZES ARE USUALLY COOKED BY ABSORPTION IN MUCH THE SAME WAY AS RISOTTO. BOTH CAN BE USED IN SALADS, SOUPS AND DISHES WITH A SAUCE.

COUSCOUS WITH ARTICHOKES

POTATO AND BOTTARGA GNOCCHI WITH TOMATO SUGO
GNOCCHI DI PATATA ALLA BOTTARGA E SUGO POMODORO

INGREDIENTS

1 kg (2 lb 4 oz) potatoes, unpeeled

200 g (7 oz) plain (all-purpose) flour

50 g (1¾ oz) grated parmesan cheese

2 egg yolks

50 g (1¾ oz) bottarga (see page 414), thinly sliced

TOMATO SUGO

½ cup (125 ml/4 fl oz) extra virgin olive oil

1 brown onion, finely diced

2 garlic cloves, minced

12–14 tinned roma tomatoes, mashed

METHOD

To make the tomato sugo, heat the olive oil in a frying pan and gently fry the onion and garlic for a couple of minutes until soft but not coloured. Add the tomatoes, mix well and add a couple of good pinches of salt. Simmer gently for 15 minutes. Adjust the salt and add some cracked pepper. Makes 2 cups (500 ml/17 fl oz).

Put the potatoes in a saucepan and pour in water to a depth of 3–4 cm (1¼–1½ in). Cover and bring to the boil, then turn the heat down and simmer for 25–30 minutes until tender. Drain and let cool a little. Peel, then mash using a ricer and put on a clean work surface. Make a well in the centre and add 1 cup (150 g/5½ oz) of the flour, then the parmesan and then the egg yolks. Season with 3 good pinches of salt and some finely ground pepper, then bring the lot together using your hands. If the dough seems a little sticky, add more flour. Flour your work surface and roll a piece of the dough into a small sausage about 3 cm (1¼ in) in diameter. Cut some 2 cm (¾ in) gnocchi from the roll. Bring a small saucepan of salted water to the boil and plunge in a couple of the gnocchi. Once they rise to the surface (1–1½ minutes), remove using a slotted spoon and put on a plate. They should be firm but tender – if they are falling apart, add a little flour to the dough. Shape the rest of your gnocchi and put them on a tray lined with a clean tea towel (dish towel). If you are not yet ready to cook, the gnocchi can be set aside, covered with a clean tea towel, for 3–4 hours but no more. Cook the gnocchi in a large saucepan of boiling salted water and serve with the tomato sugo, topped with the bottarga.

SERVES 8   WINE: Vermentino

CLAMS WITH BEANS
VONGOLE E FAGIOLI

INGREDIENTS

1 cup (200 g/7 oz) dried borlotti
    beans, soaked overnight in
    plenty of cold water

1 garlic clove

1 bay leaf

1 small brown onion, halved

4 parsley sprigs

3 ripe tomatoes, chopped

⅓ cup (80 ml/2½ fl oz) tomato
    passata

pinch of saffron threads

3 tablespoons breadcrumbs

1 kg (2 lb 4 oz) clams (vongole),
    well washed

2 red chillies, seeded and
    chopped

¼ cup (60 ml/2 fl oz) extra
    virgin olive oil

METHOD

Drain and rinse the beans, then put in a saucepan, cover with cold water and bring to the boil. Drain immediately and return to the pan. Add the garlic, bay leaf, onion, parsley, tomatoes, passata and enough cold water to cover generously. Cover and simmer gently for 1 hour, adding more water if needed. Stir in the saffron, sprinkle the breadcrumbs over and simmer for a further 30 minutes or until the beans are tender. Meanwhile, discard any clams with broken shells and put the remainder in a saucepan or frying pan. Add 1 cup (250 ml/9 fl oz) water, cover and cook over high heat, shaking the pan, until the clams open. Discard any that haven't opened and strain the cooking liquid through a fine sieve or muslin (cheesecloth). Mix the clams and their cooking liquid with the beans and add the chillies. Warm through, season with salt and drizzle the olive oil on top to serve.

SERVES 4–6   WINE: Vermentino di Sardegna

MUSSELS WITH SAFFRON, FENNEL SEEDS AND TOASTED BREADCRUMBS
COZZE IN UMIDO ALLO ZAFFERANO

INGREDIENTS

½ cup breadcrumbs

½ cup (125 ml/4 fl oz) extra
    virgin olive oil

1 teaspoon fennel seeds

2 French shallots, finely
    chopped

1 garlic clove, minced

small pinch of saffron threads

4 tinned roma tomatoes,
    mashed

1 kg (2 lb 4 oz) mussels,
    scrubbed and de-bearded

4 tablespoons finely chopped
    parsley

METHOD

Mix the breadcrumbs with ⅓ cup (80 ml/2½ fl oz) of the olive oil until well coated. Roast the fennel seeds in a frying pan on medium heat for about a minute until aromatic, keeping them moving in the pan so they don't burn. Add the oiled breadcrumbs and stir until they are crisp and toasted. Remove from the heat and set aside. Heat the remaining oil in a large saucepan and lightly fry the shallots and garlic, then add 1 cup (250 ml/9 fl oz) water and the saffron. Simmer gently for 5 minutes so the saffron colours the water. Turn the heat up to high and add the tomatoes and mussels. Mix well using a long-handled spoon, then cover and steam for about 2 minutes until the mussels have opened. Remove the lid and mix well for a minute so the mussels cook evenly. Stir through the parsley and add a few turns of cracked pepper. Serve in large bowls with the toasted breadcrumbs scattered over the top.

SERVES 4   WINE: Carignano del Sulcis rosato

SARDEGNA
SECONDI

TUNA WITH CELERY HEART AND OLIVES
TONNO AL SEDANO E OLIVE

INGREDIENTS

100 ml (3½ fl oz) extra virgin olive oil

2 French shallots, finely chopped

1 garlic clove, minced

1 celery heart (including the tender light-green leaves), finely chopped

2–3 tinned roma tomatoes, mashed

½ cup small black olives, pitted

1 tablespoon red wine vinegar

4 × 140 g (5 oz) tuna steaks

METHOD

Heat ⅓ cup (80 ml/2½ fl oz) of the olive oil in a saucepan and gently fry the shallots, garlic, celery and half the celery leaves for a minute or two. Add the tomatoes, olives and a couple of good pinches of salt and simmer for 5 minutes, then mix in the vinegar. Check for seasoning and add a little more salt, if necessary, and a couple of turns of pepper. Mix well and turn off the heat. Heat the remaining oil in a frying pan on high heat. Season the tuna steaks and sear each side for 5–6 seconds (or more if you prefer it cooked through). Put the braised celery on serving plates and the tuna on top. Scatter the remaining celery leaves over to serve.

SERVES 4   WINE: Vermentino di Sardegna

CATALAN-STYLE LOBSTER
ARAGOSTA ALLA CATALANA

INGREDIENTS

2 × 600–700 g (1 lb 5 oz–1 lb 6 oz) rock lobsters

1 large white onion, halved and very thinly sliced

¼ cup (60 ml/2 fl oz) red wine vinegar

600 g (1 lb 5 oz) ripe, sweet tomatoes, halved, seeded and cut into fillets

juice of 1 lemon

⅓ cup (80 ml/2½ fl oz) extra virgin olive oil

METHOD

Bring a large saucepan of salted water to a rolling boil. Plunge in the lobsters and when the water comes back to the boil, turn the heat down and simmer for 10 minutes. Meanwhile, put the onion and vinegar in a small bowl, cover with water and set aside for 20 minutes. Transfer the lobsters to a bowl and cool using plenty of ice on top. Remove the meat from the lobster tails and as much meat as possible from the claws. Cut the tail meat in half lengthways so you have 4 pieces, then put all the lobster meat in a large bowl. Drain the onion, pat dry with a clean tea towel (dish towel) and add to the lobster. Add the tomatoes, then dress with the lemon juice and olive oil, season and toss.

SERVES 4   WINE: Vermentino di Gallura

425

BRAISED OCTOPVS WITH CHICKPEAS

BRAISED OCTOPUS WITH CHICKPEAS
POLPO E CECI

This dish uses a large octopus that needs to be first cooked in water and then braised. If you can't find a large octopus, a smaller variety will do, but in that case the pre-cooking is not necessary and care must be taken not to overcook the octopus during the braising.

INGREDIENTS

1 × 1 kg (2 lb 4 oz) octopus, cleaned

1 brown onion, quartered

1 carrot, chopped into chunks

1 celery stick, cut into 5–6 pieces

⅓ cup (80 ml/2½ fl oz) extra virgin olive oil

4 French shallots, diced

2 garlic cloves

1 teaspoon fennel seeds

pinch of smoked paprika

300 ml (10½ fl oz) tomato passata

2 cups (400 g/14 oz) cooked chickpeas

½ cup chopped parsley

grated zest of 1 lemon

METHOD

Put the octopus in a large saucepan with the onion, carrot and celery and cover with cold water. Bring to the boil, then turn the heat down and simmer for 40–50 minutes until tender (test by cutting a little from the thick end of a tentacle and tasting). Let the octopus cool in its cooking water and store in the refrigerator if not proceeding immediately with the rest of the recipe (this step can be done a day or two in advance). Heat the olive oil in a large frying pan and lightly fry the shallots, garlic, fennel seeds and paprika for 2–3 minutes, stirring continually. Add the passata, chickpeas and a couple of good pinches of salt. Stir and simmer for a minute, then add the octopus either whole or chopped into bite-sized pieces. Simmer for 15 minutes. Add the parsley, a few good turns of pepper and more salt if needed, stir and simmer for a few more minutes. Stir in the lemon zest and serve.

SERVES 6   WINE: Vermentino di Sardegna

FREGOLA WITH SEAFOOD AND SAFFRON
FREGOLA SARDA AI FRUTTI DI MARE

INGREDIENTS

200 g (7 oz) fregola sarda
  (Sardinian couscous)

1 garlic clove, minced

⅓ cup (80 ml/2½ fl oz) extra
  virgin olive oil

500 g (1 lb 2 oz) clams
  (vongole)

500 g (1 lb 2 oz) mussels,
  scrubbed and de-bearded

pinch of saffron threads

100 ml (3½ fl oz) tomato
  passata

½ cup chopped parsley

150 g (5½ oz) cuttlefish,
  cleaned and cut into 3 cm
  (1¼ in) squares

150 g (5½ oz) calamari,
  cleaned and cut into 1 cm
  (½ in) wide strips

8 raw prawns (shrimp), peeled
  and deveined, tails left on

METHOD

Bring a saucepan of lightly salted water to the boil and cook the fregola until al dente, as you would pasta. Drain, reserving the cooking liquid, and keep warm. Lightly fry the garlic in the olive oil in a large frying pan until golden but not dark or burnt. Add the clams and mussels and a ladleful of the fregola cooking water. Stir in the saffron, turn up the heat, cover and cook until the shellfish have opened. Transfer the clams and mussels to a bowl and strain the cooking liquid through a double layer of muslin (cheesecloth) or a clean tea towel (dish towel) to remove any grit. Remove and discard the top shells of the clams and mussels. Put the strained liquid in a clean saucepan and add the fregola, passata, half the parsley and another ladleful of the fregola cooking water. Add a good pinch of salt and mix, then add the cuttlefish, calamari and prawns and simmer for 5 minutes. Add the clams and mussels and cook for 1 minute, then season and serve with the remaining parsley.

SERVES 4   WINE: Vermentino

GRILLED LAMB SHOULDER WITH ANCHOVY, OLIVE AND HERB SALSA
AGNELLO ALLA BRACE

INGREDIENTS

160 ml (5¼ fl oz) extra virgin
  olive oil

½ cup mixed herbs (parsley,
  thyme, rosemary), chopped

4 garlic cloves, minced

1 large lamb shoulder, boned
  and butterflied into an even
  piece about 2 cm (¾ in) thick
  (ask your butcher to do this)

6 anchovy fillets, chopped

1 tablespoon large salted
  capers, rinsed and chopped

½ cup chopped green olives

2 tablespoons red wine vinegar

METHOD

Combine the olive oil, herbs and garlic and season with a little salt and several turns of pepper. Rub half this mixture into the lamb and cook on a very hot barbecue grill (or in a hot frying pan) for 2 minutes on each side. Remove from the heat and let rest. Meanwhile, combine the anchovies, capers, olives and vinegar with the remaining herb mixture. Slice the lamb and put on a serving plate. Spoon on the salsa, season (if necessary) and serve.

SERVES 6   WINE: Cannonau di Sardegna

CIPOLLATA
CIPOLLATA

Cipollata usually refers to a traditional onion soup from Siena, but in this case it's a vegetable braise featuring onions. This simple dish comes from the province of Sassari and the best versions use the onions grown around the town of Banari.

INGREDIENTS

100 ml (3½ fl oz) extra virgin olive oil

8 brown onions, each cut into 8 chunks

4 potatoes, each cut into 8 chunks

3 carrots, cut into similar-sized chunks

1 celery heart, cut into chunks

4 ripe tomatoes, chopped

1 cup basil leaves

3 cups (750 ml/26 fl oz) vegetable broth or water

4 eggs

100 g (3½ oz) grated pecorino cheese

METHOD

Heat the olive oil in a large frying pan and brown the onions, potatoes, carrots and celery. Cook, stirring, for 4–5 minutes, then add the tomatoes and basil and bring to a simmer. Cook gently for 10 minutes, stirring occasionally. Add 2–3 good pinches of salt and the vegetable broth and simmer for another 15 minutes until the vegetables are tender. Break the eggs onto the vegetables and simmer until the eggs are cooked. Scatter the pecorino over to serve. Traditionally this dish is accompanied by couscous.

SERVES 4 WINE: Carignano del Sulcis Rosato

SARDEGNA DOLCI

SARDINIAN ORANGE RIND, HONEY AND ALMOND BALLS
ARANZATA

Honey is the principal sweetener used in many Sardinian sweets and the island produces many unusual varieties, none more so than corbezzolo (from the Arbutus unedo plant). This honey is almost savoury rather than sweet, and once tasted is never forgotten. It is rather rare, so if you can't find it use a good light-coloured raw honey. To help you judge how many oranges you will need to obtain the amount of rind required for this recipe, an orange weighing 250 g (9 oz) will typically yield 25 g (1 oz) orange rind (minus pith).

INGREDIENTS

250 g (9 oz) orange rind, without any white pith
250 g (9 oz) light-coloured raw honey (such as orange-flower or acacia)
2 cups (250 g/9 oz) slivered almonds, lightly toasted

METHOD

Line trays with baking paper or have ready a silicone sheet. Slice the orange rind very finely and put in a saucepan. Pour in water to just cover, then bring to the boil. Remove from the heat, drain and run the rind under cold water to refresh. Repeat this whole process twice, adding the honey with the water the final time. Bring to a simmer and cook until the water reduces to a thick syrup. Using a wooden spoon, mix in the almonds. Keep simmering until there is very little liquid left. Transfer the peel to the trays or sheet and put in the refrigerator to dry for an hour or so. Form small balls of the mixture and put in small paper containers (like those used for chocolates). Serve with espresso.

MAKES 25–30   WINE: Grappa di Vernaccia

GRAPE MUST CONDIMENT
SABA OR VINCOTTO

From Piemonte to Emilia-Romagna to Sardegna, fresh grape must (juice) is made into saba or vincotto. Like many other widely distributed Italian preparations, there are regional differences. For example, in Piemonte autumn fruits such as quince, fig, pear and apple are added and simmered down to add body and flavour. This preparation is simple and delicious and, once mastered, can be used as a base for your own additional flavours.

INGREDIENTS

10 litres (2 gallons) freshly pressed white or red grape must or grape juice

METHOD

Put the must in a stainless steel saucepan and slowly bring to a low simmer. Cook slowly until reduced to 1 litre (35 fl oz), regularly skimming off any impurities that come to the surface – this will take the better part of a day. Transfer to a bowl and rest overnight. The next day, filter through a clean tea towel (dish towel) and funnel intro a sterilised bottle. The must will keep indefinitely in the refrigerator. Use on gelato, in cakes, or in sweet and savoury sauces for game and pork.

MAKES 1 litre (35 fl oz)

ORISTANO AMARETTI
AMARETTI DI ORISTANO

INGREDIENTS

350 g (12 oz) blanched
    almonds
100 g (3½ oz) apricot kernels
1 tablespoon plain
    (all-purpose) flour
3 egg whites
500 g (1 lb 2 oz) caster
    (superfine) sugar

METHOD

Preheat the oven to 90°C (195°F). Put the almonds and apricot kernels
on a tray and dry in the oven for 10–15 minutes – don't let them colour.
Remove from the oven and let cool completely. Increase the oven
temperature to 140°C (285°F). Line a baking tray with baking paper and
sprinkle with the flour. Put the almonds and apricot kernels in a large
mortar and pound to a fine meal (this can be done in a food processor
if you prefer). In a large bowl, whisk the egg whites to soft peaks
and then whisk in the sugar until glossy and stiff. Carefully fold in the
almond and apricot meal. Take a spoonful of the mixture and form into
a large almond shape using another spoon. Put on the baking tray and
repeat until all the mixture has been used. Bake for 20–25 minutes until
golden. Cool completely before serving.

MAKES 40–50   WINE: Malvasia Dolce

RICOTTA TORTA
TORTA DI RICOTTA

INGREDIENTS

unsalted butter
1 kg (2 lb 4 oz) ricotta cheese
5 eggs
300 g (10½ oz) sugar
1 vanilla bean, split and
    seeds scraped
4 tablespoons candied orange
    peel (see page 406)
4 tablespoons candied lemon
    peel (see page 406)

METHOD

Preheat the oven to 200°C (400°F) and grease a 24 cm (9½ in)
springform cake tin with butter. Pass the ricotta through a fine sieve into
a bowl and set aside. Break the eggs into the bowl of an electric mixer,
add the sugar, vanilla seeds and a pinch of salt. Whisk at high speed
until light and fluffy. Turn the mixer to its lowest setting, add the ricotta
a spoonful at a time and mix for 3 minutes. Pour the mixture into the
cake tin and put the tin on a tray. Put in the oven, then reduce the oven
temperature to 180°C (350°F) and bake for 30 minutes. Turn off the oven
and leave the cake in it for 1 hour. Remove from the oven and turn out
of the tin. Serve immediately (or cooled to room temperature) with the
candied peel.

SERVES 8   WINE: Moscato di Cagliari

GRAPE MUST AND NUT CAKE
PANE E SAPA

This unusual and delicious cake is made using saba (also called vincotto), which is available from good providores – but if you would like to make your own there is a recipe on page 431. Clove oil can be obtained from health food shops or specialty food stores.

INGREDIENTS

1⅔ cups (250 g/9 oz) plain (all-purpose) flour

1⅔ cups (250 g/9 oz) durum wheat flour

40 g (1½ oz) fresh yeast

1 cup (250 ml/9 fl oz) saba or vincotto

1 teaspoon ground cinnamon

2 drops clove oil

1 tablespoon anise seeds

grated zest of 2 oranges

20 g (¾ oz) unsalted butter

50 g (1¾ oz) walnut pieces, roughly chopped

60 g (2¼ oz) pine nuts

⅓ cup (50 g/1¾ oz) hazelnuts, skinned and roughly chopped

80 g (2¾ oz) sultanas (golden raisins)

METHOD

Sift the flours onto your work surface and make a well in the middle. Dissolve the yeast in 4–5 tablespoons of warm water, then add to the well along with 200 ml (7 fl oz) of the saba. Mix until the dough comes together. Add the cinnamon, clove oil, anise seeds and orange zest and knead well for 10 minutes. Put in a bowl, cover with a clean tea towel (dish towel) and leave in a warm place to rise for 24 hours. When you are ready to cook, use the butter to grease a baking tray. Work the nuts and sultanas into the dough and divide it into 2 pieces. Shape each piece into a high, fat doughnut shape with a small hole in the middle and put on the baking tray to rise for another hour. Preheat the oven to 180°C (350°F). Bake the rings for 30 minutes (or until a skewer comes out clean), then remove from the oven and let cool. Brush with the remaining saba until it has all been absorbed. Serve by itself or with vanilla gelato or cream.

SERVES 8–10   WINE: Cannonau Dolce

SICILIA

SICILIA

SICILY

SICILIA WAS KNOWN TO THE ANCIENTS AS THE BIRTHPLACE OF GASTRONOMY. AT 25,000 SQUARE KILOMETRES (9650 SQUARE MILES), IT IS THE LARGEST ISLAND IN THE MEDITERRANEAN AND HOSTS THE LARGEST ACTIVE VOLCANO IN EUROPE, MOUNT ETNA, AT 3300 METRES (10,827 FEET). AS THE REGIONE AUTONOMA SICILIANA (SICILIAN AUTONOMOUS REGION), IT ALSO INCLUDES THE SURROUNDING ISLANDS: THE AEOLIANS, LAMPEDUSA AND OTHERS.

Thanks to Sicilia's rich history – it was ruled by just about every major power in the region, from the Greeks to the Ostrogoths, to the Arabs, the Spanish and the Normans – nowhere in Italy is food more varied, revered and woven into daily life.

The Greeks first named the island Trinacria, for its triangular shape, and finally Sicilia after one of its three original inhabitant races, the Siculi (the other two were the Sicani and the Elymians). The 4th century BCE Greek gastronome Archestratus was Sicilian, from the town of Gela.

The most important of the gastronomic influences on Sicilian cuisine was the Arabs, who arrived in 965 and ruled until 1072, moving the capital from the Greek Syracuse to Palermo, which became the emir's port.

One sign of Arabic influence in Sicilia is that it is the only region of Italy where any discussion of cuisine starts with desserts, or dolci. It is the home of cannoli, cassata and marzipan, and the capital of gelato: if ice cream wasn't invented in Sicilia, as gelato it was perfected there.

The island's interior is sun-baked and sparsely inhabited, while the coast is vibrant and colourful and contains most of the inhabitants and cities. The volcanic soil laid down by Etna makes for extremely fertile land, and agriculture has always been an important part of the island economy, producing excellent-quality durum wheat, lemons and other citrus, and almonds.

The other way in which Sicilia's cuisine differs from the rest of Italy is that it is fundamentally aristocratic: the great families of the interior owned large tracts of land and lorded it over the rest of the island for many years. Because of inheritance laws, only the first-born son could inherit. Second sons went into monasteries, especially Benedictine monasteries, but did not completely renounce earthly pleasures. In the monasteries they developed elaborate dishes and desserts – for example, the macaroni timbale described in the book *The Leopard* by Guiseppe Tomasi di Lampedusa was developed by Benedictine monks. As Kostioukovich writes in *Why Italians Love to Talk About Food*, the head cooks in the monasteries 'viewed culinary experimentation as a path to holiness'.

At the other end of the culinary spectrum, the ancient Arab capital, Palermo, is the Italian capital of street food. Examples are too numerous to list, but worth a mention are frittole, meatballs of seasoned pork rind; ciciri, fritters of chickpea flour; and the sfincione, a spongy, spicy pizza-like concoction covered with anchovies, olives and black onions whose name at least may go back to Greek times. In the afternoon you'll find stigghiole, intestines speared on a stick and grilled, and again for the adventurous, panino con la milza, or spleen sandwich. In the market at Catania you can try fritters of fresh ricotta called sfinci, and veal innards, or caldume.

An island surrounded by three seas – the Ionian, Mediterranean and Tyrrhenian – Sicilia has traditionally supplied an abundance of seafood. Fish including tuna, grouper, swordfish, white bream, a local mackerel and snapper all appear on plates around the island. In Palermo, tuna is marinated in wine, olive oil, vinegar and rosemary and quickly grilled. The belly (ventresca) is much prized, but so too are the testicles (lattume), eyes (occhi rassi) and, of course, roe (bottarga). Tuna is called the sea pig because, like the pig, every part is utilised – even the head, which is ground and used as fertiliser.

From the Aeolian Islands come the best capers in Italy; the best of all are from the island of Pantelleria. Pistachios are also grown here. The island of Lipari is famed for sea urchin, squid and turtle.

As there is little grazing land, there are not many Sicilian meat dishes – but there is at least one pork sausage that deserves to be mentioned: the salsiccia al finocchio, which is flavoured with fennel. In Palermo, they roast pork stuffed with a medieval mixture of pine nuts, raisins and almond paste for a dish known as braciola, and enjoy roast veal with mushroom sauce, or cuscinetta alla siciliana.

Pasta dishes include Palermo's pasta con sarde (pasta with sardines), maccherone alla paolina (macaroni with cabbage, pine nuts and raisin) and maccherone a treddita (with an eggplant and cheese sauce), and Catania's lasagne (lasagne alla catanese), which has a filling of eggplant, yellow peppers, anchovies, olives, capers, tomato pulp, garlic and chopped parsley – a medley of the Mediterranean's favourite hits.

As would be expected from an island not far from north Africa, couscous is found – in Trapani, where it is known as cuscussu and traditionally a fish stew is poured over it.

And finally – there just isn't room enough to list all of the specialities of Sicilia! – there is caponatina, a Sicilian take on a dish found all around the Mediterranean, from the Provençal ratatouille to the Italian peperonata, the Tunisian mechouia and the Mallorquin tombet. In that it fries its ingredients (eggplant, peppers, onions and celery) separately and then combines them, caponatina most resembles tombet.

The story of Sicilian wine is another case of 'What happened?' An island with arguably the most vibrant, vital and varied cuisine in Italy ended up in the 20th century with, to quote Bastianich and Lynchfrom their book on the regional wines of Italy, *Vino Italiano*, 'flabby dry whites' and 'coarse, sun-baked reds'. According to

THE CHOCOLATE OF MODICA

In 1693 an earthquake devastated the town of Modica, not far inland from Sicilia's southern coast. What arose from the devastation was the charming Baroque city that still thrives today. The tradition of making bitter chocolate survived the quake, as did using it in the cuisine of the town – a practice dating back to the arrival of chocolate with the Spanish.

And what chocolate it is and was. According to a 20th-century Sicilian writer, and forgiving perhaps a modicum of chauvinism, 'Modican chocolate is unparalleled in savour, such that tasting it is like reaching the archetype, the absolute'.

This incomparable confection is made today, as it has been since 1880, at the Antica Dolceria Bonajuto, an enterprise owned and run by the Ruta family.

Diego Planeta, the head of a large co-op who was interviewed for *Vino Italiano*: 'Whatever vine produced the most tonnage, that's what the farmers planted.'

It wasn't always the case. A Sicilian white wine by the name of mamertino (still made as mamertino di Milazzo in north-east Sicilia) was a favourite of Julius Caesar, as was tauromenitanium, from Taormina. Wine was being imported, drunk and maybe even made in Sicilia even before the Greeks arrived in 750 BCE – indeed, the first known use of the word vino, spelt viino, was found inscribed on a 5th century BCE terracotta vase at Centorbi.

Today things are improving, and many observers believe that the emphasis is less on quantity (until recently the island produced almost twice as much wine by volume as Australia, but less than 10 per cent of it went into bottles) and more on quality.

The best-known and most planted red wine grape is nero d'Avola, which is used to impart dark colour as a blending grape, most often with nerello mascalese, frappato or, often outside its own DOC, syrah, merlot and cabernet to produce wines with weight and elegance. Second to nero d'Avola among the major red wine grapes are nerello mascalese and nerello cappuccia, and then frappato di Vittoria and perricone.

The oldest white wine grape, which probably originated in Sicilia, is catarratto bianco, which over time has developed relatives such as catarratto bianco comune and catarratto bianco lucido; they are all extremely productive. Most recently catarratto bianco has been used for the making of Marsala and as a base for vermouth, and since receiving its own DOC in 1999 a small amount has been bottled as a single varietal. Less planted but more interesting are inzolia and ansonica, with inzolia playing the lead role in a number of blends, including with chardonnay.

We can't leave Sicilia without mentioning Marsala, which is made by a complex process – including barrel ageing for the best examples – from a number of grapes, including catarratto bianco, inzolia, pignatello, grillo, nero d'Avola and nerello mascalese. Marsala is traditionally a strong wine laced with a cooked must and appears to have been produced in western Sicilia since at least Roman times. Today, especially with egg added (Marsala all'uovo), it is more of a cooking wine than a drinking wine. However, good-quality Marsala is still made and is labelled Marsala superiore and Marsala vergine, for which the grillo grape is used.

And finally there is malvasia, another wine that has been made on the Aeolian Islands, especially Salina, since ancient times. It comes as a sweet wine and a sweeter wine – the latter is classed as a passito.

SICILIA
ANTI-PASTI

TUNA CRUDO
CRUDO DI TONNO

INGREDIENTS

400 g (14 oz) sashimi-grade
tuna, finely sliced

2 ripe tomatoes, peeled,
seeded and diced

2 tablespoons finely chopped
parsley

1 tablespoon large, salted
capers, well soaked, rinsed
and chopped

grated zest of 1 lemon

juice of 1 lemon, strained

⅓ cup (80 ml/2½ fl oz) extra
virgin olive oil

METHOD

Put the tuna on serving plates, then cover and refrigerate until needed.
Combine the tomato, parsley, capers, lemon juice, lemon zest and olive
oil. Spoon the dressing onto the tuna, season lightly and serve.

SERVES 4   WINE: Dry Zibibbo

GRILLED ABALONE WITH CAPONATA
ORECCHIA MARINA ALLA GRIGLIA CON
LA CAPONATA

INGREDIENTS

1 large abalone
(preferably live)

extra virgin olive oil

1 small garlic clove, minced

300 g (10½ oz) eggplants
(aubergines), cut into 2 cm
(¾ in) cubes

30 g (1 oz) brown onion, cut
into 2 cm (¾ in) cubes

80 g (2¾ oz) celery heart, cut
into 2 cm (¾ in) cubes

1 tablespoon sugar

2 tablespoons red wine
vinegar

50 g (1¾ oz) green or black
olives, pitted and chopped

50 g (1¾ oz) diced tomato

1 tablespoon pine nuts

1 tablespoon salted capers,
rinsed

2 tablespoons chopped
parsley

METHOD

To prepare the abalone, cut the muscle away from the shell by running
a small, sharp knife around the edge of the 'lip'. You will feel with the
blade of the knife where the muscle is attached. Remove any digestive
tract and slice the abalone very thinly. Put in a bowl with 2 tablespoons
olive oil and the garlic and set aside. Pan-fry the eggplant in a little
olive oil until golden. Drain on paper towels. Pan-fry the onion in a
little olive oil but do not let it colour. Remove from the heat. Blanch the
celery for 2 minutes in boiling salted water, then drain. Heat the sugar
in a small saucepan until lightly caramelised, then add the vinegar
and stir to make a syrup. Just before serving, combine the syrup with
the eggplants, onion, celery, olives, tomato, pine nuts and capers. Add
a little oil, season, add the parsley and mix again. Cook the abalone
quickly in a hot frying pan with 1 tablespoon oil and serve on top of or
mixed through the caponata, including the pan juices.

SERVES 8   WINE: Etna bianco

PRAWN AND SARDINE CAKES WITH SALSA AGRODOLCE
POLPETTE DI SARDE E GAMBERI CON SALSA AGRODOLCE

This salsa agrodolce is excellent with artichokes and other bitter vegetables and lettuces, and with strong-flavoured fish such as mackerel and sardines.

INGREDIENTS

1 brown onion, thinly sliced

200 g (7 oz) very fresh sardine fillets

200 g (7 oz) raw prawn (shrimp) meat

60 g (2¼ oz) day-old bread, crusts removed

½ cup (125 ml/4 fl oz) clear fish broth

2 eggs, whisked

2 tablespoons finely chopped parsley

plain (all-purpose) flour

breadcrumbs

extra virgin olive oil

2 cups lamb's lettuce (corn salad)

SALSA AGRODOLCE

200 ml (7 fl oz) extra virgin olive oil

2 brown onions, diced

3 garlic cloves, minced

4 tablespoons capers, rinsed

4 red chillies, finely chopped

90 g (3¼ oz) pancetta fat or lardo, finely chopped

10 anchovy fillets

100 ml (3½ fl oz) dry white wine

100 ml (3½ fl oz) white wine vinegar

½ cup finely chopped parsley

METHOD

To make the salsa agrodolce, heat the olive oil in a large frying pan and lightly fry the onion and garlic until translucent. Add all the remaining ingredients except the parsley, then simmer for 10 minutes until thick and reduced. Let cool, then add the parsley and season. Makes 600 ml (21 fl oz).

Finely chop the onion, sardines and prawn meat together. Moisten the bread in the fish broth and add to the fish mixture with the eggs and parsley. Season, then shape the mixture into 6 cm (2½ in) diameter patties. Coat lightly with flour and then breadcrumbs. Fry in olive oil until golden brown, drain on paper towels and serve with the lamb's lettuce and salsa agrodolce.

SERVES 8   WINE: Marsala Superiore Riserva

WOOD-GRILLED VEGETABLES WITH SALSA SALMORIGLIO
VERDURA ALLA GRIGLIA CON SALSA SALMORIGLIO

For this recipe the best flavour is obtained from a wood-burning or charcoal barbecue, but gas or electric will still produce great results. These vegetables are a good accompaniment to roast meat or fish.

INGREDIENTS

4 spring onions (scallions), halved

1 red capsicum (pepper), seeded and cut in 8

1 yellow capsicum (pepper), seeded and cut in 8

1 fennel bulb, trimmed, quartered and blanched

8 fat asparagus spears, trimmed

1 eggplant (aubergine), cut into 1 cm (½ in) rounds

2 zucchini (courgettes), cut into 5 mm (¼ in) rounds

1 head of radicchio, trimmed and cut lengthways into 8

¼ cup (60 ml/2 fl oz) extra virgin olive oil

SALSA SALMORIGLIO

juice of 2 lemons

zest of 1 lemon

1 cup (250 ml/9 fl oz) extra virgin olive oil

1 garlic clove, minced

1 cup fresh oregano leaves, chopped

½ cup sage leaves, chopped

1 tablespoon finely chopped rosemary

3 anchovy fillets, chopped

METHOD

To make the salsa salmorigilio, whisk all ingredients together in a bowl and season. Let sit for at least 1 hour before using. Makes 2 cups (500 ml/17 fl oz). Lightly brush all the vegetables with olive oil and season lightly with salt. Grill on a wood-fired barbecue until tender but retaining a little texture. Put on platters and dress with the salmoriglio to serve.

SERVES 6–8   WINE: Grillo

WOOD-GRILLED VEGETABLES WITH SALSA SALMORIGLIO

GREEN BEANS WITH ANCHOVIES
FAGIOLINI E ACCIUGHE

INGREDIENTS

600 g (1 lb 5 oz) green beans, trimmed

100 ml (3½ fl oz) extra virgin olive oil

2 garlic cloves, finely sliced

10 anchovy fillets

½ cup chopped parsley

1 teaspoon dried oregano

METHOD

Bring a saucepan of water to the boil and add the beans. Once the water has returned to the boil, cook for 3 minutes. Drain well. Heat the olive oil in a wide frying pan, add the garlic and fry lightly for a minute. Add the anchovies and stir until they dissolve. Turn up the heat and add the beans. Cook on high heat for 2–3 minutes, stirring, then add the parsley and oregano, season and serve hot or at room temperature.

SERVES 6–8   WINE: Regaleali Bianco

CAULIFLOWER POLPETTINE
POLPETTINE AL CAVOLFIORE

INGREDIENTS

1 cauliflower (about 700 g/ 1 lb 6 oz), leaves trimmed

2 garlic cloves

leaves from 1 mint sprig

¼ cup parsley

¼ cup breadcrumbs

2 eggs, whisked

40 g (1½ oz) grated pecorino cheese

40 g (1½ oz) grated parmesan cheese

½ cup (125 ml/4 fl oz) extra virgin olive oil

METHOD

Put the cauliflower in a saucepan with 2 cups (500 ml/17 fl oz) water on medium heat and bring to the boil. Cover, turn the heat down very low and steam for about 20 minutes until tender, adding more water if needed. Transfer the cauliflower to a large bowl and, while still hot, mash using a fork. Finely chop the garlic, mint and parsley together and add to the bowl. Stir in the breadcrumbs, eggs and cheeses, season well and mix well. Form the mixture into patties about 5 cm (2 in) in diameter and 1 cm (½ in) thick. Heat the olive oil in a frying pan and fry the polpettine on both sides until golden. Drain on paper towels and serve hot or at room temperature.

SERVES 4–6   WINE: Nerello Rosè

FRIED ARTICHOKES
CARCIOFI FRITTI

INGREDIENTS

1 lemon, halved

6 artichokes

1 egg, whisked

150 g (5½ oz) fine
breadcrumbs

200 ml (7 fl oz) extra virgin
olive oil

lemon wedges (optional)

METHOD

Pour cold water into a saucepan to fill by three-quarters, then squeeze in the lemon. Using a sharp knife, cut the top third off each artichoke and peel off and discard any tougher, darker leaves. Cut off the stalk, leaving about 5 cm (2 in) attached. Put the trimmed artichokes in the saucepan of water and put a plate on top to keep them submerged. Bring to the boil, then turn the heat down and simmer for 10–15 minutes or until the hearts are tender when pierced with a sharp knife. Drain and cool. Trim off and discard any tough leaves and the outer layer of the stem. Cut off the stems and then cut each stem into 2 pieces. Cut the artichoke hearts into quarters. Dip each artichoke piece in egg, letting any excess fall back into the bowl, then roll in breadcrumbs. Heat the olive oil in a frying pan until a piece of artichoke sizzles when dropped in. Fry the artichokes in batches until the edges start to colour and drain on paper towels. Season with salt and serve as they are or with lemon wedges.

SERVES 6   WINE: Grecanico

POTATO, MINT AND SORREL CROQUETTES
CAZZILLI

INGREDIENTS

1 kg (2 lb 4 oz) roasting
potatoes (such as sebago),
unpeeled

2 tablespoons finely chopped
parsley

½ cup chopped sorrel

2 egg whites, whisked

½ cup fine breadcrumbs

extra virgin olive oil

salt flakes

METHOD

Put the potatoes in a large saucepan and pour in water to come about one-third up their sides. Cover and cook until soft, then drain and let cool. Peel the potatoes and mash using a ricer. Mix with the parsley and sorrel and season well. Shape the mixture into croquettes 5–6 cm (2–2½ in) in diameter and 2 cm (¾ in) thick. Dredge in the egg whites and coat in the breadcrumbs, then shallow fry in 2 cm (¾ in) olive oil and drain on paper towels. Sprinkle with salt flakes and serve.

SERVES 8–10   WINE: Insolia

BROAD-BEAN CAPONATA
CAPONATA DI FAVE

This Sicilian salad usually accompanies fish or shellfish dishes, but it also makes a wonderful first course.

INGREDIENTS

300 g (10½ oz) eggplants
(aubergines), diced

extra virgin olive oil

30 g (1 oz) brown onion, diced

80 g (2¾ oz) celery heart,
diced

1 tablespoon caster (superfine)
sugar

⅓ cup (80 ml/2½ fl oz) red
wine vinegar

1 cup (185 g/6½ oz)
double-peeled broad beans,
blanched

50 g (1¾ oz) olives, pitted
and chopped

50 g (1¾ oz) diced tomato

1 tablespoon salted capers,
rinsed

1 tablespoon pine nuts

2 tablespoons chopped
parsley

METHOD

Pan-fry the eggplant in 1 tablespoon olive oil until golden. Drain on paper towels. Pan-fry the onion in 1 teaspoon oil but do not let it colour. Remove from the heat. Blanch the celery for 2 minutes in boiling salted water, then drain. Heat the sugar in a small saucepan until lightly caramelised, then add the vinegar and stir to make a syrup. Just before serving, combine the syrup with the eggplants, onion, celery, broad beans, olives, tomato, capers and pine nuts. Add 2 tablespoons oil, season, add the parsley and mix again. Serve as a first course with salad or as an accompaniment to grilled octopus, prawns (shrimp) or fish.

SERVES 6   WINE: Primitivo or Zinfandel

SICILIA

PRIMI

BORLOTTI BEAN AND MUSHROOM SOUP
ZUPPA DI FUNGHI E BORLOTTI

This recipe calls for fresh borlotti beans, but if they are not available dried borlotti beans can be used. Soak them in cold water overnight and cook as per the instructions on page 40.

INGREDIENTS

½ cup (125 ml/4 fl oz) extra virgin olive oil

1 small leek, white part only, cut into 1 cm (½ in) rounds

2 garlic cloves, minced

1 celery heart, chopped

600 g (1 lb 5 oz) mixed mushrooms (Swiss browns, buttons, shiitake or whatever is available), trimmed and cut into bite-sized pieces

1 cup (200 g/7 oz) shelled fresh borlotti beans

2 ripe tomatoes, chopped

grated pecorino cheese

METHOD

Heat ⅓ cup (80 ml/2½ fl oz) of the olive oil in a large saucepan and gently fry the leek, garlic and celery for about 2 minutes until soft. Turn up the heat and add the mushrooms. Cook, stirring, for 2–3 minutes until soft, then add the beans, tomatoes and 2 litres (70 fl oz) water. Bring to the boil, then turn the heat down and simmer for about 2 hours until the beans are very tender and beginning to break up. Remove from the heat, season and drizzle with the remaining oil. Serve sprinkled with pecorino and offer plenty of bread. The soup is even better the day after you make it.

SERVES 10   WINE: Frappato

WILD MUSHROOMS GROW IN SICILY BUT ARE LIMITED TO THE MOUNTAIN ELEVATIONS SUCH AS ETNA, NEBRODI, IBLEI, PELORITANI, MADONIE AND SICANI. THERE IS STILL A WIDE VARIETY TO BE FOUND SUCH AS PORCINI (LOCALLY KNOWN AS SIDDI), MORELS (LUGNI DI VECCHIA), CHANTERELLES (CRICCHI DI JADDU) AND THE EXCELLENT CAESAR'S MUSHROOM (FUNCIU D'OVU). IF YOU ARE AROUND THE MOUNTAIN AREAS OF SICILY IN MID AUTUMN YOU WILL NO DOUBT FIND A MUSHROOM FESTIVAL OR SAGRA.

BORLOTTI BEAN AND MUSHROOM SOUP

LINGUINE WITH LEMON, PARSLEY AND MINT
LINGUINE AL LIMONE

INGREDIENTS

juice and grated zest of
   1 lemon
150 ml (5 fl oz) best-quality
   extra virgin olive oil
500 g (1 lb 2 oz) dried linguine
¾ cup (80 g/2¾ oz) grated
   parmesan cheese
½ cup chopped parsley
¼ cup chopped mint

METHOD

Combine the lemon juice and zest with half the olive oil and leave for
1 hour. Bring a large saucepan of salted water to the boil and cook the
linguine until al dente. When it is nearly ready, heat a serving bowl for
the pasta and add the lemon-flavoured oil, parmesan, parsley, mint,
remaining oil and 5–6 spoonfuls of the pasta cooking water and whisk
it all together. Drain the pasta and transfer to the bowl. Toss with the
sauce, add freshly cracked pepper and a little salt if necessary, and
serve immediately.

SERVES 4   WINE: Carricante

PENNE WITH BROAD BEANS, ARTICHOKES AND RICOTTA
PENNE CON FAVE, CARCIOFI E RICOTTA

*This is an accompaniment to short pasta such as shells, tubes or elbows, which are popular
around Palermo.*

INGREDIENTS

¼ cup (60 ml/2 fl oz) extra
   virgin olive oil
2 garlic cloves, minced
1 teaspoon fennel seeds
200 g (7 oz) button mushrooms,
   thinly sliced
¼ cup (60 ml/2 fl oz) dry white
   wine
4 cooked artichoke hearts
   (see page 39), cut into
   bite-sized pieces
500 g (1 lb 2 oz) broad beans,
   double-peeled and blanched
150 g (5½ oz) ricotta cheese
3 tablespoons chopped parsley
½ teaspoon ground chilli
500 g (1 lb 2 oz) dried penne or
   other short pasta
grated pecorino cheese

METHOD

Heat the olive oil in a large frying pan and lightly fry the garlic and
fennel seeds for a minute. Turn up the heat, add the mushrooms and
fry, stirring, until soft. Add the wine and cook until it has evaporated. Stir
in the artichokes, broad beans, ricotta, parsley and chilli, adding a little
water if the ricotta is too dry and lumpy. Season and simmer while you
cook the pasta in salted boiling water. Drain the pasta, then toss with
the sauce and serve with plenty of grated pecorino.

SERVES 4   WINE: Insolia

SPAGHETTI WITH PORK RAGU
SPAGHETTI AL RAGÙ DI MAIALE

INGREDIENTS

½ cup (125 ml/4 fl oz) extra virgin olive oil

100 g (3½ oz) pancetta, finely chopped

1 brown onion, finely chopped

1 celery heart, finely chopped

1 carrot, finely chopped

750 g (1 lb 10 oz) pork neck, minced

1 tablespoon tomato paste (concentrated puree)

leaves from 1 rosemary sprig, chopped

2 kg (4 lb 8 oz) ripe tomatoes, peeled and pureed

1 cup chopped parsley

800 g (1 lb 12 oz) dried spaghetti

150 g (5½ oz) ricotta salata (salted ricotta), coarsely grated

METHOD

Heat the olive oil in a saucepan and add the pancetta, onion, celery and carrot. Stir on medium heat for a minute or so, then add the pork and stir for about 5 minutes until browned. Add the tomato paste and rosemary and stir well. Add the tomatoes, then simmer for about 70 minutes until the sauce is thick. Stir in the parsley and season. Cook the spaghetti in salted boiling water until al dente, then drain and toss with the ragù. Serve with the ricotta salata.

SERVES 8   WINE: Etna Rosato

TOMATO, MOZZARELLA AND ANCHOVY BAKE
POMODORI E MOZZARELLA AL FORNO

INGREDIENTS

¼ cup (60 ml/2 fl oz) extra virgin olive oil

1 garlic clove, minced

400 g (14 oz) ripe tomatoes, peeled, seeded and chopped

4 eggs, whisked

200 g (7 oz) fresh cow's milk mozzarella cheese, thinly sliced

3–4 anchovy fillets, chopped

2 tablespoons chopped tarragon

METHOD

Preheat the oven to 180°C (350°F) and grease a baking dish. Heat 2 tablespoons of the olive oil in a frying pan and lightly fry the garlic for 30 seconds, making sure it doesn't colour. Add the tomatoes and simmer for 10 minutes, stirring occasionally. Add the eggs, season and stir gently using a fork or wooden spatula, scraping the bottom. Cook on medium heat for a minute or two so the eggs begin to scramble. Transfer the tomato/egg mixture to the baking dish and cover the top with mozzarella. Scatter over the anchovies and tarragon and bake for 5–6 minutes until firm. Let cool to room temperature, then cut into wedges to serve.

SERVES 6–8   WINE: Menfi Chardonnay

PRAWN CUTLETS WITH BROCCOLI AND CAPERS

PRAWN CUTLETS WITH BROCCOLI AND CAPERS
GAMBERONI IMPANNATI CON BROCCOLI E CAPERI

INGREDIENTS

500 g (1 lb 2 oz) broccoli

160 ml (5¼ fl oz) extra virgin olive oil

1 brown onion, diced

1 garlic clove, minced

80 g (2¾ oz) plain (all-purpose) flour

2 eggs, well whisked

150 g (5½ oz) breadcrumbs

1 kg (2 lb 4 oz) large raw king prawns (shrimp), peeled (tails left on) and butterflied

6 tablespoons salted capers, rinsed and dried

METHOD

Cut the broccoli florets off the stems and separate into smaller florets. Cut off and discard the tougher parts of the broccoli stems, then cut the tender parts of the stems into bite-sized pieces. Heat ¼ cup (60 ml/2 fl oz) of the olive oil in a large frying pan and gently fry the onion, garlic and broccoli stems for 2 minutes. Add the broccoli florets and 3–4 tablespoons water and simmer for about 5 minutes until the broccoli is tender but retains some texture. Season, then remove from the heat and let cool. Put the flour, eggs and breadcrumbs on 3 separate plates. Dust each prawn in flour, then dip in egg and finally in breadcrumbs, pressing them in well. Heat the remaining oil in a frying pan until just starting to smoke. Fry the prawns a few at a time, making sure the pan is not crowded, and drain on paper towels. Carefully strain the hot oil into a bowl, discarding any crumbs, and wipe out the pan. Return the oil to the pan and fry the capers until crisp. Arrange the prawn cutlets on the broccoli and scatter the capers on top to serve.

SERVES 6   WINE: Menfi Chardonnay

EGG-SEALED STUFFED ARTICHOKES
CARCIOFI TAPPATI

INGREDIENTS

160 ml (5¼ fl oz) extra virgin olive oil

1 garlic clove, thinly sliced

1 small brown onion, finely chopped

350 ml (12 fl oz) tomato passata

1 tablespoon tomato paste (concentrated puree)

4 artichokes, tough outer leaves removed

½ lemon

½ cup chopped day-old bread (crusts removed)

50 g (1¾ oz) sultanas (golden raisins)

3 tablespoons grated parmesan cheese

2 eggs, whisked

METHOD

Heat 2 tablespoons of the olive oil in a frying pan and gently fry the garlic and onion for a minute or so until softened. Add the tomato passata and tomato paste and a couple of pinches of salt, stir and simmer for 5–6 minutes. Remove from the heat and set aside. Using a sharp knife, cut the top quarter off each artichoke to reveal the layers and heart. If there is no choke, leave the heart as is; if the choke is tough, use a tablespoon to dig it out, then discard it. Cut off and discard the stem and rub the exposed cut leaves all over with the lemon, squeezing some juice into the heart – this will stop the artichoke from discolouring. Mix the bread, sultanas and parmesan with enough oil so the mixture comes together and doesn't crumble. Season, then stuff each artichoke with this mixture and dip the top of the artichoke in the egg. Heat the remaining oil in a frying pan and fry the egg-dipped sides of the artichokes until they are sealed by cooked egg. Turn the artichokes over and pour in the tomato salsa to almost reach the top of the artichokes – don't cover them. Simmer gently for about 1 hour until the artichoke hearts are pierced easily by a sharp knife. Serve with the salsa.

SERVES 4   WINE: Etna Bianco

SICILIA

SECONDI

TUNA WITH POMEGRANATE
TONNO AL MELOGRANO

INGREDIENTS

2 tablespoons finely chopped
    parsley

2 tablespoons finely chopped
    sage

1 tablespoon finely chopped
    thyme

600 g (1 lb 5 oz) tuna fillets,
    skin removed, cut into 2 cm
    (¾ in) cubes

3 pomegranates

2 tablespoons red wine
    vinegar

½ cup (125 ml/4 fl oz) extra
    virgin olive oil

2 cups curly endive

METHOD

Combine the herbs and a few pinches of salt in a large bowl. Add
the tuna and toss so the fish is well coated. Refrigerate until you are
ready to cook. Juice 2 of the pomegranates and collect the seeds from
the third (see page 39). Mix the pomegranate juice with the vinegar
and ⅓ cup (80 ml/2½ fl oz) of the olive oil. Scatter the endive on a
platter or individual plates. Heat the remaining oil in a frying pan until
just smoking, then add the fish and fry for a few seconds on all sides.
Remove from the heat and season. Arrange the fish on the endive,
sprinkle with the dressing and scatter the pomegranate seeds over
to serve.

SERVES 4   WINE: Regaleali Bianco

GRILLED SWORDFISH ROLLS WITH
BREADCRUMB STUFFING
INVOLTINI DI PESCE SPADA

*The classic accompaniment for this dish is the Sicilian wine Passopisciaro, made from Nerello Mascalese
grapes – but a lighter-style pinot noir is also good.*

INGREDIENTS

40 g (1½ oz) breadcrumbs

25 g (1 oz) grated pecorino
    cheese

2 tablespoons finely chopped
    parsley

1 tablespoon finely chopped
    capers

1 garlic clove, minced

1 tablespoon extra virgin
    olive oil

800 g (1 lb 12 oz) swordfish,
    cut into 12 thin slices

1 cup salsa salmoriglio
    (see page 459)

METHOD

Put the breadcrumbs, cheese, parsley, capers, garlic and olive oil in a
bowl and mix thoroughly. Lay each swordfish slice on your work surface
and evenly sprinkle on 1 tablespoon of the stuffing within 2 cm (¾ in) of
the edge. Fold 2 cm (¾ in) of the left and right edges of the fish into the
centre and roll south to north, securing with a toothpick. Brush the rolls
with a quarter of the salsa salmoriglio and grill (broil) for 2 minutes on
each side. Serve with the remaining salsa and a green salad.

SERVES 4   WINE: Passopisciaro or a light Pinot Nero

DOLPHINFISH (MAHI MAHI) IN OLIVE AND CAPER SAUCE
LAMPUGA IN SUGHETTO DI CAPERI E OLIVE

INGREDIENTS

- 4 × 160 g (5½ oz) pieces dolphinfish (mahi mahi), skin removed
- 2 tablespoons extra virgin olive oil
- 1 celery heart, cut into 1 cm (½ in) cubes
- 1 large brown onion, cut into 1 cm (½ in) cubes
- 12 large green olives, pitted and chopped
- 2 tablespoons salted capers, rinsed and dried
- ⅓ cup (80 ml/2½ fl oz) tomato passata
- ¼ cup (60 ml/2 fl oz) red wine vinegar
- 2 tablespoons caster (superfine) sugar
- 100 ml (3½ fl oz) fish stock or water
- 1 tablespoon chopped parsley
- 1 garlic clove

METHOD

Put the fish in a steamer and steam for 10–12 minutes, depending on thickness, until just firm to the touch. Meanwhile, heat the olive oil in a frying pan and gently fry the celery and onion until soft. Don't worry if they colour a little – just don't burn them. Add the olives and capers and gently fry for a minute or two, stirring. Add the passata, vinegar, sugar and fish stock and turn up the heat to medium. Cook until the liquid reduces and thickens a little, then season. Finely chop the parsley and garlic together. Arrange the steamed fish on serving plates and spoon the sauce over the top. Sprinkle with the parsley/garlic mixture and serve.

SERVES 4   WINE: Regaleali Bianco

FASHION BEING WHAT IT IS, COOKS HAVE COME TO PREFER TINY CAPERS. WHILE THEIR FLAVOUR IS FINE, SUBTLE AND EVEN UNDERSTATED, THERE'S NOTHING LIKE FULL-GROWN LARGE CAPERS TO GET THAT BIG FLAVOUR PUNCH INTO A DISH. SICILY PRODUCES EXCEPTIONAL CAPERS. THEY GROW WILD, ESPECIALLY ON THE AEOLIAN ISLANDS, AND THEY'RE USED THROUGHOUT SICILIAN CUISINE AS A SEASONING. CAPERS CAN BE BOUGHT SALTED OR PICKLED IN VINEGAR. THE FORMER IS BETTER FOR FLAVOUR. IT'S IMPORTANT TO WASH SALTED CAPERS WELL, TWO OR THREE TIMES IS ALWAYS A GOOD IDEA.

SICILIAN-STYLE ROAST SARDINES

SICILIAN-STYLE ROAST SARDINES
SARDE A BECCAFICO

Caciocavallo cheese is made from cow's milk and comes predominantly from two rare-breed cattle, the cinisara and the modicana. The most famous variety is caciocavallo palermitano, which is made in the comunes of Cinisi and Godrano in the province of Palermo.

INGREDIENTS

2 brown onions, minced

1 garlic clove, minced

80 g (2¾ oz) sultanas (golden raisins)

⅓ cup (50 g/1¾ oz) pine nuts

80 g (2¾ oz) caciocavallo or provolone cheese

100 g (3½ oz) breadcrumbs

½ cup (125 ml/4 fl oz) extra virgin olive oil

16 sardine fillets

12 bay leaves

2 teaspoons caster (superfine) sugar

juice of 2 lemons

METHOD

Preheat the oven to 200°C (400°F). Put the onions, garlic, sultanas, pine nuts, cheese and breadcrumbs in a bowl and mix well. Add enough olive oil so the mixture comes together, then season. Put a little of the stuffing on each sardine fillet and roll it up from top to tail. Take 4 skewers and thread 4 sardine rolls on each skewer, alternating each roll with a bay leaf. Whisk together the sugar, lemon juice and remaining olive oil. Put the skewers in a baking dish and spoon on the dressing. Bake for 10 minutes and serve with caponata (see pages 440 or 446).

SERVES 4   WINE: Zibibbo Secco

BARBECUED PRAWNS WITH SALSA SALMORIGLIO AND SAVOY CABBAGE SALAD
GAMBERI ALLA GRIGLIA, VERZE AL SALMORIGLIO

INGREDIENTS

¼ Savoy cabbage, core and tough outer leaves removed

⅓ cup (80 ml/2½ fl oz) red wine vinegar

160 ml (5¼ fl oz) extra virgin olive oil

12 cherry tomatoes, halved

16 large raw king prawns (shrimp), peeled and deveined

SALSA SALMORIGLIO

2 garlic cloves, minced

1 cup parsley leaves, chopped

½ cup fresh oregano leaves, chopped

juice of 1 lemon

¼ cup (60 ml/2 fl oz) extra virgin olive oil

METHOD

To make the salsa salmoriglio, combine all the ingredients. Set aside. Finely slice the cabbage and put in a bowl. Dress with the vinegar and ½ cup (125 ml/4 fl oz) of the olive oil. Sprinkle with 2–3 good pinches of salt and toss well. Set aside for 30–45 minutes, giving it a stir occasionally. Add the cherry tomatoes and toss with a few turns of fresh pepper. Heat the remaining olive oil on a barbecue grill (or a large frying pan). Brush the prawns with some of the salsa and grill on both sides until they turn red (about 30 seconds on each side). Serve the prawns with the cabbage salad with the remaining salsa spooned on top.

SERVES 4   WINE: Carricante

PAN-FRIED PORK FILLET WITH CARROTS IN MARSALA
FILETTO DI MAIALE IN PADELLA CON CAROTE AL MARSALA

INGREDIENTS

700–800 g (1 lb 9 oz–
   1 lb 12 oz) small (Dutch)
   carrots or 1 kg (2 lb 4 oz)
   large carrots
¼ cup (60 ml/2 fl oz) extra
   virgin olive oil
¼ cup (60 ml/2 fl oz) dry
   or semi-dry marsala
   (or fino sherry)
12 pork fillet medallions, each
   about 3 cm (1¼ in) thick
½ cup sage leaves

METHOD

If using small carrots, trim the tops and peel them, then put in a bowl of cold water until needed. Drain and pat dry before using. If using large carrots, peel them and cut into 1 cm (½ in) rounds. Heat 2 tablespoons of the olive oil in a frying pan on medium heat. Add the carrots, turn up the heat and cook for 2–3 minutes, stirring, until softened. Add the marsala and cook, stirring, until there are only 3–4 tablespoonfuls of liquid left. Remove from the heat, season and keep warm. Heat the remaining oil in a separate frying pan on medium heat and fry the pork medallions for about a minute. Turn to cook the other side for a minute, adding the sage leaves. Season and serve with the carrots and some of the pan juices.

SERVES 6   WINE: Marsala Vergine

SWEET AND SOUR RABBIT
CONIGLIO ALL'AGRODOLCE

INGREDIENTS

1–2 rabbits (about 1.2 kg/
   2 lb 12 oz total weight)
1 cup (250 ml/9 fl oz) extra virgin
   olive oil
1 large white onion, finely chopped
3 garlic cloves, finely chopped
½ cup chopped parsley
1 celery heart, finely chopped
6 large green olives (such as
   Nocellara del Belice variety),
   pitted and chopped
2 tablespoons large capers, well
   rinsed and chopped
1 cup (250 ml/9 fl oz) pureed ripe
   tomatoes
3 tablespoons chopped fresh
   oregano
1 tablespoon caster (superfine)
   sugar
½ cup (125 ml/4 fl oz) red wine
   vinegar

METHOD

Wash the rabbit under cold water and pat dry. Joint it into pieces (you can ask your butcher to do this, if you like). Heat ⅓ cup (80 ml/2½ fl oz) of the olive oil in a large, deep frying pan and fry the rabbit pieces until well browned. Remove from the pan and set aside. Wipe out the pan and heat the remaining oil. Fry the onion and garlic, stirring, until translucent, then throw in the parsley and celery and stir for 30 seconds. Add the olives, capers, pureed tomatoes and oregano and cook for about 10 minutes, stirring. Throw in the rabbit pieces and stir everything together. Season, then cover and simmer gently for 10 minutes, stirring occasionally. Dissolve the sugar in the vinegar and add to the pan. Turn up the heat and stir until almost all the liquid is gone. Turn off the heat, put the lid back on and leave for 2 hours, mixing every 30 minutes. Serve with roast or grilled vegetables.

SERVES 4   WINE: Etna Rosso

SWEET AND SOUR CHICKEN
POLLO ALL'AGRODOLCE

INGREDIENTS

1.5 kg (3 lb 5 oz) chicken
thighs

2 brown onions

1 cup (250 ml/9 fl oz) dry
red wine

6 black peppercorns

3 bay leaves

½ cup plain (all-purpose) flour

½ cup (125 ml/4 fl oz) extra
virgin olive oil

2 tablespoons finely diced
pancetta

2 celery hearts, finely chopped

10 green olives, pitted and
chopped

1 tablespoon capers

50 g (1¾ oz) sultanas (golden
raisins)

⅓ cup (50 g/1¾ oz) pine nuts

1 tablespoon caster (superfine)
sugar

⅓ cup (80 ml/2½ fl oz) red
wine vinegar

2 tablespoons chopped
parsley

METHOD

Rinse and pat dry the chicken thighs and put them in a bowl. Thinly slice 1 onion and put it in a saucepan with the wine, peppercorns, 1 bay leaf and 1 teaspoon salt. Bring to the boil and cook for 1 minute, then remove from the heat and let cool. Pour over the chicken, cover and refrigerate for 6–8 hours. When you are ready to cook, drain and pat dry the chicken, discarding the marinade. Dust the chicken with the flour. Heat half the olive oil in a frying pan, then add the chicken and fry until golden on both sides. Set aside. Finely chop the second onion. Heat the remaining oil in a flameproof casserole dish and add the onion, pancetta, celery, olives, capers, sultanas, pine nuts and remaining bay leaves. Lightly fry for a minute, then add the chicken and a couple of pinches of salt and stir on low heat. Dissolve the sugar in the vinegar and add to the dish. Mix, cover and cook on low heat for 10–12 minutes, adding water if the mixture is too dry. Season and stir in the parsley, then serve.

SERVES 6   WINE: Cerasuolo di Vittoria

AGRODOLCE LITERALLY MEANS SOUR AND SWEET. IN ROMAN TIMES IT WAS A COMBINATION OF SWEET AND SAVOURY INGREDIENTS. IN MODERN ITALIAN COOKING IT IS USUALLY AN ADDITION OF SUGAR AND VINEGAR. THE SUGAR CAN BE IN THE FORM OF MUST LIKE SABA, VINCOTTO OR BALSAMIC AND THE SOUR IN THE FORM OF VINEGAR, LEMON OR UNRIPE GRAPE JUICE (VERJUICE).

461

BROCCOLI SHOOTS 'AFFOGATI'
BROCCOLETTI AFFOGATI

This is great as a side dish to accompany roast meats or fish, or tossed through pasta.

INGREDIENTS

1.5 kg (3 lb 5 oz) broccoli
   shoots or broccolini
⅓ cup (80 ml/2½ fl oz) extra
   virgin olive oil
3 French shallots, thinly sliced
2 garlic cloves, thinly sliced
1 cup (250 ml/9 fl oz) dry
   white wine
3 tinned roma tomatoes,
   mashed
3 anchovy fillets, chopped
16 best-quality black olives,
   pitted

METHOD

Wash the broccoli shoots well and trim the very end of the stalks to remove any tough parts. Heat the olive oil in a wide frying pan and gently fry the shallots and garlic for a minute. Add the broccoli shoots and mix well, then add the wine and tomatoes and bring to the boil. Reduce the heat, add a good couple of pinches of salt and put a lid, a bit smaller than the pan, over the top of the broccoli shoots so the liquid reduces as it simmers. Cook very gently for 15 minutes, then add the anchovies and olives. Simmer, uncovered, for 2–3 minutes. Check for salt, add a few good turns of pepper and serve hot or at room temperature.

SERVES 8   WINE: Carricante

SICILIA DOLCI

LEMON AND MINT GRANITA
GRANITA AL LIMONE E MENTUCCIA

To my mind, cold infusion, as used in this recipe, works better than heat with mint. It imparts the fresh flavour without the 'stemmy' bitterness and doesn't leach the green from the leaves. The latter also keeps this granita white.

INGREDIENTS

2 cups mint leaves, well washed and dried

1.25 litres (44 fl oz) filtered water or still mineral water

190 g (6¾ oz) caster (superfine) sugar

1 cup (250 ml/9 fl oz) freshly squeezed lemon juice

METHOD

Put the mint leaves in an airtight container with 1 litre (35 fl oz) of the filtered water and refrigerate for 24 hours. Next day, put the remaining water and the sugar in a saucepan and bring to the boil. Remove from the heat immediately and let cool. Strain the mint infusion through muslin (cheesecloth) to remove any fine particles and stir into the cooled sugar syrup along with the lemon juice. Transfer to a clean, shallow plastic container with a lid, then put in the freezer for 1 hour until it begins to freeze. Whisk quickly so the mixture forms small crystals rather than setting hard. Repeat the whisking every 15 minutes until the granita has set, which can take up to 2–3 hours.

SERVES 8–10

RICOTTA-STUFFED DATES
DATTERI FARCITI

Dates were important in the Roman cooking of Apicius. In his recipe for date sauce for fried or poached fish fillets, translated and adapted by John Edwards, we can get a sense of Roman cooking at the height of the Empire: 'In a mortar, grind together pepper, coriander, fennel, oregano and rosemary. Add chopped dates. Moisten with vinegar and olive oil, combine with (fish) stock and boiled wine. Bring to a boil and simmer for 25 minutes. Serve with cooked fish and a sprinkling of pepper.'

INGREDIENTS

2 egg whites

1 tablespoon caster (superfine) sugar

120 g (4¼ oz) mascarpone cheese

½ teaspoon grated nutmeg

115 g (4 oz) ricotta cheese

20–25 dates

METHOD

Beat the egg whites with the sugar until the mixture is glossy and forms soft peaks. Whisk in the mascarpone, add the nutmeg and gently fold in the ricotta. Put in the refrigerator for at least 1 hour to cool and harden. When you are ready to serve, make a neat slit in each date from top to bottom on one side, then carefully remove the stone. Put the ricotta mixture in a piping bag with a medium-sized round nozzle. Fill each date with the mixture and serve with strong espresso.

MAKES 20–25   BEST with strong espresso

PISTACHIO AND SESAME BISCUITS
BISCOTTI DI PISTACCHI E SESAMO

INGREDIENTS

1 kg (2 lb 4 oz) softened
 unsalted butter

1.5 kg (3 lb 5 oz) caster
 (superfino) sugar

1.5 kg (3 lb 5 oz) plain
 (all-purpose) flour

60 g (2¼ oz) baking powder

500 g (1 lb 2 oz) fine polenta
 (cornmeal)

750 g (1 lb 10 oz) pistachio
 kernels (preferably from
 Bronte, Sicily)

250 g (9 oz) sesame seeds

10 eggs, whisked

METHOD

Preheat the oven to 170°C (340°F) and line baking trays with baking paper. Using an electric mixer, cream the butter and sugar until smooth. Sift the flour and baking powder together into a bowl and mix in the polenta, pistachios, sesame seeds and ½ teaspoon salt. Add the mixed dry ingredients to the creamed butter and sugar. Using a paddle attachment, slowly mix until smooth, adding the eggs a little at a time. Shape the dough into logs about 8 cm (3¼ in) wide, 2 cm (¾ in) thick and as long as your baking trays can handle. Put on the baking trays and bake for 25 minutes until golden brown, firm and just beginning to crack. Cool. Reduce the oven temperature to 150°C (300°F). Using a sharp, serrated knife, cut the logs into 1 cm (½ in) slices and put the biscotti back on the trays. Bake for 8–10 minutes until dry and crisp. Cool before serving.

MAKES about 160   WINE: Marsala

LEMON SEMOLINA BISCUITS
BISCOTTINI AL LIMONE E SEMOLINA

INGREDIENTS

200 g (7 oz) plain (all-purpose)
 flour

100 g (3½ oz) semolina

1 teaspoon baking powder

½ teaspoon bicarbonate of
 soda (baking soda)

110 g (3¾ oz) softened
 unsalted butter

2 tablespoons extra virgin
 olive oil

260 g (9¼ oz) sugar

1 egg

1 egg yolk

½ teaspoon natural vanilla
 extract

grated zest and juice of
 1 lemon

METHOD

Combine the flour, semolina, baking powder, bicarbonate of soda and a pinch of salt in a bowl and set aside. In an electric mixer fitted with a paddle attachment, cream the butter, olive oil and 200 g (7 oz) of the sugar until light and fluffy. Add the egg, egg yolk, vanilla, lemon zest and lemon juice and mix until well combined (it may be necessary to scrape down the sides of the bowl). On low speed, add the dry ingredients and mix until a soft dough forms. Shape the dough into a flat disc, wrap in plastic wrap and refrigerate for 1½ hours. Preheat the oven to 170°C (340°F) and line baking trays with baking paper. Put the remaining sugar in a bowl. Lightly flour your fingers and take a small piece of dough. Roll it to the size of a golf ball, then roll in the sugar and put on the baking tray. Continue rolling until all the dough has been used, placing the balls about 4 cm (1½ in) apart on the trays. Bake for 20–25 minutes until lightly golden. Cool and store in an airtight container.

MAKES about 40   WINE: Liquore al Limone di Verdello di Sicilia

CLEMENTINE AND ALMOND BISCOTTI WITH CLEMENTINE RICOTTA CREAM
BISCOTTI DI CLEMENTINE CON LA CREMA DI RICOTTA

INGREDIENTS

- 425 g (15 oz) plain (all-purpose) unbleached flour
- 1 teaspoon baking powder
- 4 whole eggs
- 2 egg yolks
- 400 g (14 oz) caster (superfine) sugar, plus 1½ tablespoons for glaze
- 2 teaspoons natural vanilla extract
- 1 tablespoon anise seeds
- zest of 4 clementines
- 4 cups blanched almonds, chopped
- 1 egg white

CLEMENTINE RICOTTA CREAM

- 1 cup (250 ml/9 fl oz) thin (pouring) cream
- 50 g (1¾ oz) caster (superfine) sugar
- 200 g (7 oz) ricotta cheese
- ½ teaspoon natural vanilla extract
- zest of 4 clementines

METHOD

Mix the flour, baking powder and 2 pinches of salt to combine thoroughly. Using an electric mixer fitted with a paddle attachment, beat the eggs, egg yolks and sugar on medium speed for 2 minutes until the mixture looks curdled. Beat in the vanilla, anise seeds and clementine zest, then add the flour mixture and then the nuts until a soft dough forms. Wrap in plastic wrap and refrigerate for 2 hours. Preheat the oven to 165°C (330°F) and lightly grease 2 baking sheets or line them with baking paper. Divide the dough into 5 equal pieces. On a lightly floured surface, shape each piece of dough into a log 5 cm wide × 25 cm long (2 in × 10 in). Put 2 logs on one baking tray and 3 on the other, making sure there is at least 7 cm (2¾ in) between the logs. Using a fork, whisk the egg white until frothy. Use a brush to paint the logs with the egg white, then sprinkle the extra sugar on top. Bake for 20–25 minutes until golden brown, firm and just beginning to crack. You may have to rotate the trays halfway through to ensure the logs brown evenly. Cool on the trays for 30–40 minutes. Reduce the oven temperature to 95°C (200°F). Using a sharp, serrated knife, cut the logs on a slight bias into 5 mm (¼ in) thick biscotti. Lay them on the trays and return to the oven for 20 minutes until dry and crisp. Cool completely and store in an airtight container. Serve with the clementine ricotta cream.

To make the clementine ricotta cream, whip the cream and sugar in a bowl until the mixture is glossy and firm peaks form. Press the ricotta through a fine sieve to remove any lumps, then mix with the vanilla and clementine zest. Fold the ricotta mixture through the whipped cream. Makes about 2 cups (500 ml/17 fl oz).

MAKES about 50   WINE: Malvasia delle Lipari

CLEMENTINE AND ALMOND BISCOTTI WITH CLEMENTINE RICOTTA CREAM

PISTACHIO CAKE
TORTA DI PISTACCHI

INGREDIENTS

unsalted butter

200 g (7 oz) Bronte pistachio
kernels (or other variety)

5 large eggs, separated

80 g (2¾ oz) caster (superfine)
sugar

1 tablespoon lemon juice

grated zest of 1 lemon

2 tablespoons grappa (or
other spirit or liqueur)

1 teaspoon natural vanilla
extract

100 g (3½ oz) apricot jam

METHOD

Preheat the oven to 200°C (400°F). Butter a round 20 cm (8 in) cake tin and line the bottom with baking paper. Put 175 g (6 oz) of the pistachios in a food processor and pulse until finely ground. Beat the egg yolks with sugar until pale and creamy. Mix in the ground pistachios, lemon juice and zest, grappa and vanilla. Beat the egg whites until shiny and forming soft peaks, then fold gently but thoroughly into the pistachio mixture. Transfer the mixture to the tin and bake for 25 minutes until firm to the touch. Cool in the tin. Gently heat the apricot jam in a small saucepan until melted. Using a pastry brush, 'paint' the liquid jam onto the surface of the cake until glossy. Scatter the remaining pistachios on top to finish the cake.

SERVES 8   WINE: Passito di Pantelleria

THE **PISTACHIOS** GROWN IN BRONTE, IN THE PROVINCE OF CATANIA, HAVE LONG BEEN RECOGNISED FOR THEIR OUTSTANDING QUALITY OF FLAVOUR, COLOUR AND PERFUME. THEY ARE PROTECTED BY DOP LAW AND THEIR GROWERS – A LITTLE OVER 1000 IN NUMBER – ACCOUNT FOR A MERE ONE PER CENT OF TOTAL WORLD PRODUCTION. MOST HOLDINGS ARE ONLY A HECTARE OR SO IN SIZE.

CHOCOLATE AND WALNUT SOUFFLES
WITH CHOCOLATE AND CINNAMON CREAM
SOFFIATI AL CIOCCOLATO

This is adapted from a recipe by Andreas Zangerl of the Metropole Hotel in Taormina, Sicily.

INGREDIENTS

70 g (2½ oz) softened unsalted butter, plus extra for greasing

130 g (4½ oz) caster (superfine) sugar, plus extra for dusting

3 eggs, separated

70 g (2½ oz) dark best-quality chocolate (70% cocoa solids), chopped

140 g (5 oz) day-old white bread, crusts removed

milk

70 g (2½ oz) ground walnuts

icing (confectioners') sugar

CHOCOLATE AND CINNAMON CREAM

½ cup (125 ml/4 fl oz) milk

2 cinnamon sticks

100 g (3½ oz) best-quality chocolate (70% cocoa solids), chopped

METHOD

Preheat the oven to 120°C (250°F). Grease 4 soufflé moulds (150 ml/5 fl oz) with butter and dust with sugar. Beat the butter, 100 g (3½ oz) of the sugar and the egg yolks together until pale and creamy. Bring a small saucepan of water to the boil. Put the chocolate in small bowl that fits over the saucepan but won't touch the water. Put the bowl over the saucepan and turn off the heat. The chocolate should melt in a matter of minutes. Meanwhile, soak half the bread in enough milk to saturate for a minute or so, then squeeze as much milk as possible out of the bread. Beat the melted chocolate and squeezed bread into the butter mixture. Break the remaining bread into large crumbs and add to the chocolate mixture with the ground walnuts. Beat the egg whites with the remaining sugar to form stiff peaks, then fold into the mixture. Fill the moulds to three-quarters full with the mixture, then put the moulds in a baking dish and pour in water to come three-quarters of the way up the sides of the moulds. Bake for 35 minutes.

Meanwhile, make the chocolate and cinnamon cream. Put the milk and cinnamon sticks in a small saucepan and bring to the boil on low–medium heat. Simmer for 2–3 minutes, then turn off the heat and stir in the chocolate. Let sit for 10 minutes, then pass through a sieve. Makes about 200 ml (7 fl oz).

Serve the soufflés hot straight out of the oven dusted with icing sugar, with the chocolate and cinnamon cream. Alternatively, let them cool a little before unmoulding and refrigerating. When you are ready to serve, warm them in a microwave oven and serve with the chocolate and cinnamon cream.

SERVES 4   WINE: Passito di Pantelleria

BLACK RICE
RISO NERO

INGREDIENTS

200 g (7 oz) Italian rice
  (vialone nano or carnaroli)

1.5 litres (52 fl oz) milk

1 cinnamon stick

1 vanilla bean, split

80 g (2¾ oz) caster (superfine)
  sugar

20 g (¾ oz) best-quality dark
  chocolate (70% cocoa
  solids), chopped

40 g (1½ oz) best-quality
  unsweetened cocoa
  powder

60 g (2¼ oz) blanched
  almonds, toasted and
  chopped

1 tablespoon icing
  (confectioners') sugar

2 teaspoons ground cinnamon

METHOD

Bring 2 litres (70 fl oz) water and a pinch of salt to the boil in a saucepan. Add the rice and blanch for 2 minutes. Meanwhile, bring the milk to the boil in a separate, smaller saucepan and add the cinnamon stick, vanilla bean and sugar. Drain the rice well and add to the milk. Simmer gently for about 25 minutes until the rice is just cooked – it should be creamy and a little runny. Remove from the heat and whisk in the chocolate and cocoa until the chocolate has completely melted and all is incorporated. Transfer to individual ramekins or a large bowl and cool to room temperature. Scatter with the almonds and dust with the icing sugar and cinnamon to serve.

SERVES 8–10   WINE: Malvasia delle Lipari

IN THE CITY OF **TINDARI**, SITUATED IN THE PROVINCE OF MESSINA IN NORTH-EASTERN SICILY, THERE IS A STATUE OF A BLACK MADONNA CARVED FROM CEDRO (CITRON) WOOD. IT RESTS IN A CHURCH CALLED THE SANCTUARY OF TINDARI. BLACK RICE IS TRADITIONALLY PREPARED AS A VOTIVE FOR THE BLACK MADONNA OF TINDARI.

POMEGRANATE JELLY WITH PISTACHIO PRALINE
GELO DI MELOGRANO CON CROCCANTE AL PISTACCHIO

For instructions on juicing and seeding pomegranates, see page 39.

INGREDIENTS

100 ml (3½ fl oz) sweet white wine (such as moscato or late-picked riesling)

1 teaspoon pomegranate molasses

50 g (1¾ oz) caster (superfine) sugar

2 cups (500 ml/17 fl oz) pomegranate juice

40 g (1½ oz) gelatine sheets, moistened in water

seeds from 1 pomegranate

PISTACHIO PRALINE

450 g glucose

360 g (12¾ oz) sugar

360 g (12¾ oz) pistachio kernels

METHOD

To make the pistachio praline, dissolve the glucose in a saucepan on low heat. Add the sugar in 4 lots, mixing each time to dissolve. After the sugar has all completely dissolved, the mixture will begin to caramelise. When it has turned golden, add the pistachios and mix well. Turn out onto a tray and let cool, then chop finely or pulse in a food processor. Store in an airtight container (not in the refrigerator).

Heat the wine in a saucepan on medium heat, then add the pomegranate molasses and sugar and stir until completely dissolved. Remove from the heat, add the gelatine sheets and stir until completely dissolved. Mix in the pomegranate juice. Line a square tin (20 cm (8 in) × 20 cm (8 in) or dish with plastic wrap and tip in the pomegranate mixture. Refrigerate for at least 4 hours, then serve sprinkled with the pistachio praline and pomegranate seeds.

SERVES 4–6   WINE: Passito di Pantelleria

QUINCE WITH TAMARIND, MINT AND POMEGRANATE
MELE COTOGNE AL TAMARINDO, MENTUCCIA E MELOGRANO

INGREDIENTS

500 g (1 lb 2 oz) sugar

4 quinces, well washed

1 vanilla bean, halved

peel from 2 mandarins (mandarin oranges)

1 large pomegranate

1 level teaspoon tamarind paste

6 mint leaves, thinly sliced

lime or lemon sorbet, to serve

METHOD

Preheat the oven to 130°C (265°F). Put the sugar and 1.5 litres (52 fl oz) water in a saucepan and bring to the boil, then stir well to make sure the sugar has all dissolved. Pour the sugar syrup into a baking dish. Peel and quarter the quinces and cut the woody core from each piece of quince. Put the quince peel and cores in a piece of clean muslin (cheesecloth) and tie securely. Add to the baking dish along with the quince pieces, vanilla bean and mandarin peel. Bake for 4–5 hours until the quince is deeply coloured and tender. Remove from the oven and let cool. Roll the pomegranate on your workbench, pressing with your palm, to release the juice from the seeds inside. Once the pomegranate has softened, cut it open over a bowl and remove the seeds and juice. Make sure there is no white pith. Add the tamarind paste, mint and 200–250 ml (7–9 fl oz) of the cooled quince cooking liquid and stir to combine. Thinly slice the quince, arrange on plates and spoon the sauce over. Serve with lime or lemon sorbet.

SERVES 8 WINE: Zibibbo

PRICKLY PEAR WITH MASCARPONE CREAM AND ROAST PISTACHIO
FICHI D'INDIA CON CREMA DI MASCARPONE E PISTACCHIO

INGREDIENTS

8 prickly pears, peeled

200 g (7 oz) caster (superfine) sugar

3 egg whites

300 g (10½ oz) fresh mascarpone cheese

80 g (2¾ oz) pistachio kernels, roasted and rouhly chopped

¼ teaspoon ground cinnamon

METHOD

Puree the prickly pears in a food processor. Sieve over a bowl and separate the pulp from the seeds, discarding the seeds. Put the puree in a saucepan with 50 g (1¾ oz) of the caster sugar and bring to the boil, stirring. Turn the heat down and simmer until the liquid has reduced by half. Let cool, then refrigerate. Whisk the egg whites in a bowl, slowly adding the remaining sugar, until firm peaks form. Fold in the mascarpone until the mixture is light and fluffy. To serve, ladle some prickly pear puree into bowls, add a large dollop of mascarpone cream, scatter pistachios on top and dust with cinnamon.

SERVES 8 WINE: Malvasia delle Lipari

CHOCOLATE GELATO
GELATO AL CIOCCOLATO

INGREDIENTS

200 g (7 oz) dark chocolate
  (70% cocoa solids),
  chopped
2 cups (500 ml/17 fl oz) milk
1 vanilla bean, split and seeds
  scraped
225 g (8 oz) caster (superfine)
  sugar
8 egg yolks
300 ml (10½ fl oz) thin
  (pouring) cream

METHOD

Put the chocolate in a bowl. Heat 100 ml (3½ fl oz) of the milk until almost boiling, then pour over it the chocolate and stir until smooth. Put the vanilla pod and seeds, sugar and remaining milk in a saucepan and bring to a simmer. Remove from the heat. Beat the egg yolks in the bowl of an electric mixer until thick and pale. Pour in the milk mixture and whisk vigorously to combine. Return this mixture to the saucepan and cook on medium heat until thick and coating the back of a spoon. Strain and combine with the chocolate/milk mixture. Cool in the fridge, then whisk in the cream until smooth. Churn in an ice-cream machine according to the manufacturer's instructions.

MAKES about 1.5 litres (52 fl oz)

VANILLA GELATO
GELATO ALLA VANIGLIA

INGREDIENTS

3 cups (750 ml/26 fl oz) milk
1 cup (250 ml/9 fl oz) thin
  (pouring) cream
1 vanilla bean, split and seeds
  scraped
280 g (10 oz) caster
  (superfine) sugar
8 egg yolks

METHOD

Put the milk, cream, vanilla pod and seeds and 250 g (9 oz) of the sugar in a saucepan and bring to a simmer, then remove from the heat. Beat the egg yolks and remaining sugar in the bowl of an electric mixer until thick and pale. Pour in the milk mixture and mix to combine. Using a thermometer, cook at 80°C (175°F) for 9 minutes on the stove top, then strain and cool in the fridge. Churn in an ice-cream machine according to the manufacturer's instructions.

MAKES about 1.2 litres (44 fl oz)

PINE NUT AND ROSEMARY GELATO
GELATO AL ROSMARINO E PINOLI

INGREDIENTS

10 egg yolks

200 g (7 oz) caster (superfine) sugar

400 ml thin (pouring) cream

200 ml (7 fl oz) milk

1 vanilla bean, split and seeds scraped

PINE NUT AND ROSEMARY PRALINE

360 g (12¾ oz) glucose

360 g (12¾ oz) sugar

⅔ cup (100 g/3½ oz) pine nuts, toasted

2 tablespoons dried rosemary

METHOD

To make the pine nut and rosemary praline, gently dissolve the glucose in a saucepan on low heat. Add the sugar in 3 lots, mixing each time until it has dissolved before adding the next. When the mixture has caramelised and is golden brown, add the pine nuts and rosemary and mix well. Turn out onto a tray lined with silicone and let cool completely. Break into shards and pound in a mortar or pulse in a food processor until it resembles coarse sand.

Cream the egg yolks and sugar until pale. Put the cream, milk and vanilla pod and seeds in a saucepan and bring to the boil. Pour the boiling mixture over the egg/sugar mixture while whisking, then return the entire mixture to the saucepan or a double boiler and cook on very low heat until thickened and coating the back of a spoon. Strain and cool in the refrigerator. Churn in an ice-cream machine according to the manufacturer's instructions, then fold in 4 tablespoons of the crushed praline and set in a bowl in the freezer.

MAKES about 1 litre (35 fl oz)

BLUEBERRY SORBET
SORBETTO AL MIRTILLO

This needs an ice-cream machine to achieve the smooth texture that is a feature of a good sorbetto.

INGREDIENTS

1 kg (2 lb 4 oz) blueberries

280 g (10 oz) caster (superfine) sugar

2 tablespoons lemon juice

METHOD

Put all the ingredients in a blender and process to a puree. Strain (if desired) and refrigerate until cold. Churn in an ice-cream machine according to the manufacturer's instructions.

MAKES about 1 litre (35 fl oz)

CHESTNUT GELATO
GELATO ALLE CASTAGNE

To score chestnuts, use a very sharp knife to make a small cut through the outer skin.

INGREDIENTS
⅔ cup (150 g/5½ oz) caster (superfine) sugar

4 egg yolks

600 ml (21 fl oz) milk

CHESTNUT CREAM
300 g (10½ oz) chestnuts, scored

100 ml (3½ fl oz) milk

80 g (2¾ oz) caster (superfine) sugar

1 vanilla bean, split and seeds scraped (or 1 teaspoon natural vanilla extract)

3 tablespoons thick (double) cream

METHOD
To make the chestnut cream, put the chestnuts in a saucepan, cover with water and boil for 30 minutes. Peel the chestnuts and pass the flesh through a sieve or ricer. Wipe out the saucepan and pour in the milk. Bring to the boil, then add the chestnut puree, sugar, vanilla and cream. Simmer for 10–15 minutes until thickened. Cool completely.

Pass the chestnut cream through a very fine sieve so it is smooth, then set aside. Whisk the sugar and egg yolks together in a bowl until pale and creamy. Heat the milk in a saucepan until it almost boils, then whisk half the milk into the egg and sugar mixture. Return this mixture to the milk in the saucepan and cook on a low heat for about 10 minutes, stirring constantly, until thickened. Remove from the heat and mix in the chestnut cream. Let cool and then refrigerate until cold. Churn in an ice-cream machine according to the manufacturer's instructions.

MAKES about 1 litre (35 fl oz)

TOSCANA

TUSCANY

TRIANGULAR TOSCANA BORDERS LIGURIA TO THE NORTH-WEST, EMILIA-ROMAGNA TO THE NORTH AND EAST, LAZIO TO THE SOUTH-EAST AND UMBRIA TO THE EAST. IT HAS A WESTERN COASTLINE ON THE TYRRHENIAN SEA AND INCLUDES AN ARCHIPELAGO OF ISLANDS, THE LARGEST BEING ELBA. TOSCANA COVERS 23,000 SQUARE KILOMETRES (8880 SQUARE MILES).

Undertaking the Grand Tour of Italy from the 17th century on, after taking in the antiquities of Pompeii and Herculaneum the wealthy of Europe would make a beeline for Toscana, as much for the beauty of its countryside as for the art and architectural treasures to be found in its galleries and ancient cities, such as Florence and Pisa. It still attracts millions of tourists annually, and others, wealthier, who succumb to its charms and buy property there, hoping to absorb some of the charm of the place and its people for themselves. Built on and around the original home of the Etruscans, Toscana is seen by many as the heartland of Italy and all that is admired about Italian culture – including, of course, cuisine.

The beauty of the Tuscan countryside is a cultivated one, with meticulously tended farmlands, olive groves, vineyards and country estates dotted throughout the rolling hills, punctuated by tall, dark cypress trees. The cultivated countryside is matched by its people. In his book on Machiavelli, Giuseppe Prezzolini opined: 'the most civilized people in the world, those Tuscans; with a breeding ingrained and secular, no mere veneer or rote'.

Agriculture has dominated the Tuscan conversation for many years, which means that Florentine cuisine begins and ends with careful attention to raw materials. The simplicity of the Etruscans has travelled down the centuries to inform the cuisine of today. Sauces are practically unknown – Tuscans prefer to eat their food raw or just cooked over flames, often not even with salt (there is no salt in Tuscan bread). However, they do love their fresh herbs: in his *Natural History*, published between 77 and 79, Pliny the Elder wrote of the herbs that grew on his land:

'The meadows are jewelled with flowers, and produce trefoil and other herbs, always tender and soft, and looking as though they were always fresh.'

Ask any Italian what typifies Tuscan cuisine and the answer will be bistecca alla fiorentina, or Florentine beefsteak. No ordinary cut of meat, it is taken from the pure white Chianina, the oldest, heaviest (up to 1400 kg, or 3086 pounds) and tallest cattle in Europe. It is cut in the Florentine style as a T-bone, grilled en sangue, or rare (no arguments), over charcoal, seasoned with Tuscan olive oil, pepper and salt, and served sliced on a wooden plate with a runnel around the edge to catch the juices, which are to be soaked up with bread. Simple and rustic.

It stands to reason that the bread used for those meat juices is a very important food in Toscana. Locals eat bread for breakfast with cafè latte, and spread a crusty slice with the magnificent local olive oil and something simple, such as tomatoes, liver or olive paste, before lunch to make bruschetta. If the bread is spread only with oil, then it is called panunto or fettunta. (The nickname of Domenico Romoli, the author of *La Singola Dottrina*, or *The Unique Doctrine*, was Panunto.) Another form of bread, from Siena, is panforte: spiced bread packed with dried and candied fruit, nuts and honey. At the end of a meal, goat's cheese, figs and walnuts are often placed on a slice of bread, while pappa al pomodoro (bread and tomato soup) is served in restaurants, as are most soups, in simple and elegant ceramic bowls. And bread is an important ingredient in the famed Livornese fish soup cacciucco, which is poured over slices of bread.

The name cacciucco derives from the Turkish küçük, meaning 'not much', as it was originally made with the little fish left over after a fisherman had sold his catch. This derivation points to the cosmopolitan nature of Livorno: the Medicis designated it a free port, so it attracted inhabitants from

»

FRENCH TARRAGON

French tarragon spreads like plush pile carpet on the ground throughout Toscana. I keep snipping off stems the length of my forearm and the plant keeps increasing its diameter.

Crush the delicate leaves between your fingers and the smell is intoxicating, with scents of liquorice, aniseed and fennel. It's different from the more common Russian tarragon in several ways. The first difference is the all-important flavour: it's true to say that the flavour of the bigger-leafed Russian tarragon is in inverse proportion to that of the small-leafed French. And if you're growing tarragon, the Russian will easily sprout from seed while the French rarely does – it prefers to be propagated from cuttings. Perhaps the most pertinent difference is that Russian tarragon is easily found in many greengrocers while French is hard to get. The frustrating thing is that many store owners don't know the difference, so home cooks often end up buying Russian when they need French. French tarragon's Latin name, *dracunculus*, has always fascinated me because tarragon in Italian is dragoncello. This 'little dragon' reference comes from the much older Greek word *drakontion*, meaning adderwort, a reference to the herb's one-time use in treating the bites of venomous creatures.

all around the Mediterranean. It was also the only city in Italy without a ghetto and so became a refuge for the Jews who fled Spain after 1492. And that, in a roundabout way, is why you will find couscous in Livorno – the Jews had links with Tunisia and brought it with them. Couscous is made in Livorno in much the same way as it is in Tunisia, being steamed over mutton, lamb or beef stew and served with a fiery harissa sauce.

A fish soup made on the island of Giglio, off the southernmost tip of Toscana in the Tyrrhenian Sea, called zuppa de pesce alla gigliese is said to contain every fish and shellfish in the area, especially baby octopus. And there is a wine called ansonica, made from the ansonica grape. It was a favourite of the French novelist Stendhal, a one-time resident who called the island Mermaid Island. The locals said that after drinking enough of this wine you would see anything, mermaids not the least!

The best-known wine of Toscana, Chianti, has a varied and contested history. It was first recorded in the 13th century, as white. From the 18th century onwards it was red, and by the mid-19th century, a wine could only be called Chianti Classico if it was made from at least 70 per cent sangiovese.

Today the question has to be asked: what is Chianti Classico? The ups and downs, changes of rules and tussles over what blend of grapes constitutes a Classico have filled many pages of many wine books. What is clear is that the major grape is still sangiovese. There are 600 members of the Consorzio Chianti Classico, of which 260 bottle their own wine. You will not be lost for choice.

The clash of the Chiantis and the rebellion over the restrictions of the DOCGs led to the phenomenon known as the Super Tuscans, many of which are not produced in Chianti but in the Maremma around Bolgheri. These wines took the world by storm and there are now some 19 of them, most still using sangiovese but some having varying amounts of added syrah, cabernet sauvignon, merlot and cabernet franc, and a couple based on cabernet sauvignon blends.

So dominant is the C wine that it is easy – but a mistake – to overlook the other great reds of Toscana. One is Brunello di Montalcino, from the DOCG south of the Chianti Classico (brunello is the local name for sangiovese). Then there is the Vino Nobile de Montepulciano, the DOCG in the middle of Chianti Classico, vinified from the prugnolo grape (another version of sangiovese) and Brunello di Montalcino. Other DOCGs utilising blends highlighting sangiovese are Carmignano and Rúfina; both are close to Florence and have respectable pedigrees stretching back to the early 18th century and Cosimo III de'Medici's original production zones.

And yes, there are Tuscan whites, as any lover of the vernaccia used in the wines of San Gimignano will know. Trebbiano, although mostly used as a blending grape, does find itself alone in wines from the Montescudaio and Montecarlo DOCs especially, as well as playing a supporting role (to malvasia) in some fine vin santos – wines traditionally teamed with almond biscotti, into which they are dunked to delicious effect.

TOSCANA
ANTI-PASTI

ROAST TOMATO AND CANNELLINI BEAN CROSTINI
CROSTINI DI POMODORO AL FORNO E CANNELLINI

INGREDIENTS

8 good-sized, ripe roma (plum) tomatoes, halved lengthways

leaves from 2–3 fresh oregano sprigs

3 garlic cloves, thinly sliced

½ cup (125 ml/4 fl oz) extra virgin olive oil

16 thick slices country-style bread

½ cup cooked cannellini beans

METHOD

Preheat the oven to 170°C (340°F). Put the tomatoes on a baking tray cut side up. Scatter the oregano over, then put 2–3 slices of garlic on each tomato half and sprinkle 2 tablespoons of the olive oil over the lot. Season and roast for about 20 minutes until soft but not falling apart. Cool. Brush the bread on both sides with 2 tablespoons of the remaining oil and grill (broil) lightly. Dress the beans with the remaining oil, season and mix well. Put a piece of tomato on top of each crostino, pressing lightly to flatten it. Spoon some beans on top and serve.

MAKES 16   WINE: Bianco delle Colline Lucchesi

BAKED CHICKPEA-FLOUR TART
CECINA AL FORNO

Cecina is best described as Tuscan street food and is most satisfying eaten with your fingers as you would pizza.

INGREDIENTS

250 g (9 oz) chickpea flour (besan)

30 ml (1 fl oz) extra virgin olive oil, plus extra for brushing

100 g (3½ oz) pecorino cheese, shaved

METHOD

Preheat the oven to 200°C (400°F). Using a whisk, mix the flour and 700 ml (24 fl oz) warm water to form a smooth batter, adding the water little by little. Mix in the olive oil and season. Brush a 24 cm (9½ in) non-stick ovenproof frying pan with oil and heat until just smoking. Pour in the batter to a thickness of 5 mm (¼ in). When it has crusted up around the sides, transfer to the oven until the bottom is crisp and the top is creamy but just set. Cut into wedges and sprinkle with the pecorino and some cracked black pepper. Eat hot or cold.

SERVES 10–12   WINE: Vermentino delle Colline Lucchesi

CALAMARI BRAISED WITH CAVOLO NERO
CALAMARI STUFATI CON CAVOLO NERO

INGREDIENTS

400 g (14 oz) cavolo nero (Tuscan kale)

2 tablespoons extra virgin olive oil

1 small brown onion, finely chopped

2 garlic cloves, minced

1 chilli, seeded and thinly sliced

250 g (9 oz) calamari, cleaned and cut into bite-sized strips

1 cup (250 ml/9 fl oz) dry white wine

300 g (10½ oz) tin tomatoes, chopped

½ cup chopped parsley

METHOD

Strip the cavolo nero leaves from their stems and wash well, then chop the leaves. Heat the olive oil in a frying pan and lightly fry the onion, garlic and chilli until just coloured. Add the calamari and cavolo nero leaves on high heat and cook for 2 minutes, stirring constantly. Add the wine and cook until it has all evaporated, then add the tomatoes and a couple of good pinches of salt. Stir well, turn down the heat and simmer gently for 40 minutes, adding a little hot water if the pan gets too dry. Stir in the parsley and add a little more salt (if needed) to serve.

SERVES 6–8   WINE: Vermentino

SLOW-COOKED OCTOPUS WITH POTATOES
POLPO CON PATATE

INGREDIENTS

1 brown onion

1 celery stick

1 carrot

2 bay leaves

1 handful parsley stalks

1 × 1.2 kg (2 lb 12 oz) octopus, cleaned

400 g (10½ oz) potatoes, cut into 1 cm (½ in) dice

1 tablespoon extra virgin olive oil

juice of 2 lemons

½ cup parsley, chopped

¼ cup (50 g/1¾ oz) capers, chopped

100 g (3½ oz) taggiasche olives, pitted

METHOD

Chop the onion, celery stick and carrot into chunks and put into a large saucepan with bay leaves, parsley stalks and plenty of water. Bring to the boil, then add the octopus (add more water if necessary to cover the octopus), turn the heat down and simmer for 40–50 minutes until tender (test by cutting a little from the thick end of a tentacle and tasting). Let cool in the cooking liquid. Boil the potatoes in salted water until tender. Chop the octopus into bite-sized pieces and mix with the potatoes. Dress with the olive oil, lemon juice, parsley and capers. Add the olives and season.

SERVES 8–10   WINE: Trebbiano

TOSCANA
PRIMI

ARTICHOKE AND PECORINO FLAN
TORTA DI RICOTTA E CARCIOFI

INGREDIENTS

2 teaspoons butter

4 tablespoons breadcrumbs

1 lemon

4 artichokes, trimmed
(see page 39)

2 tablespoons extra virgin
olive oil

1 garlic clove, minced

1 red onion, very thinly sliced

⅓ cup (30 g/1 oz) grated
pecorino cheese

1 teaspoon grated nutmeg

150 ml (5 fl oz) béchamel
sauce (see page 50)

3 eggs, whisked

METHOD

Preheat the oven to 180°C (350°F). Grease 6 souffle moulds (150 ml/
5 fl oz) with the butter and dust with the breadcrumbs. Squeeze the
lemon into a bowl of cold water. Thinly slice the artichokes, putting
them in the lemon water as you go, then drain and pat dry. Heat the
olive oil in a frying pan and lightly fry the artichokes, garlic and onion
until softened. Transfer to a tray and let cool, then combine with the
pecorino, nutmeg, béchamel and eggs. Season and mix well. Spoon the
mixture into the moulds and put the moulds in a baking dish. Pour in
water to come halfway up the sides of the moulds, then bake for about
15 minutes. Cool slightly before serving with salad.

SERVES 6   WINE: Vermentino

SALT COD WITH LEEKS
BACCALÀ AI PORRI

INGREDIENTS

750 g (1 lb 10 oz) baccalà
(salt cod), soaked and rinsed
(see page 125)

½ cup (125 ml/4 fl oz) extra
virgin olive oil

500 g (1 lb 2 oz) leeks, white
part only, halved lengthways
and cut into 1 cm (½ in) slices

1 brown onion, finely diced

1 celery stick, finely chopped

1 carrot, finely chopped

2 garlic cloves, minced

4 tablespoons finely chopped
parsley

½ cup basil leaves, chopped

1 teaspoon chilli flakes

450 g (1 lb) tin tomatoes, pureed

12 slices country-style bread

METHOD

Drain the cod and cut it into large pieces. Put the cod in a large
saucepan and pour in water to cover. Bring to the boil, then turn down
the heat and simmer for 25–30 minutes. Drain and let cool a little, then
shred the cod into flakes, discarding any bones. Set aside. Heat ⅓ cup
(80 ml/2½ fl oz) of the olive oil and lightly fry the leeks, onion, celery,
carrot, garlic, parsley, basil and chilli flakes until soft. Add the tomatoes
and simmer for 15 minutes. Add the cod, stir and cook for 5–6 minutes.
Season with salt (if needed) and plenty of pepper. Grill (broil) the bread
and brush with the remaining olive oil, then serve hot with the cod
and vegetables.

SERVES 6   WINE: Vermentino

MUSHROOM AND BEAN SOUP
ZUPPA DI FUNGHI E FAGIOLI

INGREDIENTS

200 g (7 oz) fresh borlotti
    beans (or 150 g/5½ oz
    dried, soaked overnight
    in plenty of cold water,
    then drained)

2 garlic cloves

1 carrot, sliced

1 celery stick, sliced

½ cup (125 ml/4 fl oz) extra
    virgin olive oil

600 g (1 lb 5 oz) assorted
    mushrooms, thinly sliced

3 litres (5¼ pints) vegetable
    stock or water

80 g (2¾ oz) pecorino or
    parmesan cheese, grated

METHOD

Cook the beans in plenty of water until tender, then drain and set aside.
Finely chop the garlic, carrot and celery together. Heat the olive oil on
medium heat in a large saucepan and fry the garlic mixture, continually
stirring, for 3–4 minutes. Add the mushrooms and cook for 2–3 minutes.
Pour in the stock and bring to the boil, then turn down the heat and
simmer for 45 minutes. Add the beans and simmer for 10 minutes.
Season and serve with the grated cheese.

SERVES 4–6   WINE: Rosso di Montalcino

PICI WITH DUCK SAUCE
PICI AL SUGO D'ANATRA

INGREDIENTS

2 red onions

1 carrot

1 celery heart

½ cup sage leaves

500 g (1 lb 2 oz) duck legs,
    skin on

2 tablespoons extra virgin
    olive oil

1½ cups (375 ml/13 fl oz) dry
    white wine

¼ cup (60 g/2¼ oz) tomato
    paste (concentrated puree)

4 juniper berries, lightly
    cracked

600 g (1 lb 5 oz) pici pasta
    (see page 44) or thick
    spaghetti

grated parmesan cheese

METHOD

Pulse the onions, carrot, celery and sage in a food processor until finely
minced (or mince finely using a knife) and set aside. Season the duck
legs. Heat the olive oil in a heavy-based frying pan and brown the duck
well, rendering as much fat as possible from the skin. Transfer the duck
to a tray, leaving all the oil in the pan. Add the minced vegetables to the
pan and fry gently for 5–6 minutes until softened. Add the wine, tomato
paste and juniper berries. Bring to the boil, then reduce the heat and
simmer until the liquid has reduced by half. Return the duck to the pan
and pour in enough water to just cover. Season lightly and simmer for
2 hours until the duck meat comes easily off the bones. Remove the
duck and let it cool a little, then remove the meat from the bones. Chop
the meat and return it to the sauce. Check for seasoning. Cook the
pasta in plenty of boiling salted water until al dente, then drain and toss
with the sauce. Serve with grated parmesan.

SERVES 6   WINE: Rosso di Montalcino

PICI WITH DUCK SAUCE

SWEET AND SOUR PRAWNS
GAMBERI IN AGRODOLCE

INGREDIENTS

80 g (2¾ oz) sultanas (golden raisins) or seedless raisins

24 raw prawns (shrimp), peeled and deveined, tails left on

3 tablespoons rice flour or plain (all-purpose) flour

⅓ cup (80 ml/2½ fl oz) extra virgin olive oil

pinch of ground cinnamon

30 ml (1 fl oz) strained lemon juice

1 teaspoon white wine vinegar

METHOD

Put the sultanas in a bowl and cover with tepid water. Let soak for at least 30 minutes. Dust the prawns with the flour and shake off any excess. Heat the olive oil in a wide frying pan and gently fry the prawns on medium heat for 30–45 seconds on each side. Add the cinnamon, a couple of pinches of salt and a turn or two of pepper. Remove the pan from the heat. Using tongs, transfer the prawns to a plate, leaving the pan juices in the pan. Drain the sultanas and give them a good squeeze to remove any excess water. Put the pan back on the heat and add the sultanas, lemon juice and vinegar. Simmer, stirring, until the liquid has reduced to a tablespoon or so. Return the prawns to the pan for a few seconds, then serve.

SERVES 4   WINE: Bianco delle Colline Lucchesi Vermentino

CAVOLO NERO WITH GARLIC BREAD
FETTUNTA CON CAVOLO NERO

INGREDIENTS

juice of ½ lemon

leaves from 400 g (14 oz) cavolo nero (Tuscan kale), chopped

4 slices sourdough or country-style bread, 3 cm (1¼ in) thick × 8 cm (3¼ in) long

½ cup (125 ml/4 fl oz) extra virgin olive oil

2 garlic cloves, halved

60 g (2¼ oz) parmesan cheese, thinly shaved

METHOD

Bring a large saucepan of salted water to the boil, add the lemon juice and plunge in the cavolo nero. Simmer for 20 minutes, then drain, reserving ½ cup (125 ml/4 fl oz) of the cooking liquid. Preheat the oven to 180°C (350°F). Brush the bread with half the olive oil and toast in the oven until golden. Rub the bread well with the garlic on both sides and put in 4 bowls. Distribute the reserved cooking liquid evenly among the bowls. Toss the cavolo nero with the remaining olive oil and season, then spoon it onto the garlic bread and scatter the parmesan on top.

SERVES 4   WINE: Chardonnay

SECONDI

SKATE LIVORNO STYLE
RAZZA ALLA LIVORNESE

This simple dish is from the restaurant Enoteca Nardi in Livorno. It is a typical preparation of skate in western coastal Tuscany. Of interest is the pairing of fish with cheese. As well as a main course, it makes a great antipasto or first course.

INGREDIENTS

600 g (1 lb 5 oz) skate wings, skin left on

2 tablespoons extra virgin olive oil

2 garlic cloves, minced

1 handful sage leaves

juice of ½ lemon

60 g (2¼ oz) grated parmesan cheese

METHOD

Bring a large saucepan of water to the boil. Immerse the skate carefully in the water and simmer for 20 minutes. Remove from the pan and let cool a little so it can be handled. Peel off the skin on both sides and, using a sharp knife, cut the flesh in pieces from the centre cartilage. Heat the olive oil in a frying pan and fry the garlic and sage for a minute. Add the skate and fry, gently, moving the fish around, for about 5 minutes. Transfer to a serving plate, scatter the lemon juice over and sprinkle the parmesan on top.

SERVES 4   WINE: Vermentino

SNAPPER POACHED IN TOMATO WITH BASIL AND OLIVES
DENTICE IN GUAZZETTO

If snapper is not available, another thick, meaty fish such as bream or Spanish mackerel will work just as well.

INGREDIENTS

2 tablespoons extra virgin olive oil

1 small brown onion, minced

1 garlic clove, minced

24 ripe cherry tomatoes, halved

1 cup basil leaves

100 ml (3½ fl oz) dry white wine or water

20 small green olives, pitted

4 × 160 g (5¾ oz) pieces snapper, skin off

METHOD

Heat the olive oil in a flameproof casserole dish and gently fry the onion and garlic until soft and fragrant. Add the tomatoes, basil, wine and olives and a couple of good pinches of salt. Simmer for about 5 minutes until the tomatoes have fallen apart. Arrange the fish pieces on top so they are not touching each other, spoon some of the tomato sauce over the fish, turn the heat to very low and cover. Simmer for 5 minutes, then take the dish off the heat and let rest for 5 minutes. Add more salt (if needed) and a few good turns of pepper. Serve immediately.

SERVES 4   WINE: Rosato di Carmignano

SNAPPER POACHED IN TOMATO WITH BASIL AND OLIVES

BARBECVED MINVTE STEAK WITH PRESERVED MUSHROOMS

ROAST CHICKEN THIGHS WITH TARRAGON AND GARLIC
COSCE DI POLLO AL DRAGONCELLO

INGREDIENTS

8 good-sized chicken thighs, bone in and skin on

½ cup French tarragon leaves

½ cup (125 ml/4 fl oz) extra virgin olive oil

20 large garlic cloves, peeled

6–8 French tarragon stems

1 cup (250 ml/9 fl oz) chicken stock

METHOD

Preheat the oven to 200°C (400°F). Force a finger between each chicken thigh's skin and flesh to make a pocket, making sure you don't remove the skin entirely. Push some of the tarragon leaves into the pocket and spread them over the flesh. Rub the chicken thighs with some of the olive oil and put them in a baking dish. Scatter the garlic cloves around and sprinkle the remaining oil on the garlic and season the chicken skin. Roast for 15 minutes, then add the tarragon stems and stock and roast for 10 minutes more. Serve immediately.

SERVES 4   WINE: Chianti Colli Senesi

BARBECUED MINUTE STEAK WITH PRESERVED MUSHROOMS
BISTECCHINA AL MINUTO CON FUNGHI SOTT'OLIO

INGREDIENTS

600 g (1 lb 5 oz) trimmed beef fillet, cut into 4 even pieces

½ cup shaved parmesan cheese

½ cup mixed herb leaves

4 lemon wedges

PRESERVED MUSHROOMS

3 cups (750 ml/26 fl oz) white wine vinegar

2 garlic cloves, lightly crushed

10 thyme sprigs

4 red chillies, halved

peel from 1 lemon (no white pith), cut into large strips

750 g (1 lb 10 oz) mixed mushrooms, cut into bite-sized pieces

1 cup (250 ml/9 fl oz) extra virgin olive oil

METHOD

To make the preserved mushrooms, put the vinegar and 3 litres (5¼ pints) water in a large saucepan with the garlic, thyme, chillies and lemon peel. Bring to the boil, then turn the heat down and simmer for 15 minutes. Turn up the heat and add the mushrooms. Once the mixture comes to the boil again, cook for 5 minutes. Remove from the heat, pour the mixture into a large container and let cool. Strain. Put the mushrooms in a container that has a lid, then add the olive oil, season and mix well. Cover and refrigerate until needed (the mushrooms will keep for 8–10 days). To use, remove from refrigerator and let come to room temperature.

Preheat the barbecue or a chargrill pan to high. Place each piece of beef between 2 sheets of baking paper and, using a flat-sided meat tenderiser, flatten until about 1 cm (½ in) thick. Barbecue or grill the beef for 30 seconds on each side. Transfer to serving plates and scatter some mushrooms over, then some parmesan and lastly the herbs. Serve with the lemon wedges.

SERVES 4   WINE: Morellino di Scansano

PEPOSO
PEPOSO

INGREDIENTS

2 kg (4 lb 8 oz) beef cheeks, cut into 3 cm (1¼ in) cubes

4 garlic cloves, lightly crushed

1 red onion, cut into 1 cm (½ in) dice

1 carrot, cut into 1 cm (½ in) dice

2 celery stalks, cut into 1 cm (½ in) dice

1 litre (35 fl oz) Chianti or other dry red wine

1 heaped tablespoon freshly ground black pepper

1 tablespoon tomato paste (concentrated puree)

2 bay leaves

2 cups (500 ml/17 fl oz) veal stock

METHOD

Put the beef in a flameproof casserole dish with the garlic, onion, carrot and celery. Pour in enough wine to just cover the meat. Bring to a simmer, then partly cover and cook for 2 hours. Add the pepper, tomato paste, bay leaves, veal stock, remaining wine and 2–3 good pinches of salt. Simmer gently, uncovered, for at least 2 hours until the sauce has reduced and thickened. If the mixture dries out too much, add a little more stock. Check for seasoning and add a little more salt if needed. Serve with polenta (cornmeal) or crusty bread.

SERVES 6   WINE: Brunello di Montalcino

BRAISED SILVERBEET
BIETE IN PADELLA

This is a great accompaniment to a classic bistecca fiorentina cooked on a wood grill.

INGREDIENTS

500 g (1 lb 2 oz) silverbeet (Swiss chard), well washed and dried

⅓ cup (80 ml/2½ fl oz) extra virgin olive oil

1 leek, white part only, chopped

1 small brown onion, finely chopped

2 garlic cloves, minced

1–2 red chillies, seeded and finely chopped

1 teaspoon saba or vincotto

1 tablespoon red wine vinegar

METHOD

Strip the silverbeet leaves from the stems. Cut the leaves into large strips and the stems into 5 mm (¼ in) pieces. Bring a saucepan of salted water to the boil and blanch the stems for 2 minutes or so until tender. Remove using a slotted spoon and set aside. Blanch the leaves in the same water for 30–45 seconds, then drain and cool before squeezing out as much water as possible. Heat the olive oil in a wide frying pan and lightly fry the leek, onion, garlic and chilli for a minute until translucent and aromatic. Add the silverbeet stems and leaves, stir well and cook on medium heat for a couple of minutes. Combine the saba and vinegar, then add to the pan, season and stir well. Serve.

SERVES 6–8   WINE: Merlot

TOSCANA
DOLCI

RICCIARELLI BISCUITS
RICCIARELLI

INGREDIENTS

325 g (11½ oz) icing
(confectioners') sugar,
plus extra for dusting

3 cups (300 g/10½ oz)
almond meal (freshly ground,
if possible)

pinch of sea salt

grated zest of ½ lemon

grated zest of ½ orange

1 teaspoon natural vanilla extract

1 teaspoon honey

2 egg whites

METHOD

Preheat the oven to 170°C (340°F) and dust baking trays well with icing sugar. Combine all the ingredients except the egg whites. Whisk the egg whites to soft peaks and fold into the mixture. Dust your work surface well with icing sugar and roll out the mixture to 1.5 cm (⅝ in) thick. Cut into diamonds about 4 cm (1½ in) long. Using the tips of your fingers, twist one end of each diamond one way and the other end the other way to form an S shape. Put the biscuits on the baking trays and dust again with icing sugar. Bake for about 10 minutes until light golden brown. Cool before serving.

MAKES about 40   **WINE:** Vin Santo

SIENA SPICED FRUIT AND NUT CAKE
PANFORTE

There's not much use making a small batch of this – everybody loves it.

INGREDIENTS

1 tablespoon extra virgin olive oil

3 kg (6 lb 12 oz) mixed dried
fruit – apricots, sultanas
(golden raisins), candied
mixed peel, prunes, figs,
peaches

1 kg (2 lb 4 oz) blanched
almonds, roasted

1 kg (2 lb 4 oz) hazelnuts,
roasted

6 tablespoons ground cinnamon

6 tablespoons mixed spice

2 teaspoons freshly ground
black pepper

1 kg (2 lb 4 oz) plain
(all-purpose) flour

1.25 kg (2 lb 12 oz) caster
(superfine) sugar

1.25 kg (2 lb 12 oz) honey

icing (confectioners') sugar

METHOD

Preheat the oven to 170°C (340°F). Brush 2 baking trays (30 cm × 40 cm/12 in × 16 in) with the olive oil and line with rice paper cut to fit. Chop any larger dried fruits into 1 cm (½ in) pieces and mix with the nuts, spices and flour. Heat the sugar and honey in a frying pan to soft ball stage (118°C/244°F on a candy thermometer), then add to the dry mixture and quickly mix using a sturdy wooden spoon. The sugar/honey will harden as it cools, so this has to be rapid. Spread the mixture evenly on the trays and flatten using a wet hand. Don't worry too much if it is not completely even – it will spread once it is in the oven. Cover the top with rice paper and press down firmly. Bake for 25 minutes. Cool in the trays before turning out and cutting into thin slivers or 2 cm (¾ in) squares and dusting with icing sugar. Serve with espresso. The panforte will keep indefinitely if stored in a sealed container in a cool place.

MAKES a lot   **WINE:** Vin Santo

SWEET GRAPE AND ANISEED BREAD
SCHIACCIATA

This is a simple, sweet treat that is made at grape harvest time in autumn. It's best with wine grapes such as canaiolo, but table grapes such as black muscatels can be substituted.

INGREDIENTS

3 cups (450 g/1 lb) plain (all-purpose) flour

2 × 7 g (¼ oz) sachets powdered yeast

⅓ cup (80 ml/2½ fl oz) milk

50 g (1¾ oz) caster (superfine) sugar

2 tablespoons extra virgin olive oil, plus extra for greasing

40 g (1½ oz) anise seeds

150 g (5½ oz) white rock sugar

700 g (1 lb 6 oz) ripe black grapes (such as muscatels)

METHOD

Combine the flour, yeast, milk, caster sugar and olive oil with enough warm water to make a soft, easily worked dough. Knead for at least 10–12 minutes until smooth and elastic, then put in a bowl, cover with plastic wrap and set aside for 1 hour. Preheat the oven to 230°C (450°F). Divide the dough in half and roll out 2 × 5 mm (¼ in) thick circles or rectangles to fit a 25–30 cm (10–12 in) round or rectangular baking tray. Oil the tray well. Put the anise seeds and rock sugar in a mortar and crush until fine. Roll the grapes in the aniseed/sugar mixture so that they are coated. Lay 500 g (1 lb 2 oz) of the grapes on one sheet of dough and sprinkle half the remaining aniseed/sugar mixture over. Lay the other sheet of dough on top and scatter with the remaining muscatels and aniseed/sugar mixture, pressing them into the dough using your fingertips. Bake for 15–20 minutes. Cool before serving.

SERVES 6 · WINE: Vin Santo

ANISE OR **ANISEED** IS USED THROUGHOUT ITALIAN CUISINE IN MOST REGIONS. THE PLANT HAS ACCLIMATISED ON THE ITALIAN PENINSULA TO THE POINT WHERE IT GROWS WILD LIKE A WEED. IT'S THE SEEDS THAT CONTAIN THE RICHLY AROMATIC OILS WITH THE FLAVOUR ESSENCES. PERHAPS BEST KNOWN FOR PRODUCING THE POPULAR SAMBUCA LIQUEUR, ANISEED IS USED IN MANY OTHER REGIONAL DISTILLATES AS WELL AS BISCUITS, PASTRIES AND BREADS, ESPECIALLY FOCACCIA.

RICE FRITTERS WITH VANILLA CREAM
FRITTELLE DI RISO, CREMA ALLA VANIGLIA

This traditional recipe is from Gabriele Taddeucci from Lucca.

INGREDIENTS

500 g (1 lb 2 oz) Italian rice
(vialone nano or carnaroli)

1 litre (35 fl oz) milk

60 g (2¼ oz) unsalted butter

grated zest of 1 lemon

1 vanilla bean, split

2 cups (300 g/10½ oz) plain
(all-purpose) flour

200 g (7 oz) caster (superfine)
sugar

5 eggs, whisked

1 teaspoon bicarbonate of
soda (baking soda)

50 ml (1¾ fl oz) rum

VANILLA CREAM

3 eggs, separated

100 g (3½ oz) caster
(superfine) sugar

300 g (10½ oz) mascarpone
cheese

seeds from 1 vanilla bean

CINNAMON SUGAR

1 teaspoon ground cinnamon

⅔ cup (150 g/5½ oz) caster
(superfine) sugar

METHOD

Put the rice in a saucepan with the milk, butter, lemon zest and
vanilla bean and cook until soft (between 20-25 minutes depending
on the rice). Cool down mixture, remove the vanilla bean and add the
flour, sugar, eggs, bicarbonate soda and rum and mix until smooth.
Refrigerate for at least 4 hours.

To make the vanilla cream, whisk the egg whites with the sugar until
firm peaks form. Whisk the egg yolks and fold into the meringue
with the mascarpone and vanilla seeds. This will make about 2 cups
of vanilla cream. When you are ready to cook the fritters, make the
cinnamon sugar by combining the ingredients. Drop teaspoonfuls of the
rice dough in hot oil and cook until golden brown. Roll in the cinnamon
sugar and serve 4–5 fritters per diner with the vanilla cream.

MAKES about 60   **WINE:** Vin Santo

TRADITIONAL SWEET HERB TART FROM LUCCA
TORTA D'ERBI LUCCHESE

The Tuscan bread called for here is peculiar to that region, where no salt is included in the dough. This dish is usually made with assorted wild leaves but also, as here, with cavolo nero (Tuscan kale), or nettles or dandelion. Spinach can be substituted.

INGREDIENTS

1 quantity shortcrust pastry (see page 47)

150 g (5½ oz) Tuscan bread or white country-style bread, crusts removed and torn into pieces

200 ml (7 fl oz) milk

80 g (2¾ oz) raisins

1 tablespoon Alchermes liqueur

leaves from 180 g (6½ oz) cavolo nero (Tuscan kale)

2 eggs

⅔ cup (150 g/5½ oz) caster (superfine) sugar

¼ cup (40 g/1½ oz) unsalted peanuts, chopped

1 tablespoon pine nuts, toasted

½ teaspoon grated nutmeg

½ teaspoon ground cinnamon

20 g (¾ oz) unsalted butter, cubed

METHOD

Choose a 28 cm (11¼ in) tart tin with 4 cm (1½ in) high sides and a removable base. Roll out the pastry to fit the tin with an 'overhang' of 3–4 cm (1¼–1½ in), then line the tin and refrigerate it. Soak the bread in the milk and soak the raisins in the Alchermes liqueur. Preheat the oven to 170°C (340°F). Meanwhile, bring a large saucepan of water to the boil and plunge in the cavolo nero. Once the water comes back to the boil, cook the cavolo nero for 5–6 minutes until soft. Drain, let cool and squeeze out as much water as possible, then chop finely. In a large bowl, whisk the eggs and sugar together. Squeeze a little of the milk out of the bread, then add the bread to the bowl along with the raisins, cavolo nero, peanuts, pine nuts, nutmeg and cinnamon. Mix everything together by hand, then pour the filling into the tart case, spreading it evenly. Scatter the diced butter over and fold the pastry overhang onto the tart. Bake for 30–35 minutes until golden. Serve at room temperature.

MAKES 8   WINE: Moscadello di Montalcino

CHESTNUT CREPES FILLED WITH SWEET RICOTTA
NECCI

This dish is from the family of Balla head chef Gabriele Taddeucci. Necci are native to north-western Tuscany. This is the simple version, but they can be enhanced with pieces of roast chestnut or some chopped dark or milk chocolate mixed through the ricotta filling.

INGREDIENTS

2 eggs

200 g (7 oz) chestnut flour, sifted

30 ml (1 fl oz) extra virgin olive oil

300 g (10½ oz) ricotta cheese

1 level tablespoon icing (confectioners') sugar

60 g (2¼ oz) brown sugar

METHOD

Beat the eggs in the bowl of an electric mixer, then add the flour and a pinch of salt and keep beating until there are no lumps left. Beat in the olive oil. Slowly add 450 ml (16 fl oz) water in a stream and keep mixing until you have a smooth, runny batter. Put in the refrigerator to rest for at least 1 hour. Combine the ricotta and icing sugar and refrigerate until needed. Heat a 22–25 cm (8½–10 in) non-stick frying pan – there is no need to add oil or butter if the pan is non-stick. Ladle batter into the hot pan and once it starts to bubble through, flip the crepe gently to cook the other side. Repeat until all the batter has been used. If you are not serving the crepes immediately, they can be refrigerated for a couple of days and reheated in the microwave. To serve, cut each crepe in half, put a couple of spoonfuls of ricotta mixture on each half and roll up to a cone shape. Serve sprinkled with the brown sugar.

SERVES 8–10   **WINE:** Vin Santo

BAKED COFFEE CREAM
CAFFÈ IN FORCHETTA

INGREDIENTS

5 eggs

3 egg yolks

320 g (11¼ oz) caster (superfine) sugar

1 litre (35 fl oz) milk

1 cup (250 ml/9 fl oz) espresso

1 tablespoon brown sugar

1 teaspoon very finely ground coffee beans

METHOD

Preheat the oven to 90°C (195°F). Beat the eggs, egg yolks and caster sugar together until pale and creamy. Heat the milk and espresso together until almost boiling, then whisk into the egg/sugar mixture until well incorporated. Pour into 6 individual moulds (150 ml/5 fl oz) and put the moulds in a baking dish. Carefully pour in hot water to come up to the liquid level in the moulds, then bake for 35 minutes until a crust forms. Cool. Combine the panela sugar and ground coffee and sprinkle on top of each baked cream. Serve in the moulds just warm or at room temperature.

MAKES 6   **WINE:** Moscato di Pantelleria Passito

CHESTNUT CREPES FILLED WITH SWEET RICOTTA

RICOTTA, MASCARPONE AND CHOCOLATE DOME
ZUCCOTTO

The amarena cherries used here are imported from Italy and can be bought at good providores.

INGREDIENTS

⅓ cup (80 ml/2½ fl oz) marsala

100 ml (3½ fl oz) sugar syrup (see page 163)

cherries preserved in syrup (amarena or maraschino), to serve

CITRUS SPONGE

6 eggs, separated

1 cup (220 g/7¾ oz) caster (superfine) sugar

80 g (2¾ oz) plain (all-purpose) flour, sifted

grated zest of 1 lemon

MASCARPONE FILLING

250 ml (9 fl oz) thin (pouring) cream

100 g (3½ oz) icing (confectioners') sugar

250 g (9 oz) mascarpone cheese

50 g (1¾ oz) cherries preserved in syrup (amarena or maraschino), chopped

40 g (1½ oz) pistachio kernels, chopped

100 g (3½ oz) dark chocolate, chopped

RICOTTA FILLING

300 ml (10½ fl oz) thin (pouring) cream

100 g (3½ oz) icing (confectioners') sugar

300 g (10½ oz) ricotta cheese

¼ cup (40 g/1½ oz) blanched almonds, chopped

50 g (1¾ oz) mixed peel

50 g (1¾ oz) cedro (preserved citron), diced

COCOA SPONGE

400 g (10½ oz) eggs (approximately 8 eggs)

200 g (7 oz) caster sugar

80 g (2¾ oz) plain (all-purpose) flour

½ cup (60 g/2¼ oz) cornflour (cornstarch)

60 g (2¼ oz) unsweetened cocoa powder

METHOD

To make the citrus sponge, preheat the oven to 180°C (350°F). Cream the egg yolks and ⅓ cup (75 g/2¾ oz) of the sugar until thick and fluffy. Whisk the egg whites and remaining sugar until they form soft peaks. Fold the two mixtures and the flour together with the lemon zest. Spread onto two 30 cm × 40 cm (12 in × 16 in) baking trays lined with baking paper and bake until golden brown (8–10 minutes).

To make the cocoa sponge, preheat the oven to 180°C (350°F). Beat the eggs with the sugar until pale and forming a ribbon. Sift the flour, cornflour and cocoa together, then slowly sprinkle into the egg mixture and mix. Spread on a 30 cm × 40 cm (12 in × 16 in) baking tray lined with baking paper and bake until golden brown (8–10 minutes).

To make the mascarpone filling, whip the cream and icing sugar together to form soft peaks. Fold into the mascarpone, then mix in the cherries, pistachios and chocolate until well incorporated. To make the ricotta filling, whip the cream and icing sugar together to form soft peaks. Fold into the ricotta, then mix in the almonds, mixed peel and cedro until well incorporated.

Choose a stainless steel or ceramic round dome mould about 24 cm (9½ in) in diameter and line it with plastic wrap. Cut one of the citrus sponge sheets into three rounds 10 cm (4 in), 14 cm (5½ in) and 22 cm (8½ in) in diameter. Cut the other citrus and cocoa sponge sheets into triangles to fit around the sides of the mould. Combine the marsala and sugar syrup. Lay the 10 cm round sponge at the base of the mould

>>

and brush well with marsala syrup. Line the sides of the dome with alternating cocoa and citrus sponge triangles, then brush well with marsala syrup. Pipe the mascarpone filling into the mould to come about halfway up. Lay the 14 cm round sponge on the mascarpone filling and press gently. Brush well with marsala syrup, then spoon in the ricotta mixture. Cover with the 22 cm round piece of sponge, brushing it well with marsala syrup. Wrap the zuccotto in plastic wrap and leave in the fridge overnight. To serve, cut into small wedges and spoon over some cherries and their syrup.

SERVES 12–16   WINE Vino Santo

ESPRESSO AND HAZELNUT CAKE
TORTA AL CAFFE E NOCCIOLE

INGREDIENTS

200 g (7 oz) self-raising flour, plus extra for dusting

1 heaped teaspoon baking powder

180 g (6½ oz) softened unsalted butter, plus extra for greasing

200 g (7 oz) caster (superfine) sugar

4 eggs, separated

½ cup (125 ml/4 fl oz) espresso

100 g (3½ oz) hazelnut meal

1 teaspoon natural vanilla extract

⅓ cup (50 g/1¾ oz) hazelnuts, roasted, skinned and chopped

ESPRESSO CREAM

200 g (7 oz) caster (superfine) sugar

10 egg yolks

1 litre (35 fl oz) thin (pouring) cream

1 teaspoon natural vanilla extract

100 ml (3½ fl oz) espresso

2 tablespoons Cognac or brandy (optional)

METHOD

Preheat the oven to 180°C (350°F). Grease a 23 cm (9 in) ring tin with butter and dust with flour. Sift the flour and baking powder into a bowl. In another bowl, beat together the butter and sugar. In another small bowl, whisk together the egg yolks and a pinch of salt. Slowly add the egg yolks to the butter and sugar, mixing until well incorporated. Mix in the flour and baking powder, then add the espresso, hazelnut meal and vanilla. Whisk the egg whites until they form firm peaks and fold into the mixture. Pour the mixture into the mould and sprinkle the hazelnuts on top. Bake for 45 minutes. Let cool in the tin for 5 minutes before turning out onto a wire rack. Serve cold with the espresso cream.

To make the espresso cream, whisk the sugar and egg yolks until pale and forming a ribbon. Heat the cream almost to the boil, then whisk it into the egg mixture. Add the vanilla and espresso and return the mixture to a low–medium heat. Stir continuously with a wooden spoon until the custard thickens and coats the back of the spoon (a line made with your finger across the face of the spoon will remain). Transfer to a bowl and cool to room temperature. Add the Cognac, if using. Makes about 1.5 litres (2½ pints).

SERVES 8–10   WINE: Aleatico Passito

TRENTINO-ALTO ADIGE

TRENTINO-ALTO ADIGE

BORDERED BY AUSTRIA TO THE NORTH, SWITZERLAND TO THE NORTH-WEST AND LOMBARDIA AND VENETO TO THE WEST AND SOUTH RESPECTIVELY, THIS IS THE NORTHERNMOST REGION OF ITALY. ITS TWO PROVINCES, TRENTINO AND ALTO ADIGE (THE LATTER IS ALSO KNOWN AS SÜDTIROL, OR SOUTH TYROL) COVER ALMOST 14,000 SQUARE KILOMETRES (5400 SQUARE MILES), INCLUDING A LARGE PART OF THE DOLOMITES AND SOUTHERN ALPS.

The 6000 square kilometres (2300 square miles) of Trentino are mostly mountainous, with half of the territory covered in forest; it also contains the large and beautiful Lake Garda. The 7400 square kilometres (2857 square miles) of Südtirol are dominated to the north by the high Alps, with many of the mountains over 3000 metres (9840 feet). Although it can be hot in July and August – really hot in Trento (the capital of Trentino) and Balzano (capital of Alto Adige) – the climate the rest of the year is best described as icy. The biggest and most-anticipated festival is the one that marks the end of winter.

It is the cold climate that informs the cuisine. While Trentino is more Italian, with white and yellow bread, and Alto Adige is more Austrian, with black bread, both cuisines are more akin to their Austrian neighbour, but often with an Italian twist.

In the north of Alto Adige, in the valleys of the river Adige, rye for the black bread is grown, as are, some distance away, maize and wheat. To the south, maize is the most important crop. From these cereals, breads such as schüttelbrot ('shaken-up bread', so called because of the violence of its kneading), which is made from a mixture of wheat and barley, and the Tralendal of eastern Alto Adige are made. In the Benedictine abbey of Monte Maria (Marienberg) in Burgusio in Trentino, a family loaf is made that is shaped like a figure eight, of which each spouse is supposed to eat half; for widows and widowers there is a ring loaf.

On the menu in Alto Adige are dishes such as gnocchi tirolesi di magro and canederli tirolesi (canederli being an Italianisation of knödel, which can also be

Italianised as gnocchi and re-translated into German as Nocken).

As is the case with the province's northern neighbour, pork is the dominant protein. The most beloved preparation is speck; being made with Italian thoroughness, the meat is smoked for three hours a day for up to three months. The speck of the Val Passiria (Passeier Valley) is the northern equivalent of the Parma prosciutto from Langhirano.

Hearty soups are the hallmark of cold mountainous regions, and Alto Adige is no exception. Einbrennsuppe is a gruel made by first cooking flour in butter, then thinning it with hot water and wine and filling it with boiled potatoes. Use tripe instead of potatoes and vinegar in place of the wine, and it's sauersuppe.

A curious hangover from the Council of Trent (Trento), established in 1545 to stop the spread of Lutheranism, is a preponderance of meatless dishes in the local cuisine. The gathering priests and prelates loved their food, but there were many meat-free fasting days and so much of the food was cereal based, including the irreligiously named dumpling strangolapreti, or 'priest strangler'.

The invasion of priests and the proximity to Austria also explain the profusion of pastries, including some of the best strudels either side of the Alps. You'll also find delicacies such as presnitz, a marzipan with chopped walnuts, almonds and hazelnuts, and kastanientorte (chestnut tart) and erdbeertorte (strawberry tart), both of which utilise local products.

Proximity to Austria and Germany (Alto Adige only became part of Italy in 1919) means that wines here, especially whites, have much more in common with those countries than with the wines of the rest of Italy. The important wines, underappreciated outside the region, are crisp and aromatic and made from such Teutonic grapes as gerwürztraminer, Müller-Thurgau, sylvaner and riesling.

Among the mainstays of the region are the sparkling wines of Trentino, which, in spite of being made in large quantities, are made using the méthode champenoise (metodo classico) and the traditional champagne grapes, pinot noir and chardonnay. Those from smaller producers can be of a very high quality indeed.

The Trentino DOC covers 19 varietals, 10 of which are whites. Of these, the high-altitude sauvignon is well favoured. The highest-altitude grape is the Müller-Thurgau, which thrives and produces excellent wine from 500 metres (1640 feet). A local grape, nosiola, which grows mainly north of Lake Garda, is also made in limited quantities into a vin santo.

Surprisingly, more reds than whites are grown in Trentino-Alto Aldige/Südtirol, with about half the vineyards in Alto Adige planted to schiava; in Trentino, half the schiava is mixed with the lambrusco grape to make mass-market, slightly sparkling lambrusco wines. In recent years, less lambrusco and more pinot nero (pinot noir), merlot, cabernet sauvignon and cabernet franc have been made.

TRENTINO-ALTO ADIGE
ANTI-PASTI

ROAST BEETROOT, CELERIAC AND FENNEL WINTER SALAD
INSALATA INVERNALE DI BARBABIETOLE, SEDANO RAPA E FINOCCHIO AL FORNO

INGREDIENTS

- 750 g (1 lb 10 oz) small–medium golden beetroots (beets), trimmed but unpeeled
- 750 g (1 lb 10 oz) small–medium red beetroots (beets), trimmed but unpeeled
- 200 ml (7 fl oz) extra virgin olive oil
- 1 large celeriac, peeled and cut into 8–10 wedges
- 1 large fennel bulb, cut lengthways into 3 mm (⅛ in) thick slices
- 3 cups curly endive, well washed and dried
- 1 tablespoon red wine vinegar

METHOD

Preheat the oven to 180°C (350°F). Put the beetroots in a baking dish and add 2–3 tablespoons of the olive oil. Season and mix well, then roast for 15–25 minutes until tender. Let cool to room temperature. Leave the oven on. Halve the celeriac wedges. Heat 2 tablespoons of the remaining oil in an ovenproof frying pan and gently fry the celeriac for a minute on each side. Season with salt, then roast for 15 minutes until soft. Let cool to room temperature. Reserve 2 tablespoons of the remaining oil and heat the rest in a frying pan until just smoking. Fry the fennel on both sides until golden, then drain on paper towels. Combine the beetroots, celeriac and fennel in a large bowl and dress with the vinegar and remaining olive oil. Season and serve.

SERVES 4-6   WINE: Riesling

BRAISED FENNEL WITH GORGONZOLA AND HAZELNUTS
FINOCCHIO AL GORGONZOLA

INGREDIENTS

- ½ cup (125 ml/4 fl oz) extra virgin olive oil
- 1 garlic clove, peeled and halved lengthways
- 4 large fennel bulbs, trimmed (light-green fronds reserved) and cut lengthways into 5 mm (¼ in) slices
- 150 g (5½ oz) gorgonzola cheese, broken into small pieces
- ½ cup (70 g/2½ oz) toasted hazelnuts

METHOD

Heat half the olive oil in a wide frying pan and gently fry the garlic, moving it around until starting to colour all over. Remove and discard the garlic, then add the fennel and fry lightly for 10 minutes, moving the slices around carefully. Add 1 cup (250 ml/9 fl oz) water and a couple of good pinches of salt, cover tightly and cook on low heat for 15–20 minutes until the fennel is tender. Transfer the fennel to serving plates, then season with a little more salt (if needed) and some freshly cracked pepper and dress with the remaining olive oil. Scatter the gorgonzola, hazelnuts and fennel fronds on top to serve.

SERVES 8   WINE: Gewürztraminer

ROAST ROOT VEGETABLES WITH HORSERADISH DRESSING
VERDURA ARROSTITA CON SALSA DI RAFANO

Serve these vegetables as a first course or as a side dish for roast meats or fish. The dressing will keep perfectly well in the refrigerator for a couple of weeks but is at its most potent just after it is made.

INGREDIENTS

1 large celeriac

2 large carrots

2 large potatoes

4 medium–large parsnips

½ cup sage leaves

1 cup (250 ml/9 fl oz) extra virgin olive oil

8 cm (3¼ in) piece horseradish root, peeled and finely grated

2 tablespoons white wine vinegar

METHOD

Preheat the oven to 180°C (350°F). Peel the celeriac, carrots, potatoes and parsnips and cut them into 3–4 cm (1¼–1½ in) cubes. Put the vegetables in a roasting tin and toss with the sage and one-third of the olive oil. Season and roast for 30–40 minutes until golden and tender. Meanwhile, combine the horseradish, vinegar and remaining olive oil. Season and mix well. Put the roast vegetables on serving plates and dress with the horseradish mixture.

SERVES 6–8   WINE: Kerner

TRENTO-STYLE GRILLED HERRINGS
AGONI ALLA GRIGLIA

Herrings of one sort or another are found throughout the world. Agoni, a small fish found in the lower and upper alpine lakes that stretch across the north of Italy, are a type of freshwater herring much prized for their flavour. Often they are fried and doused with a flavoured vinegar solution, but another good way to prepare them is simply to barbecue them over a fire, as in this dish. Any small fish (10–15 cm/4–6 in) can be cooked in this way. The moderating effect of the large lakes on local temperatures allows olives and lemons to grow successfully around their shores.

INGREDIENTS

1 kg (2 lb 4 oz) agoni or other small fish, scaled and gutted

1 cup olive leaves

juice of 2 lemons

METHOD

Put 2–3 olive leaves in the stomach cavity of each fish. Once all the flame is gone from the fire and only the hot coals are left, put the fish on a wire grill and cook for about 15 minutes on each side, then sprinkle with salt and the lemon juice. Serve immediately.

SERVES 8   WINE: Sylvaner

ROAST ROOT VEGETABLES WITH HORSERADISH DRESSING

BUCKWHEAT AND SAUSAGE PIE
SMACAFAM

This dish has such a great name in the local Trento dialect: smacafam literally means 'hunger buster'! There are many different versions, all of which are baked. The sausage used is a luganega trentina – a kind of fermented salami that has been aged for about a month and a half. It is soft, fresh and very tasty. If fresh salami is not available, use good pork sausages.

INGREDIENTS

1 litre (35 fl oz) beef broth (see page 48)

300 g (10½ oz) luganega trentina sausage, thinly sliced

500 g (1 lb 2 oz) buckwheat flour

40 g (1½ oz) lardo, diced

80 g (2¾ oz) Grana Padano, grated

80 g (2¾ oz) butter

METHOD

Pour the beef broth into a saucepan and heat gently until just warm. Set aside 6 slices of the luganega. Transfer the broth to a large bowl and slowly add the flour, continually mixing until blended and creamy. Preheat the oven to 160°C (320°F). Heat the lardo in a wide frying pan, then add the remaining luganega and fry gently until golden, turning once. Remove from the heat and let cool. Mix the fried luganega and any pan juices into the buckwheat mixture, along with the cheese. Season. Use half the butter to grease a 24 cm (9½ in) round baking dish that will hold the mixture but not be too full. Pour in the luganega mixture and arrange the reserved slices of luganega on top. Scatter with knobs of the remaining butter and bake for 50 minutes–1 hour until golden. Slice and serve hot.

SERVES 8   WINE: Pinot nero

TRENTINO-ALTO ADIGE
PRIMI

WINE SOUP
ZUPPA AL VINO

This is a traditional soup from the Austrian heritage of Alto Adige that is great in cold weather – it's easy to make and hearty to eat. Use an aromatic white wine both to make the soup and to accompany it. Don't worry about the alcohol in the wine: it will all have evaporated once the soup is cooked.

INGREDIENTS

6 egg yolks

1 teaspoon cornflour (cornstarch)

pinch of ground cinnamon

600 ml (21 fl oz) aromatic white wine (such as riesling or traminer)

¾ cup (180 ml/6 fl oz) thin (pouring) cream

600 ml (21 fl oz) beef or chicken broth (see page 48)

50 g (1¾ oz) unsalted butter

6 thick slices bread

METHOD

Whisk the egg yolks, cornflour, cinnamon, wine and ½ cup (125 ml/4 fl oz) of the cream until well incorporated. Bring the broth to the boil in a large saucepan, then turn down to a low simmer and slowly add the wine mixture, stirring continuously. Keep stirring until thick and creamy. Whip the remaining cream to soft peaks and stir into the soup. Season. Heat the butter in a wide frying pan and fry the bread on both sides until golden brown. Put a slice of bread in each bowl and ladle the soup on top.

SERVES 6   WINE: Riesling

TURNIP GNOCCHI
GNOCCHI DI RAPE

These are known as canederli and are related to the Austrian knödel, a type of gnocchi.

INGREDIENTS

300 g (10½ oz) turnips, peeled

2 tablespoons unsalted butter

1 French shallot, thinly sliced

1 garlic clove, thinly sliced

4 sage leave, picked

½ teaspoon cumin seeds

200 g (7 oz) two-day-old bread, crusts removed, diced

2 eggs, whisked

50 g (1¾ oz) ricotta cheese

50 g (1¾ oz) parmesan cheese, grated, plus extra for serving

METHOD

Boil the turnips in plenty of salted water until tender (until a point of a knife pierces the skin easily). Drain and let cool a little, then chop and puree in a food processor. Transfer to a tea towel (dish towel) and squeeze out as much water as possible. Heat the butter in a frying pan and lightly fry the shallot, garlic, sage and cumin seeds for a minute or so. Let cool, then combine with the bread, eggs, ricotta and parmesan. Add the pureed turnips, season with salt and let rest for at least 30 minutes. Form the mixture into balls 4–5 cm (1½–2 in) in diameter and cook in boiling salted water as you would gnocchi. They are ready when they rise to the surface. Serve with burnt butter (see page 331) and parmesan.

SERVES 4–6   WINE: Grüner Veltliner or sylvaner

BREAD DUMPLINGS
CANEDERLI

These dumplings are similar to gnocchi in that they are poached and can be served with burnt butter (butter heated in a small saucepan on high heat until it is nut brown) and grated Grana Padano. They can also be served as a soup, as here – poached in a flavoursome beef or chicken broth and dusted with grated Grana. Yet another way is to poach and serve them with a cheese fondue

INGREDIENTS

500 g (1 lb 2 oz) dried bread,
  crusts removed, cut into
  2 cm (¾ in) cubes

150 ml (5 fl oz) milk

150 g (5½ oz) softened
  unsalted butter

120 g (4¼ oz) plain
  (all-purpose) flour

3 eggs, lightly whisked

2 tablespoons finely chopped
  parsley

3 tablespoons finely snipped
  chives

½ teaspoon grated nutmeg

3 tablespoons grated Grana
  Padano, plus extra for
  serving

1.5 litres (52 fl oz) beef
  or chicken broth
  (see page 48)

METHOD

Put the bread and any crumbs in a large bowl. Heat the milk to warm and pour over the bread, then let soak for 30 minutes. Add the butter and flour to the bread and use your hands to mix until incorporated. Add the eggs, parsley, chives, nutmeg and Grana Padano, then season with salt and mix well. Moisten your hands with water and roll a dumpling 4–5 cm (1½–2 in) in diameter. Bring the broth to the boil in a saucepan and drop in the dumpling. Once the broth comes back to the boil, turn the heat down to a simmer and poach the dumpling for 7–8 minutes. Remove using a slotted spoon and taste for seasoning and firmness. Add more salt to the remaining mixture if needed. If the dumpling is too soft, add more flour to the mixture; if it is too hard, add a little more milk. Shape the remaining mixture into dumplings and poach in the broth. Serve immediately with grated Grana Padano.

SERVES 6   WINE: Lagrein

SCRAMBLED EGGS WITH SALMON ROE
VOVA STRAPAZZATE CON UOVA DI SALMONE

INGREDIENTS

8 eggs

2 tablespoons thin (pouring)
  cream

50 g (1¾ oz) unsalted butter

4 slices country-style bread

4 tablespoons salmon roe

1 tablespoon finely snipped
  chives

METHOD

Crack the eggs into a bowl, add the cream and season lightly. Whisk using a fork. Melt the butter in a non-stick frying pan on low heat. Add the egg mixture and stir until firm and creamy. Grill (broil) the bread and put on 4 plates. Spoon on the scrambled eggs, scatter the salmon roe on top and sprinkle with the chives.

SERVES 4   WINE: Gewürztraminer

SPAGHETTINI WITH HOT-SMOKED SALMON AND VEGETABLES
SPAGHETTINI CON SALSA DI SALMONE AFFUMICATO

This dish calls for hot-smoked salmon, but you could also use hot-smoked river trout, kingfish or mackerel. It is also good with smoked mussels or oysters.

INGREDIENTS

- ⅓ cup (80 ml/2½ fl oz) extra virgin olive oil
- 2 zucchini (courgettes), cut into fine matchsticks
- 1 carrot, cut into fine matchsticks
- 1 small leek, white part only, cut into fine matchsticks
- 12 cherry tomatoes, halved
- ¼ cup (60 ml/2 fl oz) dry white wine
- 150 g (5½ oz) hot-smoked salmon, torn into bite-sized pieces
- ½ cup chopped parsley
- 500 g (1 lb 2 oz) dried spaghettini

METHOD

Heat the olive oil in a frying pan and lightly fry the zucchini, carrot and leek for 2 minutes until soft. Add the tomatoes and wine and simmer for 2 minutes, then add the salmon and parsley, season and stir well. Turn off the heat. Cook the spaghettini in plenty of boiling salted water until al dente, then drain and toss with the salmon and vegetable sauce. Serve immediately.

SERVES 6   WINE: Trento Brut Riserva

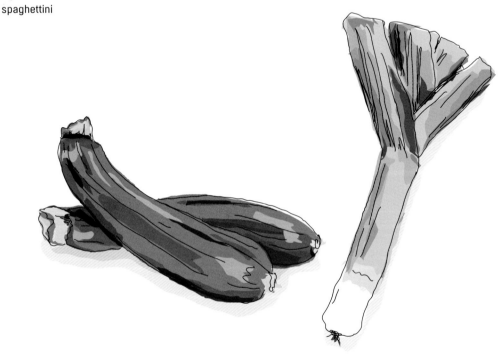

SPAGHETTINI WITH HOT-SMOKED SALMON AND VEGETABLES

RISOTTO-STYLE BARLEY WITH PORCINI MUSHROOMS
ORZOTTO AI FUNGHI PORCINI

INGREDIENTS

2 litres (70 fl oz) chicken broth (see page 518)

100 g (3½ oz) unsalted butter

1 brown onion, minced

1 garlic clove, minced

1 cup (200 g/7 oz) pearled barley, washed and drained

100 ml (3½ fl oz) dry white wine

200 g (7 oz) fresh porcini mushrooms, sliced (or 30 g/1 oz dried porcini mushrooms, soaked in cold water and drained)

100 g (3½ oz) Grana Padano, grated

METHOD

Pour the chicken broth into a saucepan and bring to the boil, then turn the heat down to a simmer. Heat half the butter in a separate saucepan and lightly fry the onion and garlic for 30 seconds. Add the barley and stir for a minute, then add the wine and let it evaporate. Ladle in enough hot broth to cover the barley, then stir in the porcini and a couple of good pinches of salt. As each quantity of broth is absorbed, add more. Keep simmering and adding broth for 30–35 minutes until the barley is al dente. Remove from the heat and vigorously stir in the remaining butter and the Grana Padano. Season and serve immediately.

SERVES 4   WINE: Lagrein

TRENTINO-ALTO ADIGE
SECONDI

POACHED SALMON WITH VEGETABLES AND SALMON ROE
SALMONE IN CAMICIA

Make sure the salmon you use here has been cut from the centre of the fish and that the pieces are all the same thickness. This is important so that the portions cook equally. Ocean trout (fish and roe) can be substituted for salmon.

INGREDIENTS

8 baby carrots

1 small fennel bulb, cut into 8 wedges

4 spring onions (scallions), trimmed and kept whole

2 radishes, quartered

4 baby turnips, halved

1 litre (35 fl oz) fish stock

4 × 160 g (5¾ oz) pieces salmon (see recipe introduction), skin and bones removed

⅓ cup (80 ml/2½ fl oz) extra virgin olive oil

2 tablespoons finely chopped parsley

2 tablespoons salmon roe

METHOD

Put the carrots, fennel, spring onions, radishes and turnips in a saucepan of salted water and bring to the boil. Turn the heat down and simmer until tender, then drain, season, mix and keep warm. Wipe out the saucepan and pour in the fish stock (the saucepan needs to be wide enough to fit the salmon without the pieces touching each other). Bring to the boil and gently add the fish. Bring back to the boil, then turn the heat down and simmer for 2 minutes. Drain and put the salmon on 4 serving plates. Distribute the vegetables evenly among the plates, then combine the olive oil and parsley and drizzle over the fish. Spoon on the salmon roe and serve.

SERVES 4   WINE: Kerner

TROUT TRENTINO STYLE
TROTE ALLA TRENTINA

Freshwater fish abound in the alpine lakes and rivers of Trento and Alto Adige. This is a simple way to prepare trout and is a perfect summer dish when accompanied by a fresh salad.

INGREDIENTS

⅔ cup (120 g/4¼ oz) sultanas (golden raisins)

6 × 160 g (5¾ oz) whole trout, trimmed

60 g (2¼ oz) plain (all-purpose) flour

¾ cup (180 ml/6 fl oz) extra virgin olive oil, plus extra for drizzling

1 rosemary sprig

1 sage sprig

2 garlic cloves, thinly sliced

1 cup parsley leaves

1 brown onion, thinly sliced

¼ cup mint leaves

400 ml (14 fl oz) white wine vinegar

grated zest of 2 lemons

grated zest of 1 orange

lemon wedges

METHOD

Soak the sultanas in warm water for 10 minutes, then drain, pat dry and set aside. Using scissors, cut the trout fins and tails, then wash the trout well (including in the cavity) and dry thoroughly. Using a sharp knife, make 4–5 cuts parallel to the head along each side (this will help the fish to cook quickly), then dust the fish with the flour. Heat ⅓ cup (80 ml/2½ fl oz) of the olive oil in a frying pan that will fit the fish snugly in a single layer. Once the oil is hot, add the rosemary, sage and trout and cook on medium heat for 2–3 minutes on each side, taking care that the skin doesn't burn (turn the heat down if it looks like burning). Transfer the fish to a terracotta or stainless steel container that is large enough to hold it in a single layer. Set aside. Finely chop the garlic and parsley together. Put the remaining oil in a saucepan on medium heat and lightly fry the onion until it begins to colour. Add the parsley and garlic, mint, vinegar, lemon and orange zest and sultanas. Bring to the boil, then turn the heat down and simmer for 5 minutes. Pour over the trout, cover and let cool. Once cooled, refrigerate for 24 hours. When you are ready to serve, drain the trout and put on plates. Drizzle with a little oil, season and serve with lemon wedges.

SERVES 6 WINE: Gewürztraminer

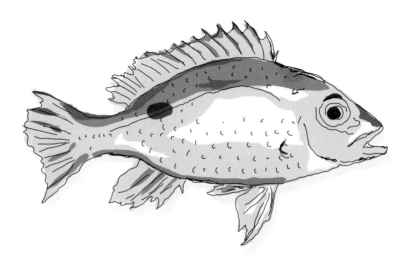

CHICKEN STUFFED WITH WALNUTS
POLLO RIPIENO ALLE NOCI

This recipe requires the chicken to be boned out. To do this, begin at the cavity end and separate the breast meat from the carcass, working toward the head. You want to leave the breast meat and skin as intact as possible. What remains is a boneless pouch to stuff. This does require some skill, but perhaps if you ask your butcher nicely ...

INGREDIENTS

4 cups chopped bread, crusts removed

100 ml (3½ fl oz) milk

40 g (1½ oz) walnut pieces

¼ cup (40 g/1½ oz) pine nuts

150 g (5½ oz) bone marrow, chopped

100 g (3½ oz) chicken livers, chopped

100 g (3½ oz) Grana Padano, grated

pinch of grated nutmeg

1 × 1.6 kg (3 lb 8 oz) chicken, boned (see recipe introduction)

METHOD

Soak the bread in the milk. Put the walnuts and pine nuts in a mortar with a couple of pinches of salt and pound to a paste. Transfer to a bowl and add the bone marrow and chicken livers. Squeeze any excess milk from the bread and add the bread to the bowl along with the cheese and nutmeg. Season, then use your hands to mix everything together. Stuff the chicken with the mixture, then sew the opening tightly with thick cotton and truss the legs. Put in a large saucepan and pour in water to cover by at least 5 cm (2 in). Bring to the boil, then immediately turn the heat down and simmer for about 1 hour, skimming the surface of any impurities. Serve hot or let the chicken cool in its cooking liquid and serve at room temperature, moistened with a little cooking liquid. (Reserve the cooking liquid, season and serve as a soup with grated parmesan.)

SERVES 4   WINE: Pinot Nero

DUCK LEGS BRAISED IN RED WINE
COSCE D'ANATRA AL VINO ROSSO

INGREDIENTS

8 duck legs, trimmed

⅓ cup (80 ml/2½ fl oz) extra virgin olive oil

1 brown onion, diced

4 rosemary sprigs

2 cups (500 ml/17 fl oz) red wine

2 cups (500 ml/17 fl oz) duck or chicken stock

METHOD

Preheat the oven to 170°C (340°F). Salt the skin of the duck legs and put them in a large frying pan on medium heat, skin side down. As the duck legs start to brown, turn the heat to low. Cook for 10–15 minutes, then transfer to a baking dish, skin side up. Discard the fat and wipe out the pan. Heat the olive oil in the pan and add the onion and rosemary. Stir and fry lightly for 2–3 minutes, then pour in the wine and stock and bring to the boil. Pour enough boiling liquid into the baking dish to leave the duck skin exposed, then bake for about 1 hour 15 minutes until the skin is crisp and the flesh is tender. Can be served with polenta (see page 41).

SERVES 4   WINE: Pinot Nero

ROAST GUINEA FOWL WITH PORCINI MUSHROOMS
FARAONA ARROSTO CON PORCINI

INGREDIENTS

3 guinea fowl

½ cup (125 ml/4 fl oz) extra
    virgin olive oil

6 fresh porcini mushrooms
    (or portobello mushrooms)

1 cup parsley leaves

2 garlic cloves

¼ cup (60 ml/2 fl oz) white
    wine

juice of ½ lemon

METHOD

Preheat the oven to 220°C (430°F). To prepare the guinea fowl, trim off the wings at the first joint, then rub the birds with half the olive oil and season the skin with a little salt. Put the guinea fowl in a roasting tin and add the porcini, sponge side up. Finely chop the parsley and garlic together, then mix with the remaining oil and spoon onto the porcini. Season. Roast for 10 minutes, then splash the wine on the guinea fowl and return the tin to oven and roast for 15 minutes. Let rest for 10 minutes in a warm place. Take the breast meat off the bone and cut the legs at the joint, then arrange on serving plates with the porcini. Sprinkle the lemon juice on the mushrooms and serve. Fennel baked with parmesan (see page 525) is an excellent accompaniment.

SERVES 6   WINE: Lagrein

KOHLRABI WITH SAUSAGE AND SPINACH
SALSICCIA CON CAVOLO RAPA E SPINACE

INGREDIENTS

¼ cup (60 ml/2 fl oz) extra
    virgin olive oil

3 kohlrabis (German turnips),
    peeled and cut into 1 cm
    (½ in) dice

600 g (1 lb 5 oz) Italian-style
    fennel and pork sausages,
    cut into 3 cm (1¼ in) pieces

½ cup (125 ml/4 fl oz) dry
    white wine

100 g (3½ oz) spinach, well
    washed and dried

METHOD

Heat 2 tablespoons of the olive oil in a large frying pan on medium heat. Add the kohlrabis and sausages and cook for 3–4 minutes, then add the wine and cook until all the liquid has evaporated. Add the remaining oil and the spinach, stir and cook for a minute or two until the spinach is tender. Season and serve.

SERVES 4   WINE: Merlot

ROAST STUFFED VEAL BREAST WITH CARROTS

ROAST STUFFED VEAL BREAST WITH CARROTS
POLPETTONE DI VITELLO

This dish needs skill in preparing the veal breast. A good butcher should be able to 'butterfly' the breast for you without leaving any holes for the stuffing to escape from.

INGREDIENTS

1 cup sage leaves

100 g (3½ oz) butter

1 brown onion, diced

4 garlic cloves, minced

2 cups breadcrumbs

100 g (3½ oz) grated
    parmesan cheese

½ cup chopped parsley

1 × 2.5–3 kg veal breast,
    butterflied (see recipe
    introduction)

⅓ cup (80 ml/2½ fl oz) extra
    virgin olive oil

2 cups (500 ml/17 fl oz) red
    wine

24 baby carrots

METHOD

Preheat the oven to 220°C (430°F) and scatter half the sage leaves in a baking dish. Melt the butter in a frying pan, then add the onion and garlic and fry lightly until soft but not burnt. Transfer to a bowl with any cooking juices and add the breadcrumbs, parmesan and parsley. Season, then mix well and let cool. Lay the veal open on your workbench. Spoon on the stuffing evenly, leaving a 3 cm (1¼ in) border. Roll up into a tight sausage and tie securely with butcher's twine. Put in the baking dish and grease the veal well with 1 tablespoon of the olive oil. Scatter the remaining sage on top of the roll, sprinkle with salt and pepper and roast for 20 minutes. Pour in the wine, cover with foil and reduce the oven temperature to 160°C (320°F). Bake for 3 hours, basting every 30 minutes or so. Remove the foil, increase the oven temperature to 220°C (430°F) and roast for 15 minutes until browned. Turn off the heat and leave the roll to rest in the oven with the door slightly ajar. Meanwhile, heat the remaining olive oil on a flat grill plate or in a chargrill pan and fry the carrots, turning, until lightly charred and soft. Season. Slice the veal and serve hot with the carrots and some of the baking juices. It is excellent cold as well.

SERVES 10–12   WINE: Lagrein

FENNEL BAKED WITH PARMESAN
FINOCCHIO AL FORNO

INGREDIENTS

½ cup (125 ml/4 fl oz) extra
    virgin olive oil

6 fennel bulbs, each cut into
    8 wedges

100 g (3½ oz) grated
    parmesan cheese

METHOD

Preheat the oven to 180°C (350°F) and brush a baking tray with the olive oil. Simmer the fennel in salted water until softened and al dente. Do not overcook. Drain and cool, then fill the folds of the fennel with the parmesan, season and put on the baking tray. Bake for 7–8 minutes until golden and serve hot.

SERVES 8 as a hot side dish   WINE: Lagrein

ROAST VENISON LOIN, PICKLED FENNEL AND BLACK OLIVE SALSA
CAPRIOLO ARROSTO CON FINOCCHIO E SALSA DI OLIVE

INGREDIENTS

- 4 × 150 g (5½ oz) pieces venison loin
- 1 large fennel bulb, halved
- ¼ cup (60 ml/2 fl oz) white wine vinegar
- 3 French shallots, diced
- 1 garlic clove, minced
- ¼ cup (60 ml/2 fl oz) extra virgin olive oil
- ½ cup good-quality black olives (preferably taggiasche or Ligurian), pitted and chopped
- 3 tablespoons chopped parsley
- 1 tablespoon good-quality balsamic vinegar

METHOD

Lightly coat the venison with freshly cracked pepper and set aside. Cut each fennel half into 6 wedges, then put in a saucepan and pour in water to cover. Add half the vinegar and bring to the boil, then turn the heat down and simmer for 15 minutes. Remove from the heat and let the fennel cool in the cooking liquid. Once cool, add the remaining vinegar. Refrigerate the pickled fennel in its liquid until you are ready to serve. Lightly fry the shallots and garlic in 2 tablespoons of the olive oil until translucent. Add the olives and fry lightly for a minute or so, then season, stir in the parsley and remove from the heat. When you are ready to serve, preheat the oven to 180°C (350°F). Heat the remaining oil in an ovenproof frying pan and sear the venison lightly on each side. Transfer to the oven for 3–4 minutes (for rare–medium rare), then remove from the oven and let rest for 5 minutes. Gently reheat the salsa and mix in the balsamic vinegar. Drain the pickled fennel, cut it into pieces and arrange on serving plates. Slice the venison and arrange on top of the fennel. Spoon the salsa over and serve.

SERVES 4   WINE: Teroldego

TRENTINO-ALTO ADIGE DOLCI

GREENGAGE AND VANILLA PRESERVE
CONFETTURA DI PRUGNE ALLA VANIGLIA

INGREDIENTS

1.2 kg (2 lb 12 oz) greengage
    plums (or other green
    or yellow plums),
    stalks removed
800 g (1 lb 12 oz) sugar
juice of 1 lemon, strained
1 vanilla bean, split

METHOD

Cut each plum in half and remove the stones. Put the plum cheeks
in a large bowl and mix well with the sugar and lemon juice, then
cover and leave for 2 hours. Tip the plums and any liquid into a large
saucepan. Bring to the boil, then turn the heat down and simmer for
5 minutes. Return carefully to the bowl, cover and refrigerate overnight.
The next day, sieve the liquid into a large saucepan and, using a candy
thermometer, bring to 105°C (220°F). Add the plums and vanilla bean
and simmer gently for 10 minutes, skimming off any impurities that form
on the surface. Transfer the hot preserve to sterilised preserving jars
and seal according to the instructions provided.

MAKES about 1.5 litres (52 fl oz)   WINE: Moscato Giallo Passito

POLENTA AND ALMOND TART
TORTA DE FREGOLOTI

*This is a version of the torta sbrisolona of neighbouring Lombardia (see page 347). It is great with either
espresso or tea, or for dessert cut into wedges and served with crema inglese (page 52).*

INGREDIENTS

1 egg
180 g (6½ oz) caster
    (superfine) sugar
225 g (8 oz) fine polenta
    (cornmeal)
1½ cups (150 g/5½ oz) almond
    meal
150 g (5½ oz) softened
    unsalted butter
30 g (1 oz) blanched almonds

METHOD

Preheat the oven to 170°C (340°F). Whisk the egg and sugar together
until pale and creamy. Add the polenta, almond meal, butter and a
pinch of salt and mix well, totally amalgamating the butter, until the
mixture resembles coarse sand. Transfer to a round, low-sided pie
dish (24 cm/9½ in). Press the almonds into the mixture and bake
for 30–35 minutes until golden and let cool to room temperature
before serving.

SERVES 6–8   WINE: Moscato Rosa

ITALIAN DOUGHNUTS
KRAPFEN

Those who have travelled and eaten in Italy often come across a dish or preparation that is similar across towns, provinces and even regions. A version of krapfen can be eaten in pastry shops, cafes and even roadhouses throughout Italy. The doughnuts are known variously as bomboloni in Tuscany and Emilia-Romagna, bombe in Lazio and graffe in Naples. Though the recipe and form may vary, the ancestor of these yeasted, fried pastries is krapfen, from the Austrian part of Italy.

INGREDIENTS

1 cup (250 ml/9 fl oz) milk

50 g (1¾ oz) fresh yeast (or 15 g/½ oz powdered yeast)

700 g (1 lb 9 oz) plain (all-purpose) flour

2 eggs, whisked

100 g (3½ oz) caster (superfine) sugar, plus extra for serving

30 ml (1 fl oz oz) grappa

100 g (3½ oz) unsalted butter at room temperature, diced

grated zest of 1 lemon

pinch of salt

extra virgin olive oil

jam or pastry cream (optional)

METHOD

Heat 100 ml (3½ fl oz) of the milk until warm (not hot) and dissolve the yeast completely in it. Put the flour, dissolved yeast and remaining milk in the bowl of an electric mixer fitted with a dough hook and mix well for 10 minutes. Cover the bowl and put in a warm (not hot) place for 1 hour to rise. Return the bowl to the electric mixer and add the eggs, sugar, grappa, butter, lemon zest and a pinch of salt and mix until smooth. Cover the bowl and return to the warm place for 45 minutes to rise again. Roll out the dough to a thickness of about 3 mm (⅛ in) and cut out discs using an 8 cm (3¼ in) cutter. Heat olive oil to 190°C (375°F) and fry a few pastries at a time, turning once, until golden. Drain on paper towels and roll in sugar to serve. Alternatively, use a piping bag fitted with a long thin nozzle to fill the pastries with jam or pastry cream. They can also be filled before frying with sweetened ricotta studded with candied fruits or chocolate pieces.

MAKES about 20   WINE: Trentino Moscato Giallo Liquoroso

THE PLUM IS A SUMMER FRUIT BUT, MORE OFTEN THAN NOT, IT CAN STILL BE PLENTIFUL WELL INTO AUTUMN. TRENTO IS ONE OF THE PRINCIPAL PRODUCERS OF PLUMS IN ITALY. WHEN THEY ARE AT THEIR BEST AND SWEETEST, A DISTILLATE IS MADE FROM PLUMS IN MUCH THE SAME WAY AS GRAPPA. IT'S SERVED IN A SMALL GLASS, WITH A PRUNE IN IT, AS AN AFTER DINNER DIGESTIVE.

APPLE AND HAZELNUT STRUDEL
STRUDEL DI MELE E NOCCIOLE

The strudels of Austrian Italy are filled with all manner of local fruits and nuts, including apples, pears, stone fruit, cherries, chestnuts, walnuts and hazelnuts.

INGREDIENTS

300 g (10½ oz) apple flesh, cut into 5 mm (¼ in) cubes

⅔ cup (150 g/5½ oz) caster (superfine) sugar

¾ teaspoon ground cinnamon

juice of 1 lemon

1 tablespoon rum

60 g (2¼ oz) hazelnuts, roasted, skinned and chopped

4 tablespoons fine breadcrumbs

1 egg yolk, lightly whisked

STRUDEL PASTRY

1⅔ cups (250 g/9 oz) plain (all-purpose) flour

1 egg

2 teaspoons extra virgin olive oil

1 teaspoon white wine vinegar

METHOD

To make the pastry, sift the flour onto your work surface and make a well in the centre. Add the egg, olive oil, vinegar, a pinch of salt and enough warm water to work the dry ingredients, using your hands, into a smooth dough. Knead firmly and knock the dough against the work surface 20 times. Shape into a ball, put in a bowl, cover with a tea towel (dish towel) and set aside for 30 minutes in a warm place. Roll out on a lightly floured surface to a paper-thin 35–40 cm (14–16 in) square. Put the pastry sheet on a large clean tea towel (to facilitate rolling) and let it air for a few minutes before filling.

Put the apple, sugar, cinnamon, lemon juice, rum and hazelnuts in a bowl and mix well. Sprinkle the breadcrumbs evenly on the pastry, then spoon on the apple mixture in a flat, even layer. Using the tea towel, roll the pastry into a log. Brush the final edge with a little of the egg yolk and carefully transfer the log to a baking tray, then refrigerate for 20 minutes. Meanwhile, preheat the oven to 180°C (350°F). Brush the top of the roll with the remaining egg yolk and bake for 35–40 minutes, until golden. Allow to cool a little before cutting and serving.

SERVES 6   WINE: Moscato Rosa

APPLE AND HAZELNVT STRVDEL

PRESERVED PLUM TARTLETS
TORTINE DI PRVGNE

INGREDIENTS

5 eggs, separated

250 g (9 oz) sugar

125 g (4½ oz) softened
unsalted butter

1 level tablespoon plain
(all-purpose) flour

250 ml (9 fl oz) greengage
and vanilla preserve
(see page 528), plus
2 tablespoons for serving

icing (confectioners') sugar

140 ml thick (double) cream,
lightly whipped

SHORTCRUST PASTRY

350 g plain (all-purpose) flour

70 g (2½ oz) caster (superfine)
sugar

½ teaspoon baking powder

grated zest of 1 lemon

170 g (6 oz) cold unsalted
butter, cut into 2 cm (¾ in)
cubes

1 egg

1 egg yolk

¼ cup (60 ml/2 fl oz) thick
(double) cream

METHOD

To make the pastry, put the flour, sugar, baking powder, lemon zest
and a pinch of salt in a food processor and pulse to combine well.
Add the butter and pulse repeatedly until the mixture resembles sand.
In a separate bowl, whisk together the egg, egg yolk and cream. Add
this mixture to the food processor and pulse until the mixture forms a
ball. Shape into a log about 6 cm in diameter, wrap in plastic wrap and
refrigerate for 3–4 hours.

Preheat the oven to 170°C (340°F). Roll out the pastry to fit 16 × 8 cm
tartlet tins or 2 × 22 cm tart tins and use to line the tins. Let rest in
the refrigerator while you prepare the filling (the pastry does not need
to be blind-baked.) Whisk the egg yolks with ⅔ cup (150 g/5½ oz) of
the sugar until light and fluffy. In a separate bowl, beat the remaining
sugar with the butter. Combine the two mixtures and beat in the flour,
greengage preserve and a pinch of salt. Whisk the egg whites until
stiff, then fold into the mixture. Spoon into the tart shells and bake
for 25 minutes for tartlets or 35 minutes for larger tarts. Cool, then
dust with icing sugar and serve with the whipped cream and extra
greengage preserve.

SERVES 16   WINE: Moscato Rosa

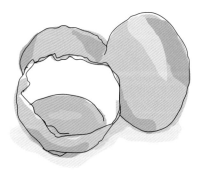

MILK AND APPLE CUSTARD
BUDINO DI MELE

The mixture can be made a day ahead and baked just before your lunch or dinner.

INGREDIENTS

1 tablespoon extra virgin
olive oil

2 cups (500 ml/17 fl oz)
non-homogenised organic
or biodynamic milk

2 eggs

50 g (1¾ oz) plain (all-purpose)
flour, sifted

grated zest of 1 lemon

small pinch of ground
cinnamon

½ teaspoon natural vanilla
extract

4 small–medium new-season
apples, peeled, cored and
cut into 5 mm (¼ in) thick
wedges

2 tablespoons caster
(superfine) sugar

METHOD

Preheat the oven to 170°C (340°F) and thoroughly grease 8 dariole
moulds (100 ml/3½ fl oz) with the olive oil. Whisk the milk, eggs, flour,
lemon zest, cinnamon, vanilla and a pinch of salt until smooth (the flour
must be completely dissolved). Ladle into the moulds and carefully
arrange the apple wedges on top. Don't worry if they float or sink – this
won't diminish the final dish. Sprinkle 1 teaspoon of the caster sugar
evenly over each pudding. Put the moulds on baking trays and bake for
about 20 minutes until just set. Let cool for 15 minutes before serving.

SERVES 8   WINE: Moscato Rosa

VMBRIA

VMBRIA

BORDERED BY TOSCANA TO THE WEST, LE MARCHE TO THE EAST AND LAZIO TO THE SOUTH, VMBRIA HAS BOTH HILLS AND MOUNTAINS. ITS TOPOGRAPHY IS DOMINATED BY THE APENNINES, WITH THE HIGHEST POINT IN THE REGION AT MONTE VETTORE ON THE BORDER OF LE MARCHE, AT 2476 METRES (8123 FEET), AND IT IS THE ONLY ITALIAN REGION HAVING NEITHER A COASTLINE NOR A COMMON BORDER WITH ANOTHER PROVINCE.

The countryside of Umbria is romantic, with gentle rolling hills dotted with lakes, hermitages and monasteries. Its 8400 square kilometres (3243 square miles) are relatively sparsely populated by about 890,000 citizens. This peaceful country, whose name is derived from the ancient Umbri tribe, was the birthplace of a number of saints, foremost among them the animal-loving St Francis of Assisi who, it is said, would pick worms from the ground so he didn't tread on them. St Benedict, the founder of Western monasticism, was born in Norcia, and St Clare, founder of the order of the Poor Clares, in Assisi. Unsurprisingly, Umbria is home to some of the most beautiful Romanesque chapels in Europe.

The cuisine of such a sparsely populated region relies heavily on food gathered from the meadows, lakes and woods, on the black truffles of Norcia and the white of Orvieto, and on the freshwater fish – carp, trout, perch and eels – of Lake Trasimeno. A Perugian dish that uses black truffles is spaghetti ai tartuffi neri, where the truffles are chopped finely and marinated in olive oil, garlic and anchovies for a day before being cooked with the pasta. Another Umbrian pasta dish is spaghetti ad aglio ed olio, spaghetti with garlic and oil, which contains one unnamed ingredient that makes it Umbrian (apart from the dialect name): ginger.

Throughout Italy, pork butchers are called norcini after the Umbrian city of Norcia; they are usually also salumiere, or salami makers. One local product of the land and the art of the norcini is the prosciutto of Norcia. Other products of the local pigs are capocollo ham, salami, head cheese and the remarkable porchetta – a whole pig boned and stuffed with its entrails and fennel and other herbs, and cooked on a spit. Also spit-roasted is lamb, as agnello all'arrabbiata, or 'angry lamb', referring to the high flame over which it is cooked; it is seasoned simply with salt, pepper and vinegar.

If you've ever fallen under the spell of a Baci (meaning 'kiss') you should know that the hazelnut and chocolate confection was first made by the Buitoni family in Perugia, and that it was originally known by the far more pugnacious title of cazzotti ('punch'). It was given its more romantic name by the poet Gabriele d'Annunzio.

Umbria came late to wine, remaining a 'home brew for the locals' region until the 1970s. There was a quick catch-up and today it ranks eleventh in Italy in the percentage of DOC-classified wines it makes. What makes this even more remarkable is that of the 13 DOCs in the region, eight were created after 1980.

The best-known Umbrian wine is Orvieto, from that DOC. It is a white wine made from the trebbiano grape but with increasingly more grechetto going into blends. Outside Orvieto grechetto has the upper hand, with many makers producing wines based on this variety – as indeed are some in Orvieto itself.

From Perugia come sagrantino di Montefalco wines – reds from the hillside vineyards near the village of Montefalco and made from the sagrantino grape, which is particular to the Montefalco DOCG. There is nothing like it elsewhere in Italy, and not much even there, with only around 160 hectares (395 acres) planted.

Although sangiovese is the predominant red wine grape of the region, there is a growing 'Super Umbro' group trying unconventional blendings such as sangiovese–canaiolo and sangiovese–cabernet.

There are a handful of DOCs making spumante wines, mainly for local consumption, but some sweet wines are turning heads and pleasing palates. Orvieto has long had a reputation for thick sweet wines, beloved of the 12th-century popes and clergy, but today the micro-climate is such that it allows for the production of late-harvest botrytis-affected or muffa nobile (noble rot) wines. Even more intense are the sweet red wines of Montefalco, made by drying the grapes – in a process called passito – to concentrate the sugars. It is recommended by the writers of wine guide *Vino Italiano* that you do not leave Umbria without trying an example of this style.

UMBRIA
ANTI-PASTi

ANCHOVY AND BEET LEAF BREAD
PANE CON LE ALICI E BIETA

Traditionally this was made as a quick snack with leftover bread dough.

INGREDIENTS

⅓ cup (80 ml/2½ fl oz) extra
 virgin olive oil
500 g (1 lb 2 oz) basic
 focaccia dough
 (see page 285)
3 cups chopped beetroot
 (beet) leaves, blanched and
 squeezed well
120 g (4¼ oz) anchovy fillets,
 drained
coarse sea salt

METHOD

Preheat the oven to 210°C (410°F) and use 1 tablespoon of the olive oil
to grease a 30 cm (12 in) pizza tray. Roll out the dough into 2 rounds
about 30 cm (12 in) in diameter and 5 mm (¼ in) thick. Position one of
the rounds of dough on the tray and scatter with the beet leaves and
anchovies. Season and drizzle 1 tablespoon of the remaining oil on top.
Cover with the second round of dough and crimp the edges together
using a fork. Press the top gently using your fingers to leave small
indentations, then drizzle with the remaining oil and scatter on some
sea salt. Bake for 15–20 minutes until golden. Let cool a little before
cutting into wedges to serve.

SERVES 8-10   WINE: Trebbiano Spoletino

SALAD OF SMOKED TROUT WITH BLACK TRUFFLE DRESSING
INSALATINA DI TROTA AFFUMICATA AL TARTUFO DI NORCIA

INGREDIENTS

400 g (10½ oz) young green
 beans, trimmed
1 garlic clove, minced
½ cup finely chopped parsley
½ cup (125 ml/4 fl oz) extra
 virgin olive oil
2 hot-smoked rainbow trout,
 skin and bones removed
1 tablespoon truffle mustard
 (see page 315)
½ cup (125 ml/4 fl oz) red
 wine vinegar
2 cups young rocket (arugula)

METHOD

Blanch the beans in plenty of rapidly boiling water for about 2 minutes
until tender but still with some texture. Drain. Combine the garlic,
parsley and half the olive oil in a large bowl. Season, then add the
beans and toss to coat. Break the trout flesh into bite-sized pieces.
Whisk together the mustard, vinegar and remaining olive oil to make
a dressing. Toss the trout with the rocket, beans and dressing and
serve immediately.

SERVES 8-10   WINE: Orvieto Classico Superiore

CROSTINI WITH TRUFFLED CHICKEN LIVERS
CROSTINI ALLA PERUGINA

Truffles, both white and black, are considered expensive, exotic ingredients the world over. Ordinarily they are out of reach of most people due to their high price, but in parts of Italy where they are found they have been used traditionally in many local dishes as just another ingredient.

INGREDIENTS

3 garlic cloves

10 sage leaves, stems removed

½ teaspoon fennel seeds

¼ cup (60 ml/2 fl oz) extra virgin olive oil

1 tablespoon capers, rinsed

300 g (10½ oz) chicken livers, trimmed

½ cup (125 ml/4 fl oz) dry red wine

40 g (1½ oz) black truffle, shaved

6 slices country-style bread

METHOD

Chop the garlic, sage and fennel seeds together on a board. Heat 2 tablespoons of the olive oil in a frying pan and add the garlic mixture and capers. Fry lightly for a minute, constantly stirring, then add the chicken livers and fry for a minute. Add the wine, a couple of good pinches of salt and a turn or two of pepper and simmer for about 10 minutes until the wine has reduced. Remove from the heat and let cool a little, then transfer the contents to a food processor and pulse a few times to make a rough puree. Reserve 8 truffle shavings and chop the rest. Stir the chopped truffle into the chicken liver puree. Grill (broil) or toast the bread and brush with the remaining olive oil, then cut each slice into smaller pieces. Gently heat the puree and spoon onto the crostini. Halve the reserved truffle shavings and put a piece on top of each crostino to serve.

SERVES 6–8   WINE: Colli del Trasimeno Gamay

IF YOU TRAVEL TO PARTS OF UMBRIA
IN THE TRUFFLE SEASON (WINTER), YOU'LL FIND THE LOCALS WILL SHAVE THEM ON JUST ABOUT ANYTHING, AND IF YOU'RE IN A TRADITIONAL OSTERIA, THE PRICE OF A TRUFFLE DISH WILL BE QUITE AFFORDABLE.

PROSCIUTTO WITH BLACK TRUFFLES AND TRUFFLE MUSTARD DRESSING
PROSCIUTTO AL TARTUFO

INGREDIENTS

14 thin slices black truffle

100 ml (3½ fl oz) extra virgin olive oil

¼ cup (60 ml/2 fl oz) red wine vinegar

1 teaspoon Dijon mustard

1 cup small salad leaves

8 × 8 cm × 3 cm (3¼ in × 1¼ in) pieces ciabatta or other bread

4 slices prosciutto, halved

METHOD

Preheat the oven to 160°C (320°F). Finely chop 6 of the truffle slices. Combine ⅓ cup (80 ml/2½ fl oz) of the olive oil with the vinegar, mustard and chopped truffle. Season with salt and mix well, then set aside. Arrange the salad leaves on serving plates. Brush the bread with the remaining olive oil and toast lightly in the oven for 8–10 minutes. Remove from the oven and, while still hot, put a piece of prosciutto on each crostino and nestle the crostino on the salad leaves. Drizzle with the truffle dressing and finish with a couple of truffle slices on each crostino. Add a couple of turns of pepper over the lot and serve.

SERVES 4   WINE: Grechetto

VMBRIA
PRIMI

CASTELLUCCIO LENTIL SOUP
ZUPPA DI LENTICCHIE DEL CASTELLUCCIO DI NORCIA

This preparation is based on Umbrian-born chef Angelo Paracucchi's dish featuring the famous lentils of Castelluccio.

INGREDIENTS

300 g (10½ oz) Castelluccio lentils (see page 36), well washed
1 carrot, finely diced
1 celery heart, finely diced
⅓ cup (80 ml/2½ fl oz) extra virgin olive oil
1 brown onion, finely diced
1 garlic clove, minced
250 g (9 oz) ripe tomatoes, peeled and chopped

METHOD

Put the lentils, carrot and celery in a saucepan and pour in water to cover. Add a good pinch of salt and bring to the boil, then turn the heat down and simmer for 10 minutes. Meanwhile, heat the olive oil in a frying pan and lightly fry the onion and garlic until translucent. Add the tomatoes and a couple of pinches of salt and pepper. Simmer for 5 minutes, then add the tomato mixture to the lentils and simmer for 20–25 minutes until rather dense and only slightly runny. If the mixture becomes too dry, add a little water. Check for seasoning and serve.

SERVES 4   WINE: Colli Martani Grechetto

UMBRICELLI PASTA WITH PORCINI
VMBRICELLI AI FUNGHI PORCINI

Umbricelli are close cousins to neighbouring Tuscany's pici. This dish is best made with fresh porcini mushrooms, but if they're not available use 50 g (1¾ oz) dried porcini (soaked and chopped) and a mixture of your favourite cultivated mushrooms.

INGREDIENTS

2 tablespoons extra virgin olive oil
100 g (3½ oz) unsalted butter
2 garlic cloves, chopped
1 brown onion, chopped
400 g (10½ oz) fresh porcini mushrooms, cut into 2 cm (¾ in) chunks
50 ml (1¾ fl oz) dry white wine
leaves from 1 thyme sprig
leaves from 1 rosemary sprig
½ cup parsley leaves
400 g (10½ oz) umbricelli pasta (see page 45)
grated pecorino cheese

METHOD

Heat the oil and half the butter in a saucepan and lightly fry the garlic and onion for 2–3 minutes until translucent. Add the porcini and cook for 5 minutes – they will release a little liquid initially, but it will evaporate. Add the wine and turn up the heat until it evaporates. Chop the herbs together, then add to the pan and remove it from the heat. Stir in the remaining butter and season. Cook the pasta in plenty of boiling salted water, then drain, keeping a ladleful of the cooking liquid to moisten the sauce if necessary. Toss the pasta in a large bowl with the porcini sauce and serve with plenty of grated pecorino.

SERVES 4–6   WINE: Sagrantino Rosso

RISOTTO WITH SAGE AND PECORINO
RISOTTO ALLA SALVIA E PECORINO

INGREDIENTS

2 litres (70 fl oz) chicken stock
  (see page 48)
50 g (1¾ oz) unsalted butter
1 brown onion, very finely
  chopped
500 g (1 lb 2 oz) carnaroli rice
100 ml (3½ fl oz) dry white
  wine
½ cup sage leaves, stems
  removed
100 g (3½ oz) salted butter
150 g (5½ oz) aged pecorino
  cheese, shaved

METHOD

Bring the chicken stock to the boil in a saucepan. Melt the unsalted
butter in a wide frying pan, then add the onion and fry gently until
translucent but not coloured. Add the rice and stir for about a minute
until the grains become translucent. Pour in the wine and stir until
it has completely evaporated. Add a ladleful or two of boiling stock
and simmer and stir until the liquid is almost entirely incorporated.
Keep adding the stock a little at a time until the rice is almost cooked.
Remove from the heat and stir in the sage leaves, salted butter, pecorino
and a little salt. Cover and let rest for 3–4 minutes before serving.

SERVES 6–8   WINE: Montefalco Rosso

FRESHWATER CRAYFISH WITH LETTUCE AND PICKLES
GAMBERI D'ACQUA DOLCE ALL'AGRODOLCE

INGREDIENTS

1 garlic clove, minced
¼ cup parsley, finely chopped
100 g (3½ oz) mixed Italian-
  style pickled vegetables,
  drained and finely chopped
1 teaspoon capers, rinsed and
  finely chopped
juice of 1 lemon
2 tablespoons white wine
  vinegar
150 ml (5 fl oz) extra virgin
  olive oil
1 small cos (romaine) lettuce,
  well washed and dried
500 g (1 lb 2 oz) cooked
  freshwater crayfish, peeled
  (or small–medium cooked
  prawns, peeled and deveined)

METHOD

Put the garlic, parsley, pickled vegetables, capers, lemon juice, vinegar
and olive oil in a bowl with a couple of good pinches of salt and whisk
energetically until well incorporated. Cut the lettuce into fine strips and
arrange on serving plates. Sit the crayfish on top of the lettuce, drizzle
the dressing over and serve.

SERVES 4   WINE: Grechetto Colli Perugini

WHITE VEGETABLE PUREE WITH BLACK TRUFFLES
PASSATO DI VERDURA BIANCA AL TARTUFO DI NORCIA

INGREDIENTS

1 brown onion, cut into chunks

1 celery heart, cut into chunks

1 leek, white part only, cut into chunks

1 potato, cut into chunks

1 parsnip, cut into chunks

1 large celeriac, peeled and cut into chunks

250 g (9 oz) Jerusalem artichokes, peeled and cut into chunks

6 garlic cloves, peeled

50 g (1¾ oz) unsalted butter

white pepper

4 tablespoons grated fontina cheese

⅓ cup (80 ml/2½ fl oz) good-quality extra virgin olive oil

15–20 g (½–¾ oz) black truffle

TRUFFLE BUTTER

250 g (9 oz) softened butter

1 × 40 g (1½ oz) black or white truffle, finely shaved

METHOD

To make the truffle butter, put the butter and truffle in a food processor and pulse until well incorporated. Transfer to a length of plastic wrap and roll up into a log. Refrigerate or freeze and use when needed. Makes 250 g (9 oz).

Put all the vegetables and the garlic in a large saucepan and pour in cold water to just cover. Bring to the boil, then turn the heat down and simmer for 25 minutes. Drain, reserving the cooking liquid, and transfer to a food processor. Pulse until well blended, then add enough of the cooking liquid to give a rich, thick but runny consistency. Add the butter and 50 g (1¾ oz) of the truffle butter, season with salt and fine white pepper and stir until well incorporated. Transfer to bowls and top with the grated fontina. Drizzle the olive oil over, shave on some truffle and serve with hearty bread.

SERVES 4   WINE: Rosso Orvietano

TRUFFLE BUTTER IS EASY TO MAKE AND AN EXCELLENT WAY TO USE UP END PIECES OF TRUFFLE. IT'S ALSO A GOOD WAY TO PRESERVE TRUFFLES AS THE BUTTER CAN BE FROZEN.

ROAST YOUNG VEGETABLES WITH TRUFFLE PARMESAN SAUCE
VERDURE PICCOLO CON SALSA DI TARTUFO NERO E PARMIGIANO

Unless you grow them yourself, you may have to go hunting for these young vegetables in markets and shops. If you can't find them, cut larger ones down to smaller sizes after roasting.

INGREDIENTS

- 6 young yellow carrots
- 6 young orange carrots
- 6 young golden beetroots (beets)
- 6 young red beetroots (beets)
- 6 young turnips
- 2 tablespoons extra virgin olive oil
- 200 ml (7 fl oz) thin (pouring) cream
- 60 g (2¼ oz) grated parmesan cheese
- 40 g (1½ oz) butter
- 10–15 g (¼–½ oz) black truffle

METHOD

Preheat the oven to 190°C (375°F). Peel the carrots and put them in a bowl of cold water until ready to cook. Wash and scrub the beetroots and turnips well, making sure all grit is removed, but don't peel them. Pat all the vegetables dry using a clean tea towel (dish towel), then put in a bowl and toss with half the olive oil until well coated. Put the beetroots in a baking dish, sprinkle with salt and roast for 12–15 minutes until tender – a sharp knife should pierce with little resistance. Heat the remaining olive oil in an ovenproof frying pan on high heat and cook the carrots and turnips for a minute or so until lightly coloured. Sprinkle with salt and put the pan in the oven for 8–10 minutes until the vegetables are tender. Remove from the oven and keep warm. Bring the cream to the boil in a saucepan, then turn the heat down and stir in the parmesan. Simmer for 3–5 minutes until the mixture thickens, then remove from the heat and stir in the butter. Grate in a third of the truffle and stir. Spoon the sauce onto 6 warm serving plates and scatter the vegetables on top. Shave on the remaining truffle and serve.

SERVES 6   WINE: Sagrantino di Montefalco

ROAST YOUNG VEGETABLES WITH TRUFFLE PARMESAN SAUCE

TOASTED FARRO WITH VEGETABLE PUREE
FARRO ARROSTITO CON PASSATO DI VERDURA

INGREDIENTS

180 g (6½ oz) potatoes, unpeeled

80 g (2¾ oz) pearled farro, washed and drained

⅓ cup (80 ml/2½ fl oz) extra virgin olive oil

1 leek, white part only, chopped

1 small brown onion, diced

2 garlic cloves, sliced

1 cup (125 g/4½ oz) cauliflower florets, blanched until tender

1 cup (250 ml/9 fl oz) chicken stock (see page 48)

METHOD

Boil the potatoes until tender, then drain, peel and slice. Cook the farro in boiling salted water for about 10 minutes until half-cooked – it should still be quite al dente. Drain, then rinse under cold water and set aside. Heat half the olive oil in a frying pan and lightly fry the leek, onion and garlic until tender. Add the potatoes, cauliflower and chicken stock and bring to the boil, then turn the heat down and simmer for 3 minutes. Season, then use a stick blender or food processor to puree until smooth. Heat half the remaining oil in a frying pan and add the part-cooked farro. Toast gently until a little crisp, then season. Heat the vegetable puree and ladle into bowls. Scatter the farro on top and drizzle with the remaining olive oil to serve.

SERVES 6 · WINE: Colli Perugini Chardonnay

BEET LEAF BAKE
TORTA DI BIETA

INGREDIENTS

500 g (1 lb 2 oz) beetroot (beet) leaves (including stalks), well washed and chopped into 2 cm (¾ in) pieces

1½ cups breadcrumbs

80 g (2¾ oz) cheddar cheese, grated

½ cup (50 g/1¾ oz) grated parmesan cheese

50 g (1¾ oz) butter

¼ cup (60 ml/2 fl oz) extra virgin olive oil

1 brown onion, finely sliced

2 garlic cloves, minced

150 ml (5 fl oz) thin (pouring) cream

METHOD

Preheat the oven to 180°C (350°F). Fill a large saucepan with water, add salt and bring to the boil. Drop the beetroot stalks and leaves into the boiling water and blanch for 2 minutes, then drain well. Combine the breadcrumbs and cheeses in a bowl. Put the butter and oil in a frying pan on medium heat and gently fry the onion and garlic for 2 minutes. Add the beet stalks and leaves and sauté for 2 minutes, then add the cream. Turn the heat to high and let the liquid evaporate until there is just enough to coat the beet leaves and stalks. Season. Spoon into a baking dish to a depth of 3–4 cm (1¼–1½ in), spread the breadcrumb mixture over the top and bake for 20 minutes until golden brown. Serve hot by itself or as an accompaniment to roast beef, pork or duck.

SERVES 6-8 · WINE: Orvieto

UMBRIA
SECONDI

STEWED SALT COD
BACCALÀ IN GUAZZETTO

INGREDIENTS

⅓ cup (80 ml/2½ fl oz) extra virgin olive oil, plus extra for drizzling

500 g (1 lb 2 oz) brown onions, thinly sliced

6 garlic cloves, minced

1 celery heart, cut into 1 cm (½ in) pieces

500 g (1 lb 2 oz) cherry tomatoes, quartered

½ cup green olives, pitted and chopped

2 red chillies, seeded and minced

1.2 kg (2 lb 12 oz) baccalà, soaked and rinsed (see page 125), cut into 4 cm (1½ in) pieces

METHOD

Heat the olive oil in a large frying pan and lightly fry the onions, garlic and celery for 2–3 minutes. Stir in the tomatoes, olives and chillies and simmer for 5 minutes until the tomatoes have broken down. Add a ladleful or two of hot water so the sauce is not too dense. Arrange the baccalà in the sauce and simmer slowly for 20–30 minutes, making sure the liquid doesn't reduce too much. Season, then serve drizzled with a little oil.

SERVES 6   WINE: Colli Perugini bianco

PRAWNS WITH ZUCCHINI FLOWERS AND CANNELLINI BEANS
GAMBERI IN UMIDO CON FIOR DI ZUCCHINI E CANNELLINI

INGREDIENTS

12 zucchini (courgette) flowers with zucchini (female)

⅓ cup (80 ml/2½ fl oz) extra virgin olive oil

4 bulb spring onions (scallions), cut lengthways into 4 or 6 wedges

2 garlic cloves, thinly sliced

6 tinned tomatoes, mashed

1 cup cooked cannellini beans

1 cup basil leaves, torn

1 kg (2 lb 4 oz) cooked king prawns, peeled and deveined

METHOD

Separate the zucchini flowers from the zucchini. Cut the rough stem-ends off the zucchini, then halve each zucchini and flower lengthways. If the flowers are very fresh, the pistils can be left – if not, remove and discard them. Heat the olive oil in a wide frying pan and lightly fry the spring onions and garlic for a minute. Add the zucchini (not the flowers) and stir gently for a minute, making sure they don't break up. Add the tomatoes, beans, basil and a couple of pinches of salt, stir carefully and simmer for 10 minutes. Add the prawns and zucchini flowers, stir carefully and add a little more salt (if necessary) and a couple of turns of pepper. Serve hot or at room temperature.

SERVES 6   WINE: Colli Martani Grechetto

VEAL WITH LENTIL CREAM
BOCCONCINI DI VITELLO ALLA CREMA DI LENTICCHIE

This is a companion dish based on an Angelo Paracucchi recipe. It uses leftover lentil soup.

INGREDIENTS

1 × 600 g (1 lb 5 oz) round of veal (from the leg)

100 ml (3½ fl oz) extra virgin olive oil

3 garlic cloves, lightly crushed but left whole

2 sage sprigs

2 rosemary sprigs

100 ml (3½ fl oz) dry white wine

3 tinned tomatoes, chopped

1 cup (250 ml/9 fl oz) hot Castelluccio lentil soup (see page 543)

METHOD

Cut the veal into 3 cm (1¼ in) cubes about 1.5 cm (⅝ in) thick. Heat the olive oil in a frying pan and lightly fry the garlic, sage and rosemary for 30 seconds. Turn up the heat and add the veal. Season and cook, stirring, for 2 minutes or so until the veal has browned. Add the wine, then turn the heat down to very low, cover and simmer for 10 minutes. Transfer the veal to a plate and keep warm. Add the tomatoes to the pan and cook until the mixture is reduced and thick. Remove from the heat and remove and discard the herbs and garlic. Combine the tomato mixture and hot lentil soup, then puree using a stick blender. Season and ladle into bowls, arrange the veal on top and serve.

SERVES 6   WINE: Montefalco Rosso

QUAILS IN TOMATO SAUCE WITH TARRAGON
QUAGLIE NEL SUGO AL DRAGONCELLO

In many ways, quails are easier to prepare than chicken. Once you take the breasts and legs off the carcass, they're very easy to cook. Both cuts remain moist and succulent simply pan-fried or grilled (broiled).

INGREDIENTS

8 quails

⅓ cup (80 ml/2½ fl oz) extra virgin olive oil

1 small red onion, finely diced

2 garlic cloves, minced

1 celery stick, finely diced

1 small carrot, finely diced

100 ml (3½ fl oz) dry white wine

1 kg (2 lb 4 oz) ripe tomatoes, seeded and chopped

½ cup tarragon leaves

METHOD

Using a small sharp knife, cut the legs off the quails at the thigh joints and cut the breasts (2 for each bird) off the breastplates. Heat the olive oil in a large frying pan and fry the quail breasts and legs until browned. Transfer to a plate and set aside. Put the quail carcasses in the pan and add the onion, garlic, celery and carrot. Stir continually for 2–3 minutes until the carcasses brown a little, then pour in the wine. Once the wine has evaporated, remove the carcasses and add the tomatoes and quail breasts and legs to the pan. Stir in the tarragon, season lightly and simmer for 15 minutes. Check for seasoning and serve with polenta (cornmeal) or crusty bread.

SERVES 4   WINE: Montefalco Rosso

WOOD-GRILLED LAMB WITH HERBS
SCOTTADITO D'AGNELLO

Scottadito has many variations across central Italy and is most often made using lamb cutlets. This version uses boneless lamb steaks instead, which are a cheaper and more abundant cut. Prosciutto fat is often available from Italian grocers and has traditionally been used, along with herbs, to 'mask' less-than-fresh meat. As is so often the case with necessity informing invention, the successful result has lived on. Cook the lamb over wood for the best result, but it can also be cooked on a gas barbecue.

INGREDIENTS

6 garlic cloves

2 tablespoons rosemary
leaves

2 tablespoons marjoram
leaves

100 g (3½ oz) prosciutto fat,
diced and softened at room
temperature

1.2 kg (2 lb 12 oz) lamb leg
steaks, cut about 1 cm
(½ in) thick

METHOD

Mince the garlic and herbs together on a board using a sharp knife. Add the prosciutto fat and chop until all is incorporated and you have a thick paste. Spread the paste in a thin layer on both sides of each steak. Once the coals on the wood grill have formed, cook the steaks for 2–3 minutes on each side, making sure they don't flare up. Season and cut into 2 cm (¾ in) wide fingers to serve.

SERVES 6   WINE: Assisi Rosso

SAUSAGES AND ROMAN BEANS BRAISED IN TOMATO
SALSICCE E FAGIOLI IN UMIDO

The beans called for here are large, green, flat Roman beans. They're meaty and tender and can take a good deal of braising.

INGREDIENTS

300 g (10½ oz) good-quality
Italian pork sausages

100 ml (3½ fl oz) extra virgin
olive oil

1 red onion, finely chopped

2 garlic cloves, minced

600 g (1 lb 5 oz) ripe tomatoes,
chopped

300 g (10½ oz) flat green beans,
trimmed and cut into 5–6 cm
(2–2½ in) lengths

½ cup chopped parsley

METHOD

Bring a saucepan of water to the boil and blanch the sausages for 2–3 minutes, depending on their size. Transfer to a plate and let cool. Heat the olive oil in a frying pan and lightly fry the onion and garlic until translucent and fragrant. Add the tomatoes and 2 good pinches of salt. Stir well and simmer for 10 minutes. Add the beans, stir well and simmer for 10 minutes. Slice the sausages and add to the pan, then stir in the parsley and simmer for a further 5–6 minutes until the beans are tender. Stir in salt (if needed) and a few turns of pepper. Let cool a little before serving with good bread.

SERVES 4   WINE: Montefalco Rosso

SAUSAGES AND ROMAN BEANS BRAISED IN TOMATO

SAVOY CABBAGE WITH POTATOES
CAVOLI STRASCINATI

This simple side dish uses ingredients that are usually at hand, and leftover bread. It's a traditional accompaniment to grilled and roast meats as well as sausages.

INGREDIENTS

- ½ large Savoy cabbage, trimmed and cut into 5 mm (¼ in) slices
- 2 cups 2 cm (¾ in) potato cubes
- ½ cup (125 ml/4 fl oz) extra virgin olive oil
- 3 garlic cloves, lightly crushed but left whole
- 1 cup 2 cm (¾ in) bread cubes
- 2 tablespoons chopped parsley

METHOD

Bring a large saucepan of salted water to the boil and plunge in the cabbage. Boil for 2–3 minutes until tender but still a little al dente. Drain and let cool a little before squeezing out as much water as possible. Bring a small saucepan of salted water to the boil and blanch the potato cubes for a couple of minutes, then drain. Heat the olive oil in a large frying pan and lightly fry the garlic until just golden. Remove and discard the garlic, then add the bread and potato cubes and lightly fry until golden. Add the cabbage, turn up the heat, season well and add the parsley. Stir gently and continually for 5–6 minutes until the cabbage wilts. Serve hot as a side dish.

SERVES 6–8

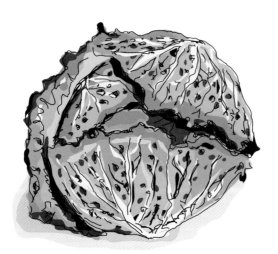

DOLCI

VMBRIA

GRAPE JELLY
GELATINA D'UVA

Black grape jelly is great with blue and aged sharp cheeses, while white grape jelly is ideal for desserts. Whichever grapes you use, make sure they are flavoursome. You need enough grapes to yield 2 litres (70 fl oz) of juice.

INGREDIENTS

black or white grapes, stems removed

500 g (1 lb 2 oz) caster (superfine) sugar

METHOD

In a juicer, juice enough grapes to give 2 litres (70 fl oz) of liquid. Pour the grape juice into a saucepan and add the sugar. Bring to the boil, then turn the heat down and simmer slowly until the liquid has reduced by half, skimming off any impurities that rise to the surface. Test the jelly by letting a couple of drops fall on a refrigerator-cold plate. If it sets the jelly is ready; if it doesn't set, keep reducing. Remove from the heat and let cool a little, then ladle into sterilised jars, seal and store in the refrigerator. This will keep indefinitely but once opened, use within a week.

MAKES about 1.2 litres (44 fl oz)

BREAD AND SUGAR FRITTERS
FRITTELLE DI PANCOTTO

The art of making something delicious out of very few ingredients is a hallmark of Italian cooking. This dish is typical of the way leftovers, especially bread, are used. Nothing is wasted.

INGREDIENTS

300 g (10½ oz) breadcrumbs

2 tablespoons caster (superfine) sugar

2 tablespoons plain (all-purpose) flour

½ teaspoon ground cinnamon

grated zest of 1 small lemon

2 tablespoons grappa

2 eggs

1 cup (250 ml/9 fl oz) duck fat or extra virgin olive oil

icing (confectioners') sugar

METHOD

Put the breadcrumbs, caster sugar, flour, cinnamon, lemon zest and grappa in a large saucepan and slowly mix in 1 litre (35 fl oz) hot water. Bring to a simmer and cook for 15–20 minutes, then remove from the heat, transfer to a bowl and let cool. Add the eggs and beat until well incorporated and the dough is neither too firm nor too runny (it should sit in a spoon easily without running). Heat the duck fat in a saucepan (of a size that will give a 2 cm/¾ in depth of melted fat) until a teaspoon of dough sizzles immediately on contact. Drop in a few tablespoons of dough at a time and cook until golden. Drain on paper towels, dust with icing sugar and serve with coffee and grappa or another liqueur.

MAKES 40–50

BEST with coffee and grappa

RICOTTA AND FARRO TART
TORTA DI FARRO E RICOTTA

INGREDIENTS

1 cup (200 g/7 oz) pearled
  farro, soaked overnight in
  plenty of cold water

2 cups (500 ml/17 fl oz) milk

grated zest of 3 lemons

300 g (10½ oz) caster
  (superfine) sugar

15 g (½ oz) butter

1 quantity shortcrust pastry
  (see page 47)

500 g (1 lb 2 oz) ricotta
  cheese

½ cup (125 ml/4 fl oz) sweet
  white wine

1 tablespoon pine nuts

1 tablespoon chopped walnuts

1 tablespoon finely diced cedro
  (preserved citron)

4 eggs, separated

icing (confectioners') sugar

METHOD

Drain the farro, then put it in a saucepan and pour in water to cover. Bring to the boil, then reduce the heat and cook for about 45 minutes. Drain. Wipe out the saucepan, then return the farro to the pan and add the milk, two-thirds of the lemon zest, 60 g (2¼ oz) of the sugar and a pinch of salt. Cook slowly until the milk has reduced and the mixture is thick and creamy. Mix in the butter and let cool right down. Meanwhile, roll out the pastry (3 mm/⅛ in thickness) to line a round 28–30 cm (11¼–12 in) tart tin and also a pastry lid for the tart. Refrigerate the lined tart pan and lid. Preheat the oven to 190°C (375°F). Add the ricotta, remaining sugar and lemon zest, wine, nuts and cedro to the farro mixture, then mix in the egg yolks. Whisk the egg whites until they form soft peaks, then fold into the farro mixture. Pour into the pastry case and cover with the pastry lid. Bake for 25–35 minutes until golden – it may be necessary to rotate or move the tart in the oven to get even cooking. Remove from the oven and let cool to room temperature, then dust with icing sugar and serve.

SERVES 8–10   WINE: Sagrantino Passito

VALLE D'AOSTA

VALLE D'AOSTA

A TINY MOUNTAINOUS REGION OF JUST OVER 3000 SQUARE KILOMETRES (1158 SQUARE MILES), THE SPARSELY POPULATED VALLE D'AOSTA HAS ABOUT 130,000 INHABITANTS AND IS TUCKED IN AMONG THE FRENCH RHÔNE-ALPES TO THE WEST, SWITZERLAND TO THE NORTH AND PIEMONTE TO THE SOUTH AND EAST. IT IS ARGUABLY THE LEAST ITALIAN PROVINCE OF ALL, AS FRENCH AS THE ALTO ADIGE IS AUSTRIAN BUT MORE SO, AND HAS A HISTORY OF STUBBORN INDEPENDENCE.

In spite of Valle d'Aosta being the only feudal territory of the Savoys, Elena Kostioukovich author of *Why Italians Love to Talk About Food*, quotes Emanuele Filiberte, one of the representatives of the Savoy dynasty in the 16th century, as writing: 'The Valle d'Aosta does not depend on us, like the others. It has its own laws and customs.'

Fiercely independent and speaking both Italian and Valdôtain (a form of Franco-Provençal), the inhabitants of Valle d'Aosta have a limited but fascinating cuisine that includes some wonderful cheeses, many of which are aged in caves in the mountains. The best known of these is fontina.

Cattle are grazed and cereals grown at high altitude. Even further up, game abounds – in particular the chamois goat, whose population, according to the official Valle d'Aosta tourism website, has in recent decades 'risen steadily, helped by the existence, in the valley, of large areas of woodland'. This is good news for lovers of mocetta, the cured and seasoned 'ham' made from the chamois goat – although you will have to go to the region to try it. Another cured pork product is jambon de Bosses, a ham cured with local herbs including sage, rosemary, thyme and juniper berries.

Speck is also made, as are boudin from local pig's blood and air-dried sausages from a mixture of lean beef, pork, fresh lard and garlic. Fondue is a popular dish, served communally with a mixture of local cheeses.

As is the case in many mountainous regions, soups and stews are at the heart of the cuisine. Some of the local soups are so thick as to be soup in name only, with the base being a beef bouillon that was in former times always simmering on the back of the stove. Such is the soupe à la vapelenentse, in which a layer of slices of wheat bread is topped by finely chopped Savoy cabbage, fontina, butter and then the bouillon. It's a dish to climb mountains on.

One item of produce worth noting, and looking out for should you find yourself in the region, is the martin sec pear. This sweet fruit is customarily baked with red wine and cloves, then served with cream and a glass of grappa.

Very little wine emanates from this mountainous province, and very little of that leaves Italy – or the valley. Most of it is consumed on the spot by locals and skiers, but if ever a region is worth a special trip, it is this one – and not just for the wine, but also for the beauty of the mountain setting, the medieval castles and the vineyards perched on hillsides. The best way to graze across the wines of the region is to visit the Ad Forum Enoteca, the wine promotion centre in the city of Aosta, and plan your trip around the wines that impress you most.

As with the food and the people, there is a distinctly French accent to both the grapes and the wines produced. In the western end of the Valle d'Aosta DOC zone (one DOC covers the entire region), in Morgex, vines are cultivated at 1200 metres (3937 feet) and higher, making them some of the most elevated in Europe. White varieties include Blanc de Morgex et de la Salle, grown in the shadow of Mont Blanc and made into

crisp, acidic still wines – or, using the metodo classico, a sparkler as crisp as the mountain air. There are also local clones of moscato that are made into both dry and sweet wines. Petite arvine makes a light wine with citrus notes. At 640 metres (2099 feet), the chardonnay made in Aymavilles may be one of the most interesting wines in the region. Also to be found are Müller-Thurgau, nus malvoisie and pinot nero, the latter vinified as a dry white wine.

Rosés (rosati) include the prëmetta, referred to as a rosato naturale as its skins are so light and thin that it can only make a pink wine, albeit a very good one.

Although it is difficult to make reds at the altitudes found in Valle d'Aosta, many are made. What they lack in weight, they make up for in brightness. Nebbiolo, here known as picotendro, makes aromatic reds, and gamay is somewhat surprisingly found but used mainly in blends. More beaujolais-like is the wine based on petit rouge, the most widely planted local red wine grape; this can also contain gamay as well as pinot nero, fumin and vien de Nus. Fumin on its own is a local grape that is attracting more attention, making as it does a peppery syrah-like wine.

Sweet wines are made with moscato and nus malvoisie, using the passito method of drying the grapes to intensify the flavour. Of particular interest is the nus malvoisie, which is one of the most enjoyably eccentric of the locals.

VALLE D'AOSTA
ANTI-PASTI

SILVERBEET AND APPLE FRITTATA
FRITTATA DI BIETOLE E MELE

Aosta has great apples. This recipe traditionally uses the renette variety, which has a wonderful tartness to balance its sugar. If renette apples are not available, use a granny smith. This frittata is cooked completely in the pan and not finished in the oven – to my mind, the oven dries the frittata too much.

INGREDIENTS

200 g (7 oz) silverbeet (Swiss chard), leaves and stems separated

⅓ cup (80 ml/2½ fl oz) extra virgin olive oil

1 leek, white part only, thinly sliced

1 garlic clove, minced

1 renette or granny smith apple, peeled, cored and thinly sliced

8 large eggs, lightly whisked

30 g (1 oz) fontina cheese, coarsely grated

30 g (1 oz) parmesan cheese, finely grated

METHOD

Chop the silverbeet leaves into large strips and cut the stems into 5 mm (¼ in) pieces. Bring a saucepan of salted water to the boil and blanch the stems for 2 minutes or so until tender. Remove using a slotted spoon and put in a bowl. Blanch the leaves in the same water for 30–45 seconds. Drain and cool, then squeeze out as much liquid as possible. Heat half the olive oil in a frying pan and lightly fry the leek and garlic for a minute until translucent and aromatic. Add the silverbeet stems and leaves and stir well on medium heat for a couple of minutes. Add the apple and cook until it is soft but not falling apart. Season and stir well, then add to the eggs with the fontina and parmesan. Season lightly and mix well. Heat the remaining oil in a 20 cm (8 in) heavy-based frying pan on high heat until it starts to smoke, then add the egg mixture. Lift the edges continually with a spatula as it cooks so the raw mixture fills the space (this will trap air and make the frittata light and fluffy). Once cooked on the bottom, turn the frittata onto a plate and then slide it back into the pan, uncooked side down. Cook for 2–3 minutes until the centre feels done – touch the centre of the frittata and if it feels too runny, cook a little longer. Slide the frittata onto a plate and let cool for a minute or so, then cut into wedges to serve.

SERVES 8

WINE: Valle d'Aosta Chardonnay

FRESH GOAT'S CHEESE WITH SALSA VERDE
TOMINO AL VERDE

Fresh goat's cheeses are common in the Aosta mountains and are quick and easy to make. They're a perfect light summertime dish served with fresh rocket (arugula).

INGREDIENTS

2 slices bread, crusts removed

⅓ cup (80 ml/2½ fl oz) milk

3 cups parsley leaves

2 garlic cloves

2 tablespoons large capers, rinsed

6 anchovy fillets

juice of 2 lemons

2 hard-boiled eggs

extra virgin olive oil

2 cups finely sliced rocket (arugula) leaves

8 × 40–50 g (1½–1¾ oz) fresh goat's cheeses

METHOD

Soak the bread in the milk for 10 minutes, then squeeze out any excess milk. Put the bread in a food processor with the parsley, garlic, capers, anchovies and lemon juice and process until gritty but not a paste. Add the eggs and enough olive oil to achieve a thick consistency. Season. Put the rocket in a large serving dish, scatter the goat's cheeses around and dress the cheeses with 1 tablespoon of the sauce. Drizzle the remaining sauce on the rocket and serve.

SERVES 8   WINE: Valle d'Aosta Pinot Gris

BAKED FENNEL WITH ROCKET AND FONTINA
FINOCCHIO AL FORNO CON RUCOLA E FONTINA

INGREDIENTS

4–5 large fennel bulbs, trimmed

80 g (2¾ oz) butter

12 slices bread, crusts removed

160 ml (5¼ fl oz) milk

4 hard-boiled eggs, each cut into 4–5 slices

4 cups chopped rocket (arugula)

250 g (9 oz) fontina cheese, grated

60 g (2¼ oz) parmesan cheese, grated

METHOD

Put the fennel in a saucepan of cold water, bring to the boil and simmer for 25–30 minutes. Preheat the oven to 180°C (350°F). Choose a baking dish with a base that will fit a layer of 4 slices of the bread and grease it well with 20 g (¾ oz) of the butter. Drain and cool the fennel, then cut it lengthways into 3 mm (⅛ in) thick slices. Lay 4 slices of bread in the baking tray and sprinkle with one-third of the milk. Add one-third of the fennel and season, then add one-third of the egg, one-third of the rocket and one-third of the fontina. Repeat until you have 3 layers of each ingredient. Distribute the remaining butter and sprinkle the parmesan evenly over the top and bake for 30–40 minutes until golden brown. Remove from the oven and let rest for 5 minutes before serving.

SERVES 4–6   WINE: Chambave Rosso

BAKED CELERY HEARTS WITH MUSHROOMS
SEDANO E FUNGHI AL FORNO

INGREDIENTS

2 celery hearts, tough outer stems removed

20 g (¾ oz) dried porcini mushrooms, soaked in cold water for 15 minutes

¼ cup (60 ml/2 fl oz) extra virgin olive oil

1 brown onion, thinly diced

2 garlic cloves, minced

100 g (3½ oz) button mushrooms, thinly sliced

50 g (1¾ oz) shiitake mushrooms, thinly sliced

½ cup peeled and chopped tomatoes

½ cup parsley, finely chopped

50 g (1¾ oz) grated parmesan cheese

METHOD

Preheat the oven to 180°C (350°F). Keep only the tender celery hearts and cut off the tops so that the hearts are at most about 20 cm (8 in) long. Remove and set aside the light-green and yellow leaves, then halve the hearts lengthways. Bring a saucepan of salted water to the boil and blanch the celery hearts for 2–3 minutes until tender but still al dente. Drain and put in a baking dish to fit snugly. Drain and chop the porcini. Heat the olive oil in a large frying pan and lightly fry the onion and garlic for a minute, then add all the mushrooms and turn up the heat. Season and stir well for a few minutes until the mushrooms have wilted. Add the tomatoes and simmer for 10 minutes, then stir in the parsley and add pepper and more salt (if necessary). Tip into the baking dish, then scatter on the reserved celery leaves and sprinkle with the parmesan. Bake for 25 minutes and serve hot.

SERVES 4   WINE: Val d'Aosta Chambave Muscat

ROAST BEETROOT WITH WALNUTS AND GORGONZOLA
BARBABIETOLE ARROSTITE CON GORGONZOLA E NOCI

INGREDIENTS

24 small–medium red and golden beetroots (beets)

2 tablespoons extra virgin olive oil

200 g (7 oz) gorgonzola cheese (or other blue cheese), broken into small pieces

150 g (5½ oz) walnut pieces, lightly roasted

METHOD

Preheat the oven to 180°C (350°F). Trim both ends of the beetroots, then use a soft brush to scrub them well under cold water. Pat dry and toss with half the olive oil. Season, then wrap in foil and roast for 15 minutes or so until tender. Unwrap immediately and let cool before peeling and quartering. Meanwhile, preheat the griller (broiler) to high. Transfer the beets to an ovenproof plate and sprinkle with the remaining olive oil. Scatter the gorgonzola over and put under the grill (broiler) for a few seconds until the cheese has melted. Scatter the walnuts on top and serve.

SERVES 8–10   WINE: Val d'Aosta Chambave Muscat

PICKLED CARROTS
CAROTE IN AGRO

INGREDIENTS

500 g (1 lb 2 oz) small
   new-season carrots

350 ml (12 fl oz) dry white
   wine

1 cup (250 ml/9 fl oz) white
   wine vinegar

1 rosemary sprig

1 parsley sprig

1 mint sprig

6 basil leaves

2 bay leaves

2 garlic cloves, peeled and
   halved

10 black peppercorns

1 tablespoon caster (superfine)
   sugar

¼ cup (60 ml/2 fl oz) extra
   virgin olive oil, plus extra
   for serving

½ cup chopped mint leaves

1 cup chopped parsley

METHOD

Trim the tops of the carrots, leaving a little of the stem on, then peel, wash well and halve lengthways. Put the carrots in a flameproof casserole dish and add all the remaining ingredients except the chopped mint and half the chopped parsley. Pour in 2 cups (500 ml/17 fl oz) cold water and bring to the boil. Turn the heat down and simmer for 20 minutes, then drain through a very fine sieve, keeping the liquid. Pick out the carrots and put them in a glass or ceramic container. Pour the cooking liquid over and add the remaining parsley. Let cool, cover and refrigerate for 48 hours. To serve, drain and dress with olive oil and chopped mint. Will last one month if refrigerated.

SERVES 8   WINE: Pinot Bianco

VALLE D'AOSTA
PRIMI

CREAM OF POTATO AND PORCINI
CREMA DI PATATE E PORCINI

INGREDIENTS

⅓ cup (80 ml/2½ fl oz) extra virgin olive oil

100 g (3½ oz) pork sausages, casing removed

1 small brown onion, finely chopped

1 celery heart, finely chopped

1 small carrot, finely chopped

¼ cup parsley, finely chopped

600 g (1 lb 5 oz) potatoes, cut into 2 cm (¾ in) cubes

2 cups (500 ml/17 fl oz) chicken or vegetable stock

15 g (½ oz) dried porcini mushrooms, soaked in cold water for 15 minutes

1 garlic clove, minced

50 g (1¾ oz) grated parmesan cheese

100 g (3½ oz) button mushrooms, diced

METHOD

Heat half the olive oil in a saucepan and gently fry the sausage meat with the onion, celery, carrot and parsley for 2 minutes. Add the potato and stock. Bring to the boil, then turn the heat down and simmer for 30 minutes. Puree using a stick blender. Drain and finely chop the porcini. Heat half the remaining oil in another frying pan and gently fry the garlic, mushrooms and porcini for 3–4 minutes, then add this mixture (including any pan juices) to the puree and heat gently. Mix in the parmesan and season, then drizzle with the remaining oil to serve.

SERVES 6   WINE: Mayolet

RED ONION SOUP
ZUPPA DI CIPOLLE

The famous red onions from Tropea in Calabria are available throughout Italy these days (even in supermarkets) and are used in many regional dishes – such as this hearty onion, bread and cheese soup from Aosta. The soup can be prepared in individual ramekins if you prefer.

INGREDIENTS

120 g (4¼ oz) unsalted butter

500 g (1 lb 2 oz) red onions (preferably Tropea), thinly sliced

3 tablespoons plain (all-purpose) flour

2 litres (70 fl oz) vegetable or beef broth

4 slices bread (1–2 days old), halved

50 g (1¾ oz) Grana Padano, grated

100 g (3½ oz) gruyère cheese, thinly sliced

METHOD

Preheat the oven to 200°C (400°F). Heat half the butter in a large saucepan and fry the onions on medium heat for 3–4 minutes until wilted. Add the flour slowly, stirring and cooking until there are no lumps. Keep stirring for a few minutes as the flour cooks. Pour in the broth and bring to the boil, then turn the heat down and simmer for 15 minutes, stirring occasionally. Meanwhile, fry the bread in the remaining butter until brown on both sides. Season the soup. Arrange the fried bread in a baking dish and pour the soup over. Sprinkle on the Grana Padano and then cover with the gruyère. Bake until the cheese has melted and browned a little.

SERVES 4   WINE: Valle d'Aosta Syrah

PARSNIP AND POTATO PASTICCIO
PASTICCIO DI PASTINACA E PATATE

INGREDIENTS

40 g (1½ oz) butter

750 g (1 lb 10 oz) parsnips, cut into 2 cm (¾ in) rounds

750 g (1 lb 10 oz) unpeeled potatoes

2 garlic cloves, peeled

½ cup parsley

leaves from 1 marjoram sprig

6 eggs

250 g (9 oz) grated parmesan cheese

¼ cup (60 ml/2 fl oz) extra virgin olive oil

½ teaspoon grated nutmeg

METHOD

Preheat the oven to 180°C (350°F) and grease a flan (tart) tin or pie dish (28 cm (11¼ in) diameter) with the butter. Cook the parsnips and potatoes separately in plenty of boiling water until soft. Peel the potatoes and put them in a large bowl. Add the parsnips and mash the lot using a fork. Finely chop the garlic, parsley and marjoram together. Whisk the eggs, parmesan and olive oil together, then add to the mash with the garlic/herbs and nutmeg. Season and mix well. Spoon into the tart tin and bake for 30–35 minutes until crispy on the outside and soft in the centre. Serve hot.

SERVES 6   WINE: Torrette

PEAR, HAZELNUT AND PARMESAN SALAD
INSALATA DI PERE, NOCCIOLE E PARMIGIANO

INGREDIENTS

3 ripe pears (packham, winter
   nelis or comice), peeled,
   cored and halved
1 tablespoon apple cider
   vinegar
juice of ½ lemon
⅓ cup (80 ml/2½ fl oz) extra
   virgin olive oil
4 slices good-quality country-
   style bread
2 witlof (chicory), leaves
   separated
½ cup chopped rocket
   (arugula)
4 tablespoons hazelnuts,
   roasted and skinned
125 g (4½ oz) parmesan
   cheese, shaved
1 tablespoon snipped chives

METHOD

Put the pears in a bowl with the vinegar, lemon juice and half the olive oil. Grind on a few turns of pepper and mix carefully using your hands. Set aside. Brush the bread with the remaining oil and grill (broil) or fry until golden. When you are ready to serve, add the witlof, rocket, hazelnuts and parmesan to the pears, season lightly with salt and toss gently. Pile neatly on the toasted bread and sprinkle with the chives to serve.

SERVES 4   WINE: Pinot Nero

VALDOSTANA-STYLE POTATO GNOCCHI
GNOCCHI ALLA VALDOSTANA

INGREDIENTS

1 quantity potato gnocchi (see
   page 359)
300 g (10½ oz) fontina cheese,
   coarsely grated
100 g (3½ oz) Parmigiano
   Reggiano, grated
120 g (4¼ oz) unsalted butter
1 garlic clove, lightly crushed

METHOD

Bring a large saucepan of salted water to the boil and plunge in the gnocchi. Once they come to the surface, remove using a flat sieve (also known as a spider) and drain on a clean tea towel (dish towel). Put the gnocchi on a large, hot serving plate and sprinkle the fontina and parmesan evenly over the top. Keep the gnocchi warm. Heat the butter and garlic in a small frying pan until the butter is bubbling and nut-brown. Remove and discard the garlic, then spoon the hot butter over the gnocchi, season and serve.

SERVES 8   WINE: Valle d'Aosta Fumin

TAGLIATELLE WITH TROUT SAUCE
TAGLIATELLE AL SUGHETTO DI TROTA

The few pasta dishes that have come north are mostly based on soft wheat tagliatelle. This sauce makes good use of freshwater fish, especially trout, which are found in abundance in mountain streams.

INGREDIENTS

2–3 trout (total weight about 600 g/1 lb 5 oz), filleted and skin removed

30 g (1 oz) unsalted butter

1 leek, white part only, finely chopped

1 garlic clove, minced

1 tablespoon capers, rinsed and chopped

2 thyme sprigs

300 g (10½ oz) tin tomatoes, mashed

1 teaspoon minced chilli

1 quantity basic pasta dough (see page 42), cut to tagliatelle size (approx. 1 cm (½ in) wide

2 tablespoons extra virgin olive oil

METHOD

Remove all the bones from the trout, then chop the flesh into 2 cm (¾ in) pieces and set aside. Heat the butter in a wide frying pan and gently fry the leek, garlic, capers and thyme. Add the tomatoes, chilli and 2–3 good pinches of salt and simmer on medium heat for 7–8 minutes until the sauce thickens. Add the trout and stir. Meanwhile, cook the pasta in plenty of boiling salted water until al dente. Drain the pasta and toss with the sauce, adding a little more salt and pepper if needed. Drizzle the olive oil over and serve immediately.

SERVES 6   WINE: Valle d'Aosta Chardonnay

OF ALL ITALY'S REGIONS, VALLE D'AOSTA HAS THE MOST TENUOUS LINKS WITH PASTA AS ITS CULINARY TRADITIONS ARE INFLUENCED MAINLY BY FRANCE, SWITZERLAND AND PIEMONTE. IT IS FROM THE LATTER, WITH WHICH AOSTA SHARES A BORDER TO THE SOUTH, THAT THE TRADITION OF PASTA COMES.

VALLE D'AOSTA
SECONDI

SALMON WITH SOUR ONIONS
SALMONE CON CIPOLLE ALL'AGRO

INGREDIENTS

¼ cup (60 ml/2 fl oz) extra virgin olive oil

4 × 200 g (7 oz) pieces salmon (2 cm/¾ in) thick), skin off

2 large brown onions, halved and very thinly sliced

100 ml (3½ fl oz) white wine vinegar

4 pinches dried oregano

METHOD

Heat 1 tablespoon of the olive oil in a wide frying pan on medium heat and gently fry the salmon for 1–1½ minutes on each side until lightly browned but still pink in the middle. Remove from the pan and set aside. Wipe out the pan, add the remaining oil and fry the onions on medium heat until soft and sweet. Turn up the heat, add a couple of good pinches of salt and pour in the vinegar. Let it evaporate, then pour the contents of the pan over the salmon. Rest for 10 minutes, then divide among 4 plates and add a pinch of oregano to each. Serve.

SERVES 4   WINE: Chardonnay

BRAISED BEEF SHOULDER WITH LEEKS AND SAGE
SPALLA DI MANZO IN UMIDO

INGREDIENTS

1 large leek, trimmed and washed

1 carrot

1 celery heart

4 garlic cloves

1 × 1.5–1.75 kg (3 lb 5 oz–3 lb 12 oz) piece beef blade, trimmed of membrane and excess fat

⅓ cup (50 g/1¾ oz) plain (all-purpose) flour

150 ml (5 fl oz) extra virgin olive oil

3 cups (750 ml/26 fl oz) dry white wine

8 tinned tomatoes, mashed

1 cup sage leaves

1 cup chopped parsley

METHOD

Put the leek, carrot, celery and garlic in a food processor and pulse until finely chopped. Dust the beef with the flour. Heat one-third of the olive oil in a wide frying pan and fry the beef on medium heat, browning both sides well, then remove from the pan. Add half the remaining oil and fry the chopped vegetables on medium heat for 5–6 minutes until softened. Return the beef to the pan and turn the heat up to high. Pour in the wine, add the tomatoes and bring to the boil. Turn the heat down and add the sage leaves, half the parsley and 2–3 good pinches of salt. Cover and simmer on very low heat for 2½ hours. Once the blade has cooked, add the remaining parsley and simmer, uncovered, for 20 minutes. Add a little more salt if necessary and a few turns of pepper, then serve in slices with some of the sauce.

SERVES 8   WINE: Val d'Aosta Syrah

VEAL CUTLETS WITH WHITE TRUFFLE AND FONTINA
COSTOLETTE DI VITELLO ALLA VALDOSTANA

With the famous white truffles of Piemonte next door, this Val d'Aosta recipe is a perfect way to showcase the precious fungi. Along with the local fontina cheese – which is used extensively in truffle dishes across the northern regions – and the delicate flavour of veal, this is a grand dish. If fresh truffle is not available, proceed without it.

INGREDIENTS

8 slices fontina cheese

4 slices leg ham

4 × 160–180 g (5¾–6½ oz) veal cutlets (2 cm/¾ in) thick)

30 g (1 oz) white truffle, thinly shaved

3 eggs, lightly whisked

⅓ cup (50 g/1¾ oz) plain (all-purpose) flour

100 g (3½ oz) fine dry breadcrumbs

80 g (2¾ oz) butter

METHOD

Trim the fontina and ham slices so they are about 2 cm (¾ in) smaller in diameter than the veal cutlets. Using a sharp knife, make an incision on the opposite side of each cutlet to where the bone is. Cut along half the circumference of the cutlet to divide the meat in half and create a pocket that is deep enough to insert the fontina and ham slices. Insert 2 slices of fontina and 1 slice of ham into each cutlet pocket, then add a few slices of truffle. Press each cutlet down firmly using the palm of your hand to close it tight. Season the eggs. Dust each cutlet with flour, dredge in egg and press into the breadcrumbs. Melt the butter in a large frying pan on medium heat until frothing, then add the cutlets. Turn the heat down a little so the butter doesn't burn and cook the cutlets for a couple of minutes on each side until golden on the outside and rosy-pink in the middle. Drain on paper towels for 30 seconds and serve.

SERVES 4   WINE: Valle d'Aosta Torrette

FONTINA IS AN ALPINE CHEESE PRODUCED IN VALLE D'AOSTA. IT'S MADE OF RAW MILK OBTAINED FROM THE LOCAL VALDOSTANA BREED OF COW. ONCE MADE, THE CHEESES ARE MATURED FOR AT LEAST 80 DAYS IN CAVES AND SOMETIMES MILITARY BUNKERS. THE RESULT IS A WHEEL WEIGHING 8-12 KG (13-17 LB) WITH A RUSSET-COLOURED CRUST AND AN INTERNAL COLOUR RANGING FROM PALE CREAM TO INTENSE YELLOW. THE TEXTURE IS SEMI-HARD AND CREAMY. IT IS PERFECT FOR FONDUE AND SAUCES. IT IS PARTICULARLY GOOD WITH WHITE TRUFFLES.

VEAL VALDOSTANA STYLE
FETTINE DI CARNE ALLA VALDOSTANA

INGREDIENTS

50 g (1¾ oz) unsalted butter

8 × 70 g (2½ oz) slices veal sirloin (5 mm/¼ in thick)

200 g (7 oz) fontina cheese, thinly sliced

1 tablespoon capers, rinsed and chopped

1 tablespoon chopped parsley

METHOD

Heat the butter in a wide frying pan and brown the veal for 15 seconds on each side. Put 1–2 slices of fontina on each piece of meat and sprinkle with the capers and parsley. Season with a couple of pinches of salt, then cover and cook on low heat for 3–4 minutes. Serve immediately with roast potatoes or other roast vegetables.

SERVES 4   WINE: Valle d'Aosta Petite Arvine

BRAISED VENISON SHOULDER IN RED WINE
CAPRIOLO ALLA VALDOSTANA

INGREDIENTS

1.2 kg (2 lb 12 oz) venison shoulder, cut into 3 cm (1¼ in) cubes

1 brown onion, chopped

1 carrot, chopped

1 celery heart, chopped

3 garlic cloves, crushed

2 bay leaves

1 thyme sprig

3 cloves

6 juniper berries

1 cinnamon stick

3 cups (750 ml/26 fl oz) red wine

50 ml (1½ fl oz) extra virgin olive oil

¼ cup (60 ml/2 fl oz) grappa

60 g (2¼ oz) plain (all-purpose) flour

300 g (10½ oz) tin tomatoes, mashed

1.5 litres (52 fl oz) beef broth (see page 48)

½ cup chopped parsley

METHOD

Put the venison in a bowl with the onion, carrot, celery, garlic, bay leaves, thyme and spices. Add 2–3 good pinches of salt and a few turns of pepper and pour in the red wine. Stir, cover and let marinate in the refrigerator for at least 24 hours, mixing every 6 hours or so. Drain, reserving the marinade and discarding the vegetables, herbs and spices. Pat the venison dry, then heat the olive oil in a flameproof casserole dish and brown the venison on medium heat for a couple of minutes. Splash in the grappa and let it evaporate (be careful that it doesn't catch fire). Sprinkle in the flour and keep cooking and stirring on low heat for 3 minutes, then add the marinade, tomatoes and broth and bring to the boil. Turn the heat down to very low, cover and cook for 70 minutes. Check the meat for tenderness – it should take another 30 minutes or so to cook but will depend on the type of venison (red deer will take longer than fallow deer to cook). Simmer, uncovered, until the liquid has reduced and thickened. If the dish becomes too dry, add a little hot water. When the venison is cooked, check for seasoning and adjust with salt and freshly cracked pepper. Stir in chopped parsley. Serve with polenta (cornmeal; see page 41).

SERVES 6   WINE: Torrette

VALLE D'AOSTA DOLCI

ALMOND AND HAZELNUT BISCUITS WITH COCOA CREAM
TEGOLE VALDOSTANE CON CREMA AL CACAO

INGREDIENTS

butter

200 g (7 oz) egg whites (approx. 7 eggs)

2 cups (200 g/7 oz) almond meal

125 g (4½ oz) hazelnut meal

90 g (3¼ oz) plain (all-purpose) flour

400 g (14 oz) caster (superfine) sugar

½ teaspoon natural vanilla extract

COCOA CREAM

10 eggs

¾ cup (160 g/5¾ oz) caster (superfine) sugar

¾ cup (80 g/2¾ oz) good-quality unsweetened cocoa powder

1 litre (35 fl oz) milk

peel from ¼ lemon, cut into strips

40 g (1½ oz) dark chocolate, broken into pieces

METHOD

To make the cocoa cream, whisk the eggs and sugar until pale and creamy. Whisk in the cocoa until the mixture is completely free of lumps, then whisk in the milk. Transfer to a saucepan and add the lemon peel. Heat slowly on medium heat, continually stirring, until the mixture thickens and coats the back of a spoon. Be careful that the eggs don't overheat and scramble. Pass through a sieve into a bowl, discarding the lemon peel. Let cool for 5 minutes, then whisk in the chocolate – the mixture should be hot enough to melt it. Transfer to small bowls or pots and let cool to room temperature.

Preheat the oven to 180°C (350°F) and grease 2 or 3 baking trays with butter. In a large bowl, whisk the egg whites to firm peaks. In a separate bowl, combine the almond meal, hazelnut meal, flour, sugar and a pinch of salt. Carefully fold the egg whites and vanilla into the dry mixture. Fit a piping bag with a 5 mm (¼ in) nozzle and fill with the mixture, then pipe 3 cm (1¼ in) rounds on the baking trays, keeping 4 cm (1½ in) between each round. Bake for 10 minutes then cool on racks. Serve with the cocoa cream.

MAKES 40–50   WINE: Petite arvine Vendemmia Tardiva (late-picked)

ONE OF THE BEST HAZELNUTS, THE 'TONDA GENTILE' VARIETY, IS GROWN IN THE NEIGHBOURING PIEMONTE REGION. FAMOUS THE WORLD OVER AND AN ESSENTIAL INGREDIENT FOR TOP PASTRY CHEFS, THIS HAZELNUT HAS ITS OWN APPELLATION, PROTECTED BY ITALIAN LAW. ONCE TOASTED IT HAS A FINE, PERSISTENT NUTTINESS AND CAN BE GROUND TO A SMOOTH PASTE FOR USE IN PASTRY, BISCUITS, CREAMS, GELATO AND CHOCOLATE.

SPICED APPLES WITH TOFFEE WALNUTS
MELE SPEZIATE E NOCI AL CARAMELLO

INGREDIENTS

1 lemon

4 large apples, peeled and
cored

80 g (2¾ oz) brown sugar

20 g (¾ oz) unsalted butter

2 star anise

½ teaspoon anise seeds

8 black peppercorns

200 ml (7 fl oz) dry white wine

⅔ cup (80 g/2¾ oz) walnut
halves

METHOD

Using a vegetable peeler, peel strips of zest from the lemon. Reserve the zest. Juice the lemon into a bowl and pour in 2 litres (70 fl oz) water. Cut the apples into half-moon slices about 5 mm (¼ in) thick and put in the lemon water. Put the sugar, butter and spices in a large saucepan and heat until the sugar has completely melted. Add the wine and reserved lemon peel and stir well. Arrange the apples neatly in the liquid and simmer for about 20 minutes until the apples are tender but not overcooked or falling apart. Transfer the apples to a bowl and strain the liquid, discarding the spices. Return the liquid to the pan and boil until it thickens. Turn the heat down to very low and add the walnuts, stirring to completely coat them with the toffee. Use a fork to remove the walnuts to a sheet of baking paper. Return the apples and any juice to the pan and stir carefully. Serve warm or at room temperature with the toffee walnuts (and cream or ice cream if you must).

SERVES 6   WINE: Nus Malvoisie Flétri

BLUEBERRY SEMIFREDDO
SEMIFREDDO AI MIRTILLI

Each year in August in the town of Fontainemore, in the Lys Valley at an altitude of 1200 km (760 miles), there is a sagra (festival) to celebrate blueberries.

INGREDIENTS

50 g (1¾ oz) unsalted butter

100 g (3½ oz) caster
(superfine) sugar

450 g (1 lb) blueberries

2 egg whites

200 ml (7 fl oz) thickened
(whipping) cream, whipped

METHOD

Melt the butter in a frying pan, then add 30 g (1 oz) of the sugar and cook until lightly caramelised. Add the blueberries and stir gently. Mix in ¼ cup (60 ml/2 fl oz) water, then remove from the heat and let cool. Whisk the egg whites to soft peaks and gradually whisk in the remaining sugar to form firm, glossy peaks. Gently fold the egg whites into the blueberry caramel mixture, then fold in the cream. Spoon into 6 moulds 150 ml (5 fl oz) and refrigerate overnight. When you are ready to serve, dip the base of each mould in hot water and the semifreddo should easily slip out.

SERVES 6   WINE: Chambave muscat Flétri

SPICED APPLES WITH TOFFEE WALNUTS

BAKED FIG CUSTARD TART
TORTA DI FICHI ALLA CREMA

INGREDIENTS

1 quantity shortcrust pastry
   (see page 47)

4 large egg yolks

2 level teaspoons cornflour
   (cornstarch)

½ teaspoon natural vanilla
   extract

100 g (3½ oz) caster
   (superfine) sugar

1 cup (250 ml/9 fl oz)
   thickened (whipping) cream

8–10 figs, stems removed,
   halved lengthways

METHOD

Preheat the oven to 160°C (320°F). Roll out the pastry to fit a 24 cm (9½ in) tart tin. Line the tin with the pastry and refrigerate while you prepare the filling (the pastry does not have to be blind-baked). Whisk together the egg yolks, cornflour, vanilla, 80 g (2¾ oz) of the sugar and a pinch of salt, then whisk in the cream. Arrange the figs cut side up in the tart shell and pour the mixture in carefully so it comes almost to the top of the shell. Sprinkle with the remaining sugar and put the tin on a baking tray. Bake for 35–40 minutes. Cool to room temperature in the tin before serving.

SERVES 8   WINE: Petite arvine Vendemmia Tardiva (late-picked)

PEACHES STUFFED WITH AMARETTI AND CHOCOLATE
PESCHE RIPIENE

INGREDIENTS

4 large yellow peaches

2 eggs

40 g (1½ oz) caster (superfine)
   sugar

30 g (1 oz) good-quality
   unsweetened cocoa
   powder

100 g (3½ oz) amaretti
   biscuits, crumbled

20 g (¾ oz) unsalted butter

METHOD

Preheat the oven to 170°C (340°F). Bring a saucepan of water to the boil and immerse the peaches, holding them under, for 30 seconds. Immediately plunge them into iced water to cool, then peel and cut in half. Remove and discard the stones. Using a teaspoon, make the cavity in each peach twice its original size. Whisk the eggs and sugar together, then whisk in the cocoa and add the amaretti biscuits. Fill each peach half with the mixture and arrange in a baking dish. Dab ½ teaspoon butter on top of each peach half and bake for 20–25 minutes. Serve at room temperature.

SERVES 4   WINE: Chambave moscato passito

CHESTNUT AND VANILLA CREAM WITH CHOCOLATE
CREMA DI CASTAGNE AL CIOCCOLATO

INGREDIENTS

300 g (10½ oz) chestnuts, scored

100 ml (3½ fl oz) milk

80 g (2¾ oz) caster (superfine) sugar

seeds from 1 vanilla bean

3 tablespoons thick (double) cream

170 g (6 oz) dark chocolate (70% cocoa solids)

200 ml (7 fl oz) thin (pouring) cream

1 egg yolk

METHOD

Boil the chestnuts for 30 minutes, then peel. Reserve 4 chestnuts and pass the rest through a sieve or ricer. Bring the milk to the boil in a saucepan and add the sieved chestnuts, sugar, vanilla seeds and thick cream. Simmer for 10–15 minutes until the mixture thickens, then set aside to cool. Roughly chop 120 g (4¼ oz) of the chocolate and put in a small metal bowl. Heat ½ cup (125 ml/4 fl oz) of the thin cream in a saucepan on medium heat until hot to touch (70°C/160°F), then pour it over the chocolate and rest for 1 minute. Stir with a whisk until very smooth, then add the egg yolk and whisk to combine. Cool. Grate the remaining chocolate, whip the remaining cream and chop the reserved chestnuts. Spoon some chestnut cream into dessert glasses, then some chocolate cream and then more chestnut cream. Finish with a dollop of whipped cream, some grated chocolate and a sprinkle of chopped chestnuts.

SERVES 6–8   WINE: Petite arvine Vendemmia Tardiva (late-picked)

VENETO

VENETO IS THE EIGHTH-LARGEST REGION IN ITALY, WITH A TOTAL AREA OF AROUND 18,000 SQUARE KILOMETRES (3089 SQUARE MILES). IT IS IN THE NORTH-EAST, BORDERED TO THE EAST BY FRIULI-VENEZIA GIULIA, TO THE SOUTH BY EMILIA-ROMAGNA, TO THE WEST BY LOMBARDIA AND TO THE NORTH BY TRENTINO-ALTO ADIGE. AT ITS NORTHERNMOST CORNER IT SHARES A BORDER WITH AUSTRIA.

Veneto can be divided into four areas: the northern alpine zone, the hill zone, the lower plain and the coastal territory. By area, 29 per cent of its surface is mountainous. The Po Valley covers just over half of Veneto, and is divided into the higher plain (which is gravel-strewn and not very fertile) and the lower plain (which is rich in water sources and arable terrain). The lower plain is both a mainstay of agricultural production and the most populated part of the region.

Veneto is among the wealthiest, most developed and most industrialised regions of Italy, and has among the richest of the country's historical, natural, artistic, cultural, musical and culinary heritages. The contrast between the ancient, canal-carved city of Venice, with its 15th- and 16th-century palazzi and general air of decadence and languor, and the green hills of the Veneto, with its neat towns and occasional white Palladian villas, is stark.

Venice's fish and seafood are at the heart of its cuisine, and that is why the fish market of the Rialto is known as the cuore della città, the heart of the city. There you will find caragoi (sea snails), caparossoli (clams) and cape longhi (razor clams). Sardines are fried and marinated with onions and vinegar to make sarde in saòr, a method of preserving the fish; this was an important dish for sailors and fishermen, who carried it with them packed in barrels.

One of the eccentricities of Venetian cuisine is that when you order baccalà, you will get not salted cod, as you would in the rest of Italy, but dried cod, called elsewhere stoccafisso. The locals know the difference, but stick stubbornly to the Venetian way.

Other Venetian classics include the humble risi e bisi, or rice with peas, and the similar-sounding but very different risi e bisati, or rice with eel; fegato alla veneziana, veal liver with onions; and a dish invented in Venice in the famous Harry's

Bar some 50 years ago: carpaccio, or thinly sliced raw beef dressed with oil and lemon. Carpaccio was named after the 15th-century Venetian painter Vittore Carpaccio, and was first served to the countess Amalia Nani Moncenigo.

Choice seasonal produce from the region includes the cherries of Marostica, the peaches of Verona, chestnuts from the Trevisan mountains, and the white asparagus from Bassano del Grappa. Then there are the famous purple artichokes from Sant'Erasmo in the Venetian lagoon. In their youthful incarnation they are called canarini, the fruit of the second cutting is called castraure, the third cutting produces a true artichoke, and from the fourth come the bottoms.

The risottos of the Veneto are many and famed, among them risotto with asparagus, pumpkin, frog's legs, treviso radicchio, and seafood. They are traditionally made all'onda, or wavy – more liquid in consistency than the risotto of some other regions.

Outside Venice, especially in Verona, you will find dishes made using meats that may give you pause for thought even if you are a convinced carnivore: cavallo (horse) and asino (donkey). Horse is served as sfilacci, or strands, dried and sometimes smoked, often over a bed of rocket (arugula), or as a bistecca di cavallo, or horse steak.

In addition to being the home of horse meat, Verona is the site for Vinitaly, the largest and most important wine show in Italy. It is Italy's answer to France's Vinexpo, which is held in Bordeaux; this is apposite, as Verona has been called the Bordeaux of Italy.

Veneto has long been famed for its wines, with the Romans enthusing about reticum and acinaticum 2000 years ago. Today, the province is the third- or fourth-largest producer in Italy after Emilia-Romagna, Puglia and Sicilia, but the largest, in terms of numbers of bottles, of DOC wines. There are 23 DOCs in the region, but 30 per cent of the classified wine comes from one zone: Soave, near Verona. Here the white wines are made based on the garganega grape. The red wines of the area are bardolino and valpolicella, which are both blended but based on the corvino grape.

A relatively recent addition to the list of DOCs is Garda, which admits many local and foreign varietals, including corvina, garganega, pinot noir, the cabernets of Bordeaux, riesling italico and others. It is worth seeking out.

SATAN'S DRINK

Although the Arabs had first introduced coffee to Sicily in the 10th century, it wasn't until around this time that Italy's long and ardent love affair with coffee began.

The Venetians re-introduced it through their trade with the Turks in the early 17th century. At first, because of coffee's association with Islam, the Christian church had denounced it as a 'Satanic threat to the soul' – but it was irresistible.

In 1600 Pope Clement VIII responded to pressure from his prelates to ban coffee by pronouncing: 'Why, this Satan's drink is so delicious it would be a pity to let the infidels (Muslims) have exclusive use of it. We shall fool Satan by baptising it, and making it a truly Christian beverage.'

According to the book *Caffeine* by Weinberg and Healer, there is an unconfirmed story of a coffee house opening in 1645 somewhere in Italy. But the first historically verifiable date for a coffee house in Italy is for one in Venice, name unknown, in 1683. Less than 40 years later, in 1720, Caffe Florian opened; it soon became the most famous coffee house in Europe, attracting such illustrious patrons as Casanova, Rousseau, Byron and Georges Sand, and is there to this day.

VENETO
ANTI-
PASTI

PICKLED SEASONAL VEGETABLES
GIARDINIERA

Pickled vegetables can be found throughout Italy, with local flourishes. This basic method can be added to any vegetables, including celery, zucchini (courgette), celeriac, red and yellow capsicums (peppers), chillies and red onions. Serve the pickled vegetables as an antipasto or with terrines, salumi and boiled meats.

INGREDIENTS

4 litres (7 pints) white
   wine vinegar

200 g (7 oz) sugar

220 g (7¾ oz) salt

5 black peppercorns

5 small red chillies

5 juniper berries

5 cloves

5 bay leaves

florets from 2 kg (4 lb 8 oz)
   cauliflower

2 kg (4 lb 8 oz) green beans,
   trimmed and cut into
   3–4 cm (1¼–1½ in) pieces

2 kg (4 lb 8 oz) carrots, cut
   into sticks 3–4 cm long ×
   1 cm thick (1¼–1½ in × ½ in)

2 kg (4 lb 8 oz) baby onions,
   halved

METHOD

Put the vinegar, sugar, salt, peppercorns, chillies, juniper berries, cloves, bay leaves and 2 litres (70 fl oz) water in a large saucepan and bring to the boil. Turn the heat down and simmer the vegetables one variety at a time until tender but still slightly crunchy. As each vegetable is ready, remove it from the liquid using a sieve and transfer to a large bowl. When they are all done, mix well. Pour in hot cooking liquid to cover and let cool, then transfer the vegetables and liquid to a container, seal and refrigerate for 3–4 days before using. (To preserve the pickled vegetables, drain and put in preserving jars, cover with extra virgin olive oil, seal and sterilise. They will keep indefinitely.) To serve, drain your desired quantity of vegetables, toss with olive oil and chopped parsley, and season.

MAKES about 10 litres (17½ pints)

SWEET AND SOUR CARROTS
CAROTE IN AGRODOLCE

INGREDIENTS

50 g (1¾ oz) sultanas (golden
   raisins)

⅓ cup (80 ml/2½ fl oz) sweet
   white wine

2 tablespoons extra virgin olive
   oil

1 kg (2 lb 4 oz) carrots, cut into
   5 mm (¼ in) slices

2 tablespoons duck fat

30 g (1 oz) pine nuts

120–160 ml (4–5¼ fl oz) red
   wine vinegar

METHOD

Put the sultanas and sweet wine in a small saucepan on a low heat until the sultanas swell 5–10 minutes, then drain and set aside. Heat the olive oil in a deep frying pan and add enough carrots to cover the base. Dot with duck fat and add another layer of carrots. Repeat until all the carrots and fat have been used. Sprinkle with a couple of pinches of salt, then cover and simmer gently for 20 minutes or until the carrots can be pierced with a fork. Add the sultanas and pine nuts, turn the heat up to medium and mix gently. If there is too much fat, drain it off. Add the vinegar and mix well. Cook on high heat until the liquid has evaporated and the carrots are browned. Can be served hot or at room temperature.

SERVES 6–8   WINE: Valpolicella Classico

SALMON CRUDO
CRUDO DI SALMONE

Crudo, which you often see on restaurant menus, simply means 'raw' in Italian. Occasionally there is a whole crudo section on a menu. Rather than carpaccio, the correct description of raw seafood is crudo.

INGREDIENTS

480 g (1 lb 1 oz) very fresh salmon, skin off

2 small cucumbers, trimmed and quartered lengthways

leaves from 150 g (5½ oz) large-leafed rocket (arugula), thinly sliced

½ cup (125 ml/4 fl oz) extra virgin olive oil

1 lemon

METHOD

Cut the salmon into 5 mm (¼ in) cubes and put in a large bowl in the fridge, covered. Cut the cucumber into thin wedges and toss in a bowl with a pinch of salt. Leave for 20 minutes, then rinse with cold water and pat dry using a clean tea towel (dish towel). Add to the salmon with the rocket, olive oil and a couple of pinches of salt and mix well. Carefully remove the rind from the lemon using a vegetable peeler so no white pith is attached, then cut the rind into thin strands. Juice the lemon and toss the juice with the salmon and vegetables. Check for seasoning and arrange on plates. Finish with a turn of pepper and strands of lemon rind.

SERVES 6–8   WINE: Garganega/Trebbiano blend

FRITTATA WITH WILD GREENS
FRITTATA ALLE ERBE DI CAMPO

Wild greens have been gathered for generations throughout Italy, not only for their taste but also from necessity. In the Veneto, especially, there are many unusual 'weeds' that grow in open pastures and paddocks. I particularly like sgrizoi, or sculpit, a little-known weed that grows abundantly in many parts of the region where there are mountain pastures. Its top shoots and leaves are often pickled and served as antipasto.

INGREDIENTS

2–3 cups mixed wild greens – such as dandelion leaves, borage, wild rocket (arugula), cime di rapa (broccoli raab), wood sorrel and sculpit

1 French shallot, finely diced

1 garlic clove, minced

2 teaspoons extra virgin olive oil

6 eggs

2 tablespoons grated parmesan cheese

METHOD

Wash the wild greens thoroughly. Bring a large saucepan of salted water to the boil and plunge in the wild greens. Blanch for a minute, then drain well. Heat half the olive oil in a frying pan and lightly fry the shallot and garlic for 30 seconds to soften, then add the wild greens. Fry on medium heat for a couple of minutes and season lightly. Whisk 2 of the eggs in a bowl with half the parmesan and a little salt and pepper. Heat the remaining olive oil in a 15–18 cm (6–7 in) heavy-based frying pan and pour in the whisked egg. Move the egg around the pan to cover the base. It will take less than a minute to cook through, and should still be a little creamy. Spoon one-third of the greens on top, then transfer to a warm plate and quickly repeat the whole process to make 2 more frittatas. Cut in half and serve immediately.

SERVES 6   WINE: Custoza Bianco Superiore

SALMON CRUDO

BRAISED ARTICHOKES
CARCIOFI ALLA VENETA

INGREDIENTS

juice of 1 lemon

12 artichokes, trimmed
  (see page 39)

1½ cups parsley leaves

2 garlic cloves

100 ml (3½ fl oz) extra virgin
  olive oil

100 ml (3½ fl oz) vegetable
  stock (see page 49)

METHOD

Put the lemon juice in a large bowl with 2 litres (70 fl oz) water. When trimming the artichokes, leave 2 cm (¾ in) of leaves above the heart and cut the stems so the artichokes can sit with the hearts facing up. As each artichoke is prepared, put it in the lemon water to prevent discolouration. Finely chop the parsley and garlic together. Heat the olive oil in a saucepan that is large enough to hold all the artichokes and lightly fry the parsley and garlic for a minute. Add the artichokes and fry on medium heat for 2–3 minutes, continually stirring. Add the vegetable stock and a couple of pinches of salt and pepper. Turn the heat down to low, cover and cook for 20–30 minutes until the artichokes are tender. Transfer the artichokes to a serving plate and dress with the cooking liquid. Serve warm.

SERVES 6   WINE: Pinot Bianco

VENETO
PRIMI

RADICCHIO AND POLENTA SOUP
ZUPPA DI POLENTA E RADICCHIO

INGREDIENTS

120 g (4¼ oz) dried cannellini
    beans, soaked in plenty of
    cold water overnight

1 carrot, cut into chunks

1 small brown onion, halved

1 celery stick

1 bay leaf

1 tablespoon extra virgin
    olive oil

80 g (2¾ oz) pancetta, finely
    chopped

3 heads of radicchio

1.5 litres (52 fl oz) vegetable
    stock (or water)

100 g (3½ oz) fine polenta
    (cornmeal)

METHOD

Drain the beans, then put in a large saucepan with the carrot, onion, celery and bay leaf and pour in water to cover. Bring to the boil, then turn the heat down and simmer for about 2 hours until the beans are tender. Drain and discard the vegetables. Heat the olive oil in a frying pan and gently fry the pancetta for a couple of minutes. Drain on paper towels and set aside. Parboil the radicchio heads in a large saucepan of water for 15 minutes, then drain, cool and chop finely. Wipe out the saucepan, pour in the vegetable stock and bring to the boil. Add the radicchio and when the stock comes back to the boil, sprinkle in the polenta in a fine stream, stirring constantly. Simmer for 10 minutes, then add the pancetta and beans. Stir well and cook for 15–20 minutes. Season and serve.

SERVES 4–6   WINE: Breganze Rosso

CHICKEN AND CABBAGE SOUP
ZUPPA DI POLLO E VERZA

INGREDIENTS

6 chicken drumsticks, skin on

⅓ cup (80 ml/2½ fl oz) extra
    virgin olive oil

2 leeks, white part only, halved
    lengthways and cut into
    1 cm (½ in) slices

1 brown onion, chopped

4 garlic cloves, chopped

1 celery heart, chopped

½ Savoy cabbage, tough outer
    leaves discarded

5 cups cavolo nero (Tuscan
    kale), finely chopped

300 g (10½ oz) tin tomatoes,
    mashed

grated parmesan cheese

½ cup (125 ml/4 fl oz) extra
    virgin olive oil

METHOD

Sprinkle the chicken with salt. Heat the olive oil in a saucepan, add the drumsticks and fry until well browned, turning often. Remove from the pan and set aside. Put the leeks, onion, garlic and celery in the pan and lightly fry for 2 minutes, continually stirring. Add the cabbage and cavolo nero and stir well, then pour in cold water to cover. Add the tomatoes and chicken, season with 2–3 good pinches of salt and stir well. Bring to the boil, then turn the heat down and simmer for 1 hour. Turn off the heat and taste for seasoning, adjusting if necessary. Leave for 1 hour, then serve (one drumstick per person) with grated parmesan, a drizzle of the olive oil and plenty of crusty bread. The soup tastes better the day after you make it, and better the day after that.

SERVES 6   WINE: Valpolicella

TAGLIATELLE WITH RABBIT, OLIVE AND TOMATO
TAGLIATELLE CON SALSA AL CONIGLIO, OLIVE E POMODORO

INGREDIENTS

240 ml (8 fl oz) extra virgin olive oil

1 rabbit, jointed into pieces (you can ask your butcher to do this, if you prefer)

1 large brown onion, finely diced

3 garlic cloves, minced

½ cup chopped parsley

1 celery heart, chopped

6 large green olives, pitted and chopped

2 tablespoons capers, rinsed and chopped

450 ml (16 fl oz) tomato passata

3 tablespoons chopped fresh oregano

1 tablespoon caster (superfine) sugar

½ cup (125 ml/4 fl oz) red wine vinegar

800 g (1 lb 12 oz) basic pasta dough (page 42), cut to tagliatelle size (approx. 1 cm (¼ in))

grated parmesan cheese

METHOD

Heat one-third of the olive oil in a large, deep frying pan. Fry the rabbit pieces until well browned, then set aside. Wipe out the pan and heat the remaining oil. Fry the onion and garlic until translucent, then throw in the parsley and celery and stir for 30 seconds. Stir in the olives, capers, tomato passata and oregano and cook for about 10 minutes. Throw in the rabbit pieces and stir everything together. Season, then cover and simmer gently for 10 minutes, stirring occasionally. Dissolve the sugar in the vinegar and add to the pan. Turn up the heat and stir and cook until the liquid has reduced by half. Turn off the heat, put the lid back on and leave for 2 hours, mixing every 30 minutes. Remove the rabbit and let it cool enough to handle, then remove the flesh from the bones. Cut the flesh into bite-sized pieces and return to the sauce. Cook the tagliatelle in plenty of boiling salted water, then drain and toss with the sauce. Serve with grated parmesan.

SERVES 8   WINE: Breganze Bianco

SKEWERED SCALLOPS AND PANCETTA
SPIEDINI DI CAPPESANTE E PANCETTA

This recipe is based on a dish I had at Hostaria Via Caprera in the town of Vittorio Veneto, province of Treviso.

INGREDIENTS

8 slices pancetta, halved

16 scallops

¼ cup (60 ml/2 fl oz) extra virgin olive oil

1 red capsicum (pepper), cored and chopped

1 small potato, sliced

1 brown onion, finely chopped

2 garlic cloves, minced

METHOD

Have ready 4 skewers. Roll a piece of pancetta around each scallop, then thread 4 scallops onto each skewer and refrigerate until you are ready to cook. Heat 2 tablespoons of the olive oil in a frying pan and fry the capsicum, potato, onion and garlic on medium heat, stirring, for 2–3 minutes. Pour in water to cover, add a couple of pinches of salt and simmer for 15–20 minutes until the potato is tender. Transfer to a blender or food processor and blitz to a thick but runny sauce. Season. Wipe out the pan, then fry the scallop skewers in the remaining oil, turning, until the pancetta is crisp. Spoon the sauce onto serving plates and arrange the skewers on top to serve.

SERVES 4   WINE: Soave Superiore

CHICKEN LIVERS WITH ROAST BEETS
FEGATINI DI POLLO CON BARBABIETOLE ARROSTO

Lamb's tongue lettuce, or lamb's lettuce (corn salad), is called mâche in French and valeriana in Italian. In the province of Brescia it is known as grassello.

INGREDIENTS

8 plump lobes of chicken liver, trimmed of fat and sinew

8 small beetroots (beets), trimmed but unpeeled

⅓ cup (80 ml/2½ fl oz) extra virgin olive oil

30 g (1 oz) butter

2 tablespoons red wine vinegar

12 clumps lamb's lettuce (corn salad), trimmed

1 tablespoon finely snipped chives

METHOD

Preheat the oven to 180°C (350°F). Put the chicken livers on a plate, cover and refrigerate. Put the beetroots in small baking dish or ovenproof frying pan and toss with half the olive oil and a little salt and pepper. Bake for 15–20 minutes until tender. Remove from the oven and set aside in the dish. In a frying pan, heat the butter and half the remaining oil until foaming. Sprinkle the livers with salt and pepper and fry for 3–4 minutes, turning once. Remove from the pan and keep warm. Return the pan to medium heat and add half the vinegar, scraping the bottom of the pan using a wooden spoon as the liquid bubbles. Once it has reduced to a couple of tablespoons, turn off the heat. Slice the chicken livers. Toss the lamb's lettuce with the remaining oil and vinegar and arrange on a plate with the beets and chicken livers. Spoon on the reduced pan juices and sprinkle with chives to serve.

SERVES 4   WINE: Custoza Superiore

PORK HEAD TERRINE
TESTA IN TERRINA

INGREDIENTS

2 pig heads, well washed and
  any bristles removed

2 pig tongues (optional)

3 carrots, each cut into
  4–5 pieces

3 celery sticks, cut into
  large pieces

3 brown onions, quartered

1 garlic bulb, halved

15 thyme sprigs

5 black peppercorns

3 bay leaves

1 teaspoon fennel seeds

1 handful parsley stalks

3 cups (750 ml/26 fl oz)
  white wine

¼ cup (60 ml/2 fl oz) red
  wine vinegar

METHOD

Put the pig heads and tongues (if using) in a large saucepan with all the other ingredients except the vinegar. Pour in water to cover. Bring to the boil, then reduce the heat and simmer very gently for 5 hours or until all the meat is tender (the tongues should be removed after 1–1½ hours). Remove the pig heads from the pan and let cool slightly. Peel away and set aside all the prime sections of meat, such as the cheek and near the brains. Put the heads back into the pan along with any bones that may have come loose, and simmer for 3 hours. Remove the heads from the pan again and strain the cooking liquid through a sieve lined with a double layer of muslin (cheesecloth). Spoon a little of the stock into a small bowl or plate and chill to check the gel. It should be firm but not too rubbery. If it doesn't set, reduce the liquid by a quarter and retest. Set aside.

Remove all the remaining meat and skin from the pig heads. Remove the ears and snout and cut them into 1 cm (½ in) cubes. If you cooked the tongues, cut them into 2 cm (¾ in) cubes. Line a terrine mould (or two) with plastic wrap, leaving enough overhang on the two long sides to fully cover the mould. Put all the meat in a bowl and use your fingers to mix gently, then add the vinegar and mix. Transfer to the terrine mould and pour in enough of the reserved cooking liquid to just cover. Fold the plastic wrap over the top and press down on the mixture to make sure it fills the entire space of the mould. Refrigerate overnight or for up to 2 weeks. Cut into wedges and serve with young salad leaves and pickled vegetables (see page 587).

SERVES 12–18

WINE: Valpolicella

BRAISED SALAMI WITH CARROTS AND POTATOES
SALAME IN UMIDO

This recipe calls for 'small fresh salame', which is a soft, usually small salame that is often found in Italy's northern regions. Substitute with large Italian fresh sausage if salame is not available.

INGREDIENTS

2 potatoes, cut into 2 cm (¾ in) cubes

½ cup (125 ml/4 fl oz) extra virgin olive oil

150 g (5½ oz) small fresh salame

8 small carrots, cut into 5–6 cm (2–2½ in) pieces

250 g (9 oz) large carrots, cut into 1–2 cm (¾ in) slices

1 garlic clove, minced

1 rosemary sprig

300 ml (10½ fl oz) clear chicken or veal stock

2 teaspoons chopped rosemary

METHOD

Put the potatoes in a bowl and cover with cold water. Set aside until needed. Heat the olive oil in a heavy-based saucepan and gently fry the salame for a minute or so, turning once. Transfer the salame to a plate. Drain the potato and pat dry, then put in the pan and fry on all sides until golden. Add the carrots, garlic, rosemary sprig and a couple of pinches of salt and turn the heat up to high. Pour in the chicken stock and gently stir. Bring to the boil, then turn the heat down and add the salame. Cover and simmer for 10 minutes until the potatoes and carrots are tender but not overcooked. Add a few turns of pepper, mix well and serve hot sprinkled with the chopped rosemary.

SERVES 4   WINE: Valpolicella

WHILE THE **SALAMI** KNOWN OUTSIDE ITALY ARE USUALLY THE AGED, FIRM TYPE, WITHIN THE COUNTRY MOST REGIONS ALSO USE VERSIONS THAT ARE SOFT OR FRESH AND NOT OVERLY DRIED. ONE FAMOUS EXAMPLE IS CALABRIAN 'NDUJA WHICH IS FINELY MINCED AND MIXED WITH A LOT OF DRIED CHILLI. IT IS LEFT IN ITS GUT FOR UP TO A YEAR BUT IS ALWAYS LIKE A SPREADABLE PASTE. OTHER SOFT SALAMI CAN ALSO BE COARSELY MINCED; SOMETIMES SLICED AND EITHER FRIED OR BRAISED; SOMETIMES REMOVED ENTIRELY FROM THEIR SAC AND USED IN PASTA SAUCES, PIZZA OR EVEN SOUPS.

BRAISED SALAMI WITH CARROTS AND POTATOES

POLENTA WITH SAUSAGES AND TRUFFLE
POLENTA CON SALSICCIE E TARTUFO

INGREDIENTS

1 cup (190 g/6¾ oz) good-quality polenta (cornmeal) (such as polenta di Storo or Mulino Marino)

1 tablespoon butter

1 tablespoon extra virgin olive oil

1 brown onion, chopped

500 g (1 lb 2 oz) Italian sausage

½ cup sage leaves

15 g (½ oz) black truffle, thinly sliced

METHOD

Bring 1.25 litres (44 fl oz) water and 1 teaspoon salt to the boil in a saucepan that has a tight-fitting lid. Slowly add the polenta, stirring constantly using a wooden spoon or a whisk until it comes away from the sides of the saucepan and thickens. Turn the heat down to very low, cover and simmer for at least 1 hour, stirring well every 5 minutes until the polenta is soft and tender but not runny. (The longer it is cooked, the thicker and more flavoursome it will be.) Heat the butter and oil in a frying pan and gently fry the onion for 30 seconds. Add the sausage and fry gently until the sausage is almost cooked, then add the sage leaves and cook until they are crisp. Remove the pan from the heat. Chop the sausage into pieces and return to the pan with any juices. Season. Spoon the polenta onto plates and arrange the sausage, sage and pan juices on top. Finish with truffle slices.

SERVES 6   WINE: Ripasso

VENETO
SECONDI

POACHED MEATS WITH BONE MARROW AND PEPPER SAUCE
BOLLITO MISTO CON LA PEARÀ

Bollito misto is popular all across the northern regions and can be very elaborate, with as many as 12–15 different poached meats – including various special cuts of beef, tongue, ribs, chicken, duck, cotechino sausage and the like. This is a simple, manageable recipe. More cuts can be added once you are confident and if you have a lot of people to feed. Around Verona the sauce, which dates back to medieval times, is called pearà, *from* pear *(pronounced PEH-ar), the local dialect's word for 'pepper'. It is made using a terracotta cooking pot, but care must be taken that the pot is well seasoned and will not crack. Terracotta is preferred because it allows food to cook slowly and evenly.*

INGREDIENTS

1 large brown onion, halved

1 celery heart

4 garlic cloves

6 parsley stalks

1 × 1.2 kg (2 lb 12 oz) piece chuck steak

1 × 500 g (1 lb 2 oz) calf tongue

1 × 2.2–2.5 kg (5 lb–5 lb 8 oz) chicken

1 × 300 g (10½ oz) cotechino sausage

BONE MARROW AND PEPPER SAUCE

1 litre (35 fl oz) broth from bollito misto (see method)

1½ cups fine dry breadcrumbs

150 g (5½ oz) unsalted butter

1 × 50 g (1¾ oz) piece bone marrow

½ tablespoon finely ground black pepper

1 teaspoon ground cinnamon

80 g (2¾ oz) Grana Padano, grated

METHOD

Pour 8 litres (1¾ gallons) cold water into a large saucepan and add the onion, celery, garlic and parsley stalks. Bring to the boil and boil for 5 minutes, then turn the heat down and gently add the beef, tongue and chicken. Bring back to the boil, then turn the heat down, cover and simmer for 1 hour. Put the cotechino in a separate saucepan with plenty of cold water and bring to the boil. Immediately turn the heat down and simmer gently for 1 hour. Remove the chicken from the first saucepan and transfer to a large stainless steel or ceramic bowl with a little of the cooking liquid. Cover and keep warm. Check the tongue by piercing it with a sharp knife – if it is tender, transfer to the bowl with the chicken; if not, keep cooking until tender, then transfer to the bowl. Cook the beef for 2–2½ hours altogether. Drain, reserving 1 litre (35 fl oz) of the broth to make the bone marrow and pepper sauce.

To make the bone marrow and pepper sauce, heat the reserved broth gently in a saucepan, then slowly add about three-quarters of the breadcrumbs, whisking constantly so there are no lumps, until the mixture starts to boil and thicken. Turn the heat down to very low and whisk in the butter and bone marrow. Once they have both melted, stir in the pepper and cinnamon. Cook for about 1½ hours until the sauce is the consistency of runny polenta, stirring using a wooden spoon as if making polenta, and scraping the bottom and sides so the sauce doesn't stick. If necessary, put a simmer mat under the pan to keep the sauce from sticking. If it gets too dry, add a little more hot broth; if too wet, add more breadcrumbs. When it is ready, a little fat should be developing on the surface. Mix in the Grana Padano and season with salt.

Slice all the meat and serve with the bone marrow and pepper sauce and other accompaniments such as mustard fruits, salsa verde, olive tapenade and freshly grated horseradish.

SERVES 8–10   WINE: Colli Euganei Cabernet

FISH 'IN CARPIONE'
PESCE IN CARPIONE

Once upon a time this was an efficient way of preserving excess fish. It was perfected by the Venetians and spread to neighbouring regions to be used for freshwater and saltwater fish alike. The frying oil can be reused a few times as long as it is strained between uses.

INGREDIENTS

1.2 kg (2 lb 12 oz) fish fillets (snapper, bass, kingfish, perch or similar), cut into 40–50 g (1½–1¾ oz) pieces

½ cup (75 g/2½ oz) plain (all-purpose) flour

1 litre (35 fl oz) extra virgin olive oil

MARINADE

1 litre (35 fl oz) dry white wine

100 ml (3½ fl oz) white wine vinegar

2 large brown onions, thinly sliced

4 celery stalks, thinly sliced

3 carrots, thinly sliced

3 garlic cloves, lightly crushed

2 bay leaves

1 green chilli, halved lengthways

1 teaspoon salt

METHOD

To make the marinade, put all the ingredients in a saucepan and bring to the boil, then turn the heat down and simmer for 20 minutes. Meanwhile, dust the fish with the flour and heat the oil in a large, wide frying pan to 170°C (340°F) (to test the temperature, drop in a cube of bread – it should turn golden in 20 seconds). Gently drop in the fish pieces and cook until golden. Remove with tongs and transfer to a large bowl. Slowly ladle the hot marinade carefully over the fish, then let cool to room temperature. Serve the fish with wilted greens, such as broccoletti or cime di rapa (broccoli raab).

SERVES 4–6

WINE: Cartizze Brut

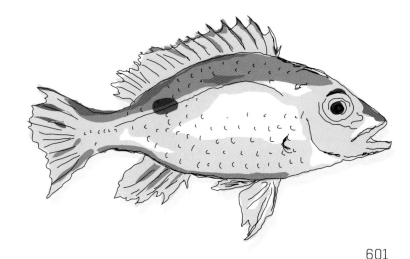

DUCK BREAST WITH GRAPES
PETTO D'ANITRA ALLA GRIGLIA ALL'UVA

This is a restaurant dish but is very easy to make as long as the duck breast is not overcooked. It can just as easily be done with quail, which is a lot more forgiving than duck.

INGREDIENTS

4 duck breast fillets, skin on

1 cup (250 ml/9 fl oz) chicken or duck stock

1 cup grapes (either red or white or mixed), halved lengthways

1 tablespoon redcurrant or lambrusco jelly

1 tablespoon extra virgin olive oil

1 tablespoon good-quality balsamic vinegar

METHOD

Preheat the oven to 220°C (430°F). Salt the skin of the duck breasts well and put them in an ovenproof frying pan on medium heat, skin side down (no oil). Brown the skin, letting the duck fat render out (you may need to turn down the heat if the duck begins to brown too quickly). Once the skin is crisp, drain the fat from the pan. Put the pan in the oven for 3 minutes, then transfer the duck to a warm plate to rest and wipe out the pan. Pour the stock into the pan and reduce on high heat by two-thirds. Add the grapes and jelly and simmer until the jelly has dissolved. Season and stir in the olive oil. Slice the duck breasts and arrange on plates with the sauce and grapes. Sprinkle with the balsamic vinegar to serve.

SERVES 4   WINE: Amarone

DUCK IN ITALY IS COOKED IN THREE MAIN WAYS. THE FIRST IS SLOWLY SIMMERED IN ITS OWN FAT AND THEN PRESERVED UNDER THAT FAT. THIS IS KNOWN THROUGHOUT THE WORLD AS DUCK CONFIT. IT CAN THEN BE USED IN SALADS, SOUPS AND THE LIKE. NEXT IS CUT INTO JOINTS AND SLOWLY BRAISED IN A LIQUID. IT CAN THEN BE SERVED AS A SOUP, IN WHOLE PIECES WITH THE LIQUID REDUCED TO A SAUCE OR SHREDDED TO ACCOMPANY PASTA. THE THIRD, ROASTING, GRILLING OR PAN-FRYING, USES DRY HEAT AND IS PERHAPS THE MOST DEMANDING OF SKILL ON THE PART OF THE COOK.

DUCK BREAST WITH GRAPES

GRILLED PORK CHOP WITH BRAISED DANDELION
COTOLETTA DI MAIALE ALLA GRIGLIA

Dandelion grows like a weed in many gardens, but in some restaurants it's a much sought-after ingredient. If dandelion is not available, substitute radicchio, treviso lettuce or even spinach leaves. A wood-burning grill will give the best results here, imparting a smoky flavour to the pork. If this is not available, then a gas barbecue or large frying pan will do.

INGREDIENTS

6 × 160–180 g (5¾–6½ oz) pork chops

⅓ cup (80 ml/2½ fl oz) extra virgin olive oil

300 g (10½ oz) dandelion leaves, well washed

2 French shallots, minced

1 garlic clove, minced

2 teaspoons good-quality balsamic vinegar

METHOD

Rub the pork chops with half the olive oil and season lightly on both sides. Cook on a hot grill or barbecue for 2–3 minutes on each side, then rest in a warm place for 10–15 minutes. Meanwhile, blanch the dandelion leaves for 30 seconds in boiling water. Drain and squeeze out any excess water. Heat the remaining oil in a frying pan and gently fry the shallots and garlic for a minute until soft. Turn up the heat and toss in the leaves. Fry for 2–3 minutes, stirring, then turn off the heat and add the balsamic vinegar. Season. Serve the pork chops on the braised dandelion leaves.

SERVES 6   WINE: Bardolino

CRUMBED VENISON CUTLETS WITH CABBAGE SALAD
COTOLETTE DI CAPRIOLO CON INSALATA DI VERZE

INGREDIENTS

8 venison cutlets

1 cup breadcrumbs

¼ cup grated parmesan cheese

4 tablespoons chopped sage

¼ Savoy cabbage, thinly sliced

¼ cup (60 ml/2 fl oz) red wine vinegar

160 ml (5¼ fl oz) extra virgin olive oil

½ cup (70 g/2½ oz) plain (all-purpose) flour

2 eggs, whisked

50 g (1¾ oz) butter

METHOD

Press each venison cutlet gently between 2 pieces of plastic wrap, flattening a little to 1.5 cm (⅝ in) thick. Combine the breadcrumbs, parmesan and sage and season. Toss the cabbage with the vinegar and half the olive oil, then season and set aside. Dust each cutlet with the flour, dip in the egg and press with the crumb mixture. In a large frying pan, heat the butter and remaining oil until foaming. Add the cutlets and cook for a couple of minutes on each side until golden brown. Drain, season with salt and serve with the cabbage.

SERVES 4   WINE: Valpolicella Ripasso

ROAST PUMPKIN AND CHESTNUT PUREE
PURÈ DI ZUCCA E CASTAGNE

This is a great accompaniment for roast pork, turkey, chicken or duck.

INGREDIENTS

500 g (1 lb 2 oz) chestnuts, scored

500 g (1 lb 2 oz) pumpkin (such as Marina di Chioggia variety), cut into 2 cm (¾ in) cubes

½ cup sage leaves

80 g (2¾ oz) pancetta, thinly sliced

¼ cup (60 ml/2 fl oz) extra virgin olive oil

vegetable or chicken stock

METHOD

Preheat the oven to 180°C (350°F). Cook the chestnuts in boiling water for 5 minutes until tender. Drain and peel as soon as they are cool enough to handle, making sure both the skin and the fine inner pellicle are removed. Put in a baking dish with the pumpkin, sage and pancetta and toss with the olive oil. Season and bake for 30 minutes. Set aside 2–3 roast chestnuts and a couple of crisp sage leaves that are intact. Set aside the pancetta. Put the remaining roast pumpkin, chestnuts and sage in a food processor and blend, adding enough stock to make a thick puree. Check for seasoning and adjust if necessary. Garnish the puree with the reserved chestnuts, sage and pancetta to serve.

SERVES 6

WINE: Breganze Rosso

VENETO

DOLCI

CHERRIES IN GRAPPA
CILIEGIE SOTTO GRAPPA

All good grappa is different and expresses the quality of the initial fruit used. One of my favourite producers, Gianni Capovilla, makes grappa and distillates of extreme quality. Use as good a grappa as you can afford for this recipe.

INGREDIENTS

1 kg (2 lb 4 oz) cherries, pitted

50 g (1¾ oz) caster (superfine) sugar

200 ml (7 fl oz) best-quality grappa

½ cup mint leaves

METHOD

Put all the ingredients in a bowl, stir well and refrigerate for 3 hours. Every 30 minutes, stir well. Transfer to sterilised small preserving jars and seal. The cherries will impart more of their flavour to the grappa the longer they stay sealed. Serve in individual bowls with mascarpone cream (see page 52) or gelato, with the cherries and some of their juice spooned over.

MAKES 1 kg (2 lb 4 oz)

PANETTONE WITH CHERRIES IN RECIOTO AND MASCARPONE CREAM
PANETTONE CON CILIEGIE AL RECIOTO

Recioto di Soave is an exceptionally good sweet wine made from garganega grapes. Any late-picked sweet white wine can be substituted.

INGREDIENTS

1 kg (2 lb 4 oz) cherries, pitted

60 g (2¼ oz) sugar

150 ml (5 fl oz) Recioto di Soave

8 slices panettone, each cut into 3

MASCARPONE CREAM

3 egg whites

⅓ cup (75 g/2½ oz) caster (superfine) sugar

300 g (10½ oz) mascarpone cheese

METHOD

Put the cherries, sugar and Recioto in a saucepan, cover and simmer gently for 5 minutes. Transfer the cherries to a tray and let cool. Boil the cooking liquid vigorously until it reduces by half. Cool, then combine with the cherries and refrigerate overnight. To make the mascarpone cream, whisk the egg whites until soft peaks form. Slowly add the sugar, whisking continually until firm peaks form. Fold in the mascarpone and refrigerate until needed. To serve, layer the panettone with the mascarpone cream and cherries and spoon on some of the juice.

SERVES 8   WINE: Recioto di Soave

CARMELISED PEAR CUSTARD TART

CARAMELISED PEAR CUSTARD TART
CROSTATA DI PERE ALLA CREMA

INGREDIENTS

juice of ½ lemon

4 large ripe but firm winter nelis or bosc pears

100 g (3½ oz) caster (superfine) sugar

4 × 65 g (2¼ oz) egg yolks

2 level teaspoons cornflour (cornstarch)

½ teaspoon natural vanilla extract

1 cup (250 ml/9 fl oz) thickened (whipping) cream

SWEET SHORTCRUST PASTRY

350 g (12 oz) plain (all-purpose) flour

70 g (2½ oz) caster (superfine) sugar

½ teaspoon baking powder

grated zest of 1 lemon

170 g (6 oz) cold unsalted butter, cut into 1 cm (½ in) cubes

1 egg

1 egg yolk

¼ cup (60 ml/2 fl oz) thick (double) cream

METHOD

To make the sweet shortcrust pastry, put the flour, sugar, baking powder, lemon zest and a pinch of salt in a food processor and pulse until well combined. Add the cold butter cubes and pulse repeatedly until the mixture resembles sand. In a bowl, whisk together the egg, egg yolk and cream, then add this mixture to the food processor and pulse until the mixture forms a ball. Flatten the dough to a disc and refrigerate wrapped in plastic wrap for 3–4 hours.

Preheat the oven to 160°C (320°F). Roll out the pastry to a thickness of 2 mm and use to line 8 × 12 cm (4½ in) tart tins. Refrigerate the lined tins. Pour 2 litres (70 fl oz) water into a bowl and add the lemon juice. Peel the pears, then cut them in half lengthways and remove and discard the cores. Put the pears in the lemon water to prevent them going brown. Whisk 80 g (2¾ oz) of the sugar with the egg yolks, cornflour, vanilla and a pinch of salt, then whisk in the cream. Remove the pears from the lemon water and pat dry with a clean tea towel (dish towel). Slice each piece into 3 and then cut each slice across into 3 cm chunks. Arrange in the tart tins, then carefully pour in the batter until almost full – you should be able to see pear chunks poking through the batter. Sprinkle with the remaining sugar and put the tins on a tray or trays. Bake for 35–40 minutes. Cool to room temperature in the tins, then serve.

SERVES 8

WINE: Recioto di Soave

PUMPKIN AND AMARETTO PUDDING WITH ANISE CREAM
BUDINO DI ZUCCA E AMARETTO

INGREDIENTS

300 g (10½ oz) pumpkin (winter squash) flesh, sliced

2 cups (500 ml/17 fl oz) milk

1 vanilla bean, split and seeds scraped

100 g (3½ oz) sugar

1 teaspoon amaretto liqueur

2 eggs, whisked

15 pieces of soft eating liquorice, cut into 1 cm (½ in) slices

ANISE CREAM

250 ml (9 fl oz) thick (double) cream

3 cups (750 ml/26 fl oz) milk

1 tablespoon anise seeds

1¼ (275 g/9¾ oz) cups caster (superfine) sugar

12 egg yolks

METHOD

To make the anise cream, combine the cream, milk, anise seeds and 1 cup (220 g/7¾ oz) of the sugar in a saucepan and bring to a simmer, then remove from the heat. Meanwhile, whisk the egg yolks with the remaining sugar in a heatproof bowl until thick and pale. Add the hot milk mixture and whisk to combine. Put the bowl over a saucepan of boiling water (or use a double boiler) and cook, stirring, until thick (12–15 minutes). Strain, then cool in the fridge. Makes about 1.5 litres (52 fl oz) and can also be used as custard.

Preheat the oven to 120°C (250°F). Put the pumpkin, milk, sugar and vanilla pod and seeds in a saucepan and simmer until the pumpkin is soft. Add the amaretto and eggs and whisk well. Remove and discard the vanilla pod, then push the pumpkin and all the liquid through a fine sieve into a bowl. Spoon the mixture into 100 ml (3½ fl oz) moulds and put the moulds in a baking dish. Pour in water to come halfway up the sides of the moulds, then bake for 50 minutes. Cool before unmoulding onto plates. Serve with the anise cream and a slice of liquorice.

MAKES 12–15 depending on size of mould   **WINE:** Torcolato

CHOCOLATE PUDDING
BUDINO DI CIOCCOLATO

INGREDIENTS

2 cups (500 ml/17 fl oz) milk

100 g (3½ oz) caster (superfine) sugar

2 eggs

2 egg yolks

¼ cup (30 g/1 oz) good-quality unsweetened cocoa powder

METHOD

Preheat the oven to 130°C (265°F). Put the milk in a saucepan and bring almost to the boil, then remove from the heat. Whisk the sugar, eggs and egg yolks in large bowl until fluffy and the sugar has completely dissolved. Mix in the cocoa, then slowly pour in the hot milk, mixing well so there are no lumps. Pour into 6 moulds 100 ml (3½ fl oz) and cover each mould with plastic wrap. Put the moulds in a baking dish and pour in water to come halfway up the sides of the moulds. Bake for 45 minutes. Cool to room temperature before placing in the refrigerator for at least 4 hours. Unmould to serve.

SERVES 6   **WINE:** Grappa

TORRONE AND CHOCOLATE TARTUFO
TARTUFO AL CIOCCOLATO E TORRONE

INGREDIENTS

½ cup (70 g/2½ oz) raw peanuts

⅛ cup (80 g/2¾ oz) blanched almonds

1 kg (2 lb 4 oz) hard Italian torrone, roughly diced

1 cup grated chocolate

GELATO BASE

1.5 litres (52 fl oz) thin (pouring) cream

200 g (7 oz) honey

100 g (3½ oz) sugar

12 egg yolks

CHOCOLATE CREAM

200 ml (7 fl oz) thin (pouring) cream

300 g (10½ oz) best-quality milk chocolate, cut into small pieces

METHOD

To make the gelato base, put the cream, honey and sugar in a saucepan and bring to a simmer, then remove from the heat. Set aside to cool. Beat the egg yolks in the bowl of an electric mixer until thick and pale. Pour in the cream mixture and mix to combine. Churn in an ice-cream machine according to the manufacturer's instructions.

To make the chocolate cream, heat the cream until almost boiling, then remove it from the heat and whisk in the chocolate. Set aside to cool.

Preheat the oven to 100–120°C (200–250°F). Roast the peanuts and almonds until lightly browned (10-15 minutes), roughly chop them then let cool and mix thoroughly with the chocolate cream. Add to the gelato and mix in the torrone, then spoon into 16 individual moulds (150 ml/ 5 fl oz) and freeze overnight.

When you are ready to serve, unmould the tartufi, roll in the grated chocolate and serve.

MAKES 16   WINE: Colli Euganei Fior d'Arancio Passito

THE HUMBLE INGREDIENTS OF HONEY, EGG WHITES AND ALMONDS, WHEN MIXED AND THEN COOKED, FORM ONE OF THE CLASSIC ITALIAN CHRISTMAS TREATS. IT'S DIFFICULT TO ASCERTAIN THE ORIGINS OF TORRONE, OR AS THE FRENCH CALL IT, NOUGAT. ALTHOUGH IT WAS THE ROMANS WHO FIRST MADE MENTION OF THE SWEET, ONE OF THE OLDEST AND FINEST EXAMPLES IS THE SICILIAN CUBBAITA, OF ARABIC ORIGIN. THERE'S A LOT OF GOOD TORRONE MADE IN ITALY BUT ONE OF MY FAVOURITES IS SCALDAFERRO, MADE IN DOLO, A CHARMING TOWN BETWEEN VENICE AND PADUA.

BAKED QUINCE WITH POLENTA SHORTBREAD AND MASCARPONE CREAM
MELE COTOGNE ALLA SBRISOLONA

INGREDIENTS

500 g (1 lb 2 oz) sugar

4 quinces, washed

1 vanilla bean, split

peel from 2 mandarins

2 star anise

⅓ cup (80 ml/2½ fl oz) thin (pouring) cream

50 g (1¾ oz) caster (superfine) sugar

80 g (2¾ oz) mascarpone

icing (confectioners') sugar

POLENTA SHORTBREAD

125 g (4½ oz) plain (all-purpose) flour

80 g (2¾ oz) fine polenta (cornmeal)

1 cup (100 g/3½ oz) blanched almond meal

80 g (2¾ oz) caster (superfine) sugar

1 egg yolk

juice of ½ lemon

grated zest of 1 lemon

60 g (2¼ oz) butter, melted

50 g (1¾ oz) duck or goose fat, melted (or 50 ml/1½ fl oz extra virgin olive oil)

1 teaspoon natural vanilla extract

METHOD

Preheat the oven to 130°C (250°F). Place the sugar and 1.5 litres (52 fl oz) water in a saucepan and bring to the boil. Stir well to make sure the sugar has all dissolved, then pour the syrup into a baking dish. Peel and quarter the quinces, cutting out the woody cores. Put the quince peel and cores in a piece of clean muslin (cheesecloth) and tie securely. Add the quinces, muslin bag, vanilla bean, mandarin peel and star anise to the baking dish and bake for 4–5 hours until the quinces are deeply coloured and tender. Remove and let cool in the cooking liquid (the baked quinces will store well in the fridge).

Adjust the oven temperature to 180°C (350°F). To make the polenta shortbread, combine the flour, polenta, almond meal, sugar, egg yolk, lemon juice and lemon zest, then mix in the butter, duck fat and vanilla. Roll out the mixture to about 5 mm (¼ in) thick and use an egg ring or an 8 cm/3¼ in cutter to cut out rounds. Arrange on a non-stick or greased baking tray and bake for 30 minutes until golden but not dark. Let cool on the tray before moving.

When you are ready to serve, whip the cream and sugar to firm peaks, then fold into the mascarpone. Layer the polenta shortbread with the mascarpone cream and sliced quince and dust with icing sugar.

SERVES 8–10   WINE: Recioto di Soave

BAKED QUINCE WITH POLENTA SHORTBREAD AND MASCARPONE CREAM

ACKNOWLEDGEMENTS

To Julie Manfredi-Hughes, my business partner and ex-wife who supports all my varied endeavours.

To the entire team at Manfredi at Bells. Thanks to Cameron who runs the kitchen and his team supported by Duncan. Thanks to Shady, extraordinary pastry chef and baker whose contribution to the recipes in this book is immense. Thank you Brian and Karina and John Singleton for the opportunity.

To the team at Balla. Thanks Gabriele for your impeccable organization and leadership in the kitchen. Grazie to Francesco and Riccardo who make up the triumvirate to lead the large kitchen team. Grazie to restaurant manager Luca and to Fabio, our sommelier, who has carried my idea of an all-Italian list and made it his own.

Special thanks to the many quality importers of Italy's food and wine treasures: Gianmarco Balestrini at Lario; Michael Trembath and Virginia Taylor at Trembath and Taylor, and the many more providores of Italy's unique culinary and vinous patrimony who make our jobs as Italian cooks pleasurable.

Thank you to the producers here who continue the Italian tradition. Thanks Pino and Pia Tomini Foresti for spectacular salumi.

Thank you Fairfax for the extended opportunity to write about food and cooking for all those years.

Thank you John Newton, friend and collaborator, I really couldn't have finished the book without you.

And finally to Tracy O'Shaughnessy at Allen & Unwin who proposed this book and made sure it was published on time.

Stefano Manfredi

PICTURE CREDITS

INDEX

A